PRAISE FOR *I WILL TEACI*
WRITERS, TEACHERS, AN

Charles Guittard's history of his grandfather and his family is enchanting. I loved the format he used, popping backward and forward in time via the peanut gallery. It gave the various generations a real sense of connection with each other. A daring and thoughtful approach making the story so accessible.

KATHI APPELT: Author of more than 30 books, co-authoring *Down Cut Shin Creek: the Pack Horse Librarians of Kentucky,* winner of the Texas Institute of Letters Award and the annual PEN Award for *The Underneath.*

The biography of famed Baylor professor Frank Guittard is really the biography of an era, or several eras. Charles Guittard does a remarkable job, not only relating Frank's life, but also revealing those time periods and imagining how they influenced Frank and helped to make him the unforgettable teacher he was.

PATRICIA BERNSTEIN: Author of *The First Waco Horror: The Lynching of Jesse Washington and the Rise of the NAACP; Ten Dollars to Hate: The Texas Man Who Fought the Klan*; and many articles for periodicals including *Texas Monthly* and *The Smithsonian.*

Charles Guittard's book is delightful—actually, extraordinary. The final sentence of this remarkable 600-page book voices a wish: "May we all live in good health long enough to tell our families' stories, including our college family..." Charles Guittard has done exactly that in this biography of his grandfather, Frank Guittard, who taught history at Baylor University from 1902 until 1950. The book fulfills the promise of its subtitle as it recounts not only the life of its protagonist but also the times in which he lived, strove, and endured. Any person interested in Baylor or in higher education in Texas will be captivated by this book's terrific stories, and it is chock-full of them.

TED L. ESTESS: Dean Emeritus and holder of the Jane Cizik Chair, the Honors College of the University of Houston; professor of English Literature, the University of Houston; and author of *Elie Wiesel, A Monograph*; *Fishing Spirit Lake*; and other works.

Part family memoir, part institutional history, part biography, with a dash of imaginative reconstruction and narration, this book is a labor of love that has been in process for nearly 45 years. Charles Francis Guittard tells the story of his grandfather, Francis Gevrier Guittard, partially inspired by Charles's own feelings for Baylor University and the department of history his grandfather virtually founded. As a former chair of history, I myself am indebted to Francis Guittard, as are all who have passed through our department, and now we all owe a debt of gratitude to Charles Guittard for this splendid history.

BARRY HANKINS: Professor of History, Baylor University; author of *Woodrow Wilson: Ruling Elder, Spiritual President*; *God's Rascal: J. Frank Norris and the Beginnings of Southern Fundamentalism*; and other volumes.

Drawing upon his passion for history and story-telling, Charles Guittard has produced an eminently readable and relatable biography of his grandfather, Francis Gevrier Guittard, faculty member and long-time chair of the history department at Baylor University. More than a traditional biography, I Will Teach History offers valuable insight into Frank Guittard's life and family, as well as the history and traditions of Baylor University and Waco, Texas.

KIMBERLY R. KELLISON: Associate Dean for Humanities and Social Sciences and Professor of History, Baylor University; author of *Forging a Christian Order: South Carolina Baptists, Race, and Slavery, 1696-1860* (forthcoming).

If history doesn't repeat itself, it sure comes close. Charles Guittard's loving journey through his grandfather's life and times reminds us that cultural battles over evolution, the Bible, race and the role of women persist, even if in new forms. Guittard revisits a Texas that is all-too-recognizable: Journalist W.C. Brann, slashing Baptist Baylor U. about sex; fundamentalist preacher J. Frank Norris, attempting to chill academic freedom; the KKK, on the march – an event Guittard retells in part through the eyes of my great aunt, a Baylor senior. Frank Guittard, Charles's paterfamilias and a scholar, worries that reactionary forces will zap the modest salary that sustains his passion for teaching. If past echoes seem familiar, that's because they are. There's a wealth of research here, strikingly presented.

ROBERT T. GARRETT: Austin Bureau Chief, *Dallas Morning News*; multiple awards for reporting, including from the Association of Capitol Reporters and Editors; John S. Knight Journalism Fellow, Stanford University (1993-94).

Filled with humor and punctuated by imaginative recreations of scenes from an era over a century ago and questions from a peanut gallery of the author's grandchildren, this "life and times" of Frank Guittard is a profitable read for anyone interested in the history of Texas, Baptists, higher education, Baylor, or just what American life was like back then. I WILL TEACH HISTORY is also deeply researched, drawing from a rich source base of documents and oral histories.

ANDREA L. TURPIN: Associate Professor of History and Director of Graduate Studies, Baylor University; author of *A New Moral Vision: Gender, Religion, and the Changing Purposes of American Higher Education, 1837-1917.*

I WILL TEACH HISTORY is a fascinating family story reaching from generation to generation with wisdom and charm.

JULIA MARKUS: Professor Emerita of English, Hofstra University; author of *Dared and Done: The Marriage of Elizabeth Barrett Browning and Robert Browning,* and *Lady Byron and her Daughters.*

The Frank Guittard saga is both lively and surprising as a clear and challenging portrait of American society and higher education. It offers many stories that are relevant to our own rapidly changing times.

T. MICHAEL PARRISH: Linden F. Bowers Professor of American History, Baylor University; author of *Richard Taylor: Soldier Prince of Dixie,* and *Brothers in Gray: The Civil War Letters of the Pierson Family.*

I thoroughly enjoyed reading this book, especially for the style in which it is written. I liked the conversational tone with which the stories of Frank, Baylor, and Waco are presented through dialogues with the author's own grandchildren aka the peanut gallery. But more than style or tone, America loves to root for the underdog and Frank Guittard had to overcome many obstacles in his life. It is an inspiring tale of one man's resiliency, dedication to hard work and family, and strength of moral character. A great American story.

CARSON MENCKEN: Professor and Chair, Department of Sociology, Baylor University; author of *Paranormal America: Ghost Encounters, UFO Sightings, Bigfoot Hunts and Other Curiosities in Religion and Culture (with Christopher Bader and Joseph Baker).*

Charles Guittard has written an expansive and intriguing biography of a key academic leader in the growth of Baylor University intertwined with an engaging portrait of a contemporary family (the Guittards) bound together by an ambitious research endeavor.

JUDY JOLLEY MOHRAZ: Former president of Goucher College; former associate provost of Southern Methodist University; author of *The Separate Problem: Case Studies of Black Education in the North, 1900-1930.*

At last, the long-awaited memoir of a noted historian by his grandson, Charles Guittard...Those who are contemplating a memoir should take a look at this one.

DARWIN PAYNE: Professor Emeritus of Journalism, Southern Methodist University; author of *The Man of Only Yesterday: Frederick Lewis Allen, Owen Wister: Chronicler of the West, One Hundred Years on the Hilltop [the story of SMU]*, and other works.

I found I WILL TEACH HISTORY compelling both for its story and for its sense of experimentation. Charles Guittard's passion for chronicling Francis Gevrier Guittard's life and times has delivered to the reader not only the account of one outstanding man and instructor, but also an epic of the age he lived through. Equally fascinating is the way in which the story's telling is placed in conversation between generations of Guittards.

STEPHEN M. SLOAN: Associate Professor of History and Director of the Institute of Oral History, Baylor University; co-editor of *Listening on the Edge*; author, with S.K. Sielaff, M.L. Holland, and A.A. Cain, of *Oral History at a Distance* (forthcoming).

I WILL TEACH HISTORY

The Life & Times of Francis Gevrier Guittard, Professor, Baylor University

An unconventional biography narrated conversationally in dialogues with the author's grandchildren; the final volume of a trilogy chronicling a Ph.D.'s journey.

Francis "Frank" Gevrier Guittard

Charles Francis Guittard

Illustrations by Amanda Hope Smith

Edited by Cole Niles

I WILL TEACH HISTORY, The Life & Times of Francis Gevrier Guittard,
Professor, Baylor University

ISBN 978-1506-907-96-3 PBK
ISBN 978-1506-910-67-3 MT-AMZ

LCCN 2022908599

June 2022

Published and Distributed by
First Edition Design Publishing, Inc.
P.O. Box 17646, Sarasota, FL 34276-3217
www.firsteditiondesignpublishing.com

I'm late, I'm late! For a very important date! No time to say 'hello, goodbye,' I'm late, I'm late, I'm late!
Lewis Carroll

Procrastination is the thief of time. Collar him!
Charles Dickens

There is no book so bad…
that it does not have something good in it.
Miguel de Cervantes Saavedra

I am a part of everything that I have read.
Theodore Roosevelt

In life, as in a football game, the principle to follow is this: Hit the line hard.
Theodore Roosevelt

When you reach the end of your rope,
tie a knot and hold on.
Theodore Roosevelt

What a fool, quoth he, am I, thus to lie in a stinking Dungeon, when I may as well walk at liberty!
John Bunyan

The hill, though high, I covet to ascend;
The difficulty will not me offend.
For I perceive the way to life lies here.
Come, pluck up, Heart; let's neither faint nor fear.
Better, tho' difficult, the right way to go,
Than wrong, though easy, where the end is woe.
John Bunyan

Dedication

This volume is dedicated to Patricia Ann Verlander Guittard, my dear late wife, who was my love and companion for over three decades and passed away in early 2021. Then, to my wonderful partner and love of my later years, Nancy Davis Labastida, whom I met and married in late 2021. Both listened to me often talk about this project, which I began in 1978. I'm sure both wondered if it would ever see its completion day.

Secondly, to my four grandchildren, Miles, a recent graduate of the University of Texas in Austin; Charlie, a junior at the Gymnasium Art School of Austin; Finn, a freshman at City College Business School in Austin; and Katie, an AP student in psychology in Irvine, California. They all appear in this volume individually and collectively as the peanut gallery. Having four grandchildren has served as an inspiration to complete a project begun decades before, but occasionally flagging for want of time and focus.

Finally, to seventy-five former students of Frank Guittard, many of whom were history majors, and to faculty colleagues of Frank Guittard, all of whom sent their reminiscences, suggestions, and words of encouragement. The detail and effort that went into their letters after so many years proved impressive. The earliest letter came from a student who entered Baylor in 1910 when Frank first became history chair, the student offering his observations from over one hundred years ago! One student said she had retained her textbooks and papers written in her history courses with Frank Guittard. Some had diaries or scrapbooks of their college days. The correspondences triggered their recollections and their reduction to writing before they were lost forever. In some cases, students remembered the names of their teachers at Baylor after fifty years. Where Frank's classroom was concerned, they recalled their classes, the classrooms including Room 202 in Old Main—Frank's room for decades, the classroom windows, the bells, the fire escape, the professor's elevated desk, where they sat, the map case, the class routine, the unusual events, the homework, something of the courses, and the course textbooks. They also recalled the professor's method, his pocket watch, the notebooks he used, and his demeanor, appearance, personality, and personal characteristics. They remembered the context of their Baylor years, Professor Guittard's house on South 8th Street, his wife Josie, and some even remembered their sons, Francis and Clarence. Amazing.

It has taken me a little over four decades to produce this volume, and most, if not all, of the students who sent me their memories have unfortunately departed this world. Although they will not be able to read this volume, I am confident the final result will be a better book because of the passage of time, and those looking down will understand.

Finally, we dedicate this book to the current Department of History of Baylor University; also, to those legendary professors of times past, the late Ralph L. Lynn and Robert L. Reid. We hope they also will be pleased with the ultimate results of their words of encouragement.

Acknowledgments

This volume represents the third work of a trilogy pertaining to the life & times of Francis Gevrier Guittard ("Frank Guittard"). I gratefully acknowledge everyone along the way who has inspired, encouraged, or made this effort feasible and even enjoyable. The first volume was *A Ph.D.'s Reverie* consisting of a short biographical poem with notes composed three years ago; the second, *A Ph.D.'s Reverie: The Letters,* arising primarily from Guittard family correspondences found in storage over forty years ago and supplemented with Baylor context; and the third volume, the current piece—*I WILL TEACH HISTORY: The Life & Times of Francis Gevrier Guittard, Professor, Baylor University*—completing a project started forty years ago, but certainly not as the lifetime project it has become.

The first volume, and indeed all three, were initially inspired decades ago by Baylor History professors whose courses I took during my Baylor years—the late Ralph L. Lynn, who punctuated his provocative points by laughing to himself while banging his head on the blackboard, his class looking on in shock, amazement, or curiosity; and the late Robert L. Reid, whose specialty was humorous impersonations of historical figures. Dr. Lynn made a special point of telling me in 1978, a la Oliver Cromwell, "Write it, warts and all." Professor Guy B. Harrison, Jr., Director of The Texas Collection and protégé and student of Frank Guittard, sounded a note of urgency in his letter early on, saying "you are just in time before all who had close personal contacts with him are gone." Professor Harrison was probably referring to interviewing faculty members who knew Frank Guittard rather than students in his classes. However, I did my best to locate and find former students, resulting in seventy-five writing me a total of one hundred letters conveying their reminiscences about Frank Guittard and his history classes. I was interested in discovering what his students thought of him as a teacher and his teaching method.

In more recent years, current members of Baylor's Department of History have supported and provided encouragement for these efforts, including Professors Jeffrey Hamilton, Kimberly R. Kellison, and Barry Hankins, all former or current DOH chairs. In addition, Professors T. Michael Parrish, Stephen M. Sloan, and Andrea L. Turpin have all provided input and feedback. Baylor professors George Gawrych, Thomas S. Kidd, and Joseph Stubenrauch read proofs of the second volume and gave their thumbs up. With respect to the inputs of History professors Hamilton, Kellison, Hankins, Parrish, and Sloan, changes were made which improved the final product. Additionally, English professors Linda Bunnell, Greg Garrett, and Elizabeth Dell have all been consulted on one or more works in the trilogy.

Because this project was inspired initially by batches of Guittard correspond-dences, I want to thank my first cousins Stephen Wood Guittard and the late Philip Alwin Guittard, both Baylor graduates and the oldest of Frank Guittard's five grandchildren. I have freely consulted with both, not only about the letters and Frank's life, but about the particulars of the Guittard house at 1401 South 8th Street in Waco before it morphed into a student parking lot. Since Steve is the oldest of the five, I have naturally asked him the most questions, and, although in his 80s, he has retained a number of detailed memories about Frank Guittard, the Guittard household, and the house itself from his occasional visits to his Guittard grandparents when his parents were traveling. The Guittard with the most memories was my father Clarence Alwin Guittard, who wrote out in longhand his recollections of life growing up in Waco with Frank, Josie, and Francis and also sat for more than one recorded interview in Dallas. I was not able to interview my uncle Francis Gevrier Guittard, Jr., who died before I was even aware of the letters, but I have the letters which include those to and from Francis. The fourth grandchild was my brother John, whose many contributions to this project included providing technical expertise to various aspects of the project and being available from time to time to talk through what I was learning, giving me his take on certain points. The fifth grandchild was my sister, Mary Guittard Voegtle, who has continued to be a strong supporter of these projects and is always interested in hearing about Frank and Mamie as well as about Frank and Josie.

Before turning to those seventy-five students and others who shared their recollections of Frank Guittard and his classes with me, I want to thank all of those who have been helpful in providing access to trustee and faculty records in the Baylor University Archives kept by The Texas Collection ("TTC" herein). I wish to thank John S. Belew, Vice President for Academic Affairs; Kent Keeth, TTC Director, and Ellen Kuniyuki Brown, TTC Head of Historical Manuscripts, in connection with my research in the 1970s and 1980s. As to my most recent research commencing ten years ago, I am grateful to John Wilson, TTC Director, former TTC University Archivist Amanda K. Norman, and TTC Special Collections and Manuscripts Archivist Benna Vaughan, TTC Processing Archivist Paul Fisher, and TTC Archival Assistant-Digital Input Specialist Thomas A. DeShong. Tommy DeShong deserves a special second mention since he was my research assistant and editor for the first two books in the trilogy. Thomas L. Charlton, formerly Director of Baylor's Program for Oral History (PFOH), provided tape recording equipment for interviews with faculty members in the 1970s; current PFOH Director Stephen Sloan has generally supported my efforts to complete the trilogy over the last ten years. For the current volume, my assistants have been Baylor students Cole Niles, a perceptive but diplomatic editor, and Amanda Hope Smith, the talented illustrator of this volume. I am very grateful that Cole, a millennial, and Amanda, a Gen Zer, pitched in enthusiastically to help this Baylor traditionalist—only three to four generations apart between us—get this ball finally across the finish line.

As to my efforts to find Frank Guittard's former students, the seventy-five that responded to my requests were found looking through *Baylor Round-Ups* for history majors and by placing an ad in *The Baylor Line*. I looked for students who had taken courses from Frank Guittard between 1910 and 1950. I queried my correspondents, many by multiple letters, on a number of topics but primarily relating to their classes with Frank Guittard. An astounding number of my correspondents became teachers of history, and a fair number were Frank's graders. I also received some responses from Baylor faculty and a few cousins and others who knew Frank Guittard. The responses to the detailed questions were consistent and illuminated unambiguously what Frank was like as a classroom teacher and his lasting effect on his students. The responses of some forty or more students are incorporated in the chapter entitled "The Professor Who Put 'Sys' in 'System'"; their names are shown directly following their inputs.

Finally, I want to thank my writing consultant, Georgette Taylor of Plano, Texas (*Taylor Your Writing*), who patiently took my final edited drafts of the chapters and copy edited, scrubbed, and polished them for publication in a way I could never have done. I also finally want to acknowledge the invaluable help of all those not named here who read all or portions of the manuscript before publication. I also appreciate the moral support of those in Baylor Development, including Jordan Hannah, Kelli Edmond, David Cortes, Rose Youngblood, and Professor Michael Parrish, all of whom encouraged these writing projects. Of course, the responsibility for any errors or omissions is mine alone.

I WILL TEACH HISTORY

The Life & Times of Francis Gevrier Guittard, Professor, Baylor University

Charles Francis Guittard

Illustrations by Amanda Hope Smith
Edited by Cole Niles

Contents

Foreword

by Jeffrey Hamilton

The "life and times" genre is often turned to when there simply isn't enough to say about the subject of a biography, and yet, in the case of Francis (Frank) Gevrier Guittard, there is such an embarrassment of riches that a would-be biographer need not stray too far from the reconstruction of the facts of his life. It turns out that Frank Guittard bequeathed some thirty-seven storage boxes containing everything from the mundane—reading notes and class materials—to the highly personal—diaries, letters, photos, etc.—all the way to autobiographies (Plural!). More than any would-be biographer could possibly hope for. And yet, Charles Guittard wanted still more, and he got it through interviews and correspondences with some seventy-five former students of Frank Guittard. Much was learned about the professor's teaching method of recitation (or, if you prefer, inquisition), and an equal amount about the system and style of higher education in the United States—from Baylor to Chicago to Stanford—in the late nineteenth and first half of the twentieth centuries.

So much, then, for Frank Guittard's life. Thankfully, Charles Guittard has placed this life into its times which enrich our understanding of that life, which in turn illuminates the times. Controversial topics such as the Ku Klux Klan and the controversy surrounding the theory of evolution could not be sealed off from the so-called "ivory tower" any more than the impact of two world wars and the Great Depression. The intersections of Frank's life with other figures who would be notable not only at Baylor University, in Texas, and beyond is remarkable. That, in 1895-96 while both were teaching at the newly founded Southwestern Academy in Magnolia, Arkansas, he should have roomed with Pat Neff who later served as governor of Texas, president of Baylor University, and president of the Southern Baptist Convention seems more providential than coincidental. They would, of course, be reunited and work together in Waco many years later to even greater effect.

The great American medievalist and contemporary of Francis Gevrier Guittard, Charles Homer Haskins (1870-1937), remarked in the course of his Colver Lectures at Brown University in 1923 that the medieval university "had no student societies...no college journalism, no dramatics, no athletics, none of those 'outside activities' which are the chief excuse for inside inactivity in the American college." And while Frank Guittard made very little allowance for inside inactivity in his rigorous classroom, his story overlaps with the birth and growth of American institutions such as college football, homecoming parades, and academic freedom on campuses. These were part and parcel of his life and times.

In combining the history of an era with a rich and detailed personal portrait of a man who helped to shape, and was himself shaped by, this same era, Charles Guittard has produced a highly readable, entertaining, and enjoyable window into a not-so-distant, but often forgotten, past.

Jeffrey Hamilton, Professor of History and Vice-Provost for Global Engagement; Jo Murphy Chair in International Education; former chair of the Department of History, Baylor University, Waco, Texas; and author of The Plantagenets: A History of a Dynasty (2010).

Introduction

Dear Reader,

Do you have a mysterious ancestor—maybe a grandparent you may have met but never really knew—whose life history, personality, and character are mostly unknown to you? Moreover, did your grandparent, unfortunately, not leave a clear path for you or another family sleuth to follow if someone wanted to know more about their forebear? Or was there a path left, but the tracks were confusing to read or contradictory? Or, perhaps you made a genuine effort to find your forbear's trail, but, ultimately, despite finding some clues—possibly many clues—you eventually gave up the search as a bad job; there were too many loose ends to chase, or too much time was required, and you left it for a younger researcher to tackle later.

If any of those scenarios sound familiar, then read on for the results of my investigation following the trail of the schoolman who was my paternal grandfather, Francis ("Frank") Gevrier Guittard. The trail starts with his birth in Ohio on January 7, 1867, two years after Robert E. Lee and the forces of the Confederacy surrendered to U.S. Grant and the Union Army. This book reports on what I could discover by the time the trail reached its end in Dallas, Texas, in 1950.

Unlike *The Hoosier Schoolmaster* (1871) by Edward Eggleston, this volume is not a work of fiction written in "a white heat" and completed in ten weeks. Work commenced investigating Frank Guittard's story in 1978 with the idea of a possible book and pursued in fits and starts after that. It is also essential to acknowledge that I barely knew my grandfather. I was seven when he died at eighty-three years of age, and I rarely saw him except at Christmas and on a few Baylor University homecoming weekends in Waco, TX. The only memory I have of any interaction with him is one occasion when he read me *The Katzenjammer Kids* from the Sunday funnies. *Kids* was a comic strip in which the characters spoke a hybrid sort of German-English, likely made up by the strip's author to enhance its odd humor. Who were these strange un-Disney-like, not charming, and unfunny comic characters, and why was my grandfather reading to me about their juvenile misadventures, usually involving pranks and some degree of cruelty? I had no idea. For the rest of his grandchildren and me, Frank Guittard was a private and remote character. I can't say at the time I was conscious of missing a deeper connection. Years later—I don't remember when—I came into possession of several tangible items of his. Those included a pair of rimless metallic spectacles, a 1901 tuxedo, a grandfather clock from his family's home in Ohio, a copy of *Richardson's Free Masonry*, and the raggedy Ph.D. academic robe he wore when he received his doctorate in 1931. As for his library in Waco, someone disposed of the books after his death in 1950. Unfortunately, I wasn't old enough to ask for any of them.

But let's fast-forward to the mid-1970s, over two decades after Frank Guittard's death, when I came across a package of family letters from the 1920s. Before opening those letters, what I knew about him could be reduced to a handful of basic facts: Frank Guittard came to Texas from Ohio a long time ago; he was a teacher of history at Baylor University for almost a half-century; after my biological grandmother ("Mamie") died, he married a good-natured, humorous, and affectionate woman we all called "Mama Josie"; he and Josie lived in a large two-story frame house on South 8th Street across from the Baylor campus; and, finally, late in life, he earned a Ph.D. at Stanford in California. Of course, he enjoyed playing golf on weekends, and during the week, taking naps after lunch before returning to campus. That's it—I knew nothing of his private side known only to his wives and children, what he was like as a teacher for almost a half-century, anything about his family of origin, and most other facets of his life, not to mention his times.

That first package of letters opened windows to his personality. It inspired my desire to find out more about this reserved grandfather who was neither talkative, huggable, nor the type to get down on the floor and play marbles with his grandchildren. Then, not long after reading that first package of letters, I received the second package of letters. Together with the first group of letters, the second package suggested that Frank Guittard, once anyone got to know him, was an intriguing guy. Maybe he was someone whose life might even be interesting to people not in his immediate family. These thoughts all assumed sufficient additional information was available and could be collected. Fortunately, I learned that Baylor's Texas Collection had preserved thirty-seven storage boxes of his papers. The papers contained several Frank Guittard autobiographies, ledgers, diaries, letters, essays, handwritten notebook summaries of texts he used in his history classes, materials on his Ohio family, family photographs, and much more. The Texas Collection held copies of the student newspaper (*The Lariat)*, copies of student yearbooks (*Baylor Round-*

Ups) going back to 1896, and a 75-page master's thesis on Frank's life by Professor Louise Moore Cagle, one of Frank's students.

Also, early on, and at the suggestion of Professor Guy B. Harrison, Jr., one of Frank's students, I corresponded with seventy-five of Frank's former students. One of those students took Frank's courses and was his grader sometime between 1910 and 1914—more than a century ago. All in all, I received one hundred letters from those seventy-five students. It finally dawned on me that I had enough details and facts along with Frank's own words to turn his life's twists and turns into compelling reading for other people. I had the general feeling that if enough detail could be collected about nearly any ordinary person, then that person's story could be compelling reading for unrelated readers.

The packages of letters represent only the first stages of my research into his life & times. The research phase lasted for over forty years and ultimately included a beginning bibliography of over six hundred volumes and research materials collected in fifty boxes and stored in Dallas. As I looked at the number of sources I consulted over the years, I was hopeful the result would be a richer and more engaging final product than one which skipped over the times and context of the letters. I also began to think of the life & times almost like a Christmas tree to which could be added ornaments, lights, and other decorations, Frank's life being the tree and the events and context of his times being the ornaments and decorations. However—and the reader may have guessed this already—my research process became so broad that it was difficult to conclude the research and to strip away the unessential. I realized I had enough material for a three-volume biography. Still, at seventy-eight years of age, with neither the stamina nor the patience to complete such a work, the crucial question was how to reduce the material to just the topics most worthy of inclusion. The number of books, boxes of notecards, and research folders became so intimidating that I decided to postpone the writing process by composing a narrative poem to regain control over the project and its direction.

However, once I had the poem out of the way—"A Ph.D.'s Reverie"—I continued to struggle with how to regain control over the project and resume writing. Luckily, before long, I stumbled upon the central paradox of Frank's story as well as the peculiar "twist of fate" which figured crucially into the way his life played out. The central paradox was that Frank, a person who left nothing to chance and was famous for being systematic in everything, often could not avoid riding the winds of chance, concluding himself in 1928 that he had just "blundered" along. The "twist of fate," about which we will make much of later on, was that unpredictable turn of events set in motion by a college prank played on Baylor President Cooper in 1902, the prank leading to Frank's accepting a teaching job at Baylor.

Suffice to say, the family letters, the students' letters, the written archival materials, the central paradox, and the twist of fate all reinforced my feeling that a life & times, although still a daunting task, should be resumed as soon as possible. But now, the challenge was how to reduce the project to a manageable size. After puzzling over how to do this for months, I arrived at what seemed to be a promising solution. Instead of attempting a comprehensive work about Frank Guittard's life & times—my first inclination and a completely unrealistic one—I would try something different. My notion was to structure most of the work around a series of questions which would pull out anything from my research worth memorializing. But how would this process work in practice? What questions would guide the structure and content of the book?

To this last question, the answer, which came from who knows where, was...drum roll, please...a peanut gallery. I would create a peanut gallery—that is, a small group of interested interlocutors. Some older readers may remember the peanut gallery from the 1950s Howdy Doody Show and emcee Buffalo Bob saying, "Hey kids, what time is it?" and the kids shouting on cue, "It's Howdy Doody Time!" Accordingly, I assembled a peanut gallery composed of my four grandchildren (Miles, the oldest; Charlie; Finn; and Katie, their first cousin and the youngest). I hoped, after providing them with basic information about Frank Guittard and reading them the poem, they would come up with questions they would like answered about their great-great-grandfather Frank Guittard and respond with a comment or two. Thus, the peanut gallery would supply the initial questions that I would attempt to answer, supplemented by whatever other questions and answers would be needed to better complete the picture on any topic. I might even address my questions exclusively on some possible topics if none were forthcoming from the peanut gallery. The final result, nevertheless, would be a work inspired first and foremost by my grandchildren's curiosity. The peanut gallery would also serve as stand-ins for readers who might have questions or comments. Maybe readers at some point would identify with my grandkids and their attempts to peel the onion of Frank's life and times.

Katie: (*speaking for the first time*) I wish I could have been on that television show.

Pops: Hi, Katie. The others are around here somewhere. Have you seen them?

Katie: I think they are finishing up their Grape-Nuts. Finn may still be eating Froot Loops.

Finn: Nope, no more. I'm onto Wheaties and Skinner's Raisin Bran. They were huge at the dorm.

Pops: (*pausing as Miles, Charlie, and Finn join Pops and Katie*) In addition to the central paradox and the twist of fate, it was inevitable that my research would strongly suggest several extended metaphors about Frank Guittard's life. These figures of speech represent some ways readers might use in thinking about Frank's life and making some themes in his life—all of our lives have themes—more understandable.

So, what possible metaphors could help readers think about Frank's life & times? Frank himself uses the mountain metaphor for his almost Sisyphean struggle to earn his Ph.D., and the related "Fool's Hill" metaphor for the fruitless efforts young adults may attempt before obtaining maturity. The knight in armor or medieval metaphor from the days of King Arthur was suggested by an observer of Frank's participation in one of Baylor's first homecoming parades. Frank's letters discussing the library basement dungeon at Stanford, in which he reviewed archived documents, suggest the Inquisition metaphor. In addition to those metaphors, another category of metaphors includes those helpful in notifying the reader concerning the author's progress or lack of progress in finding answers: "rabbit holes"—the subjects often murky but with possibilities that I felt obliged to follow Frank's trail down into; "black holes"—those subjects or periods I could find little or no path to follow; and "briar patches"—those prickly topics I could not skip despite their sensitive nature. This last category of metaphors is related to the questions from the peanut gallery that remain unanswered at the end of this volume.

Charlie: Knights in armor are cool. Have you watched that program, *Forged in Fire*? I would like to have one of their swords.

Pops: No, I haven't seen it. We will have more to say about metaphors and paradoxes in Frank's life. As to the facts of Frank's life & times, I had a gratifying amount of first-hand information from family members. These family members were familiar with Frank as a person, husband, and father; I also have information from many of his students conversant with his characteristic teaching style and classroom persona. In a few instances, I have attempted to recreate scenes from his life with dialogue and context. One example is a recreated classroom scene featured in the prologue in which Frank conducts a History 105 class using his recitation interrogation style. No, I did not have a time machine to pull this off, but I had many, many letters from former students describing his technique in detail, giving examples of how he would ask questions; I also had his handwritten notes from every class he taught and the textbook from which he taught History 105.

To illustrate Frank's sense of humor, which provided an occasional diversion from the facts of history (the terms of peace treatises, the causes of wars, and so on), the divider pages preceding the "books" will include excerpts from Frank's "Funny-Book" along with some of his favorite words and phrases. In his "Funny-Book," Frank compiled off-the-wall and wrong-headed answers ("bone-heads") students had offered on written history exams, either to be funny or just hoping for the best and coming in on a wing and a prayer.

Finn: Were the answers really funny or just kind of lame?

Pops: You'll have to wait and see. The peanut gallery will undoubtedly pose many questions, including those along these lines:

- Could Frank ride a horse? Would he need a pistol or Bowie knife after arriving in Texas? Were there outlaws in Texas?
- Was Frank's family home in Ohio a hard or fun place to live?
- Did Frank do farm work in Ohio? What kind? Why didn't he stay in Ohio and become a farmer?
- Why didn't Frank's family follow him to Texas? What was wrong with Texas?

- Was Frank Guittard a tough teacher? Did he require homework? How many subjects could he teach? Did he tell jokes? Was he funny?
- Did Frank have any girlfriends as a young man? Any crushes on girls?
- Could Frank play a musical instrument or sing? Did he ever play in a band?
- What was in the attic of the house at 1401 South 8th? Where did the disappearing staircases lead to?
- What was Frank like behind closed doors with only family around?
- Why did Mama Josie sell eggs from their backyard chickens?
- Why did Frank walk around the house with a sandbag on his head?
- Was Frank good at golf? Who taught him to play?
- Why did Frank dye his hair? Why did his students talk about his hair?

And for the benefit of the reader, on each of the ten book divider pages are sample questions for the peanut gallery's consideration so that the reader can see where the conversation may go in particular books and chapters.

Coming attractions for this volume will include the following topics not necessarily in order: the train trip to Texas, Frank's game plan, the prank and the offer, Frank's teaching method, the battle with bees, Christmas in Huntsville, summer salesman, rooming with Pat Neff, flirtations and courtships, the health crises, the Student Self-Government Experiment, the years in a Palo Alto dungeon, and many others.

In addition to the narration of the facts of the life & times of Frank Guittard in response to the questions posed by the peanut gallery, we have opted to stretch the traditional definition of biography. As indicated above, we have included several scenes supported by solid historical research that begged to be recreated. Our goal is to produce these scenes with enough detail to transport readers back to the times and places in question. We will identify these scenes with an explanation for how we built them.

The Scholar-Pilgrim

Young Frank from Ohio
Bad weather, worse times
the young Scholar-Pilgrim
to Piney Woods propelled.
Fifteen years passed;
Chicago's courses completed.
A scene surreal in Baylor chapel
(a window open, a hound, then horrors!)—
a capricious Twist of Fate
from mercurial Providence
returning him to Texas terrain.
In time Duty issued
one late-life, last siren call
to the Pilgrim now grown gray--
not to sleep or slumber yet,
but rather resume ascent
toward the terminal degree,
his ultimate mountain Grail.
Professor Frank from Waco
to Stanford's Dark Dungeon came.

Note to the Reader

This work is divided into thirty-eight chapters, not counting the appendices and other pieces we have included. Some chapters are long, most of them medium-length or happily short. We decided not to try the average reader's patience and put a few of the longer chapters on a diet. We doubt there will be any complaints.

We admit that in several respects, this life & times has been an experiment. First, we characterize several chapters, starting with the "History 105 Class" scene in the prologue, as "imagined." Nevertheless, we painstakingly constructed these scenes from family and student letters, family documents, and other books and records in The Texas Collection. We believe these chapters to be fair depictions of scenes that would inevitably have taken place in Frank's story. The reason for the construction of these scenes was to animate the narrative in a way that is still faithful to the story of Frank Guittard and to the underlying facts.

Second, it was an experiment to bring in the peanut gallery with questions and comments from the author's grandchildren; they participate in most of the chapters but not all, owing to their busy schedules. The peanut gallery did two valuable things: they helped me, against my natural inclination to embellish and protract, to simplify and shorten Frank's story overall through their questions and comments; and second, in certain contexts, they did help flesh out some of the material through their requests for missing information or for clarification of certain points. Because they were partially aware of the plan for the book before we started, including some of Frank's history, they could be a little sharper in their feedback, which was usually constructive. I suspect their questions in many instances are ones that you, Dear Reader, might have yourself as Frank Guittard's story unfolds. Thus, the peanut gallery is a stand-in for you and your questions. One more thing: the peanut gallery also serves to connect the goings-on that form the context (the "times") to the spine of Frank's story.

Third, in one or more chapters, I attempt to draw conclusions about Frank's thinking from the "mental furniture" we know he had. After all, we all have "mental furniture" of the same sort—the books we have read, for example—which becomes an integral part of who we are and influences our thinking and, thereby, our actions. I attempted to do this conservatively and each time with a solid basis of fact. With any luck, this approach to help tell Frank's story may prove to be a good idea, but the reader will decide for himself.

Fourth, in at least two of the chapters, I may reference two periodicals that Frank read during certain periods of his life. We can't be sure exactly when these periods began or ended. We know he read *The Youth's Companion* growing up in New Bedford, Ohio in the 1880s and *The Literary Digest* at Stanford while working on his doctorate in the 1920s. I have acquired three or four issues of these periodicals in proximity to actual dates in Frank's life—his enrolling as a student at Baylor University in Waco in January 1890 and accepting a position as instructor in the preparatory department in the spring or summer of 1902. In 1902, Frank was either still at the University of Chicago or back home in New Bedford, Ohio, tending to family business after his father's death. Though we can't say for sure whether Frank received or read the particular issues I've found, the topics in these issues still serve to inform the reader's understanding of Frank's interest in these publications and a little of what he learned by reading them. These issues also served to transport the author back 130 years ago to Frank's time and place. We hope the reader will have a similar experience.

Fifth, occasionally some chapters in this volume will echo each other. Why this might be so is explained—and we hope satisfactorily—in the third chapter, which explores the mind of a bookworm.

Sixth, in some chapters we refer to Frank's second wife, Josephine S. Glenn Guittard, as "Josie" and in others as "Mama Josie," which was the name used by both family, including the author, and faculty. In the earliest chapter, "Along Comes Josie," and in "Private Sides," "Josie" is used almost predominantly. Frank sometimes called her by both names. In the chapter "Failure Is Not an Option," "Mama Josie" is used almost exclusively. Josie's middle initial apparently stood for "Swaim," which was her mother's maiden name.

Finally, after the initial submission of I WILL TEACH HISTORY to my publisher, it has very recently been reported that Baylor University's Board of Regents has voted to rename Burleson Quadrangle the Quadrangle and to remove President Burleson's statue to another location on campus. These changes, and many others, come in the wake of the June 2020 Regents' "Resolution on

Racial Healing and Justice" and the December 2020 final report of the Commission on Historic Campus Representations, the unjustified killing of George Floyd by police having occurred in May of 2020 in Minneapolis, Minnesota. These anticipated changes in the campus have suggested supplementary comment in the epilogue relating to the following topics: President Rufus C. Burleson's legacy, Frank Guittard's guided tour of campus for Mamie Welhausen, and Frank Guittard's emphasis on teaching the facts of history.

Charles Francis Guittard

Peanut Gallery Orientation Session

The conversation below occurred between your author ("Pops") and his grandchildren, Miles (the oldest), Charlie, Finn, and Katie (the youngest). Pops is wondering to himself, *this peanut gallery thing sounded like a good idea at first, but I haven't seen them in a while, and I'm worried that the embers of sibling rivalries between Miles, Charlie, and Finn may be distracting. I hope not, but I'm keeping my fingers crossed. I'm also unsure how patient they will be with this process. I will have to keep the sessions short and moving along to keep their attention as well as yours, Dear Reader.*

Pops: Is everybody ready to go? I can start here in Dallas if everybody is connected on Zoom. I don't see Katie.

Miles: We're ready in Austin, Pops. (*To his brothers not on camera*) Hurry up, Charlie and Finn. Pops is ready to start. Let's keep the chatter down.

Charlie: (*sitting down*) Speak for yourself, Miles. Miles is always trying to speak for all of us and tell us what to do. I want to get a cup of coffee first.

Pops: Somebody please turn off that TV. I can't hear you with that thing blaring.

Finn: It's off now. The dog is outside, too.

Pops: Katie, can you hear me in Irvine? Can you see me?

Katie: (*looking up from her notepad*) Yes, and Mom and Dad are here with me, too.

Miles: *(impatiently)* So what is it you want us to do? (*Looking over at Charlie and Finn)* You guys knock it off. I've got to leave in a little while.

Pops: Before getting into that, let me catch up a little with you guys first. Okay? I know Katie is in high school. What happens after high school, Katie?

Katie: Finn, stop making faces at me. It's very distracting (*laughing*). Well, Pops, college somewhere, maybe UCLA. Then to law school. Maybe Baylor if I can get a scholarship; I would be an out-of-state student.

Pops: Law school?

Katie: Right. I want to help women.

Finn: (*smiling*) Women need help. But they'll never admit it.

Katie: (*ignoring Finn*) There's still discrimination against women. And abuse. Somebody in this family should do something, and it's obviously not going to be the men. There's still a glass ceiling in lots of places.

Pops: Okay. Charlie?

Charlie: Pops, I'm a junior at the Gymnasium here in Austin.

Finn: (*grinning*) well, la-de-dah. That's costing Mom and Dad a small fortune.

Pops: (ignoring Finn) what's the Gymnasium? I haven't heard of it.

Charlie: It's an artsy-fartsy college for students who want to be designers or engineers. I like to design and build stuff: gadgets, toys, kitchen stuff, musical instruments, whatever. Maybe I'll be an inventor and patent stuff.

Finn: So how much money can you make doing that? Five dollars says Charlie's going to have to move home and live with Mom and Dad.

Charlie: (*annoyed*) Buzz off, Finn. Finn never could figure out how to play a snare drum. I used to drive him to early band practice.

That's the easiest instrument there is. You have to be a complete spaz if you can't play the drum.

Finn: I *could* play the drum, but my lawn business was starting to make serious bucks, and I had to drop out so I could mow lawns.

Miles: (*staying aloof from the Charlie-Finn dust-up*) By the way, Pops, one of my friends is picking me up in a little while. We're going to a pre-game tailgating party. The Horns are playing TCU in Darrell K. Royal at two. Everybody's predicting we're going to beat the Frogs like a redheaded stepchild. Poor Froggies.

Pops: Okay, fine…This first session won't take too long anyway. But tell me, Miles, where are you now and what are you up to?

Miles: I'm still in Austin. I graduated from UT last year with a degree in city planning and design. I have my application in with several cities, preferably Austin, but some smaller places, too.

Pops: I'd like to see some of your designs sometime.

Miles: Sure, no problem. And I'm pretty good with numbers, too. I like to think about what cities need. In the meantime, I am making a little money as a tennis pro—

Charlie: *Assistant* tennis pro.

Miles: (*giving Charlie a steely look, but otherwise ignoring him)*—and playing some amateur baseball. I teach kids and middle-aged women mostly. Their serves and backhands are jokes.

Katie: (*ignoring Miles's dig at women*) Well, I think it's great that you are helping women improve their games.

Miles: Yeah, I guess. The pay sucks, but there are girls in shorts everywhere, so I shag balls for them when I'm not teaching their grannies how to hold the racket.

Pops: Tennis is a great sport. In Frank Guittard's day, nobody wore shorts. There is a photo somewhere of Frank playing tennis at Baylor behind Burleson Hall. He was all dressed up in a vest and tie and wearing a hat like he had just come from the classroom, only taking off his coat so he could serve. He even had a favorite partner on the faculty. A Miss Parker, I believe—I forget what she taught. He switched over to golf later after his oldest son Francis started playing golf. Harder game, totally, just less running. In some ways, you remind me of Francis.

Miles: How do I remind you?

Pops: You and Francis are both the oldest son in a family of sons, and you are also good at tennis. So, Finn, what about you? Where are you now?

Finn: Pops, I'm a freshman at City College B-School. I'm going for a marketing degree. I know I can make money—everybody tells me I'm a natural salesman—so maybe a lot of money. See if I don't. Everybody knows Medicare is on life support, and it's going to take a lot of money to buy healthcare. I also can draw and write well. Maybe I'll be a writer for a newspaper or draw political cartoons. I may have to support Miles and Charlie from what they just said (*laughing*).

Pops: Okay, thanks for catching me up. Here's the way it will work and how you can help me. I'm going to be talking through pieces of the book I'm working on about my grandfather, your great-great-grandfather, Frank Guittard, and I was hoping you could ask me questions or make comments on what you are hearing. Please, though, let's keep your comments focused on Frank Guittard's story and let's not get off on tangents, okay? You have already heard an outline of his story in that little poem, "A Ph.D.'s Reverie." Today we'll put some real meat on the bones of that poem.

Finn: Is that the poem Dad read us a few years back? Those were outstanding drawings in that little book. Did you do them?

Pops: No, a Baylor art student named Grace Daniel did the drawings. But to preview where we will go as we walk and talk through the book, we'll cover Frank's trip to Texas on the train, those early teaching days in Texas, and his early girlfriends. We'll include the books and the comic strips he read, the dormitory he stayed in at Baylor that had no bathroom or shower, and the house where he lived for thirty years in Waco with disappearing staircases between floors and chickens in the backyard. You'll learn about the sandbag he used to improve his posture, health tips to avoid colds, the watch he won selling books to farmers' wives despite barking dogs, and the student prank that led to his job at Baylor. And finally, the 1904 World's Fair he attended in St. Louis, the method he used to teach history to his students, his advice to himself on how to succeed as a teacher and faculty member, his advice to his sons on how they should prepare for careers as attorneys, and much more.

Miles: I don't think we can do all of that today, Pops.

Pops: No, no, I know that—we'll have to do many Zoom meetings. We'll keep them short, though, and not try to do too much at any meeting.

Katie: So, how will these meetings with us help you tell Frank's story?

Pops: Good question. The book is going to be a life & times, so you may be asking why I don't write a biography of his life like any other biography.

Katie: So why don't you, Pops?

Pops: The best answer is that Frank's story is just as interesting for the times he lived in as for his own life. However, making it a life & times added greatly to the research I have had to do. The book has grown like Topsy in the last forty years, and I have far too much material to put in one book. But one book is all I'm going to do, which means I need to shrink the book drastically. Your questions will help me do that by helping me get to the essential parts of his story and then clarifying points that may not be clear.

But there are two other significant things that you can help me do: first, tell Frank's story more entertainingly, and second, ask any questions that you may have and which many readers may have as they read the book. You will help those readers by standing in for them to ask the questions they may have themselves. You have all been fishing and had to bait your hooks. Your questions will be like baited hooks; you guys will be like fishermen, and the answers you bring up will be the fish. You will be dropping your lines in all of this research I've accumulated. Oh, I forgot to mention, all of you will be in the book.

Miles: Okay, Pops. I hear a horn outside. I have to go.

Pops: I'll email everyone the time of the next meeting after you send me your schedules. Please do that right away.

Miles: Everyone get that?

Katie: Bye, Pops.

List of Illustrations & Photographs

All of the hand-drawn illustrations were created by artist Amanda Hope Smith based on the sources furnished to her by the author, including a number of photographic images. The illustrations are the property of the author of this work.

All of the photographic images of the Guittard family are from the archives of the family of Francis Gevrier Guittard.

All of the photographic images relating to Baylor University published herein, including early views of the campus and its buildings and the first four of the university's presidents in Waco (Burleson, Cooper, Brooks, and Neff), are published in the instant work of scholarship with the assistance and permission of Baylor University and The Texas Collection, Baylor University, Waco, Texas.

The Primary Characters, Onstage and Off

Family Members
Francis Joseph Guittard, Lydia Myers Guittard, Francis Gevrier Guittard, Mamie Welhausen Guittard, Francis Gevrier Guittard, Jr., Clarence Alwin Guittard, Josephine ("Mama Josie") Glenn Guittard, Captain Charles Welhausen, Eliza Amsler Welhausen

Baylor Presidents
Rufus C. Burleson, Oscar Henry Cooper, Samuel Palmer Brooks, Pat M. Neff

Others (selected, in alphabetical order)
Horatio Alger, Jr., A.J. Armstrong, Sam Bass, William Cowper Brann, Frank Bridges, Georgia Burleson, Sallie Canon, Benajah Harvey Carroll, Francis Lafayette Carroll, George Washington Carroll, Grove Samuel Dow, Charles S. Fothergill, W.W. Franklin, Geronimo, John Wesley Hardin, William Rainey Harper, Samuel Porter Jones, David Starr Jordan, J. Frank Norris, Annie Oakley, Kate Ross Padgitt, Leopold von Ranke, Edgar Eugene Robinson, John D. Rockefeller, Theodore Roosevelt, A.G. Shortle, M.D., Joseph Warren Speight, Amos Alonzo Stagg, Jane Stanford, Leland Stanford, T. DeWitt Talmage, Antonia Teixeira

Narrator and Peanut Gallery
"Pops" (the author, Charles Francis Guittard)
Miles, Charlie, Finn, and Katie Guittard (the author's grandchildren)

I WILL TEACH HISTORY

The Life & Times of Francis Gevrier Guittard Professor, Baylor University

Charles Francis Guittard

Illustrations by Amanda Hope Smith
Edited by Cole Niles

PROLOGUE

"Master of the Recitation"

I keep six honest serving-men
(They taught me all I knew);
Their names are What and Why and When
And How and Where and Who...
The Elephant by Rudyard Kipling

There is no better way to answer the peanut gallery's questions about Professor Frank Guittard as a teacher of history than to eavesdrop on one of his classes. His classroom for many years was No. 202, located on the northwest corner of the second floor of Old Main. The desks were double-style and students were seated alphabetically. In the winter, the open radiators and unwrapped pipes clanged and rattled noisily, while students near the uninsulated windows could feel the cold air leaking in. During the summer, windows were open with only the slight benefit of two or three overhead ceiling fans humming and blowing the hot air around. One student noted that classroom 202 "was about as disagreeable as is possible to imagine."

I have chosen to reconstruct Frank's History 105 class from Monday morning, November 13, 1930. Using the recitation method, Frank would assign 15-18 pages of the course text for each class, at which time he would proceed alphabetically down the row, asking questions from his "Ancient Notebook." Frank used his handwritten notes from the text to guide him in pulling out the facts from the students' reading of the assigned materials. More about his use of the recitation method will come out later when we attempt to appraise his teaching style from one hundred years of hindsight, but for the time being, the recreated scene in this chapter must suffice. Frank was the expert in the recitation method of teaching, not your author (who has never taken a history course in which the recitation method was used), although your author has undertaken the task of reconstructing an example from one of Frank's classes ninety years ago.

The support for the credibility of this reconstruction includes correspondence with seventy-five former students, nearly all of whom describe his teaching method and are unanimous in their accounts; Frank's detailed handwritten notes in his notebook outlining David Savile Muzzey's text, which he used to teach History 105; David Savile Muzzey's 1927 textbook, *The American People*, published by Ginn and Company, Boston; the input of Baylor history professors Ralph Lynn (a student and later colleague of Frank's), Robert Reid (another student of Frank's), Guy B. Harrison, Jr. (a third student who took twelve courses from Frank and was one of his graders), and Jefferson Davis Bragg (successor to Frank as history chair); the 1931 *Baylor Round-Up* with its account of the 1930 football season; and a 1980 interview with Clarence A. Guittard.

In the construction of this scene, mindful of the reader, I shortened it drastically, as a transcript of a 50-minute class session would have been impractical. To connect the scene with his dissertation at Stanford (Roosevelt and Conservation), I chose Chapter XVI, "The Roosevelt Era," for the day's assignment. This chapter would have been especially appropriate; one student said that when the course reached this topic, Frank at some point would drop the recitation process and speak passionately on the importance of conservation and Roosevelt's accomplishments. However, we will reserve the substance of those remarks about Roosevelt and conservation for the chapter entitled "Failure Is Not an Option: The Struggle for the Ph.D."

We selected the students' names in the scene randomly from the 1930 *Baylor Round-Up*. The author has no proof that anyone by any of their names took any history course with Frank.

THE SCENE: At the stroke of 8:00 a.m., Frank Guittard enters room 202 on the second floor of Old Main Building, mounts the dais, takes his seat, and places his pocket watch in its accustomed cushion of Tyrolean purple. Guittard, nattily attired as usual in his accustomed three-piece pinstriped suit, celluloid collar, and tie, gazes out over the sea of some thirty faces. The Saturday before class, Baylor's football team, despite a strenuous effort, lost its homecoming game 14-0 on Carroll Field to its arch-rival, the University of Texas Longhorns; the class seems to be less animated than usual. Guittard begins after rapping on his desk with his pencil and clearing his throat.

Guittard: May we have your attention, please? Thank you. Who is willing to give us a report on Saturday's game? What the Sam Hill happened? Did Jake get hurt? Couldn't Botchey tackle those guys?

Ragsdale: Dr. Guittard, it was a very bad day at Carroll Field.

Guittard: Professor Guittard, Mr. Ragsdale, please. It won't be official until next year. The chicks are all still in their unhatched state.

Ragsdale: Point taken, Professor. It was a sad outcome given that it was one of the nicest homecomings we've ever had. Everyone said so, and we had to lose to the Longhorns. No, Jake didn't get hurt, and no, Botchey couldn't always tackle Koy and Stafford, at least by himself.

Guittard: But why did we lose? We have such a good team.

Maloney: Professor, Coach Jennings said after the game that the Tea-Sips have the finest team he has ever seen in this part of the country. They have the deepest bench we've faced and just kept putting in fresh players who were as good as or even better than those they took out. It was just terrible luck to be embarrassed at our homecoming.

Kerr: I think it was the same thing that happened in Lafayette against the Boilermakers. The Bears put up a good fight, but it just went against us with those long passes for touchdowns and Jake's long run for a TD being called back for someone being offside. That really hurt.

Guittard: Well, we will have to come back twice as hard on Saturday, shake this thing off, and play in earnest. (*Frank pauses and looks down at his notebook and pocket watch.*) Today the reading assignment is Muzzey's chapter sixteen, and we are still studying Theodore Roosevelt's era. We left off with Mr. Butler on Friday. Mr. Campbell, can you tell the class Roosevelt's corollary to the Monroe Doctrine and how it originated?

Campbell: Professor, I believe, and I could be wrong, but wasn't that the "speak softly and carry a big stick" policy Teddy announced in 1904 after Santo Domingo went bankrupt and the US had to intervene to prevent chaos?

Guittard: Yes, but what did Roosevelt have in mind by "big stick policy," and what was the "big stick"?

Campbell: (*looking puzzled*) Professor Muzzey doesn't explain that part.

Guittard: Can anyone help Mr. Campbell here? Miss Hatchett?

Hatchett: I think the "big stick" is not expressly stated but is implied. Before this time, under the Monroe Doctrine, we had only forbidden Europe to step into the affairs of the republics of the New World, and now we were coming in ourselves to protect Latin American republics.

Guittard: You said, "implied." Can you expand on that, Miss Hatchett?

Hatchett: (*brightly*) Well, we did have an army, and both Santo Domingo and Europe knew that. They also knew Roosevelt was no pantywaist. He was, after all, the hero of San Juan Hill.

Guittard: Miss Hatchett, can you help us with the geographical location of Santo Domingo? Where is Santo Domingo?

Hatchett: Yes, indeed. Santo Domingo is the eastern half of an island about nine hundred miles, give or take, southeasterly from the Florida Keys. Haiti takes up the western half, with the Atlantic Ocean on the north and the Caribbean Sea on the south. Islands Cuba and Jamaica are to the west and Puerto Rico to the east.

Guittard: (*smiling*) Correct and good work. You cracked open your atlas last night, I can see. (*Hatchett also smiles.*)

Hatchett: Professor Guittard, I've heard from my older sister that one of your sons used to come to class and answer geography questions from the students. He knew more geography than most of your students.

Guittard: Yes, that was a few years ago when Clarence was eight or so and got hold of a geography text when he was down with pneumonia. He's thirteen now, and I'm afraid he's more interested in *Tom Swift and his Airship* and Jules Verne stories these days—fiction. He did like to perform, though.(*Professor Guittard pauses and looks at Mr. Simmons.*)

Mr. Simmons, getting back to the subject, Miss Hatchett has pointed to Roosevelt being a pretty feisty character. Do you think Roosevelt was always ready to fight or help other countries fight? What say you?

Simmons: No, I don't agree with that statement at all. Professor, unless I am very much mistaken, the Nobel committee awarded him the Nobel Prize for his efforts on behalf of international peace. One reason was his work in negotiating arbitration treaties with European countries. Another was getting Russia and Japan to the bargaining table at Portsmouth, New Hampshire, to resolve those countries' arguments over Czar Nicholas II's refusal to evacuate Manchuria.

Guittard: Miss Hatchett, did Mr. Simmons leave anything out?

Hatchett: Well, I think Mr. Simmons's statement is correct as far as it goes, but I think we should also point out that both Japan and Russia were tired of their war. Too many people had already died, and both countries wanted it to end, but they had their reasons for keeping it going.

Guittard: Reasons?

Hatchett: Yes, Nicholas II was afraid that if his armies withdrew or were perceived to have been defeated, that would encourage the anarchists in Russia to overthrow him. There were many people in Russia who didn't like Nicholas's autocratic rule. And the Japanese naturally were concerned not to lose face and appear weak by agreeing to meet to discuss peace.

Guittard: Mr. Simmons, anything you might want to add to that?

Simmons: Yes. It's also important to mention that Roosevelt would not have been able to do what he did to get the parties together except that there was a thing called the Hague Convention of 1899 that supported neutral countries offering to mediate a dispute between belligerents. The Japanese-Russian conflict was an obvious situation begging for a neutral country to intervene and mediate.

Guittard: Miss Hatchett, anything that you might want to include to finish this subject?

Hatchett: Yes, surely. The only reason Roosevelt was as prominent as he was in resolving this dispute was that Secretary Hay was fatally ill when the conflict needed fixing. Roosevelt decided he had to take over the diplomatic role.

Simmons: (*excitedly*) I beg to differ. I think Roosevelt was looking for an opportunity to take over the state department—he could have let an undersecretary handle the entire thing. Just look at the course of his presidency. And insofar as Roosevelt taking the role of peacemaker, I think what he enjoyed was not so much peacemaking, but rather power politics and wielding power. After all, the point of "carrying a big stick" is using power to bend others to your will! In a good cause, sure, but Roosevelt loved the "big stick" part. Loved power. Not your classic mediator by any stretch of the imagination.

Guittard: (*chuckling*) Well, that's an interesting comment, Mr. Simmons, and undoubtedly worthy of more attention than we have time to give it. We'll have to take that under advisement for the time being, as we have a lot more to cover before the bell, including Roosevelt's policy on conservation (*pausing and looking toward Mr. Walker*). Mr. Walker, do you agree with Senator La Follette's comment that Roosevelt's most outstanding contribution as president was the conservation of our natural resources? If so, why?

Walker answers, giving a brief overview of Roosevelt's policy on conservation. After his answer, Guittard supplements Walker's answer with five minutes of off-the-cuff remarks drawing on his research at Stanford for his Ph.D. For more on Frank's views on the subject, see the chapter on "Failure Not an Option."

Frank Guittard's class continues for another thirty minutes until the bell sounds. Frank closes his notebook, picks up his watch, placing it carefully back in its cushion and then in his pocket, and with the Muzzey text, quickly strides to the door and turns back to greet the students as they file out. The class spills down the stairs of Old Main and out to the walkways crisscrossing Burleson Quadrangle. The following yells can be heard from nearby Carroll Field behind Carroll Science:

B! B! B-ay!
L! L! L-o-r!
U! U! Un-i-v!
V! V! Var-si-ty!
Baylor! Baylor!
U! U! U! of B!
Bay-lor! Var-si-ty!
Ki-gar! War-hoo!
Zip-boom! Baylor U!

Hi! Ru! Ke!
Hi! Ru! Ke!
B. U.! B. U.! Varsitee!
Varsity-re! Varsity-ra!
Rah! Who! Rah!
Rah! Who! Roh!
Rah! Who! Rhe!
High-up! High-up! Varsitee!
Varsity Baylor!
Sis! Boom! Bah!

BOOK ONE

New Bedford, Ohio—Frank Guittard's Story Begins

Sample questions for the peanut gallery's consideration in this book's chapters:

How did the idea of Frank leaving Ohio for Texas come up? Why had Frank's father immigrated to Ohio from France? Wasn't Texas a rough place known for outlaws and lawlessness? Did Texas still have cowboys? What were the conditions in Texas as contrasted with those in Ohio? What kind of education did Frank receive in Ohio? Did he decide to be a teacher before leaving for Texas? How big a reader was Frank growing up, and what kinds of books did he read?

Excerpts from Frank's "Funny-Book of Student Bone-heads" from student examinations:

Question: "How did Luther defend himself at Worms?" Answer: Luther said, "I am here for no otherwise, so help me, Lord. Amen."

Question: "Who was Demosthenes?" Answer: "Demosthenes was a philosopher he went around carrying his clothes in a tub. When anyone asked him what they could do for him, he only asked them to get out of his sunlight."

Examples of Frank's favorite words and phrases from his letters:

"fine" or "finely" — "Today I am feeling finely" or "They are all fine girls."
"been seized" — "Today I have been seized with a great longing to see you."
"arduous" — "This has been the most arduous year of teaching."

CHAPTER 1

Father Disinherited in Alsace; a Decision in Ohio

We touch on many topics in this first chapter. To simplify our task, I am asking each peanut gallery member to request any topic he or she is especially interested in. But first is a mini-summary of Frank's story without elaboration, of which some details will emerge later with the peanut gallery's help. Katie and Charlie will start off with me as we begin talking through this chapter, and Finn and Miles may join in later.

Charlie: Excuse me, Pops and Katie—before we all get too far into this, can I ask about one thing?

Pops: Sure.

Charlie: Well, if it's okay with you, can we just skip over all that ancestry stuff, all the begats, the names of all the children, when they married and when they died, where they went to school, and what they did, what crops did well and what crops didn't, you know, that kind of thing, and maybe just begin with Frank Guittard leaving home and starting to struggle? When I read a biography, I just skip over the early part and then I read up until whoever reaches that sweet spot in their life where they've made it and are just writing letters to their friends who've made it and congratulating each other—that part is usually pretty boring—and then when I've finished, I box it up to take to Half Price Books.

Pops: (*smiling*) Yes, Charlie, sometimes I do the same thing to avoid getting bogged down in the weeds—don't tell anybody. Maybe our challenge for today in this first chapter is to make the early years at least thought-provoking, and then, when we get to them, do the same drill with the later years. For sure, nothing dramatic happened in Frank and Mama Josie's last two decades—the sweet spot, as you called it—but there's good news. Those years are the ones for which we have stories and anecdotes; they are about Frank in the classroom, his class routine, students' misbehavior, including answering roll and reciting for a buddy, the funny moments, and a few incidents of cheating. We can also share with the world for the first time what was going on behind closed doors at 1401 South 8th. I think you are going to like those. So how does that sound?

Charlie: Okay. That seems pretty cool.

Pops: As to those years leading up to leaving home—the part you said you skip over—including the "ancestry stuff" and the background for Frank's story as a young man, let me ask you a question. Did you like the history courses you've taken?

Charlie: Well, I did when my teacher was interesting.

Pops: Of course. What if I were to tell you the lifetimes of Joseph Guittard and Catherine Genereuse Guittard, Frank's grandparents, and Francis Joseph, Frank's father—who lived in Alsace, France—spanned the regime of Louis Philippe I, known as the King of the French? What if I added that Louis Philippe, who was a monarchist and whose own father was guillotined by French revolutionaries, had actually sympathized with the French Revolution, but opposed the executions of Louis XVI and Marie Antoinette and married Marie Antoinette's niece? What if you knew that Francis Joseph and Joseph and their families immigrated to Ohio during the last few years of Philippe's regime (1845-1848) which saw wave upon wave of dire agricultural, economic, and financial crises? Would any of that make the Guittards' ordinary lives as French citizens more intriguing to you?

Charlie: Sure would. Sounds like living in France in those days would have been very stressful, regardless of which political party one belonged to.

Katie: I can see why people would be leaving France for America. I would like to know more.

Pops: You and Charlie might also be interested to know that Philippe survived multiple assassination attempts—seven by one count—and traveled under at least three aliases while he was in exile. Also, for a number of years, to make a living, he taught mathematics, history, geography, and modern languages. He also spent several years in the US and met people like Alexander Hamilton, John Jay, and George Washington. That was all before he became king in France.

Katie: He must have had some fascinating conversations considering his divided sympathies in France between those who wanted a more liberal monarchy and those who wanted a republic and considering who he was introduced to in America—like Alexander Hamilton.

Pops: There is much more that can be said, but, unfortunately, we have to leave it there and move over to France's neighbor, Germany. Things were not going well there either, and certainly not in Hanover, Germany, where the Welhausens lived, including Mamie's father, Captain Charles Welhausen and his parents. Captain Charlie immigrated with his parents to Texas in 1846, when he was nine. At the time, Hanover was known as the Kingdom of Hanover and had its own throne. In 1837, the Gottingen Seven—seven professors including the brothers Grimm—protested the ascension of Ernest Augustus, a son of George III of Great Britain, to the Hanover's throne. Their primary objection to Ernest was that he had said he was not bound by Hanover's 1833 constitution. Although Ernest Augustus would become king, his reign was anything but tranquil, and various revolutions broke out in Germany in 1848 and 1849. In 1866, Hanover was annexed by Prussia after the Austro-Prussian War.

Katie: So, it sounds like it was a good time for the Welhausens to find their passports and get out.

Pops: Absolutely, and especially to the US, which was a functioning republic. I think all of you will be interested to know that the opposition of the Gottingen Seven to Ernest Augustus's abrogation of the Hanover constitution is credited, at least in part, with leading ultimately to the modern republic in Germany after World War II, over a hundred years later.

Katie: So, getting back to the Guittards, with all those adverse conditions in France you mentioned which had been going on for a while, what finally triggered their decisions to immigrate to the US?

Pops: The causes were likely multi-fold, starting with Francis Joseph's parents disinheriting him, apparently leaving him on his own in France with a deteriorated economy and poor prospects for employment. This would have given Francis Joseph a lot of time to knock around and see what other French citizens were doing, which he did. Francis Joseph's months or years on his own, away from priests, school, and family, were the crucial turning point for him and the Guittard family as he would decide that the US was the future for himself and his family. His family followed.

Katie: I wonder why his parents saw fit to disinherit him. That seems pretty extreme. And also whether and when they may have later buried the hatchet.

Pops: The family's original plan was for Francis Joseph to become a Catholic priest. He had been studying for the priesthood, possibly at the expense of his parents. However, something about the priesthood didn't agree with him—the priesthood is not for most people for obvious reasons—and he refused to go through with the plan to have a priest in the family. His refusal is the apparent reason for being disinherited. Francis Joseph, not long afterward upon the advice of some people he met in Paris—more about Paris later—emigrated in 1847 from France at nineteen with his older sister Mary Catherine, thus serving as the family scout to the US and ultimately Ohio. They left behind their father Joseph Guittard, mother Catherine Genereuse Gevrier, younger sister Rosine Philomene, and younger brother Francois Xavier, who all followed Francis Joseph and Mary Catherine a few years later to Ohio. Apparently, the family rift caused by Francis Joseph refusing to become a priest was patched up at some point, and it was in the interest of the entire family to follow him to the US.

Now, for a short summary of what happened after Francis Joseph arrived in Ohio as we work toward a family decision concerning Texas. Francis Joseph married Lydia Myers; she was from a Pennsylvania Dutch family. Lydia's sister, Parmelia Myers Pomerene, was married to an Ohio physician named Joel Pomerene. After working for a time as a clerk in a dry goods store in Mt. Hope, Ohio, Francis Joseph started his medical studies under Dr. Pomerene, possibly meeting Lydia through his relationship with the Pomerenes. In April 1856, after he finished his medical training with Dr. Pomerene and had opened his own medical office in New Bedford, Francis Joseph wrote Lydia, "I long to see you, press you to my heart. Life, without you, would seem a dreary waste. Write soon. Meanwhile I remain, truly yours, F.J. Guittard." In time, Francis Joseph would have both a busy medical practice and a farm requiring the assistance of a large family—his wife Lydia, five sons, and two daughters. During the Civil War, Guittard family legend had it that he helped train Union soldiers in marching. However, since he was a trained physician, he likely served primarily as a Union doctor, helping to clean and suture wounds, stop bleeding, and amputate limbs.

Over twenty years later, in 1886, because of hard times in Ohio and elsewhere in the US during what is sometimes ironically referred to as the "Gilded Age," the Guittard family decided to send Frank to Texas. The purpose was for Frank to scout the land for a possible farm and determine a good place for Francis Joseph Guittard to restart a medical practice. The quality of land and life in Texas had been touted fifty years earlier by the legendary Davey Crockett, who came to Texas but did not get out of the Alamo alive. In early 1836, two months before the climactic battle at the Alamo, Crockett wrote a letter excerpted as follows: "I must say as to what I have seen of Texas, it is the garden spot of the world. The best land and the best prospects for health I ever saw...and I do believe it is a fortune to any man to come here. There is a world of country here to settle...I have taken the oath of government [to the Republic of Texas] and have enrolled my name as a volunteer...I am rejoiced at my fate. I had rather be in my present situation than to be elected to a seat in Congress for life. I am in hopes of making a fortune yet for myself and family, bad as my prospect has been." Crockett's view of Texas as a garden spot would have been music to Lydia Guittard, who had a garden in New Bedford that had to endure Ohio winters.

While Texas was being puffed and promoted by Crockett and others as a paradise and garden spot, most of the US was suffering during the Gilded Age. The term the "Gilded Age" referred to the period following the Civil War from the late 1860s to the late 1890s. It implies that a cheaper metal has been covered over with a thin layer of gold and comes from the book *The Gilded Age: A Tale of Today* by Mark Twain and Charles Dudley Warner (1873). The book called attention to the small number of Americans who lived lives of affluence and ease as contrasted with the much greater number who struggled to live at or below the poverty line. In the 1880s, almost ten thousand strikes and lockouts occurred, and nearly 700,000 workers struck in 1886 alone. Had Francis Joseph read it, *The Gilded Age* would have been an interesting and cautionary tale. Twain and Warner's tale took as its central theme the lust of many people to speculate in land and thereby derive wealth, which represented a curse upon those infected with this passion.

As reported in the *Cincinnati Enquirer* of May 5, 1886, the historic Haymarket Riot occurred in Chicago on May 4. Following the riot, four labor organizers who had protested in favor of an eight-hour workday were tried for conspiracy to murder, convicted, and hanged. Among these organizers was Albert Parsons, a former moral philosophy student of President Rufus C. Burleson at Waco University. The widely publicized incident occurred four months before Frank left for Texas. The case against Parsons was weak, but cooler heads did not prevail. When he was charged, he declined on principle to admit guilt and took the opportunity to justify his political and economic positions, explaining why he was an anarchist. He also declined to appeal his case, choosing to stand on principle. We will come back to the subject of hard times and workers' plight when we address the state of the national economy in the 1890s when Frank dropped out of Baylor to find employment.

Texas was still a wild place in the mid-1880s; the Civil War and Reconstruction period had ended by law only sixteen years before Frank left Ohio. Though long trail drives of herds from Texas to Kansas became a thing of the recent past, towns along the cattle trails were still rambunctious, semi-lawless destinations. Dime novels featured tall tales about true Texas outlaws like John Wesley Hardin and Sam Bass. On the other hand, newspaper readers in Ohio were able to read stories about the quality of life in Texas designed to lure readers into resettling in the relatively new state. Frank and his parents ultimately decided for him to go to Texas and investigate whether Texas offered more to the Guittard family than staying put in New Bedford.

So that's the brief summary. How about giving me some feedback on the topics you want me to include?

Charlie: I want to know about those outlaws and cowboys, but also what was wrong with Ohio, and why were people leaving for Texas?

Finn: Outlaws. John Wesley Hardin. Sam Bass. And what the heck happened to the cowboys?

Katie: I'm interested in Mrs. Guittard and her garden. I'm reading *Little Women* at school. Did she ever read *Little Women*?

Pops: Miles?

Miles: I want to know more about Francis Joseph coming to America and his medical practice. Since he was French, how could he understand those medical books? Weren't they written in English?

Katie: And I would like to know about Francis Joseph being disinherited and how he came to be a Methodist.

Pops: Okay. We'll get to all of that. But first, let's start with the beginning of the Guittards in America, which means we have to get them over to America from Alsace. Francis Joseph Guittard, the father of Francis Gevrier Guittard, was born at Montreux Vieux in the Haut-Rhin department of Alsace, France, on September 27, 1828, to a saddle maker—and later deputy mayor—and his wife. Alsace is a largely Roman Catholic region where a mixture of the French language—which predominated—and Alsatian language, a German dialect. Francis Joseph attended school at Mulhouse in Alsace in preparation for the priesthood.

Alsace is on France's northern border adjoining Germany and on the west bank of the upper Rhine. Although he was French, young Francis Joseph had learned some German due to spending time at the home of a German farmer. Having abandoned any intent he may have had to go into the priesthood, he was drafted into the French army and served out his term of conscription. After that, Francis Joseph went to Paris and reportedly supported himself in part as a wine taster. In Paris, he met certain devout church people who influenced him to go to America because of France's poor economic conditions and the uncertainty of living next to the Germans. Lack of work, housing shortages, and hunger led many French citizens to leave Alsace, some for Paris, others for various locations in the United States.

On the voyage across the Atlantic, Francis Joseph began to learn English. After he arrived in America in 1847, he settled at Mount Hope, Holmes County, Ohio. While at Mount Hope, he worked for a George W. Slutz who was engaged in the dry goods business. Around 1854, he began his study of medicine with Dr. Joel Pomerene at Mount Hope, which he continued until the day Pomerene died. Then, around 1855, he moved to New Bedford, Coshocton County, Ohio, where he would practice medicine until shortly before his death in 1902. Francis Joseph's marriage to Lydia Myers, daughter of George and Sarah Myers of Berlin, Ohio, occurred on October 2, 1856. Little is known about Lydia other than that she was Dr. Pomerene's sister-in-law, had literary tastes, and provided a pleasant and comfortable home for her large family.

Located on the north side of New Bedford, the Guittard home was a large two-story wooden building, the ground surrounding it planted with trees including mountain ash, Scotch fir, white pine, Arborvitae, and spruce. Frank recalled that the home was plainly but amply furnished and supplied with papers, periodicals, and a library of carefully selected books to read, as well as an organ, and later a piano. In the US, Francis Joseph joined the Methodist church and remained an active Methodist for the rest of his life. The Guittard family household, as a part of its routine, maintained prayer times and devotionals. The Methodist Episcopal Church split into two parts at the time of the Civil War, the northern part known for supporting the radical Republicans and its hard line toward the South. We don't know exactly where Francis Joseph stood on the Civil War. Still, we believe he would have been anti-slavery and pro-Union, as Ohio was a free state and he was a physician to the Union army and a northern Methodist.

Charlie: Pops, can you tell us more about Francis Joseph and life in New Bedford? And did Frank Guittard play a musical instrument? It seems that many later generation Guittards could play them.

Pops: All right, we'll get to that. Francis Joseph was academically gifted and an unusually deliberate and contemplative person. He did not complete his medical education and receive his degrees until considerably after starting his practice, graduating from the Charity Hospital Medical College in 1868 and the medical department of the University of Wooster in 1871, both located in Cleveland, Ohio.

He was a lifelong learner whose curiosity would be equaled only by that of his son, Frank Guittard, decades later. Francis Joseph worked long hours as a physician-farmer to support his large family and had little time to play or relax other than working in his garden, reading, or playing around on one of those old horns we will mention later.

When his younger sister Rosine, who had followed him to the United States, announced her intention to get married, he advised her with due gravitas: "You are going to make a step that decides much [of] the current of a person's life, but I will do you the justice of believing that you have reflected well upon it, as one ought not to become engaged without deliberation..."

Having an excellent small library, he was undoubtedly torn between the time required for his exhausting medical practice and the time he needed for mental contemplation and stimulation. These tendencies he passed on to his son Frank. In 1896, he wrote Rosine: "Mrs. Harbaugh sends you her respects and her regards...You would know them, well, they are people of simple life and manners, and, as we say at our place, 'stout folks.' Their company is agreeable enough. But you know well their thoughts do not stray off from outside the circle of the condition of life for the farmers. When I am tired of the discussion of the weather, the working of the crops, the horses, cattle and chickens...I...go off to find the company of my books and journals...I do not have any desire to go into crowds and meetings of people. I like much better the tranquility of home."

Francis Joseph was also a skilled extemporaneous speaker and often served as chair for July 4th celebrations. He invariably read the Declaration of Independence in addition to his other duties as chair. Regarding the July 4, 1885 celebration he organized for New Bedford, he wrote his eldest daughter Rosalie that five bands from nearby communities took part, coming in from different roads and being met by red-sashed mounted marshals who escorted them to Shauwecker's Woods, the place selected for the celebration. Francis Joseph noted that "The strains of music breaking out upon the ear simultaneously from all the points of the compass, made an exceedingly animated and stirring scene. After all the bands were in, the line of march for the grove was taken with colors in front followed by the six bands one after the other, when the first band dropped the strain the next one took it up...the Bedford Choir sang a piece...Dr. E. Luke read the Declaration of Independence."

Katie: Pops, I have to ask, are we about to learn about Frank Guittard and the Guittards' home life? And did Frank like doing homework?

Pops: Katie, Francis "Frank" Gevrier Guittard was born in New Bedford, Ohio, on January 7, 1867, during the administration of President Andrew Johnson. Frank shared the same birthday as President Millard Fillmore, born in 1800. 1867 also saw the births of celebrated figures Madame Curie, Wilbur Wright, Arturo Toscanini, Florence Ziegfeld, Jr., and William "Pudge" Heffelfinger. Frank was the middle child of seven surviving children, the oldest sibling ten years older, and the youngest nine years younger. An older brother and a younger brother became physicians like their father. Frank's parents encouraged him, his brothers, and sisters to read Shakespeare, Milton, Bunyan, and Gibbon. Frank additionally read the periodicals the *Youths' Companion* and the *Cincinnati Inquirer* which were available in the home. He especially liked biography. Because his father was away from home most of the time seeing patients, Frank's early training came primarily from his mother. One of his most cherished memories was that of his mother teaching him at his bedside the simple prayer, "Now I lay me down to sleep."

The two-story wooden Guittard home often vibrated with music from five boys and two girls, all of whom liked to sing. The Guittard organ was the first in the community. Frank's oldest sister, Mary Catherine, especially liked music and took organ lessons from a teacher who lived in the Guittard household and came to be regarded as a family member. The Guittards would gather around the organ or piano and sing hymns and college songs. Neighboring boys and girls would also come over and join these family entertainments. In addition, social life in that small community included the young people's parties where they played games like forfeits. Occasionally there was a taffy pulling, but the highlight of the social season was the tacky party when each couple tried to best the other couples in dressing up in ridiculous clothing. The older couples among the young people sometimes had a dance and joined in with the married people for a polka, a schottische waltz, a Virginia reel, or a square dance. Frank recalled these times fondly in his later years, adding that "there were, of course, some pious people who held to that idea that dancing in any form was one of the cardinal sins, and their social pleasures were of a more sedate type, such as discussion of the latest scandal." Frank attended Sunday school and sang in the church choir. The choir practices were usually held in the homes of choir members, and Frank was impressed by the effect they had in drawing minds and hearts together. Frank later recalled that the results of the choir meetings were "not unusual and was due doubtless to the emotional influence of music."

Frank's school days began in his seventh year, and he attended the village school for six to eight months each year. He noted that his teachers could be classified as good, bad, and indifferent. He remembered with pleasant feelings one of his first teachers who gave him a prize for the highest number of head marks given to the top students in spelling class. Another teacher he remembered with loathing gave Frank a severe flogging for pushing a little girl playmate into the creek. In Frank's mind, this punishment was overly harsh considering that the water was only a couple of inches deep, and he had already been pushed in several times himself. Corporal punishment was a given in country schools in the nineteenth century, at least where young men and boys were concerned. Edward Eggleston, who drew upon his brother's experiences teaching in Indiana during the same period that Frank received the severe flogging, captures in *The Hoosier Schoolmaster* the prevalent attitude toward flogging, thrashing, or licking. One of the book's characters tells the schoolmaster, "Boys won't l'arn 'less you thrash 'em, says I...Lay it on good is what I says to a master...Don't do no harm. Lickin' and l'arnin' goes together. No lickin' no l'arning', says I. Lickin' and l'arnin,' lickin' and l'arnin', is the good ole way." It often fell to a new teacher to lick or whip the toughest boy in the country school to establish order and achieve respect from the class. In *The Hoosier Schoolmaster*, a tough student who claims he had thrashed the last master tells the new master Ralph Hartsook, "I could whip you in an inch of your life with my left hand, and never half try." There is also an amusing chapter in which Hartsook dramatically competes in a spell-down with the students in his class while dreading his inevitable loss of prestige if he should be easily spelled down.

Despite his aptitude for reading and learning, Frank disliked school until he was fourteen. That year a young teacher took a particular interest in him and persuaded Frank "to go to work in earnest"—a phrase which would become second nature for Frank and would be reprised almost fifty years later when he received his Ph.D. from Stanford and made it clear that he didn't intend to retire. After that young teacher's taking an interest in Frank, Frank didn't miss a single day of school and made the best record for behavior and study for any session that he attended. Frank said he owed much to this teacher, having lost count of the floggings received from his predecessors. His favorite studies were history, geography, and grammar.

By 1884, when he was in his seventeenth year, and Presidents Grant, Hayes, Garfield, and Arthur had come and gone, Frank made what turned out to be a momentous decision: he left the public school and decided to try teaching. When he obtained his teacher's certificate, he secured a teaching assignment at the Pleasant Hall School in Holmes County, and for three months had his first taste of professional accomplishment. He would later report: "I was quite elated over my success in getting a certificate from the Board of Examiners and not long afterwards succeeded in making a Board of Trustees believe I could manage their school...My first term [as teacher] gave me reason to think I could succeed as a teacher." Frank also recorded that in that district, arithmetic was thought to be the only path to success in life, so he spent most of his time teaching arithmetic. At the end of his first term teaching, he decided to prepare himself for a better position and, during the summer of 1885, he attended Mount Union College in Alliance, Ohio.

During the winter of 1885-1886, Frank remained at home working on the sixty-acre family farm, and in the summer of 1886, he attended the Teacher's Institute at Millersburg, Ohio. Throughout the winter of 1885-1886 and the following summer, Frank held to his ambition of obtaining a college education as he took his turn managing the farm, his two older brothers having already left home. His oldest brother Alwin had already left for medical school and then started a practice in a neighboring town; the other brother, Victor, had left to prepare himself for a position as a railroad station agent. On the farm, Frank made some improvements by draining a portion of the lowlands not suitable for farming and introducing rotation for crops' fertilization. He also initiated a more practical breed of cattle for home dairy purposes, improved a breed of hogs, and obtained a good team of horses along with an acceptable buggy horse for his father. As a result of doing farm work, he became sturdy physically, measuring five feet eleven inches in height and weighing 150 pounds. His hair was dark brown, nearly black; his face was of an oval type, but not very full; his eyes were light blue, and he had a straight nose and a fair complexion. Frank took a break from farm work at noontimes to play checkers—a game some say is thousands of years old—and also play around on some old brass horns, including a cornet and alto and tenor horns. He was fascinated by the harmony that these antiquated horns could produce. The horns were probably relics of those militia and community bands in Ohio that were common during the Civil War. Francis Joseph had probably collected, and could play, these old horns himself, an interest he passed down to Frank and his son Clarence, who played French horn in high school and college. Clarence would pass that interest in horn-playing on to his son Charles (Sousaphone and trombone), who passed it to his son Jim (trombone).

Throughout the summer of 1886, Frank was seized with a restlessness to get his higher education back on track and anxiously awaited his turn to go to college following his two older brothers. He had done all he could to distract himself with newspapers, books, magazines, and games. He told his father and mother he wanted to return to Mount Union College the next year to continue his education, as he had been out of high school for two years as of the summer of 1886. However, Frank came to a painful realization that summer: although his father had been able to send his two older brothers Alwin and Victor and his older sister to good schools, he could not help Frank. Frank's future would now depend solely on himself, as federal loans and grants did not exist in that day. Frank was disappointed and upset, but he began to form a plan.

At this time, many boys Frank's age were going to Kansas, Nebraska and other western states. Around that time, a resident of Chester, Tyler County, Texas, wrote a letter to the *Cincinnati Inquirer* giving an enthusiastic account of the local possibilities for a practicing physician and the opportunity to invest in cheap land. The Guittards discussed the letter, and Frank suggested that he go to Texas, scout the land, and report back. Francis Joseph had already been corresponding with a friend in Texas regarding Texas land. Francis Joseph had grown weary of the unrelenting demands on a country doctor, especially riding on horseback to see patients whatever the weather. Frank's mother wanted to live where there would be no more long, sick winters with seasonal illnesses and confinement to the house. She loved to work in her garden and desired a milder climate.

Though Francis Joseph had a large and busy country medical practice in a cold northern state, it is not surprising that he had grown tired of it. His life was a hard one, especially in winter. At this time of year, there was much pneumonia and diphtheria with no modern remedies for treatment. He would sometimes start out on horseback to answer a call and would not be back for days. Often, when he would visit a patient, other calls had to be made as well. In those days, a physician in desperate cases had to be a nurse as well as a doctor. The entire Guittard family would often be waked from sleep by a shout and hello from a rider on horseback. The rider's cries often meant that his pregnant wife was in distress, it not mattering to the rider how many children had already appeared in the family. The husband was just as insistent that the doctor make the greatest haste possible. Usually, Frank or one of his brothers saddled the horse while their father assembled his equipment. All preparations having been made, the husband and doctor would start off at high speed, the sounds of hoof beats and mud splashes being heard thereafter in the distance. Sometimes, after a long ride home the morning after a call the night before, Francis Joseph would appear with his long beard white from his frozen breath. Occasionally, Frank would accompany his father on a house call. Though Francis Joseph had a large and busy country practice, Frank observed first-hand the hardships of a country physician. Although Francis Joseph had substantial accounts receivable for his services owed him by his patients which were never collected, he never refused a call from a needy patient.

Texas's broad allure to Ohio residents like Francis Joseph arose from several factors. The city of Cincinnati and its citizens had bonded with Texas in connection with Sam Houston's defeat of Santa Anna at the Battle of San Jacinto in 1836, fifty years before Frank took the train to Texas. To support Texas's revolt against Mexican authority, Cincinnati citizens had raised funds to purchase two cannons for shipment to Texas. The Ohioans delivered the cannons to Galveston Island, where they were presented to Texas forces by the twin daughters of a physician moving to Texas. The two cannons were named the "Twin Sisters," and thus, there were two sets of twins in the presentation. The guns reached General Sam Houston's forces ten days before the battle of San Jacinto and were used to shoot at the Mexican soldiers to confuse them. However, because the Texans had no proper cannonballs, the cannons' gunners had to make do with horseshoes, broken glass, and musket balls.

Then, too, several publications vigorously promoted the positive aspects of settling in Texas; these included William Kennedy's *Texas: The Rise, Progress, and Prospects of the Republic of Texas* (1841) and *Burke's Texas Almanac and The Immigrant's Handbook 1883,* published in Houston, Texas. *Burke's Texas Almanac* contained the kind of information business owners and other residents of the Lone Star State wanted publicized to attract immigrants to Texas, including: "[Texas is] by far the largest State in the Union...larger than France or Great Britain...The eastern portion of the State...is heavily timbered, and from here are drawn nearly all the immense supplies of pine lumber required in the prairie portions of the State...The natural resources [include] vast deposits of iron ore of excellent quality, and extensive beds of lignite. Large crops of cotton, corn, and other grains are grown in its valleys, and its lands are noted for the production of fruits and vegetables. It is generally well watered by streams and springs...On the score of health, Texas will compare favorably with the healthiest portions of the United States.

Consumption—that dreaded disease of the eastern and some of the northern States—is almost unknown here, at least very few, if any cases have originated here, but on the contrary, afflicted persons from other parts have been much benefited in health by residence in Texas. ... [As to agriculture] Nature has been extremely lavish in making Texas one of the most varied in her products of all the States in the Union. Such is the adaptation of her soil and climate to the production of cotton—ranking in staple the finest in the world's markets—that one-fifth of her territory could produce an annual crop greater than is now gathered from all the cotton fields on the globe."

Burke's Almanac also detailed the crops of peaches, grapes, pears, apples, figs, wheat, and corn grown in certain sections in Texas and promoted Sam Houston Normal Institute in Huntsville where Frank Guittard would spend at least a year between 1887 and 1888. The *Almanac* advised prospective immigrants: "Among the advantages that Texas offers to immigrants is a most delightful and salubrious climate. It is true that in some localities along our rivers near the coast in wet years, people are occasionally subject to chills and fevers, but these readily yield to ordinary treatment. Rarely do we have pneumonia and lung diseases, though hundreds, if not thousands, afflicted with pulmonary complaints have here found restored health and long life. More, and more, Texas is becoming a health resort for invalids from northern climes. Formerly we were liable to visitations of yellow fever in our coast cities, but of late years an effective quarantine has restricted the fatal epidemic to very narrow limits, and no fears are now entertained of its general prevalence."

Frank would have been especially interested in Texas's colleges and railroad build-out, especially the connections between Ohio and the Lone Star State. As to educational opportunities, *Burke's Texas Almanac* affirmed: "For higher education our State University will soon be organized and open for instruction, and we have our Agricultural and Mechanical College. Then, in all the cities and larger villages, there are high schools and academies and every leading denomination of Christians has church schools for both sexes." Then, as to the crucial issue of employment opportunity: "Texas offers remunerative employment to all who seek homes in her borders. Agriculture is our leading business. Let a family desiring work on a farm arrive almost anywhere in Texas, and they need not remain unemployed twenty-four hours...There is also room in Texas for those in the learned professions—lawyers, doctors, dentists, teachers, preachers, etc., albeit there is not so urgent a demand for men of these classes as there is for laborers on the farm, in the shops and on the ranches, but Texas is an imperial State, that still offers desirable homes to the millions." The almanac writer concluded that residents of other states should consider moving to Texas: "Our patrons will learn that since the issue of our last Annual, Texas has largely increased in population and wealth. The immigration to the State during the past twelve months has exceeded by many thousands that of any former year. New towns are springing into existence as if by magic, throughout this vast domain. Every branch of industry is in a thriving condition. No inhabitant willing and able to work need remain poor." In addition to opportunities for obtaining education, the following language would have drawn Frank's interest, the almanac concluding: "According to the Chicago Railway Age, the total construction of railroads in the United States, for the first six months of the year, was 3,480 miles. Of this number, 734 were in Texas. The state ranking next to Texas was Colorado with 253 miles. In Texas the railroad boom still continues."

Finn: I'm curious why, if Texas was this great, all the people from the cold northern states weren't flocking to Texas. What was holding them back?

Pops: I'm not sure I can answer that question, except that for a family to pull up stakes and move from Ohio or from any state to Texas would have been a huge deal. Most people right down to today don't seem to make big changes unless they absolutely have no choice or are almost guaranteed to be better off. Texas did historically have some detractors, including British lawyer Nicholas Maillard who made several trips to Texas during the era of the Republic of Texas (1836-1845). Maillard asserted that Texas was "filled with habitual liars, drunkards, blasphemers and slanderers, sanguinary gamesters and cold-blooded assassins; with idleness and sluggish indolence, two vices for which the Texans are already proverbial; with pride, engendered by ignorance and supported by fraud." In an 1849 account of his travels through Texas, German scientist Ferdinand von Roemer claimed that the early settlers of Texas had included "the most degraded riff-raff, adventurers, gamblers, swindlers and murderers—the scum not only of the United States but of all nations." There was one anonymous detractor in Texas the year after Texas gained independence from Mexico who strongly cautioned visitors to be careful about what they eat in Texas, as "fish in the heat of summer are evidently unwholesome" and that the effect of peaches on the system tended to bring on "bilious attacks." Finally, this detractor advised settlers to settle west of the Brazos—which runs through Waco—preferably on the Colorado or Guadalupe.

Then too, when Frank left home, Texas was still trying to overcome its reputation as the most lawless of all the states. One authority noted that "For almost three decades after joining the Union in 1845...Texas became a magnet for fugitives from every other part of the country...towns and ranches were terrorized by packs of armed thugs who broke laws with impunity because there was no one to stop them." Another claimed "Texas had within its borders eight thousand known outlaws, most of them fugitives from other states." The solution in 1874 was to reorganize the Texas Rangers with the appointment of Captain Leander H. McNelly, whose task was "eliminating the threat of outlaws—murderers, mercenary fighters, rapists, and most especially, rustlers, who were decimating the herds of honest ranchers."

So, against all of the generally rosy description of life in Texas, along with some negative reports, let's go back to Charlie's question—how were things back in Ohio in the late 1880s, and what were Francis Joseph, Lydia, Frank, and the rest of the Ohio Guittards reading in the *Cincinnati Enquirer* about conditions close to home? To begin with, on April 6, 1886, Ohio experienced in Sandusky—97.5 miles from New Bedford—a "super snowstorm" according to the National Weather Service. The storm represented a massive late-season weather event impacting the entire state. This storm could not have been encouraging to someone in Ohio or Michigan thinking about moving to a warmer climate. The Ohio employment picture was even grimmer for a nineteen-year-old like Frank Guittard. The ads in the *Cincinnati Enquirer* of men looking for work were not encouraging. Here are a few examples from the January 1, 1886 issue: "WORK—inside or out, by a young man, stout married man; would sooner work cheap than be idle." "WORK—by a sober, industrious man to carry coal and work about house for board and washing." "WORK—in a store by a young man who is willing to do anything." And the want ads in the same issue of the *Enquirer* were similarly depressing: "BOYS—five, to bunch kindling." "BARBER—boy with some experience preferred; must know how to shave." "MAGICIAN—must have first-class apparatus for...a show going south." "STONE-MASONS—and cutters, eight or ten good ones." As to available land for purchase, on February 20, 1886, this ad appeared in the *Enquirer*: "LAND—Four hundred acres of the richest land in Texas, all tillable, well-watered; three miles from Dickerson's Station, on Galveston and Houston Railroad."

<u>Charlie</u>: Finn and I would like to hear more about those unemployed cowboys, Sam Bass and John Wesley Hardin.

<u>Pops</u>: Yes, with those guys, I'm reminded of that line, "Live fast, die young, and leave a good-looking corpse." As we've already discussed, in the popular literature at least, Texas had secured the reputation of being a lawless territory. Outlaws like Bass, Hardin, Bill Longley, and others like them, sometimes Confederate army deserters, often hid from the law in wooded thickets outside towns, inflicting their depredations on innocent citizens at their leisure. Bass, one of the worst, inspired an anonymous poet to compose a poem that included the following lines:

> Sam Bass was born in Indiana--'twas his native home.
> And at the age of seventeen young Sam began to roam.
> Sam first came out to Texas a cowboy for to be,
> A kinder hearted fellow you seldom ever see...
> Sam used to coin the money and spent it just as free,

He always drank good whiskey, wherever he might be.
Sam met his fate at Round Rock, July 21,
They pierced poor Sam with rifle balls and emptied out his purse.

And one other thing—there were those lethal feuds among families living in communities—Frank's parents may have wondered, wasn't there a danger to Frank of getting between two feuding families and getting peppered with buckshot? The bloody Sutton-Taylor feud produced litigation until 1899, thirteen years after Frank arrived in Texas. And what about those vigilantes and vigilance committees that hanged suspected horse thieves in the 1870s? Sometimes ordinary citizens had to hire their own lawmen called regulators.

Finn: So, what's the answer? Was Frank at risk at all? Maybe ordinary citizens could just hire their own lawmen like those regulators in that movie *Missouri Breaks*.

Pops: I wouldn't be surprised about there possibly being regulators in Texas, but I really don't know. I do know that the activities of feuding families and the vigilantes—inevitable in the aftermath of the Civil War—were mostly wound down by Frank's trip to Texas. However, as will be clear later—especially in connection with the incidents in Waco involving W.C. Brann and his enemies—there were still many Texans who thought no more of strapping on a pistol than attaching a pocket watch to a vest. Numerous deadly feuds in Texas continued through the 1890s, although not on the same scale as in the 1870s. Likely going armed in Texas and in the South decades after the Civil War was a direct consequence of post-Reconstruction lawlessness. Sam Bass's legend lived on in Waco and elsewhere, even into the twentieth century. Bass had been in Waco the week before the bloody gunfight with Texas Rangers at Round Rock, succumbing to his wounds two days later on his twenty-seventh birthday in 1878. Bass proved that all it took in the 1870s to become a Texas legend was to rob banks and trains, demonstrate proficiency with a pistol, shoot a lot of people, die before reaching the age of thirty, and have a catchy ballad written about him.

Charlie: You were going to tell us more about Texas cowboys.

Pops: So, let's talk a little about cowboys' way of earning a living in September of 1886 when Frank came to Texas. Although cattle was still an essential agricultural industry, large trail drives and the need for cowboys to drive the cows to northern railheads had become a thing of the past. The cattle industry had suffered greatly during the winter of 1886-1887, which saw hundreds of thousands of cattle starve because of overgrazing. But more importantly, trail drives were disappearing because of barbed wire fencing interfering with driving cattle up the

Chisholm and other cattle trails and because of increased shipping of cattle to northern locations by rail, including by rail from Waco.

However, the mythology of Texas cowboys still intrigued northerners who read about them in dime westerns that featured tales of capture and rescue, disguise and revelation, pursuit and escape, and card games generally ending in gun-play. In Texas, men from many walks of life commonly wore cowboy hats, vests, boots, and often pistols as insurance against confrontation with a lawbreaker, to protect the wearer's honor, or defend his women-folk. Lee Rutland Scarborough, later an Erisophian Society brother of Frank Guittard at Baylor University, grew up on a ranch and was a trail-tested cowboy as late as 1886. Later, Scarborough would attend Baylor and ultimately become president of Southwestern Baptist Theological Seminary in Fort Worth. Don't ask me whether he wore a pistol in his days as a cowboy because I don't know. Frank himself enjoyed wearing a western-style Stetson and boots at least as late as the late 1890s, even keeping a horse in Waco after returning to teach at Baylor. However, there is no evidence he ever owned a pair of leather chaps, bandanna, leather gloves, spurs, or sturdy jeans of the kind cowboys required. He did pick up a Colt Model 1860 Army Revolver, which his grandchildren discovered in the attic at 1401 South 8th, but there is no evidence he was ever required to use it.

But let's go back for a moment to that other prominent Texas outlaw, John Wesley Hardin, killer son of a Methodist preacher. Hardin was a skillful practitioner of the road agent spin of his pistols, by which he supposedly got the drop on Wild Bill Hickok himself. However, in 1886, he was still serving time at Huntsville State Penitentiary; his subsequent history and eventual fate we will mention later. Moreover, we'll get to Hardin again when we talk about Frank's game plan.

Finn: Okay, Bass was dead and Hardin was in jail in 1886, but we know Frank still caught the train to Texas. How did that come about?

Pops: So how did Frank happen to come to Texas when it was such a wide-open place? Well, on September 20, 1886, Francis Joseph wrote a letter of introduction for Frank to a Reverend Canon of Chester, Texas: "Dear Sir: These lines will be presented to you by my son, Frank G. Guittard, who is visiting in your neighborhood. Would it be presuming too much to ask you to befriend him? Any attentions he may be the recipient of will be duly appreciated and gratefully remembered. His object is to become acquainted with that part of the country, and, if he can, find some employment to turn his hand to, [that] he may remain in your neighborhood for some time. May the peace and good will signified in that grand and glorious angelic proclamation of 2000 years ago...be yours."

Armed with this letter and supplied with lunches packed by his mother, Frank said farewell to his mother, brothers, and sisters, not knowing he would never see his mother again. He expected to spend a year or more in Texas but was taken aback by his mother's parting words that she would be glad to hear that he had done something of note in Texas. Frank took this to mean that she thought he was leaving for good and expected him to make Texas his future home. Since he had understood the original purpose of the trip was to do a survey and report back, her message was confusing and upsetting when he was already feeling anxious about when he might return to Ohio. Nevertheless, he put up a bold front to hide his heartache and set out with his father for the railroad station in Coshocton, twelve miles away, where he intended to board the Pennsylvania Railroad. If a horse reportedly can walk at 3-4 miles per hour and trot at 8-10 miles per hour, Frank's ride in a horse-drawn buggy with his father at maybe 6 to 7 miles per hour would have taken about two hours. Two hours would have provided Frank and his father time to share thoughts and feelings regarding this momentous leave-taking destined to change the lives of both men, Frank especially.

Katie: I would have liked to know what they said to each other on their ride to the station in Coshocton.

Pops: So, what could Frank and his father have chatted about on the way to the railroad station? Because almost forty years had passed since Francis Joseph at the same age had embarked on his own life-changing voyage to the United States, one cannot help but wonder whether father or son would have brought up the elder Guittard's trip to a strange new land when he was the same age. There is nothing from which to draw a firm conclusion here. Still, it appears, given the Guittard men's apparent resistance to expression of emotions—and neither was loquacious under normal circumstances, that the subject of Francis Joseph's trip from France likely never came up. If it had, Frank, always a preserver of history, would have recorded it.

But there were many other topics Frank and his father could have talked about. Perhaps most of them they had already been exhausted back home in New Bedford in the months, weeks, and days leading up to the trip. For example, would he need to buy a horse and saddle to get around, and how soon? How much would Francis Joseph be willing to pay per acre for a farm, and how many acres did he think he might want? What crops would he be interested in growing? How far from a town should a farm be? How many people live in the community surrounding any particular farm, and how far away would the nearest doctor be? How about the average rainfall and average temperature? What flowers and other plants fared well in Texas? If Francis Joseph's medical practice turned up in Ohio, might Frank return to Ohio and receive assistance with college expenses? Unfortunately, Frank left no record of his last conversation with his father before boarding the train.

Soon after saying goodbye to his father at the station, Frank was surprised to meet several neighborhood boys who were going to Kansas, all of whom were land prospectors like himself. One of these, Jake Lower, was his traveling companion as far as St. Louis. On the train, these young adventurer-travelers improvised beds in the day coach by pushing seats together and using their bags as pillows. Jake Lower's interest in Kansas land could have stemmed from the Homestead Act of 1862, which for a time made cheap land available and drew a lot of attention to Kansas.

Finn: One last question. Early on you mentioned "Pudge" Heffelfinger as a famous person born the same year as Frank. Who was that?

Pops: Heffelfinger is regarded as the first professional football player in America. He was a three-time All-American guard at Yale who played from 1888 to 1891. At Yale, he was 6'3" and weighed 196 pounds. He died in 1954 at the age of eighty-six.

Katie, as to your questions, I would have to believe that Frank's mother and sisters, who all loved to read, would have read *Little Women* by Louisa Mae Alcott. It was first published in the late 1860s and continues to be an important novel that women and girls love. It has been made into a movie several times. I think I sent you a copy of the book for your birthday several years ago.

Katie: I remember; I read it, Pops. What's next?

Pops: Next we talk about Frank's college days before Baylor, and you'll hear about how Frank enjoyed the Christmas program at the Huntsville penitentiary chapel put on by the inmates.

CHAPTER 2

Frank's Early Schooling; College Days Before Baylor

This chapter concerns Frank's student experiences in high school and his earliest attempts at higher education after graduating from high school: Mount Union College in Alliance, Ohio; the Teacher Institute at Millersburg, Ohio; and Sam Houston Normal School in Huntsville, Texas. These last two were training schools for teachers and not colleges or universities. Charlie says he is interested in this topic.

Pops: So, Charlie, you have a question or two about Frank's endeavors for education before Baylor?

Charlie: Yes, but I'm also interested in his high school days. Frank must have really sailed through high school. After all, he had to be a good student to eventually earn a Ph.D.

Pops: He was a good student, but school wasn't always pleasant for him. Up until the time he was twelve or thirteen, his teachers didn't think his behavior was acceptable, and he said he lost count of the floggings he deserved, as well as those he did not deserve. He could still remember at twenty-seven some of those floggings. But something good eventually happened. He had one teacher who was kind and motivated him to go to work on his studies in earnest. At the close of the term in this teacher's class, Frank noted in his 1894 autobiography: "I remember...I could say that I had not missed a day of school and that I had made the best record for behavior and study of any previous session that I had attended."

Charlie: When did Frank get out of high school? What did he do then?

Pops: When Frank finished high school in 1884, he decided he would try teaching, so he obtained his teaching certificate in Ohio and taught arithmetic for a while. Frank liked teaching and resolved to prepare himself for a better teaching job. The next year, he attended the summer session at Mount Union College in Alliance, Ohio.

Charlie: Was that a good college?

Pops: It's hard to say, but in the 1870s, it was the second-largest college in Ohio, second only to Oberlin. It had a commercial department and a museum. The museum contained an Egyptian mummy, a gorilla, and other popular oddities. Perhaps the mummy and the gorilla helped draw parents and their kids to visit the school.

Charlie: I would have liked to have seen that mummy. Everybody's seen a gorilla. They didn't have anything that cool at my school. Didn't he go back to Mount Union in the fall?

Pops: No, he did not go back to school anywhere until the summer of 1886, when he spent one month at the Teacher's Institute at Millersburg, Ohio. That was it for Frank's further education until after he arrived in Texas and enrolled at Sam Houston Normal School in Huntsville. He studied there from the fall of 1887 through December 1888. Sam Houston Normal is considered the first state-run normal school in the southwestern US.

Charlie: What's a "normal" school?

Pops: "Normal" schools taught high school graduates what they needed to know to teach students in the primary grades according to normal teaching standards and appropriate curriculum. For the 1887-1888 school year, Frank had saved enough money teaching in small schools to attend Sam Houston Normal, and while he was there, he reached his twenty-first birthday. His birthday inspired him to write home on January 7, 1888:

> Today is my twenty-first birthday, so I thought I could do nothing better than write home. Like Al and Vic, I don't happen to be home at the [moment]. Although it is an important day..., I almost forgot about it until I began writing a letter and put down the date. The holidays are past, and everything is moving along smoothly again...Xmas [sic] is celebrated differently here from what it is at home; if it were not for the Xmas [sic] trees it would be more like the Fourth of July. I don't believe I ever heard such a shooting of crackers, rockets, Roman candles, etc. as they had Christmas Eve, Monday, and Mon. night. Even Sunday the pop, pop by fits and starts could be heard now and then...
>
> In Sunday school, one of the little boys happened to shoot off a firecracker, accidentally, of course...New Year's Day passed off like any other day. I went to an entertainment in the Penitentiary chapel. It was good, especially the music. A fine young man played

> the piano; by inquiring I found out that he was a graduate from some eastern college and having a life sentence. The manager, a convict as well as all who took part in [the program], was formerly...a professor in some college...

Charlie: Pops, what would a college professor be doing in the pen?

Pops: Well, we don't know. Maybe he was desperate for money and stole somebody's watch and was caught trying to pawn it. Money was tight in those days. Here's the rest of Frank's letter:

> Nearly all of the students who left since the holidays are taking themselves through on their own means and...this gives out sometimes... The way the course is arranged a great deal is lost by not taking the whole year as each student is expected to go the whole year and the course is arranged accordingly, and only those that do get [teaching] certificates. I want to take the whole year if possible. Like some of the rest I will soon scratch the bottom of the pan; I will need some money next month, in all about fifty dollars perhaps more, perhaps not as much...This may come at a bad time since you have had to pay off that old claim but if I can go the whole of the year, I think I can get along myself awhile again...
>
> How are you all standing the winter? Does Mother still wish to move to the sunny south? I will send you some circulars soon that may interest you...Respectfully, F.G. Guittard

Frank signed up for the two-year program but may not have finished it. However, he was busy accumulating the funds to enroll at a college somewhere. Between 1888 and 1890, he taught for twenty-three months and in at least six schools in different small Texas towns.

Charlie: Wow! He would have been moving nearly all the time and sending home his new addresses.

Pops: I'm sure he was accustomed to traveling light and could put all his stuff in one or two bags he could walk on the train with.

Charlie: Couldn't he take the bus?

Pops: Nope; a bus was a kind of automobile, and even automobiles were not around until the early twentieth century.

Charlie: So, Frank really liked to read?

Pops: Yes, indeed. Reading was a large part of his life from an early age. We will focus on that in the coming chapter and go at it from several directions—from Shakespeare to dime novels to comic strips.

CHAPTER 3

A Bookworm's Mind: Influences, Interests, & Books

Dear Reader, if you are asking yourself, why this chapter? Our broad answer is that it may serve, paired with the chapter on Frank Guittard's "Private Sides" later, to provide a few fragmentary glimpses of his mental landscape and furniture, however incomplete and imperfect. I will explore several categories of Frank's reading with Finn.

Pops: Candidly, Finn, Frank Guittard would have disliked the term "bookworm." However, he would have admitted he preferred reading and study over nearly every other activity, golf being an exception in his later years. In Frank's case, a description of a bookworm's mind cannot be contained in one chapter, as some topics in this chapter will inevitably be echoed in later chapters. Then, too, this book's chapters are not always tightly tied together; in some respects, they represent a series of essays, more or less chronological, on related subjects. My intent is to draw the big picture here about Frank's preoccupation with reading and then, in the coming chapters, add bits from the big picture to some of the smaller pictures for context. The nature of the book as a series of related essays applies to the entire book, a book written in fits and starts since 1978. So, if occasionally the reader should say to himself, "Hmm, that sounds familiar," then he will be right, but he will also know why. There's one other possible reason for inevitable echoing, namely, that the author is talking to his grandchildren and sometimes repeating himself, as grandparents sometimes will, to make sure they are heard by their grandchildren.

So, why attempt to sketch the invisible brain of a bookworm, an uncertain exercise at best? To understand in small measure Frank's view of things based on what was stored in his brain starting in New Bedford, Ohio. The more challenging question is, since we know he read constantly almost from the moment he held that first McGuffey Eclectic Reader, how do we go about doing this? To start with, we know that Dr. Francis Joseph Guittard, an overworked, underpaid physician-farmer with an energy-draining practice and little time to read, was able to build an excellent small library. His book buying probably started in the nine years he was learning English between his immigration to the US in 1847 and his marriage to Lydia Myers in 1856. That library is where Frank started reading, following his father's example, perhaps with a book in hand, sitting in an easy chair in front of a fire, lying in his bed, or in a shady spot outside. So, beginning with the books Frank remembers reading in his father's library, how do we then identify, in a broader way, the other volumes, magazines, or even comic strips he read beginning in New Bedford, which would have possibly influenced him? This is one of the questions you and I will work through.

Finn: So, Frank liked to read a lot. What kinds of books did he read? Are any of the books ones I would like today? Or were they old, weird books of poetry like Chaucer that would be hard to understand? Shakespeare is hard to read, too, even though English teachers make you read him.

Pops: Finn, let's start with three categories of books. First, the books and other things we know he read—we know he read the books in this category either because he listed them specifically as books or authors in his father's library or because he mentions them in his autobiographies, essays, or correspondence. Those in his father's library that he specifically cited as being familiar with include *The Arabian Nights* (unknown authors), *The United States Dispensatory for 1854 (*a medical encyclopedia), *Robinson Crusoe* (Defoe), *Don Quixote* (Cervantes), *The Decline and Fall of the Roman Empire* (Gibbon), *A Pilgrim's Progress* (Bunyan), *Paradise Lost* (Milton), Shakespeare (including *Hamlet, Macbeth, King Lear, Othello,* and *Romeo and Juliet,* as well as the principal comedies), and *Uncle Tom's Cabin* (Stowe). Nine storytellers, novelists, historians, playwrights, poets, and other writers in all.

At Baylor, Frank served as a librarian for The Erisophian Literary Society, and according to the records kept by Frank as librarian, he checked out the following books from the society's library in Main Building: Augusta Wilson's *Macaria*; J.L. Adams's *American Statesmen*; Porter's *Science and Sentiment;* Holmes's *The Professor at Breakfast*; Holmes's *Medical Essays*; book by Prince Bismarck, volume II; Victor Hugo's *By Order of the King*; Roosevelt's *The Naval War of 1812*; House Reports; *Chamber's Encyclopedia*, and *The Annual Cyclopedia Year 1888.*

The second category is books by authors he must have read, given their preeminent place in Western literature and his inborn inclination to read all the great works of literature. Those would have included works by American authors James Fenimore Cooper, Sir Walter Scott, and Mark Twain (Samuel Clemens).

A third category is books and other things he must have read, including comic strips, either because of their popularity and cultural omnipresence or because they addressed his interests, longstanding or transient, or his sense of humor. This category would include the several nonfiction works by Horatio Alger, Jr., biographies of James Garfield, Daniel Webster, and Abraham Lincoln; also, dime novels by various authors with western or Texas settings, popular in the 1880s—Frank must have read some out of curiosity or because many were set in romantic Texas. Of course, this category would also include works of fiction like *The Swiss Family Robinson,* written primarily for young men.

Now let's briefly mention three other categories of books or periodicals: books he must have read in his studies at the University of Chicago, including those in French and German, given his concentration in history. Then, books he must have read and later found in the library of his son Clarence, who inherited some of Frank's books. This category would include books by David Starr Jordan (*Book of Knight and Barbara,* 1899), Lew Wallace (*Ben-Hur: A Tale of the Christ,* 1880), and Edward Noyes Westcott (*David Harum,* 1898). Finally, other books or periodicals, some of which he would have read starting in Ohio: *The Bible (King James Version), The Baptist Standard,* and other publications of Southern Baptists; and after 1886, *The Youth's Companion, The Farmer's Almanac, The Literary Digest, National Geographic, Readers Digest,* and *Time* magazine.

Finn: That sounds like a lot of books to get over in this little chapter, Pops.

Pops: You are so right, so I will not attempt to go over each of these categories in detail but pick some representative books in most of them and jump around. We might as well start with one of the most impactful books he read early in his father's library, John Bunyan's *A Pilgrim's Progress.* I've excerpted in the prior volume, *A Ph.D.'s Reverie: The Letters,* a handwritten essay Frank wrote at Baylor in Bunyan's epic allegory style. This essay strongly suggests his then personal philosophy for getting on in the world and the virtues one should aspire to, e.g., punctuality, prudence, toil, knowledge, honor, and the contentment that comes from striving and hard work. If Frank had attached a name to his essay, that title could have been "Life's Journey Across the Land of Toil."

Finn: That's heavy. It sounds like Frank identified with that Bunyan guy or his pilgrim. But did Frank ever write essays on subjects that would have been more personal to him? *Pilgrim's Progress* is an allegory; it's not about real flesh-and-blood people like you and me.

Pops: Okay, here's another essay of Frank's regarding a book he read back in Ohio that later inspired him to write a theme at the University of Chicago. Tell me what you think. This is what Frank wrote in July 1900 for his English III course:

Charles Dickens's *David Copperfield*

> I read this book when a boy and I do not remember any other story that I have read that took such hold of me as this did. I do not think David is an ideal character [but] what he does is always of interest. His hardships and sufferings enlisted my full sympathy and his triumphs caused me to rejoice with him...

> Another reason why I have always retained my liking for this one of Dickens' books is because it portrays one of the finest characters I have ever met in fiction. This is the character of Agnes. Somehow the fact that she loved David yet took a real interest in all his love affairs without any sign of jealousy produced an impression on my youthful mind that has caused her character to stand out from those of other women I have met with in fiction. Of the other characters, I admired David's aunt for her generosity and affection for David, as well as for her numerous peculiarities.

Finn: Yes, that's more like what I was talking about.

Pops: Actually, the stories of David Copperfield and his creator Charles Dickens, the story of David Copperfield being partially based on his creator's life, would have resonated with Frank Guittard. The theme of being taken from home or having to quit school when the father in the home was strapped financially and fending off creditors would have felt familiar. Dickens's father—think Mr. Micawber—was forced to sell the books in his tiny library, those which Dickens read as a child. In *Copperfield*, Mr. Micawber's books had to be sold to a bookstall for whatever they would bring, a disturbing scene for Frank to contemplate, given his passion for reading.

The problems with creditors, both for Mr. Micawber and Dickens's father, would also have resonated with Frank. He occasionally remarked on his father's debts and kept a careful record of his debts to his brothers, with entries showing his repayments. Of course, Francis Joseph's financial issues arose overall from being in a low pay and sometimes pro bono public service profession—a country medical practice. Micawber's financial problems stemmed from being a poorly paid clerk whose expenditures inevitably exceeded his income, causing him to take various desperate measures. At the same time, Micawber was always whistling a happy tune, hoping things "would turn up." Reading of the distress caused by debt in the Micawber family would have only reinforced Frank's desire to finish his education and obtain suitable employment before taking on a wife and potentially a family. Copperfield notes that "I have known him [Micawber] to come home to supper with a flood of tears, and a declaration that nothing was left but a jail; and go to bed making a calculation of the expense of putting bow-windows to the house, 'in case anything turned up,' which was his favourite expression."

Finn: You know, most of these books you're saying he read sound like the ones he would have had to read in high school English class. I'm wondering if he read any books that wouldn't have been required reading in high school.

Pops: Really good question. We know from his family that he read the Sunday funnies, although Frank doesn't himself record all the popular literature he read. But let's for a moment consider the books of Horatio Alger, Jr. *Britannica Encyclopedia Online* states that Horatio Alger, Jr. was "one of the most popular American authors in the last 30 years of the nineteenth century and perhaps the most socially influential American writer of his generation." Although Alger's more than one hundred books would not have been on the shelves of the Guittard library in New Bedford, Frank could not have escaped reading one or more volumes even if he had wanted to. The target audience of Alger's stories was young men drawn to stories about other young men dealing with adversity where money or making a success of themselves was concerned. Typical plots involved scheming butlers, stolen inheritances, orphans as victims, and lost identities, all of which would be extraordinary events by any measure. Nevertheless, the power of these books to speak to and inspire young men in that time is well known; the unidentified author of the introduction to the 1878 publication of *The Western Boy or The Road to Success* states:

> Horatio Alger, Junior, gave me heroes and words to live by. He created idols to emulate. That they were only thinly fleshed didn't matter to my untrained mind...With the scanning of each volume [each Alger novel] I could almost feel my psyche being molded. I was actually able to sense the concrete forming in my backbone. I acquired honesty and ten logical reasons why it was better than dishonesty. Breathing in slogan after slogan, I became the perseverant, steady, pluck [sic], attentive, sympathetic, logical, and kind.

Although the Alger novels presented formulaic and repetitive melodramas, they inspired a publishing cottage industry for authors of similar books. A prominent example was Oliver Optic (real name, William Taylor Adams). Some of Optic's one hundred plus titles between 1853 and 1897 were *Work and Win; Now or Never; Try Again, or, The Trials and Triumphs of Harry West (aka The Boy Who Did Right); Little by Little; Poor and Proud;* and *Breaking Away, or, the Fortunes of a Student* (also known as *The Way to Succeed*).

Alger, the father of a publishing phenomenon, was a precocious Phi Beta Kappa Harvard graduate, recipient of Bowdoin awards, and a well-read student of good literature. In his novels, Alger included references to Cicero, Shakespeare, the Bible, Raphael, John Milton, Jenny Lind, and "Il Trovatore." The best regarded of Alger's novels is his first, *Ragged Dick* (1868), the story of a poor fourteen-year-old orphan and shoeshine boy against whom the odds were stacked but who, through honesty, pluck, and luck, rises to middle-class respectability. Since Frank was in his late teens in the late 1880s, he was five or more years beyond the usual age for reading Alger's simplistic novels about bootblacks or paperboys on their own in the big city, trying to rise in the world by working at beggarly wages and being squeakily honest. However, he would have surely appreciated the positive messages for young boys on their own out in the world and must have absorbed some of them before heading to Texas.

Another reason Frank would have encountered Alger's writing is that Alger, in addition to the formulaic stories like *Ragged Dick*, *Mark the Match Boy* (1869), *Ben the Luggage Boy* (1870), *Paul the Peddler* (1871), *Phil the Fiddler* (1872), *Do and Dare: Or a Brave Boy's Fight for Fortune* (1884), and many more, also authored several serious biographies for younger readers; those included biographies of James Garfield (1881), Daniel Webster (1882), Abraham Lincoln (1883), and Edwin Forrest (1877). Frank would have been interested in all of these. Garfield, in particular, would have been fascinating to Frank since Garfield was the unusually brilliant son from an Ohio family in Moreland Hills, about ninety miles due north of New Bedford. Garfield's story as a young man would have been compelling for Frank because of several points of similarity between the difficulties in their paths as teachers. More about the Garfield biography in a moment.

Finn: So, the Alger novels were everywhere, and Frank probably read a few.

Pops: There are at least several more reasons we suspect Frank read at least a few of the Alger novels and may have been influenced by the themes of the Alger books. First, we know he was a fan in the 1920s and 1930s of the Sunday comic strip "Ben Webster." In this strip, a squeaky clean but poor young man and his dog companion Brierley had numerous adventures, all involving strange or dangerous situations. Further, the strip was published under the name Edwin Alger, Jr., a pseudonym for Jay Jerome Williams. Because of the striking similarity of the names and the squeaky-clean heroes both in Alger's novels and in "Ben Webster," it appears that Williams intended in his comic strip melodrama to capture the themes and central character archetype that had made Alger's novels so successful.

A final reason for believing Frank was exposed to Alger's novels is that one cultural impact of Alger's novels was to inspire the myth of the self-made man and the loner hero. This myth, however, was a distortion of the usual Alger storyline in which there was nearly always a wealthy or powerful older man who takes the young hero under his wing and facilitates his rise in the world. Frank would have read "Ben Webster" in the mid-1920s to late 1930s. Ben Webster would have represented youthful aspiration and struggle against dark forces arrayed against young Ben and his faithful canine companion. In the 1920s, being reminded of Ben Webster's ongoing battles with villains in dark plots would have been comforting to Frank, considering his struggles at Stanford. Frank probably pulled for Ben Webster just as he pulled for David Copperfield over three decades earlier. Frank's son Clarence said growing up, he was mystified by his father's interest in the fortunes of Ben Webster. Still, Frank's long identification with the stories of earnest young men like David Copperfield, Ben Webster, and probably the Alger heroes, explains it. Frank always had a soft spot in his heart for underdogs, especially small town or country boys like himself who sought to improve their chances in the world. Whether or not Frank saw himself as a loner hero, he was an introverted bookish sort who knew all too well he was on his own in the world with little or no help from anyone. Frank's life story, however, is only a partial confirmation of what's been called the Horatio Alger myth's false promise that with study, hard work, and playing by the rules, one can become financially secure. Only partial because, although Frank followed the rules, the noble path he chose of teaching was longer and less economically secure than those of the Alger novel heroes who all bettered themselves substantially, if not actually becoming millionaires.

Finn: I'm not convinced from what you said that Frank actually read any of Alger's novels, but maybe he probably read Alger's biographies of historical figures like Garfield and Lincoln. I will buy that part.

Pops: Well, Frank's likely interest in James A. (Abram) Garfield deserves special mention. Yes, Garfield was from Ohio, and yes, he was elected president, and, of course, he was assassinated. Lincoln was shot twenty-one months before Frank's birth, Garfield was shot when Frank was fourteen, and Frank was thirty-four when McKinley was assassinated. Frank would have been vitally interested in the lives of all three assassinated sitting presidents, but perhaps none more than Garfield. There were many points of similarity between Frank and Garfield's lives: their pleasure in reading; their mothers' hopes for them; neither wanted to work on a farm; both recognized the importance of staying healthy; both were born to be teachers; both had to work; both debated for their college literary societies; Garfield was born in 1831 and was a contemporary of Frank's father who had emigrated from France; both were raised on Ohio farms, and each had one parent who died early; and the passion of both for reading and learning defined their lives.

Finn: You mentioned dime novels a while back. What about dime novels? Didn't Frank read them before getting on that train for Texas? I'll bet the ones about Texas would have been interesting to a teenager like Frank sent to Texas to check things out for his family.

Pops: I think they would have been. Dime novels were trendy in the US from around 1860 to 1900, and later as well. Frank's son, Clarence, said Frank did not read pulp fiction as an adult. However, it seems reasonable that when Frank was thinking about going to Texas, or sitting on a train headed toward Texas, he may have had a copy of a dime novel in his hip pocket. The dime novels were originally pocket-sized, hundred-page books with woodcut illustrations on the covers, and they cost between five and twenty-five cents. Their formulaic adventure themes included capture and rescue, disguise and revelation, pursuit and escape, and then repetition until the story's conclusion. Men resolved their disputes with violence rather than courts, judges, juries, or negotiations, and card games generally ended with revolvers drawn and shots fired. According to an anthology of dime westerns, Irwin Beadle and Company published over seven thousand dime novels between 1860 and 1897. Some of Beadle's authors, grinding away in a writing factory, could produce a book in twenty-four hours.

Finn: Maybe Frank could have told himself he was researching Texas.

Pops: I doubt dime novels set in Texas would have had much research value on the new land he was traveling to, but it would have made for entertaining reading on the train. Dime novels, all with their well-drawn cover art, were a literary phenomenon of the 1880s; a budding historian would have felt obliged to be informed about local culture.

Finn: What were the dime novels in Texas about? Can you give some examples?

Pops: Here is a title with its featured articles, publisher's name, and dates of issuance leading up to Frank's train trip to Texas in September 1886:

> *Texas Jack the Prairie Rattler; or the Queen of the Wild Riders* by Buffalo Bill, Hon. Wm. F. Cody, Beadle's New York Dime Library, August 20, 1884. The cover shows a mounted horseman, presumably Texas Jack, with sombrero, rifle, and lasso, at a full gallop.

Finn: That sounds like something I would like to read.

Pops: Here are a couple more. Their covers were all illustrated by excellent artists:

> *Mad Tom Western, The Texan Ranger* by W.J. Hamilton, Beadle's Pocket Library, February 4, 1885. The cover shows a young woman with a dagger standing over the body of another woman.

> *The Dread Rider, or The Texan Duelist* by Geo. W. Bowne, Beadle's Pocket Library, February 17, 1886. The cover shows a mounted horseman with a rifle studying a shooting target in the company of two other men; all three have mustaches and short beards.

It wouldn't take but an hour or so to read one of these, and there would always be time later to get back into one of those serious books he may have borrowed from his father's library.

Finn: You mentioned some other books and plays in his father's library. I'm curious what he would have thought of those, and which ones may have affected him the most. You already mentioned *David Copperfield.*

Pops: Yes, *David Copperfield* must have had quite an impact on the young Frank. As to the other books Frank mentions as being in his father's library, we make the following comments, book by book:

> Harriet Beecher Stowe's *Uncle Tom's Cabin* published in 1852: After the Bible, this novel was the best-selling book of the nineteenth century and the best-selling novel. The central theme was the evil and immorality of slavery and the laws that supported it, like the Fugitive Slave Act of 1850. President Lincoln reportedly said to Mrs. Stowe, "So this is the little lady who started this great war." The character Eliza, a slave and personal maid to a Mrs. Shelby, was based on a real person who escaped across the Ohio River from Kentucky into Ripley, Ohio.

> Daniel Defoe's *Robinson Crusoe* published in 1719: Defoe's best-known novel is about a castaway on a remote tropical island who is able to survive in a mostly solitary existence despite cannibals, mutineers, and other dangers before being rescued. To stay alive, Crusoe had to become unusually self-reliant and resourceful. Interestingly, Crusoe's parents wanted him to pursue a career in law, but he went against their wishes by setting out on a sea voyage in 1651. In East Texas and later in Palo Alto, Frank may have occasionally thought to himself, *Well, I shouldn't complain; this is bad, but Crusoe had it much worse.*

> John Bunyan's *The Pilgrim's Progress* published in 1678: The fact that Frank was impressed enough with this work that he wrote an

> autobiographical essay in the style of this poem has already been mentioned. Bunyan's work has been translated into more than two hundred languages and has never been out of print. The names of the places and the names of the characters in the poem may have seemed applicable to some of those Frank encountered in Texas, including: the Slough of Despond, the Hill of Difficulty, the Valley of Humiliation, Vanity Fair, Giant's Doubting Castle, and The Delectable Mountains, the City of Destruction, and the Celestial City; and for people he encountered, Ignorance, Mr. Worldly Wiseman, Formality, Hypocrisy, Mistrust, Lord Hate-Good, Pagan, and Christian, Evangelist, Faithful, Goodwill, Prudence, Charity, Piety, and many others.

Finn: Yes; I wish he were here today to see if he remembers thinking about some of those names in connection with his travels around Texas or the people he met.

Pops: Then we have Cervantes. Miguel de Cervantes Saavedra's *Don Quixote* published in two volumes, the first in 1605 and the second in 1615, is perhaps the most influential work ever written by a Spaniard. The novel features the loony Don Quixote, who imagines that he is a knight on a medieval quest and that a local farmer who has agreed to accompany him will serve as his squire. Quixote is obsessed with books of chivalry, and his overzealous reading of such books has led him to rename himself "Don Quixote." Quixote bizarrely wears a suit of armor, imagines a local farm girl to be his lady love, arranges for a "dubbing ceremony," and decides to become a knight-errant searching for adventure. Frank must have sympathized with Quixote's desire to live a blame-free life and pursue adventures while recognizing that Quixote was a more than a little off upstairs. Frank was also aware that the practical side of life meant "getting there and staying there," not riding cross-country tilting at windmills.

> *The Arabian Nights: One Thousand and One Nights*, a collection of folk tales from the Islamic Golden Age published in English in the early eighteenth century: The major themes in these tales would have been attractive to Frank as a young man eager to be out on his own. Many of the tales, which are forerunners of the Horatio Alger, Jr. stories but were critically acclaimed as literature incorporated many of the same themes as the Alger stories, including men rising from poverty to wealth and prosperity, those involving luck and good fortune and the importance of cleverness, perseverance, daring, or thirst for adventure. Stories include "Aladdin's Lamp," "Ali Baba and the Forty Thieves," "The Three Apples," "The Seven

> Voyages of Sinbad the Sailor," and "The Fisherman and the Jinni." Of these particular tales, those with Sinbad would have been especially memorable to Frank since, in his travels, Sinbad faced many obstacles like shipwrecks, giant eagles, strange beasts, and giants. Despite these dangers, Sinbad continued on his voyages until he had the wealth he needed to settle down.
>
> William Shakespeare's tragedies, *Hamlet* and *Macbeth*, written around 1599-1601 and 1606 or 1607, respectively. Both offer the reader disturbing explorations of themes relating to dysfunctional family relationships and conflicts related to struggles for temporal power. When Frank's father remarried after his first wife died and difficulties ensued, as noted elsewhere, one wonders whether Frank's feeling of loyalty to his father reminded him of Hamlet's devotion to his mother Queen Gertrude, who remarried after Hamlet's father was murdered. Perhaps Frank wondered whether the conflict of the Guittards with Francis Joseph's mentally disturbed second wife had unpredictably played a part in triggering her suicide somewhat as the family conflict in Hamlet's household had led to inadvertent tragic consequences. Hamlet killed Polonius by mistake. What do you think?

Finn: I don't see the connection, and I don't think Frank would have either. That's pretty far-fetched.

Pops: On the other hand, Macbeth is a twisted story of human evil represented in Macbeth's murder of the Scottish king, Duncan, and that murder inevitably giving rise to further evil deeds. As a possible template for understanding European history, one might ask whether certain murders led to other murders. The French Revolution comes to mind and the execution of Louis XVI of the House of Bourbon. Also, the murders of Czar Nicholas II and his family by the Bolsheviks.

Finn: It does sound like Frank read a lot. He must have read a lot more than what we've talked about so far.

Pops: Frank was a bookworm. He read the *Literary Digest* in bed at night because it was dull. After *Literary Digest* was discontinued, he read *TIME* magazine. He also read *Readers Digest*, *National Geographic*, and some professional materials, including *The American Historical Quarterly*. He would read best sellers with Mama Josie, who would read aloud to him. When he was working on his Ph.D., he read textbooks and French and German books to keep up his language facility. He kept a list of the books he read over and above professional periodicals between 1931 and 1947, one hundred twenty in all. In the category of "heavy" books were the *Rise of the Republic of Germany* by Daniels, *The Robber Barons and Great American Capitalists 1861*-1901 by Josephson, *The Challenge to Liberty* by Hoover, *My Battle* by Adolph Hitler, *One World* by Wilkie, and *The Russian Enigma* by Sumner.

Frank categorized as biography twelve books he read, including *Aaron Burr: A Romantic Biography* by Stryker, *The Raven: A Biography of Sam Houston* by James, *Voltaire: Genius of Mockery* by Thaddeus, and *Benjamin Franklin* by Van Doren. The books he read that he categorized as "light" offer a small window into that playful, curious inner child described more at length elsewhere herein: *Coronado's Children* by Dobie, *Golf Made Easy* by Martin, *A New Way to Better Golf* by Morrison, *A Parody Outline of History* by Stewart, *A Vaquero of the Brush Country* by Dobie, *Bambi* by Salten, *French Short Stories* by Buffum, *And Quiet Flows the Don* by Sholokhov, *Good-bye Mr. Chips* by Hilton, *For Whom the Bell Tolls* by Hemingway, *A Tree Grows in Brooklyn* by Smith, *Cass Timberlane* by Lewis, *Pleasant Valley* by Bromfield, *The Egg and I* by MacDonald, *The Farm* by Bromfield, *Lydia Bailey* by Roberts, and *Hackberry Cavalier* by Perry.

Finn: I wonder if those books on golf improved his golfing. And I wonder if he ever broke 100.

Pops: It's hard to get better at golf by poring over the books written by tournament champions describing how they did it. Frank played a lot of golf after Francis taught him how. We are confident he never shot in the 70s, perhaps never in the 80s. Rumor has it he shot straight from the tee but short. Though he might have been interested in a book on speed reading.

Illustrations 1-8

Making railroad ties before his teaching job started.

Attempting to move swarming bees back to their hive.

Sleeping under mosquito netting at Maggie Houston Hall.

Practicing small talk at a Burleson Hall soiree.

Selling books door to door to farmers' wives

Discussing approaches to the opposite sex with Pat Neff.

President Cooper removing an unfortunate dog from chapel.

Instructing students on Baylor's first homecoming parades.

BOOK TWO

From Ohio to Texas to Waco

Sample questions for the peanut gallery's consideration in this book's chapters:

What were the conditions in Texas after Frank's arrival? Did Frank already know how to ride a horse? How did Frank support himself in Texas? Had Frank heard about Baylor University in Ohio? What did the railroad network build-out have to do with the original Baylor at Independence? What lands did Baylor in Waco acquire for its campus? How was Waco "wild and woolly?" What were "bawdy houses?" What happened to the Waco Indians? How did the city of Waco try to attract new residents? Could Frank have supported himself as a cowboy if he had wanted to? What was Frank's game plan, and what were his student days at Baylor like? Why was the dormitory for poorer male students called "Maggie?" How strict was President Burleson with Baylor students?

Excerpt from Frank's "Funny-Book of Student Bone-heads" on student examinations:

Question: "What lasting contribution did the Olympic Games make to Greek life and the Greek civilization?" Answer: "The games always attracted great crowds and from mixing with each other they would become enlightened as to civilization, and another was that the trade that they started between each other brought them into commercial civilization and from such things as these, mixing with other people and trade and the enlightenment they got among themselves by getting together and talking to each other had something to do with their civilization and enlightenment."

Examples of Frank's favorite words and phrases from his letters:

"not overly confident" — "I was not overly confident to begin with."
"don't care much about" — "I don't care much about being one of many..."
"in earnest" — "I will feel like taking a holiday in good earnest"

CHAPTER 4

Train Trip to Texas to Enrollment at Baylor (1886-1890)

Frank Guittard's initial adventures in Texas command our attention here, beginning with his 1886 seventy-hour train trip from Coshocton, Ohio, to Chester, Texas, and concluding after we get him enrolled at Baylor University in 1890. Nineteenth-century cracker barrel humorist and lecturer Artemus Ward (Charles Farrar Browne) is reported to have said: "It ain't so much the things we don't know that get us in trouble. It's the things we know that ain't so." Whether this aphorism applies to Frank's trip to Texas is an open question for the peanut gallery and the reader. Miles will accompany me today, and the others may chime in at some point.

Pops: Before getting into that train trip, let's first talk generally about the United States in the last two decades of the nineteenth century. In 1886, the following states still awaited admission to the Union: North Dakota, South Dakota, Montana, Washington, Idaho, Wyoming, Utah, Oklahoma, New Mexico, Alaska, and Hawaii. Frank's destination was Chester, Texas—Texas having been admitted to the Union as the twenty-eighth state in December 1845—which the city's founders had named for Chester A. Arthur before becoming President. Within a month of Frank arriving in Chester, the Statue of Liberty was dedicated by President Cleveland, the newly merged Baylor University at Waco, Texas, began classes, and the State Fair of Texas opened in Dallas. Other events during 1886 included Sigmund Freud starting his practice in Vienna, Karl Benz patenting the first gasoline-driven car, and US workers forming the American Federation of Labor. The year before Mark Twain had published the *Adventures of Huckleberry Finn*, French scientist Louis Pasteur successfully tested an anti-rabies vaccine, and German Chancellor Bismarck took possession of Cameroon and Togoland. John L. Sullivan fought Dominick McCaffrey in boxing's first heavyweight title fight with three-ounce gloves and three-minute rounds. Riots broke out in Montreal to protest against compulsory smallpox vaccination. 1886 and the year before were eventful years.

Charlie: You quoted Artemus Ward at the beginning of this chapter. Was the Guittards' decision to send Frank to Texas based on falsehoods? I'm also curious whether Frank ever thought his coming to Texas had been a mistake.

Pops: We will gradually get to all of that, and you can make up your own mind. The reality of life in Texas when Frank left home did not live up to the promoters' promises—and there was no way it could have. The promises were so exaggerated. Texas was different from Ohio; it presented a different climate and different challenges from the ones Frank was used to. But I'll get back to you later on when we talk about what you think of the Guittards' decision to send Frank to Texas to scout land.

Charlie: So Frank just got on a train in Ohio and headed to Texas. Did anyone know he was coming? When would he go back home to New Bedford? What did he have to eat on the train? Did anyone meet him at the train station? Did he already know how to ride a horse?

Pops: Lots of good questions; Frank would have had many himself. Such a trip required plenty of preparation, and no one believed in preparation more than Frank did. When he boarded the train for Texas, Frank carried with him his teaching certification that he earned in Ohio, lunches prepared by his mother, and a letter of introduction from his father to Reverend Canon. No doubt he took with him as many books and other reading materials as he felt like lugging around in his bag. Books are heavy, so there could not have been but a few. Although he was venturing into a reportedly wild and woolly state, we doubt he had any weapon for self-defense, such as a derringer, bowie knife, or even a walking stick he could use as a club if need be.

Before relating the events of Frank's train trip, in retrospect, there was a potential irony in sending Frank to Texas. First, in connection with determining whether it would be a good place to relocate the Guittard household and restart a medical practice, and also as to whether it would be a better place for Frank to make a new start in life. Of course, the Guittards could not see into the future, nor did they have access to modern-day information and communication sources to compare Ohio versus Texas's prospects for Frank. All the Guittards knew is that the economy and employment situation in Ohio were miserable, Dr. Guittard having difficulty collecting payment of his medical fees. On the other hand, there was an opportunity in Chester, Texas, for a physician to set up a practice. In addition, Lawrence Sullivan Ross, the candidate for governor of Texas in November 1886, advocated the sale of agricultural land to settlers and then decisively defeated his opponent with 73 percent of the vote. After his election, the legislature "carried out Ross's policies on land sales, permitting sales only to settlers." We doubt the Guittards knew anything about Ross's candidacy before Frank's trip. However, we know now that one of the greatest depressions in US history was rapidly approaching in the late 1890s. Texas experienced a crippling drought from 1884 through 1886, "causing most of the farmers to fail and return to the East."

If Texas during the 1880s was—based on hindsight—not an especially good relocation choice for a physician-farmer with a large family, Ohio was by some standards an even more economically stressed place. Unemployment had become so bad in Ohio by 1894 that bands of Ohio men were marching on Washington, "composed mainly of hardworking and serious men...to demand relief...The most famous group was an army led by an Ohio businessman Jacob S. Coxey. Coxey and five hundred volunteers descended on the capital to demand that President Cleveland put unemployed men to work" constructing useful public improvements. When the army arrived in Washington, D.C., the president ordered the marchers to stop, "calling out the entire city police force and a body of federal troops to halt them."

Looking back, the decision to send Frank to Texas draws mixed marks. It certainly made sense to send Frank to investigate whether Texas would be a suitable place for relocating the Guittard household, depression or no depression. Whether Texas was a promising place to send Frank in consideration of the devastating drought in Texas, the answer is problematic. We have concluded that whatever the conditions were in Texas at the time, assuming the Guittard household knew as much as we know today, conditions in Texas could not have been, even with the drought, worse than those in Ohio. But if the question of whether Frank should immigrate to Texas was a coin-flip, his parents' decision to stay in Ohio was a wise one.

Pushing past the decision to send Frank to Texas, once he was on the train with his traveling companions, he was up for an adventure of the sort that a nineteen-year-old young man might crave. If we suppose he was aware of the ongoing Orphan Train Movement in which 200,000 orphaned, abandoned, or homeless children were relocated by trains to foster homes by the Children's Aid Society, he must have suppressed any feelings he may have had about that phenomenon. He, too, in a sense, was now a homeless child on a train. He would not have a real home in Texas until many more years had passed.

On September 25, 1886, after a tiresome three-day, seventy-hour trip, interesting because of novel sights more than for the scenery, Frank arrived at Chester, Tyler County, Texas. As of 1890, just a few years later, Chester was reported to have "a sawmill, a school, two gins, and two churches," the population in 1904 reportedly being 176. Chester was blessed with fine black land soil and surrounded by prime pine forests. After arriving in Chester, Frank posted a long letter home to his father:

> I left...in such a hurry after the train came that I did not have much time to think of leaving home. I must say that I did not feel very cheerful for a while after leaving...After the train started, Jake Lower and I arranged our sleeping quarters, and I tried to compose

myself to slumber...I would go off in a doze, but when the engine gave a blast, I would be wide awake again. It went this way until we came to Indianapolis at midnight...My [companion] had snored like a good fellow all the way. After leaving Indiana's capital, I did not try to sleep but amused myself the best I could thinking of home and dreaming of the future...Occasionally I would raise the window and take a peep into the darkness but the night air was so cool that I was glad to keep the window closed and content myself with my own thoughts, the snores of the sleeping passengers, and the rumblings of the train...I arrived at Union Station in St. Louis at 8:40 Wednesday morning...I inquired at the information booth about the next train to Texarkana. The official smilingly informed me, "I suppose you mean Tex-r-kan-a, that train will leave in a few minutes from track number 12"...I boarded the train and sat there feeling somewhat lonesome for I had cut my last connection with home when I said goodbye to the prospectors...

We came to Little Rock at night. During a stop for several minutes I ate the last of my lunches which mother had so carefully prepared for my trip, and while the train was speeding on its course across the Arkansas River, I opened the window and dropped fleeing chicken bones and saw them splash on the lighted surface of the river many feet below...We arrived at Texarkana in the morning...Thereafter, I was to change trains at Trinity, but when we arrived there I was so sound asleep that I did not hear the station called and was taken on some distance before I was conscious of what had happened and to get off the train at Dodge. I was informed that the next train back to Trinity was due at 9:00 a.m., but for some unknown reason, it did not arrive until evening. After a tedious all day delay at this desolate place, I backtracked to Trinity. I informed the conductor what had happened and that I was carried past Trinity due to the fact that the conductor had not waked me. The ticket puncher was not in the least sympathetic and threatened to stop the train and put me off if I did not pay my fare from Dodge back to Trinity. I decided that the conductor had the best end of the bargain and paid the fare which after all was not much.

When the train came to Trinity, I learned that I had missed the train going south and that there was no way to get out of Trinity until the next morning. So I located a lodging place for the night and was soon in the land of dreams. In the morning I started on my last lap to Chester, and I arrived there at noon, went to what they

> called the hotel. We had a southern dinner composed chiefly of chickens fried to a crisp, baked sweet potatoes, topped off with corn bread and biscuits. It was raining when I came to Chester...and getting around was very disagreeable. The mud clung to your shoes until they felt like weights on your feet.
>
> By inquiring I learned of a man, who on the way home, was going as he said a short distance from Mr. Canon's farm and would take me with him in his wagon part of the way. He assured me that by a short walk I could easily find the destination that I had been looking forward to for so many days. I started out with my new found friend after the rain checked up somewhat. We went through pine woods country most of the way until we came within a mile of the Canon farm. My guide gave me what seemed to be very clear directions and I started out on foot. But there seemed to be too many right hand and left hand turns and I became confused as to which one to take and soon found myself out in open pine woods without a very definite roadway in any direction. In other words, I was lost. To make matters worse, the rain began to pour down in sheets and added to all this darkness was coming on. If you have ever been lost in a boundless forest, as it seemed to me, you can imagine what a feeling of desolation and even despair took possession of me. If it had not been that I purchased a yellow 'slicker' from my recent friend, I would have been in a very sorry plight wandering here and there following roads that generally led nowhere. All this time it rained ceaselessly. Finally, I got in a cleared out roadway that led to an open field at the edge of which stood a good sized cabin with a welcome light in the window.
>
> In spite of a barking dog, I approached the house and found that its occupants consisted of a man, his wife, and two children. I inquired the way to Mr. Canon's. 'Mr. Parson Canon lives some way from here, it's raining hard and it's getting mighty dark, if it suits you and you can put up with our fare, you can stop with us tonight, and I'll take you over to Brother Canon's in the morning.' I was only too ready to accept this kind hospitable offer. (FGG letters home, October 4, 1886 and a subsequent letter)

In the morning after a breakfast of cornbread and bacon, Frank's host guided him to Parson Canon's place.

The Canons received Frank with open-hearted hospitality; he liked them immediately. Mrs. Canon was a gracious, motherly woman and Mr. Canon a combination of preacher, planter, scholar, and southern gentleman. The Canons had eight children, including a striking blue-eyed blonde daughter of eighteen years named Sallie. One day, Mr. Canon took Frank on a long walk to inspect one of the tracts adjoining the Canon farm. This tract was for sale and Frank's father and Mr. Canon had corresponded about it. As a land prospector, Frank was interested in everything Mr. Canon had to say about the land, the forest trees, the plants, and wildflowers. Frank initially viewed Texas as offering an opportunity for his family to acquire a piece of land at a reasonable price, and to furnish employment for a bunch of boys. His mother had often said she wished they had something to interest the boys and keep them busy at home.

Just before Christmas, Frank's father wrote him: "About the last we heard from you, you were in a log school house endeavoring to promote the mental culture and development of a lot of young Texans...by way of apology...having lost a couple of nights' sleep neither my head nor stomach are in condition to write anything elegant or interesting. We were glad to hear that you are pleased with your surroundings & that country generally...Keep an eye out and learn all you can about the quality of the soil and [what grasses] will grow there if cultivated as it is done here. It would be a good idea for you to keep a record of the weather, especially with reference to rain, its amount...As to investing, we think it very likely between this & next spring. Meanwhile, look out & gather all information that you can & do not seem to be anxious. After I get matters so arranged here as to be ready for purchase, it is likely that I will visit that country myself."

Frank completed his land survey not long after arriving in Texas. While the family was digesting the land information, Frank opted to spend at least a year in Texas before returning to Ohio. He and Jobe, the oldest Canon boy, went to the railroad station in an ox-drawn wagon to pick up his trunk and deliver it to the Canon home, where he had made arrangements for board and lodging for an indefinite period. When Mr. Canon asked him what he intended to do in Texas, Frank informed him that he had taught school in Ohio. After that, Mr. Canon made inquiries among his acquaintances as to possible teaching prospects for Frank.

In early October, Frank took Mrs. Canon's saddle horse to ride out to visit with the trustees of the Myrtle Springs District approximately ten miles from Chester. The three trustees approved his application unanimously, and a conditional contract was drawn up to pay Frank thirty-eight dollars a month. Thirty-eight dollars a month was better than the pay for a comparable teaching job at country schools in Ohio. The next step was to get his teaching certificate in Texas so that his contract would be valid. He went out again the following Saturday; this time to Woodville, the county seat. He first called on Judge West, the county school superintendent, who told him where the three examiners lived. He discovered that one of them was sick with chills and a fever, another was out of town, and the third was a lawyer who said he could not do anything by himself. Not wanting to ride back twenty miles to Chester without a certificate, Frank returned to confer with

Judge West, who advised him to stay over in Woodville for the night and that next day, a Sunday, something might be done. That night, he took a room at the local hotel where a crowd was gathered in connection with the session of the court that week. Those at the hotel were markedly different in appearance from the men Frank was accustomed to seeing, and he found them interesting to study. He joined a long, crowded eating table abundantly supplied with food at suppertime, with several waitresses hovering about. When one waitress asked, "Will you have some coffee?" each of the men answered, "Yesum, please." When the waitress came over to Frank, who did not drink coffee, he also replied, "Yesum, please," so that he might fit in with the others.

In the morning, after a good night's rest, Frank was able to round up the three examiners for a meeting in the county judge's office. The judge issued a permit for the examiners to hold an examination, and, with that authority, the group proceeded to the courthouse. The examiners asked Frank whether he had ever taught school. He said that he had and showed them his teacher's certificate from his home county. The examiners inspected his certificate and spared him the necessity of a formal examination, deciding they would use the same grades shown on his certificate from Ohio. The process went swiftly, fees were paid, and Frank received his certificate. Frank felt good being certified quickly without any hard questioning, which gave him a high regard for Texans.

However, since Frank's new school did not begin until after cotton-picking season was over in mid-November, he needed something to do in the meantime. At the time, two other young men who were also boarding with the Canons worked making railroad ties in the piney woods not far from the Canon farm. Frank already knew how to handle an ax and one end of a crosscut saw and got a job from these tie makers at one dollar per day. In Chester, he invested in the clothing he would need as an assistant tie maker: a wide-brimmed white hat, brogan shoes, and work shirt. The next day, in his new clothes, he was ready for work as an apprentice tie maker. Handling a broadax, however, was new for Frank and he badly blistered his hands learning this new skill. Eventually, his ties were almost as smooth as if he had planed them, and his fellow tie makers commended his work.

The tie makers stacked the ties they had prepared to await the coming of the inspector who made monthly trips along the railroad. The inspector would generally point to a few ties as unfit, paying for the rest, but would have his men haul off all ties. After paying the owner of the timber and the hauler of the ties, he paid the tie makers twenty cents apiece. An average day's production for two tie makers was twenty ties, for which they earned one cent per tie. Despite the low pay, Frank enjoyed his work making ties and liked the employers who were patient with his early efforts. He was also struck by the fact that they rarely used profanity, their chief cusswords being "dad gum it" and "dad blame it." Frank, in future years, would never be much of a "cusser." As a tie maker, Frank earned barely enough to pay for room and board with nothing left over.

There were nights when he occasionally went with the older Canon boys on a possum or coon hunt. Sometimes a fire hunt for deer was organized: One boy would carry a torch made of lighted "fat pine" splinters; another boy would follow carrying material to replenish the torch; a third boy (the marksman) held a gun and would watch for the shining eyes of a deer staring curiously at the torch.

Sundays were rest days. On Sunday mornings, there was a preaching service at a nearby church. Songs were from the "Sacred Harp" songbook, which used a four-note system: *do, me, sol, la.* There was no organ or piano. Frank liked these singing sessions primarily because Sallie Canon was available to accompany him to church. The Guittards in Ohio were not timid about singing in groups, and Frank liked to sing bass. Before school began, Frank made arrangements to board with the Roper family who lived about only two miles from the schoolhouse. Frank shared a room that was adjacent to the front porch. The room was furnished with a minimum of basic furniture and an oil lamp. In the early evenings, the family assembled around the open fireplace where they burned wood and pine knots.

In the mornings after breakfast, with his lunch basket in hand, Frank walked through the piney woods to his school. On the way, he would see deer skipping across the trail, chattering squirrels, and scared rabbits. Students generally had to walk to school and tended to show up with rashes, head lice, impetigo, and pinkeye. Students with rashes were sent home, and the teacher treated the rest. Parents were often opposed to vaccination against disease, fearing the vaccination more than the disease. The teacher often boarded with a nearby family since generally there was no teacherage.

The first order of business after arriving at school on cold mornings was building a fire, the fuel being pine knots and logs. The schoolhouse was built of split pine logs. The cracks between the logs were covered by light timber strips, and there were no windows; some cracks were left open to allow the light to come in. The furniture was extremely primitive by Frank's standards: a table and a rawhide-bottom chair for the teacher, and long benches for the pupils. The writing desk was a heavy plank twelve inches wide that extended the entire length of one end of the room. To furnish light for writing, the plank was placed parallel to the crack between two logs of the building. When the desk was not in use, a long board suspended by leather hinges covered the long open window. Children took their places at this desk, seating themselves on a long bench. On a cold day, the children's fingers would become numb in ten or fifteen minutes, and they had to take time out to thaw their fingers before completing their assignments. There was no blackboard, slates and tablets being required during arithmetic and grammar recitations. The three R's—reading, "riting," and "rithmetic"—were supplemented by spelling, geography, and United States History. *Webster's Blue Back Speller* was standard in the schools, along with *McGuffey's Readers*. The teacher's desk was set on a platform elevated some eight inches above the floor. Behind the teacher was a wall cabinet of large pull-down maps and often a standing United States flag. On the teacher's desk was a hand-held school bell and beside it, a wastebasket. Heating was provided by a potbellied stove. Often there was a framed print of Gilbert Charles Stuart's portrait of George Washington.

Recitations were sing-song in spelling, arithmetic, and geography, with students reciting verbatim in unison words in their texts. As documented and criticized in Cincinnati's school system, sing-song recitation tended to "deaden the soul and convert human beings into automatons." A teacher in the public school of a midwestern state once said that "anyone equipped with a knowledge of the three R's, a sound pair of lungs, and a stout rattan is able to compel children to memorize words."

Frank had no problem with student discipline during the entire five-month term. The average number of children in the ungraded country school was about twenty-five, and they all seemed eager to learn. He was flattered when they addressed him as "Professor," which was standard for addressing the teacher. Discipline was strict. Boys caught fighting would be whipped. According to one student of that era: "[The teacher] would send both boys who had been in a fight out to cut switches and then she would use those switches either on the one who cut them or the other party. The offenders never knew whether they were cutting switches for themselves or their enemy." As to one of Frank's favorite subjects—geography—everyone liked the study of geography, although no one liked carrying geography books that were larger and more difficult to carry. The students brought their lunches to school in syrup buckets and "punched nail holes in the tops to prevent condensation of moisture." Usually, each student had several biscuits apiece, one of which might be sweetened, and another student might have a fried egg. Apples were unusual; sometimes there was a cold potato and often deviled eggs. Once the students got to school, before lunchtime, they would trade items with other students. Pocket knives were popular with the boys, each boy carrying several knives for trading, sometimes knives that were broken. There were also several games boys played with knives, including "mumble peg." One top-rated game was "popping the whip," with the bigger boys swinging a line of boys linked together until it "cracked" the smaller boys off the other end of the "whip."

The children Frank taught in these country schools sometimes had unusual health problems. Frank was concerned about three children from one family whose sallow complexions concerned him. Asking the Ropers about these children, he learned they were "clay eaters," which meant literally that they were addicted to eating dried bits of clay found around the fireplace in their home. If children were not carefully observed during the creeping stage when they were inclined to put anything in their mouths, they formed the habit of eating clay. As they grew older, clay-eating children would pick lumps of clay out of the chimney and carry them around in their pockets to satisfy their cravings, like an average child's craving for candy. It was practically impossible to break a child of the habit. Clay eaters rarely lived to maturity and were always in poor health. Today, clay-eating is classified as an eating disorder and called geophagia.

The damp, cool days passed rapidly and Frank had no time to be homesick. He played outdoor games with the Roper children, who often chased rabbits with the Roper dog. When a rabbit finally escaped temporarily into a hollow tree, it was usually all over as Frank or one of the Roper children would insert a forked switch into the opening, twisting it into the rabbit's fur and gradually drawing him from his hiding place. That night, the Ropers would have rabbit stew for dinner. The other reason Frank had no time to be homesick was he was now contracted to teach the children in the area. Once a month, Frank had to travel twenty miles to Woodville to draw his teacher's salary. If the weather was terrible, he usually spent the night in town and came home on Sunday morning. He met some of the town boys this way, who would invite him to some of their parties, games of charades, and square dances. Frank considered that "he was readily adapting himself to the customs and ideas of the people with whom he had cast his lot."

<u>Charlie</u>: Why did Frank say "cast his lot?"

<u>Pops</u>: Yes, that's pretty dramatic, almost ominous, isn't it? It must mean Frank believed—at least at that moment—he was fated to head down a path requiring him for a beggarly wage to teach the children of poor country people. Those country people would primarily be farmers scrambling to put food on the table and ensure their children were exposed to the three Rs. Sundays provided breaks in the hard lives of country folk, Frank accompanying the Ropers to Sunday services in a country church, which was miles away from the Ropers' house. The family would make the trip in the farm wagon, and the Ropers' youngest child sat in the spring seat. Frank and other members of the family sat on rawhide-bottom chairs in the back of the wagon bed. As their wagon progressed toward the church, Frank was aware of every root and rut in the crude road. Later, on the way back home, the Ropers would warmly praise the preacher's sermon. Frank was usually not as impressed, but he kept his thoughts to himself. On Sunday afternoons, he would often visit the Canons. The younger children would run up to meet "Mr. Frank" when they saw him coming through the front gate. Miss Sallie was more reserved, but she appreciated his visits.

<u>Miles</u>: If Frank was, as you say, only paid a beggarly wage in Texas to teach school, wouldn't he have had to have some help from his parents?

Pops: I don’t think so, Miles. In Texas, Frank was totally on his own. Dispatched to Texas with only a letter of introduction and a sack of lunches, he struggled to determine how and where to complete his higher education for a teaching career. His family's only influence on him with respect to getting a college education or choosing a career were the examples of his father, brothers, and older sister. In Frank's case, the choice of a professional career was not, in all likelihood, addressed at any length, given that his father could not even help him get a college education. However, Frank had tried his hand as a public-schoolteacher in Ohio and seemed to like it; the family probably assumed, as did Frank initially, that he could always fall back on teaching in a public school. What was missing from Frank and his parents' thinking was any realistic understanding of the best choice of temporary employment to make money for his higher education. Also missing was the number of years it might take him to complete his education, what kind of career he could prepare for so that he and any family of his might have a reasonably comfortable life, and what the costs of that preparation might be. Apparently, there was no out-front recognition that teaching school was more of a low pay means to an end than an ultimate goal. An additional drawback to teaching public school was that it was not the fastest way to put himself through college, just an option he was comfortable with. An optimistic Frank wanted to give Texas time for something good to happen. As Mr. Micawber might have said, "Something will turn up." As it turned out, by heading to Texas, Frank would spend sixteen years earning a four-year bachelor's degree by working his way through, primarily teaching school.

During the school months, Frank corresponded with his parents concerning the opportunity at Chester for a country doctor and the land available for purchase. Francis Joseph eventually decided that, despite his original sentiments and intentions, he could not afford to give up an established, but not overly lucrative, medical practice to start a new one in an unfamiliar state when he was close to sixty years of age. He had possibly become aware that as of 1890, reportedly two-thirds of all homesteaders in the US failed to make a go of it. Perhaps there were too many farmers trying and too many failing. Then too, land values in Ohio had been falling precipitously, making it more difficult for Francis Joseph to sell the house and farm for enough to make the moving proposition workable. Frank's mother was more reluctant to give up her dream of moving to a warmer climate, but finally concluded that pioneering was for younger people—a fortunate decision for reasons that will become apparent. There is no record that Francis Joseph ever made the trip to Texas he mentioned earlier wanting to make.

Despite his parents' understandable yet disappointing reaction, Frank was not ready to go back to Ohio and was determined to give Texas a thorough test. He planned to find some kind of employment for the summer months, and with his hoarded school salary plus the money he would make during the summer, he hoped to attend a Texas college for at least one session. After his school closed for the summer, Frank had no trouble getting a job with tie makers working near Chester. His prior apprenticeship tie making in the fall now came in handy, and, in a few days, he was again swinging an ax, maul, and broadax just as well as the old-timers. Frank did, in time, change his initial impression about the location, deciding it was not suitable for his family. Most of the region was a pine forest thinly settled—not promising for a new medical practice, and the land was not especially productive—not encouraging for a prospective farmer.

Frank was, nevertheless, irresistibly drawn to this new land, despite his view there was no part of the United States where people lived more primitively than in East Texas. Later, at the University of Chicago, he recalled: "One is deeply impressed with the stillness while walking through the woods. This silence is still more impressive in the primitive pine forest. The great size and the height of the trees, quietness disturbed only by the melancholy soughing of the branches high above the head inspires one with a feeling of awe and insignificance. While looking in the distance, one gets the impression of being under a vast canopy of green supported by immense pillars." Then, too, he was attracted by the lifestyle of the logrollers. "The night after a hard day's work was over, old and young joined in the cotillion. Violinists furnished peculiar music called the 'breakdown.' An accompanist would sit by the violinist and, with two light pine sticks, beat a tattoo on the sounding board above the musicians' fingers, which was considered to add a desirable quality to the instrument's tone. People generally seemed to take life easy, and no one was in a hurry. When men came into the country village on Saturday, they stayed the whole day. There was a general exchange of gossip and opinion about crops; some engaged in a game of 'pitching dollars' or horseshoes. Anything [that] didn't require much effort."

Frank also noticed a general similarity in the appearance of the men. He recalled: "They are tall and not very muscular, wear broad-brimmed hats and high top boots with spurs. The most striking facial feature is a long mustache. All use tobacco; and when one member of a company feels it necessary to satisfy his craving for the weed, he first offers it to each one before partaking of it himself. Frequently some target is selected to which they direct their attention between remarks. In order to keep their flowing mustaches from interfering with their aim, they place two fingers to the lips and, by spreading them a little, make an aperture through which the load darts with lightning rapidity to the target. A little practice in this piece of marksmanship, they acquired such a degree of skill that they can hit a spot at a distance of six or eight feet with remarkable accuracy."

Yet Frank was appalled by the high level of ignorance in matters of general interest. A story of unknown origin and likely apocryphal was told about a traveler passing through one of the most backwoods districts of East Texas who stopped at a house along the road to inquire the way. The woman who came to the door could not give him any very definite directions beyond the corner of the farm. The traveler was led to believe she knew little of anything out of the immediate neighborhood from her conversation. To satisfy himself, however, he asked her several questions on general topics. Finding that she was in ignorance in that regard, he ventured to ask whether she had even heard that the war had ended. "No, I hain't hearn of it," she replied, "and it's all my John's fault, I've been wanting him to describe for a newspaper this long time and now all this has done happened and we hain't hearn a thing about it."

Frank taught at numerous country schools between the end of the 1887-1888 school year at Sam Houston Normal School working on a higher-level teaching certificate and February 1890, when he enrolled at the newly merged Baylor University at Waco. These schools included the Crawford School, Tyler County, for four months; the Chester School for two months; the Thomas School, Jasper County, for two months; the Cairo School, Jasper County, for nine months; and the Sherlock School, Alma, Tyler County, for two months. By February 1890, Frank had been able to hoard enough out of his meager teacher's salary to feel that he could justify taking more college courses. We don't know why Frank chose to enter Baylor University rather than return to Sam Houston for another session. Baylor's preeminent place among the educational institutions in Texas—chartered at Independence, Texas in 1845—and its status as a four-year college were necessarily significant factors in his decision. It was also widely known that Baylor's President Burleson had been behind securing the founding of Sam Houston Normal for teacher training. Frank enrolled at Baylor for the 1890 spring term. He returned for the eight-week summer term in 1891, 1892, and again in 1893. In 1893-94, Frank attended Baylor the entire session of ten months. By the spring of 1894, Frank left Baylor without a degree, his funds exhausted after spending almost two years in Waco. Now there would be another long delay to earn money before resuming his college education in 1897 at the University of Chicago and the road to obtaining his A.B. degree in 1901 at thirty-four.

As to Frank's final recommendation to his parents on moving to Texas, Frank's advice was likely even-handed, neither pressing hard for them to come to Texas nor discouraging them from making such a drastic change. In that respect, his advice differed from the advice that the notorious Texas outlaw Sam Bass gave his brothers in 1878 regarding following him to Texas from Indiana. Sam advised his brothers to stay in Indiana, that "Texas was a wild state yet, and being a cowboy wasn't as much fun as it might appear from Indiana." Sam spoke with authority, as he was no cowboy but rather in the process of becoming a celebrated bank and train hold-up man. On the other hand, John Wesley Hardin, another romanticized Texas outlaw who was in the penitentiary studying law, might have advised a person like Frank that making a living practicing law was certainly doable at his age. A law school degree was not essential, and Hardin had been able to commence law practice after spending a decade in prison where he read law.

After Frank left Baylor later his first year, he taught at schools in Tyler and Magnolia Springs, both in Texas, starting in the summer. We don't know where he spent Christmas 1890, but we have a copy of the 1890 Christmas edition of *The Youth's Companion*, a periodical Frank read in Ohio, and the peanut gallery is looking it over. Miles, is there anything in that issue you think would have interested Frank if he had read that issue?

Miles: That's a good question. The print is tiny and the stories all seem to be preachy or pretty lame. Here's a feel-good story about a disabled boy on Christmas Eve. Seems to be a combination of *The Christmas Carol* and a Horatio Alger story. Here's one called "Cindy's Discovery"—I'm surprised to see this kind of language—here's the beginning sentence: "Now be good chilluns, while I'm gone, an' doan' let dat kittle ob hominy squorch," said Mammy Kershaw." Definitely Uncle Remus-y.

Katie: And look at those illustrations! Very racist depictions of African-Americans, and this was twenty-five years after the end of the Civil War. The hair on that kid's head is sticking up like Buckwheat's in *The Little Rascals*.

Finn: The ads back then were interesting. Here's one advertising Diamond Dyes with information about how to make any color you want. President Brooks, like other students at Baylor, dyed his pants when he couldn't afford to buy a new pair. I wonder if Frank Guittard dyed his pants too. He was strapped for cash—that's why he kept dropping out of Baylor.

Miles: Here's one on page 703 that he certainly would have been interested in, pushing Pond's Extract for hoarseness and sore throat. An unnamed "prominent physician from New York" supposedly said, "Aside from throat trouble caused by infection, sore throat results from overwork of vocal cords, from being exposed to moist, raw air, and from many other causes."

Pops: Yes, that ad would have resonated with Frank in 1890 and afterwards.

Katie: Here's a great one for the hair and the skin, Barry's Tricopherous for the Hair and Skin established 1801: "removes all impurities from the scalp, prevents baldness, and gray hair...Infallible for curing eruptions, diseases of the skin, glands and muscles, and quickly healing cuts, burns, bruises, sprains." Pops, is this on the level?

Pops: Probably not as to many of those claims. I don't think anyone today could get approval from the FDA for all of those claims. Many salespeople back then could get away with saying or printing almost anything. The Pure Food and Drugs Act was not passed until 1906.

<u>Miles</u>: I got another good one. On page 707, Scott and Bowne, New York chemists, announce Scott's Emulsion of Cod Liver Oil with Hypophosphites as the "great remedial agent for wasting diseases," and say "for the early stages of consumption it is the most effective remedy, and if it will not absolutely cure, will give comfort and prolong life in the latter stages of the disease." Wait, there's more. "It is a most perfect specific for Colds and Chronic Coughs, Relieving the cold at once and building up the system when ordinary cough remedies fail. The most sensitive person can take it."

<u>Pops</u>: We haven't gotten there yet, but later we will talk about your great-great grandmother Mamie getting really sick—she was only thirty-seven—no telling how many popular "cures" Frank would have read about and even said to himself, if only momentarily, "*I know this must be greatly exaggerated, perhaps completely fallacious, but I wonder if we should give it a try? A bottle of Scott's Emulsion of Cod Liver Oil only costs $16.99.*"

<u>Katie</u>: (*brightly*) Today we don't have as many quack medical cures, at least in the US. Just quack political cures.

<u>Pops</u>: My guess is there are still a lot of medicines out there making exaggerated claims for their effectiveness, just not sold at CVS or Walgreens. Ever hear of the dark web?

CHAPTER 5

Short History of Baylor University (1845-1947)

This chapter will flesh out several strands of Baylor University's history, perhaps unknown to many, including the students currently entering Baylor in Waco. Finn and I will sort through this part together.

Pops: Any questions before we start?

Finn: If you were a new student entering Baylor today and not even minoring in history, why would you need to know anything about Baylor's history?

Pops: Not to dodge the question, but it all depends on the student. If a student likes to know the history of things, then that's the answer. If the student couldn't care less, then that's the answer for that student. For me, I like getting under the surface of things and finding out how people of long ago brought about the institution we chose to attend for four years. I want to know about the difficulties they had along the way. Struggles and conflicts get my attention. When things are in doubt, I am curious to find out how they were, or will be, resolved.

Finn: Okay. I am curious about one thing. I don't understand the difference between Baylor in Waco and Baylor at Independence, or where Waco University comes into all of this. Rufus C. Burleson seems to be all over the place—what's going on there?

Pops: Finn, I graduated from Baylor in Waco and didn't know any of what I'm about to tell you. I even grew up in a Baylor family interested in history. Though Baylor's history is complicated, I will move through the high points to put it all together for you. So, if you are ready...

Finn: Okay, shoot.

Pops: Baylor University at Waco is the oldest university in Texas, chartered February 1, 1845, as Baylor University at Independence by the Republic of Texas. Baylor is the only university in Texas to be chartered by the Republic to survive in continuous operation to the present day. When Baylor was at Independence, it had several presidents, the most noteworthy being Rufus C. (Columbus) Burleson, who served from 1851 to 1861 when he and the male faculty members relocated to Waco. In Waco, he would establish and become president of a college named Waco University. Burleson's distinguished successor as president of Baylor at Independence and formerly a friend—William Carey Crane—would compete with Burleson for students and financial support from Baptists for their respective institutions for over two decades. Crane served Baylor at Independence from 1864 until his death in 1885. In 1886, with Cranc out of the picture and after protracted negotiations, Baylor at Independence merged with Waco University to become Baylor University in Waco. Rufus C. Burleson took the reins of the new Baylor in Waco. In a sense, Burleson was back in the saddle again at Baylor. That's the story in a nutshell. Got it?

Finn: I think so.

Pops: Before talking more about the 1886 merger, Professor Frederick Eby, formerly on the Baylor faculty in Waco and an authority on how higher education developed in Texas, tells us:

> The early institutions of Texas bore many pretentious names. The terms "university," "college," "academy," "institute," "seminary," "collegiate institute," and "high school" were rather promiscuously employed. Some of these high titles must be understood to designate their aspirations rather than any standard which they could hope to realize. There was no real appreciation of the significance of these terms. The people were generally devoid of a sense of educational standards...Rarely was any protest raised against the bombastic claims. The people in the towns proudly referred to the "college on the hill," though none of its students could pass the sixth grade of a modern school.

Interestingly, when Frank applied for admission to the University of Chicago in 1897, he explained that his inability to supply a complete transcript of his courses was that Baylor had not kept a record of the earliest classes he had taken. That circumstance, along with others, must have made him uneasy about the wisdom of finishing up his course work at Baylor if he had better prospects elsewhere, which it turns out he did by the time he was ready to return to college. But we haven't gotten to the part where he dropped out of Baylor yet. That's for a later chapter.

Finn: I'd like to back up some. What led to the merger? Did Baylor at Independence gobble up Waco University and move to Waco?

Pops: It was more like Burleson and Waco University opportunistically gobbled up the floundering Baylor at Independence. The merger, which had become increasingly inevitable, was occasioned by the shrinking student body at Independence, coupled with the fact that the city of Independence had refused to be included as a railroad stop when the railroads were building out their lines. As a result, Waco would be more favorably located for students who could come in by train. Rufus C. Burleson strongly maintained that as a result of "a fatal blunder of the citizens," the towns of Washington and Independence were left off the railroads and became inaccessible. Baylor University in Waco opened on September 20, 1886, in the Waco University campus buildings near 5th and Webster. The first building on Burleson Quadrangle, called Main Building and located a mile or so away from the old Waco University campus, would open for classes a year later in September 1887.

At the time of the merger, Waco University had nineteen professors for three hundred and eighty-five students. Baylor at Independence in its last year (1885-86) had only sixty-three students. Burleson served Baylor as president at Waco from the merger in 1886 until he stepped down in 1897 to become president emeritus. Burleson had thus served Baylor in Waco or the two merging Baptist institutions for over forty-five years. Independence went from being a thriving small community to being little more than an interesting historical tour stop for those interested in Baylor University's history.

Finn: So, who did Baylor put in charge after President Burleson finally stepped down?

Pops: After Burleson became president emeritus, faculty chair John C. Lattimore served as acting president for several years until the trustees named outstanding Yale graduate and native Texan Oscar Henry Cooper as president in 1899. First in his class at Yale, Cooper was a recognized expert in university standards and was exceptionally well-equipped to help Baylor improve its university standing at the time of his appointment. His achievements at Baylor were significant despite what would be a relatively brief tenure. Notwithstanding his qualifications to help Baylor concerning its standards and its standing, a critical challenge for him, as it was for President Crane at Independence before him, was raising sufficient funds to keep Baylor afloat. He was not too proud to beg on Baylor's behalf. On one occasion in 1900, he declared Baylor required $15,000 and that "we have no Baptist wealth here" unlike that available to fund the University of Chicago, and that "the feeble churches" [in Texas] could not stand another year's strain. Baylor had already "touched the extreme limit of waiting."

Finn: That was fortunate that Baylor was able to secure President Cooper as president considering how small Baylor was at the time.

Pops: True enough, but unfortunately, President Cooper served only until early 1902 when he resigned following a student protest against him in the wake of an unfortunate student prank. We'll get to that prank in a later chapter. After Cooper's resignation, the trustees sent a telegram to New Haven informing Baylor graduate and former faculty member Samuel Palmer Brooks—who was well known to the trustees and the faculty—that they had elected him as Baylor's new president and that he should "come at once." Although stunned by Baylor's offer, Brooks accepted promptly and served with distinction, greatly enlarging and adding university departments and buildings until he died in 1931. In 1931, W. Sims Allen was made acting president and served until 1932 when Pat M. Neff was elected president during the Great Depression. Neff served until 1947 when he became president emeritus.

Finn: It sounds like Brooks had huge shoes to fill. How did he measure up?

Pops: Well, and then some. Brooks would prove himself to be a highly progressive, visionary, and able administrator. He would perform service to Baylor not excelled and perhaps never equaled from Baylor's earliest days in Independence to the present. But it is interesting that Oscar Cooper's career as a college president was not over, and he went on to have a distinguished career as a schoolman, university president, and potent force in Texas education. He had been Phi Beta Kappa at Yale and then spent a year after graduation studying at the University of Berlin, all before becoming Baylor's president. Cooper was almost uniquely qualified to be a force for bettering secondary and higher education in Texas, whichever institution he decided to serve. Most importantly, Cooper is credited with being the primary instigator and supporter of the proposal for a single state-supported, state-controlled university in Texas. This proposal directly resulted in creating the University of Texas and was appropriately recognized by Governor O. M. Roberts. Dr. Eby proclaimed that Oscar Cooper was "The greatest living educator that Texas has ever produced" and "did more to establish state and Christian education in Texas than any other single man." Notwithstanding Cooper's strengths and undoubted contributions to both Baylor University and the founding of the University of Texas, there appears to be a consensus that no other person following Cooper's departure could have served Baylor as ably as President Brooks. We have included a separate chapter devoted to Brooks elsewhere within.

Finn: I'm curious about how Baylor's campus in Waco was put together, particularly Burleson Quadrangle and all the other lands around the Quadrangle.

Pops: They came from certain large donors, from Baptists, and from citizens of Waco. Among Baylor's early financial benefactors were Joseph Warren Speight and John Camden West. Their properties (Oak Lawn and Minglewood Park, respectively) became the basis for Baylor's initial campus in Waco and Burleson Quadrangle. Speight had served as chair of the board of trustees of Waco University for its entire existence (1861-1886) and was instrumental in bringing Rufus C. Burleson and his male faculty members from Independence to Waco in 1861. West, for a brief time, served as principal of the Trinity River Male High School, which evolved into Waco Classical School and then, under President Burleson, to Waco University. The citizens of Waco purchased the Oak Lawn and Minglewood Park properties, which covered altogether twenty-three acres, for Waco University to hold in trust for Baylor University at Waco after it was chartered under the plan for the merger. More than ten years later, Francis Lafayette Carroll and his son George Washington Carroll were responsible for the large gifts that made possible the Carroll Chapel and Library and the Carroll Science Building. The evidence also indicates that some funds for the construction of Main Building and Georgia Burleson Hall on the Oak Lawn property were provided by Texas Baptists and the citizens of Waco.

Finn: Where did Frank Guittard become a student? Waco or Independence?

Pops: Frank Guittard enrolled in Baylor at Waco as a student in 1890, almost four years after the merger, earning only two years of course credit over four years. He later served on Baylor's faculty for nearly five decades (1902-1950). Frank knew Presidents Rufus C. Burleson, Samuel Palmer Brooks, Pat M. Neff, and W.R. White. Frank attended Baylor University in Waco as a student off and on between 1890 and 1894 during the tenure of President Burleson. He returned in 1902 with two degrees from the University of Chicago to teach in the Baylor Academy at the request of President Brooks. Several years later, he was promoted to the collegiate department. Two decades later, he earned his Ph.D. from Stanford during the last eight years of Brooks's administration, mostly during six summers. He trained future historians during the entire tenures of President Brooks and President Neff and died two years after Neff retired. Did you get all that?

Finn: Most of it, I think. Since Waco University was doing well under President Burleson and Baylor at Independence was on its last legs, I don't get why they didn't call the merged institution Waco University or Waco-Baylor University or even Burleson University.

Pops: The reason is that Baylor at Independence and Waco University, in a sense, were family, with Baylor at Independence having bragging rights to being the oldest university in continuous operation founded by the Republic of Texas. Waco University could not make that claim since it came about when Burleson and his male faculty splintered off from Baylor at Independence in 1861 to transform what had essentially been a private Waco high school into a college. Calling the merged university "Burleson University" would have been a non-starter as the merged institution's founders intended to maintain Baylor's unique identity as having been chartered in 1845 under the Republic of Texas.

Finn: Hey, here's a thought. In hindsight, wouldn't naming a university after its president been kind of risky anyway? If the president resigned under pressure or under embarrassing circumstances, I think that would be awkward for the university to continue to bear his or her name. A university might have to change its name while doing a lot of explaining.

Pops: I hadn't thought of that, but perhaps it's just as well Baylor was named after one of its early founders without any known baggage.

Finn: Are you certain that Judge Baylor had no baggage associated with his name?

Pops: Actually, I'm not. Humans are all fallible. Perhaps William M. Tryon would have been as good or better choice than Judge Baylor for the naming honor. We will talk about how the founders decided to name the new university after Baylor rather than Tryon in a later chapter.

CHAPTER 6

Wild & Woolly Waco, McLennan County, Texas

Today we have a hodgepodge of curious and colorful topics pertaining to Waco and McLennan County, and the entire peanut gallery has questions. The topics would all have been of interest to the squeakily upright Frank Guittard, who was interested in history, sanitized and un-sanitized. They provide the necessary context for Frank's and Baylor's stories. We want to show how Waco originated and grew, and we want to dig into its compelling narrative, not all of which boosts the city of Waco.

Pops: Since all of you wanted to participate in rolling out this chapter, I'm going to briefly mention a number of the topics we can cover today. You all be thinking about which ones you want to get into during the next hour or so. But, first, since Frank enrolled in Baylor in 1890, some background about 1890s Waco may be helpful.

There are many things about 1890s Waco that differ from today. Although Waco had its first electric lights beginning in 1886, the trolleys around Waco in 1890 were powered by mules, not electricity; electrified trolley cars were not used until 1891. Telephones were not yet in general use in Waco, people used iceboxes and washboards, most people did not have showers until the 1920s, and there were still outhouses, just to name a few things. Thus, when Frank first stepped off the train in 1890, he would have taken a trolley pulled by mules to transport him to the Baylor campus where the primitive Maggie Houston Hall for less-affluent male students awaited him. Waco, by comparison to many other Texas cities of that era, was a bustling and enterprising town. It was trending upwards and possessed a hard-working, church-going citizenry. The city's suspension bridge across the Brazos connected Waco with the big world out there, and multiple railroads came into and went out from Waco's centrally located train stations.

However, when Frank checked into Maggie Houston Hall, vice in Waco was a serious problem. Prostitution had just been formally legalized by the city fathers and was not just winked at and ignored, as in the recent past. This state of affairs was occurring as President Burleson, a conspicuous paragon of personal rectitude in a Prince Albert suit, hat, and cane, conducted frequent chapel sessions, seeking to teach moral philosophy to college students. Baylor's campus presented a stark contrast with downtown Waco: on the one hand, the sheltered, nominally co-educational campus and its Bible-reading students and the sheltered, prim and proper young Baptist women sequestered in the partially fenced-off Georgia Burleson Hall; on the other, the legally protected area for bawdy houses, eventually called "Two Street," a quick bike ride or walk from Maggie Houston Hall, and near the city square with its teeming saloons and gambling parlors. These dubious attractions continued to flourish well past the last days of the cattle drives that came up the Chisholm Trail. Maggie was originally part of the Waco University campus when Rufus Burleson was its president. For a number of years following 1886, Baylor's male students of lesser means, initially mostly ministerial students but also including students like Samuel Palmer Brooks, Pat M. Neff, and Frank Guittard, called Maggie home at some point while in Baylor. Though the bawdy houses, saloons, and gambling houses were close to Maggie, First Baptist of Waco was also close at 4th and Mary (from 1857 to 1906). Frank Guittard lived in Maggie beginning in early 1890, probably during his first quarter at Baylor and continuing for several quarters, and then sometime later before he left school. From what we know about Frank's upbringing in Ohio, he must have been appalled by the number of Waco's vice emporiums and other dubious goings-on. And then, too, he may have been simultaneously curious.

Charlie: Okay, Pops. Will there be anything about cowboys in this chapter?

Pops: Indeed, there will. Cowboys had been important to Waco, but we'll get to that. Here are many of the topics which we can touch on. We can talk about the Indians who were in Waco when it was Waco Village; or the Reconstruction era outlaws; the Modocs and the ex-Texas Ranger Sul Ross, who cleared them from East Waco; the trail drives up the Chisholm Trail; the Waco Suspension Bridge across the Brazos River, which the Waco Indians called the Great Tohomoho; Kate Ross Padgitt, the first white child born in Waco Village; and there's also Lover's Leap in Cameron Park and the Indian legend that goes with it.

Waco was also a city of churches—many churches—including First Baptist Waco, as well as colleges and charitable institutions. Surprisingly, despite the strong church presence in Waco and, of course, on the Baylor campus, the activities we just mentioned and would consider vices today were flourishing. Initially, they were tolerated, but they were later licensed to make money for Waco and their business owners. Other topics we might cover are Camp MacArthur and the Spanish Influenza of 1918–some might say a cautionary story for the pandemic we are currently experiencing. The story of Waco also cannot be told without telling the story of cotton, cattle, and the railroads with five depots, as shown by the 1892 map. Then too, we can't leave out General Joseph W. Speight, George B. Dutton, and John C. West, or the architect William Larmour. Okay, Charlie says he wants to hear about cowboys in Waco. What about the rest of you?

Finn: I'd like to hear about Lovers' Leap and the Modocs. Those sound good.

Katie: I want Lovers' Leap too. I'd like to hear about the Indian tribes and Kate Ross Padgitt.

Miles: Pops, I'm curious about the saloons, gambling, and bawdy houses, but I'm not sure what "bawdy" means exactly, or what exactly went on in those places, although I have a general idea.

Pops: According to the dictionary, "bawdy" means indecent or obscene. Other words for bawdy house are: brothel, cathouse, whorehouse, and disorderly house. Bawdy houses are illegal in most places today. Generally, a bawdy house was where men paid money to have sexual relations with women who were employees of the bawdy house. Have you seen those massage parlors in some of our cities? Some of those may be bawdy houses or may be connected to prostitution. The sex business, human trafficking of minors, and prostitution are alive and operating in shadowy corners of our cities and on the internet.

Miles: Ever been to a bawdy house yourself, Pops?

Pops: Nope, but I knew a student at Baylor who said he had—although he could have been enjoying telling me a tall tale. You definitely don't want to go near those places. Creepy. There were lots of bawdy houses in Waco for many years, including when Frank was a Baylor student. They were generally located on North First, Second, Third, Fourth, and Fifth streets, and other streets, including Washington. Perhaps the best-known bawdy house was Mollie Adams's house at 408 north Second Street, which was recorded in the 1910 census as having seven residents. Waco was not unusual insofar as having its share of bawdy houses. In the 1890s, most towns of any size had bawdy houses, saloons, and gambling parlors.

Frank may have been curious about them for all I know, but I suspect not enough to go near them. He was a conventional, old-fashioned kind of guy from a strong Methodist family in Ohio. Besides, Frank had his head in the books with a firm game plan for his life that did not permit risky diversions. He would have been leery of having any connection with the abused young women—often listed as "actresses" in the city directory—who worked in those places. Believe it or not, there was rumored to be at least one bawdy house between Penland Hall and the Brazos River when I went to Baylor in the 1960s, but it must have disappeared during Waco's urban renewal. I'm not sure where it was, somewhere around there. My grandfather on my mother's side, who went to medical school in Dallas around 1915, would occasionally be called out to Dallas's protected area for prostitution to tend to an "actress" who was in distress from attempting to terminate an unwanted pregnancy.

Katie: I'd also like to know whether people talked differently in the 1890s, 1900s, and so on. Did they use the exact words we do today? Or did they use the same words but just pronounce them in a way it would be hard to understand what they were saying?

Pops: That's an interesting question. I think I have an answer when we get to that.

Charlie: Okay, Pops. I've got another topic I want to hear about—what downtown Waco was like. Did it have any tall buildings other than the ALICO [Amicable Life Insurance Company] Building? Why didn't that tornado knock it down when it came through? Didn't somebody have an office there? And why do you call this chapter "Wild & Woolly Waco?"

Pops: Let's start with the Indians, Lovers' Leap, and some early Waco background, and then we'll hit the rest of those topics. The name Waco comes from the Indian tribe that lived in an area of Waco called Indian Springs. What were the Wacos like? The Waco Indians practiced extensive body tattooing of their short, stocky bodies, including their eyelids and the corners of their eyes. The Wacos called themselves the "raccoon-eyed people." The springs were important; the Indians believed they had magical power. Following the drilling of the first artesian well, there were places in downtown Waco that tapped into sources of artesian water; these waters were selling points for hotels because of the alleged healing properties. The Natatorium is an example of an 1890s hotel and spa erected with access to subterranean waters.

Returning to the Indians, the Wacos were friendly with some other tribes but not all. You're familiar with the play *Romeo and Juliet*? Or the movie *Thelma and Louise*? The Lovers' Leap legend was about a Waco Indian girl in love with a young man from an enemy tribe, the Apache. When the couple realized the tribal elders had discovered their plan to elope, they went to a high point overlooking the Bosque River in an area now known as Cameron Park. They leaped to their deaths there. Here are a few lines from the conclusion of a poem chronicling their sad story:

> Thus is told the wondrous legend / Of the cold and barren chalk-cliff / Known as Lovers' Leap; this chalk-cliff / Where the noble Indian lovers leaped and lost their lives together / On the river known as Bosque.

Katie: What happened to the Wacos? Are any of them still in Waco?

Pops: I don't think so. About one hundred ninety years ago, a tougher tribe, the Cherokee, moved into Waco on the other side of the Great Tohomoho, or the Brazos River, and drove the Wacos out. The Cherokees scalped between fifty and fifty-five Wacos in 1829. I assume the descendants of the Wacos are still out there somewhere, but not in Waco.

So, what was the city of Waco like in the 1890s when Frank enrolled at Baylor? People referred to Waco by several names, such as "the Athens on the Brazos," because of Baylor University and other educational institutions. Charles Carver, the biographer of W.C. Brann, the famed critic of Waco, said, "Thus the Waco that Brann found in 1894 may have been a small town, and it may have been a prairie town, but it was also a religious and education center bursting with intellectual as well a physical energy as witnessed by all the schools and the more than fifteen periodicals that were being issued in 1894."

Waco was also called "Geyser City" because of the artesian waters drawing visitors to its hotels, "Central City" because of its location in Texas, and "Six-Shooter Junction" because of people carrying pistols around and firing them off in the city. Certain storied gunfights involving Baylor and Waco are detailed later; some people in this era considered Waco an armed camp. Waco had a reputation in 1886 as a place where you could get shot or scalped, or, failing that, get to see somebody else shot or scalped. However, that is an exaggeration, undoubtedly fostered by the writers of dime novels, with an element of truth mixed in. Resident journalist W.C. Brann, in an article entitled "The Six-Shooter," argued that "We have a drastic anti-pistol packing law—enacted by Legislators half of whom at the time had six-shooters in their hip pockets...[Nevertheless] the law prohibiting the carrying of concealed weapons has ever been a dead letter and must so remain until men feel that gun powder is no longer necessary to the protection of their purses."

Waco of that era might have been called "the vice capital" of Texas because of its many saloons, gambling parlors, and bawdy houses. According to one historian, "By the late 1800s, the vice capitals of the Lone Star State would bow to an emerging city in the heart of central Texas—Waco." Even with its numerous profitable destinations for vice, Waco could also have touted itself as a mecca for the godly because of the abundance of houses of worship and the high percentage of church-going Christians. According to the census of 1890, the following faiths or denominations flourished in Waco: Baptists, Methodist Episcopal Church South, Disciples of Christ, Methodist Episcopal Church, Cumberland Presbyterian Church, German Evangelical Synod, African Methodist Episcopal Church, Roman Catholic Church, and Protestant Episcopal. The Methodists and the Baptists competed in numbers for the largest congregations, the Methodists supposedly having more people on its rolls, though not necessarily more church-attending members. The 1900 Waco city directory lists forty-three churches, including Jewish synagogues.

We're going to talk about the Waco business community's boosterish view of Waco, but first let's finish answering Charlie's question about why we're calling this chapter "Wild & Woolly Waco." We already talked about Waco as arguably the vice capital of Texas. Let's look now at a slice of the legal framework for life in 1890s Waco when Frank entered Baylor. This information is from *The Ordinances of the City of Waco for the Year 1890.* The ordinances I'm about to mention were in place in 1890, some funny, others odd, and others brutal or strange. We've already mentioned the licensing of bawdy houses, prostitutes, and businesspeople making money from vice in downtown Waco, or on Two Street, and we will talk more about that in a moment. But the *Ordinances* that specified other activities requiring a licensing fee or occupation tax were as follows:

> $25 annually from every clairvoyant or mesmerist and $500 annually from every fortune-teller; $5 per performance from every sleight-of-hand or legerdemain exhibition; $250 for every performance of a fight between man and man, or between men and bulls, or between dogs and bulls, or between bears and dogs, or between bulls and other animals, or between dogs and dogs; $10 annually from every person exhibiting any electrical machine, lung-tester, or other machines of like character; and $5 annually from every person canvassing for the sale of lightning rods, and $8 annually from every velocipedrome, flying-horse, or amusement of like nature.

Charlie: What was a velocipedrome or a flying-horse entertainment?

Pops: The first was an entertainment in which the audience watched races of people on bicycles. The State Fair of Texas used to have one in the 1950s, only the riders rode motorcycles instead of bicycles and would ride upside down in spherical metal cages. I'm sure you've been on a flying-horse kind of entertainment—they are usually called merry-go-rounds or carousels—where the public buy tickets to sit on mechanized horses that go up and down on poles while the round floor revolves to the strains of a calliope.

When Waco's 1890 ordinances were not raising money by licensing various activities, they were banning a long list of other activities. Here are some of those:

> Hogs and goats could not run at large and could be impounded and sold.

> Doorbell ringing and pulling doorknockers or bell pulls was declared malicious mischief if done mischievously.
>
> Boisterous conduct such as loud hallooing, stamping, dancing, skating, sliding, cursing, swearing, or other vociferous or unusual noises that were annoying were prohibited.
>
> Naked bathing or swimming in the Brazos, pond, or pool during daylight hours was declared to be a misdemeanor.
>
> No one could operate a locomotive, engine, or car at a greater rate of speed than four miles per hour.
>
> No one could dig any pit for use as a privy.
>
> No one could drive any beast of burden without using reins in any public place or without a bell or bells attached.

Waco also had an ordinance declaring various persons who strolled around town without visible means of support, who were not attempting to become gainfully employed, or who were prostitutes, professional gamblers, beggars, habitual drunkards, and others as vagrants. However, prostitution confined to Two Street ["The Reservation"] was lawful and licensed. Local citizens strolling into bawdy houses were not interrupted since bawdy houses represented protected activities as long as the required licenses were paid.

For the business community's view of Waco promised earlier, we can turn to the boosterish 1901 publication, *Waco, Texas—the Central City of the Lone Star State (Illustrated Twentieth Century Edition)*—published by Knight Printing in Waco, Texas. This publication touts itself as providing:

> A Review of her [Waco's] Commerce, A description of her Enterprises, With Illustrations of her Public and Private Buildings, Her Steady Progress, Her Manufacturing and Railroad Facilities, Her Wonderful Resources, and Fertile Farming Country. Waco, Texas—the Land of Cotton, Corn, Wheat, Fruits, and Timber.

Although Waco had a population of 14,445 according to the 1890 census, McLennan County, by 1900, had a population of 75,000. The reader is also told:

> Waco, the Central City of Texas, is the Capital of McLennan County. It is located practically in the geographical center of the state, with the Brazos River dividing it into two parts, the river being spanned by a suspension bridge which is a monument of engineering skill. A new courthouse is now being built on Washington Street at a cost of $300,000. The Missouri, Kansas, and Texas Railway has just completed a large, handsome brick and

> stone depot at a cost of $50,000. Waco is already a large railroad center, and she must, by virtue of her location, become the commercial emporium and industrial metropolis of Texas. No city has a more commanding and attractive position, for no city on earth has such a great country surrounding it. There is no guessing about it...This book with its evidences of public spirit, generosity and prosperity, will tend to show that Waco possesses another element in the contexture of her greatness, and is her enterprising business men...Such men as have produced this book are capable of making a great city of Waco, and they will conspire to do so, and ere another decade they will have steamers playing in the waters of the Brazos River from the Gulf of Mexico to Waco.

Among the different industries Waco boasted in the 1900s, the cotton industry was especially significant:

> Waco is the largest inland cotton market in the south, having wagon receipts amounting to over 60,000 bales a year, and four compresses with an annual output of 200,000 bales...Two large [cotton-seed manufacturing] plants with a joint capacity of 275 tons of seed per day are operated for twenty-six weeks every year...A state which had one crop of such magnitude, and whose soil produces almost every other crop known to a temperate climate, and whose mineral and timber resources are sufficient to create even more wealth than its agriculture, is a State which must be reckoned with in forecasting the future of our country.

Dorothy Scarborough, the most distinguished female graduate of Baylor at Waco in the nineteenth century and who earned degrees both at Baylor and the University of Chicago, noted in her 1923 novel *In the Land of Cotton:* "Yet cotton is the master of them all, in spring as well as autumn, in winter as in summer. Yellow or white or black, all men in the south are slaves of cotton, subject to its power, prospering as those white fields flourish, and failing as they fail. King Cotton may be cruel or benign, but he wields his mighty scepter over the whole south."

Local Waco historian Roger Conger also referred to the importance of cotton to Waco leading up to the Civil War, saying: "By 1859 Waco had become a community dependent quite largely on the rich plantations of the Brazos Valley, and almost all of her leading citizens were quick to side with the heated agitation for secession from the Union. Waco's population...numbered 749, but in the County there were 1938 slaves constituting a property value of at least $1,000,000. The mention of abolishing an investment of this extent, without remuneration to the investors, was nothing less than fighting talk." McLennan County voted 586 to 191 for secession, and after hostilities commenced, 900 men out of a total of 6,200 volunteered to fight for the Confederate States of America.

According to the booklet, Waco's schools and universities were also described with pride, including thirteen district schools, two business colleges, the Academy of the Sacred Heart, Paul Quinn College, Add-Ran University, and Baylor University. Yet, Waco also had many other assets potentially of interest to prospective families or businesses. By 1900, the US Government engineer had reported to Congress the results of its survey of the Brazos River, which included its recommendation that the Brazos be made navigable from Waco to the Gulf of Mexico. An appropriation for such purpose was on the calendar for 1901-1902. This booklet goes on to extol the numerous attributes of Waco—the large number of passenger trains, streetcar system, double system of sewers (sanitary and storm), the hospitals, parks, newspapers, Anheuser-Busch brewing business, paved macadamized streets, five "magnificent hotels," its various factories, coupled with a strong pitch on why everyone should want to live and work in Waco and waste no time getting there.

What the booklet fails to say is that the Great Tohomoho tended to overflow its banks during heavy rains and flood downtown Waco, primarily East Waco, which is lower than the part of Waco on the southwest side of the Brazos. Waco had seriously flooded in May 1885. It would flood again in July 1902, December 1913, and in September 1936, when two thousand citizens were left homeless and the city manager would declare martial law. Professor Archer, in her work on the unruly Brazos, stated: "Refusing to bend to any single interpretation of itself, the Brazos is a river that becomes swollen then waterless, hostile then motionless, docile then boundless. This is a river of many faces, one that enjoys a gluttonous feast of water or no water at all."

The 1906 *Baylor Round-Up* would, in turn, echo the boasts by the business community, claiming that "Waco has become a city of 30,000 inhabitants," that it is "conceded by all to be the fastest-growing city in the south," and that "one of the greatest men ever engaged in building railroads in Texas predicted...that Waco would be the leading city of the...State...that Waco would be the great railroad center of Texas." The *Round-Up* went on to declare that "Waco has already twelve railway outlets, and the promise of four more in the near future," and that "Waco [was] the most prominent cotton concentrating center in the state."

If this booklet represented the majority report, or the business community's view of Waco, there was an extremely irritating minority report, not necessarily fact-based but composed of soaring, inimitable rhetoric. Conspicuously vocal journalist W.C. Brann—the brilliant but unremittingly savage critic of Waco, Baylor University, President Burleson, and whatever else if he thought it would sell his publication, *The Iconoclast.* Well-named "The Wizard of Words," Brann declared in the mid-1890s after moving to Waco:

> Saintly Waco fairly ruptures a blood vessel trying to hermetically seal the saloons on Sunday, yet permits the licensed house of prostitution to do business seven nights in the week. But then the law permits the necessaries of life to be sold on Sunday, and in the eyes of the professional godly, drinking a glass of beer on the Lord's Day were emphatically more wicked than dallying with abrasive broads.

Brann on another occasion, with his usual brutal sarcasm, advised his readers:

> Of course, Waco, like other places, has its drawbacks; but, taken by and large, there is no better. While it is true that you cannot secure a bath, shave or clean a shirt here on Sunday, the saloons and churches are open and the Reservation [area in which the vices of drinking, gambling, and prostitution were permitted] hath all seasons for its own. Waco [has perhaps] two or three society women who do not chew gum, straddle a bike nor drink gin rickeys. There be several men here who could safely be left alone with a blind orphan girl, or a corpse whose eyes were covered with coppers...All trains stop in Waco. You will recognize the place by a structure which resembles a Kansas section house that has been hailed by the vandal time or criminally assaulted by a cyclone.

There are so many "Brannisms" from the Wizard of Words that choosing among them is almost impossible. However, we must include this one: "Waco is the only town in Texas of any consequence where men are boycotted in business for questioning the Immaculate Conception."

Talking about Waco saloons in the early 1890s, there were fifty or so, and also bars in the hotels. Some of the names were the Red Front Saloon, Little Red Front Saloon, Blue Front Saloon, Shannon & Nalley, Harmon's Brazos Bank Saloon, Bell & Doud, Kentucky Saloon, Anderson's Saloon, St. Charles, George Williams's Saloon, and many others. But Brann wasn't the only person complaining about the protected vice activities [saloons, bawdy houses, and gambling emporiums]. An article and related letter to the editor in the *Waco Evening News* on January 2, 1894, when Frank was still in Baylor, gives the flavor of what went on nightly in downtown Waco. The letter's writer, one Vorley Wright, an overnight guest in Room 35 on the third floor of the downtown McClellan Hotel, complained that he couldn't sleep because of drunken songs and yells and vomiting, rattling dice, quarreling hack drivers and lewd women and a constant five-minute service of hacks from one night resort to another; and further claimed these are "the concomitant features that go to make up the nightly carnival of disturbance on Austin Street." In one instance, Wright was kept awake from three o'clock in the morning until daylight by boisterous singing, shouting, swearing and dice throwing, coming from a saloon at Third and Fourth Streets. Another time, two hack drivers contended alternately with oaths and horsewhips uninterrupted for a half or three-quarters of an hour.

Miles: That would make it hard for me to sleep, but Charlie can sleep through anything. How did Waco citizens like Brann's articles? It doesn't seem like they would have.

Pops: No, many of them didn't since they were proud of their hometown and were trying to build a larger and more prosperous Waco. They also resented all the attacks on Baylor and the aspersions Brann had cast on Baylor women.

Miles: Sounds like he might have been happier in another city, assuming he could have held back from publishing attacks on his neighbors.

Pops: Maybe, but before long, Brann's unpopularity in Waco would reach a violent climax. The October 1897 issue of *The Iconoclast*, after referring to Baylor as a "manufactory of ministers and Magdalenes," had announced: "It is devoutly to be hoped that the recent expose of Baylor's criminal carelessness will have a beneficial effect—that henceforth orphan girls will not be ravished on the premises of its president, and that fewer young lady students will be sent home enceinte ...Probably Baylor has never been so bad as many imagine, that the joint keepers in the Reservation have been mistaken in regarding it as a rival, [and] that the number of female students sent away to conceal their shame has been exaggerated." The high level of local animosity toward Brann reached its conclusion when a Baylor student's father, who resented Brann's attacks on the character of Baylor women as promiscuous, shot Brann in the back. After taking his assassin's bullet, however, Brann was able to put a lethal bullet into his attacker.

Miles: I don't understand why Brann would have been knocking Baylor women.

Pops: I'm not sure I understand that either, except that Brann was a professional scandalmonger, his specialty being attack journalism. His grandson, one hundred years later, admitted that "[his] grandfather had a vitriolic pen. It got him fired from a lot of jobs...He was a sensationalist. But boy, could he write." So why did Brann go on the attack when he moved to Waco? When Brann initially arrived in Waco, he was reportedly broke and needed to do what came naturally, namely writing savage stories that would build circulation and support him and his family. That style would prove to be successful financially, and within several years, he had achieved circulation to over 100,000 readers.

However, where Baylor was concerned, his attack primarily targeted President Burleson in connection with the alleged rape of a young Brazilian girl sent to him by a Baptist missionary. It was undisputed that the fifteen-year-old girl, who lived under the care of the Burlesons, became pregnant by a brother of Burleson's son-in-law. The accused denied the charge of rape on the basis of consent, and Burleson and his wife Georgia claimed that the girl, Antonia Teixeira, was morally loose, undisciplined, and a problem. Grand jury proceedings were instituted against the accused, who was ultimately acquitted. Burleson himself was called upon at some point to explain his own actions in connection with Miss Teixeira's care. The authorities eventually dropped all charges and all proceedings. However, the proceedings and Brann's articles in *The Iconoclast* had been bad publicity for Baylor. The controversy was reportedly one of the factors leading to President Burleson's decision to step down as president.

Brann's relentless attack on Baylor, Burleson, and Baylor women in connection with the Teixeira episode was highly upsetting to many, if not most, Wacoans and the Baylor community. His harsh treatment of Baylor and Burleson made him the target of those willing to sanction him for his opinions. On October 2, 1897, an angry group of Baylor students, reportedly members of Baylor's two male literary societies, brought Brann forcibly to the Baylor campus for public shaming and discipline to be meted out without the sanction of law. Fortunately, faculty members intervened and defused the situation, and Brann escaped to write more attack articles. The kidnapping and transport of Brann to the Baylor campus where Baylor men could express their displeasure with his writing, while regrettable, is interesting. It started with the collaboration of the Erisophian and Philomathesian Literary Societies, which under normal circumstances were bitter rivals, but on this occasion, they came together in common cause—perhaps reminiscent of their temporary truce during the Civil War—to protect the holy grail, namely, the reputation of Baylor women—and their presence in sufficient numbers on the Baylor campus. Three or more students from the literary societies, who were later prosecuted for their actions and pled guilty to aggravated assault, went to downtown Waco. There, they kidnapped an unarmed Brann in his office in the Providence Building, loaded him into a horse-drawn hack waiting in an alley, and took off for the Baylor campus. Reportedly, once on Fifth Street and headed toward the campus, one student took the reins from the hack driver and drove at full speed to Baylor, where about two hundred boys were waiting.

The initial motivation or intended resolution of Brann's kidnapping, other than sticking up for Baylor and Baylor women, is unclear. There was some suggestion that tar and feathering may have been in the minds of some of the students. Afterward, Brann might possibly be tied on a mule backward and turned loose. Although it is clear from all reports that the objective was not to hang or kill Brann but to bluff him into changing his writing about Baylor and Baylor women, the situation was so volatile that Baylor faculty and others were concerned that hot-headed male students might end up harming Brann.

Anyway, after the students reached the campus with their prisoner, a document was presented for Brann to sign which retracted his comments about Baylor women in Burleson Hall. Brann signed the document after initially hesitating. Then, after considerable commotion, several Baylor faculty members finally arrived, including Professors Brooks and Lattimore, who declared that the students should return Brann to his office in downtown Waco. Accordingly, he was placed back in the hack and delivered back downtown.

There was one other incident involving Baylor students and Brann that preceded the kidnapping episode. In 1958, First Baptist Church pastor J.M. Dawson wrote a piece entitled "Image-Breaker Six Decades After" in which he reported that an unnamed Baylor trustee told him that George Scarborough, son of another trustee, on reading one of Brann's incendiary attacks on the Baylor women, took an oath to kill Brann. According to the first trustee, Judge Scarborough said he made a deal with his son George that if George would resist the urge to kill Brann, he [Judge Scarborough] would hold Brann while George horse-whipped or caned him. According to Dawson, after the Scarboroughs administered the punishment to Brann, Brann was undeterred and renewed his attacks on Baylor's women, which led to students from the literary societies combining to discipline Brann further.

Charlie: Pops, can we turn the page a minute? What about cowboys? You said you would talk about them.

Pops: Yes, I did, and this is as good a place as any, but we have to go back to a time twenty or twenty-five years before Frank became a student at Baylor, say 1865 to 1890. To talk about cowboys, we will cover cows, cattle drives, the Chisholm Trail that ran through Waco up to a railhead in Abilene, Kansas, and all the questionable activities in Waco that cowboys indulged in, as well as businesspeople, including some church-goers who profited from these activities. To start with, at the end of the Civil War in 1865, cows were running loose all over Texas. So, to deliver cows to northern and northeastern markets, cowboys called drovers were initially needed to collect those unbranded longhorns into herds and drive those cows in all kinds of weather along several trails to the north. One of those trails, the Chisholm Trail, came through Waco on the way to Abilene, and saw heavy use beginning several years after the Civil War. The trail was later made famous by the Tex Ritter/Moe Bandy song about the Chisholm Trail.

However, during certain times of the year, there was a problem with cattle crossing the Brazos on the trek north as the water might be too high to drive the cattle across to the other side. Captain Shapley P. Ross's ferry connected the people of the small community on the west bank of the Brazos with the east bank "from which landing the Stage Road lay eastward to Waxahachie and Dallas." Then, General Joseph Speight and others proposed the idea of a suspension bridge over the Brazos connecting the south and north banks and allowing herds of cattle to be driven across the river and up north along the trail to towns like Wichita and Abilene, Kansas, in the case of the Chisholm Trail, and St. Louis and Kansas City, Missouri, in the case of the Shawnee. Trail drives up the Chisholm and other trails gradually wound down by the early to mid-1890s due to the introduction of barbed wire across routes obstructing their use and due to the increasing availability and use of railroads to transport Texas cattle to Kansas markets. After barbed wire fences made it increasingly difficult in the 1880s to drive cattle north to Kansas, the Waco Suspension Bridge made it possible to transport cattle to the eastern and northern side of the Brazos to East Waco, where rail could transport cattle to Kansas.

Before barbed wire, as long as it was possible to drive the herds north to Kansas, driving the cattle to markets was cheaper than shipping them by rail from East Waco. When the drovers and their herds arrived in Waco, they would camp outside Waco, their drovers heading into town. The cowboys were thirsty, lonely, hungry, sex-deprived single men who wanted a break from the hard, boring work of driving cows. A substantial number of Waco businesspeople were only too happy to furnish activities for the cowboys, including alcohol, gambling, and sex for hire. These businesses tended to be all around the city square (the saloons) or within a matter of a few blocks (the bawdy houses) from the suspension bridge.

At some point, Waco's city fathers, including those with a personal business interest in protecting vice revenue, decided—their wives, mothers, and daughters not having a vote except indirectly—that if these forms of vice (drinking, gambling, and whoring) were going to exist, Waco might as well make some money from them. As an example, Waco began to license bawdy houses and prostitutes and afford them protection from arrest, provided the businesspeople paid the required fees to the city. Brann asserted without proof that "Waco...is the only municipality, the majority of whose citizens are church communicants, which has licensed houses of prostitution." The Reservation, called by many "Two Street," covered by ordinance the area from Washington Avenue on the southeast to the Brazos River to the east and north, and on the south and west by North Second Street. Prostitution was first legalized in 1889, the year before Frank Guittard enrolled at Baylor.

There were several arguments for permitting and licensing bawdy houses as long as they stayed in one part of the city: first, that having bawdy houses protected the virtuous women of Waco; second, that the bawdy houses would be easier to monitor and control if they were limited to one small section of the city; third, that keeping the bawdy houses separate avoided mixing legitimate businesses and law-abiding citizens with bawdy houses which would have normalized them; and fourth, that if bawdy houses and prostitution could not be eliminated, then the city might as well make some money off them. One additional reason for creating the Reservation and limiting prostitution within the Reservation's borders was to deal with the fact that bawdy houses were all over the city, some of them across the street from college dormitories, thus disturbing parents who might otherwise be willing to send their children to college in Waco. By the time the Reservation was fully established in 1905, it had been nicknamed "Two Street."

Miles: Are all of those saloons and bawdy houses still there on Two Street?

Pops: Nope, and they haven't been for a long time. During World War I, the US Army made Waco a deal it couldn't refuse. It needed to establish an army base near Waco, but the condition was that Waco had to eliminate the Reservation, or Two Street, as a protected area for prostitution since venereal disease would constitute a health risk to soldiers who would be stationed on the base. Waco accepted the Army's proposal and thereafter, Waco benefited from lawful commerce with soldiers at Camp MacArthur rather than fees from the Reservation's resident prostitutes. No doubt the wives of the city fathers were happy with the new arrangement, even if all the owners of bawdy houses in the Reservation were not. The prostitutes were given until August 4, 1917, to pack their bags and clear out, and a police sweep was planned for August 11 to catch any madams still on the Reservation. However, establishing Camp MacArthur in Waco had an unintended consequence. The next year after the end of World War I, soldiers who came back to Camp MacArthur brought the Spanish swine flu back to Waco residents. Over seven hundred cases of flu and 153 military deaths occurred, along with other deaths in the community. The US as a whole experienced 675,000 deaths from the Spanish flu pandemic.

As for the saloons on Bridge Street west of the Brazos, around the square, and in every hotel, according to the 1896 city directory, there were over fifty with addresses in the directory. According to W.C. Brann, saloons were "in every block." There is no indication that the bars went out of business until Prohibition became law in McLennan County in 1917. Thus, external forces—the war, the US Army, and the Prohibition movement in McLennan County—teamed up to deal Waco's vice district and the saloons a mighty blow. Of course, the blow wasn't fatal since we know that Prohibition was openly flouted until it was repealed over a decade later. However, once saloons and the Reservation were outlawed, the gambling parlors no longer had their friendly business partners next door.

Katie: Tell us more about Kate Ross, Pops.

Pops: I definitely don't want to forget her. Kate Ross Padgitt was an 1867 graduate of Waco University under President Burleson. Kate was a prominent Waco philanthropist, a mover and shaker from a prominent Waco family. Her father, Shapley P. Ross, had been a legendary Indian fighter who tracked down the infamous Comanche Big Foot who had been stealing horses. After neither Shapley nor Big Foot could fire their weapons, they both drew their knives, and Ross was able to subdue and scalp the Indian. On her nineteenth birthday, January 6, 1870, Kate led a procession across the Waco Suspension Bridge at its official opening. The bridge used cables provided by John A. Roebling and Son, which would build the larger and more famous suspension bridge, the Brooklyn Bridge, a few years later. In 1875, Kate was also instrumental in making it possible for steamboats to attempt to navigate the Brazos to Galveston. Unfortunately, the Brazos lacked enough water to get the first steamboat—named the Kate Ross—past Calvert, Texas, which was some 178 miles upriver from Galveston.

Pops: What have we forgotten to cover, anyone?

Katie: You haven't gotten to my question about the words people used in those days and whether it would have been hard to understand people because of how they talked.

Pops: Okay, I'll answer that second question first. I don't think you would have any problem understanding people living in the 1890s in Waco or afterward. There may have been some regional accents in East Texas or central Texas, but I don't think you would have any problem there. As to the words they used, as you can tell from the language in the chamber of commerce publication, the vocabulary used in 1901 was very close to that we use today. To be sure, some words were common then and they are not as common today, including:

> drought, parlor, mantel board, porch, stoop, chifferobe, chiffonier, highboy, bureau, divan, bath rag, hydrant (inside), privy, outdoor toilet, toad frog, peckerwood, grub-worm, wiggler, roasting ears, thicket, blinky, blue-john, cold drink, boogers, pulley bone, reared, part-time preacher, and granddaddy

Ever hear anybody say any of those?

Finn: I have—blinky and boogers. Everybody has heard of those.

Charlie: Me too—and cold drinks and granddaddy.

Pops: Yep, those are still around.

Finn: What about the Modocs, Pops? You haven't gotten around to them yet.

Pops: Whoops, I almost forgot the Modocs. We are not talking about that small Indian tribe who lived in northeastern California and southern Oregon. Our Modocs, who resided in and around McLennan County, were the drifters, thieves, and murderers who had fled into Texas during Reconstruction. They claimed squatters' rights to the 1830 Tomas de la Vega Land Grant (eleven leagues, ca. 816 square miles) from Mexico across the Brazos from Waco. The grant would have included what came to be called East Waco. The Modocs were so numerous and entrenched that their hide-out area became a lawless no man's land, perhaps similar to Butch Cavendish's hide-out in one of those Lone Ranger movies where the gang was a law unto itself within their protected territory. Arrests by the local authorities of Modocs were useless as these outlaws intimidated witnesses or suborned perjury, or, failing in those efforts, broke their fellow troublemakers out of jail. Sul Ross we already talked about. After serving as a Texas Ranger, he chased the Modocs out of the thickets around East Waco when he was sheriff of McLennan County. Ross is credited with jailing seven hundred outlaws during his two-year term as sheriff.

One other thing, Charlie, you asked about cowboys. You're not old enough to remember movie star Tom Mix, a real cowboy who made silent westerns in the 1920s. I never saw his westerns, but I listened to his radio show. Anyway, Mix visited W.C. Brann's grave marker in Oakwood Cemetery in Waco in 1929 and laid a wreath on Brann's tomb. At the time, Mix said, "I am a great admirer of the man and his writings. I have all his books at home."

Finn: I liked Brann's line "a corpse whose eyes were covered with coppers." Alliteration, right?

Pops: Sure is, and that's a good line; I have all of Brann's *Iconoclast* essays, too, if you want to read some. Or, you can just read Charles Carver's biography which excerpts many of his best essays. Carver also relates that gunfight at the end, destined to be Brann's last and only gunfight.

Katie: If any of you guys want to see a Tom Mix film, they're on YouTube.

CHAPTER 7

Rufus C. Burleson, His Universities, and Waco (1851-1897)

There could be no bigger subjects to discuss in Baylor's history than two of its most illustrious presidents, Rufus Columbus Burleson and Samuel Palmer Brooks, sometimes referred to as Burleson and Brooks. We will start with Burleson because he came before Brooks; Brooks will have several chapters later. The entire peanut gallery wants to be in on this one; whoever has a question or comment can break in anytime.

Katie: I have one before you get started. I've seen that large standing statue in Burleson Quadrangle of President Burleson holding his hat and cane, but there is an even more enormous sitting statue of Judge R.E.B. Baylor on Founders Mall leading up to Pat Neff Hall. If Judge Baylor's statue could stand up, it would be taller than the Burleson's. So how did Judge R.E.B. Baylor get a more prominent statue than President Burleson? It seems like someone is claiming that Judge Baylor was more important than President Burleson.

Pops: Interesting question. Judge Baylor was one of three men credited as Baylor University's founders, the others being William Milton Tryon and James Huckins, both pastor-missionaries, both of whom have monuments on either side of Judge Baylor's statue. Baylor is the one whose name ended up on the founding documents, although there was a feeling initially that the name for the new institution should be Tryon University. Tryon, who had originated the idea of there being a Baptist university chartered by the Republic of Texas, in a generous gesture, wrote in Baylor's name instead of his own on the founding documents. Tryon became the first chair of Baylor's board of trustees.

Finn: Too bad Tryon's contribution is forgotten today.

Pops: Once the founders of an institution have departed the scene, they tend to be overlooked. But not so fast—Tryon is not entirely forgotten at Baylor as the oldest of the men's social clubs, Tryon Coterie, was named after him. Your late cousin Phil was a member. Burleson, however, continues to loom large at Baylor. His role in Baylor's story began six years after Baylor's chartering, first at Baylor at Independence, Baylor's original location, then at Waco University in Waco; and finally at the merged Baylor University at Waco. I suppose the size difference in

Baylor's and Burleson's statues was decided by a committee that thought the Founders' Mall location demanded a more prominent statue for Baylor than Burleson's in the Quadrangle. After all, Baylor's name was attached to the university, not Burleson's. However, in terms of relative importance to Baylor University, there can be no doubt that while Judge Baylor may or may not have been the best pick for the naming honor at the time Baylor was chartered, Burleson is the giant figure in Baylor's early history.

Finn: I think it would have been funny if the university had been named Huckins University after that other guy. All the Tea-sips would have loved that. I can just hear them saying "Yuckins University" and laughing themselves silly.

Charlie: Yeah, Baylor dodged a bullet there, for sure.

Pops: A little background to get us up to Burleson's entrance on the scene. For several years in the 1880s, a far-ranging campaign had been maintained in Texas for a great central Baptist university, arguing that none of the existing Baptist colleges could be made to meet the needs and demands of Texas Baptists. Two of the essential Baptist institutions of higher learning were Baylor University at Independence and Waco University in Waco. Baylor University at Independence had declined since Independence failed to secure a stop on the Houston and Texas Central Railroad. That decline accelerated rapidly upon the death of Baylor President William Carey Crane in February 1885. By June of the same year, there were only sixty-four students and one graduate student. Texas Baptists' one great school campaign further undermined Baylor at Independence.

President Burleson's Waco University, on the other hand, was prospering. During its entire history from its founding in 1861, it had maintained a strong faculty and grown numerically and financially. Its report for 1882 stated: "We're glad to say that Waco University has just closed the most prosperous session ever enjoyed by her in all her history, having matriculated nearly 400 people in its various departments, and now has an able and experienced faculty ready to enter upon the coming session...In the last eleven years, in the liberal arts department alone, there were one hundred fifty graduates, fifty-five men, and ninety-five women."

The history of Waco University and its eventual merger with Baylor at Independence is a story of intra-denominational competition and compromise beyond the scope of this work. However, the basic outline can be sketched quickly. Reverend N.T Byers came to Waco in the early 1850s and organized the First Baptist Church. In 1854, Reverend S.G. O'Brien graduated from Wake Forest College and was called to First Baptist Church. In 1855, the Trinity River Association passed a resolution creating a school for boys; the following year, this institution was opened in the church building, and Pastor O'Brien was president. After he resigned three years later, the school was chartered as the Waco Classical School under the Waco Association. In 1861, Rufus C. Burleson left Baylor University at Independence, where he had been president for ten years, to take over the Waco Classical School, immediately re-chartering and renaming it Waco University. President Burleson made the school coeducational so that the instruction of men and women in the same classes could be allowed. Burleson's stated theory was that coeducation is more economical. I wonder if part of his motivation was also to avoid the kind of turf war he had with Horace Clark at Independence, who was in charge of the female department of the university.

Miles: The turf war with Clark sounds interesting.

Pops: It is certainly interesting, but unfortunately is not on our dance card for today. In 1869, a crucial event occurred in the history of Waco University and eventually Baylor University at Waco: Benajah Harvey Carroll was called to pastor First Baptist in Waco. According to Frederick Eby, Dr. Carroll accomplished four crucial tasks making possible the survival and success of the Waco school. Carroll created a dominant Baptist environment around Waco University, certainly without parallel in Texas. By being instrumental in the consolidation of Baylor and Waco Universities, he endowed the surviving Waco school with the prestige of old Baylor. Together with George W. Truett, he rescued Baylor from a load of debt crushing her very life. Finally, by making Baylor the head of the coordinated system, Carroll ensured its dominancy among Baptist colleges in Texas. More about Truett later, by all accounts a spell-binding preacher and Baylor's extraordinary early fundraiser.

On December 10, 1885, the year before the merger of Burleson's two universities—the one Burleson had led in Independence and the one he had commanded in Waco, Frank was still in Ohio working on the family farm, trying to distract himself from thinking about his future. At that moment, completely unknown to Frank, events that would change things forever were afoot in Texas. Pastor Carroll, the spokesperson for the Committee of Ten, a joint subcommittee appointed by the respective committees from the Baptist State Convention and the general association, made the recommendation that Waco and Baylor Universities be consolidated, the name of the school shall be Baylor University, and that Baylor University shall be located at Waco. Then, at the first meeting of the newly consolidated Baptist General Convention on June 29, 1986, the consolidation of schools and the two general bodies of Baptists was consummated. The new school was named Baylor University in Waco, Texas.

On September 29, 1886, five days after Frank arrived in Chester, Texas, to prospect land, the newly merged and expanded Baylor University opened in Waco with three hundred thirty-seven students. Two years later, its enrollment would be four hundred twelve. Waco, McLennan County, the home of the new Baylor University at Waco, Texas, had also experienced rapid growth. In 1850, there were only a few hundred people in the entire county. By 1860, McLennan had 6,200 people and Waco Village had eight hundred. In 1870, McLennan had 13,500 and Waco Village had 3,613. In 1890, McLennan had 39,204 and Waco Village had 14,445. By 1890, McLennan County was one of thc five most populous counties in Texas, exceeded only by Dallas, Grayson, Bexar, and Tarrant Counties.

When Frank stepped off the train in Texas, he knew very little about Texas and next to nothing about Waco. Waco, he would quickly learn, really turned out for church. Churches of all faiths proliferated, with the Baptists having the edge in numbers. However, not all of Waco's church-going people were especially pious. Samuel P. Brooks observed in the *Baylor Literary Magazine*: "In the country, there will be found near the church door, knife swappers, whittlers, and ignoramuses...In the city as you [enter] into the church house, you pass a crowd [for] which there is no name in the books. Among them are little dudes in knee breeches, big dudes with high collars, old dudes with neglected, dejected characters; everybody twirling his cane, and puffing great clouds of smoke, while many incessantly pull a few feeble mustaches...These are the skunks that stand by the door, in the door, in the vestibules and cast their loathsome odor over ladies as they seek egress."

At this time, Waco Baptists were still embroiled with "Martinism" which resulted in a heresy trial called "churching." Heresy trials were still in use to punish and brand those with off-brand religious beliefs. Martinism was a doctrine named for a recently discharged assistant minister at First Baptist Waco who had strongly advocated the principle of "Absolute Assurance." Anyone who doubted his conversion, so the doctrine went, had never been converted in the first place. A great mathematician and reasoner, Martin was no ordinary preacher and swept many people off their feet with his mathematical demonstrations of his odd beliefs. Even though they knew Martin had to be wrong, few men could stand up to him in an argument. As his appeal was great, other preachers began to imitate him. However, his mathematical demonstration of the doctrine of absolute assurance puzzled and troubled many in his congregation. During B.H. Carroll's years as pastor of First Baptist Waco, where Rufus C. Burleson was a member, Martin, a credentialed Baptist pastor, was charged in 1889 with heresy, and church conferences were convened to consider the matter. Martin was eventually adjudged a heretic by a vote of about three to one, and his credentials as a pastor of the Baptist denomination were withdrawn by First Baptist Waco. Martin would move on to First Baptist Marlin, Texas, where his credentials would be restored.

<u>Miles</u>: Pops, I thought this chapter was going to be about President Burleson and his universities. Are we getting there?

Pops: I was just about to talk about how Baylor's history includes both Baylor's men on horseback and its gadflies. Perhaps the foremost gadfly was J. Frank Norris, who will come up again in a later chapter. Among the men on horseback who served Baylor, either at the helm of the institution or outside during periods of severe crisis—men like Rufus C. Burleson, Benajah Harvey (B.H.) Carroll, George W. Truett, Samuel Palmer Brooks, and Pat M. Neff—none is a more colorful character than Dr. Rufus C. Burleson. Since Burleson was president of Baylor when Frank Guittard enrolled in 1890 and served during the entire time that Frank was a student at Baylor (1890-1894), special attention is appropriate.

Burleson was a force of nature, a man of titanic energy, aspiration, and dedication. He had the singular distinction of having served as president of both universities merged into the current Baylor University at Waco in 1886. He was president of Baylor at Independence from 1851 to 1861, then president of Waco University from 1861 to 1886, and finally president of Baylor University, Waco, Texas, from 1886 through 1897. Burleson's wife, Georgia J. Burleson, had said that her husband's favorite quotation was "paint me as I am." Born in 1823 in northern Alabama, he attended the University of Nashville for about a year and a half before he withdrew because of broken health. He attributed the break in his health to his zealous study habits. Later, he attended Western Baptist Theological Seminary at Covington, Kentucky, for a year and a half, and then he was chosen to succeed Tryon at a small church in Houston which had been cut down by yellow fever, Tryon himself succumbing to the disease. In 1851, Burleson was elected president of Baylor at Independence. He was also mindful of his lack of fitness; he wrote his brother Richard: "You ask how it is that I hold such a prominent position among such men? Well, I assure you it is not from superiority but from my sleepless vigilance and untiring energy."

If Burleson's formal education—a total of about three years for college and theological school combined—was limited by the standards of his day, nevertheless, he is reported to have "conceived a profound contempt for David's messenger, who ran before he got his tidings ready." Burleson accordingly spent seven years in arduous study, finally graduating from the Literary and Theological Institute of Covington, Kentucky. According to legend, Burleson spent seven months thereafter deeply studying the lives of Romulus, Alfred the Great, Roger Williams, John Calvin, and John Wesley, and also outlined in his notebook the plan for his life's work, which he pursued for forty-four years.

Charlie: Have you seen that notebook?

Pops: I don't think I have, but I would like to. Burleson was one of those unforgettable people. The popular perception of Burleson during his day is suggested by the following excerpt from McLennan County history: "He had never used tobacco nor intoxicating drinks, was never seen in a ballroom, a theatre, nor on a race track. He knows nothing of cars, billiards, or chess, and never swore but one oath in his life." Adjudged by Baptist chroniclers as temperamental, sometimes unreliable, and inclined to be headstrong and self-centered, he was adored by those who worked with him, but was abhorred by many others. He was capable of 'prodigious labor' but had to be in charge. He was unusually efficient but offended others by his boastfulness. He was a man of burning ambition who once said that his "great life purpose seemed like fire in his bones."

Finn: Do we know what the one oath he swore was? Or what would have made him swear it?

Pops: Sorry, neither his wife Georgia nor his biographer Harry Haynes thought it necessary to preserve it for posterity. I would guess the oath was a fairly mild one, since even mild cussing would have been burned Burleson's ears. Perhaps he got irked over some random act of student misbehavior. Burleson's tremendous energy was often directed at monitoring students' leisure activities, and he took a dim view of many popular pastimes of the day. In a chapel talk entitled "Do Thyself No Harm," he advised his audience: "The mania of card playing, when it gets a firm hold, is just as fatal as intoxicating drinks. It hardens the heart and blots out all the nobler sensibilities of the soul...I know a learned preacher in Texas who has acquired such a passion for dominoes that when sent for to see a dying lady—a member of his church—he said, 'I have a special engagement and will come as soon as I can.' But alas, the lady died while her...pastor was playing dominoes...All games of hazard... such as dominoes, checkers...burden the heart and deaden all the nobler feeling of the soul when played to excess."

Katie: I didn't realize that dominoes and checkers were bad for you. Or card playing.

Pops: It seems that Burleson felt activities like dominoes and checkers could become manias that would interfere with students living blame-free, productive lives. Burleson had firm opinions, and some were definitely out of touch with the times. He also showed a definite aversion to hazing students, secret societies, and certain other forms of student foolishness. In an address to the Texas State Teachers Association in 1898 he stated: "I am convinced that many of our great universities are sewing the tares of lawlessness and anarchy. I refer especially to the brutal habit of hazing, or dragging the students out of their beds at the hour of midnight, tying their hands, blindfolding them, drenching them in mud or water, encasing them in coffins, and other things that would disgrace Comanche Indians. I also refer to stealing chickens and turkeys, robbing Bee-gums, tearing down gates and sign boards, hauling away buggies and carriages, et cetera..., which are tolerated and laughed at as college tricks in many of our great institutions...Secret societies are justly regarded as the chief...fountain of many of these degrading habits in college life...I declined ever to inaugurate a secret society in any college where I presided."

<u>Finn</u>: I've seen a photograph of President Burleson. He looked really tired.

<u>Pops</u>: I'm sure he was. Frank Guittard's last year at Baylor was 1894, when Burleson was seventy-one. It was said that ten years more could be added to his actual age on account of the hard life and exposure he suffered during his early years in Texas. As an itinerant preacher, Burleson rode horseback, swam creeks, slept in swamps, went without food, and endured other hardships. Those hardships reportedly impaired his constitution, which had not been robust since his hard study at Nashville in 1840.

<u>Finn</u>: It sounds like being president of Baylor in its early days took a lot out of you. I would imagine by the time President Brooks became president, it was a lot easier.

<u>Pops</u>: Hold that thought. Being president of Baylor was no cakewalk for Brooks either, even if he never swam in a creek or slept in a swamp. We'll get to all of that before long.

CHAPTER 8

Frank's Game Plan: Education, Career, and Family

(1885-1931)

Frank's evolving plan for his life is key to understanding his story. He was, from early on, a patient planner and systematizer. I will be going through this chapter with Katie.

Pops: Katie, I am going to throw a lot of stuff out there in this chapter; if you have a question, please ask and I will try to clarify. We start this chapter with the view that although Frank was anxious at times to move forward in his life, he was not ordinarily in a hurry; when he had no choice but to wait, he could wait. He had to bide his time for many of the good things in his life, yet he was never standing completely still; instead, he was usually walking steadily forward, sometimes side to side as he pondered his path *forward*, but always in motion. Frank's plan for his life—which he tweaked from time to time but never really abandoned after realizing there were no funds for medical education—included obtaining a university education and then selecting and fitting himself for a professional career. His father and two brothers were physicians, but medicine was not in the cards for Frank. An essential down-the-road piece of his plan was to meet and marry a cultured woman of common interests and faith with whom he could combine romance and family; if possible, one who liked to read.

He was eventually able to do all these things despite some difficult bumps in the road along the way. Those bumps were occasioned by what he euphemistically called the "winds of chance"—including the economic conditions in the country between 1885 and 1900, which affected the dollars in the pockets of farmers, farmers who were patients of his father; the resulting lack of sufficient funds for his education that would have allowed him to go straight through college and university; the lack of any real mentoring or career information from his parents or anyone else as to suitable careers paired with Frank's own reluctance to ask others for advice; the prevalence of tuberculosis and other infectious diseases affecting his family; and the absences from his family necessary to earn his Ph.D.

In the absence of funds for a medical education or other education, Frank decided while still in Ohio he could at least be a teacher, teaching being the career he adopted by default. After that, he progressed, usually ploddingly, toward a teaching career without serious consideration of a career in any other profession, including the legal profession, for which he appears to have been well suited. As we will discuss, decades later he would ensure that both of his sons went to law school and commenced careers in the law.

Frank's general plan for education, career, and family was certainly in his mind before leaving Ohio for Texas. In his 1894 autobiographical sketch while a Baylor student, he recorded: "If I keep my health, I intend to complete my college degree. I have had much to discourage me, but I still hold to this one aim of my life." However, there was always an uneasy tension between his plan and the pursuit of his goals and the reality of where the winds of chance might take him, especially as long as a teaching career was his objective. At some point, as time wore on, Frank began to think he had made some "mistakes" or "blunders" in navigating between his plan, on the one hand, and where chance might be taking him on the other. What those errors may have been in his own mind and whether his life was any less rewarding in any sense because of any self-perceived "blunders," we will speculate about later. Sometimes good things do happen by chance.

Katie, any questions about what we will talk about today?

Katie: I have a few. You say he lacked any real career advice, but didn't he have the example of his father practicing medicine?

Pops: Yes, of course, he had his father's example, but that's not the same as actual career counseling or mentoring. In his 1906 treatise, Professor Gowin at New York University got to the heart of the problem when he stated: "In choosing his life work the young man faces a problem of vital importance, and he should act upon the best possible information and counsel. It is no satisfactory solution to leave him with the vague statement 'The world lies before you,'...The young man learns after a time that the real test lies not so much in ambition and upward looking as in effort well directed. He then wants to know what may be done and where to take hold."

However, finding a suitable career, Professor Gowin advised, was not to be accomplished by merely dreaming, but rather upon the investigation of many vocations before selecting a life calling. Gowin's advice was to study the careers of others, to learn from the people one meets, visit places of vocational interest, and read vocational books and magazines. Gowin then discussed the requirements for entering many vocations, including teaching, and offers advice about using teaching as a stepping stone. This advice would have been interesting and potentially important for Frank Guittard to consider. Professor Gowin stated: "The caution must be given...that in using teaching as a stepping stone, one should not lose sight of the larger ambition [if one has one]. Too many have drifted into teaching as a temporary occupation and have continued in it for life...The young man who goes into teaching simply for the money he can get out of it will likely be disappointed."

Katie: I think Frank wanted to go to medical school, but he couldn't, and so he shifted his dream to get a college education, which would have been helpful preparation for several professions, not just teaching. Couldn't he, as Professor Gowin said, have used preparation for teaching and then teaching as stepping stones to another career, for example, the law? I am also wondering if he ever considered going into a business of some sort. He could still have read as much as he had time.

Pops: Let's hold your question for a minute. I have with me today the November 22, 1890, issue of the *Literary Digest.* Let's go through a few pages and see if we can answer your question. The front page has an ad for a set of the *Encyclopedia Britannica* for $25. In line with your question, Frank could have earned $25 doing something and invested in the *Britannica* in twelve double volumes, thereby acquiring plenty to read for a lifetime. Let's look at the people writing articles for the *Digest,* and I'm sure for the *Britannica,* as well. Here are some book ads—a book by Carlos Martyn, D.D.; a book by Wendell Phillips, who gave a Phi Beta Kappa oration at Harvard; and one about Professor Koch's discovery relating to tuberculosis bacilli. Okay, does this information help you with your answer?

Katie: Maybe. But now I'm thinking Frank possibly wasn't interested in simply knowing things scholars and professionals knew; he wanted to *be* one of them with a degree or degrees after his name. What do you think?

Pops: I think you are on the right track. He wanted to be one of those degreed teacher-scholars who could write articles for the *Digest* in their spare time. He didn't want to be someone focused on markets, money, and business who just read scholarly articles on the side. He wanted to do his passion full-time—read and teach history. As for being an attorney, I don't think he thought about it seriously except in retrospect much later when Francis was about to graduate from Baylor and was thinking about his career options. At all times when it mattered, Frank did not have an ambition other than being a teacher and scholar—certainly not after giving up his dream of being a medical doctor. You had another question, though?

Katie: (*smiling*) Yes, Pops, you're going to think this one is completely off the wall, but since Frank came to Texas and there were still some cowboys in Texas, did Frank ever think about being a cowboy and driving cows up to Kansas? Did he know any cowboys or cowgirls?

Pops: This is going to be a long answer. Although the long trail drives were rapidly disappearing and cowboys a vanishing breed by the time Frank came to Texas, some cowboys were still needed to manage and drive herds. At one point earlier on, cattle had been driven across the Brazos via the Waco Suspension Bridge and then up the Chisholm Trail to Kansas. Can you imagine the racket on the bridge as the cows were driven across? As for Frank being a cowboy in Texas, he could ride a horse and had a horse for a time after he moved back to Waco to take the Baylor job. We have no idea where that horse might have been stabled; surely not in the garage! We have an 1890s photo of him in a Stetson hat and boots, but I don't think he would have enjoyed sitting in a saddle all day. We know he was not afraid of being by himself, but he may not have wanted to be outside and sleep under the stars in all kinds of weather. He was unusually cautious about catching a cold. A saddle and a scratchy saddle blanket for a pillow at night? I don't think so. Anyway, that alternative was a moot point after the cattle drives were broken up by barbed wire across the open ranges and there were just fewer cowboys needed.

Even if cattle owners had still needed cowboys, cowboys' ideas of fun at the end of a long trail ride would have been foreign to Frank—going into town, drinking, gambling, and riding while firing off their pistols at the moon, loud hallooing, and frequenting bawdy houses. Drinking bad whiskey and dealing with B-girls and prostitutes would not have appealed to him. Even eating beans around a grub wagon, singing and telling stories around the campfire, hanging out with rough men without a high school education, some of whom could scarcely have written a letter back home to family, would have gotten old quickly for Frank. And there were no libraries or bookstores on the trail. And no Sunday services to take a girl to. No Sacred Harp singing sessions. Really no girls except in the bars along the trail, or, worse, in the bawdy houses.

Katie: Somewhere, I heard about a president of Southwestern Seminary in Fort Worth being a cowboy when he was young.

Pops: Yes, believe it or not, sometimes educated young men, even from eastern universities, took a wild fancy to working as cowboys, a romantic notion fostered by dime novels. Frank's fellow Erisophian, Lee Scarborough, actually worked as a cowboy before enrolling at Baylor. Scarborough ultimately became president of Southwestern Theological Seminary. When your dad, Jim, obtained his diploma from Southwestern a few years back, the faculty all marched into that auditorium in their academic robes wearing black cowboy hats. Maybe that's because Lee Scarborough had once been a cowboy. Maybe you could research that.

Katie: What did a cowboy wear on a trail ride?

Pops: A big hat or sombrero to shade him from the sun, a box-toed boot, a shirt and jeans, a slicker, and chaps.

Katie: Wouldn't a slicker have kept Frank warm if he had wanted to be a cowboy?

Pops: Dry but not warm. Historian Ramon G. Adams claimed that one cowboy humorously complained a single slicker wasn't enough to keep him warm, but if he had had two slickers, he would have frozen to death. Realistically, in 1886, when Frank came to Texas, being a cowboy was a doomed occupation. Big cattle drives up the Chisholm Trail—which went through Waco—had drastically declined. Barbed wire fences and the build-out of railroads killed trail drives, cattle being increasingly shipped to Kansas by rail.

Katie: What about cowgirls? Did they go on trail drives with the men? I hear today that truck drivers' wives sometimes go on the road with their husbands.

Pops: There were probably a few, and there were definitely women in those days who could ride and shoot as well as the men. Annie Oakley, who came from Ohio, could shoot better than any man of her era. Frank saw her when Buffalo Bill staged his Wild West Show in Chicago. I don't even think Buffalo Bill—who was a crack shot—would have stood a chance against her in a shooting contest. There were also women who could ride and shoot but who were on the wrong side of the law, outlaws like Belle Starr, Calamity Jane, Pearl Hart, and Big Nose Kate.

Katie: Why did they call her Big Nose Kate?

Pops: Her nose must have seemed large to somebody writing a dime novel, or maybe that made for better newspaper copy. I found a picture of her online and it didn't look so big to me. But let's go back to Frank's game plan for his life. It seems Frank evolved his plan over time to meet the challenges cropping up along the way. We will discuss what appears to have been his evolving game plan for his education, career, and family in stages.

Katie: I'm not sure how you know what Frank was thinking over a century ago.

Pops: That's a fair comment. Cloudiness of motives of persons long deceased is always a challenge for the biographer. We have to admit that our grasp of another person's history, particularly his motivation at a particular moment, is always fragmentary at best. Fortunately for us, in Frank's case, we have many clues; he left us letters, diaries, autobiographies, essays, ledgers, and other writings. He clearly said what he was thinking at certain times. For example, when we get to his self-assessment of how he had planned out his life, we will use his own words in his letters to his oldest son Francis where he speaks of having made "mistakes" and having "blundered" in his planning. He was trying to put Francis on the right path at a law firm and hoping he would benefit from mistakes Frank thought he had made.

So, let's start with that evolving plan, which I will try to sketch out roughly from the facts and events in his life based on a significant number of archival sources. The terms "Plan A," "Obstacle," "Challenge," and so on are my own, but I believe they fairly represent Frank's perspective and intent at the time, as well as important context for the plan and its chances of success.

Frank's Evolving Game Plan for Education, Career, and Family

1886: Plan A—Attend the teacher's institute in Millersburg, Ohio, hoping for his father's encouragement and financial assistance for further schooling, probably undergraduate courses, and then medical school.

> Obstacles: the weak economy in Ohio and nationally, his father's struggling medical practice, and his inability to assist Frank.

1886: Plan B—Take the train to Texas as a land scout to find a location for his father's medical practice and family relocation, hoping to improve his family's financial prospects and his chances of parental financial assistance for more education.

> Obstacles: family's change of heart regarding the feasibility of Frank's father starting over in Texas, probably also realizing that Texas had its own problems, the national economy still being depressed.

1887 or so: Plan C—Stay in Texas, family staying in Ohio, and thereafter support himself by teaching in country schools, saving money to attend Sam Houston Normal to improve his marketability as a teacher in public schools; as soon as possible, to take college courses toward a college degree. He taught at, or was principal of, six or more country schools.

> Inspiration for the plan to teach: While at Sam Houston, Frank would have been fortified in his plan to teach. The January 1890 *Texas School Journal* edited by O.H. Cooper, State Superintendent of Education and president of Baylor in Waco in 1899, not only spoke of the nobility and loftiness of teaching and the feeling of value teachers experience, but the view that the "educating influence, or educator, is God, represented by Nature." Further,

Cooper claimed the would-be teacher should be on guard against impure motives [making money], which may interfere with the humanitarian spirit needed to animate a teacher.

Reason for change of plan: after a year at Sam Houston, Frank felt he had acquired sufficient funds to enroll at Baylor, a degree from which being the next step upward. Frank's reason for moving from school to school is not recorded in his diaries, but likely was his need to earn as much as possible to support his plan to get a college degree.

1890: Plan D—Enter Baylor in Waco and make a determined effort to work his way straight through Baylor as rapidly as possible. Having entered Baylor, Frank identified his life's goals in his 1893 essay "Life" composed in the fall of 1893 in the Giant Rhetoric class. Those goals were "Getting an Education, Choosing a Vocation, Choosing a Wife, Making a Success of one's Vocation, and Living Uprightly."

Obstacle: After four years of alternating studies at Baylor with teaching in small schools, Frank's funds ran out, and he had to return to teaching after a summer selling books.

1897: Plan E—Enter the University of Chicago and take courses during the summers, returning to Texas or Arkansas to teach, principally at the Southwest Academy at Magnolia, Arkansas, and finish up his initial bachelor's degree.

Reasons for deciding against returning to Baylor: In addition to the University of Chicago opening as a world-class university and being closer to Ohio than Waco, Chicago also provided plentiful opportunities for students to work and pay for their education. It assisted one-fourth of its 2,000 students, and students enjoyed all the cultural attractions of a large city. Years later, Frank would speak to students on the topic "Students Who Work to Get through College." In this speech, Frank would list eleven specific jobs for students at the University of Chicago and twelve jobs on the outside, including waiters at boarding clubs. Waiting at a boarding club is one job we know Frank had in Chicago.

Challenge: Again, insufficient funds to go straight through.

1902: Plan F—Having earned two degrees at Chicago (including a Master's in History), accept President Brooks's invitation to teach in the Baylor Academy and advance as quickly as possible; perhaps pursue a Ph.D. as soon as feasible, preferably at Chicago; pursue his interest in Mamie Welhausen as a potential marital partner.

> Challenge: achieve promotion to Baylor's collegiate department and thereby enhance his faculty position; acquire the funds needed to purchase a home (1905) so that he and Mamie would not have to start their married life in a boarding house; maintain Mamie's interest over the protracted courtship period and work to solidify the approval of her prosperous banker father, Captain Charlie Welhausen, and her mother, Eliza Amsler Welhausen.

Katie: So Frank decided to teach history while a student at Chicago. Did he ever say why?

Pops: Not in so many words. But others have offered their reasons for studying history. Here are a few reasons that would seem to fit Frank and his approach to the world and learning:

- George Santayana: "A country without a memory is a country of madmen."
- Shailer Mathews: "When a historian enters into metaphysics, he has gone to a far country from whose bourne he will never return a historian."
- T.F. Tout: "We investigate the past not to deduce practical political lessons, but to find out what really happened."
- Charles Seignobos: "History is not a science; it is a method."
- Herbert Hoover: "The supreme purpose of history is a better world."
- Edgar Saltus: "Skepticism is history's bedfellow."
- Leo XIII: "The first law of history is to dread uttering falsehood; the next is not to fear stating the truth; lastly, the historian's writings should be open to no suspicion of partiality or animosity."
- Arthur M. Schlesinger, Jr.: "The passion for tidiness is the historian's occupation disease."
- Hippolyte Taine: "After the collection of facts, the search for causes."
- Archbishop Leighton: "The only true knowledge of things is the knowledge of their causes."

Pops: Do you like any of those?

Katie: I liked Santayana's about a country without a memory is a country of madmen.

Pops: Me too. Let's continue with Frank's evolving game plan.

1906-1916: Plan G—Having gotten the job in the Academy, then a promotion to Baylor's college division, a home, the girl (Mamie), a promotion to history chair: to start a family while working steadily at Baylor; to progress in income and responsibility under the presidency of his college colleague, Samuel Brooks. One of the two most fulfilling and happy periods of his life.

> Intervening tragedies: illness and death (1916) of infant son Charles and illness of Mamie.

1916-17: Plan H—Survive the separations from Mamie and the grief associated with the deaths of Charles and Mamie in 1916 and 1917.

1917-1920: Plan I—Focus on teaching, be a father to Francis, see Clarence in Shiner, TX, as often as possible, and find a suitable marriage partner who could mother Clarence.

1920-1923: Plan J—Buy a larger house to live in with Josie Glenn, secure her agreement to marry, pick up Clarence from relatives in Shiner, and return to a more stable life with all family members together in the same house. 1920-1923 is the second very happy period.

> Challenge: President Brooks expressed his intention that all department chairs have doctorates and go back to school to earn them.

1923-1931: Plan K—Obtain a Ph.D. in history at Stanford University by taking courses primarily in the summers, returning to Baylor before the fall semester. Beginning in the mid-1920s, steer oldest son Francis into studying law and advise him concerning his preparations for that course of action.

> Challenges: the strenuous, grinding nature of studies at Stanford, particularly in fulfilling the requirements for demonstrating proficiency in two foreign languages; the feeling of loneliness and isolation from his family, his friends, and colleagues on the Baylor faculty.

1931-1950: Plan L—Teach at Baylor and serve as history chair as long as possible; guide his sons as needed, particularly Clarence in his career planning. A third happy period and possibly the most satisfying.

> Challenges: the lack of a Baylor retirement program and Frank's inability to afford retirement. To hold on to his position as chair and administrator of the history department as long as possible, leave sufficient assets for Josie to live on, and establish a fellowship for graduate history students.

Pops: Any questions to this point?

Katie: Yes. I want to know what he was thinking about as a young man, what his goals in life were before he got on the train for Texas. I would like to know, for example, whether he had read books about Texas. Had he read Horatio Alger, Jr. books? I would also like to know what had happened for Frank to say he had much to discourage him.

Pops: Well, Katie, as to that last question first, we don't know specifically what may have discouraged Frank, but we can guess. Running out of money at Baylor before he completed his degree, or having to make decisions without help or advice from home, or having to constantly find new teaching jobs where he could make the money he needed to go back to school—all of those would have caused him to worry. One other thought that may have disturbed him was what would happen if he became sick and could not take care of himself? His mother was gone, his family was dispersed, and his father seemed to have his hands full taking care of himself during the hard times of the mid-1890s. What would become of Frank if he got sick in Texas and needed care from others and couldn't pay for it? The 1890s was not a good decade to become ill without financial resources or be unable to find work. There were shelters called poor houses and infirmaries for the poor in Ohio and elsewhere. There was one in Holmes County north of New Bedford, as well as one in Coshocton County, where New Bedford was located. Oftentimes, mentally ill people lived in such facilities with the sick and unwell and the poverty-stricken elderly.

Frank would have learned rather quickly that Texas, too, had its share of poor farms or poor houses; at least sixty-five of Texas's 254 counties had established poor farms. "The dream of finding a new life, the belief if a man worked hard, he could 'make it,' drove settlers to the cheap land in Texas. But if illness, death of the breadwinner, drought, or crop failure forced a family into poverty, they and their neighbors believed that the need to accept public assistance was a form of moral failure...To be on charity, to be a public charge—this held a special dread in pioneer times."

The prospect of being buried in one of those pauper's cemeteries around the state would have been depressing to Frank had his mind dwelled on it. The Kaufman County poor farm, which opened five years before Frank arrived in Texas, housed paupers who were expected to support themselves by working on the farm until they were financially able to leave or until they died, whichever occurred first. Virtually all of Ohio's counties had poor farms. When the residents were able to work, "on one county poor farm, residents in the 1930-1940s time frame were lured out of the residential facility to play dominoes and eat ice cream while fumigators sprayed their living quarters."

Whether the following was accurate or was a satirical dig isn't clear, but on March 25, 1906, the *Sunday Gazetteer* [a Texas newspaper] allegedly reported: "It has been discovered that eating small particles of wood is very healthy. This is a hint to City Jailor Tom Wright...of the poor farm, to maintain their inmates on a diet of shredded shingles or hashed fence posts. A very considerable saving in the annual budget could be made." Also disturbing was the fact that during the 1900 smallpox outbreak, the poor farm served as the epidemic camp and previously had been used as the typhoid fever epidemic burial site. According to Dana Goolsby, "Poor farms...were society's dumping grounds for outcasts. Those who were insane, tubercular, deaf, imbecile, criminal, aged, or poor, were often placed together on county poor farms. They were viewed as hopeless and useless."

Katie: That poor farm stuff would have been pretty scary to a guy like Frank who didn't have a financial cushion to fall back on; he knew his parents were having a hard time making it themselves. I'm wondering if there were books or magazines that Frank could escape into and distract himself from the hard realities of making a living during a depression.

Pops: We don't know of any books specifically about Texas that he read. However, he must have read some, including possibly some of the many popular dime westerns about Texas that made Texas seem both exciting and dangerous because of its publicized lawlessness. Of course, newspapers and periodicals carried stories about Texas, too. We have talked about such stories in the chapter called "A Bookworm's Brain." More importantly, we know that young men and women, especially young men, were given to daydreaming about their futures and what adventures may be in store for them. The books in his father's library may have also encouraged in Frank some wanderlust or an appetite for adventure as well as providing relief from melancholy thoughts. We know *The Arabian Nights*, *Robinson Crusoe*, *Don Quixote*, and *A Pilgrim's Progress*, along with many other books in the house in New Bedford, could have taken his mind off his concerns.

Although we don't think he would have read many of the Horatio Alger, Jr. books since they have never been considered good literature despite Alger's Harvard degree, nearly all of them featured adventures of young men out on their own with little or no support from friends or family. Decades later, we know Frank was reading the comic strip *Ben Webster* by Edwin Alger. *Ben Webster* was a take-off on the Alger books starring an earnest young man striving for the American dream who was involved in one adventure after another.

I may have just left off one of the most important factors possibly influencing his goals before the trip to Texas. In 1847, Frank's father, when he was a young man of Frank's same age, immigrated to the United States from France as a land scout, accompanied by one of his sisters, pursuing a mission for his family to canvass opportunities for a family move to the US. His family, including his father, mother, and another sister, followed him several years later. And now, Francis Joseph Guittard was discussing with Frank that he accomplish a somewhat lesser feat, land scouting in Texas, and Frank would not even have to learn a new language.

So, what were Frank's goals, originally? All we know is that early on in New Bedford he wanted a college education, a career in one of the usual professions, preferably medicine, and marriage and family. Moreover, Frank was a voracious reader who wanted to read books in many fields to broaden his knowledge and understanding of the world.

<u>Katie:</u> So, what other career options, including teaching, do you think he had in mind between 1886 when he originally came to Texas and 1902 when he returned to Texas with two degrees from Chicago?

<u>Pops</u>: No doubt he had many options, but few would have appealed to him. We already discussed being a cowboy, which would have been a non-starter. Then, no doubt he could have worked in some sort of business or a government office. These wouldn't have worked for him since he had his heart set on a career as a professional of some kind. Professional careers included church pastor, church music minister, dentist, pharmacist, engineer, medical doctor, orchestra or band musician, geologist, accountant, college professor, and attorney. Frank made a firm decision to be a college teacher while he was at the University of Chicago working on his undergraduate degree between 1897 and 1901. Below are perhaps some reasons he didn't pursue some of the other options mentioned:

> *Dentist, engineer, pharmacist, medical doctor, geologist, and accountant*: Of these, medical doctor was the only option that he desired to pursue since his father and two brothers were doctors; these callings required money for tuition, and that was in short supply. His desire to be a physician was despite the "vast number of

incompetents, large numbers of moral degenerates, and crowds of pure tradesmen [the medical profession still contained in 1900]." The medical profession in the 1890s was [also just emerging from] the boom of homeopathic, eclectic, and botanic colleges, which "invaded the country after 1830 and did battle with 'regular' schools of any type." Medical professionals, in general, were held in low esteem because of the low level of medical education in the late 1800s. The "botanics" depended on vegetable drugs and represented a rival profession to the regular doctors. Since Frank had his heart set on being a physician, we doubt whether a career devoted to teeth, building things, dispensing pills, reassuring neurotic patients, studying rocks, or adding up or subtracting numbers would have appealed to him. As to dentistry, it was reported that "dentistry is one of the first areas...cut back in a recession... unless [people] have a toothache." No doubt he would have been a good doctor like his father and brothers, but his father's financial fortunes sagged, the struggling economy intervened, and he was dispatched to Texas.

It is also certainly possible that limiting his reading to the ills and functions of the human body would have been frustrating. Going on house calls in a horse and buggy, or in an automobile, and then sitting up all night with sick patients like his father had to do would have gotten old quickly. Although the University of Texas had opened a medical branch in Galveston in 1890, either its expense, admission requirements, inadequacy of its facilities, or all of these combined weighed against this path for Frank. We also doubt Frank would have wanted to learn medicine by working in the office of a doctor as his father did in Ohio or reading medical books at night by candlelight as Abe Lincoln read law books. He would have wanted to go to a regular medical school, but that door was closed to him.

Pastor: Frank was a strong believer in the Christian faith and the Baptist denomination; however, like President Brooks, Frank's call was to teach and enlighten students as to history so that they could adequately evaluate people and events of the past to make good decisions as citizens. There is no mention of him leading public prayer, which seemingly would have been an activity at which a pastor would be expected to be proficient. Frank also didn't like spending any more time in meetings than was absolutely necessary, and a pastor of a congregation could not avoid attendance at a great number of lengthy conferences as well as meetings with those in his congregation.

Orchestra or band musician: Frank must have liked playing the cornet, but he either doubted his ability to take his skill to the professional level, or doubted whether the money and the required travel would support his goal of having a family. Then, too, making money buzzing his lips and blowing air through a mouthpiece while his fingers worked valves was not the kind of intellectual challenge that would have appealed to him. He did like playing in a small orchestra at Baylor after he first joined the faculty. There is also a question about whether the last two fingers on his right hand would have been a problem playing the cornet professionally.

Attorney: Frank does not appear to have thought seriously about law as a career until sometime after 1902, likely in the early to mid-1920s when he enrolled Francis in the Baylor Law School. We don't know what specific objection or reservation he would have had to becoming an attorney himself, other than the expense of going to law school and the fact that lawyers were generally at a lower rung of the social ladder than medical doctors. In Texas, a person could apply for a law license if he had attained the age of twenty-one, resided in the state for six months, and had a good reputation for moral character and honorable deportment. The licensing procedure required appearing before a district judge and passing an oral examination conducted by three attorneys. We suspect that Frank's serious consideration of law as a career for a young man was delayed until the 1920s by his initial interest in medicine in Ohio, followed by his immigration to Texas with only a teaching career on his mind, teaching becoming his career by default as time passed. We will talk later about the great essayist and lexicographer Samuel Johnson wishing he had been an attorney.

It is clear that teaching, especially teaching history, was his passion and that Frank chose to pursue his passion as his career rather than a career that would make his goal of family more affordable. It is also clear that while law practice would have been a more lucrative profession than teaching, for many attorneys, law practice can be unsatisfying and burdensome due to lawyers graduating law school needing to work hundreds of hours monthly to stay afloat. It would have been frustrating for Frank to have no choice but to shrink or eliminate time reading history for the relentless and mind-numbing grind of reading law cases and statutes. How well he would have adjusted to dealing with clients

> and speaking on their behalf is also open to question given his personality, but there is no one personality for a successful attorney.
>
> *Businessman or entrepreneur*: Waco had a well-regarded business college founded by Edward Toby, Jr. called Toby's Practical Business College of Waco. The school opened in Toby's Waco residence around 1890 and fielded a football team that played against Baylor's team. Baylor President Brooks even recommended Toby's to Baylor students. Although Frank believed that the skills Toby taught (such as shorthand, book-keeping, and typewriting—which he recommended to son Francis) were essential for a young lawyer-to-be, he was never interested in pursuing money for its own sake or in the world of commerce. Neither his father nor brothers were primarily motivated by making money. Money was necessary to live, but its accumulation was not.
>
> If Frank had been debating between academia and a business career, Francis Joseph likely would have supported either choice and not offered the kind of advice John Graham offered son Pierrepont as a Harvard freshman: "No, I can't say that I think anything of your postgraduate course idea. You're not going to be a poet or a professor, but a packer [in Chicago] and the place to take a postgraduate course for that calling is in the packing-house."

As to the feasibility of Frank reading law in a lawyer's office instead of going to law school, that path was open to him. He could have taken this course but may have felt—we can't say for sure—that he would emerge as a lawyer with a second-class education, which would not have appealed to him. Have you ever heard of John Wesley Hardin?

<u>Katie</u>: Wasn't Hardin a big Methodist?

<u>Pops</u>: No, he wasn't a big Methodist, just named for a big Methodist by his Methodist parents. Even if he was a Methodist, John Wesley Hardin was not a good guy at all—he was a convicted stone-cold killer with at least twenty notches on his gun belt. He read law in prison and started practicing law after being pardoned by Texas's governor J.S. Hogg. He was sent to the pen in 1878, being sentenced to twenty-five years with hard labor for second-degree murder. He served over fifteen years before being released in 1894—the same year Frank dropped out of Baylor. In the pen, Hardin studied law, theology, and arithmetic; he was superintendent of the Sunday school; and he had been elected president of the debating society. By the time he was released, he had been studying law for eight years.

Katie: Strange story.

Pops: After Hardin was released, he practiced law for a while but spent too much time gambling in saloons and getting into trouble, eventually being shot in the back of the head by lawman—and sometimes outlaw—John Selman in 1895. Selman himself was later shot and killed in a gunfight by U.S. Marshal George Scarborough (not related to the Baylor Scarboroughs).

Katie: So, you are telling me this because...?

Pops: Because Frank must have known Hardin's history in 1894 when Frank dropped out of Baylor. Hardin was a celebrity who had read law in prison and been licensed to practice law. If he had wanted to, Frank could have read law and obtained his law license.

Katie: Why didn't Frank go to law school like Pat Neff?

Pops: It was a matter of time and money, and Frank had neither the time nor the money. If he had followed Pat Neff's path into the law—which path they surely discussed during the two years they roomed together, those years being the subject of a later chapter—that would have meant Frank finishing up his undergraduate degree at Chicago in 1901 and then taking another estimated five years to work his way through the University of Texas Law School. If he had been willing or able to do this, it would have taken him potentially until 1906. At that point, he would have been thirty-eight by the time he could have started practice, which would have been three years after he started his teaching job at Baylor in 1902. On the other hand, if he had been able to read law with an attorney beginning in 1886 at age nineteen and secured a legal apprenticeship lasting seven years, he would have been ready to practice law at age twenty-six, a full nine years before being able to make a living as a Baylor professor of history. However, Frank's personality and commitment to an undergraduate degree and formal schooling foreclosed the possibility of any shortcuts to establishing a career.

Katie: I'm getting dizzy. I'm not sure what you are saying.

Pops: Okay. The point is that hindsight is 20-20. If he had known from the beginning that his best shot at quick financial independence as an adult was reading law, he would have had to give up his goal of obtaining a bachelor's degree. His best path going forward to accomplish all of his goals starting from his arrival in Texas was, at best, problematic. So Frank opted, without financial resources or the input of a judge, attorney, or other mentors, to work his way through the University of Chicago and obtain two degrees to prepare him for a teaching career. It took him a total of sixteen years to accumulate his bachelor's and master's degrees, which delayed when he could get married and start a family.

Katie: College students today can go straight through college in four years and then on to professional school if they want to. Either their parents help them, or they get loans or grants.

Pops: That's right. We live in a different time.

Katie: I'm wondering how Frank felt about taking so much time to go through school.

Pops: I'm sure it must have been discouraging to see his contemporaries, or even a younger man like Pat Neff, getting ahead of him. If we use Francis Joseph Guittard's lifespan (September 3, 1827-June 11, 1902) as one measuring stick for Frank's feelings of progress or frustration, we may be able to gauge his feelings of being behind people like Brooks and Neff. We may get a sense of where he would have liked to have been in his life had he not been challenged by lack of financial support from his parents and, of course, the lack of grants and loans. I used a single 24-hour day as a metaphor for the length of anyone's life. I also assumed that Frank might have thought he could not count on living any longer than this father, who lived to be seventy-three and approximately nine months. So, I took his father's lifespan and called that a 24-hour day to make my calculations to measure Frank's possible feelings of progress or lack of progress. Although my math is pretty loose and I ignored leap years, here are the results:

- When Frank left for Texas on September 23, 1886, at nineteen years of age, it was 6:25 a.m. of the metaphorical 24 hours, his day was already 1/4 gone and his life 27% spent.
- When he ran out of money in April 1894 and had to leave Baylor without a degree, it was 8:52 a.m., and he was twenty-seven. His life was 37% spent.
- When he started at the University of Chicago in the summer of 1897, it was 9:54 a.m., and he was thirty. His life was 41% spent.
- After his father died and Frank had finally completed his A.B. and A.M. degrees in Chicago, and President Brooks had offered him a job at Baylor, it was 11:11, almost noon. He was thirty-five. His life was 49% spent, and he had yet to teach his first day as a college teacher—his professional career goal.

- When he married Mamie on December 24, 1906, it was 1 p.m. and he was almost forty. His life was 54% spent.
- When Mamie died on May 17, 1917, and Frank obliged to re-enter the dating game, it was 4:23 p.m., and he was fifty. His life was 68% spent.
- When Frank reluctantly commenced his Ph.D. at Stanford in June 1923, it was 6:21 p.m., and he was fifty-six. His life was 76% spent.
- When Frank at long last received his Ph.D. on June 16, 1931, it was 9 p.m.–3 hours before midnight, and he had not yet taught one day with his Ph.D. degree. He was sixty-four and his life was 87% spent.
- When Frank died on April 28, 1950, at eighty-three, it was 3 a.m. of the next 24-hour day. It turned out he lived as long as his father, plus almost another ten years.

Katie: You mentioned when we started talking earlier that Frank decided later he had made some mistakes and had blundered along. What is that about? After all, once President Brooks hired him, Frank stayed at Baylor the rest of his career and earned a doctorate in the 1920s. He was a respected history teacher, never had to go anywhere else, lived in a big two-story house in Waco for three decades, and had two sons who gave him five grandchildren.

Pops: Yes, but it is also clear that Frank faulted himself severely, and, perhaps to some extent by implication, his overworked, underpaid father for insufficient planning and guidance in the matter of his education and career, at least up to the time he secured his position at Baylor in 1902 at age thirty-five. In 1926, he wrote Francis from Stanford at age fifty-nine before Francis entered Baylor Law School:

> Then while I have a little leisure, I should like to suggest something else for you to think over. I am writing from my own experiences in life. *No one advised me or suggested what I should study for or take up as a life work.* As a result when my judgment was immature as it is with everyone before coming in contact with the practical affairs of life I can look back now and see that *I made some very serious mistakes...I would regret for you to blunder along as I have done* and be driven by circumstances instead of making out a line of action and working to it. That is make everything contribute directly [or indirectly] to the plan of action. (emphasis supplied; FGG letter August 26, 1926, to Francis).

Frank's use of the word "blunder" seems to be significant. Nineteenth-century humorist Josh Billings once said that most men would rather be accused of a malicious act than to have committed a "blunder." Frank did not want to be guilty himself of failing to give [Francis] sufficient guidance at the crucial age Frank had needed it—when he was nineteen—but did not receive it. He did not want Francis to commit the same "blunder," whatever that was in Frank's mind. Perhaps Frank felt like he had been too single-minded or narrowly focused in search of the Holy Grail of higher education and had, in the process, ignored other viable career options until it was too late.

Frank's advice to Francis is consistent with earlier advice he had given others on choosing a career. In a speech entitled "Specialization in College Work," probably made shortly after his return to Waco in 1902, Frank told his audience:

> I believe that a student makes a great mistake who waits until he graduates before deciding definitely what occupation to engage in. This should be determined early in his college course and studies taken such as to give him special preparation. This will lay a foundation of his work later on in life that will prove invaluable in ensuring his success. I have in mind a young man who was in Baylor while I was a student here whose work in college and subsequent career illustrates what I have been saying about specialization with a view to taking up a certain line of work after leaving college and to success in this work.
>
> [Here Frank makes the note 'Give the example of N.'—apparently referring to Pat Neff who had been his roommate in Magnolia, Arkansas, before Neff enrolled in law school at the University of Texas.]

Katie: Do you think Frank just said that to Francis because was he was depressed and lonely from all the pressure at Stanford and missing Mama Josie and Waco?

Pops: I don't think so. On March 11, 1928, eighteen months later, he wrote Francis instructing him how to prepare for his life work after he graduated from Baylor, telling him: "*The time has come when you should begin to plan definitely for your work after you get through school and not leave it to chance or the urge of conditions at the time, which has been the bane of my life.*" [Emphasis supplied] Frank's advice was the result of mature reflection over many years and calls to mind two anecdotes involving Samuel Johnson. The first anecdote has Johnson telling his biographer James Boswell, "It would have been better that I had been of a profession. I ought to have been a lawyer," and Boswell responding, "I do not think it would have been better, for we should not have had the English Dictionary," to which Johnson responded, "but you would have had Reports." In the second anecdote, Boswell relates: "Sir William Scott informs me...he said to Johnson, 'What a pity it is, Sir, that you did not follow the profession of the law. You might have been Lord

Chancellor of Great Britain, and attained to the dignity of the peerage; and now that the title of Lichfield, your native city, is extinct, you might have had it.' Johnson, upon this, seemed much agitated; and in an angry tone, exclaimed, 'Why will you vex me by suggesting this, when it is too late?'"

Katie: I'm surprised Frank was so impressed with the law as a profession, considering how familiar he was with Dickens's novels, which were pretty dark where lawyers and the English legal system were involved.

Pops: That's a good point. Dickens, intimately familiar with the English legal system and its abuses, made villains or crooked lawyers important characters in novels like *Bleak House, The Pickwick Papers,* and others. The case of Jarndyce v. Jarndyce is one of the most famous in Western literature and does not show the English system in a good light. But at the time, there were debtors' prisons like the Marshalsea and workhouses employing young boys. I think the answer is that by the time Frank was advising Francis about going into law, fifty or more years had passed after the abuses in England, and considerable ameliorating changes had occurred, at least in England.

Katie: Okay, I get that part, but what is he saying he didn't do but should have done where planning his career was concerned?

Pops: The comments from those letters from over ninety years ago are vague as to specifics, and Frank has left us to read between the lines. He couldn't foresee that he would have descendants who would talk about this years in the future. But having been through his many letters and all the available evidence, I think I can give you a good answer to that one. Frank, early on, not having received advice on careers from a knowledgeable mentor, had not fully recognized the mismatch between his goals of professional success as a teacher and having a wife and family with the limited earning potential of a teaching career at a Baptist college in Waco, Texas, in that age and time. His income would be forever limited, as would the opportunities for him and a family to travel and enjoy the material comforts of this world. Taking care of a wife and family would be extremely challenging on a teacher's salary. He obviously, early on, did not realize how long it would take him to obtain the two degrees necessary to obtain a college teaching post. He also did not think about when he might retire, or whether he would have to teach until he dropped. That is exactly what happened, although he lived fourscore and three years.

Katie: Do you think he blundered in his planning?

Pops: I'm not persuaded that "blundered"—which is Frank's word—is fair to Frank. The main mistake he made, as he himself admits, in pursuing his education and selecting a career, was in failing to seek advice from people who could have helped him think through obtaining higher education and then settling on a career thoughtfully. If he had, he wouldn't have felt later that he missed receiving the advice he needed when his judgment was immature.

Secondly, the evidence does suggest that since the medical career option was not feasible, Frank should have chosen the legal profession. However, by 1902, maybe if he concluded he had made a mistake in the choice of a career path, nevertheless, it was too late to change course. We know that he liked to read the antics of George Bungle *in The Bungle Family* comic strip—maybe that humorous strip reminded him of his feelings of having "bungled," and he derived some *schadenfreude* from following the ups and downs, mainly downs, of Bungle.

But then, if Frank had chosen the law, the inescapable ironies are that his two successful marriages to Mamie and then Josie may never have taken place, as well as the family that he had with Mamie. He and Mamie were an excellent match where intelligence, interests, and shared values were concerned. Mamie's family set up trusts that provided a house and a stipend for the benefit of the two boys, likely because the Welhausens, while they were pleased that Frank and Mamie were finally tying the knot, realized that Frank would probably never be well compensated as a teacher and would have difficulty affording his children. Also, if he had chosen the law early on, it is highly doubtful he would have met Josie, to whom he was happily married for almost thirty years and who supported him in every way possible. Maybe the reason Frank didn't provide specific mistakes in his letters to Francis is that absent such mistakes, perhaps Francis and Clarence never would have existed. Of course, if Frank had acknowledged this irony, some of the urgency of his advice to Francis would have escaped from the picture he was trying to paint for Francis's urgent consideration.

There are other inescapable ironies as well. Although Frank regretted being driven by circumstances, chance, and temporary conditions, he did, from time to time, benefit greatly from important events riding on the winds of chance. First, the twist of fate resulting in the resignation of President Cooper and the resulting election of Samuel Palmer Brooks as Baylor president, and Brooks's hire of Frank. Second, the oil discoveries in Texas in 1901 facilitating the gift by George W. Carroll to Baylor which, along with that of his father, F.L. Carroll, led to Baylor's campus expansion in 1902 and 1903, and arguably indirectly to Brooks's offer to Frank.

Katie: Okay.

Pops: But you might consider also that whatever Frank's feelings may have been in those letters to Francis, those letters were written for the specific purpose of guiding Francis, and they are not the end of the story. If he was really disturbed about his own "mistakes" when he wrote those letters, we doubt they represented his perspective long term. After all, having influenced and encouraged both of his sons to become attorneys, their successful legal careers and marriages must have been highly satisfying to Frank and mitigated any residual feeling of having blundered where his career path was concerned.

Similarly, Frank's feeling of having been at the mercy of the forces of chance, even if that feeling persisted for many years, we suspect had largely dissipated by the time he achieved his Ph.D. in 1931. After all, he had achieved a Ph.D. and was receiving the additional respect, although without additional compensation; and Francis was already in law school. Later, when Clarence was thinking about being a law school teacher rather than a practicing attorney, Frank would head that off by talking to the dean of Baylor Law School. Thus, he had successfully intervened in the lives of both sons so that they might avoid what he considered his own mistakes. Both interventions not only did not backfire, but they led to positive results in both sons' lives.

Katie: Did Frank ever take a trip to Europe? It seems like he would have wanted to see the countries whose histories he was teaching.

Pops: No, he never got there. A teacher, even a department chair at Baylor, didn't make much money in those days. Frank and Mamie, because of help from Mamie's parents, and afterward Frank and Josie, were better off than most faculty members at Baylor. Professor Armstrong was another exception—he had a highly successful summer tour business taking students to Europe. Frank and Josie's residual estate went into a fellowship for history students. Armstrong's monies went into buying Browning letters, manuscripts, art, and the like for the Armstrong-Browning Library.

Katie: Was Frank able to provide for Josie after his death?

Pops: Yes. Although Frank and Josie's will, signed in 1947, provided for an endowed history fellowship, it was not to be funded until both Frank and Josie were gone. Josie died in 1958 after returning from a trip to Europe in 1953. The first fellowships were awarded for the 1959-1960 school year to two master's students.

Katie: Josie must have thought every day on her European trip that it was a shame she and Frank hadn't traveled there together.

CHAPTER 9

Frank's College Days at Baylor (early 1890s)

Frank's college days in Waco are the subject of this chapter; Finn will be helping me explore the events of this period. Frank enrolled at Baylor in February 1890 and would work off and on, teaching at small schools or attending classes at Baylor, until April 1894, when his lack of funds forced him to drop out, never to return as a student.

Finn: Why did Frank pick Baylor for his college education in Texas?

Pops: He never said, but his decision must have had something to do with Rufus C. Burleson, a legendary longtime college president, Texas college pioneer, and Southern Baptist. Another consideration could have been that Baylor was a well-known Baptist school. Or possibly his choice had something to do with Oscar Henry Cooper, who had played a leading role at Sam Houston Normal before Frank enrolled there. Rufus Burleson is a good place to get into Frank's Baylor days as a student. So, what was Frank's view of the venerable Dr. Burleson after he arrived at Baylor? Frank recorded his impressions of Burleson in an essay at the University of Chicago ten years later:

> As he stood there reading the scripture lesson, I felt I was in the presence of a great and good man. I observed that he was tall, slender, slightly stooped, and about sixty-five years of age. Although not of robust physique, he was well proportioned and gave one the impression that, in his prime, he had been a fine-looking man. His black diagonal suit with a coat of Prince Albert cut showed the effects of time and wear. Still, his linen was faultless. Burleson's large dark expressive eyes, shaded by shaggy iron-grey eyebrows and a medium-sized nose of the Greek type, were the most striking features. His mouth was hidden behind a full iron-grey beard, which he wore short and well-trimmed. When his face was in repose his expression was somewhat sad; but when talking to the students, this gave way to one of kindness; and those eyes would at times twinkle while he was telling a joke or anecdote. Yet he made me feel that he could be very firm if necessary.

Finn: It sounds like President Burleson was a good and kind man, but almost worn out when Frank was there.

Pops: Burleson had slowed down; however, something of the old fire remained.

Finn: Were there any students of note the year Frank enrolled?

Pops: You could say so. The *1890-1891 Baylor University Catalogue* shows over 650 students in the collegiate department, including Pat M. Neff, R.A. Burleson, Lee Carroll, Josephine Jenkins, Myrtle Mainer, Carl Lovelace, Douglass Scarborough, Dottie Scarborough, G.M. Scarborough, L.R Scarborough, J.S. Tanner, and F.G. Guittard. Several hundred students are also shown in the preparatory department.

Finn: So, I would like to know more about the President Burleson Frank would have known.

Pops: The best way to get a feel for Burleson as a man at any age, his passionate advocacy of Baylor, and his outspoken leadership and hands-on management—he designed Old Main—is to hear his voice from one of those Baylor catalogues Baylor published in the 1890s:

From the 1890-1891 Catalogue featuring a brief history of the relocation of Baylor from Independence to Waco occasioned by an unfortunate mistake. Burleson claimed: "For many years [Independence] was the great educational center of Texas. Its trustees were prudent and liberal men and did all in their power in selecting competent teachers and providing buildings. But by a fatal blunder of the citizens, the towns of Washington and Independence were left off the railroads and became inaccessible...Dr. Burleson and faculty foreseeing this, removed to Waco and inaugurated Waco University in 1861. [Baylor at Independence] was diminished from 250 students in 1861 to 32 in 1886... [immediately before the merger with Waco University]. In 1890, [Baylor University in Waco] has enrolled twenty-six professors and teachers and 705 students."

Freshman courses for the 1891 fall term included Algebra and Geometry, Xenophon and Anabasis, Allen's Greek grammar and composition; spring term courses included Algebra and Trigonometry, Cicero's *Orations*, Rhetoric [W.W. Franklin's course], and Homer's *Iliad.* Sophomore courses included Physics, Horace's *Odes*, Greek histories, Physiology, and Physical Geography, Analytical Geometry, Chemistry, Xenophon's *Memorabilia*, Aeschylus's *Prometheus*, and Ancient History. Junior and senior courses included more Greek and Roman poetry and literature, geology, calculus, botany, English classics and literature, Moral Science, and Logic. The curriculum also offered practical courses such as arithmetic, music, penmanship, bookkeeping, composition, reading, and orthography—perhaps to prepare female students to be wives and mothers and run a family household.

President Burleson, who taught the courses in Moral and Intellectual Philosophy, reminds the reader that "the Bible and Christian morality are founded upon the eternal rock of Truth." He cautions that "progress...begets in superficial reasoners a tendency to skepticism and universal anarchy, threatening the very foundations of all government and civilization."

Finn: That's pretty scary language. I don't follow why President Burleson is talking about anarchy. Was there anarchy on the Baylor campus or in Waco?

Pops: No, but he was a forceful leader with many rules for the young men and women, especially the young women, which he employed to market Baylor to the parents of prospective Baylor students. There's one thing further that might have been in the back of his mind: a former student of his in moral philosophy at Waco University, Albert Parsons, had been convicted of being part of an anarchistic riot in May 1886 in Haymarket Square in Chicago. In the riot, a dynamite bomb thrown by someone killed seven policemen. Although the convictions of Parsons and seven others were criticized in later years for insufficient evidence, Parsons was hanged by the State of Illinois in 1887.

Finn: Burleson must have regretted one of his students being hanged.

Pops: You would think so, for a number of reasons. Parsons had dropped out of Waco University about twenty years earlier and had not completed his work. Burleson's only reported comment on Parsons was that he had fallen in with the wrong kind of people and been led astray. Parsons was a charismatic socialist reformer determined to press the causes of labor, including the eight-hour workday. The event started in Chicago as a peaceful rally, and no one knows who threw the bomb killing the policemen. Parsons was in the wrong place at the wrong time with the wrong people, and his visible participation, along with his reputation as a fiery speaker, enhanced the impression that he was there with others to stir up trouble.

Finn: Gosh.

Pops: But back to Baylor and its emphasis on a classical education for freshmen. Professor of Classics, W.H. Long, noted in the same catalogue that:

> In our experience, we have found so few young men who have made any preparation in Greek when they come to enter college,

> that we think it best to begin the Freshmen year with Xenophon's *Anabasis* and continue the Greek to the Senior year...We firmly believe that the old college curriculum, which requires a thorough course in Latin, Greek, Pure Mathematics, the fundamental branches of the Natural Sciences, and Belles Lettres, will prepare the mind for the various professions and occupations of life better than the modern elective courses...Each recitation will continue one hour—a portion of which will be occupied in reviewing the recitations of the previous day...Immediately after the daily recitation of the student, the professor shall affix a numerical mark to his name...For a perfect recitation the number shall be five...for a failure, zero.
>
> Miscellaneous expenses for five scholastic months included boarding in Georgia Burleson Hall, tuition, a foreign language, a library fee, fees for instruction on the piano, guitar and vocal; fees for instruction for drawing in pastelle [sic], crayon, and pencil.

As to Georgia Burleson Hall, named for President Burleson's wife, Burleson published many rules governing the lives of its female occupants, apparently formulated by President Burleson in consultation with Georgia. The catalogue advised that:

> All Ladies not living in Waco are required to board in Georgia Burleson Hall, a magnificent building with seventy-five rooms...The advantages of boarding [in Georgia Burleson include]: The watchful care and counsel of the lady teachers in all the details of general deportment and social etiquette. No private family can afford equal facilities or study and general improvement. The young ladies are required to study two hours at night and one hour before breakfast in the morning, in the study hall, under the direction of the governess...Parents are earnestly requested not to send bundles or boxes of...edibles...Hereafter no student will be permitted to receive such boxes...
>
> No letter or note shall be sent to or from the boarding house without the approval of the governess. Any student sending or carrying communications, except through the presiding officer, will be liable to suspension. Each young lady must attend Sunday school and church under the supervision of the governess...
>
> Young ladies slightly unwell but too unwell to attend public exercises will assemble in the study hall and devote church hours to reading the Bible and receiving religious instruction.

> Winter costumes [for young ladies] must be black...not trimmed with silk or satin, but plain...[and] required for all public occasions...Passion for dress is as ruinous to a young lady's progress in study as drunkenness or gambling is to a young man. And one extravagant young lady will demoralize a dozen others. A passion for dress among girls is as contagious as small-pox. We want no young lady in Baylor University who wastes her time on dress and demoralizes...others...Extravagant display is a blighting curse on our country, and the seeds are often sown in a boarding school by the mistaken tenderness of...parents...Each student must be provided with an umbrella, thick shoes, and India-rubber over-shoes, and slippers. To crush this monstrous evil [extravagant dressing] we are compelled to...adopt the...uniform for every-day wear...[Parents] can keep their daughter at home...if they want her to squander money and craze her brain about dress and foolish display...The uniform for every-day will be black checked calico and a plain, white apron and linen collar. No ribbon of any shade or description will be worn. Every young lady must have a sun-bonnet to be worn at all times, except when walking on the streets.

Finn: Burleson could really get on a tear there on girls' clothes.

Pops: Or his wife, Georgia. He definitely could get wound up on certain subjects. Another example was health. President Burleson advocated for Waco as a healthy location on the western bank of the Brazos River to counter the narrative of "evil surmisers [who] have whispered...there is more sickness in Baylor University than in any other institution in Waco. Monthly statistics show that Waco is healthier than these great cities [Boston and San Antonio], considered the healthiest in the United States. And with Waco's recently developed artesian wells her health will be increased at least five per cent." President Burleson also challenged "a comparison between [Baylor's] students and those Texas students educated in other institutions. Not less than three hundred students are sent out of Texas annually...and abundant facts show that young men and ladies educated in Texas are every way equal to those educated in other states [including at Yale or Harvard]. But this evil has well-nigh run its course. Experience is a dear school, but a certain class of the human family can learn in no other way."

Toward the end of the 1890-1891 catalogue, Burleson appealed to former students [not to] "allow the drummers of third and fourth-rate schools from other states to come in and carry whole carloads [of students] out of Texas when your Alma Mater is prepared to give them better and cheaper education...I call attention of our old students and friends to the fact that our new site [of the merged institution Baylor at Waco], 'Oak Lawn' and 'Minglewood Park,' is unsurpassed in Texas for beauty, health and accessibility. Don't forget that the next session begins on Monday, September 14, 1891, and that we want to open with 850 students. Your Devoted Friend and Old Teacher, Rufus C. Burleson."

In connection with the moral environment Baylor provided, Burleson affirmed that "all secular studies, reading and correspondence are forbidden on the Sabbath...All reading of novels is forbidden as an unmitigated evil." Although Burleson opposed nearly all interactions between the sexes other than the highly regulated soirees, he strongly believed in everyone's participation in one of the five literary societies at Baylor. Burleson believed the purpose of the societies was "to awaken and cultivate a love of reading and literary taste, and to drill the student in oral debate and writing essays and a profound practical knowledge of parliamentary usage in conducting deliberative assemblies."

In August 1891, Frank wrote home from Waco to one of his sisters:

> News from home is getting to be a scarce article down here. I take *The Plain Dealer* but it is seldom if ever that it contains any New Bedford items. School closed here last Friday. I have decided to teach again next winter and have accepted a good position that was offered to me by one of the teachers here in the Institute this summer...I will stay here until school opens.
>
> Have a good boarding place [212 Webster Street] with one of the Profs of Baylor University who is worth only a hundred thousand; he is one of the few teachers who have made a financial success of the business. He has several farms near the city on the Bosque River. I frequently drive out with the children to fish and get watermelons. I am getting pretty well acquainted here in the city and don't lack for social enjoyment of the best quality.
>
> I had decided once to go home and help Claude [one of Frank's younger brothers] to make hay but decided that I could spend the time more profitably going to school but it has been so warm that I hardly think I will try another summer school in Texas but go where the climate is not quite so tropical after this. P.S. I sent Claude a small specimen of horned toad. I have some curiosity to know if it went through alive.

In W.W. Franklin's Giant Rhetoric class, Frank composed an essay entitled "The Events of a Day" excerpted as follows:

> When I awoke on the morning of Dec. 5th, 1893, the sunlight was streaming in through the window of my room. Upon looking

> out, I saw the sky was clear, so the prospects were favorable for having an agreeable day. The bell called me to breakfast which was dispatched with the usual skill and rapidity necessary at Maggie Houston Hall. In chapel Dr. Burleson read one of his favorite texts: 'Let everything be done in decency and order.' So he then made an appropriate talk, and announced that the students should form in line, march down to the old McClellan House, take their stand, see the Trades Display—then march to Padgett's Park, hear the orator of the day Ex-Gov. Hubbard and disband. After the exercises, the Literary Societies formed in line, with the ladies ahead and marched to the appointed place. The line attracted universal attention. Crowds of people were already on the streets, uniformed officers were riding here and there, and all Waco was decorated for a holiday. It consisted of floats each representing some business house and the variety of goods sold. Other industries were also represented. The useful, the agreeable, and the beautiful were blended in such a way as to show what Waco is and can be. At the park we listened to the eloquent address of the orator of the day. He compared Waco of early days with Waco of today, pictured a bright future for her, and concluded with some advice to the young ladies and an exhortation to the young men. The president of the board of trade then awarded the prizes for the most novel and beautiful displays. In the afternoon I visited the woolen mills and saw the whole process of making cloth. Going home I felt that the day had been well spent.

Frank again spent the 1893 Christmas holidays in Waco, describing how the holidays went for him in an essay entitled "How I Spent the Christmas Holidays":

> As I had heard much about Christmas time at Baylor University and knew that I would be here during the holidays, I look forward to the adjournment of school with a great deal of pleasure. I felt as though I could enjoy a few days of relaxation after laboring with Latin, Greek, Science, and Literature for four months. The time came at last. Dr. Burleson announced in chapel Friday morning that we could have a soiree that night from 7:30 to 10:00 p.m. and also that there would be no school Monday and Tuesday. At the appointed hour the students assembled in the chapel. To use the expression of a rural journalist it was a time when 'delightful conversation was rapidly engaged in.' The soiree broke up after many good-byes and kind wishes for a Merry Christmas.

While watching the happy throng, my mind was carried back to many Christmas times spent at home with father, mother, brothers, and sisters, and it seemed to me that if it were possible once more to pass the holidays in that dear old home as it used to be, it would be one of the sweetest enjoyments that could be granted to me. I also thought that those who have a happy home where they can go to spend the holidays and who know how to appreciate such a blessing have something they may be truly thankful for.

Saturday, I read most of the day and did some review work in my studies. That night after prayer meeting I went with several of the boys out to the Christian church. When we arrived, the entertainment, consisting of a play, songs, and tableaux had already begun. The last act of the play was the most interesting. When the curtain rose, there on the stage stood a large windmill resembling the one Don Quixote tackled, imagining it to be a giant. Around the windmill barrels with paper heads, were scattered...Santa Claus looked out of the window of the mill and said that if a breeze did not soon come up, he could not grind out these presents. At this, out of each of the barrels popped a boy with a small bellows. They proceeded to raise a breeze; the arms of the mill begun to move and the presents to come out of an opening in front and roll down a trough to the foot of the stage. Two men caught the presents and began calling the names, whereupon the boys who were fantastically dressed, dropped their bellows and delivered the presents to the eager recipients, but the mill continued to run until all the presents were given out.

The next day, Sunday, although rather dreary on account of so many of the boys having gone home, I passed very agreeably reading, going to church and visiting the other boys. I don't think I ever met with a more hearty and good-natured crowd than the students who remained at Maggie Houston Hall during the holidays. One source of great pleasure were our prayer meetings which were held each day after supper in one of the rooms. The meetings did much to make the holidays pass by pleasantly.

Christmas morning, we had a merry time at breakfast as all received some kind of a present. The next important event during the day was dinner which received due consideration by all present. In the evening, I called at Georgia Burleson Hall where we enjoyed ourselves for a few hours getting acquainted with our co-workers. That night we had a moot court at Maggie Houston Hall. The most important events of Tuesday were calling and serenading that night.

As to Frank's comments about his enjoyment of soirees, considering that he was an introverted sort and largely spent his time in serious reading, not likely to facilitate conversation at a soiree, we take them with a grain of salt. Other students expressed a different opinion of soirees, such as one student attending one Thanksgiving afternoon, saying that after he was almost unable to get any words out of his mouth, the young woman he was paired with said, "Well, this looks like a monkey show," to which he replied, "I believe you." Then our awkward student was interrupted by another student also wanting to talk to his partner, and accordingly he had to move on to another, saying, "May I hold a few minutes' conversation with you?" The new female student's response, "just come back in a few minutes," was discouraging, perhaps because his prior conversation partner had not defended him against the earlier interruption. Another male student had a similarly frustrating experience, saying: "At one of these soirees I got a partner and around and around we marched in utter silence, [until] finally the girl cruelly remarked, 'I believe I'll quit.'"

Pat M. Neff originated a verbal gambit intended to keep a man from having to talk to a homely girl all evening at a soiree. Neff used the gambit when he felt like he had been overlooked (presumably in the matching process) by the introduction committee and desired to move on to another female. Neff reportedly would extricate himself from a conversation with one female by rising from his chair and declaring in a dignified manner, "Madame, I have nothing else to tell you," whereupon he would excuse himself. Soirees came only four or five times a year, and there were few opportunities outside of them to talk to young women, thus making it critical to circulate at soirees. "Not allowed to associate or even speak to their fair friends without being presented with an abundance of demerits, except on the occasion of a 'soiree,' the soiree assumed monstrous importance in the life of the Baylor men." Another student recalled: "When we first came out here in 1918, we could not walk across the campus in front of Georgia Burleson Hall. That was against the law because that was sacred to the women. We had to march from the Main Building out to Fifth Street, or from Carroll Science Hall out to Fifth Street, go down Fifth Street and go in the front door of the Carroll Library Chapel." Although President Burleson was gone from the scene by 1918, something of his "imaginary line,"—explained more fully elsewhere—or the boundaries separating the sexes, still existed for some time during President Brooks's administration.

It is not surprising that a young man, if not also a young woman, might become tongue-tied at a soiree while dressed to the nines when there was almost no other opportunity sanctioned by the university to practice the art of conversation with young women. Samuel Palmer Brooks remembered: "In my day as a student in Baylor, a man was not allowed to speak to a woman. I thought the rule was absurd. I thought so then. I think so now. However, I did not pay tuition to a faculty in order to talk to the girls. I came to learn certain lessons in the curriculum which I thought would help me. Except as the rules were waived on certain occasions, I obeyed them. If I had not been willing to obey them, I would have quit this school and gone to another."

Finn: You mentioned the Giant Rhetoric class and W.W. Franklin. What kind of class was that, and who was he?

Pops: It's easier to explain who Franklin was than what the Giant Rhetoric class was about. Professor Franklin was an original on the faculty, and, in some ways, entrepreneurial, a forerunner of Professor A.J. Armstrong of the English department. Franklin carved out some turf for himself beginning in 1885 at Waco University under the presidency of Rufus Burleson. He taught rhetoric, elocution, and related courses at Waco University and then at Baylor until 1895, after which he disappeared from history. While at Baylor, Franklin was the primary supporter of the debate activities of the men's literary societies and provided awards for winning debate teams.

Now the hard part—describing what the elocution and rhetoric classes were about since they can't be easily pigeonholed into modern college course categories. They seemed to be about training the voice and the body—the body, in Franklin's view, being plastic and revealing of the inner man. There was strong emphasis on elevation and spirituality in Franklin's courses, which would have fit in with Baylor's emphasis on imparting education in a Christian atmosphere. The Giant Rhetoric class also required writing essays in an exact and detailed way. According to *Franklin's Outline of Advanced Rhetoric and Essay Book: A Guide to the Systematic Study and Investigation of the Most Interesting and Useful Science and Art—Practical Rhetoric,* Franklin had seventeen separate rules for preparing a manuscript—just the manuscript—after the student had finished writing the essay. The rules included writing it on a good quality of foolscap, tearing the sheet apart so as to furnish two leaves, and folding the essay according to a multi-step protocol requiring a ruler, a pen, red ink, black ink, and proper backing of an essay.

The 1890-91 Baylor Catalogue affirmed that the purpose of the Lone Star School of Oratory included: "healthy, vigorous bodies; bright, active, clear, strong minds and a natural pleasing, easy, powerful expression. To prepare the teacher for successful work which will be...productive of great good...To enable the minister to use his God-given powers in such a way that his work may show the greatest results. To make lawyers and politicians masters of themselves and their surroundings. To give ladies and gentlemen the power of being pleasant and agreeable conversationalists and thereby influential members of society."

Baylor's 1893-94 Catalogue stated: "The Lone Star School of Oratory [Franklin's department] offers a complete course in every department of the science and art of expression. The analytic or Rush method of voice culture is used, while in gesture, the synthetic method is taught, together with all that is practical of the Delsarte system." The Delsarte system, which Professor Franklin used to design his courses in elocution, rhetoric, and oratory, had more than a touch of the airy fairy in it. A review of students' notes in Franklin's classes reveals they were taught a peculiar mixture of Egyptian, Greek, and other metaphysical notions, along with Christian theology. Student Douglass Scarborough recorded Delsarte maintained that, among other propositions, "the source of all manifestations, both in the universe and its epitome, is essence, spirit or soul."

Finn: So, I'm not getting what Delsarte meant by that.

Pops: Sorry, it's either deep or insightful, or a just lot of hooey; you pick. At best, it was vague. But it worked for Franklin. Franklin had carved out a small teaching realm inside Waco University under President Burleson and then moved it over to Baylor with the 1886 merger. Franklin's department had a Baylor degree of Bachelor of Oratory (B.O.) issued under its name for those students completing the three-year course. The catalogue describes Franklin's department in detail, stating: "The complete entire course in elocution and oratory requires three years of 40 weeks each, 1-1/2 hours per day. A student may, by devoting 5 hours per day, complete the course in two years."

Finn: Did Frank like the Giant Rhetoric class?

Pops: I'm not sure whether he liked it or not, but he was conscientious in following Franklin's rules for essays, and his handwriting was better than his sons'. Those essays served as practice for all the letters he would write to his family and friends later. Of course, Frank was not in Baylor on his father's dime, and that may have increased his seriousness in all of his course work, including handwriting. Frank, however, was not pursuing a B.O. (Bachelor of Oratory) degree but rather the Classic Course in order to get a Bachelor of Arts, not a degree in oratory.

Finn: Did Professor Franklin have a Ph.D. to teach all of those courses?

Pops: I don't believe so. In 1893-94, the collegiate department only had eight professors, and only one had his doctorate and he taught Greek. It wasn't Franklin. Here are the eight members of faculty: Rufus C. Burleson—Professor of Mental and Moral Philosophy, Logic, and Evidences of Christianity, Pastoral Duties and Church Government; James F. Greer, Professor of Latin and French; W.A. Harris, Ph.D., Professor of Greek; J.C. Lattimore, Professor of Mathematics and Pedagogy; W.W. Franklin, Professor of Belle Lettres; O.C. Charlton, Professor of Natural

Sciences and Curator of Museum; H.L. Hargrove, Professor of Latin, History and Literature; and B.H. Carroll, Department of Bible Teaching.

President Brooks recalled that when he entered Baylor's preparatory department in 1887 en route to his graduation in 1893 from the Collegiate Department, "every professor taught more than one subject. There were few students. There were few well-defined departments. There were no electives. The basis of every A.B. degree was Latin, Greek, and mathematics. These courses were taught thoroughly and over a wide field. There was very little English taught. The professor of English was also professor of History and of Elocution." A year later Brooks added, "When I began teaching in Baylor...all teachers taught substantially all day. They were required to come to eight o'clock chapel in addition. Even college teachers taught six classes per day of sixty minutes each...If it was found that any teacher...had a vacant period during the day, he was expected to take on another course no matter whether it was his specialty or not. Teachers taught classes in both academy [preparatory department] and college. Teachers of English had no false pride in having a course in the history of English literature at one hour and English grammar in another."

Finn: Pops, I have a question. When Frank ran out of money and dropped out of Baylor, do you think he intended to go back after he had worked a while like he had before?

Pops: I doubt it. By the fall of 1892, the University of Chicago had already opened its doors. It offered a student like Frank a world-class university with an exceptional faculty. It was also a good choice for students who needed to work their way through. No more "Maggie" for Frank—you'll hear a lot more about Maggie in the next chapter. We will talk about Frank's Chicago days in another chapter.

CHAPTER 10

"Maggie" for Students of Lesser Means

Frank resided at Maggie Houston Hall (Maggie) during his freshman year at Baylor. Samuel P. Brooks and Pat M. Neff also lived at Maggie for a time and were roommates. Maggie did not constitute sumptuous accommodations but was available to students who could not afford to live in the private boarding houses, often ministerial students enrolled in Baylor on a shoestring. The later constructed, more attractive Brooks Hall and Kokernot Hall did not yet exist. Finn has volunteered to assist me with this chapter.

<u>Finn</u>: So Pops, what was dormitory life like when Frank Guittard went to Baylor? Was it noisy? Was the food terrible?

<u>Pops</u>: Frank worked for room and board at Maggie Houston Hall, living at the back of Maggie and likely in one of the least desirable rooms. If he had been a ministerial student, his tuition would have been free, and the charges for room and board would have been at lower rates. But since he was an ordinary student without a special break on tuition and fees, he was obliged to pay full price. Maggie, located on Fifth Street near the intersection with Webster Avenue, was twelve blocks from Burleson Quadrangle. In 1890, the university campus consisted of only Georgia Burleson Hall and the Main Building, presently called Old Main. Maggie, which was downtown, was eight blocks from Waco's city square with its many saloons and a stone's throw from other temptations for Baylor students.

<u>Finn</u>: Did they have to walk twelve blocks from Maggie to the campus and back?

<u>Pops</u>: Most students living at Maggie had bicycles. It was the cycling era everywhere back then.

<u>Finn</u>: Was there a Maggie Houston? Who was she?

<u>Pops</u>: Yes. Margaret "Maggie" Lea Houston was General Sam Houston's second or third wife, depending on whether you want to count the Indian woman Houston married when he lived with the Indians. He also had a daughter named Maggie who had been a student at Baylor at Independence. President Burleson baptized Houston, and they had a special connection.

Finn: Why was Maggie so far away from the campus?

Pops: It was twelve blocks away because it was a part of the campus of the old Waco University that merged with Baylor at Independence. It was used in the early days after the merger until housing on campus could be provided for the men. Girls lived on campus in Georgia Burleson Hall, which was a nice place back then. The girls were always looked after more carefully than the men in Maggie.

Finn: What about the food at Maggie? Was it horrible?

Pops: Oh, the food. There were no pizzas, tacos, or hamburgers, and Dr. Pepper hadn't been formulated yet at Morrison's drugstore. No sushi. No salad wraps.

Finn: What did they eat?

Pops: Basic things like meat, potatoes, and biscuits. On Thanksgiving, they had turkey. Strawberries when they were in season—they didn't have frozen food back then, and fresh food had to be refrigerated in big iceboxes.

Finn: Anything sweet to eat?

Pops: Well, they had muffins and preserves occasionally, but not too often, and sometimes fish. There was a lot of hash, which Maggie's residents called "Chinese stew," made up of chopped-up leftovers from previous meals. It was served on Saturdays made from chopped-up Monday through Friday leftovers. A popular dessert was sweet milk and warm biscuits, and there was ice cream that the cooks made with hand-cranked ice cream makers.

Finn: Anything else?

Pops: Prunes, and occasionally steak and packing-house sausages when visitors were present. Eggs for breakfast. And they had milk from a cow a student was responsible for milking. The student who owned the cow paid reduced tuition.

Finn: Did the men complain about the food?

Pops: Yes and no, depending on the offering of the day, and I suppose most of them were grateful for anything that kept body and soul together. If they had a little more money, the men in Maggie would probably have been staying at one of the private boarding houses that some of the professors owned near the campus. Frank

Guittard had to leave Baylor before finishing his degree because he ran out of money for tuition and board, even at the inexpensive Maggie Houston Hall.

Finn: What were their rooms like? Did they each have a room, or did they have suitemates? I'm getting the feeling that the rooms were not that fancy. Where was the toilet?

Pops: Maggie had room for eighty-five men. Men slept four to a room, and these rooms were furnished with two double beds, a table, four chairs, an oil lamp, and a wood burning stove. The men's trunks served as additional chairs. They had no real bathtub, no plumbing, no running water, and no electric light. President Brooks said when he first arrived on campus as a new student that he was taken to a second-hand furniture store and bought a bedstead, a shuck mattress, a chair, a cedar water bucket, a tin wash pan, a mirror, and other items for his room at Maggie. Pat M. Neff, who would room with Brooks at Maggie, noted that "there were no screens, no water system, no sanitation, no electric lights, no bathtubs in those days...No bath[s] except when the months were warm...we could draw water out of a deep well on the old Maggie Houston campus and bring in the little tin washtub that was held in common by about 50 students for bathing facilities...Tuition was five dollars per month payable in advance with a two dollar and fifty cents incidental fee. Sometimes students paid their tuition in promises only, and teachers could not be paid in full. The affluent male students often boarded in big brick houses several on Third and Fourth streets."

Finn: That sounds terrible. Why didn't the men protest the living conditions? Go on strike?

Pops: They didn't protest because, in most cases, the conditions were as good as those in the homes from which they came. They knew they were fortunate to even be in college rather than feeding the chickens or slopping the hogs. A lot of those men were really from farming families struggling to make it.

Finn: Did they have a bathroom? Toilets? Did they have a shower?

Pops: Yes, but Maggie's "bathroom" was very basic; there was no sewerage connection and someone had to empty the chamber pots.

Finn: Couldn't they just flush the toilet?

Pops: Nope—there were no flush toilets in dormitories or for the general public until years later.

Finn: Wonder who had to empty those pots.

Pops: Students like Frank Guittard.

Finn: Well, couldn't they at least take a shower or a bath if they needed to?

Pops: I'm afraid not. You couldn't take a shower—there were none—and baths were infrequent and accomplished with large wash basins made of tin in each room. Warm water for a bath would have been scarce and would have had to be pumped from a deep well and then heated in pails on small fires outside Maggie. Students often had to share bath water with other students, so baths were a lot of work and a mixed blessing at best.

Finn: Eeeewwwww!

Pops: Yep. President Brooks, who lived at Maggie when he was a student, said conditions for students were a little better than what the Indians were used to in their villages.

Finn: Wasn't it hot at night sometimes?

Pops: Hot, yes, and there could be mosquitoes buzzing around. When it was colder, you could hear axes chopping firewood for the wood burning stoves in the rooms at night.

Finn: What happened when the men got sick?

Pops: That was a problem, and many did become ill, at least in the view of President Brooks. According to Brooks, "the men nursed each other and only went for the doctor when one was needed since there were no telephones. The doctors would come in their buggies with cheery smiles and terrible medicines. Some of us lived. [It was not the fault of the doctors or their terrible medicines but] it was the flies, the mosquitoes, the unsanitary conditions under which we lived, though it was not much [worse] than anywhere else in Texas."

Finn: How good was the food, Pops? It must have been okay.

Pops: Well, Maggie's residents boarded on what was called the club plan. One boy was given his board for collecting the money. Another was given board for buying the groceries and was called the steward. There were two long tables where the boys ate. At intervals along the table were plates of bread, meat, gravy, and vegetables. Big pitchers of syrup also accompanied each meal. The boys liked hot biscuits and did not like bakery bread since they could sop molasses better with biscuits than with bakery bread. Brooks served as steward for four years at Maggie and recalled that if the boys ever got a tough piece of meat, he was "cordially abused." On one occasion, he was confronted by a new student who thought he had more experience in the world than some of the rest of the students. The student informed Brooks that the table fare [would] be more pleasing if the boys could be supplied with condiments. Since Brooks did not know what "condiments" were, he looked it up in the dictionary and immediately went forth and laid in a supply of pepper sauce.

Finn: Did the food ever make the students sick?

Pops: It possibly did on occasion, although we have no proof of that. However, Maggie did have its own hospital. According to the 1896 *Round-Up*: "the health [at Maggie] has been so good the last two years, there has been no occasion to use it, so the room has been let to some of the gentlemen." However, Brooks's recollections throw that statement—no doubt penned by President Burleson, Baylor's foremost marketer—into doubt. According to Brooks, measles and mumps broke out among the student body practically every Christmas; students would go home, and they would bring back one or both diseases. The medical care available to the boys was inferior, and while some boys developed "congestive chills," no Baylor student was ever operated on during the years Brooks spent at Baylor.

Finn: That sounded pretty good until that last part.

Pops: Right. If the health conditions at Maggie were questionable, the cost of boarding was about right. Boarding for the boys cost $7 per month. Room rent was $1 per month. Oil was 25 cents per month, and coal and other odds and ends about 50 cents per month. A room could be furnished for about $10 per occupant. This made the average cost for room and board nearly $10 per month for the entire ten months. Because heating in Maggie's rooms was accomplished by a wood burning stove in each room, in cold weather the yard outside Maggie was covered with small woodpiles, there being as many piles as there were rooms of boys. Some of the boys bought cordwood and an ax, saving money by chopping it themselves.

Maggie's boys had little money to spend on haircuts or anything else. Now and then, someone might pay 25 cents downtown for a bath in a bathtub. Boys rarely ever shaved more than once a week on Sunday, and they saved money by cutting each other's hair. Brooks recalled that one boy who cut hair developed a following. However, at one point, he became exasperated with the pair of old, dull scissors he had been using and bought a pair of regular barber shears. After that, he attempted to charge 15 cents for a haircut to pay for the shears. The boys quit him flat as they felt they might as well go to a professional barber if they had to pay for a haircut.

However, Professor Poole recalled in a humorous vein that there were always some of Maggie's monitors who were slipshod in reporting conditions at Maggie: "It made no difference if large barrels of oil cans became peripatetic and would chase Professor Brown [down] the stairways frantically in the still, small hours of the night, as he perambulated about the building. It made no difference if, at the midnight hour, the old college bell was heard tolling fearfully...The uniform report usually sent up from these rooms was 'all present, order good.' Also, a great number of incidents, both humorous and pathetic, occurred in the old chapel in Maggie. One night two Erisophians were up there looking at a book they needed for an argument they planned to use in an upcoming debate. There they found an old fellow who had come over to Baylor from East Texas...He was moving around up there all by himself and they asked him what he was doing, he said that he was writing a poem and would come around the next day and say it to them. He did come around as promised and one of the Erisophians remembered a couple of its lines which ran: 'Oh, thou pale and yaller moon, what makes thou rise and sot so soon?'"

Although Maggie was dilapidated in the 1890s, Maggie's boys were—at least according to the official view, which was President Burleson's—very loyal to her. According to the 1896 *Round-Up*: "When a great calamity, changing of the waiters or the failure of the cook to make chili on Saturday night occurs, the event is properly observed by tolling of bells, singing of dirges, and speeches from the leading orators of the day. Should any grand addition be made to the conveniences of the hall, as a new oilcloth for a table, a new barrel for ice water, spoons or a dinner bell, a mass meeting is called and the joyous occurrence celebrated by music, songs and speeches that make the ashes of Cicero and 'Demmy' shift about, causes spirits of Clay and Calhoun to heave a sigh, and Hogg and Hedley turn green with envy."

Frank could not afford to return to Ohio for the Christmas holidays during his student years at Baylor, and he stayed at Maggie with the other young men of "lesser means," taking part in such entertainments as were available to Maggie's boys. It was not wholly depressing to remain at college during the Christmas holidays. However, we conclude this chapter on Maggie by mentioning that, regardless of the reduced boarding fees and the rosy depiction of life at Maggie, Frank, at some point, perhaps after his first term at Baylor, decided to board elsewhere.

<u>Finn</u>: Maybe he got tired of sharing bathwater with other boys and chopping wood...especially sharing bathwater.

<u>Pops</u>: It's hard to believe students actually shared bathwater and had just a tin tub for baths, but I guess they did. Frank certainly would have wanted to be closer to campus, as well, to live in a boarding house less basic than Maggie. At some point, he resided in another boarding house, although later he would return to Maggie.

<u>Finn</u>: I wonder why he went back to Maggie if it was as bad as all that.

<u>Pops</u>: It was cheaper, and a mosquito net would be worth the investment. You asked early on about noise. It must have been extremely noisy. You know what men's dormitories are like, don't you?

CHAPTER 11

President Burleson's Rules, Chapel, and Discipline

Rules, chapel, and discipline at Baylor during President Burleson's administration were front and center when Frank Guittard attended Baylor as a student. Though Baptists continued to support Burleson's firm framework of rules for students, the world was changing. By the 1890s, voices of many college authorities could be heard criticizing disciplinary approaches like Burleson's as being outdated and excessively paternal. Miles will be exploring this area with me.

Pops: Baylor was a Baptist institution. Parents had to be satisfied that their children would be safe from all manner of harm and nurtured appropriately in the Christian faith and values during their college years at Baylor. For this reason, President Burleson believed in rules, lots of them, to protect his students, especially females. Daily morning chapel was compulsory for all students and faculty, and two religious services were required on Sunday for all female students.

Miles: Why weren't male students required to attend two services on Sunday?

Pops: I don't know, but that would have increased the likelihood of unsanctioned interaction with the women who would be going to church. I think the main reason was really the double standard that existed for maintaining the morals of men versus those of women. President Burleson was firm in clearly saying he wanted "none, but good students, no loungers, no swearers, no scoffers, no spendthrifts...The vicious and idle are reformed or quietly sent home." Yet two services for the men on Sundays were not a requisite in his playbook. Burleson also came down hard against the primarily male vice of profanity, "nocturnal disorders," and drinking liquors, and he let it be known that he had "not had time to smoke a cigar, to take a chaw of tobacco or a dram of whiskey; [he] never was in a ball-room or theater, or on a race-ground." Baptists generally strongly supported Burleson's moral positions.

For views similar to Burleson's, we might turn to Reverend Thomas Shephard's advice to his son upon his admission to Harvard College in 1672: "Dear Son,...Remember now to be watchful against the two great Sins of many Scholars; the first is youthful Lusts, speculative wantonness, and secret filthiness, which God sees in the Dark, and for which God hardens and blinds young men's hearts, his Holy Spirit departing from such unclean Styes. The second is malignancy and secret distaste of Holiness and the Power of Godliness...for there are and will be such in every Scholastical Society for the most part, as will teach you how to be filthy and how to jest, and Scorn at Godliness...whose Company I charge you to fly from as from the Devil."

Miles: Gosh, I didn't think UT was all that bad when I was there. So, how many rules did Burleson have at Baylor?

Pops: I have not counted them, but here are examples of some of his rules found in the early 1890s Baylor catalogs:

- Any student who shall ring the university bell, not directed to do so by the proper officer, shall be suspended or otherwise punished.
- Any student guilty of playing cards, or any game of hazard, shall be suspended or otherwise severely punished.
- Any student who shall be guilty of licentiousness, using ardent spirits, or visiting drinking establishments, shall be suspended or otherwise punished.
- No student shall be guilty of nocturnal disorders or reveling, nor become connected with a dancing school society or social club without the approval of the faculty; and for violation of this rule, such a student shall be suspended or otherwise punished.
- Each student is required to attend Sabbath-school and also some religious worship twice on the Sabbath. [*Author's note: Apparently interpreted differently where men and women were concerned.*]
- When the demerits of any student, for any term amount to twenty, it shall be the duty of the president to inform his parent or guardian of the fact; and when his demerits amount to fifty, to dismiss him from the University, or otherwise punish him.
- Any student who shall be guilty of talking in school shall receive two demerits; in recitation, four.
- For leaving seat or desk during study hours, two demerits.
- For leaving room during study hours, three demerits.
- For lounging on streets or about stores or college building, four demerits.
- No young lady of the institution, boarder or day student, shall receive the attention or escort of young men. A violation of this rule will incur a heavy penalty...Books and beaux never go together.
- Young men must not visit or in any way intrude upon the chapel, study hall, recitation rooms or campus of the young ladies.

Boys did not have to sign in or out of their dormitory, but they had to be back by dark. Two boys received demerits for attending an opera at night. Boys were also frequently caught for writing, receiving, and carrying notes, and one boy was suspended for "clandestine communications with young ladies." Sometimes young women threw notes out the window to young men standing below.

Miles: What was behind these rules from President Burleson? What was he worried about?

Pops: Several things. To begin with, he believed that the nation's political and social systems were corrupt and that society and the nation's youth were at risk from lawful saloons, gambling houses, and brothels. Before World War I and Prohibition, these kinds of seedy businesses proliferated in Waco, especially downtown around the city square in the general area of the Waco Suspension Bridge. President Burleson would have been especially aware of these businesses because before the 1886 merger and the creation of Burleson Quadrangle, the old Waco University campus was just blocks from brothels, gambling emporiums, and saloons. Putting more distance between the campus and the seedy downtown area had been one of the plusses Burleson would have seen in the more residential campus on the Oak Lawn and Minglewood Park properties. Burleson believed strongly in separating students from bad places and bad people. He thought that students at Baylor were immature and needed close monitoring, guidance, and protection while still in a formative stage. On occasion, that could mean a whipping would follow an infraction of rules, although the exact details of this sort of punishment are not available. It appears that Burleson's rules for Baylor in Waco were more or less the same rules he enforced at Waco University and before that at Baylor at Independence.

Miles: Did Burleson administer corporal punishment himself?

Pops: We don't know for sure, but I think he did, starting in Independence when he was not only the president but also in charge of the male department. He may have used his cane, or perhaps a buggy whip. So, I suppose that cane in the Burleson statue was not just to help him walk or used as a fashion accessory. I also believe that some faculty members, on occasion, attended to this distasteful task. Corporal punishment in the nineteenth century was widespread in the elementary grades through high school and relatively common at the college level, although not to the same degree as in the prior grades, but I can't imagine that any of the young women in Georgia Burleson would have ever been whipped or caned; if there was a serious problem with a young woman's behavior that couldn't be resolved by demerits or restrictions, she was just sent home.

Miles: If he had ever caned a girl, he might have had a father show up to cane him.

Pops: Surely. As for women and men getting together on campus, the rule from Independence against "sociables" was partially relaxed, and faculty permission was granted for certain receptions, teas, and picnics and usually convened in the chapel or Georgia Burleson Hall. The soiree was always the primary social event; when the boys arrived, they would be received by a committee as they came through the door. Then, they would wait together for the girls to come down from their rooms, taking seats in the parlors. The boy would indicate which girl he would like to meet and then be presented. After that, the evening consisted of the conversations occurring between the matched-up couples. Boys could change partners by asking permission from the girls they wanted to chat with who might say yes, no, later, or whatever. A girl might also request a boy to move on to another girl. There was absolutely no dancing at soirees—dancing was verboten for Baylor students to engage in anytime, anywhere, and was considered the "devil's pastime." Although some Baptists, but not all, saw no harm in "square dancing," ballroom dancing was called "round dancing" and was the primary type to be concerned about. One story that circulated featured a young man who died of exhaustion on the dance floor. The story's narrator commented that the dance floor was entirely the wrong place to receive the final summons. Apparently, when one is called upon on judgment day to account for the way one has lived his life, a record of social dancing will not be to the good.

Besides dancing, drinking, gambling, and consorting with prostitutes, Burleson also drew the line at many activities that would be considered harmless today, including all athletic contests. Football, basketball, and baseball, as well as boat racing, card games, and theater-going, were all prohibited. Burleson thought athletics were detrimental to scholarship and culture, which is what Burleson wanted his students to concentrate on, along with growing in their faith. According to Pat Neff, Burleson initially opposed the introduction of football and sometimes whipped students he caught playing with a ball. One day, the story goes, he noticed some students playing football outside the boys' dormitory (apparently Maggie Houston Hall), stopped his buggy, got out, and went over to the fence and waited. When the ball came within reach, he confiscated the ball and drove away. Another time, he supposedly took out a knife and stabbed the ball. Card playing was against Burleson's moral code because it was considered equivalent to gambling, and the penalty was twenty demerits if a student was caught. Even reading novels—most novels were considered to have no redeeming value—was considered such a dangerous habit that Baylor trustees listed it as one reason for suspension.

On the other hand, debating was encouraged, and sword drills (competitive Bible drills) would not have been a problem. I'm kidding about sword drills since college-level students would not have been competing in sword drills. Burleson's goal was to fully occupy a student's attention so "that he or she would have no time for college revelry and crime." The college's role in laying out rules and enforcing discipline was crucial because, in Burleson's view, in many schools, teachers were not "profoundly penetrated with their sublime and glorious mission." Consequently, teachers often lacked the kind of parental love and watchful care for students needed from them.

Where mandatory chapel was concerned, Burleson was nothing if not organized. Catching and correcting misbehaving students, sometimes in a humorous way, sometimes in a physically painful way such as by whipping, had been in style since Independence. At Baylor in Waco, students served as monitors who prepared and delivered written reports read aloud in chapel. The monitors could use their duties as excuses for not preparing for their classes or for missing classes. Supposedly, the position of chapel monitor was a highly desirable appointment, and it ironically allowed male monitors to flirt and talk to girls. Students received demerits for disorder in chapel, refusing to attend chapel, picking a banjo in chapel, failing to rise during singing, gathering in groups, and laughing in chapel. Where church attendance on Sundays was concerned, the Baptist view was that "every city or nation that openly or habitually tramples on the God-given law... of...the Sabbath degenerates into anarchy, Sodomy, and social ruin." Monitors also made reports on students outside chapel and noted instances of talking and scuffling in the hall, being late, loitering on the campus, and leaving campus.

Far and away, Burleson's most crucial task was strictly regulating and limiting social interactions between men and women. Burleson favored coeducation at Waco University and Baylor in Waco, but that meant only being together in the same classes and occasional chaperoned gatherings (soirees) where the sexes were at last allowed to talk to each other. He was determined to keep the girls away from the boys and had an intricate system of rules for the girls and another set of rules, much less stringent, for the boys. Unless the girls lived in Georgia Burleson Hall, they lived with their parents or close relatives in Waco. Any pregnancy of a Burleson girl would be a serious blow to Baylor's reputation where young women were concerned and could discourage parents from sending their daughters there. Antonia Teixeira's pregnancy in the late 1890s, which we talk about elsewhere in connection with W.C. Brann's attacks on Baylor, was not the message Burleson wanted going out to parents.

When Frank Guittard enrolled at Baylor, there was a seven-foot fence in front of Georgia Burleson, and boys were forbidden to walk on the ground between Fifth Street and the fence. The enclosed area was known as the "Angels' grounds," and Burleson Hall was known as "The Angel Inn." The rules required the girls to study their Sunday school lessons and prohibited them from borrowing pencils from their next-door neighbors. Any notes from the girls to boys had to be sent to Burleson, who would read them aloud in chapel the next day.

Miles: How was Burleson trying to keep men and women apart?

Pops: With his personality and the imaginary line he forcefully drew for students.

Miles: Imaginary line?

Pops: Imaginary line. Burleson was a very forceful character and, with the help of wife Georgia in some things, was in charge of everything. For example, "On the first day of each session [he] drew an imaginary line down the aisle of the chapel with his umbrella. He said that this line extended all the way across the campus and that the boys were to stay on the Waco Creek side of the line and the girls on the Georgia Burleson Hall side." Girls were forbidden to interact with boys or be escorted by them. Boys could not converse with girls on campus and had to sit on opposite sides from the girls in classrooms and chapel, and no talking between recitations.

A sea change in approaches to student discipline was evident at the turn of the twentieth century, as not all college administrators agreed with Burleson's interpretation of "*in parens patriae*," which means standing in place of parents. President David Starr Jordan of Stanford asserted five years after taking the helm at Stanford that American colleges were removing restrictive rules and placing upon the student the responsibility for his or her conduct.

Among the reasons for Burleson's pressured resignation in 1897 was the faculty's feeling that his resignation was required for the "harmony and well-being of the school." The faculty took objection to Burleson's publicly remanding faculty members in front of the students, the students occasionally attempting to set aside the faculty's decisions on student discipline by appealing to Burleson. The faculty also claimed that after the resignation of Burleson as president to become president-emeritus, student discipline improved. It is also instructive that the faculty abolished the chapel monitor system, and students were no longer expected to watch and write up other students.

Miles: Did Frank have any opinion about mandatory chapel?

Pops: Actually, yes, after he returned to Baylor to teach. Frank was appointed to a faculty committee that reported back their recommendations excerpted as follows: "Longer scripture reading occasionally; occasional community singing...led...by some capable student; sing more of the great hymns of the Church and less ragtime; a band concert occasionally."

Miles: That's predictable he would have recommended a band concert, but I'm not sure that's consistent with opposing ragtime.

Pops: Yes, you have a point. Since the entire faculty had to sit through the chapel services along with the students, a band concert and a little ragtime might have been welcome to many of those attending chapel.

Miles: Listening to a band would have been fun and maybe singing too, but longer scriptures and longer prayers? I don't think many students would have been up for that. And I like ragtime!

Pops: One thing I forgot to mention. The problems with Burleson were apparently so serious that the faculty pressured him to resign without already having someone lined up to take his place as president.

Miles: Sounds like they were really ready for him to step down.

Pops: Sometimes it's hard for a top executive to step down, especially for one as important as President Burleson to the Baylor we know today.

CHAPTER 12

Literary Societies: Debates, Not Bats and Balls

Organizations called literary societies were common phenomena on America's college and university campuses in the nineteenth and early twentieth centuries. Baylor's literary societies existed before fraternities, sororities, and other organizations took their place and before intercollegiate sports competitions became popular. They arose in Independence, flourished at Waco University, and were an integral part of institutional and university life at Baylor in Waco from 1886 through the late 1920s when they began to lose popularity. I have asked Miles to walk with me through some of the highlights and ask any questions he wants to ask.

Pops: Both Frank Guittard and his oldest son, Francis, were active members three decades apart during their days at Baylor. Francis missed the societies' heydays, and younger brother Clarence missed them altogether. Frank was an associate editor of the *Baylor Literary* publication representing the Erisophian Literary Society (ELS), one of the two leading literary societies for men, and he also served the ELS in other capacities. The societies would play a significant role in one or more controversial episodes in Baylor's history in Waco, most notably the kidnapping of Baylor journalist-Baylor tormentor William Cowper (W.C.) Brann in the late 1890s.

The five societies (including the Erisophians and Philomathesians) had their yells and songs, much like sports teams today, as well as their written constitutions, colors, flags, and society secrets which they swore to protect against falling into the hands of the rival society. These secrets and private domains included pledge recruitment strategies, society pins, entertainments and elegant dinners with printed programs and musical accompaniments, public debate competitions, and private libraries and society rooms in the Main Building. In addition, the men's societies rushed incoming freshmen, trying aggressively to attract the more competitive students to their ranks. It might seem to have all been friendly competition, except it wasn't that friendly. The rivalry was usually cantankerous, and occasionally so bitter that some of the usual debate competitions had to be canceled. Many male members were destined for law school and paid close attention to any administration rulings they perceived to favor their competition. Victory and bragging rights for one's society ("we're the best because we win most of the competitions," et cetera) were crucial to recruit new members.

Quoting the 1909 *Baylor Round-Up*, "The most potent power in Baylor's existence has been that of her literary societies...In the days when students were few, these societies were the agents that replenished the student ranks; in the days when funds had to be had or the school should perish, the enthusiastic society workers came to its relief; and throughout the course of the institution no other force has contributed so much to its spirit and made its progress possible along so many lines as have these bodies of young men and women banded together for literary and social purposes...But it is in oratory and debate that the benefits of society training are most gratifying, and that have been most conspicuous. Baylor stands without peer in oratory and debate in Texas...Baylor has won a series of debates from the two other foremost colleges of Texas, and is now planning for larger contests in the future."

Miles: Okay, but I don't understand the "debates, not bats and balls" thing you said at the beginning of this chapter.

Pops: Miles, when you went to UT Austin, did you go to football games?

Miles: Of course; I wouldn't have missed them. We'd go on the frat bus with our girlfriends and other frat guys and their dates. It was very intense, and it was important that UT whip the other team's a—.

Pops: Well, just as you might go today to watch Texas play Baylor at McLane Stadium or Royal Stadium, if you were in college over a century ago, you might have gone to see Texas debate Baylor in an auditorium. Some say that debating was the most popular "sport" in America in the 1890s. In 1893, Baylor challenged the University of Texas debating team to a debate sponsored by Baylor's Lone Star School of Oratory. At that time, Baylor and Texas did not play each other in football, and Baylor did not start playing other schools at all in football until 1898. The best Philomathesian Society debater that year was Pat M. Neff, who joined forces with Tom Connally, the best Erisophian debater. Later, Neff would become governor of Texas and then president of Baylor. Connally later served first in the US House of Representatives and then as US Senator from Texas for decades. The 1893 debate with Texas created such intense interest among Baylor students that they chartered a special train to Austin to support their team.

Over five thousand people turned out for the return match held at the Cotton Palace in Waco the following year. The Calliopeans and RCBs were all there to support the Baylor societies' combined teams. The Calliopeans were normally the sister organization to the Philos and the RCBs the sister organization to the Sophies.

Miles: Why did it take so long for Baylor to play other schools in football? I heard somewhere that Princeton and Rutgers played their first intercollegiate game in 1869. Why did it take almost thirty years for the news to get to Waco?

Pops: I think the game back then, which was a more rugby-like game than football today, got its start in the Ivy League. The Ivy League paid more attention to sports in England, like rugby, than schools in Texas. To add to that, President Burleson opposed all intercollegiate sports and most games of all kinds, not just athletic ones, as he felt they just distracted students from their studies.

Miles: How could a debate team have a yell? That doesn't make sense to me. It seems like yelling while students were debating would have been distracting.

Pops: Hold that thought. Here are a few yells for the Philos and the Sophies from the 1915 and 1917 *Round-Ups*:

Philomathesian Yells

"I'd rather be dead than not be a Philo, Philo, Philo.
Esse quam videri malo.
Zip, Rah, Rhu! Zip, Rah, Rhu!
Watch us, watch us, when we're through,
Where'll we go? What'll we do?
We'll eat oysters. What about you!"

Erisophian Yells

"Hunt your holes and hide, Philos,
Hide Philos! Hide Philos!
Hunt your holes and hide, Philos,
Hide, Hide, Hide.
Rip-saw! See-saw!
What are the Philos here for?
Nothin' at all, nothin' at all!
Put 'em away in alcohol!"

Miles: Those are pretty funny. But did they really do those yells?

Pops: Well, I doubt those yells were heard very often, but there was nothing funny at the time about the societies' hyper-rivalry and the bitterness that would inevitably break out. There were times when Burleson must have wanted to pull his remaining hair out. As evidence of the lingering hostility created by the rivalry—despite that the Philos were no longer active on campus by 1930—the Sophies took a grim pleasure in chortling about the death of the Philos and bragging that they were the only surviving society on the Baylor campus.

Miles: Pops, what were those Philomathesian and Erisophian clubs like at Baylor? Why were they called literary societies if all they did was just argue with each other?

Pops: The best explanation I have is that the Philos and the Sophies both had libraries with thousands of books. That by itself was important because Baylor did not have much of a library back then. Members would use their societies' books for quotes to support their arguments in debates. So, in a way, it was still about debating.

Miles: So literary societies were not really about literary things like poems, plays, and novels?

Pops: Not so much about those things per se, but about words and the power and use of words in speeches, sermons, and debates, and that educated people had to be able to debate, and how to advocate effectively, especially before an audience. But to a limited extent, "literary" also meant cultural and that meant music, art, and poetry.

Miles: Music? Did they debate to music?

Pops: Very funny. No, but they put on formal programs in which musical interludes were incorporated to add a dash of refinement to what would otherwise have just been an hour or more of take-no-prisoner oratory and debate.

Miles: But what were those days like back then? What was the big deal about which fraternity a new student joined? Was it about which society had the best or most extensive library?

Pops: Being a member of the society with the best win or loss record was critical, arguably a predictor of future success at the practice of law. Intercollegiate debates between Baylor and the University of Texas, for example, were really big deals. Inter-society competition for the best student debaters was intense. In 1893, the Philo summer committee told their members to come back on different trains with these instructions: "Propose to a prospective member a boarding place, get his check for his trunks; if you can, try in every way to impress him with the fact that you want to help him & that it is as a Philo that you do this." Maybe the best way of understanding the Philo-Sophie rivalry is this excerpt from the 1902 *Round-Up* of a conversation between a Philo and a freshman named Jones during a membership drive:

Jones: (*somewhat bewildered—"New boy" written in every crease of his clothes, matriculation card in his hand, and responding to an inquiry by a Philomathesian he had just met*) "Yes sir, I just got in last night."

Fulbright: *(affably)* "You took the most important step in your life when you came. Baylor's the school of the South-west. Did you know any of the students before you came?"

Jones: "Yes, sir—J.W. Wayman. He's a junior, I believe."

Fulbright: "Oh yes, he's a junior. Jimmy's a mighty fine fellow. Got into the wrong society when he came down here though...I want to help you in making your decision. I'm a Philo, you know. This is our assembly hall [in Main Building]. That picture over there is Prof. Tanner's—you know he died last year. One of the brainiest men the South ever produced too. That fellow with the bushy hair is R.H. Hamilton. He's one of our professors now. Oh, Robert Houston is a war-horse I tell you. And there's Johnson; mathematics, you know. And those over there are other Philos, too. Taylor, Waller Baker. Oh yes, Sul Ross was a Philo. The Sophies can show some mighty fine men, but we'll show records with them any day. Have you met many Philo boys?"

Jones: "I've met so many fellows I can't keep 'em apart."

Fulbright: "I want you to meet all of 'em. They are a fine set, hardworking and stick together like brothers. I'm sure you'll want to be with the hard-working crowd too. A fellow's associates determine a great deal about his college course. By the way, have you seen our library?"

Jones: "I saw the one on the second floor."

Fulbright: "Oh, that's the Sophies'. They've got a few pretty good books down there, but they are in no order. Chaos reigns supreme. We just had our library re-catalogued. Sent a man off to study the system. It's in fine shape now, too. In fact it's the only library in the University that's in shape for use."

[Later]

Crouch: (*an Erisophian, at his politest*)—"Mr. Jones, I believe? Crouch is my name."

Jones: (*resignedly*)—"Glad to meet you, Mr. Crouch."

Crouch: "About got your work decided on? Can I help you with your course?"

Jones: "I believe I'm through until recitations begin."

Crouch: "You're from [name of town] I believe. Wayman told me about you. We've been expecting you in for a day or two. Never would do for you not to join the [Sophies.]. Everybody from down there is an Erisophian. Anybody can't help being one if he keeps his eyes open. Why one glance at our record proves our superiority. We've won the Inter-Society debate nearly every time, and our men have won two State oratorical medals...Then our men have been champions in the successful debates against the State University [UT Austin]. And we stand even on the DeGraffenreid debate, about the only thing they are even with us in. I believe they claimed a larger membership last year than we had. But they are nearly all 'preps.' Haven't got but a few upper-class-men. Prince and Dancer—have you met them?"

Jones: "Isn't Dancer a slender man, with black hair, a bald spot and a Roman nose?"

Crouch: "Yes, that's Dancer. Sure is a brilliant man, too. He and Prince won us the Philo-Sophie debate last June. Prince won the Skinner medal, too. Here's a little book that shows our records. We got it out just so the new men might understand things. 'Ten Years in Baylor.' Shows we've got 137 decisions in the past ten years to the Philos' 17."

Jones: "Is the Philo library any better than yours?"

Crouch (*mockingly*)—"Well, I should hope not. Stuck off up there in that recitation room where they couldn't use it if they wanted to. Did you see ours? Nice, quiet, cool place. Nobody ever loafs around there, either. Good order all the time. Philos been doing a lot of work on theirs, I believe. Lots of good it will do 'em...Besides, they're away deep in debt on it and the new boys with have to pay it out."

[*Later Jones, the new freshman, is in a bedroom at his boarding house...rubbing his temples and talking deliriously to himself.*]

Miles: Did President Brooks or President Neff debate when they were at Baylor?

Pops: For sure. They were both very effective debaters but had different debate styles. In 1892, while Frank was in the Erisophian Society, President Brooks was the Philomathesian champion with his partner, winning the 1892 joint debate. Neff, a peerless debater with a sarcastic attacking style, would have squared off against fellow-Philo Brooks in many debate practices, later poking fun at Brooks for Brooks's debating eccentricities. Brooks claimed that Neff always selected the books he would quote from by the brilliant, beautiful colors of the backs of the books. Neff admitted the truth of Brooks's charge but said that Brooks selected his proof books by their weight. If a book was hefty, Brooks would come into the debate and lay all the books he wanted to use down on the table. He never picked them up or read from them, just pointed at them. In each debate, according to Neff, Brooks claimed that whatever the opposite side was contending for was the cause of the downfall of the Roman Empire; that usually helped Brooks clinch the debate.

Miles: You said Frank was an Erisophian?

Pops: Right. The Erisophian Literary Society played a significant role in Frank Guittard's student days. After he came back to Baylor in 1902, he made a speech to a meeting of the Sophies which I've excerpted as follows: "During the period of about three years while I was an active member of this society, I had the honor of holding some official position for the greater part of that time. You can find in some of the old records the minutes I spread upon the books while I was recording secretary written in a much better style of penmanship than I am able to command at present. I have sadly neglected that area...Not only in an official capacity but also in a semi-official capacity, I had the honor and strenuous pleasure of serving my society. For more than once I blistered the tender portions of my pedal extremities hurrying from my boarding place on Speight St. to meet all incoming trains to get ahead of the Philos. And we did generally get ahead of them."

For a detailed account of one desperate race to get ahead of Philos determined to board the southbound Katy Flyer for Waco in Hillsboro and then to proselytize the new students coming from Dallas and Fort Worth, Sophie Jesse Guy Smith set the record straight. In the Sophies' race to beat the Philos to the prize [the new students], the Sophies headed to East Waco without tickets and caught a slow-moving northbound freight, jumped aboard an empty car while dodging train employees, planning to bribe the conductor if necessary. The result of Smith and his fellow Sophie Albert Jones's scheming and quick action resulted in corralling the incoming students and having them safely under their control before the Philo canvassers realized they had been outsmarted. Sophies no doubt bragged about that coup for months, if not years.

As bitter as their rivalry was in the early decades of the twentieth century, the 1896 *Round-Up* explains how, for a limited time after the conclusion of the Civil War, the Philos and Sophies, who had generally sided with the Confederacy, united (temporarily in 1868) under the banner of the Philomathesians. However, in time, the Erisophians reorganized and built their numbers back, emerging once again to challenge their adversaries and compete for the favor of Baylor women.

Miles: So, it took the US Civil War to get the Philos and Sophies at Baylor at Independence to bury the hatchet.

Pops: Yes sir. But the truce didn't last for long—it was all about the "Yankees are-a-coming" and all-hands-on-deck against the common enemy.

BOOK THREE

An Eventful Intermission

Sample questions for the peanut gallery's consideration in this book's chapters:

What was Frank's experience like selling books door to door? Was he good at it? Why did Frank wait so long to return to Ohio for a visit? What happened to his father's second marriage? What sort of tips did Frank give Pat Neff when they roomed together in Arkansas? Who did Frank date before Mamie? What did his students think about his unmarried state? Why was President Burleson's position changed to president-emeritus? When did President Burleson have his Robin Hood moment?

Excerpts from Frank's "Funny-Book of Student Bone-heads" on examinations:

Question: "Who was Saladin?" Answer: "Saladin became Pope. I don't know much about him, although his doctrines were much like Gregory the Seventh's."

Question: "What led to the Crimean War?" Answer: "The cause of the Crimean War was an effort to force the opium of India upon the Chinese; it was thought that China could make but little resistance and it would be a before breakfast affair."

Examples of Frank's favorite words and phrases from his letters:

"deeply wounded" — "I never felt offended at what you wrote, only deeply wounded."

"developed a suspicious tendency" — "I have developed a suspicious tendency to get fat."

"taken into consideration" — "All things taken into consideration, you made a good purchase."

CHAPTER 13

Dropping Out & Selling Books to Farmers' Wives

(1894; reconstructed)

In this chapter, we address the months after Frank Guittard dropped out of Baylor at the end of the spring quarter in 1894 and before he joined the faculty of Southwestern Academy in Magnolia, Arkansas, in December. That summer, he joined the ranks of the widely disliked, if not universally distrusted, summer book salespersons recruited by publishing companies. The following is my conversation with Miles.

<u>Miles</u>: Pops, I know you said Frank Guittard dropped out of Baylor. What happened? Did he decide college wasn't for him?

<u>Pops</u>: No, Miles, in the spring, Frank ran out of money for college. His parents couldn't help him as there was a depression and panic in Ohio and everywhere else. The depression started in 1893 and lasted four years. Frank may have intended to resume his schooling at the small sectarian school on the banks of the Brazos, and he could not have known that his days as a Baylor student were over, or that in a few years, a new chapter would begin for him in Waco that would last forty-eight years. The 1893 depression and its aftermath was the worst in the history of the US to that point. One hundred fifty banks, two hundred railroads, and fifteen thousand small businesses failed. The year before, 100,000 desperate land-seekers had rushed to Oklahoma to claim land. In 1894, unemployment worsened and climbed to 25 percent, and bands of unemployed men began to march on Washington.

To draw attention to economic conditions in Ohio, Jacob Coxey led a group of unemployed protesters walking from Ohio to Washington, D.C. Coxey's march began in March 1894, just days before Frank dropped out of Baylor. Professor Carlos A. Schwantes notes in his volume *Coxey's Army* that "people who believed themselves disinherited saw in the Coxey crusade [to Washington] an agency for their redemption; and members of similar agencies—the Populist party and organized labor—provided the movement its primary institutional support, especially in the region west of the Mississippi. There the popular crusade might have served as inspiration for L. Frank Baum's The Wizard of Oz, published years later...During the fall and winter of 1893, the time was ripe for any crusade that portrayed Uncle Sam—Congress or President Cleveland—as a wizard, who by inaugurating a program of public-works would free the American worker frozen into idleness by hard times."

Coxey's march would reach D.C. in late April. Further, by April it was clear that the Chicago world's fair, which had opened in 1893 and featured the spectacular White City was an illusion, just like Dorothy's hallucination of Oz occasioned by the bump on the head from a Kansas tornado. The United States's problems were severe and deep, capital and labor had declared war, and the Pullman employees were on strike in twenty-seven states and territories in May 1894. President Cleveland put down the strikes by sending in federal troops and arresting the president of the American Railway Union, Eugene V. Debs.

The story of what happened in Frank's life for those seven troubled months between his first stint at Baylor and his teaching job in Arkansas is an interesting one. Frank tells the story in an essay he wrote later at the University of Chicago: "At the end of this time my financial resources were at a low ebb and I accepted an agency from a book company. I traveled Hunt County enlightening the natives as to the value of good literature and especially of the lasting benefits to be derived from an investment in a copy of 'Talmage's Trumpet Blasts.' Although I was met by many varieties of dogs at the front gates, only one had the unbridled audacity to seize one of my pedal extremities and stay my progress for a few seconds. Only one man who had gone back on his subscription, threatened to get his gun, to obtain retribution for his wounded honor, when I told him that he had not acted the gentleman. In general, I was politely treated and the people were glad to look at my book."

Frank's comment about "enlightening the natives" is obviously tongue-in-cheek—I have my own copy of *Talmage's Trumpet Blasts* and have sampled its contents. The stated aim of this 1892 collection of lectures and sermons is to awaken readers to the evils and degeneracy in American society that are the missions of the "Army of Satan." The typical Talmage sermon in the volume attempts to elevate and ennoble readers through flowery language and phrase-making rather than by appeals to specific Bible verses. We will get into that in a minute.

It is interesting that at the same time Frank was dropping out of Baylor, Samuel P. Brooks was finishing up a year at Yale, which would entitle him to boast an Ivy League undergraduate degree. However, Brooks was stressed financially and borrowing money from his struggling minister father, his friend and fellow Yale student James Cantwell, and from wherever he could get it. The monies he borrowed allowed him to finish his year at Yale, but he was conscience-stricken about taking money from his father, whose resources and income as a minister were limited. In a letter to his father in the spring of 1894, Brooks—who was famous as a Baylor student for wearing worn-out clothes—reported that he was forced to spend $25 for a suit of clothes since "I cannot go to see sister, & Savannah with my patched pants, worn elbows, & shining old clothes," but that "if my health holds out, your standing by me so now shall cause me to make the effort of my life to redeem the cost to you." For Brooks, like Frank, maintaining one's health was crucial to getting on in school and repaying loans.

Miles: Where did Frank get the idea of selling books to make money?

Pops: Oh, I'm sure he had seen the ad in the *Baylor Literary* for April 1894 soliciting book agents to sell Talmage's *Trumpet Blasts* since he was an associate editor for the Literary. The Southwestern Publishing Company periodically advertised it was hiring recent graduates. A typical Southwestern ad said: "Since you have graduated, you will want money. You can make it by selling subscription books. You will next want a wife. You can win her by presenting your sweetheart with one of Southwestern's beautiful books. Money and wife mean a home. Then you will want a library. Secure it by buying a few standard books each year from the Southwestern Publishing Company, Chalmer's Block, Waco, Texas." Although Frank had not graduated, Southwestern's ads would have always secured his attention, for they addressed his need for money to continue his education, his desire eventually to marry, and his longing for a library of his own.

Miles: Well, as to the Talmage book, what was it like? What did Frank think of the book he was selling, and did he make enough money to go back to Baylor?

Pops: Answering that last question first, no, he did not make enough money selling books that summer to go back to college. He did win a pocket watch, though—valued at $75—for having sold the most books in his sales group of six students. As to the Talmage book, there may be a difference of opinion on the "lasting benefits" (Frank's words) obtainable through purchasing a copy. The Southwestern Company claimed in its 1894 ad in the *Literary*, which Frank would have seen, that "The Great Demosthenes was no more a master of eloquence in ancient Greece than is Talmage in Modern America. Graphic in illustration, splendid in imagery, exhaustless in resources, comprehensive as a thinker, the most wonderful word painter of the century, Dr. Talmage is everywhere recognized as a man of colossal intellectual proportions. We have secured his latest and best book, 'Trumpet Blasts,' or 'Mountaintop Views of Life'...If you want to make money fast and any young man of average ability can make from $75.00 to $125.00 per month...We would like to tell you about what some of our agents have done and are now doing. A number of the students from the University with whom you are acquainted...cleared above all their expenses over $100.00 a month."

Talmage's sermons in *Trumpet Blasts* are divided into sections. First, the section on the doctrine of evolution—he was adamantly against it, saying he had put scientists living and dead on the witness stand, and they all denied believing in the

Holy Scriptures and the Garden of Eden. Second, the curse of strong drink—he was strongly opposed and called it an "invisible caldron of temptation." Third, in the section on dress and dissipation—Talmage inveighed against tight boots and men who bought expensive clothes and looked like "animated checkerboards," and the men who wore padded clothes or corsets. Fourth, the section on dancing—Talmage decried those who indulged in "late-suppers... and... [who stepped from] the ball-room into the grave-yard." He also lets fire at bad pictures, bad books, attacks on the Bible, and the national perils—unhappy homes, divorce, polygamy, libertinism, and the "Club House" with its telling vile stories and filthy conversations. Talmage also fulminated against the burden of debt despite the fact that the last of his three churches, which burned in 1894, was burdened with crushing debt incurred to create the spectacular performance auditorium he required to deliver his sermons. A London newspaper referred to him as the "best-paid pastor in the universe" and a New York newspaper said "Talmage [with the exception of Henry Ward Beecher] had a more widespread reputation than any other American preacher of the gospel."

Reverend Talmage, however, was not without detractors, including one in Waco: the savage wordsmith and fiery editor/owner of *The Iconoclast,* William Cowper Brann. Brann castigated Talmage as a "wide-lipped blatherskite and religious fakir," and time and again beat Talmage like a redheaded stepchild in passages like: "*The Iconoclast* will pay any man $10.00 who will demonstrate that T. DeWitt Talmage ever originated an idea, good, bad or indifferent. He is simply a monstrous bag of fetid wind. The man who could find intellectual food in Talmage's sermons could acquire a case of delirium tremors by drinking the froth out of a pop bottle." Brann claimed Talmage's sermon entitled "Bricks Without Straw" was a "rambling fragmentary piece of mental hodgepodge, in which scraps of schoolbook Egyptology, garbled Bible stories, false political economy and fragments of misapplied history tumble over each other like specters in a delirium." At times, Brann referred to Talmage as "Talmage the Turgid."

What Frank, and possibly Brann, did not know and the Southwestern Company did not mention in its promotions of the *Trumpet Blasts* was that Talmage's tabernacles burned down three times, the last time on May 13, 1894. That day, a fire beginning in the organ engulfed the entire church building. Talmage was delivering his final sermon to a congregation already weighed down by tremendous church debt to build his performance tabernacles when the fabulous organ went up in flames. Nor did Frank's summer employer mention that Talmage, while a talented pulpit performer, did not enjoy the whole-hearted support of his congregation in 1894, and had been tried ("churched") on several allegations of untruthfulness, although the charges were eventually dropped.

<u>Miles</u>: I don't think you answered what Frank thought of Talmage's book.

Pops: No, I haven't, but my feeling is that Frank used the Talmage volume as a sleep aid after a long day of ringing doorbells, if he needed one. But having looked through the volume myself, it makes me wonder about that trite adage that a salesperson, to be effective, must firmly believe in the product he is selling. Perhaps Frank developed some uneasiness that his customers did not need the book he was selling, except to use as a paperweight. Perhaps not. Anyway, more about what Frank thought in a little bit.

Miles: So how did the summer selling go for Frank? What was the selling experience like for a quiet book lover like Frank? And was he trained on how to sell that book?

Pops: Excellent questions. First, I thought it would help to recreate a scene of Frank pitching the book to a farmer's wife in Greenville, the county seat of Hunt County, where he was sent to sell books. I've based this scene on my research, including the written accounts of other summer book salespeople of that era, from Mortimer's *Confessions of a Book Agent* to the Boyce Brothers' *Get-the-Hell-Off-My-Porch: Adventures in Door-to-Door Sales*, and other books featuring door-to-door book selling.

Imagined Scene: Frank and Mrs. Franklin, Greenville, Texas

It is about half-past four on a hot July day in one of Greenville's country neighborhoods. Frank is wearing light-colored summer suit pants without his coat, green and gold suspenders holding up his pants, a white shirt, and a nondescript striped tie. His face is sunburned, and perspiration shows on his forehead and upper lip. The armpits of his shirt are dark with sweat. He walks up to the front door of a medium-sized wood cottage set back from the road. The houses are in a neighborhood where the lots are an acre or so in size. He looks for the doorbell and, seeing none, knocks on the screen door, holding a fan in one hand and a small grip and straw hat in the other. A slightly built middle-aged woman in a blue dress and apron appears in the screen.

"Yes?"

"Ma'am, I hope I didn't disturb you. I'm a Baylor student off for the summer. Name's Frank Guittard."

"No, young man, I've just finished fixing a little supper for the family. They'll be here directly. What do you need?"

"Ma'am, I'm calling on church folks here in your neighborhood. (*Frank wipes his head with a handkerchief*) You go to Pastor Anderson's Baptist church down on Wesley Street?"

"Um-hum. Every time they ring the bell." (*She laughs*)

"You know, it's awful hot—maybe I could trouble you for a glass of water...I'm staying down at the widow Sloane's boarding house on Park Street."

"Why certainly. Just a moment; I think I have some cold lemonade in the icebox you might like better."

"Yes, Ma'am, that would be fine, but don't go to any special trouble on my account."

The farmer's wife disappears from view but soon returns and steps out on the porch where there are several rocking chairs. She is carrying a tray that holds a tall green glass of lemonade and a plate containing a large cornbread wedge left over from the evening meal the night before. She motions for Frank to sit down, saying, "Thought you might be hungry—this cornbread of mine was going to go to waste if it don't get eaten up today. My husband Dan won't eat leftovers, and my children won't neither. Hate to throw out almost fresh cornbread to those hogs yonder. They're not picky."

(*Frank gazes thoughtfully at the hog pen across the way, remembering his days with the hogs on his father's farm; he takes the refreshments offered him and starts munching on the slice of cornbread.*)

"Really good cornbread, Ma'am...I like Pastor Anderson. He can sure keep a body warm and awake on a cold night when he talks about hellfire, but he saves most of his shouting until the last five minutes. Pastor B.H. Carroll in Waco shouts the whole sermon. I don't know where he gets the energy. *(Both Frank and the farmer's wife chuckle)* I may be stretching it a little, but Pastor Carroll starts off loud, and he just get louder toward the end."

(*The farmer's wife interrupts at this point...*)

"Now, young man, be sure and ask Mrs. Sloane—that's where you're staying, right? —if she could let you taste, afore you leave town, some of that blackberry cobbler of hers. It's the best. She always brings it up to our church potlucks, and it's always gone at the end of the evening. I tell Dan to leave it alone, but he won't pay me no mind. I guess he wants a bigger pot than he has already." (*smiling ruefully*)

"This cornbread is just unusually good, Ma'am. My mother was a good cook—I really miss her. (*Frank pauses for a few seconds to gather himself.*) May I ask you how old your children are, Ma'am?"

"Well, my oldest, Leroy, is fourteen, and he'll be thinking about what to do with his life in a few years, maybe one of those colleges that teach bookkeeping and stenography or maybe the Bible. My youngest, Mildred, is ten, so we'll have her around here for a while. We'll sure miss them when they're gone off to make their way in the world. I'm too old to have more children. Guess we'll have to find us a puppy or a kitty. Don't think I could stand to look at one of those little potbellied pigs in the house." (*chuckles at her own joke*)

"You must be really proud of Leroy and Mildred."

"Yes sir, I am. I think they are both a little exceptional—I mean in a good way—if I say so myself; I know I shouldn't because bragging on your children's a sin in some people's eyes. That's what the pastor says."

"You know I never got your name, Ma'am."

"Oh, I'm sorry. I'm Wilma Robertson Franklin, of the Caddo Mills Robertsons, and my husband, who's over at the cotton gin office today, is Dan Franklin. Dan's a deacon, takes up the collection on Sunday mornings and nights—not on Wednesdays though, since he has his Grange meetings early Thursday mornings."

"You must be thinking about what Leroy and Millie will be doing one day. You mentioned college a moment ago."

"Yes, we are. Leroy is already talking about preaching in some little church somewhere. I don't know where he got that idea—I guess from above. He's already testified before the whole congregation, done it two times already. They gave him a special Bible with his name printed in gold on the cover and Jesus's words in red inside. Then the Pastor baptized him, even laid hands on him afterwards, and blessed him to the Lord's service. Leroy always wants us to call on him for the blessing at mealtimes. He's got a real passion for it."

"That's just wonderful. You know, I had a thought—it would be such a blessing if Leroy could come down to Waco sometime and meet our President Burleson, especially if Leroy would like to preach one day. Mrs. Franklin, did you know Baylor educates more young men to be preachers than anywhere else in Texas? President Burleson says it's not enough for a young man just to know the Bible and quote scripture. I'm going to be a teacher myself, but I know lots of Dr. Burleson's students, and they are really fine. President Burleson, Mrs. Burleson too, would treat him just like family, introduce him around, take him through Main Building and through the campus, let walk inside Maggie Houston Hall and talk to some of the men. Maggie was named for our great Sam Houston's wife. I stayed there myself and survived it just fine; I never got sick once." (*Frank laughs to himself and continues*). "Course, the food is not going to be as good as what Leroy gets around here if it's as good as this cornbread. But he would always remember meeting President Burleson, I promise you."

"That does sound nice. I will talk to Dan about maybe doing that."

"Something else, Mrs. Franklin, if you would permit me, is to ask you about the Bible library which you have in your house for Leroy and Millie."

"Well, we have the *King James*, of course, and some pamphlets they gave us up at the church. I don't think you would call it a library, though."

"That's a good start, Mrs. Franklin, but it sounds like, having two children around here and with Leroy interested in preaching and all, if you don't mind me saying it, you might want the book I'm showing right now to your neighbors and fellow church members. I've already visited with your pastor, and he said it is a powerful work."

"What book is that?"

(*Frank, with a practiced flourish, removes the copy of* Trumpet Blasts *from his small grip, unwraps it from its velvet covering, and carefully places it exactly halfway between them on the table.*)

"You know, people have been saying for years that there is no replacing the Bible; I believe that one hundred percent if you are talking about the *King James*. But the Bible is not enough to have in your house to support your young-uns. The Bible must be supported by powerful testimonies in modern, down-to-earth language that everyone can understand. I love the *King James* just like you; I might read a chapter at night before I turn out the light. Still, this book here—which just came out two years ago—may be the most important book there is next to the Bible—important because it makes that great old book accessible to hundreds of millions, maybe billions, who might not have made it through that old-timey English from centuries ago...actually, from Shakespeare's time. You know I love Shakespeare—I'm sure you do, too—but I must confess he's hard for me, even with some college, to get through since I don't understand what all of his words and phrases mean. After all, he was from another country and another time, and he died almost three hundred years ago. It figures anything that out of date would have to be a little hard to understand."

"Frank, we have *Shakespeare's Complete Works*. They are in the cabinet over there behind the chaise lounge. A salesman passed through here a couple of years ago, and we bought them. We thought we could read from them to the children and they could pick up some culture."

"How has that worked out?"

"We've tried to read them a little *Hamlet* and maybe a little of that *Macbeth*, but, like you say, it's not easy for us country people to make heads nor tails of, and after a hard day working the farm feeding the animals, planting the south forty, and doing farm chores, Dan and I are just too blamed tired to read that old fogey language to our kids, especially when we don't know what much of it means, anyway. Beautiful language, though, but all that killing Shakespeare puts in those plays of his! I don't know about that part."

"Uh-hum."

"You say Talmage would be easier to understand than Shakespeare?"

"Oh, much easier. Take Dr. Talmage's sermon on the demon rum. Dr. Talmage's powerful words will help keep your Leroy on the edge of his seat and on the straight and narrow after that. (*Frank reads a short passage from Talmage's sermon on drinking.*)

<u>Pops</u>: At this point, assuming Mrs. Franklin is warmed up to acquiring this handsomely bound leather volume to keep Leroy on the right path, Frank can now proceed to close Mrs. Franklin on the issues of cost, delivery, time of delivery, and,

importantly, permission to include Mrs. Franklin's name on the subscription list to show other prospective purchasers. Throughout the closing, Frank might often insert the phrase "whatever is best for you, Mrs. Franklin," where appropriate to close the deal and get a down payment.

Miles: So if *Trumpet Blasts* was as preachy and hard to get through as you are telling me, how did Frank get himself psyched up to sell this book? It sounds like he would never have wanted a copy himself.

Frank: Frank needed money, and money is always a powerful motivator. The US was still in the grip of the 1893 depression. The country did not return to normal for four more years. Then the book—although it is hard to imagine that Frank would have found it inspiring instead of over-wrought, fantastical, and strange—was in appearance an extremely handsome volume; Talmage, the author, was a popular pastor and almost a household name. As for Frank, we know that he disliked pastors who released "pious gas." On the other hand, it is unlikely that Frank knew that three of Talmage's tabernacles had burned and that his Presbyterian church had brought him up on charges for a church trial, thereby "churching" him. Moreover, although Frank was an introverted and low-key person, his need to make money in May and through the summer was the priority over most other considerations. To that end, he would have been determined to work hard selling Talmage's book of sermons to make as much money as his ethics and the hours of the day allowed him.

Miles: Selling books during a depression doesn't sound like easy work; wasn't it hard getting people to buy it? What kind of training did agents receive before going into the field?

Pops: Selling books door to door was tough, but agents received some training in making the most of any open door or receptive face and not being easily discouraged. So, we think Frank likely received most of the standard tips I'm about to mention. I do doubt whether he could have made himself do all of them, especially the ones involving an element of deception.

Miles: What tips?

Pops: First, a salesman was to be nicely dressed and look like the college student he was. He should mention that he was calling on church folks in the neighborhood; accordingly, he was required to know the names of the pastors of churches in the area, which he would have to dig out beforehand. Third, his presentation should feature Talmage's book as a weapon in the perpetual war against evil and Satan's struggle for a man's soul; he could mention that its use could ensure that, along with the Bible, any children in the house would receive the necessary nurturing and strengthening of their faiths. Fourth, the agent should endeavor to connect with the prospect by indicating that he was just like them and had grown up on a farm. Fifth, the agent's own story of his struggle to earn money for college was an essential part of the presentation, along with the agent demonstrating through his words that he was intelligent, educated, and upwardly ambitious. Sixth, though he was in the process of improving himself, he was still from a similar background as the prospect and understood their needs and situation. Seventh, he had been converted by whatever pastor converted him, in Frank's case, by Reverend James Milton Carroll, brother of Benajah Harvey Carroll, pastor of First Baptist Church of Waco. Eighth, and very important, that the book was handsomely bound—it had black leather beveled boards with red leather corners and a red leather spine with a gilt title on the front cover and gilt title on spine. It had decorative paper inside the front and back covers, many excellent black and white and colored illustrations, 588 pages, and 10.5" x 7.75" in size. It would not fall apart like some books.

Ninth, the agent should hold the book in such a way as to be able to demonstrate the beauty of the book while being able to turn its pages to point out its unique features. Tenth, the agent should not be discouraged by people saying no but persist in offering more information about the book until the sale was accomplished and the prospect's name secured for the subscription list. Eleventh, if the prospect emphatically told him no, then thank her for her time and move to the next house. Twelfth, because selling books could be discouraging, the agent had to talk to himself constantly between sales calls, telling himself that he liked to sell books, that he was making money, and that he just needed to rely on the law of averages to produce the commissions he needed. Thirteenth, if the prospect hesitated to write a down payment check, saying she didn't have the money at the moment, the agent should promise the prospect he wouldn't cash the check until the following month, "if that would work better for you, Mrs. Prospect." Fourteenth, although it might seem that selling books in hard times to farmers barely scraping along might be almost impossible, it could be done through persistence. It was true that there was a category of prospects one could call "book poor" since they had already spent all of their available assets on books. These "book poor" prospects probably couldn't be persuaded to buy additional books at any price. Fifteen, the salesperson could always play the "resemblance card," namely that the prospective buyer reminded him of his mother, grandmother, relative, or aunt he greatly admired or was from the same part of the country, or whatever. Sixteen, one could use the appeal to sympathy— "Mrs. Smith, I'm here in Greenville today calling on church folks to raise the money so I can go back to college and get my degree. I had to drop out to work for a while."

There were definite techniques agents might employ which might offend the consciences of some. For example, sometimes an agent was instructed to conceal the purpose of canvassing the church people in the neighborhood and both the book and any book prospectus until he was inside the prospect's house. The purpose was to establish some rapport and trust with the prospect. Initially, he had to sell the idea of working with church folks and the prospect's neighbors, implying that the neighbors had already blessed his enterprise. Sometimes agents tended, with or without training, to adapt as needed to any situation; for example, if the prospect's relatives were of German or Swedish heritage, the agent should also claim to have Germans or Swedes in his bloodline. The benefit from recruiting college students is that they were more credible and appealing than, say, the local barber looking for extra cash to supplement the income earned from cutting hair. Sometimes, agents who were not college students might be inclined to work a fraud on prospects such as by making extravagant claims for the sales of a book or the names of local citizens who had supposedly purchased the book. There were also door-to-door con men, not even agents for a book company, just going from house to house obtaining down payments on books that would never be delivered.

The most problematic aspect of selling books had nothing to do with the literary or spiritual merit of the work, whether the complete works of William Shakespeare, those of Sir Walter Scott (referred to by summer book salesmen as the "Sir Walters"), or Talmage's *Trumpet Blasts*—even if the farming family could afford the book or books in a depression year. It had to do with whether the book or books would ever be opened and read, or, if opened and read, how much use was ever likely to be made of them. Or whether a family in the cold light of the day after an order had been taken would regret placing the order, or the husband would come home to learn that a book had been purchased for a princely sum that he had not been asked about.

Miles: That reminds me of a scene in *Glengarry Glen Ross* where the wife of a customer demanded that her husband cancel his purchase of real estate.

Pops: That's a great scene; Pacino is so smooth and slippery as the salesman trying to hold on to his crooked deal.

Miles: Do you think Frank would have had to struggle with his conscience in order to sell *Trumpet Blasts*?

Pops: We will never know. There were salesmen—perhaps because of their training, or perhaps because of the particular book—who felt that "there was never a day in which [they] felt [they] could be honest…it meant wearing a mask every minute on the job." As to Frank, I believe if he had ever thought he might be taking advantage of someone because the book would receive little or no use, or perhaps the family was scraping along and barely making it, he would have gone on to the next house. I don't think that his own disdain, however, if had he had any for the book, would have been a problem. T. DeWitt Talmage was an extremely well-known pastor and highly regarded in some quarters. There is no accounting for other people's tastes or spiritual stripe. It was estimated that Talmage's sermons were heard or read by ten million people every week and his readers literally spanned the globe. Based on the excerpt from Frank's essay at the outset of this chapter, we suspect that Frank left it to the prospect to decide if the book would be of any benefit to the prospect or her family. High-pressure and deceptive sales tactics would have run against his basic personality and moral instincts. There was always the doorbell percentage to rely on for sales.

Of course, there would have been more than one reason for a farmer's wife to buy Talmage's *Trumpet Blasts*. If it is correct, as some sales professionals say, that the main thing the salesman is selling is the customer's experience with the salesman—a hopefully pleasant experience with a young man working his way through college, converted by a well-known or local pastor, from a farming family like themselves, et cetera—then that means that after selling himself to the prospect, the salesman should simply tell no lies and make no extravagant predictions about saving Leroy and Mildred's immortal souls; he should just stick to statements about the beautiful binding, the exciting career of Preacher Talmage, that many millions read his sermons, that the agent is talking to other church folk and several people have subscribed, and so on. It would not be necessary to add that Talmage's sermons saved the cost of sleeping pills or that some people found them gaseous. These statements would have been interesting but personal to the agent and not material to the sale.

Miles: From what I've learned about Frank so far, he doesn't sound like the type that would have been good at door-to-door selling.

Pops: He doesn't, does he? But he did well and was presented with a watch for outstanding sales. You may wonder how he did it. I have two thoughts that may explain his success. First, he may, like a stage actor, have been able to reach down deep and temporarily adopt a slightly different personality, one more confident, more personable, more charismatic, and more in control than what came naturally. The other thought is more mundane: the doorbell theory.

Miles: You've mentioned the doorbell theory several times. What's that?

Pops: That's the idea that sales success is ensured more by the number of doorbells a salesperson rings than by having a special winning sort of personality.

Miles: Did anything funny ever happen when he was selling books?

Pops: It must have, but Frank didn't record it for us. To me, the idea of selling Talmage's *Trumpet Blasts* to anyone, especially if you've ever cracked it open, is a funny idea; it is funny that people would buy it, but they did. It was a different time and place. There was a humorous novel by Ellis Parker Butler about a book agent named Eliph' Hewlitt who sought love while selling a volume entitled *Jarby's Encyclopedia of Knowledge and Compendium of Literature, Science, and Art, Comprising Useful Information on One Thousand and One Subjects, Including a History of the World, the Lives of All Famous Men, Quotations from the World's Great Authors, One Thousand and One Recipes, et cetera*. Gilt-edged and Morocco bound, *Jarby's Encyclopedia* sold for one dollar down and one dollar a month until paid.

Miles: That would be great if you could buy a one-volume encyclopedia and that would be the last book you would ever had to buy.

Pops: (*laughing*) Miles, you understand there was no *Jarby's Encyclopedia,* then or now. That was just a book title made up by Butler. However, a line actually used in the past century by some encyclopedia salesmen was, "When you have this book, you need no others. It makes a Carnegie library of the humblest home." Although Frank never sold encyclopedias, we know he bought one comprising more than twenty volumes.

Miles: Wasn't selling books a pretty easy way to make some cash? All he had to do, like you say, was walk from house to house, ring doorbells, and make pitches to farmers' wives who might invite him in for home-cooked pie and coffee.

Pops: No, it was very hard, stressful work for six twelve-hour days a week, pretty hot during summer days at that, and it came with inconveniences. We don't know of a single house where Frank was offered pie or coffee or the house's bathroom. One door-to-door salesman said a salesman in his group hated it when people would say come in before realizing he was a book salesman, and then, understanding the situation, would yell at him to get out! He also hated having to ask to use the bathroom. It worked better to pee under a bridge, in some bushes, or behind a vacant house or a barn before ringing that doorbell.

Miles: That would be pretty awkward being refused use of a bathroom. Have you seen the movie about Morman missionaries who asked to use a woman's bathroom? I think it's called *The Home Teachers*. It's a really goofy movie.

Pops: Yes, I've seen it, but movie reviews are conversation for another book.

CHAPTER 14

Summer 1895 & a Family Crisis in Ohio (1895)

This brief, unhappy chapter pertains to the March 23, 1889, death of Frank's mother, Lydia Myers Guittard, and to the tragic ending in 1895 of Dr. Francis Joseph Guittard's second marriage over protests from both families to a widow he met after being single for five years. We will call the widow "Mrs. Smith" because of the circumstances of her demise. I will work through this material with Miles and Katie.

Katie: Pops, you haven't told us much about Frank's mother, Lydia, or her life with Dr. Guittard after Frank left home for Texas. What became of her?

Pops: Unfortunately, all we know is she died in New Bedford in 1889 at fifty-eight years of age. Frank had not seen her since leaving for Texas in September 1986. He had intended to return home during the summer of 1887, but he kept putting off going home because of school and teaching commitments. You will remember that when he said goodbye to his mother and headed to the station with his father, he thought he would see them again in about a year. He never dreamed that his mother's parting words, "God bless you, Frank," would be the last he would hear her speak. We think Frank was able to return home in September 1889 after his mother had already passed, making for a sad homecoming with his father.

Miles: That does sound sad and lonely. Wonder why Frank waited so long to go home since he had intended to go home in a year?

Pops: No doubt he was asking himself the same question on the train back to Ohio. There is no good answer to that question; he had no idea that his mother was seriously ill until after her death. If he had known earlier, he would have wanted to be at her bedside with his brothers and sisters. He did have those obligations in his new state, though.

Katie: I'm wondering about the cause of his mother's death.

Pops: I don't know that, or how long she had been sick.

Charlie: Pops, I know Miles and Katie are on today, but I see on my phone where Uncle Roscoe [Pops's brother John Roscoe Guittard] just emailed us all a translation of a letter from Francis Joseph written in April 1889 to someone.

Pops: (*While studying the translation*) Yes, this letter explains some things. Francis Joseph is telling his sister Rosine Guittard Duprez that Lydia's final illness began shortly into January 1889, that she couldn't eat, and that she had heart palpitations indicating congestive heart failure which required her to go to bed. He adds that for two years she had been struggling to walk and became out of breath when walking upstairs or uphill; he also added that she had gained too much weight in her last few years. Oh, it also says here that she had a premonition of her death in her last days and made him promise her she would be placed above ground in a vault and not buried.

Katie: I wonder why it mattered to her whether her body was above or below ground level after she died.

Charlie: Maybe she had a touch of claustrophobia.

Miles: Or maybe she worried about being accidentally buried alive. Seems like I read a scary short story by Poe about premature burial.

Finn: The worms crawl in, the worms crawl out...

Charlie: The worms play pinochle on your snout...

Miles: Your back caves in, your eyes pop out...

Finn: Your stomach explodes and your guts roll out...

Pops: (*Amused but sternly*) Okay, okay, guys, enough of that. To answer Katie's question, we'll never know what Lydia's thinking was behind her request not to be buried in the ground, but it seems that there was a lot of fear out there in the nineteenth century about being buried alive despite being only unconscious or comatose. Anyway, Lydia's body was enclosed above ground in a vault as promised and Francis Joseph was placed next to her thirteen years later. We'll talk more about that mausoleum in a minute.

Katie: Since Frank was in Texas, what did he know about all of this?

Pops: Frank did not learn of his mother's death until days and possibly weeks after her death, but a telegram finally reached him. We suspect he was completely out of the loop where his mother's health problems were concerned and thus would have been shocked to hear of her death. The fact that their last parting had been emotionally disturbing for Frank would have meant that he felt her death even more keenly.

Katie: Didn't you say Francis Joseph remarried and it didn't work out so well?

Pops: Yes, that is a sad fact. When Frank made a trip home in June 1895, his father was already remarried to a woman he met the year before. According to family legend, Dr. Guittard met Mrs. Smith at a resort on Mackinac Island, Michigan, where he went every summer for his asthma. Further, word had it that Mrs. Smith was lovely, but she was not prepared to deal with the family of her new husband. She didn't seem to know how to make them like her, and they didn't seem to understand how to give her affection, or perhaps they were unwilling. The story goes that she was especially aggravated by the family's emphasis on ancestry and family tree, evidenced by numerous family portraits hanging on the wall. Most of these portraits, in the style of the times, were quite austere and devout in appearance, the family members looking like they would in their caskets except with their eyes open. Supposedly, Mrs. Smith expressed her dissatisfaction—whatever the cause of her dislike of the portraits—by turning them to the wall. Apart from this legend, there could have been other bees in her bonnet; for example, the imposing mausoleum constructed a short walk from the Guittard homestead for Francis Joseph and Lydia Myers's interment as well as their infant son Cyril, who died at just thirteen months old. It is possible that seeing that mausoleum nearly every day may have indirectly exacerbated the insecurities she may have had about fitting in with her new family.

Family legend further has it that Frank, home from Arkansas on a visit that summer, took Mrs. Smith to task for changing up the family portraits hanging on the walls. Frank's son, Clarence, recalled Frank saying that Dr. Guittard's second marriage was a mistake, and the stepmother had either turned the family pictures around or taken them down. An interview with a cousin over eighty years later substantially confirmed the story about the portraits, but added that the stepmother responded to Frank's disapproving comments by hurling a hatchet at him, cutting him badly above the elbow. According to this cousin, who apparently heard the story from other Guittards, Frank bled profusely and ran to his sister's house, whose doctor husband bound up his wounds. Family legend says that this incident contributed to the ultimate unhappy conclusion of Francis Joseph's new marriage to Mrs. Smith. In any event, later that summer, not long after this alleged incident,

Mrs. Smith committed suicide by poisoning herself. The local coroner confirmed the death as a suicide.

If the hatchet incident actually happened, or if it was in any way tied to an incident involving the portraits, Frank never mentioned it to his own family, nor did Clarence ever mention it. Clarence recalled that the last two fingers on Frank's right hand were disabled and there was a scar on his wrist. Frank's scar was not above the elbow, but below. According to Clarence, the injury to Frank's wrist, from whatever cause, had severed the tendons, thereby impairing the use of the last two fingers on that hand. The wrist and fingers are likely places for wounds had Frank raised his hand defensively to protect himself from a hurled hatchet. Frank's explanation to Clarence of his scar and disabled fingers was that he had hurt his hand in farm machinery when he was young. That ended the discussion.

<u>Miles</u>: I'm just thinking Frank lost both his mother and a stepmother in a relatively short period. That was a lot to carry around.

<u>Pops</u>: I agree. Your comment suggests a question: could Frank's feelings toward his mother have been a factor in the way events played out that summer? At the time of his mother's death, those feelings were probably unresolved. To feeling upset at being separated from her and his surprise at her seeming to close the door to his returning to Ohio was now added remorse for postponing his return to Ohio. He also would have been likely upset with her leaving this world before he had an opportunity to apologize or make up for certain things he had said or done. Only five years later, in his last year as a student at Baylor—the same year Francis Joseph married Mrs. Smith—Frank was still plagued with painful feelings concerning his mother. Frank recorded in his 1894 autobiographical sketch: "Like a great many boys, I did not always heed my mother's kind precepts and admonitions. I can recall many times, now, when I know my words and actions sent a thrill of pain to my mother's heart. Could time turn backward and make me a child again with the experience I have had in life to profit by, what [a] different life mine would be." With unresolved feelings of depression and remorse in connection with his mother, Frank might have had words with his stepmother for showing disrespect to the family pictures as well as the memory of his mother.

<u>Katie</u>: So, what do you think happened?

<u>Pops</u>: We will never know the full story, and the bits and pieces we do know are complicated. The circumstances leading to the suicide of Frank's stepmother appear more nuanced than either family legend or recollection might suggest. A review of the available evidence shows there are two main interpretations of the sad conclusion to her life. One view that gained some publicity at the time of Mrs.

Smith's death was based primarily on letters written in her hand before her death, including a suicide note she intended to publish in a local newspaper. It was reported that Dr. Francis Joseph Guittard and Mrs. Smith, a cultured widow, met and were married in early 1894. It is also unclear where the couple met. As previously mentioned, family legend said they met at a resort on Mackinac Island where he vacationed because it relieved his allergies and asthma. However, a news report after her death, without citing its source, claimed that the pair met in the same town where Dr. Guittard was allegedly undergoing treatment for morphine addiction.

Whether Dr. Guittard had a morphine problem when the couple met or whether they were both possibly being treated for addiction, it is clear that in the late nineteenth century, a very large percentage of medical professionals in the United States were addicted to morphine, as high as forty percent according to one authority in 1883. There was no shame in taking opium, and it was considered "a vital means of coping with cholera, dysentery, and tuberculosis and reduced diarrhea and coughing associated with these diseases." Morphine was popularly used to ease pain and promote sleep and calm. Most morphine addicts in the nineteenth century were initially given the drug for medical reasons, and "in the sickrooms of middle-class homes, it was prescribed as an analgesic and cure for rheumatism, headaches, women's complaints, and a variety of other ills." It became a significant problem in the medical profession, as "doctors had a steady supply of drugs, their hours were long, the conditions were stressful, and they saw the relief that morphine could provide firsthand." Dr. Guittard could easily have fallen off a horse or wrenched his back being a farmer or a horseback-riding country doctor. However, there is no information which we have been able to discover confirming whether the couple met on vacation on Mackinac Island or in a treatment facility in Ohio.

Miles: Well, what do you think happened that summer?

Pops: I don't know for sure. In any event, regardless of where or under what circumstances Francis Joseph met Mrs. Smith, no doubt a lamentable family conflict arose starting in June after Frank and one of his brothers arrived back in Ohio to spend the summer with their father. The sons' relationship with Mrs. Smith was rocky, the specific causes of the problem hidden from outsiders. In July, Frank wrote to Pat Neff, his roommate in Arkansas, confiding: "My first duty on arriving here was to get used to a stepmother, I have succeeded partly, and now think I can get used to almost anything." Frank didn't disclose to Neff what it was about his stepmother he was trying to get used to, or what kind of progress he felt he had made. In any event, the conflict became so extreme after some incident in

August that Dr. Guittard, in his desperation to resolve the conflict, barred Mrs. Smith from the family home.

Miles: I wonder why Dr. Guittard would not have sought the help of a professional to deal with the conflict. Perhaps a local minister.

Pops: Miles, unfortunately, in that day, family therapists and conflict resolution professionals were not available to a family in crisis, nor were modern medicines for treating depression and paranoia. Psychiatry as a branch of medicine was neglected until the scientific revolution in the twentieth century. As late as the early 1930s, there were fewer than 500 psychiatrists in the US.

Katie: Why didn't Mrs. Smith go live with her own family in Ohio?

Pops: That's an excellent question I can't answer. Reportedly she did had a son and daughter living in Ohio, not too far from New Bedford. After leaving the Guittard house, she began living first at a hotel and then with friends. Then, according to the local newspaper, on August 23, when her hosts were absent from the residence where she was living temporarily, Mrs. Smith carried out a plan to kill herself, secretly taking strychnine. Sometime later the same day, when it was too late to take an antidote, she advised the household that she had taken poison because the Guittards, Dr. Guittard and Frank in particular, had, in her view, acted in a shameful way toward her. She had already prepared three letters explaining her view of the circumstances leading to her demise, the one for publication seeking both a measure of revenge and justification. Her family was notified of her passing and arrived the following day. The official finding of suicide was delivered at the inquest.

Miles: That's tragic.

Pops: Yes, for several reasons. The newspaper provided a short account of the Guittard family's account of the crisis in an interview with Dr. Guittard. Dr. Guittard said that his late wife had contemplated suicide and doing something desperate for a long time and had even purchased rat poison in May before the boys arrived home in June. He said there were no rats in the house when Mrs. Smith bought the poison and that her conflict with his sons was regrettable, but it was not sufficient to explain her destroying herself. Dr. Guittard added she had a very violent temper, and there were times he thought her mind, although he was a country doctor and not a psychotherapist, was not rightly balanced. Beyond these basic contentions, he did not believe any valid purpose would be served by dwelling on the details of the unfortunate situation.

The reporter was unaware of all the facts surrounding her demise and the family rumor regarding Mrs. Smith hurling a hatchet at Frank. The reporter did not provide any information that could possibly have verified or rebutted the rumor of the hatchet injury to Frank's right hand. Some years later, Frank Guittard told his own sons that he had sustained the injury to his hand because of an accident with a lawnmower or farm equipment.

Katie: Did Frank ever say anything about his stepmother to anyone later?

Pops: Very little that we know about. It was a painful subject for the Guittard family, not one that anyone would want to talk about. However, this episode may partially explain Frank's being careful that his own sons, Francis and Clarence, were considerate of other family members, particularly their stepmother Josie, and do what they could to make home life more harmonious. Three decades later, Frank reminded Francis of this duty while on one of his sabbaticals to Stanford: "Dear Francis...Well, I am glad to know that you are taking some pride in your individual initiative. I hope it will extend and take in some of the little things that go to make home an agreeable place. It is of course an old truism that little things go to make up life. These cannot be neglected without making life a real tragedy. A thoughtless word, an act of neglect to those who are interested in you and love you, leaves a wound that does not heal for days... Lovingly, Papa" (August 31, 1926, Tuesday)

As to what person Frank was concerned about wounding, he was obviously talking about Francis's stepmother, Mama Josie. Perhaps his advice to Francis on living harmoniously with Josie was somehow related to his feelings about his mother upon hearing the news of her death and his feelings on hearing that Mrs. Smith had taken her own life. Regarding the latter, Frank must have felt terrible—a mixture of anger and horror mixed with understandable soul-searching—when he learned, as we must assume he did, of Mrs. Smith's letter to the newspaper and the reporter's interview with Dr. Guittard.

Miles: No wonder Frank didn't want to talk about it, even to family.

Katie: Sad.

Pops: Yep.

CHAPTER 15

Two Bachelors in Arkansas; Rooming with Pat Neff

(1895-1896)

Rooming together for two school years in Arkansas is the subject of this chapter. The roommates were Frank Guittard (age twenty-seven), who had dropped out of Baylor in 1894, and Pat M. Neff (age twenty-three), who had graduated in 1894 and would ultimately become president of Baylor over three decades later. Charlie will be going through this part of Frank's life with me.

Pops: Charlie, I'll start with a bit of background for the Arkansas interlude in Frank and Pat Neff's lives. James W. (William) Cantwell, a Baylor colleague of Samuel Brooks, Pat Neff, and Frank Guittard, was the first principal of the newly opened Southwestern Academy in Magnolia, Arkansas. The school opened in a brand new, attractive two-story building. The citizens of Magnolia, Arkansas, were proud of this private college preparatory school, which taught the first seven grades, high school grades 8th through 11th, and an ungraded group of students. The school had departments for music, art, physical culture, moral culture, elocution, a literary society, and a library of four hundred volumes. Students in need of boarding, usually young men, boarded at the houses of private families. Teachers, including Frank and Neff, often lived at one of Magnolia's hotels. The number of students was usually somewhere between two and three hundred and school began around September 14 of each year. Monthly fees ranged from $1.50 to $4 per month, with additional fees for music, art, and elocution.

Charlie: So, how did Frank go from dropping out of Baylor in the spring of 1894 to teaching at a private school with Neff, who had already graduated from Baylor?

Pops: Yes, Frank did not get his college degree until 1901 at Chicago, which would have been seven years after Neff earned his bachelor's from Baylor. What's odd about that is that Frank was almost five years older than Neff. If Frank could have gone to college at the same pace as Neff, he would have finished college somewhere around 1889 or 1890.

Charlie: That's curious. How did Frank, who was so much older than Neff, get so far behind him in getting his college degree?

Pops: Charlie, that is something I talked about with Katie's help in an earlier chapter, the one where we went into Frank's game plan for his life.

Charlie: Okay, I remember. There were so many steps in Frank's plan. It kept changing.

Pops: But here's how teaching in Arkansas came about. While Frank was still traveling as a book agent during the summer of 1894, he received a job offer. Baylor acquaintance James W. Cantwell, a colleague of Samuel P. Brooks with degrees from Yale and Baylor, offered Frank a position teaching in Southwestern Academy in Magnolia, Arkansas. Cantwell was principal of the newly opened academy. Frank accepted and joined Pat Neff, who likewise taught at the academy from December 1894 through May of 1896. Frank and Neff roomed together and, at some point—at least according to Neff—shared the same bed, unless Neff was just trying to get a laugh. Neff often said things for effect, humorous, dramatic, or otherwise.

Charlie: I didn't like it when I had to share a bed with Miles or Finn, especially Finn. He fidgets all night long.

Pops: Right. I have to believe that arrangement, if it occurred, was temporary.

Charlie: So Frank and Neff were both unmarried?

Pops: Both Frank and Neff were single men playing the field, although Neff still had a special girlfriend in Eagle Springs whom he eventually married. It also seems that Frank connected with an Arkansas girl sometime between 1894 and 1900, whom he later may have featured, based on the available evidence, in a 1900 essay he wrote at Chicago [excerpted in the chapter on "Early Flirtations"]. The fictionalized essay centered on a double date excursion on horseback to nearby Magnesia Springs. The evidence suggests that Neff and his date may have been the other dating couple, although they were not named in the essay. More on the "Arkansas girl" later.

Charlie: That Arkansas girl thing of Frank's is surprising.

Pops: Why? Frank didn't meet Mamie until 1898, when he took the job in Shiner. Until then, he was un-entangled romantically insofar as we have been able to determine. To be sure, though, the record is confusing here. Frank met his future wife Mamie during the 1898-99 school year in Shiner, Texas, but apparently was still corresponding with the Arkansas girl after his relationship picked back up again with Mamie in 1902. The surprising thing about Frank's dating is that Neff, in early 1895, wrote his mother that Guittard, who was almost five years older than Neff and introverted, had been instructing him by example on his approaches to women in Arkansas. I believe Neff's claim means he had observed how Frank would send a short, written note to an Arkansas girl to set up a date to church or some other excuse to get together, like a concert, picnic, or potluck supper.

Charlie: Frank Guittard giving tips to future prosecutor, governor, and Baylor President Pat Neff on dating? Hard to imagine.

Pops: Agreed. Maybe selling books in Hunt County and cold-calling on hundreds of farmers' wives boosted Frank's confidence with the opposite sex.

Charlie: Didn't you say Neff had a longtime girlfriend back in Texas? How did she react to Neff dating Arkansas girls?

Pops: Yes. Neff's Texas girlfriend was a Baylor music major from Eagle Springs named Myrtle Mainer. I mentioned her earlier. We don't know how she would have reacted to Neff's dates with other women, and we strongly suspect that Neff told his mother things he didn't tell Myrtle. Myrtle and Neff married in 1899 after Neff's teaching days in Arkansas. Here are a number of letters as excerpted from or to Neff, including a letter from Frank Guittard, all written in the1890s.

Neff to Myrtle July 27, 1892, before he graduated Baylor in 1894

"If you feel that you would like to marry me, I want you to take me strictly on the hypothesis that I would have nothing but myself. I would promise you no handsome mansion, but only a cottage by the roadside."

Neff to Myrtle July __, 1892

"I can almost agree with Talmage; he said for each person there is born a companion & they gradually approach each other from the cradle, getting nearer & nearer each other until finally they meet & join hands...I have never passed a note to anyone except you & I do not regret it in the least."

Neff to Myrtle December 9, 1894, from Magnolia, Arkansas

"Let me tell you I have been out in the rain all evening. Two of the young men offered to take Mr. Guittard and myself up to Magnesia Springs this evening, they are seven long miles from here, and just as we got there it came up a shower then it quit for a while, but just a little while after we started back it commenced raining, and rained for two hours and a half, hard and heavy...The place we went to was in a real nice place fixed up for having picnics and camp meetings—almost several different kinds of springs."

Neff to Mother Neff [Mrs. I.E. Neff] March 3, 1895, from Magnolia, Arkansas

"Dear Ma: It has been several weeks since I last wrote...I know of nothing of special importance...about and around which to vent my feelings, except that I have just sent my first note to an Arkansas girl to know if I can have the unbounded & unlimited pleasure of escorting her along winding ways & over the uneven spaces that exist between her father's mansion and the Lord's House. Prof. Guittard is getting me into these enchanting & captivating habits; he instructs me in these untrodden ways mostly by example—we have been waiting all winter for spring to come & grass to rise for us to make our debut among the unappreciated Arkansans. We have both felt a great responsibility, for the harvest here is ripe & the gatherers are few. Attended a real nice social—a select crowd of only about eight couples—we had the nicest kind of a supper, consisting of those things that suit the taste of the most delicate epicurean—for example we had salt sea oysters, several steaming smoked sausages strongly seasoned, sandwiches,...specialty selected coffee, steamed and strained, sipped from solid silver spoons.

But the funniest thing was this. Mr. Cantwell was also going with one of the teachers and on the way that night while walking along down the R.R. track, it being dark, they came to where there was a large square hole that had been dug on the track for the purpose of assisting in cleaning out the engine, let the ashes tar & such like run into it—and Cantwell & girl both tumbled into it about five feet deep—I was only a short distance behind them, got there in time to assist him in getting him pulled out—slightly hurt—her evening dress very much soiled—had to go back home & did not get to the supper. We sure had a good laugh on them, they didn't want us to tell it but we went on to the supper & told all about it. School is flourishing with about 215 students, of all sizes, ages, forms, dispositions, abilities & habits...We have a good literary society organized here now. Prof. C. [Cantwell] & myself were in for a debate last night and I did him 'up.' I must close as I want to write Brooks."

Neff to Myrtle Mainer March 24, 1895 from Magnolia Arkansas

"Magnolia is under strict quarantine. We do not allow anyone to come here either on the train or even the dirt road. The small pox is in one town about thirty miles from here and in several others in the state. Though the almond-eyed Chinaman may travel from the empire beyond the sea to where the Magnolias bloom, we meet him without the city and say, 'Thou cannot enter here.' The hotel has looked forsaken for several days. I was vaccinated last week but it didn't take. I think I shall have myself worked on again sooner for at a hotel is an easy place to catch any...Prof. Guittard & myself bought an Encyclopedia the other day just like the set you have in your parlor."

Frank Guittard from New Bedford, Ohio, to Neff in McGregor, Texas July 21, 1895

"Dear Neff, This is somewhat late to redeem my promise to write but I have been relaxing generally this summer...What a quiet restful feeling one has when at home and nothing special is to be done: no thought of what would be the best plan to handle a large Arithmetic class, to create a sentiment of honor in examinations, the best plan to avoid Arkansas rocks and brickbats coming from somewhere out of the darkness, etc.

It was six years ago when I was here last. I am now almost a stranger in my own village. Nearly all my old associates are either married and following the scriptural injunction, 'Replenish,' etc., or have emigrated to the west. I almost feel as though I had been negligent of duty when I see one of my old schoolmates with two, three or more of his young progeny tagging around after him. My first duty on arriving here was to get used to a stepmother. I have succeeded partly, and now think I can get used to almost anything. Home is not very homelike without mother, this is why I have not been home for such a while. My brother who finished a course at the State University last year is staying here with me. We have a good horse and buggy and are making good use of them. So I am passing the time quite agreeably. Father has a large library but I haven't much desire for reading of any kind just now... I think I will remain here until fall...If suitable as well as agreeable I would like for us to room together again next year [in Magnolia]. If you have not buried yourself too completely in Blackstone or some other work of legal lore, I would like to hear from you again soon."

Neff to Myrtle Mainer September 15, 1895, from Magnolia, Arkansas

"I am boarding at the hotel [Custer Hotel] you see again—All the teachers are here except Guittard. I do not know what is detaining him, he ought to have been here a couple of days ago..."

Frank Guittard in Magnolia, Arkansas January 17, 1897, to Neff in Austin, Texas

"I know what I write about affairs here will be perhaps stale to you as I have no doubt you keep pretty well informed about happenings in Magnolia but I will give you a few points. Firstly, I myself to my own wonder am still enjoying single blessedness. Miss S., secondly, your girl with whom you used to trip along so lightly over the rippling waters of the 'Amazon,' is now a resident of Waldo whither she has gone to cheer the home of Charles Clark. I was at the wedding as a special guest. I can also say that I had the melancholy pleasure of taking her out to her last party a week before she was married.

It makes a fellow feel like getting married himself when these fine girls begin to go. I am still 'working at it' and don't get a bit tired...[Miss] S's brunette milliner is now boarding with him and the 'Auburn haired gentleman' is not as attentive a caller at the parsonage as he might be, so I think it is my duty to call around there sometimes and inquire about the general health of the family. My high sense of duty allows me to call at several other places occasionally but I have not expanded my circle of friends among the ladies; perhaps contracted it.

Miss R is still the same fine girl. I am not so devoid of conscience as you were to 'spark' one of your own students so as a teacher in the same school I do not go down there very often. I think 'sister A' is well. The primary department is doing nicely which is quite a natural result. I have not taken out any widows lately. The one I did got married I am glad to say...I spent the holidays here again this year. Had a very jolly time. I suppose you took another trip in search of a lamp-shade. In regard to that story about you and Miss J, you know that when you first started out here you began with Miss J, and for some time went with her more than with anyone else. But when you organized your Shakespeare class and got your circulating library in operation, your calls became less frequent across the Amazon. This of course was rather bitter to a girl of Miss J's disposition who was used to thinking and being told that she was the peerless one among many.

I suppose you are delving in legal lore these days to your heart's content. I wish you success in the Oratorical contest...Give my regards to the Old Baylor boys and write me how you are progressing generally."

<u>Charlie</u>: Tell me more about Pat Neff.

Pops: Neff is a fascinating and somewhat enigmatic character who was of great importance in Baylor's history. Baylor historians generally credit Neff with instituting the draconian measures that kept Baylor viable in the 1930s, thus preserving Frank's job teaching at Baylor. However, here are a few other Neff facts: Neff was born November 26, 1871, and grew up on his family's cotton farm where he picked cotton and worked with the hogs. He entered Baylor in 1889, selling the cotton produced on the family farm to defray his tuition. During his five years at the university, he gained prominence as an unusually effective debater and speaker, participating in 1893 in the first intercollegiate debate between Baylor and the University of Texas. Between 1906 and 1912, after being elected as the attorney for McLennan County, Neff made a reputation as a brilliant, relentless prosecutor and tried 422 defendants, winning convictions in all but sixteen cases. Where marriage was concerned, Neff was in no hurry. He and Myrtle went through a drawn-out nine-year courtship before tying the knot. For several years, Neff maintained that he wanted to get through law school and become self-sufficient before getting married. Neff also wrote Myrtle that he didn't feel ready for marriage. He finally gave in after calling the situation "inevitable" and agreed to get married. The ceremony was on May 31, 1899, in Lovelady, Texas.

As president of Baylor, Neff showed the same firmness he had displayed as a criminal prosecutor. One Baylor faculty member recalled an early meeting with Neff after he became president: "Governor Neff came in, and without the opening prayer that we normally had at faculty meetings, he strode to the platform and addressed the faculty. And his first words were, 'You're a dime a dozen. I can replace you any minute. And I believe in the policy of two for the price of one.' That meant for any married faculty member who was married, [Neff would hire his wife at half-price if she could do anything]. So you can see how popular he became with the faculty." However, despite considerable success as president of Baylor in rescuing Baylor from the prospect of bankruptcy and adding to enrollment, acreage, and endowment during his tenure, Neff was ultimately viewed by many Baylor supporters as too rigid a disciplinarian, one who lacked the modern approach to education. In 1947, when he was seventy-six, Neff finally resigned under pressure to become president emeritus.

Charlie: I see what you mean about Neff being interesting. It sounds like he had one or two personality characteristics in common with President Burleson. And that part about dating—do you think Neff was joking about learning how to date from Frank?

Pops: He was either joking or trying not to talk too much about his own skills with the opposite sex—maybe he was afraid his mother would let it slip out to

Myrtle. Either way, it's pretty funny. But hold that thought; in the next chapter, we get into Frank's early love life.

CHAPTER 16

Early Flirtations, Romances (1886-1903)

In this chapter, we dive into the sketchy subject of Frank's early encounters, even romances, with the opposite sex, which he, despite the fact that he was a history professor, omitted to document satisfactorily in his diary, gallantly discarding all related correspondence. We were, however, able to piece bits of it together, at least after he arrived in Texas, from *Baylor Round-Ups*, a letter from Pat M. Neff, *Baylor Lariats*, an oral memoir, and from some of Frank's own writings, which helped us to connect some dots. The following is my conversation with Charlie and Katie.

Charlie: When did Frank start dating? Where did he meet girls?

Katie: Was he serious about any girls before he met Mamie? Did he go on hayrides or take girls to square dances?

Pops: I don't know about hayrides, but he went to square dances in Texas. We don't know much about Frank and girls before Texas. All we know is that the family's home in New Bedford was a gathering place for neighborhood kids, and that Frank attended a Methodist church and local schools. Because we know his personality as an adult, we can assume that as a young man, he was a fairly quiet guy who liked to read and go off by himself, and he was never the life of any party. So it seems reasonable that he did not have a serious girlfriend when he came to Texas; he certainly never mentioned one in his correspondence back home.

Charlie: So he started dating after he got to Texas?

Pops: Yes, but in those days, dating was often more informal, and there were no restaurants or movie theaters in Chester yet. The Canons were his host family in Chester because his father corresponded with friendly Methodists in Texas. Preacher Canon, Frank quickly learned, had an attractive daughter named Sallie who accompanied Frank to local church services. On Sunday afternoons, he got to know Sallie better while discussing the romantic novels she liked to read.

Katie: What did she like to read, Pops? Did he like the same books?

Pops: As to your second question, the answer is Frank simply enjoyed spending time with Sallie, not necessarily the popular romantic novels she liked. Frank spent most of a Sunday afternoon with Sallie in a shady spot on the back porch where they would discuss the last book she had read. Her favorite authors, whose works tended toward moral and sentimental themes, were Edward Payson Roe, a clergyman and former US Army chaplain, and Augusta Evans Wilson, one pillar of Southern literature during the Civil War. Frank must have read some of these formula romances himself to help him get on Sallie's wavelength since talking about the books he had read in his father's library would not have helped to connect with her. Though he was not interested in Sallie's reading choices, spending time with her provided a welcome break from the rigors of teaching in an ungraded country school.

Charlie: So, what were those books about? Would I enjoy reading them?

Pops: Charlie, I don't think you would finish a single chapter, perhaps not even a single page, although I have one at home you could try to read if you wanted to. If either you or Katie can finish one, I'll give you a dollar. They were all pretty much the same; all were written for young women of those times. For example, Roe's *A Young Girl's Wooing* from 1884 features a girl named Madge who falls in love with Graydon, a wealthy, handsome bachelor, but she temporarily loses her health. After she regains her health, she finds she has a rival for Graydon's attention. The novel goes on to its predictably happy conclusion. There is a lot in the story about innermost feelings and yearnings and wanting to express them but being afraid to.

Katie: Yuck.

Pops: Augusta Wilson, a romantic moralist who produced *Vashti*, *An Original Belle*, *Infelice*, *He Fell in Love with his Wife*, and many more similar novels, was the most successful Alabama writer of that period. A committed secessionist before the Civil War, she is said to have corresponded with Confederate General P.G.T. Beauregard. In time, she became an evangelical Christian; in *St. Elmo*, her biggest hit, she focused on the themes of the struggle between good and evil, and the change of heart in a cruel man transformed by his love for a virtuous woman.

Charlie: When did he have a real date, not just going to church and singing hymns or talking about mushy novels?

Pops: Okay, we'll get to that, but before we leave Frank's time with Sallie, we didn't get to one painfully funny experience he had. Sometimes, trying to impress a girl or her family can be risky. One spring Sunday afternoon was not as pleasant as usual. According to Frank, "While all nature seemed serene and flies and bees were buzzing about, one of the Canon boys gave the alarm, 'The bees are swarming.' Mr. Canon, who normally handled the bees, was not at home and Ms. Canon appealed to Frank: 'Mr. Frank, have you ever had any experience swarming bees?' He confessed hesitantly that he had managed several swarms back home in Ohio although he had never acquired a liking for it. This was to say too much and there was no way now to back off graciously. Ms. Canon stressed to Frank regretfully that a large swarm of bees was about to be lost. Reluctantly Frank took charge. Noticing that the bees had settled on a branch of a wild cherry tree along the fence of the back yard about fifteen feet up the tree, he improvised a plan. Jobe, the oldest boy, would climb the tree with some light rope, attach the rope to the branch where the bees were, saw the weighted branch off carefully, and lower it to Frank perched on the fence under the tree. Frank would then carefully take the swarm to the hive. Unfortunately, the execution of this ostensibly feasible plan proved faulty. With most of the Canon family and some of the neighbors looking on with interest, Frank and the other boys proceeded to show how skillfully they could handle a swarm of bees."

Frank later described the conclusion of this incident as follows: "Jobe climbed the tree, attached the rope, and began to saw on the branch. Just as the branch was nearly separated and was coming down slowly, the bees began to rise and buzz around Jobe's face. That was beyond human endurance, he lost all sense of caution, gave a last yank at the saw, off came the branch with its load, it fell until eight or ten feet...the sudden jerk [of the rope] spilled the greater part of the swarm on Frank's head and shoulders. [Frank's] first idea was to remain perfectly quiet; perhaps the honey maker would innocently leave him unscathed. But the proceedings had irritated the little fellows; suddenly, they gave out the peculiar scent of angry bees. In the next second, they punctured Frank's face unmercifully. That was the signal for him to beat a hasty retreat to a neighboring cornfield. He did not stop running until he was sure none of the little rascals were following him. Jobe had also descended hastily from the tree and made a similar retreat to the cornfield. All of those looking on, including Sallie...were swept away by the hilarity of it all. Frank's face was so swollen that he could barely see. Ms. Canon bathed his face with cool water, punctuated by bursts of uncontrollable laughter."

Now for maybe one of Frank's first actual dates. The first one we know about was at Sam Houston Normal School in Huntsville, where Frank was working on a teaching certificate during the 1887-1888 school year. We don't know how he and Lucie Meusebach [later Marschall] met, but we know he was fond of Lucie and that they had at least one date. Lucie's daughter, Baylor Professor Cornelia Marschall Smith, recalls one story, apparently from her mother Lucie, in which Frank was courting her mother. On this occasion, Frank asked a young boy to climb a magnolia tree to cut a blossom for Lucie. We suppose it wasn't too serious a relationship since Frank wasn't close to finishing his education and Lucie married Cornelia's father the next year. Frank did not enroll at Baylor until 1890; in 1888, it would be almost another eighteen years until he was ready to marry.

Katie: Well, he must have some dates later when he and Pat Neff taught at Southwestern Academy in Arkansas and roomed together. There had to have been women teachers there he would have met and wanted to spend time with.

Pops: Yes, there were, but Frank left us few details. You will remember in the prior chapter Pat Neff giving Frank credit for his instruction in dating and Neff's letter to his mother about his and Frank's romantic adventures in Magnolia, Arkansas.

Charlie: Yes, but I would like to know more about Frank's dating. How did he meet girls and set up dates? Was it all about writing notes? I guess writing notes would have been the way to go for him since he was a quiet, bookish guy, apparently without the gift of gab that I have. And when he arrived in Texas, he was straight off the farm.

Pops: Right, but the times were different, too. There were no telephones, and you couldn't just call up a girl and say, "Hi, Amanda, remember me from Sunday School? Charlie—the guy in the blue jean jacket?" If Amanda says, "uh hum," you say, "Want to go to that new movie *Jaws* at the Majestic?" And then Amanda might say, "Okay, I guess so. When?" And you say, "Friday night, and come hungry—we'll grab burgers and fries at that new Dairy Queen on the way—you're not a vegan, are you?"

Charlie: You're making me hungry.

Pops: That's maybe the way it's done today, but it was different in the 1890s and early 1900s, especially for a guy like Frank who would have been eager to follow established rules of protocol for relationships with girls. According to one of the *Redbooks* of that day, there were detailed rules governing relationships starting with the initial connection initiated by a young man toward a young woman, sometimes followed by "calling" on the young woman at her place of residence. Frank had to have been aware of such rules early on.

Charlie: What were the rules?

Pops: Well, we don't have time to cover them all. But we can start with the rule about men's hats. The practice was: "When making a call, a gentleman will carry his hat into the parlor [of the woman's lodging]. If his call is a prolonged one, he may place his hat on a table, but he should not allow his hostess [the person making the introduction] to attend to this."

Charlie: Hatsmanship.

Pops: Formal calls at a young woman's dwelling were supposed to not exceed a quarter of an hour. When calling, the man should turn down a corner of the card to indicate the purpose of the call. For example, turning down the upper right corner showed a visit. The lower right corner, adieu. Lower left corner, condolence. Writing "R.S.V.P. meant "please answer."

Charlie: Cardsmanship.

Pops: If a young man was making a formal call, a Prince Albert coat with light trousers was indicated and gloves were required. When the gentleman wanted to take a young woman to a dinner party or some other place, he sent a handwritten invitation as follows:

Mr. Charles Slaton Guittard
Requests the pleasure of your presence on
Thursday evening, December 25th
At half-past eight o'clock
Dancing—3000 Versailles Dr.

Charlie: Didn't President Burleson wear a Prince Albert coat for everyday dress? And he was famous for using a cane. Could young men carry canes when they went on dates? Those fancy canes were cool and could be handy for self-protection if needed.

Pops: Burleson did use a cane, and his statue on the Quad includes his cane. There is nothing about using a cane in the *Redbook* for that era, but I think in the 1890s, a cane would have been optional at best and probably an affectation. Over the top.

Charlie: I'm wondering what they talked about on dates in the 1890s, and what they were not supposed to talk about.

Pops: According to one *Redbook*, young men were cautioned: "Avoid anything… calculated to excite unfavorable remarks. Boisterousness is especially to be avoided; so is over-loud talk, whisperings, criticisms on religious subjects and political disputations." And it says, "It is exceedingly ill-bred to repeat scandal or discuss people or topics of questionable character." Run-of-the-mill gossiping would have been okay, and talking about other people, in general, would have been acceptable. If one is interested in complying with social conventions for dating, Emily Holt's book was really on manners for everyday use—what to do, what to say, what to write, and what to wear. Ms. Holt gave some advice Frank could have used upon finding that someone sitting near him at an opera was talking during a singer's aria. Ms. Holt said the offended opera-goer should turn and quietly say: "Will you, as a great favor, not speak quite so loud?"

Other than going to church, the primary dating activity in those days at a small sectarian college was simply walking around with a member of the opposite sex, sometimes called "promenading."

Charlie: What about at the University of Chicago starting in 1897?

Pops: Well, if Frank thought he could afford some time away from his studies, the University of Chicago would have been an excellent place to meet a young woman, perhaps from a wealthy family. But Frank's nose was to the grindstone during his Chicago days, either working at one of the men's residence halls, in class, or studying for class. That left little time for women. Fortunately, in his English III class, he submitted the essay excerpted below. Although the theme as assigned was to be ostensibly a work of fiction, Frank undoubtedly wrote it primarily out of his own experience, but slightly disguising the participants' identities. The Frank character was named Frank Burton; the female character was called, for whatever reason, Bessie Westbrook, and she lived on the Westbrook farm. In a subsequent rewrite of the theme, the Frank character was renamed Ralph Burton, a name Frank used for himself in one of his several autobiographies. At the time, the town of Magnesia Springs was about eight miles north of Magnolia, Arkansas. It is important to note that Frank wrote the theme after commencing his teaching position in Magnolia, Arkansas, at the Southwestern Academy, where he would room with a fellow teacher, Pat M. Neff.

We believe Frank's essay at Chicago could have been based on a relationship he had with an Arkansas girl, possibly named Bessie Westbrook, while he was teaching at the Southwestern Academy. While teaching in Magnolia, he certainly would have gone on an excursion to Magnesia Springs at some point, possibly with a female companion, perhaps double-dating with his roommate Pat Neff and his date. Add to that picture the *1903 Round-Up* reporting that Frank had persuaded an Arkansas girl to correspond with him, someone Frank must have met while teaching in Magnolia. However, there are several interpretations of Frank's essay we will discuss shortly.

The Camp-Meeting at Magnesia Springs

Sunday was to be the great day of the camp meeting at the springs [Magnesia Springs]. It had been announced that Sam Jones the great evangelist was to preach in the morning. All Caney Creek settlement had made preparations to go and hear the great preacher. Not all people, however, go to camp meeting for spiritual instruction. Neither was this Frank Burton's chief object in going. Early in the morning he was riding over to the Westbrook farm. He had been a frequent caller at the mansion there of late and it was whispered around the settlement that he was the favored one of Bessie Westbrook's suitors.

Those interested in such affairs said that he would be mighty lucky too, to get Miss Bessie. She was the pride of the settlement; no social event was considered complete without her presence. She was one of those girls who cause you to think that she would be as much at home in a fashionable drawing room as in the parlor of a country mansion. Frank was thinking deeply as he was riding along. He was now the owner of a large plantation and thought that if he could bring a girl like Bessie as a bride into his home, life would be all that he desired. He resolved that this day should decide whether or not his dream would be a reality.

When he rode under the sweet-gum trees in front of the gate he saw the object of his thoughts walk out over the gallery for him. He felt a thrill of pleasure at the thought. To him she looked like the culmination of all the graces as she came along to the gate; but a less partial eye than Frank's would have paused to admire her. Bessie thought as Frank was riding up that she had never seen him look handsomer. He made a fine figure in the saddle, had dark hair and eyes, and a manly face. They were soon on their horses, cantering briskly along the road to the springs.

After a ride of a few hours they came to the campgrounds. Among the stalwart pines stood the white tents of the people who had come from a distance, and were prepared to stay for several weeks. Men, women, and children were seen in every direction going toward the great shed under which the services were to be held. [Everyone hurried in order to get their seats and eat their picnic lunch.] [The program beginning] the choir of over a hundred voices rose and began to sing; the music swelled and resounded under the immense roof, and floated out through the pine forest. It seemed to cast a spell over the audience, and even the waving and fluttering of the fans almost ceased. Then the preacher rose and in his peculiar style addressed that great audience...Frank's mind inclined to wander...he wanted to have a quiet talk with Bessie & thought of a plan...

[Frank gets his feelings hurt] when two young men arrive unannounced from Magnolia, two new friends of Bessie and her girlfricnd...Frank & Roy [apparently accompanying Bessie's girlfriend] failed to enjoy the company of the two new men and the attentions they are paying to Bessie & Minnie [Bessie's friend] and wander down the hill leaving Bessie & Minnie to the two men. Frank speculated that the girls had arranged the meeting with those town chaps beforehand. They greeted them with such suspicious cordiality and Bessie was so reluctant about going up on the hill. But no, he did not believe Bessie would treat him that way. He resolved to go back; perhaps she was thinking strangely of his staying away so long. Coming near to where he had left them he heard them laughing. Doubtless, thought he, they are laughing at my expense, and he turned away.

He wandered around aimlessly all afternoon until four o'clock when they were to start for home. He found the girls still with their friends. Roy soon joined the party and the two friends expressed their appreciation to the boys for the sacrifice they had made in order to allow them a pleasant afternoon and took their departure. On the way home, Frank made no allusion to the events of the afternoon but he resolved that his calls should cease nor would he give Bessie another opportunity to play that kind of game with him.

Just as they had crossed Caney Bridge and entered a narrow road, they saw a runaway team coming at breakneck speed toward them. 'Ride up close in the corner of the fence and get down,' cried Frank. He dismounted and waited for the frantic team.

'Let them go, Frank,' entreated Bessie, 'you will be sure to get hurt.' But he stood determined. The horses came with such force that he was powerless to check them and was hurled to the ground. Bessie ran to his side, took his arm, and helped him to a bank at the side of the road.

'Are you much hurt?' she said tremulously.

'Not much, but my head feels a little dizzy. I think I shall be all right soon.'

'Oh, it was awful! I shall not get over my fright in a hurry. I thought you were killed and a thousand things came to my mind. You had such a troubled look all the way home. I know you thought

I was to blame for those boys staying with us, but I could not well help it. I was anxious all afternoon at your not coming back.'

'Then you did care after all,' said Frank thoughtfully.

'Care for what?' exclaimed Bessie with an expression of surprise in her pretty brown eyes.

'Well, you see I thought—I want to say that I have been a gump and that you are one of the sweetest girls in the world.'

There was a pause, each one busied with his own thoughts.

'Bessie, I have loved you for a long time—ever since we were schoolmates. For me to know that you love me would make me one of the happiest of men.'

Bessie's face dropped.

'Do you Bessie?' She raised her eyes full of love to his and he knew his answer.

'But I am not satisfied with your love only. I want you for my own Dear Bessie.'

'Frank, I love you devotedly.' He took her in his arms and kissed her passionately.

'Oh, Frank, let's go; someone will be along.'

'I believe I'm ready. In fact I feel a great deal better than I did before I got that fall.'

The End.

Katie: So, Pops, is the Frank Burton in Frank's essay our Frank?

Pops: There are at least three interpretations of the story in the essay. You tell me which one you like best. The first is that Frank Burton is our Frank and Bessie is our Mamie; he would have met Mamie in 1898 while teaching in Shiner before going back to the University of Chicago for the 1899 summer session; however, remember that Frank and Mamie were never schoolmates. Second, the essay is entirely fictitious, but based on similar but unknown experiences with unknown people while Frank was in Texas or Arkansas. In the third interpretation, Frank Burton is Frank Guittard, and Bessie, possibly not her correct name, is a girl he met while teaching in Arkansas from 1894 to 1896. So, which do you like?

Charlie: I like the Arkansas girl one, the third one.

Katie: I like the Mamie one. Which is it?

Pops: We can only speculate, but I think it's the third one because Magnesia Springs was a site for camp meetings in Arkansas not too far from Magnolia, where he taught. Also, although we haven't talked about it yet, he did know and correspond with a girl in Arkansas. The scene and the dialogue is believable to me and sounds like Frank. We know that he wrote essays about himself but sometimes tried to disguise that fact by simply changing the central character's name to Ralph Burton. In fact, in a rewrite of this essay, Frank changed the name Frank Burton to Ralph Burton.

Charlie: Was Frank corresponding with two girls at the same time? Was the Roy in the story Pat Neff?

Pops: I can't say I know about that. But there were at least two girls he was interested in between 1899 when he met Mamie and 1902 when he visited her in Shiner after President Brooks hired him to teach at Baylor. Roy certainly could have been Pat Neff, as he and Frank roomed together for two years and undoubtedly participated in some of the same extracurricular amusements and outings that were available in a small town. And we know that the three Baylorites—Cantwell, Neff, and Guittard—did all hang together on occasion in Arkansas.

Katie: What about the girl in Arkansas? What do we know about her?

Pops: We know about Frank's dating activities only because he and other unmarried teachers at Baylor, particularly the men, were the subject of amused gossip back on the Baylor campus and entertainment for curious students. We know this from the references and poems in *Baylor Round-Ups*. Here are the ones I've found so far:

While the personal experiences of the faculty last summer are in vogue for Chapel talks, the following topics are suggested...Prof. Guittard—How I induced an Arkansas girl to correspond with me...

—*Baylor Lariat*, December 13, 1902

Said Professor Guitard [sic]:
"It is so very hard,
The girl I saw
In Arkansas
Wrote me a postal card."
—*1903 Round-Up*

At last the auction waxed warmer and boys were sold like hot tamales. The following girls bought the following boys at the following prices: Miss Randolph (for herself) [bought] Prof. Guittard for a sofa pillow.

—1903 Round-Up

There's young Mister Guitard [sic],
With words as soft as lard;
But it's no go;
The girls all know
He's only a canard.
—1904 Round-Up

Bachelor Degrees.
Conferred by a Beneficent Providence and
Based on Merit
Prof. F.C. [sic] Guittard...
—1904 Round-Up

There is a young teacher named Guittard,
By a girl in South Texas he's smit hard;
And all of us guess,
Unless she says, "Yes,"
This dapper young man will be hit hard.
—1905 Round-Up

A young teacher of hist'ry
Has a girl near Corpus Christi;
Why do they tarry?
Why don't they marry?
To us is still a myst'ry.
—1905 Round-Up

Guittard who taught in the Prep,
Prayed, "O Lord, please give me your he'p,
I can't get a wife,
To save my life,"
Then loudly and sorely he wep'.
—1906 Round-Up

Charlie: What was so hard about the postcard from the Arkansas girl Frank received in 1903?

Pops: My guess is that with his education completed at the University of Chicago and now teaching in the Prep at Baylor, Frank had already decided Mamie in Shiner was the one for him. We don't know whether Mamie was similarly minded, but wc suspcct shc was. The hard part was how to deliver the news to Miss Whomever that he was promised to another rather than simply terminate the correspondence without explanation. From his taking a job at Baylor in the fall of 1902, Mamie appears to have been his only romantic interest until her passing in 1917.

Katie: So maybe Frank could get pretty mushy where girls were concerned?

Pops: You could say so. Although Frank was usually a man of few words, scratch the surface and there was a romantic. His son Clarence said that in the 1930s, one day in chapel Frank read the students Robert Burns's poem "A Red, Red Rose." Reportedly his reading created quite a sensation among the students since it was so unexpected coming from the starchy, reserved Professor Guittard, usually a man of few words. Here is the first quatrain:

> O my Luve's like a red, red rose,
> That's newly sprung in June;
> O my luve's like the melodie,
> That's sweetly play'd in tune.

Charlie: That's pretty mushy stuff.

Pops: Our next chapter won't be as mushy. President Burleson's "melodie" at Baylor was no longer resonating with many Baptists' ears.

CHAPTER 17

President Burleson's Last Days at Baylor (1895-1901)

The last days of Rufus Columbus Burleson as president of Baylor at Waco are an important part of our story. Without President Burleson, one could strongly argue there would have been no Baylor University at Waco, Texas. Unfortunately, Burleson's last days do not reflect as well on his mythic standing in Baylor history. Perhaps they do not because of his reluctance to surrender the reins when it was finally time to do so—sometimes turning over control to a successor is a problem for commanders-in-chief after long years of service. Perhaps those last days do not serve to burnish Burleson's reputation also because of a certain inflexibility of personality and policy, which may have served him well in earlier times as an educator, administrator, and leader in Baptist circles. I have asked Charlie to run with me through the events leading up to Burleson's last days and afterward.

Pops: Charlie, before we get to President Burleson's last days, we need to go through some history of Burleson and his times.

Charlie: I know little about President Burleson. I think I'll hold my questions until the end.

Pops: Okay, I'll get back to you in a few minutes. President Burleson faced many challenges during his tenures as a president, first at Baylor at Independence, then after he relocated to Waco to become president of Waco University, and finally at Baylor in Waco. Many colleges after the Civil War had to be closed since the war lasted much longer than supporters of secession had wishfully predicted. Albert Parsons, a student of Burleson's at Waco University, said that his guardian, the leader of the secession movement in Texas, had boasted that the war would all be over in sixty days and even claimed, "it's all bluster anyway." Parsons concluded he needed to sign up for the Confederacy while he still had the chance. Twenty years after the Civil War, the dying Baylor at Independence avoided collapse only because of its 1886 merger with Waco University. Waco University was a thriving university which Burleson led in his second tenure as a university president, having prudently withdrawn from Baylor at Independence decades earlier.

In short, for many, many years, even starting before taking the reins at Baylor at Independence in 1851, Rufus C. Burleson had been an undeniable force of nature and "preached in every old town in Texas and held protracted meetings in all the great cities...He gave up his desire to become a lawyer...under a profound sense of 'Woe is me if I preach not the gospel.'" Coincidentally, Burleson's onetime student Albert Parsons was also a powerful speaker whose oratorical abilities had only increased over the years. "Parsons could speak for two to three hours at a time, and, for at least a portion of that time, could hold the attention of the uninitiated as well as true believers." Parsons, unlike Burleson, agitated for the cause of workers' social issues, not for the salvation of their souls.

Besides preaching the gospel, Burleson was also a longtime leading advocate in Texas educational circles, as was Oscar Henry Cooper, his successor, for the cause of higher education in Texas. For that as well, Baptists and all Texans must be grateful. Burleson is famous for many sayings attesting to the firmness of his personality and his strong emphasis on determined upright conduct, including: "Never get mad, never get scared;" "A resolute mind is omnipotent;" "Owe no man anything—death and debt are kindred calamities;" and "Never hear, tell, read or do anything [you] would blush to tell [your] mother." Burleson's early years as pastor of First Baptist in Houston during the yellow fever scourge and later the cholera scourge attest to his strong character when other preachers and their congregations fled the city. Burleson remained and ministered to the afflicted, regardless of their religious convictions.

When the first railroad entered East Waco in September 1872, Mrs. J.W. Baker recalled Dr. Burleson's role in the *Galveston Tri-Weekly News*: "Dr. Rufus Columbus Burleson of Waco Baptist University marched his students across the suspension bridge [which crossed over the Brazos] to old East Waco [where the new railroad depot was located and little else]. A cheering crowd was on hand. The notable citizens made speeches. There was free barbeque for all." The good that Burleson did was not interred with his bones, including his support of the new bridge. The coming of the railroad, foreseen by Burleson, was important in the transformation of Waco, which more than doubled its population by 1880.

So it is unfortunate that his last days as president created a sour taste at the end of a long distinguished career in service of Baptists and education. Burleson, called by education historian Frederick Eby, the "stormy petrel of Baptist education in Texas for fifty years," died in Waco on May 14, 1901. He had taken the reins of the newly merged Baylor in 1886 and remained president until 1897. However, because of a combination of factors, Burleson had little choice that year except to resign, grudgingly. The Board of Trustees retired President Burleson despite having no one in mind to take his place, simply choosing Professor John C. Lattimore as Chairman of the Faculty, after which the search for a new president continued. The terms for Burleson's retirement were relatively generous, including the title of president emeritus, an annual salary to be paid as long as he was alive, and a continuing role at Baylor tending to ministerial students.

Burleson's loss of influence and control at Baylor at Waco climaxing in 1897 is reminiscent of the factors leading to his departure from Baylor at Independence. According to John Robert Guemple in his 1964 Master's thesis, Burleson's bitterness against the Board of Trustees at Independence propelled him to write the new president of Baylor at Independence, William Carey Crane, that "the fact is the Board of Trustees and the State Convention were the pliant tools of your wiley [sic] associate Horace Clark [head of Baylor's Female Department], and they left me to struggle on and sink or swim as best I could...Just at a time when I had got everything ready to make money and pay my debts...secret combinations were made to expel me from the institution...I was summoned repeatedly before the board and catechized and finally impeached on rumors the most vague until self-respect, peace, and usefulness demanded my removal to Waco."

From the Trustees' point of view, the case for Burleson to step aside and take a well-deserved rest was more than compelling. Burleson, at seventy-four, was no longer the vigorous man who had led Baylor in Independence, the same man who moved to Waco to take the position of president of Waco University, or even the man who became president of the new Baylor at Waco. Baylor's trustees had several pressing reasons for his removal. Besides Burleson's loss of vigor was the dark cloud hanging over Baylor and its ability to attract female students arising from the Antonia Teixeira scandal. The scandal concerned the fifteen-year-old Brazilian girl (Teixeira) who lived with the Burlesons and became pregnant by an in-law of Burleson, namely Steen Morris. Morris was the brother of Burleson's son-in-law. The situation resulted in a criminal trial that failed to get a unanimous guilty verdict, Morris raising the defense of consent. Nevertheless, under all the circumstances, the publicity generated by W.C. Brann's merciless and serial flogging of Burleson and Baylor in *The Iconoclast* inevitably created a foul stench on Burleson Quadrangle, resulting in the loss of over thirty female students. Students' parents were concerned about their daughters' virginity and general safety at Baylor under the Burlesons' care. Brann had warned parents against entrusting their daughters to Baylor, calling it a "pestiferous plague-spot" and "running sore upon the body social." Brann's evidence? One young woman from Brazil, pregnant and unmarried.

Other reasons also indicated it was time for Burleson to step aside. Burleson's resolute opposition to Baylor men competing in intercollegiate athletics also showed that the times had left him in the rearview mirror. Perhaps most important was the inevitable emergence of the final power struggle between Burleson and the trustees. Burleson, however well he may have gotten along with others in Independence or in Waco before returning to Baylor in Waco, apparently did not understand that, at least as of the time of the merger in 1886, he no longer had unfettered authority to run the university as a proprietary school. Baylor belonged to the Baptist General Convention of Texas, not Burleson. After all, the *B* in *BU* stood for Baylor and not Burleson. As a result of the perceived crisis in presidential leadership, the trustees decided for Burleson to step down and negotiated the terms already mentioned with him. However, in an attempted reversal, Burleson sought to change the deal he agreed to. He met a stone wall, however, and the trustees under board president B.H. Carroll and ten more trustees, including J.B. Scarborough, W.H. Jenkins, and F.L. Carroll, emphatically declined to renegotiate.

Burleson's appeal to the trustees for a change in the terms of his departure, which they rejected, was a serious miscalculation on Burleson's part since it resulted in a detailed and well-written thirty-page statement by B.H Carroll explaining the trustees' reasons. After making clear that the trustees had the full authority under Baylor's charter to take the action it had taken regarding President Burleson and that no self-appointed popular assembly of Baptists could tell the trustees who should be president of Baylor, the trustees were just getting warmed up in their attack on Burleson. They stated that Burleson, at the board's meeting in June, had not been re-elected president, but rather named president emeritus with a salary of $2,000 for the year, which Burleson had already accepted, although not graciously. Subsequently, the trustees argued Burleson had himself nominated Professor John C. Lattimore as chairman of the faculty and that the trustees accordingly made an offer to Lattimore which Lattimore had already accepted. From the trustees' point of view, the change at the top was already a done deal, and it was too late for Burleson to reopen negotiations.

Among other things, the trustees noted that Burleson's supporters argued that the 1886 consolidation had been conditioned on Burleson being made chancellor for life of the consolidated Baylor and that such condition was added "to placate Dr. Burleson who was opposing consolidation." However, the trustees noted that the resolution containing this condition was not agreed to by all parties before the final vote on consolidation and was never presented for consideration by the Baptist State Convention.

As part of the statement, Baylor's faculty went on record that the trustees' action "was necessary for the harmony and well being of the school" and that the president himself had conceded as much. They said that President Burleson had reprimanded faculty members and the faculty as a whole before the students, which was not the prerogative of the president. As a result, students had already lost respect for the discipline of the faculty and "would constantly annul Faculty action through the President." The faculty also noted that Burleson's teaching ability had declined, as noticed by his classes, and that even his chapel talks were hurtful to the students and the school. He had also abused his power of nominating teachers to "force subserviency to himself." Further, that since Burleson was no longer serving as president, fewer absences from classes were recorded, discipline at school was much better, and attendance at chapel improved with greater respect for announcements by teachers.

In any event, President Burleson's long years of service to Texas Baptists, to three educational institutions, and the cause of education generally in Texas largely ended when he was deposed by board vote in the fall of 1897. Returning to the words of Professor Eby in 1936: "Due to his [Rufus Burleson's] restless energy, his pioneering spirit, and unwonted pertinacity, Burleson accomplished a great work in Texas. He was temperamental, sometimes unreliable and inclined to be head-strong and self-centered. He was adored by those who worked with him, but abhorred by many others. He was capable of prodigious labor but could only serve as leader. In some ways, he was the most efficient educator in Texas but was always too boastful. Those who knew him well and were unbiased in their judgment honored him for many sterling qualities which counterbalanced his other characteristics...He was a rugged individualist."

Burleson would serve Baylor for another three and a half years. You may be familiar with the story of the final days of the legendary Robin Hood of Locksley and his final act of shooting an arrow, with the assistance of his men, through an open window to mark where he wanted to be buried. If you are, the death of Dr. Burleson may sound familiar. According to the Haynes's biography, on May 14, 1901, "Dr. Burleson took to his bed and died. Stretched on his couch, with every fiber and filament of that old body that had felt the blasts of seventy-eight winters, quivering with pain, he begged the watchers to turn his bed so he could see the University one more time."

Charlie: That does sound like the Robin Hood story.

Pops: Yes, it does somewhat. But Burleson is buried in Oakwood Cemetery in Waco, which was not visible from Burleson's home.

Charlie: I am confused about something, though.

Pops: What's that?

Charlie: I'm confused about how the Baylor trustees could have been so callous to depose President Burleson. He would only live another four years, anyway. Surely it could have waited, and he apparently wasn't in good health when the board pushed him out—the board must have known that.

Pops: You've made a couple of good points, but it appears the board had very good reasons to remove Burleson as president and to give him a new title and a diminished role. All the reasons I've already mentioned—his personality, which made it difficult for the board to work with him; his declining health and the deterioration in his teaching ability; the scandal involving the Brazilian ward in the

Burleson household; his apparent view that Baylor was his to run as he pleased; his hiring of faculty he believed would be subservient to him; and the breakdown in student discipline caused by students appealing to Burleson the measures meted out by the faculty. Of all of these, it seems the most critical was determining whose prerogative it was to make the major decisions for the school, whether it was the board or Burleson. For the board, the issue was really about Baylor's stagnation or decline vs. survival and growth. Seen in that light, the trustees' decision was unavoidable. It was a difficult decision because of Burleson's long history of building and supporting Baylor. And, no doubt, any number of the trustees had been longtime colleagues and supporters of Burleson.

Charlie: Still, it was too bad his presidency ended that way.

Pops: Yes, perhaps, but only temporarily. Baylor in Waco will forever have President Burleson to thank for its very existence. And there's Burleson Quadrangle, the most beautiful and historic part of the campus, and that nice statue. Remember, too, that Burleson's removal was followed a few years later by the arrival of Samuel Palmer Brooks and the transformation of a small sectarian college into a true university.

Charlie: So I guess it turned out for the best. It was time.

BOOK FOUR

Chicago, a Twist of Fate, Mamie, & Health Crises

Sample questions for the peanut gallery's consideration in this book's chapters:

Did Frank take a class from John Dewey at Chicago? Did he become interested in Darwinism? On what did Frank spend his money while in Chicago? What happened to the little dog tossed out the window during chapel at Baylor? Where did Frank meet Mamie? How long did they date before getting married? What was Captain Charlie Welhausen like and did he see action during the Civil War? How many years were Frank and Mamie married before she became ill? What did Frank and Mamie have to do with the first Baylor homecoming? How did epidemics affect the lives of Frank, Mamie, and their family?

Excerpts from Frank's "Funny-Book of Student Bone-heads" on examinations:

Question: "Give a description or provide an explanation for the Battle of Hastings." Answer: "The Battle of Hastings was begun by a Norman juggler riding along leisurely pitching up s sword and catching it. The English made a good fight but were defeated."

Question: "Explain the circumstances of the crowning of Charlemagne." Answer: "Charlemagne was crowned in Westminster by the Pope on Christmas day 800 B.C."

Examples of Frank's favorite words and phrases from his letters:

"to a fine point" — "They have all the details worked out to a fine point."

"to the fullest extent" — "The courses are all fine and I am enjoying them to the fullest extent."

"somewhat" — "The terrors are somewhat subsided and then is when I lose heart somewhat."

CHAPTER 18

Chicago Days (1897-1902)

Today we will look at the five years beginning in 1897 when Frank attended the University of Chicago (often referred to simply as "Chicago") off and on while teaching in Arkansas and, at some point, corresponded with Mamie Welhausen in Shiner, Texas. He married Mamie in 1906. Katie will be assisting me in exploring this chapter of Frank's life.

Katie: Pops, I still don't understand why Frank didn't return to Baylor after he left in 1894. At some point, he had the money for Baylor tuition, right?

Pops: Not sure, Katie. We don't know exactly since Frank never wrote about his reasons. However, he had several good reasons to transfer to Chicago. First, when he initially enrolled at Baylor, the University of Chicago had not yet opened its doors. Second, when it did open in 1892, it boasted a top faculty to teach the arts, history, literature, math, and science with departments for undergraduate and graduate studies. Chicago, funded by wealthy Baptist layman and monopolist tycoon John D. Rockefeller, became, nearly overnight, a world-class university ranking with Harvard and Yale. Baylor graduates almost immediately started enrolling there to complete graduate work to upgrade their teaching credentials. On the day it opened, the first faculty of the University of Chicago was considered the strongest faculty in America and included eight former college and university presidents. William Rainey Harper, Chicago's new president, aggressively pursued faculty members from other Ivy League schools, and "Yale and Cornell were especially depleted." Chicago also attracted students like Frank Guittard because it was organized on the quarter system, allowing students to take a regular term during the summer.

In those days, Baylor was still a small Baptist college whose degrees lacked any real credibility in the academic world. On the other hand, Chicago had first-class programs where students like Frank could finish their degrees or upgrade their academic credentials with a second degree from Chicago; President Brooks did the same thing at Yale. It should be evident that Baylor's donors and philanthropists of the late nineteenth century—Speight, West, and the Carrolls—were not in Rockefeller or Stanford's leagues. George W. Carroll, who funded the George W. Carroll Science Building and who had struck it big in the Texas oil boom, died without any fortune. Frank Guittard said Carroll could look back with satisfaction on the building he paid for. At the time of his death, Carroll had reportedly given away his fortune to worthy causes and lived in a modest room in the Beaumont YMCA, for which he had funded the construction.

Katie: I've heard some bad things about John Rockefeller and Leland Stanford. Did Frank feel guilty studying at these colleges built through contributions from these two white-collar outlaws? I've read that Rockefeller was unscrupulous, if not crooked, in the way he made his fortune from oil. He crushed a lot of people and their companies along the way and didn't feel bad. The US government had to pass the Sherman Antitrust Act to slow him down.

Pops: Yes, Rockefeller drew a lot of justified criticism because of how he built his oil empire. The magazine *Arena* affirmed that "there is probably not one [among the robber barons] ...who in the public mind so typifies the grave and startling menace to the social order." However, I don't think Frank felt guilty attending Chicago or Stanford, as much as he would have abhorred Rockefeller and Stanford's single-minded acquisitiveness. These two men's philanthropy changed our country for good in ways that only mega-millionaire business people could have done. Rockefeller was not only responsible for funding the University of Chicago with millions and millions—reportedly 24-35 million dollars—but reportedly gave away 500 million to foundations and other organizations. Those included the Rockefeller Foundation, the Rockefeller Institute, the General Education Board that benefited colleges and universities, and the Laura Spellman Rockefeller Memorial. Further, a new era in American and world medicine began with the creation of the Rockefeller Institute for Medical Research. This institute "became to the public and the medical profession alike what the Pasteur Institute was to France." But beyond Rockefeller's conspicuous unequaled philanthropy, Frank would not have been fully aware of Rockefeller's dubious business practices until after he graduated in the spring of 1902. Ida Tarbell did not begin her serialized exposure of Rockefeller attacking the Standard Oil Trust until November 1902, after Frank had his degrees, and did not complete her series until 1905.

Katie: What about Stanford?

Pops: Leland Stanford is an interesting case. Because Frank did not enter Stanford until 1923, we can assume he knew the basic facts about Stanford's rise to power and wealth and the creation of Stanford University. Although he and his wife Jane created the world-class Stanford University to honor their deceased son, Leland Jr., their philanthropic vision does not seem to have had the breadth or depth of Rockefeller's. There is no doubt that when Stanford sat in the governor's chair in California, he took multiple opportunities to enrich himself at the public's expense.

Additionally, he was vulnerable to the charge of being a white racist. Stanford took no interest when young Indian women and children were kidnapped and sold for profit. However, in a sense, his business accomplishments arguably had larger impact on Frank Guittard's life and on all of America as compared to Rockefeller's. The story of America is in part the story of its industrialization and the building of modern America. The key to that growth was the railroad network connecting all the United States and Stanford's leadership as president of the Central Pacific Railroad in building the first transcontinental railroad, Stanford tapping in the last spike—a golden spike—connecting the western and eastern stretch of tracks.

So back to your question about Frank's decision to go to Chicago for his undergraduate work rather than return to Baylor. In 1897, Frank was thirty years old and teaching at Southwestern Academy in Magnolia, Arkansas. We know that he enjoyed being a single man with relatively easy access to attractive young women without having a university chaperone reminding him to change partners or having to comply with President Burleson's strict rules. There was no imaginary line between the women's dormitory and where the men could walk. Those rules would have been intolerable for a young professional of thirty years earning his living teaching in an environment without such regulations. Frank enjoyed Baylor, but it would not have appealed to him in 1897.

Fourth, Chicago was a major city and had a broad array of cultural attractions to choose from—music, theater, symphony, ballet, opera, band music, and all the rest of the cultural scene, plus competitive collegiate sports teams. Fifth, Chicago was much closer to his family home in Ohio, his father, brothers, and sisters, than Waco. Last, the University of Chicago catered to students working their way through during the summers and who needed campus jobs. So, picking the University of Chicago in 1897 would have been almost a no-brainer for Frank.

Katie: And there was no girlfriend back in Waco drawing him back?

Pops: None.

Katie: So he worked his way through the University of Chicago?

Pops: Yes. His four brothers (Alwin, Virgil, Victor, and Claude) lent him a few dollars from time to time to supplement his savings from Southwestern Academy or earnings from campus jobs in Chicago, and he paid them back. He kept a careful record of the small loans and his repayments.

Katie: So, the University of Chicago just popped up on Frank's radar at some point?

Pops: Pretty much. He may have heard about the University of Chicago through the Baylor or Baptist grapevine, as Baylor graduates started early on enrolling there to upgrade their degrees. An earlier University of Chicago, which the Baptists had supported, went bust and was no longer operating after 1886. Baptists, including John D. Rockefeller, had wanted to start another university. Rockefeller tapped William Rainey Harper to be the new school president, and Harper went to work spending Rockefeller's money hiring faculty, principally established scholars at other universities who were attracted by the high salaries Harper was offering. Harper was quite effective raiding other universities' talented faculties. The new university in Chicago opened for its first students in October 1892 while Frank was still a Baylor student.

Katie: So Frank transferred to Chicago. Did Chicago give him credit for all his work at Baylor?

Pops: Yes, or nearly all of it. For Frank's last year at Baylor, Baylor certified to Chicago all of the following courses: Greek Orators, Horace Satires & Epistles, Zoology, Geology, Rhetoric, General History, and Mythology. Frank's grades were reported to average 95.57, with his highest grade of 98 in general history.

Katie: I assume Frank liked the University of Chicago and Chicago.

Pops: He loved it. Although he was nearly always working, the challenge of the courses and the lure of available entertainment must have been incredibly tempting. He wrote to a relative in August 1898: "I suppose you have heard that I am attending the University of Chicago. This is a great school. There are about fourteen hundred students here this summer."

Katie: Did Frank take any courses from the faculty President Harper had recruited?

Pops: All of his courses, presumably, would have been taught by teachers Harper recruited. His best-known teacher would have been education reformer John Dewey. Frank's ledger shows that he purchased a syllabus for Dewey's class for fifteen cents. Dewey would have been interesting to Frank because of his Laboratory School, his ideas for educating children, and his thoughts about the use and conduct of recitations. Where recitations were concerned, Dewey had his own theory about how recitations should be conducted in a democratized manner; Dewey's ideas were poles apart from the style of recitation Frank had used before entering Chicago, or what he would use afterward. Dewey neither lectured nor called upon students to repeat what they had read in the text the night before. Instead, he directed students' attention to specific questions Dewey wanted them to think about for the next meeting, at which time he would gather the students' opinions. One student of Dewey's recalled that "unlike every other course...in Dewey's class the students did not raise their hands, they simply engaged in conversation." Dewey would also possibly have been of interest to Frank because of his reputation as a Darwinist.

Katie: I didn't know Frank would have been interested in Darwinism.

Pops: Slightly interested perhaps, but we don't think that Frank would have been sympathetic to Dewey's views there. Despite starting as a theologically moderate Methodist from Ohio, Frank was now a Southern Baptist and likely would have seen no benefit in naturalistic theories about the origin of humankind. Moreover, Darwinism was too remote in time to be of any use in learning about the facts of history, and that was Frank's mission—to learn and teach the facts of history.

Katie: Did he have any teachers in his history major he liked, or who would have inspired him?

Pops: Frank would probably have liked most of them—Professors Fellows, Sparks, Schevill, and Thompson—although he never wrote any essays about his teachers at Chicago. I think Professor Schevill, who taught European History, would have been high on Frank's list. Schevill's brother-in-law Karl Bitter was a master sculptor of massive human figures and responsible for the sculptures decorating three world exhibitions starting with the Columbian Exposition in Chicago (1893), the Pan-American in Buffalo (1901), and the Louisiana Purchase Exposition in St. Louis (1904). We know Frank attended the 1904 St. Louis exposition and must have heard a lot about Bitter and his impressive contributions to statuary from Schevill in history class. Too bad Bitter's career was cut short.

Katie: What happened to him?

Pops: As Bitter and his wife were coming out of the Metropolitan Opera in New York on their way to catch a streetcar, a car jumped the curb on Broadway. Bitter pushed his wife (Schevill's sister) out of the way, but the vehicle struck and killed him. Bitter was born the same year as Frank and was only forty-seven.

Katie: Too bad. Bitter was so talented—I've seen pictures of his sculptures. What was it about Professor Schevill's history class Frank would have liked?

Pops: Schevill's specialty was European history. He published his *History of Modern Europe* in 1898 and after that continuously revised it. What we suppose Frank would have appreciated about Professor Schevill's course was that it was designed to expose students to "the cultural history of mankind as a continuum and as a whole." Students in his classes read authors like Shakespeare, Rousseau, Goethe, Voltaire, Chaucer, Luther, Herodotus, and many others. This approach certainly would have appealed to Frank, who wanted to know everything and read everything. Frank's students at Baylor remember him as wanting them to be familiar with art, music, and culture generally, and not just the facts of history. Professor Schevill would have approved.

Other history courses Frank took at Chicago were Medieval Europe from Thompson, Europe in the 17th and 18th Centuries from Catterall, Rise of Prussia from Schevill, Age of Renaissance from Thatcher, Europe in the Nineteenth Century from Schevill, History of Rome to Antonines from Goodspeed, Aspects of European History and Culture from Renaissance to French Revolution from Bourne, and History of the US Civil War and Reconstruction from Sparks. Frank, although a fact-based teacher of history, would have appreciated Schevill's view that history is literature and not science. Schevill noted that Leopold von Ranke of the University of Berlin had been the head of the German history movement. At the time of the formation of the American Historical Association in 1884, its members adopted Ranke as their first and only honorary member. We will discuss Ranke further in the chapter covering Frank Guittard's studies at Stanford.

Fifty years later, a later president of the AHA, Charles A. Beard, repudiated Ranke's views, at least according to Schevill. Beard argued that although Ranke contended that the mission of history was only to find the facts, nevertheless, he was always "ruled by his undeviating faith...that for Ranke God was always a God of love." Ranke, in Beard's view as interpreted by Schevill, "was moved to ignore, or at least lightly to pass over, the more cruel and disturbing aspects of the human scene." Another historian who attacked Ranke was the German historian Friedrich Meinecke. Meinecke criticized Ranke strongly after the Second World War, and "attributed the national disasters of the past forty years to a series of accidents, the vanity of the Kaiser, the election of Hindenburg to the presidency of the Weimar Republic, Hitler's obsessional character, and so forth." Frank would have been interested in the problem of the accidental in history—the shape of Cleopatra's nose, Bajazet's attack of gout, the monkey bite that killed King Alexander, the death of Lenin—these were the accidents which arguably modified the course of history. Frank, in his last ten years when he came to feel even more strongly that chance had played a crucial role in his life, may have found Meinecke's late-life views intriguing.

Katie: So Frank was obsessed with history. Do we know why he preferred to study history and teach it as his life work rather than say math, English, or philosophy?

Pops: We only know Frank decided while he was at Chicago that teaching history would be his life's work. Why he chose history to study and teach is unknown. The only answer may be that he was, at heart, a historian for whom, as Ranke claimed, "the first demand is pure love of truth." However, though the discovery of truth was for the historian the Holy Grail, the quest itself is what attracts historians to the field. The search, perhaps more than the destination, is what invigorated readers of history. This must have been the case for Frank, who continued to spend long hours in study even after he was already thoroughly prepared for all his classes.

Katie: The new president, Harper—why did Rockefeller pick him? And did Frank know Harper when he was at Chicago?

Pops: Frank knew Harper—to what extent we don't know—either at Chicago or in Waco when Harper came to Waco for the dedication of the completed Carroll Science Building. There is a photo of Harper, Brooks, G.W. Carroll, Judge W.H. Jenkins, George W. Truett, and the entire Baylor faculty, including Frank, on the steps of Carroll Science. But Frank and Harper probably also knew each other as cornetists in connection with the Chicago University band. Harper was a proficient cornetist and years before led the New Concord Silver Cornet Band. At Chicago, Harper was generally credited with the formation of the Chicago marching band. He would occasionally sit in with the band playing his cornet. Frank, who also played cornet, played with a band at Chicago for two years, probably starting during the 1900-1901 school year while he was finishing up his A.B. degree. However, we don't think he played with the marching band because of the time required for football games and other events. The University of Chicago's *1901 Cap and Gown*, which shows Frank as a senior, reported that the University Band played for dances, smokers, balls, receptions, initiations, and various parties.

Katie: So Rockefeller chose Harper because...?

Pops: Rockefeller picked Harper because he had an impressive academic background and was unusually self-assured and charismatic in projecting a vision of the future of a new Chicago University that resonated with Rockefeller. Rockefeller felt it was his Christian duty to do some good with the money he had accumulated. Harper was an acknowledged prodigy and had received his Ph.D.

from Yale at age 18; his dissertation was entitled, "A Comparative Study of the Prepositions in Latin, Greek, Sanskrit, and Gothic."

Katie: Yikes!

Pops: Yes, pretty technical, maybe good bedtime reading if you need to sleep. But Harper's vision for the new university is what grabbed Rockefeller's attention. Harper said, "I have a plan which is at the same time unique and comprehensive, which I am persuaded will revolutionize university study in this country." The University of Chicago would say that Harper "imagined a university that would combine an American-style undergraduate liberal arts college with a German-style graduate research university," and that Chicago had quickly become a national leader in higher education and research. Although initial funding and support came from Baptists, including Rockefeller, Harper's concept was that Chicago would serve as a nondenominational and non-sectarian university. Further, it would hold classes year-round. This scheduling would be convenient for summer-only students like Frank, who would only attend in the summers for several years while he worked teaching the rest of the time.

Katie: I guess Frank also liked Rockefeller's connection with Baptists.

Pops: Perhaps, but Harper, who was building the university according to his own vision, believed that denominationalism had become a stigma in progressive educational circles. They did not wish to emphasize what they referred to in private as "the Baptist side" of their institution. They welcomed breadth of support, as did Rockefeller himself. Jewish donors had also been prominent in supplementing Rockefeller's gifts to the university. Harper's religious convictions were consistent with an increasingly secular age.

Katie: Did Chicago have a good school song?

Pops: Chicago had many school songs. Here is a fight song that captured the school spirit when Frank was a student:

Wave the flag for old Chicago
Maroon her color guard
Ever shall our team be victors
Known throughout the land
Zumm rah rah
With the Grand Old Man to lead us
Without a peer we'll stand
Chicago, GO, G.O., Go

The "grand old man" must have been Amos Alonzo Stagg, the legendary football genius, College Hall of Fame inductee, and coaching phenomenon. President Harper hired Stagg in 1892 as director of Chicago's Department of Physical Culture and Athletics. Opponents never knew what to expect from Stagg's unpredictable teams. He invented numerous offensive and defensive formations, many of which are the original inspirations for many plays used by today's teams.

Katie: Back to Frank, I would like to know more about his time as a student in Chicago between 1897 and 1902. Any more letters from this period?

Pops: No more letters, but what we do have may be as good as letters, perhaps even better—the expense ledger he kept in his handwriting between 1896 and 1902. We know what he spent during his last year on clothes and his appearance, on entertainment, books for school, room rent, breakfasts, lunches and suppers, library fines, tuition, school supplies, transportation, medicine and medical supplies, magazines, repayments of small loans from his four brothers, and other items. He recorded expenses as large as monthly tuition ($13.33) and as small as pins ($.05). To itemize a few of these, here are some of the recorded expenditures for his personal appearance and clothes:

Hat	2.00	Shoes Mended	.05	Haircut	.25
Tailoring	.75	Pants dyed	.90	Sox 2 pair	.25
Collars (2)	.25	Suspenders	.19	Drawers (2)	2.50
Tie (1)	.25	Pants pressed	.15	Shoestrings	.05
Nightshirt	.50	Shirt	.48	Thread	.10
Garters	.29	Hair tonic	.50	Laundry	.37

Frank's expenses for tickets to various entertainments included:

"Uncle Tom's Cabin"	.35	"Ben-Hur"	.50
"As You Like It"	.50	"Way Down East"	.50
"King Dodo"	.50	"Price of Peace"	.35
Buff. Bill's Show	2.30	Stock show	.25
"The Merchant of Venice" starring Henry Irving and Ellen Terry			.60
"Francesca da Rimini" starring Otis Skinner			.35
"Magda" starring Mrs. Campbell			.60
Paderewski's Recital	1.00	"Carmen" grand opera	1.00
Sousa's band	.60	Opera singer Anna Held	.50
"Sultan of Sulu"	1.50	Kubelik's concert	.50

Frank's expenses for medicines and health supplies included:

Arnica	.15	Nitric acid	.05	Witch hazel	.10
Vaseline	.05	Muriatic acid	.10	Boric acid	.10
Shaving soap	.10	Lithia tablets	.25	Ointment	.45
Dentistry	4.00				

Frank's miscellaneous expenses included:

Elevator fee	.10	Knife	.25	Magazine	.10
Bicycle tire	2.13	Trip to L. Park	.90	Fountain pen box	.40
Music Lessons	2.00	Lemons	.13	Picnic	.25
Umbrella checked	.05	Library fine	.15	Pocket mirror	.25
Typewriter	.35				
Garters	.29				

Katie: I can see why Frank must have loved the opportunities for shows and entertainment he would not have had in Waco or anywhere in Texas. What were Chicago's football teams like when Frank was there?

Pops: Chicago's Maroons played fifteen games in 1900, thirteen of them on Marshall Field, Chicago's home field, and finished sixth place in the Western Conference, nine of its games against non-conference opponents. We believe that Frank attended some of these games. However, we know for certain that Frank attended Chicago football games in 1901, including the games on October 17 and 18; November 15, 27, and 30; and baseball games on April 10, 19, and April 24 in 1902.

I mentioned earlier that during Frank's years in Chicago, he continued to pursue his relationship with Mamie Welhausen. Frank records he traveled to Corpus Christi between May 31 and June 6, 1902, presumably to visit with Mamie, although he doesn't mention her by name.

Katie: Back to Mr. Rockefeller. Maybe you can explain how he acquired his wealth and earned his tycoon reputation yet gave so much money to the University of Chicago, which helped aspiring academics like Frank.

Pops: Primarily from oil. Rockefeller got into the oil business during the Civil War and formed Standard Oil not long afterward. At one point, Standard Oil Trust owned the overwhelming majority of the nation's refineries and pipelines. Then two things happened. First, Congress passed the Sherman Antitrust Act prohibiting trusts and combinations in restraint of trade. Later, the US Supreme Court ruled that Standard Oil of New Jersey was in violation of antitrust laws and broke it up into more than thirty companies. The second was Rockefeller's retirement during the 1890s, in which he gave away a substantial portion of his fortune to worthy causes, including the University of Chicago. He died in 1937 at the age of 97. More questions?

Katie: This question doesn't have anything to do with Rockefeller or Stanford, but how tall was Frank? How big a guy? Was he big enough to play on one of Stagg's teams? I'm also wondering whether he was athletic enough.

Pops: When he enrolled at Chicago in 1897 at the age of thirty, Chicago's Physical Culture Department [Staggs' department] measured him as follows: 148.2 pounds, 69.7 inches tall, and waist 30.5 inches. His weight and waist in later years expanded substantially. One of his grandchildren thinks he was at least six feet tall and that Chicago's height measurement is wrong. However, even at 69.7 inches, he would still have seemed a giant next to Mama Josie, who could not have been more than five feet one inch. Could Frank have played on one of Stagg's teams? Big enough, perhaps, but not nearly athletic enough. Frank's thing was books and history, not balls and sports. In time, however, Frank would, with diligent effort, became both a mediocre tennis player and then a mediocre golfer.

Katie: One last question. I am curious whether he planned on returning to Waco as a college professor after finishing his degrees at Chicago.

Pops: I don't think so. Frank could not have known he would have a chance to return to Baylor until he received a letter in the spring of 1902 offering him a job. The circumstances leading to that offer were capricious and bizarre.

Katie: So, Frank earned his bachelor's and master's degrees at Chicago and loved Chicago but decided to enroll at Stanford decades later. I don't understand why he didn't return to Chicago for his doctorate.

Pops: Sometimes lives go in unpredictable directions. Just wait for the next chapter.

CHAPTER 19

The Twist of Fate, President Cooper Resigns, & a Job Offer

(1902)

This brief chapter concerns the strangest yet unquestionably most far-reaching event in Frank Guittard's story, one too sensitive for some people's ears. It led to Frank Guittard's return to Waco and Baylor after dropping out eight years earlier. We will mention the incident again in the next chapter which features the guided tour of campus Frank must have given his sweetheart Mamie while courting her. I've asked Charlie to ask any questions he may need for clarification.

Pops: Ready to go, Charlie?

Charlie: Ready, Pops, locked and loaded.

Pops: Okay. In March 1902 in Baylor chapel, a bizarre incident occurred, although slightly predictable given the prank-inclined nature of some college students not emerged from their adolescent states. Baylor's distinguished but high-strung president, Oscar H. Cooper, was presiding as usual at morning chapel in Main Building when he heard a small dog whimpering, placed on stage by prankish students. We don't know whether the students were in the prep or the collegiate department, and the record prudently does not disclose their identities. But to make a short story even shorter, President Cooper snapped when he heard and then saw what was disturbing his service. He reached down, grabbed the unfortunate hound, and heaved it out one of the chapel's third-story windows, the dog being heard from no more.

President Cooper came to Baylor with outstanding credentials as an educator—first in his class and a respected tutor at Yale, post-graduate studies in Berlin, Germany, and the first native Texan to graduate from Yale. Since his appointment as president in 1899, he had served Baylor University with distinction; Baylor, by all accounts, was much the better because of his diligent efforts, even if he had not always received the proper amount of respect from the students. The unfortunate incident in chapel occurred when Cooper was in the third year of his presidency. The timing of this incident, which brought unwanted negative publicity to Baylor still struggling for its survival a few years after the 1886 merger, resulted in a student protest and Cooper's resignation. It could not have come at a worse time. A year earlier, Cooper had written the letter excerpted below to President William Rainey Harper at the University of Chicago, which had been funded primarily by John D. Rockefeller:

> This school, Baylor University, is an interesting study. It inherits...the traditions of crude scholarship which have been handed down for many years...The denomination seems to be waking up to the possibilities of a well-equipped college, but of course the great mass even of those who are interested have not the faintest conception of the resources necessary to do the work which they think ought to be done here...We have no endowment, we have no science hall, we have only a few thousand books that have been thrown together in a sort of haphazard way, and nearly everything which is necessary to make this school a college remains to be done, but there are a spirit and purpose here which money could not buy, but money would be a very great help now.

This incident would not have helped Baylor raise money to meet the school's crucial needs. Perhaps that is the reason, not just the students' ensuing protest, that prompted Cooper's resignation. On March 31, 1902, the following letter [as excerpted] from Cooper was read to the trustees: "It has been my privilege...to witness the marvelous growth of the school in numbers, in financial strength and in public confidence...Conditions have now arisen which...seem to indicate that I should ask you to allow me to lay down the authority which three years ago you asked me to assume and I make this request. Let the duty and responsibility of the presidency pass on to another man of your choice. May God's blessing rest on Baylor in all the years yet to be. Sincerely and faithfully, Oscar H. Cooper."

Seventeen days later, the trustees voted unanimously that Samuel Palmer Brooks be invited to assume the presidency of Baylor, sending him a telegram to come at once to Baylor at Baylor's expense to discuss the matter. Brooks appeared before the trustees on April 21, asked for time to consider the offer, and on April 24, 1902, accepted the trustees' offer at an initial annual salary of $2,500. More about this historic telegram in the later chapter describing the chain of events characterized as a "twist of fate." Promises having been made, Brooks returned to New Haven, completed his Master of Arts, and was back in Texas by mid-summer to take up his duties as the new president.

President Brooks had to have been excited for both him and his wife and quite busy before heading back to Texas. Among the things he did while still in New Haven was to write to Frank Guittard in Chicago and offer him a position teaching in the Preparatory Department at the beggarly wage of $75 a month ($900 per year). Brooks's letter offering a position to Frank was as follows:

Dear Mr. Guittard:

As you may have learned, I have been elected President of Baylor University. I need a man for the Preparatory Department (to assist). The position pays only $75 (seventy-five). I am ashamed to offer it to you but it is the best I can do now. I very much want you in school there with us next year. I believe it would be better for you than more money in a public school for with your scholarship I feel sure we could give you a better position & better salary in the near future—in fact increases in the salary after a year.

I wrote Cantwell [Baylor graduate, colleague of Brooks, and Frank's principal at Southwestern Academy in Arkansas] where you could be found & he gave me the address. If you give satisfaction (as I am sure you will) I will see that your salary is advanced as fast as possible. I think I am offering you a place where you can make a record, although it is a petty salary for the first year... It is all I can promise now for the Board so acted when they allowed us another man.

I will help you in every possible way to get before the people, to cultivate the students & reach a maximum of opportunity for you to develop in. Kindly write me at once if you will take it or not & I will nominate you to the Board by letter, for action at the first meeting.

I hope you will sacrifice enough to do it. Baylor pays cash now you know!

You are a Baptist I believe & a graduate of Chicago University?

Hurriedly but truly, S. P. Brooks

Frank, having no other offers in hand and with good feelings for Baylor, Brooks, and his own student days in Waco, accepted Brooks's offer, and taught at Baylor for almost forty-eight years. He would meet and court two women to be his wives—one (Mamie Welhausen) he already knew but possibly would not have married if Brooks's offer had not brought him back to Waco, and another (Josie Glenn) he would never have known if he had not taken the job at Baylor. These events arguably came about because of a twist of fate, namely, the mischievous prank which should never have happened. The future of President Brooks, Baylor University, and Frank Guittard would never be the same.

Charlie: So maybe there's a crazy moral to this story.

Pops: What do you think that might be?

Charlie: Beware of a dog barking in chapel during March.

Pops: (*smiling*) Good one. Let's all try to remember that.

Charlie: (*grinning*) So Pops, you think you and I both are only here because of a goofy prank by students who should have been expelled a century ago? Or at least suspended?

Pops: That could be. One of those questions which are difficult to answer. It all depends on things we don't know and can never know. The prank did get Frank back to Texas, where he visited and corresponded with Mamie Welhausen for more than four years before they married. If he had accepted a teaching position in Chicago, for example, who knows who he have might have met at church or the opera or a football game? Chicago must have been well-supplied with attractive, intelligent college women from prosperous families who might have liked a presentable young scholar with two degrees from the University of Chicago.

Charlie: He could look pretty sharp in a tux and bowtie, and he played the cornet!

Pops: Yes, but could he have afforded one of those Chicago girls on a teacher's salary?

Charlie: No way, José—right, Pops?

Pops: Hold on to that question, Charlie. We'll come back to it.

CHAPTER 20

Frank Gives Mamie a Guided Tour of the Campus

(imagined)

This chapter is not just about facts from the author's research, but also presents an imagined recreation of a scene which could have happened on April 19, 1903—a nice day for a guided tour to occur—and which would inevitably have happened at some point, although the date is unknown. The scene is based on the facts we know about Frank and Mamie's relationship, the configuration of the Baylor campus, and the author's other research. On April 19-21, President Brooks presided over a three-day dedication ceremony for the Carroll Science Building on Burleson Quadrangle. Frank and Mamie's relationship was on Frank's front burner when he went to Shiner for a special visit in August of 1902 after accepting President Brooks's job offer. Katie may have a question or comment after the imagined tour.

Pops: Before that imagined tour of the Baylor campus, some background on the Burleson Quadrangle. Building out Burleson Quadrangle was a monumental achievement in Baylor history considering there was no family of extraordinary wealth like the John D. Rockefellers or the Leland Stanfords to pour money into Baylor buildings or faculty salaries. Initially, Burleson Quadrangle consisted only of the Oak Lawn acreage previously owned by General Joseph Speight on which Main Building (1887) and Georgia Burleson Hall (1888) had been erected. The new buildings—G.W. Carroll Science Building and the F.L. Carroll Chapel and Library—were completed in 1903 after the Carrolls each donated $75,000. Carroll Science was dedicated in April, the occasion signifying a major milestone for Baylor. The Quadrangle continues to be a significant part of what pulls graduates back to campus and their university today.

The Carrolls were father and son. Francis Lafayette Carroll (F.L.) had been a treasurer of Baylor and reportedly had given more money to Baylor than any other person in Texas. F.L. Carroll had formed the Long Shingle and Sawmill in Beaumont. He and his son George Washington Carroll ("G.W.") founded the Beaumont Lumber Company. Additionally, G.W. had invested in the Gladys City Oil Company, which proved lucrative when the Spindletop oil field was discovered. By the time of his death in 1935, G.W. had given away most of his money. G.W. Carroll also personally supported the efforts of B.H. Carroll—no apparent relation—to establish a theological department at Baylor.

President Oscar Henry Cooper, during whose tenure (1899-1902) the Carrolls' gifts were put in motion, was absent at the dedication ceremony. However, by that time, President Cooper had gone on to become president of Hardin-Simmons University, doing so within a few weeks after leaving Baylor. The circumstances of his leaving we talk about elsewhere. President Cooper was a significant facilitator of the Carrolls' gifts to Baylor. Likely, both Carrolls realized that President Cooper had a well-thought-out plan to elevate Baylor's college standing in relation to other colleges in the US.

The dedication of Carroll Science would have been an obvious time for Frank to show off Burleson Quadrangle and Baylor University to his girlfriend and unannounced fiancée, Mamie Welhausen. One can imagine Frank and Mamie walking through the Quad, Frank telling stories about President Burleson and Baylor, relating his work teaching in the academy, showing Mamie his classroom in ivy-covered Main Building, and strolling around the entire campus. The afternoon of April 19 was chosen as a logical time for Frank and Mamie's walking tour of the Quad and the larger campus since it was a Sunday. We assumed that the academic procession on that Sunday would have already occurred after church let out and everyone had eaten lunch. The procession would have continued to the steps of Carroll Science, where appropriate remarks were made by President Brooks. At some point, Frank was on Science's steps with the rest of the faculty and dignitaries, and Mamie would have been under one of the oak trees in Burleson Quadrangle.

As to sites left off the tour, there were several. Frank would not buy his first house on 7th Street near the campus until 1905, which was before he and Mamie married. He would have only mentioned Maggie Houston Hall, the dorm for young men of lesser means that was over a mile away. Maggie was not the kind of place visitors would want to walk through unannounced. We assume the same for touring Georgia Burleson Hall, although Mamie would have been interested in seeing the girls' rooms and the parlors used for the popular soirees with young men. We have left Carroll Chapel and Library off the tour because we can't confirm it was open to the public at the time of the dedication of Carroll Science.

The Guided Tour

Frank: Well, Mamie, are you up to walking around a little more to see our little campus? Not tired out from all those speeches? Baptists like to go on a while. I wish I had timed Truett's closing prayer. Seems like it went on forever.

Mamie: Oh, no, I'm a Methodist; I'm used to windy prayers by pastors, deacons, Sunday school teachers, circle leaders, choir directors, you name it. By the way, it may be tacky to say so, but I do think two of those men on the first row of the steps could have tidied up their beards a bit for the photographer.

Frank: Not so loud, Mamie; I'm trying to get on with these people here. And if you are talking about George Washington Carroll next to George W. Truett in the front row on the right, he's the "G.W. Carroll" whose name is on the building. But yes, I agree, his beard looked pretty ragged and could have used a good trim.

Mamie: I did find those speeches inspiring, mostly. The one by President Brooks, of course. It was an informative introduction to Baylor.

Frank: Really? I'm glad. I have heard so many of that kind I can almost make them myself. I admit my mind was wandering as we all stood there for photographs on the steps of Carroll Science with G.W. Carroll and Presidents Harper and Brooks. I could see you out in the Quadrangle with Mrs. Brooks. I'm glad it didn't rain; that would have been awful.

Mamie: What were you thinking about while you were on the steps for the photographer?

Frank: I was wondering whether Harper brought his silver cornet with him—but thought probably not. Also, whether Harper is following those recent articles by Ida Tarbell that started in November in *McClure's* attacking Rockefeller's monopolistic practices. I would imagine he is aware of them, but I'm glad I didn't ask him. Her articles are continuing. I'm also curious about whether our President Teddy Roosevelt is reading Ms. Tarbell's articles and what he thinks can be done about monopolies under the Sherman Antitrust Act. He's been president now for a year and a half. If the situation is as bad as Ms. Tarbell says it is, it's high time for someone to do something.

> *(Frank pauses as he decides to keep his other thoughts private from Mamie, including: I wonder how long it will take to be promoted to the Collegiate Department or become the senior man in my subject. $75 a month will sound like chicken feed to a girl like Mamie. Can I propose to Mamie while living in a hot boarding house with all those mosquitoes, or will I need to buy a house first? Brooks was pretty vague in that letter about how fast my salary might get increased; he hasn't said anything since. Maybe I could get a bank loan to tide us over, even though I don't have much in the way of collateral. They'd laugh if I offered my cornet. I'm pretty sure I'll have to break down and go into debt to buy a house—but the house could be the collateral—otherwise,*

> *with no house, she's sure to turn me down flat. Or maybe she would say she needs time to consider my proposal but really wants to wait for a better offer—girls like Mamie can do that if they want to. How long will it be before I see her again after today? Are other guys taking her to church on Sundays in Shiner? Do they try to kiss or hug her sometimes? I'm sure they want to. What kinds of jobs do they have—can they buy a house whenever they want to and not even have to raise cash for a down payment? Are any of them professional men, maybe doctors? Dentists? Lawyers? Or sons of wealthy fathers who will help them get married? Maybe Mamie's mother or one of her brothers will wise me up to what I need to know).*

Mamie: Okay. Sorry. I'm ready. Now I'm wearing my walking shoes.

Frank: Let's do the Quad first, and then if you feel like it, we can branch out and walk around the entire campus. They don't expect us back at my boarding house for supper until 5 p.m., so that gives us a couple of hours; that should be enough time to do it up finely.

Mamie: What will be on the menu tonight?

Frank: Oh, on Sunday nights, there's no telling. Whatever it is, there will be more of Hattie's fresh lemonade. She may make some of those hot biscuits of hers, and there will be sweet cream to sop them in, and maybe some fried chicken since this is a special weekend. The biscuits are delicious, fattening, I'm sure.

Mamie: All right. I'm ready to walk. I have my umbrella if it rains. So, what's first?

Frank: Let's just start with the Main Building so I can take off this hot gown and leave it in my classroom. (*pausing*) Main Building was the first building completed in the Quad. Burleson planned the building and paid the prominent local architect William W. Larmour to design it. It was already on Burleson's drawing board before the 1886 merger with Waco University. Larmour designed both Main and Burleson in an Italianate style, updated with those turrets and trim you see up there. Those towers are the best-loved feature of these buildings. Larmour called the resulting look "High Victorian Eclectic." I call them "Italianate Villa/American Victorian" in style. Larmour knew that Italianate was going out of style, so he added the updated features. He also designed over fifty homes, including the Cameron House here in Waco. Burleson and Larmour anticipated building a boy's dorm on the other side of Main, but it never happened, so Maggie Houston and Cowden Halls near the church still house young men of limited means—I stayed at Maggie a while myself, and so did Brooks and Neff. Main was completed in September 1887, a full year after Baylor at Waco began classes in the old Waco University buildings.

Mamie: You mentioned a merger.

Frank: Yes, Baylor at Independence merged with Waco University. President Burleson was the first president of the merged university, but he had been president of both Baylor at Independence and then Waco University before the merger. Oh, one other thing before we go inside. Larmour also designed the building for the Waco Female College in the same style as Burleson and Main. Strange to say, Waco Female College went bankrupt, and TCU, then named Add-Ran College, moved to Waco and into the Waco Female College Campus. So, for a while until 1910, when TCU's Waco campus burned, Baylor's campus buildings and TCU's were similar architecturally. And, since both campuses were in Waco, it was convenient for Baylor and TCU to play football against each other more than once annually for a number of years, beginning in 1899. Let's go inside and walk up to the chapel. It's on the third floor. Are you good with stairs?

Mamie: Frank, for goodness' sake, I'm only twenty-two. I climbed a lot of steps with Papa on our trip to Europe last year, and he said I did well, considering how bad I sometimes felt on the ship. Have you ever been on an ocean liner, Frank? You can get sick being pitched about. I felt terrible. But enough about that. Where's the chapel?

Frank: Nope, I've never been on a big ship or been across an ocean. I hope to someday. The chapel is right through here. Chapel is required Monday through Friday, and President Brooks usually conducts it. Something awful happened in chapel here early last year. President Cooper, who's gone now, was presiding, and some mischievous students had put a small dog on the stage, and the dog started barking. President Cooper grabbed up the poor dog and pitched it out one of those open windows there.

Mamie: Ye gods, that's terrible.

Frank: Yes. When I heard about it, I felt sorry both for the dog and for the president. The students provoked him, and he snapped. (*pausing*) If you look out one of those windows, you can see Carroll Field, named for Lee Carroll. It was a football field in the 1890s, but President Burleson hated football and banned it. In 1902, President Cooper opened it up again for football several years after President

Burleson supposedly grabbed a football away from some students. One story was that he stabbed it.

Mamie: Why did you feel sorry for President Cooper?

Frank: President Cooper was a good man, and he was an excellent scholar, first in his class at Yale. He was also taking care of his sick wife, and he was our president when the Carrolls' gifts to Baylor were secured for Baylor. He did much to raise Baylor's stature as a university. He was an essential part of why we're here today at this dedication. But the students—you know how students get riled up by things—raised such a ruckus over the dog that Cooper resigned, and Baylor lost him. Another time, a few years back, some students, including some from my literary society I'm ashamed to say, almost lynched that journalist Brann, but thank goodness Brooks and Professor Tanner—he's gone now—stopped them.

Mamie: That sounds like a good story, too. Were you here at the time?

Frank: No, but I heard about it. It happened outside, near where we are standing right now. Brann eventually got himself shot after what he said about Baylor women and President Burleson—not by students, thank God—but that's a story for another day.

Mamie: Maybe that's why people called Waco "Six-Shooter Junction."

Frank: Oh, that was a long time ago when the cowboys were driving their herds across the Suspension Bridge, but first they were looking to have a hot bath in a Waco hotel, get tooted, and naturally let off a little steam. I guess being on a horse all day long for weeks at a time would have been hard. By the way, one of my Erisophian friends, Lee Scarborough, was an honest-to-God cowboy for a while and then went on to become president of Southwestern Baptist Seminary after finishing Baylor.

Mamie: (*smiling*) Ever thought about being a cowboy yourself?

Frank: Nope (*chuckling*), I guess I missed my moment. But really, "cowboying" must have been just too dull, too hard on the rear end, and there's no future in it. And how do you hold a book and ride a horse at the same time? Speaking of cowboys, though, that reminds me of Indians, the Hueco Indians, that is. There was a big spring somewhere near downtown Waco. The Indians liked to drink its waters, thinking it would keep them healthy. There is also a place called Lovers' Leap we might visit sometime. According to legend, the daughter of the Hueco chief named Wah-Wah-Tee fell in love with a young brave from an enemy Apache tribe. When the Huecos discovered them, the young Indian couple leaped to their death into the Bosque River far below them. There's a poem dedicated to a little Indian maid, perhaps the same one who made that desperate leap with her boyfriend, which goes:

My little Wahco maid—while I sing this serenade,
The stars that watch o'er you
Reflect a heart that is tender and true
Meet me at Proctor Spring,
I will have the Wedding ring—
My love cannot be stayed,
Little Wahco Maid.

Mamie: I don't know whether that story or the one about the dog is sadder. The story about the dog, I think. By the way, I didn't see President Cooper at the dedication today.

Frank: No, but Chicago's Harper was here. The academic procession today reminded me of the academic procession with John D. Rockefeller and Harper a couple of years ago when I was at Chicago. Today's dedication would have been bittersweet for Oscar Cooper, who is now president of Simmons College in Abilene. Cooper was at the laying of the cornerstones for both the Carroll buildings last year. Let's continue and I'll show you my classroom while we're still here on this floor. The prep courses are taught in these rooms. (*walking*) Here is the room assigned to me. We had about half of all the students in the prep. To pass the exam to get into the collegiate department, they have to make sufficient scores in orthography, reading, composition, English, Latin, Greek, higher arithmetic, elementary algebra, and ancient and modern geography. I had to teach many of those courses. I wasn't up for Greek, though. I'm glad Poole didn't ask me to teach it.

Mamie: Did the Carrolls have oil money?

Frank: Not sure about old F.L. Carroll, the father. He made his fortune in the timber business, but his son G.W. definitely benefited from the East Texas oil boom. The Spindletop gusher came in January 1901, and the *Baylor Bulletin* reported on G.W.'s gift in July 1901. The Carrolls' contributions and the plan for the new buildings were important to me when I accepted Brooks's offer. Baylor was on an upswing started by President Cooper, and I wanted to be part of it. And I needed a job.

Mamie: (*after walking into Frank's classroom*) Is that your desk?

Frank: Yes. I share it with one of the other teachers here in the Preparatory Department.

Mamie: What courses do you teach here?

Frank: Whatever Brooks or Professor Poole asks me to teach to get the prep students college-ready, from Latin to geometry or arithmetic to history to grammar, whatever.

Mamie: How can you teach so many courses? Aren't your degrees from Chicago in history?

Frank: I don't know how I've done it, but when it's do or die, somehow you just do it. This has been the hardest year of my life, harder than any year at Chicago, since I've had to look like I knew something every day in courses outside my field. It wasn't like in Chicago, where only your test paper or your essay would expose your ignorance.

Mamie: How do you conduct recitations here? Do you make the students stand up? Is it mostly students just repeating what they had memorized the night before?

Frank: No, these are college prep students, and many of them are as old as our college students. Brooks started in the prep and was a pretty old guy, almost thirty, when he graduated from the college—nearly as old as I was when I graduated from Chicago. No, I just let them do their recitations at their desks, and I stay seated as well. There is a lot of memory work in all of the courses. Memorization is one way students learn, but I like to ask them questions about their reading rather than ask them to just repeat the text verbatim. I think it makes it stick in their minds if they have to think. Memorization does work for poetry since the exact words in the precise order matters and because rhythm and rhyme matter in poetry. On the other hand, if you don't memorize poetry, you won't remember it. It's just the opposite of the way you learn other courses.

Mamie: What do you do if they don't know their lessons? Do you punish them in any way? Make them clean that blackboard over there or the erasers?

Frank: (*smiling*) Oh, no. You must be pulling my leg. That's kids' stuff. These are serious students wanting to be admitted to our collegiate department. All I have to do is make marks by their names in my grade book. They get their course grades at the end of each quarter.

Mamie: (*back out in the hall and now walking up to the second floor with Frank*) Is there a library here somewhere?

Frank: There are several libraries, but nearly all the books belong to the literary societies. The men's organizations, the Philomathesians, and the Erisophians, each society has its own room and library in Main. I think the Erisophian room is open; we can walk in there a minute and take a look. There's only one student in there right now, maybe preparing for an upcoming debate.

Mamie: (*after looking in the Erisophian room*) That's a beautiful room. I like the curtains, that wall of bookcases, those portraits on that other wall, and that large desk. A solemn room indeed for serious debating by serious students. I get a little nervous just looking at it. I'm not much of a public speaker. Didn't you get anxious when you had to stand up and debate in front of a room full of people?

Frank: Yes, I did. Speaking in public is not my favorite thing either, but debaters are allowed their notes, which helped me with the butterflies. I had my notes all written down on steno pads. I also practiced by myself sometimes, since I wasn't as fluent as some of the other men, like Neff. I could walk around jabbering to myself and trying out some of the gestures I'd learned in Professor Franklin's Giant Rhetoric Class. (*walking*) The mathematics, science, literature, and oratory departments are all also on this floor.

Mamie: You mentioned Pat Neff?

Frank: Pat Neff, himself. Neff was one of Baylor's best debaters. (*Back on the first floor of Main Building*) That office there was President Burleson's when he was here, and there was also a small library in there. I don't know if the students were allowed to use it or not. Now it's President Brooks's office.

(*Back outside and in front of Burleson Hall*) We won't be able to go inside Georgia Burleson without special arrangements, so let's just stop here a moment. Burleson and Main Building were built on a 50-acre portion of General Speight's 100-acre farm, which included what's known as Oak Lawn. Burleson Quadrangle sits on Oak Lawn. General Speight was a quite a guy. He was made an honorary Brigadier General for his service to the Confederacy in the Civil War. He recruited President Burleson and 15,000 other men for the Confederate cause; Burleson served as a chaplain for a short period. After the war, Speight was twice president of the Texas Baptist General Convention. He was instrumental in Burleson's relocation from

Baylor at Independence to Waco University. And he was also a lawyer who wrote the charter for the Convention.

I believe Burleson Hall today is located more or less where Speight's large house was. The beautiful oak trees for which Speight's tract was named are still all around here, and there are also live oaks and pecan trees providing shade to strollers. All of Burleson Quadrangle is situated on Oak Lawn. Burleson Hall was called the Angels' Inn, and that fence there is to keep the young women in and the young men out. One of these days it will be torn down, and I will be glad when that day comes. The girls' rooms are very comfortable and pleasant, I'm told, and they're lit by electricity. Speight originally owned the property bounded by Speight Street on the southeast, 7th Street on the southwest, Waco Creek on the northwest, and 5th Street on the northeast.

Burleson Hall was opened in the fall of 1887 and was surrounded by an area enclosed by a seven-foot fence. The place was called Angels' Grounds. It has multiple uses. In its three stories, there are eighty-five rooms with nearby bathrooms for the young ladies, plus a dining room and library rooms for the Calliopean and RCB Societies—those are the women's literary societies, and a Young Ladies' Reading Room. Additionally, there are practice rooms for use by the Music Department, and parlors for occasional soirees with the men. And of course, there is a sewerage connection, and the rooms are kept warm in the winter by coal stoves.

Mamie: Other than study, eat, take baths, read the Bible, and sleep, what do these girls do with their time?

Frank: Not much else. I'm told that Ma Greer, who was in charge with Professor Greer, said that "the most important thing that the women did...was to obey rules." There were lots of rules, although Ma was not sure whether there were eighty-one rules or one hundred eighty-one. I think Mrs. Greer was trying to be funny. Other than the rare soirees, Sunday was and is the big day for the women. Following roll call floor by floor, Burleson's various matrons, with their girls in tow, walk down Fifth Street to attend church at First Baptist Church. They all sit together, and the boys are supposedly not allowed to get close enough to even tell what color their dresses are. Then, after the final prayer, they return to Burleson Hall, sometimes on a streetcar.

Mamie: I think you mentioned a problem a few years back with that Brazilian girl under the Burleson's care who stayed in Burleson Hall and became pregnant. Did Burleson lose any residents after that? Did parents pull their girls out?

Frank: Yes, some of them did, and the occupancy dipped a little initially, but today I don't think there is any problem. An unfortunate situation; no doubt she was taken advantage of, and there is no excuse for that, but the girl was not one of our regular students.

Mamie: I'm dying to know what the girls' rooms are like. I know you said we can't see any of them today.

Frank: I've never been inside, but I am told that each room has two or more beds and a small stove. The coal and kindling are cut and brought into the dormitory, and the first thing the girls do each morning in the winter is to build a fire to heat their room. Each woman furnishes her own towels, soap, combs, brushes, pillow slips, sheets, two blankets, and napkins. She also brings her own spoon, knife and fork, saucer, and goblet for use in the room. All her clothes must have her name legibly marked on them. And the girls must bring their own wraps, rubbers, and umbrella.

Mamie: Like going to camp.

Frank: Right. Let's walk down this way to Speight and, if you are still game, we will just walk the outer border of the campus, turning right off Speight onto 7th Street. Then we can proceed on 7th over Waco Creek until we reach Dutton. At Dutton, we'll go right, staying on Dutton until we are back to 5th, and from there, it is only a short walk to my boarding house. I'll tell you a little about John Camden West, whose house we'll see after we cross the creek. His property, Minglewood Park, on the northeast side of Waco Creek, mostly finishes out our present campus. Before West transferred the property legally, he allowed citizens of Waco to use Minglewood Park for recreation, whatever. Judge West is a member of First Baptist, an attorney, a Latin and Greek scholar, and a writer. In 1861, he was the schoolmaster at the Waco and Trinity River Classical School, which became Waco University. West fought for the Confederacy at both Gettysburg and Chickamauga before being discharged in 1864. After the war, he practiced law in Waco before becoming a judge. He was elected Waco's mayor in the 1870s and published a chronicle covering two months (April 9-June 9, 1863) of his service in the Confederate Army.

Mamie: Such an unusual background.

Frank: Yes, and I was going to say that West mentions in his book all the classic poems and books he was reading while he served in the Confederacy whenever he had the chance, such as Lycidas's "L'Allegro" and "Il Penseroso," "The Autocrat of the Breakfast Table," *Les Miserables*, and Milton's *Paradise Lost*. He also talks about the bullets that came his way, including one that only passed through his beard and grazed his ear. Many around him were not as lucky. If we're lucky, when we walk up 7th past Waco Creek, you will see kids up in trees lining the creek, watching students playing football in a big field between the creek and Dutton.

(*the imaginary tour concluded...*)

Pops: (*pausing*) Katie, that's the imagined guided tour. Any questions or comments?

Katie: I know you mostly made all of that up, but how did you do it?

Pops: Well, so that the imagined tour would be believable, I started with several things, first my knowledge of Burleson Quadrangle, the campus generally, and its history. I also had some maps. Then I assumed Frank must have given Mamie a tour of the campus sooner or later, and then I relied on all my research for the stops along the tour, and also for my comments as to Baylor history. Did you like it?

Katie: Yes, but I, like Mamie in your tour, would have liked your imaginary tour to have included Georgia Burleson Hall and the girls' rooms. Maybe you could have imagined a conversation between Mamie and one of the girls living at Burleson; she could have talked about what it was like to live in Burleson, what the Baylor boys were like, and whether there were any boys who were not going to be ministers or lawyers, and just what it was like for women to go to Baylor in the early 1900s.

Pops: Maybe you could do some new research and rewrite this chapter someday, filling in all the gaps.

Katie: Maybe I will, Pops. I would like to know more about President Brooks first, since he was Baylor's president at the time of the tour.

CHAPTER 21

Samuel Palmer Brooks, a Primer

(President of Baylor, 1902-1931)

The chronicle of President Brooks is related to Frank Guittard's story because of three topics all developed in other chapters, namely, Frank's hire by President Samuel Palmer Brooks in 1902, Frank's role in early Baylor homecoming parades delegated to him by Brooks, and his involvement in both the creation and the demise of the Student Self-Government Experiment. Finn had shown an interest in President Brooks, perhaps because Brooks was at Baylor's helm when football was in trouble in the early 1900s.

Pops: Ready, Finn?

Finn: Yep. Brooks and Guittard sound a bit like Brady and Gronkowski. Frank joined Brooks at Baylor in Waco, and Gronkowski joined Brady in Tampa Bay with the Buccaneers. Did you see the Super Bowl yesterday against the Chiefs? Gronkowski made Brady look really good.

Pops: Yes, or Brady made Gronkowski look really good, and yes, Frank Guittard played a vital role in the Brooks's years at Baylor. The Brooks years are also necessary to an understanding of Frank's years at Baylor from 1902 on, especially through 1931, and what it must have been like to have been a member of Brooks's faculty. Samuel Palmer Brooks's administration (1902-1931) is a rich and diversified subject, and we are calling this chapter a primer, an inadequate one at that. A book devoted to Brooks's life & times is ninety years overdue.

Finn: What else you think we should know about President Brooks besides his connection to Frank Guittard?

Pops: Finn, the "what else" is what this entire chapter will be about, and it's going to take a while to cover it, so be prepared to ask any specific questions that come to mind. To begin with, I'm sure you will want to know the nitty-gritty of Brooks's style. Let's start with his speech to new first-year students, which will frame his style for us. Brooks had set speeches that he delivered to audiences on certain occasions. Incoming first-year students at Baylor would hear Brooks's set words of welcome, encouragement, advice, and gentle warnings along the lines of the remarks below, which he used in the fall of 1926. That year, Brooks, looking out over the sea of new faces, in a friendly but straight-from-the-shoulder manner, advised the newcomers:

> Members of the freshman class, were you sent to Baylor or did you come voluntarily? Do you regard yourself a freeman or a slave? Do you think of teachers as enemies or as friends? Do you expect to fritter away the years of your college life or to grow into men and women of merit and strength for service to the world? If you did not want to come and you will not work hard, then you ought to retire now. By all means do not register. If you did not want to come but are willing to try it out, then buckle down to the tasks assigned you. Work hard. Your reward will come. Everything and everybody are new. What if they are? You will get acquainted. You will make many everlasting friends—that is—if you are any account yourself. Your teachers will help you...They will not coddle you. They will be partners with you. They will not carry your loads for you. However, you may depend on them to the last ditch.
>
> Upper-class students are just folks. They did not know everything. Some of them are learning as fast as they can. Some who were freshmen last year are not with us this year. Brazos water, Baylor courses of study—something did not agree with them. The last year students who would not work are this year where the 'Whang doodle mourneth.'

That was most students' introduction to the tall figure with the bushy mustache.

Finn: Pops, I don't understand a couple things. Why is Mr. Brooks trying so hard to tell first-year students he wanted them to work hard? Wouldn't they know that anyway? And what's a "whang doodle?"

Pops: "Whang doodle"—I've never heard that before either. I think Brooks was trying to be funny while simultaneously being deadly serious; that was often his style. Brooks had good reason to impress students with the need to bear down in their studies. So few people went to college in those days, and many of the students who did go just used daddy's tuition and board money to goof off, have fun, and live it up. Then too, they could do things they weren't allowed to do back home with their parents breathing down their necks. Many students at some colleges came to hang out with their friends, stay up late, play card games, play golf or tennis, strum the banjo or mandolin, dance, go into town or on other excursions where they could party, drink beer, or kill time until they had to go back to work in their fathers' businesses.

Finn: So, what did President Brooks do when they goofed off or didn't obey the rules?

Pops: For starters, if a student was caught, it meant demerits. If what the student did was very serious, he or she would be invited not to return. I don't think Brooks liked the word "expel." And he would call them into his office and talk to them or write them or their parents letters. He seemed to prefer writing letters to face-to-face tongue lashings. Here are excerpts from a few of those letters:

January 2, 1923—"Dear Miss E: In...light of your many social duties as indicated in your record which I have, from November 29 to December 20 inclusive, wherein it is shown that you were out of town three days and withal had 22 dates, it does not appear that your social duties will allow you to do any studying, and you are therefore advised that you cannot enter the winter Quarter. This is final, and hope you will at once arrange your plans to this end. Very truly, President"

June 5, 1924—"Dear Mr. L: In conference with the Dean today, we have suspended you indefinitely from Baylor for your conduct. You hired a car downtown and had it charged to me, thus committing fraud which we cannot overlook. Surely you would not expect to remain in the school under these conditions. Very truly yours, President"

March 3, 1926—"Dear Miss M: I am embarrassed to give you this advice. In the first place you came into chapel this morning late, then haughtily walked with a radiant smile to your place, attracting a great deal of attention. I then observed that practically the whole time the man [speaker] was speaking, you were adjusting your hair or in some other ways beautifying your face. Somehow it was done in a way that attracted attention and girls all around were looking and smiling, causing considerable disorder...If I am wrong in any particular regarding this, bring this letter with you and come to see me. Yours sincerely, President"

And, finally, Brooks wrote this letter to help a student remember why his parents sent him to Baylor:

January 16, 1920—"Dear Mr. B: I have observed you now for many days around the campus, never with a book in your hand, but always with a girl close by...you are losing time, and ruining your prospects for doing the things you can do and ought to do and for which you are paying us money to have done. This is a suggestion as your friend. I have no criticism of the young men concerning the friendship of the young women or the converse, but it makes one a little weary to feel that a man can't study for bowing at the shrine of Venus."

Finn: Funny. He used a lot of words in those letters.

Pops: Brooks's letters of reprimand were always tactful to soften the blow. One student recalled that "he [Brooks] was never unduly unkind, but he apparently could say some things while smiling at the same time, that caused the guilty a great deal of discomfort." Sometimes letters were firm like those I just read and occasionally humorous like this one he wrote to the Pullman Company, which made sleeping cars for railroads: "December 30, 1925—Dear Sir: In some of the newest cars, when the berth is made up, the back of the seat that in the old cars, when raised, hung at an angle of about 45 degrees, now hangs substantially horizontal. I am 6 ft. 2 inches; weight around 240 lbs. and sleep on both pillows. When I do so I frequently bump my head on the headpiece in getting in the berth or getting out of it. This may bring a laugh to you, as it does to me when the bump is not hard, but I am wondering if you cannot tighten up a wire or insert a bolt or in some way bring that headpiece back to its former angle when fat men like myself can get in and out as formerly."

Pops: As long as we are on the subject of Brooks's size and physique, we'll stay on that and his physical appearance for a while longer. Pat Neff, who roomed with Brooks at Maggie Houston Hall, loved to talk about the way Brooks looked, especially when they were both students: "When he [Brooks] entered Baylor the thing of which he had the greatest pride was his long moustache. It had a double twist and he could touch his ears with it." You may think that Brooks's mustache in that era resembled that of those Mexican revolutionaries Francisco "Pancho" Villa or Emiliano Zapata, take your pick, but without the crossed cartridge belts and sombrero Villa was usually shown with. However, mustaches like that were popular with a lot of men.

Neff described how Brooks supposedly looked on his graduation day from Baylor: "It was a great day. I speak truthfully, Brooks owned that year just one suit of clothes. It was a long Prince Albert. And getting ready for graduation he had no money with which to buy another suit. He was paying 10 percent interest then for borrowed money. So a few days before graduation he decided he would have his Prince Albert dyed. It shrunk up. The arms of the coat and the pants leg struck him about his boot-tops, it was a sight for the gods...It became necessary for Brooks to patch the seat of his pants after he had them dyed. We just had one needle between us, one big thread that looked like what farmers sew sacks with. He patched his pants. He had to. When he showed me his deft and delicate work, I said, 'Brooks when you make your senior oration you be careful to stand still. Don't you move around on the platform or you will develop an embarrassing situation.' He stood still and was getting along nicely but he forgot his graduating oration. He was about two-thirds through and his oration left him. He stammered and stuttered and after a while said, 'Well, if I have it not in my head, I have it in my pocket,' and he went...and pulled out his manuscript to refresh his memory and went on."

Even though Brooks, who debated for the Philomathesian Literary Society, did not have a single decent suit in which to debate students with sharper creases in their pants, he nonetheless debated very well. Professor and Sociology Chair C. D. Johnson would observe three decades after Brooks's death that "Brooks never worried about his personal appearance. Neither was he one to be certain that his trousers were recently pressed, or that he was immaculately dressed...He once invited a group of students to a social gathering with 'just come in your old clothes. I'll be there, and you know how I'll be dressed.'"

Finally, Dr. Burleson presented Brooks with his diploma upon graduation and uttered an appropriate saying in Latin; Brooks, wearing his dyed, shrunken, and ill-fitting suit that he would later wear in New Haven, responded with, "*Accipio hoc diploma multis cum gratis.*" Finn, can you translate that?

<u>Finn</u>: I haven't taken Latin, but it sounds like "I accept this diploma with much gratitude"?

<u>Pops</u>: That's it. Speaking again of the suit Brooks wore at his graduation, Neff remarked, with evident admiration and some amusement, "As he delivered his graduating address, [wearing] a pair of pants that I had seen him patch with his own hands, a suit of clothes, old and faded...with that same suit of clothes, shrunk and threadbare, with no apologies to all this world, he entered Yale." Fine clothes were not affordable for Brooks when he was a student. When he entered Baylor's Academy years before he enrolled at Yale, other students made fun of him because of his general country appearance, which included a brass watch fob in the shape of a peanut. It did not make for a classy look.

<u>Finn</u>: (*smiling*) Maybe he liked eating peanuts like President Jimmy Carter. Wasn't Carter from Plains, Georgia?

<u>Pops</u>: Everyone loves eating peanuts; I do. Here are the bare-bones facts of Brooks's life before and after Baylor. Born in 1863 in Milledgeville, Georgia, Brooks was partially home-schooled by his parents. He dropped out of school to work as a section hand for the Santa Fe Railroad. Finn, do you know what a section hand did?

Finn: Not really.

Pops: A section hand's job was to maintain or build a particular section of railroad track. Neff said that Brooks shoveled dirt as a section hand. After that period, Brooks entered Baylor's Academy in Waco in 1885, working off and on, and finally graduating with a bachelor's degree from the collegiate division in 1893 when he was nearly thirty. He then enrolled at Yale as a senior and earned a second bachelor's degree in 1894, thus upgrading his bachelor's degree. He returned to Baylor to teach Latin and mathematics in 1897, and he was given charge of the newly created Department of Economics and History. He returned to Yale in 1901 for a master's degree, but his master's work was interrupted on April 17, 1902, or the day after, by a telegraph from Baylor's trustees telling him, "YOU HAVE BEEN ELECTED PRESIDENT OF BAYLOR UNIVERSITY. COME AT ONCE."

The telegram would have given Brooks a lot to think about. At the time, Baylor only had two buildings on its campus, with two more to be constructed. I am not counting the ramshackle Maggie Houston and Cowden Halls over a mile away, the Waco University leftovers. Baylor had 242 students of college grade and 518 students in the preparatory department. Of the twenty-nine members of the faculty, only five held a Ph.D. Except that Brooks saw a tremendous amount of potential for Baylor and was a graduate of Baylor with a deep feeling for the school, it was utterly problematic what action Baylor's trustees could have taken if Brooks had declined their offer. It was common knowledge that the last president, Oscar Cooper, had been run off by the student body's reaction to the unfortunate chapel incident.

Finn: Did Brooks have any other offers?

Pops: Not that I know of. Then, also, the terms "university" and "college" had no precise definitions and there was no impediment to calling a school a university regardless of the courses taught or the faculty's degrees. When Brooks accepted the trustees' offer, he was not taking the position of president at a recognized university. The term "university" as part of Baylor's name was more aspirational than real, and the use of the word "college" was thrown around loosely at the time by many small "colleges," including Baylor. If a Baylor student or graduate wanted to upgrade her educational credentials by seeking a bachelor's degree from an eastern university, the eastern university might only give a Baylor graduate three years credit for the four-year program and degree at Baylor. Brooks, still in his course work at Yale seeking his master's, knew he had his work cut out for him to improve Baylor's standing.

Back on campus for the trustees' meeting on April 21, San Jacinto Day, Brooks informed the meeting that he was so surprised he hardly knew how to reply except to say that he desired to do what was best for Baylor and needed time to think about his decision. Over the next several days, Brooks visited with various trustees regarding his decision, finally deciding "somewhat against my wishes and certainly against my judgment, that I ought to accept." On April 24, Brooks advised the trustees that although "he was overwhelmed with the magnitude of the work offered to him—and the grave responsibilities of the position...but accepted, with the clear, full understanding that he is to have the hearty cooperation of the Board and all parties in interest."

Once we get beyond those few facts, Brooks becomes more interesting, and we learn much more about the man and his vision for Baylor. Part of Brooks's appeal to Baylor students was that he believed in communicating with his students and ex-students. In communication, he manifested a caring and somewhat humorous personality coupled with a no-nonsense demeanor. He might also address the students on subjects that their parents had neglected to inform them, such as sex education. Professor Guy B. Harrison, Jr., in an oral history interview, claimed: "Once each year, we would have a big celebration in chapel, maybe several days in a row. And, women would always be excluded. We would take down our hair, you might say. And Dr. Brooks would counsel the boys about sex, life and about venereal diseases. In those days, no mother or father told their son or daughter about sex...You just had to go...get it [sex education] wherever you could. And usually it was something with the kids in school or out behind the barn or someplace like that. So we were tremendously benefited and excited considerably. This great man was standing there just like our father and counseled us, maybe 300 or 400 men in such intimate detail. Then after he finished up, the girls would be brought in to have their session. The deans of women and chaplain would give them serious lectures on sex...The University of Texas at this time did not give any such lectures."

He welcomed interaction with students and wrote a "President's Page" which was published from time to time. In one of those columns, he reported to the students: "One summer before graduating [Brooks's graduation from Baylor], President Burleson invited me to canvass for students at fifty dollars per month and expenses. I needed the money, and I accepted. He suggested I go by horseback. I bought a horse and saddle on credit. On sending in my first bill of expense and salary it was promptly paid. The trustees told the President to stop the expense of the student agent. I knew nothing of this. Dr. Burleson told me to 'go on and press the work.' This I did to the chagrin of the Trustees when I showed up in school the following fall with another bill for payment."

In another column, Brooks reported that: "I traveled over Johnson, my home county, and the adjoining counties. I was often charged seventy-five cents for staying all night at farmhouses where night overtook me. For this amount I was fed well, as was my horse. I often slept with the hired man in a shed room or the attic.

Sometimes from such a home students came to Baylor from my passionate appeal for the advantages of an education. Sometimes I was regarded as a sort of worthless peddler, was fed and bedded and gladly allowed to go my way next morning. As I look back upon my temerity, I am amazed. To tie one's horse to a fence, cross over and stop a farmer, and propose that he send his son or daughter to school seemed the limit to the farmer then and to me now. Yet some actually came from just such an appeal."

In addition to his canvassing for prospective Baylor students, Brooks traveled far and wide, giving speeches, including commencement addresses. Regarding those efforts, Brooks recorded: "In my time I have made many 'commencement addresses.' They have often been in rural schools, or at most railroad flag stops. One of my first such speeches was soon after I married. The principal of the school, a Baylor man, is now a prominent physician in a central Texas city. He took up a collection to pay the visiting orator. The amount was handed to me. It covered one dollar and seventy-five cents railroad fare and gave me a clear profit of thirty-five cents."

Finn, I will get to your question in just a minute, but I've somehow skipped over something that would be a roadmap to Brooks's presidency—his inaugural address. In his speech, he expressed the desire to "come into contact with every alumni, not only of Baylor University, but of Waco University and Baylor University at Independence." Brooks followed up his address with a letter to all the graduates of these three schools, now merged, to support the newly merged school. Brooks also requested graduates to send him brief biographical sketches of themselves to be published in a book. Thus, contact with ex-students from the beginning of his administration was central to Brooks's plan for Baylor. But Brooks especially wanted a record of the men who were the giants in Baylor's history, from the presidents and faculty at Independence to those at Waco University and Baylor at Waco.

By publishing such a record, Brooks hoped to develop a bank of information he could access to build friendly feelings for the alma mater. Those warm feelings could be tapped to build Baylor into a real university and not just more buildings and a more extensive faculty. Brooks dreamed of an institution supported by loyal alumni bound by their love of the university, its people, and traditions.

In his inaugural address, Brooks additionally pledged to honor the founders, requested alumni support, affirmed a desire to cooperate with other Baptist schools in Texas, promised to place greater emphasis on academics than on social life, and to develop a program of athletics consistent with the school's educational mission. He committed himself to addressing Baylor's needs for endowment, new dormitories, a girl's gymnasium, a law school, departmental expansion, summer sessions, and campus beautification. Above all, Brooks appealed for cooperation from Wacoans, Texans, and Baylor students, present and past, to join together in putting Baylor upon a sound and enduring foundation that would allow Baylor to continue going forward providing a Christian education. Brooks, as of the time of his death in 1931, had not only achieved all of the objectives cited in his inaugural address, but much more than he promised. Brooks provided the leadership needed to make a real university of Baylor, one that today rests on a solid financial foundation. Those additional accomplishments are detailed in *A Ph.D.'s Reverie: The Letters*, in the epilogue to that work.

Finn: What you've told us about Brooks really makes me wonder why no one has written his biography. There are biographies of the three founders, of R.C. Burleson, William Carey Crane, B.H. Carroll, Pat M. Neff, and A.J. Armstrong, but none of Brooks.

Pops: I don't know the answer, but that omission, along with his hire of Frank Guittard, is the reason this volume gives special treatment to President Brooks. Your great-grandfather Clarence, who knew both Brooks and Pat Neff, stated in 1940, "Frank had great respect and admiration for Brooks. Frank's family [members] visited Brooks's home. Brooks was warm and friendly. Brooks's persona was distinctly different from Neff's; Neff was prosecutorial, aggressive, and authoritarian. When Brooks chuckled, his stomach would shake. I thought Brooks was a great man at the time." Frank and Clarence's views of Brooks were based on Brooks's record of building a university without Rockefeller-sized gifts; the numerous testimonies as to Brooks's personality, character, and leadership; the loyalty he exhibited to his underpaid faculty; and his firm but tender-hearted interest in his students for almost three decades. And, yes, from time to time, Brooks had his detractors, but the only ones I could find after years of research were a few 1920s fundamentalists who read *Genesis* literally. We will talk about that later in the chapter on the evolution controversy at Baylor.

Finn: I don't get it when church people argue. I always thought people were supposed to get along at church.

Pops: Sometimes church is the place where people argue the most passionately. Now, we have to get into some heavy topics, and then we'll follow those up with some lighter ones.

CHAPTER 22

Mamie—Marriage, Family, & Sad Passing (1906-1917)

Today we will focus on Frank's first lasting romance and marriage to Mamie Welhausen of Shiner, a small town in south Texas, which resulted in three sons, two surviving: Francis and Clarence. Katie will help me sort through this part of the story—a chapter that will end in heartbreak.

Pops: Frank and Mamie met in 1898 when he assumed the position of principal at the Shiner School in Lavaca County; in September of that year, Mamie was not yet eighteen. They then said goodbye to each other in May 1899 when Frank left Shiner for Chicago to continue working on the bachelor's degree he had started at Baylor. In August 1902, after he finished his second degree at Chicago and had accepted President Brooks's offer to teach, Frank paid Mamie a visit in Shiner. She was then twenty-one, and he was thirty-five.

We don't know to what extent Frank and Mamie had been in contact between May 1899 and the visit three years later. We know they kept in touch, although we mostly have her letters rather than his. We also know he visited her on at least four Christmases between 1899 and 1904; however, we have no direct evidence of what they may have discussed that August or those Christmases, except certainly they talked about Frank's job as a college teacher and how much time he was spending cracking the books, getting ready to teach Prep classes. They likely also discussed what Mamie was reading for her classes, how she occupied her time when she wasn't studying, what her brothers and parents were doing, and what entertainments were available to residents of Lavaca County. Polka dancing in lederhosen? Eating strudel? Polishing off German sausage with German beer while listening to an accordionist play the "Rosamunde, Roll out the Barrel Polka"?

Katie: So, tell me about my great-great-grandmother, Mamie Welhausen Guittard. Do I look like her? Am I like her?

Pops: I don't know about looking like her; you look like your mother Katia to me. But, yes, you are very like Mamie in your love of reading. Here's what we know about her: Mamie Welhausen was the only daughter of Captain Charles Welhausen and Eliza Amsler. Captain Welhausen, a local banker and farmer, owned all or a substantial portion of Shiner National Bank. Mamie was attractive and well read, and she loved musical, literary, and other cultural entertainments. She and Frank were attracted to each other and married eight years after their initial meeting.

Katie: Pops, if they liked each other, why did they wait so long to get married? And did she go to college?

Pops: It took a while for them to get to know each other, and neither of them had finished their education when they met. Perhaps they had a mutual understanding about completing their educations first. We also know that marriage and family was always part of Frank's game plan, but he wanted to be in a better position financially before he asked Captain Welhausen for Mamie's hand. There's that ancient nursery rhyme which would not have been comforting to Frank: "Hark, Hark, the dogs do bark/ The beggars are coming to town/ Some in rags and some in tags/ And one in a velvet gown." Frank, at times, would have felt like a beggar in a velvet gown who was not prepared financially to get married. He had been pursuing his higher education, a bachelor's and then a master's degree, which he needed to secure a teaching position at a college or university. The money paid to an elementary school teacher was barely enough to pay for his room and board at a noisy boarding house. Mamie did have several other eligible young men in Shiner who were interested in her, but Frank and Mamie's mostly long-distance relationship persisted through Frank's years teaching in Magnolia, Arkansas, and his summers studying in Chicago.

Within a year after becoming principal of the Shiner School and having met Mamie, Frank purchased an endowment policy from the Security Trust and Life Insurance Company of Philadelphia, Pennsylvania. Although he had neither wife nor children and did not make enough money to support a wife, the policy must have been important to him psychologically. With a life insurance policy, he was no longer a penniless, struggling teacher or a beggar in a velvet gown but a struggling teacher whose life was insured. For a modest amount no doubt, but insured.

The earliest written communication discovered between Frank and Mamie is the following note, apparently composed in the same style as the notes he wrote to girls while teaching in Arkansas: "Miss Mamie, May I have the pleasure of taking you out to the rehearsal tonight? Respect. F.G. Guittard. May 13th, 1899." At the end of the school year, on June 15, 1899, he sent the following message to her: "Miss Mamie, as I shall say farewell to Shiner tomorrow, I would very much appreciate the pleasure of calling tonight. Sincerely, F.G. Guittard. June 15th, 1899." Frank was leaving to attend the summer session at the University of Chicago. He would return to Southwestern Academy at Magnolia, Arkansas—not to Shiner, Texas— to resume his teaching duties for another year. After that, he would return many times to Shiner, but never again to teach.

Katie: Why not to teach?

Pops: I'm not sure; maybe he was paid better in Arkansas and could save more for his college tuition at Chicago. Then Mamie, almost twenty-one years old and during the three years for which we have no correspondence between the two, took a trip with her father. Mamie and Captain Charlie Welhausen left from Galveston on the steamer Borkum for a three-month dream trip to Europe during the summer of 1901. Mamie kept a detailed shipboard diary touching on the highlights of whatever what going on around her. Frank also kept a diary for 1901, mentioning that summer only that he had gone to see the Buffalo Bill Wild West Show. Neither Mamie nor Frank mentioned the other in their diaries for that summer.

Mamie Welhausen's 1901 Shipboard Diary as Excerpted

Mamie refers to her father as either "Papa" or, in one place, "Captain Papa." The diary is a red cloth-bound volume inscribed in Mamie's hand. The following is a best-efforts transcription of her handwritten account of their twenty-four days on the steamer Borkum.

The trip began at 10:00 a.m. Monday, June 10, when Mamie and her father left their hotel in Galveston and traveled the short distance to the Galveston docks. There, Mamie and Papa boarded the steamer Borkum which set sail for Europe. After a rough trans-Atlantic voyage, especially difficult for Mamie, and a more pleasant tour of points in Europe, they boarded the SS Anchoria in Glasgow on September 1, heading to New York and ultimately home.

The reason for the trip is not stated in the diary, but it may have been Mamie's health and her father's desire to expose her to healthful sea breezes and a change of scene. Or the trip may represent a parent's gift to broaden her education, or a reward for her past studies, most recently at the state university. Or it may have been an early birthday present for Mamie, whose 21st birthday was October 11, 1901, occurring shortly after her return to Shiner.

The excerpts below have been selected because they reflect on Mamie's health during the trip. Most of the lighter, happier sections of her travel diary, of which there were many, have been deleted because they do not bear on Frank and Mamie's story.

Diary aboard the Steamer Borkum

Monday, June 10. At ten o'clock, we started from our hotel in Galveston, Texas, for our steamer "Borkum." On arriving at the docks where she lay at anchor, we boarded and were shown our staterooms where we deposited our luggage. We then took a survey of our surroundings. Workmen were loading freight: cotton bales, cottonsccd meal, and barrels containing different kinds of exports.

Tuesday, June 11. The sea was beautifully smooth with little ripping waves. We began to wonder why people complained of seasickness—surely it must be a delusion for could anyone ever feel better? Our food was wholesome, we were all in good spirits, and the day passed quickly and pleasantly.

Wednesday, June 12. I awoke this morning with a peculiar feeling of dizziness in my head. The air in my stateroom was heavy and oppressive. The night had been uncomfortably hot. I dressed quickly so as to go on deck and get fresh air. There were only a few out who sat around as if the last visage of happiness had fled forever. I sank in my chair, my head was whirling around like a cyclone. The waters were no longer rippling smoothly, but plunging, dashing, leaping, and soaring. The boat was tossing like a feather in the breeze. I found myself leaning over the railing and committing my troubles to the briney deep. I looked helplessly about me and there was some assurance at least to see everyone else in the same condition. The steward came around several times to suggest something to eat. I did not wish him any harm, but I am afraid my looks betrayed me. All that day I was wondering why I ever desired to leave home and take up such a journey.

Thursday, June 13. If you ever wish to know what seasickness is, I mean the genuine article, by all means go to sea and see for yourself. There are no words in any language that can ever give you the faintest idea. Well, today we felt better; we proceeded further to become acquainted with one another and found ourselves in an agreeable crowd. Yesterday if all the crowned royalty of Christendom had been sitting around, it would not have made the slightest difference to any of us.

Papa escaped being sick. I believe the only one on board. We got out our reading matter and sank in our steamer chairs with a peculiar feeling of resignation. Our appetites were reviving, and most of us went into the dining salon for meals. The waiters were polite. After supper, we all stayed on deck till late and used our vocal organs to our utmost possibilities.

Wednesday, June 19. Two of the officers Herr von Thulen and Mr. Praesent made a kite to fly to the amusement of those on deck. After soaring over the dark blue waves for a while, the string broke and it was buried in the sea. I have suffered all this day with a severe headache and could not join in any activity. We passed the Bermuda Islands but could not see land...

Thursday, June 20. Still a headache. Miss Anthony of F. Smith Ark. came in my cabin this early a.m. and read me the "Borkum Herald," a clever and witty sheet brought out by the intellectual ability of those on board, namely, Miss Anthony, Miss Courts, and Miss Punge. It was hugely enjoyed, and we tender our deepest respects and thanks to these bright young ladies...

Friday, June 21. This is the day of all the days for me. After a restless night, I awoke and found myself frightfully ill. A regular Texas Norther was blowing and we attired ourselves just as we do at home on a cold December day. I never wore such clothes in the middle of June before. At about ten, I had a chill, after which I was thrown into a burning fever. To be at home under such conditions would be far from pleasant but in a two by four state cabin and the boat straying like a feather! Papa spent most of the day with me, but I know that day was two weeks long.

Saturday, June 22. I feel some better today but as dull as a rail after such a siege as yesterday. I take my meals in the dining room and try my utmost to appear cheerful, but my spirits are far from being in the highlands. My head is as large as a washtub. I cannot read a line. The Doctor took us into his cabin and showed us his maps...Papa bought me a bottle of champagne to drink. Think of me resorting to anything of that sort.

Sunday, June 23. At the dinner table I feel suddenly very cold, it is that dreadful chill again. I go to bed and shake for an hour and a half, after which I am thrown into a violent fever that lasts all afternoon and night. I feel like my fever is at the highest possible point and am frightfully agitated. Papa reads four chapters from the Bible to soothe my inmost feelings.

Monday, June 24. My temples are still throbbing violently as if to keep time to hum of the machinery; my head is about to burst. My spirits are at lowest tide. I cannot sleep, the passengers seem to be holding a 'Dutch Concert.' I feel as if I am a victim of insanity and spend a most horrible day which seems a year in duration. My fever is slight, but my pulse is violent. Faces of my home people rise before me until I am quite confused, and I can see them in all attitudes and positions. Papa is always beside me, seems very much worried while I feel strangely helpless and forsaken. I can eat nothing though I have tried ever so hard. My senses are dulled by quinine.

Tuesday, June 25. I awoke this morning and find myself very weak but much improved. The breakfast is somewhat palatable. I go on deck at about twelve and sit around weak and helpless. Two whales were seen at a distance while I was still in my cabin…

Wednesday, June 26. I feel much improved in health. It is colder on deck than it has been heretofore. Very few people are out, and nearly every person on board has contracted a cold. Papa, having failed to take his overcoat as we had suggested, is almost frozen to death. Nearly everyone remains in their cabins. We had Boston Baked Beans and Bacon for lunch at 12, which was something new…Papa makes a comical picture with two coats on under one projecting about four inches. This would be one of our coldest winter days.

> *Mamie's diary entries continue until they ceased after July 28, whether because the author's copy did not contain the full diary or some other reason. We know that she and Captain Papa remained abroad, somewhere in Europe, from July 28 until September 1, when they boarded the SS Anchoria in Glasgow for New York, where they then could take passage on a ship to Galveston.*

Katie: Pops, what do we know about Frank and Mamie's courtship? When did it become serious? Did they both write letters to each other?

Pops: We don't know when Frank began courting Mamie seriously. However, the correspondence establishes that it started well before his visit to Shiner in August 1902 after he had accepted a full-time position as an instructor in Baylor's Academy. Since they were interested in each other and Frank was courting her, it may be interesting to consider what Frank may have been reading in advance of that special trip to Shiner that may have provided topics for conversation after the customary topics had been exhausted. Yes, he was a professor of history and read for his living as well as for pleasure, but what could he and Mamie talk about that wouldn't put her to sleep? Or if Frank already had a concern about Mamie's health, he may have felt he needed to entertain her or lift her spirits.

Katie: I would like to know what they could have talked about on their dates.

Pops: (*looking at a copy of an August 1902 issue of the Literary Digest*) Well, let's see what possible topics he could have used to load his conversation tool belt for their first get-together after he returned from Chicago with two degrees. Perhaps you will remember he had primed himself to talk about certain popular romantic novels of the day when he was spending afternoons with Sallie Canon sixteen years previously. Mamie was a completely different person, older than Sallie, better read and more sophisticated, with more formal education, perhaps a college degree. Mamie, too, was interested in serious subjects such as politics, literature, and music, not in discussing those popular romantic novels Sallie liked. Assuming Frank had a copy of this issue, for example, there are twelve listed topics of the day—maybe Frank thought as he glanced over this issue, *I might ask her how long she thinks the coal strike will last? How about Kaiser William's proposal to decorate three hundred Americans for entertaining Prince Henry on his trip to the US? Or his offer to send a statue of Frederick the Great to Washington? Hmm, I wonder if she thinks Dr. A.F.A. King's suggestion of using darkness to cure malaria sounds promising. Here's an article about alcoholism in children—wonder what Mamie might think of the case for congenital and hereditary alcoholism in children, whether breastfeeding from an alcoholic mother results in an alcoholic newborn?*

If all of those topics in the *Digest* would have been too heavy or pedantic, Frank could always lighten it up by remarking on the inspiring poem in the issue by Edwin Markham, "Freedom," with its references to bluebirds, wild birds, Leonidas, and Lexington. Then Frank might have been thinking about some ads at the back of the *Digest* which might be good for a laugh—*Here's an ad for a "Sanitary Still which will make the foulest water palatable and absolutely pure, no germs lurking"; not sure how that would work though; the ad doesn't say, just wants people to send for a booklet. Or this ad might draw a smile from Mamie—Dr. Deimel's Underwear—"cool, porous, ventilating"—"Wearers of ordinary underclothing cannot appreciate what real comfort means during summer."* There were certainly a lot of potential conversation starters there for Frank, and that's not covering the articles under the categories of Letters and Art, The Religious World, or Foreign Topics.

The first preserved letter to Frank from Mamie, who was thirteen years younger than Frank and sick with fever at the time, shows their relationship in 1902 was already advanced in terms of feeling and commitment:

> My dear Sweetheart, Your visit seems like an entrancing dream. I cannot realize that it is really true that I have seen you. The short time you were here was the happiest I have ever known. I was unconscious of all pain. I did not know that I was sick. Dearest Sweetheart, I don't see how I could love you any more, there never could be another man who I could love even one little portion as much as I do you…
>
> I am feeling better since you were here if I could only lose that dreadful fever, it nearly burned me up today, though the weather has been decidedly cooler…I know I shall be well soon I will do everything to get cured as speedily as possible. There is nothing like

> perfect health; about eight months ago, I felt as if I never could be sick again; I wish I felt like that now.
>
> The doctor will not frighten me again. I should not have been so foolish in the first place. Do you know my voice was clearer while you were here than any other time? (MW letter to FGG, September 1, 1902)

Katie: Did Mamie ever say what she needed a cure for?

Pops: She didn't. But her obvious concern about her health was a theme that comes up again and again in her letters, along with her feelings for Frank and hopes for the future. Mamie's September 1 letter to Frank following their meeting in August continues: "Dear Frank, You don't know how handsome you have grown, you were always fine-looking, but now you couldn't be handsomer...How proud I am of you. I am the happiest girl in all the world tonight. With truest love, Mamie"

Pops: The year following Frank's visit, Mamie, who was not well at the time and was living at a boarding house in Corpus Christi, would write a letter suggesting she feared her health issues would cloud their future:

> My darling Frank, I am just recovering from the blow of your departure. All day yesterday, my feelings were strangely depressed, but my spirits are on the ascend today. I am so happy as it is possible, I suppose, for we mortals to be; still, I feel a strange sadness which I cannot fully explain. It is a longing to reach the perfect, to rise above my surroundings into a higher sphere, mentally, morally and spiritually advanced from the one in which I live...
>
> I have been with the poor sick woman most of the time since you went away. I believe I never saw so sad a case—yet there are conditions like this which confronts us each day and everywhere. Life has so much in store for me, and I am so happy that I feel anything I could do for her would not be enough. The doctor warns me to keep away, but I feel confident I will not experience any harm, I don't think I am running much risk, for I am so improved...
>
> I am afraid I can't enjoy anything thoroughly without you, my dear. There was a time when such things were possible, but now, when I am to indulge in merriment, my thoughts turn to you, and then a longing for your presence takes possession of my soul.
>
> The moonlight was not half so entrancing last night. I sat on the porch upstairs and while I looked over the beautiful moonlit bay, I lived the past week over again. I wondered if we would always be so

> happy as we were the night before when we were down on the beach [Corpus Christi] and with our arms around each other looked into the future so bright—so full of promise, hope, and aspirations. With many kisses from your devoted, Mamie. (MW letter to FGG, June 8, 1903)

Pops: It is unfortunate that, although the risk of contracting tuberculosis through close contact with an infected person had been understood for three decades by the best-informed physicians in 1917—the year of Mamie's death, its means of transmission was not clearly understood by the public. There was no mass media, no internet. The general public did not fully understand how important it was to avoid catching it from another person's coughs and sneezes or that repeated or extended exposures to a sick person increased the risk dramatically. *The (Old) Farmer's Almanac of 1890* pointed out to its readers that "worth knowing—Consumption. [According to medical doctors in New York] tuberculosis is a distinctly preventable disease; ...it is not directly inherited; it is acquired by the direct transmission of the tubercle bacilli from the sick to the healthy, usually by means of the dried and pulverized sputum floating as dust in the air." That warning does seem clear enough if Mamie or her parents had been thinking about it.

Katie: Did Mamie have tuberculosis in 1903 when she wrote that letter to Frank? I understand her death was not until fourteen years later. Was she concerned she might have it? Was Frank concerned?

Pops: Possibly yes to both questions because of the tendency of the disease often to continue over a long period before resulting in death; we will talk about this tendency in another chapter. Mamie was an intelligent woman and may have been fully or partially aware of the seriousness of her condition. No doubt she did not want to believe she had an incurable disease, especially when she was in love and the best part of her life was just beginning.

Frank, too, would not have wanted to believe Mamie had tuberculosis, both because he loved Mamie and because it had taken him a long time to reach this point with his career in place and marriage a real possibility. Frank was progressing steadily at Baylor, and in 1904 he was promoted to the college department where he was elected Instructor of History and Political Science at an annual salary of $1,100, his future at Baylor all but assured. Moreover, Frank's superior, Professor Robert Hamilton, who had been a popular professor, had fortuitously resigned to enter law school. Professionally, Frank's path forward was clear. The best explanation for Frank waiting to get married is that he was saving his money to purchase a house. He did not want to return from a honeymoon and be obliged to carry his bride over the threshold of a Waco boarding house.

Frank received occasional inquiries from friends and faculty members asking when the wedding was going to take place and why he didn't go ahead and get married. Considering that Mamie was usually living hundreds of miles away in Corpus Christi or Austin, possibly socializing with other admirers for a prolonged period, Frank must have been frustrated with the time needed to prepare financially for marriage and anxious because of the distance between them. Mamie would write from Shiner shortly after his promotion:

> My dearest Frank, What can I say to you to take that disconsolate tone from your letters, Sweetheart? I believe you have the "blues" and need a little petting and caressing. Now, if you were here, it would be so much easier to do, but as you are so far out of reach, I'll just have to talk in a long distant way...
>
> Why, from the tone of your letter one would almost think I didn't love you any longer and that surely couldn't be possible. No, I think you need petting, as I said before, and I assure you I am more than willing to do it, just as much as you can endure until you are ready to defend yourself in almost any old way.
>
> Have you had any professional worries? I believe a man needs more sympathy then than at any other time. The fact is I have been out of sorts myself this week for two days. I suffered with a sick headache until I became desperate and took a dose of morphine. Immediately sank into a deep heavy sleep, but as soon as I lost consciousness, I would dream of you. Of course, I like to dream of you pleasantly, but I had such awful vision of you in such agony and distress that I would awaken with a start, then go back to sleep and dream it all over. It was a relief today at noon when your letter came; I could not shake the influence of my bad dreams...
>
> Now, my dear boy, lay aside those foolish fears and don't let anything ever allow you to mistrust my love even for a minute. I am sure this letter wouldn't take a place among the classics in literature, but sweetheart, I've been on my feet all day and am so sleepy that I can't do any better—the idea of writing like this to a professor, well good night and kiss from Mamie (Letter MW to FGG, April 28, 1904)

In July, Mamie stayed home from a summer baseball game in Shiner to write Frank a long letter.

> [Dear Frank] Everybody has gone to the baseball game to be played between Shiner and Houston but some way I couldn't create

> enough enthusiasm to be a witness on the grandstand. From appearances, the whole town is out—even Mama went, and she has been ill in bed for three or four days. Peck [one of Mamie's brothers] thinks I must be hopelessly stupid not to take more interest in the matter, but there are so many games to pass within the next few weeks that I may be able to redeem myself in my athletically inclined brother's eyes...
>
> I thought I would make some fancy work for our church bazaar and incidentally a little for our future home, but my eyes failed me in my purpose, and I had to give it up. They have not yet recovered entirely from the mumps. I don't want our home to look like a boarding house or an abiding place. Pretty dainty things are so cheerful and homelike in a house, and when made by oneself and one's friends, they are actually a part of a home...
>
> [Regarding the characteristics of a good housekeeper] I think a well-rounded mind and a sunny temperament are requisite. A happy heart and a sense of humor are greater pearls than fine china and costly furnishings. Then a woman should have a practical knowledge of household duties and have house-keeping reduced to an artistic science. If there is anyone who is in need of a scientific knowledge, it is certainly a housekeeper...
>
> I certainly didn't mean to give you a page from a woman's magazine, but I was in several homes in the neighborhood last week that put me in a thinking frame of mind along these lines...Well, the baseball game is ended. I see some buggies passing. I wonder who was champion. Ah. I hear the Shiner boys cheering and being cheered, they must be the victors. I feel just as well in having talked with you. With love from Mamie (MW letter to FGG, July 20, 1904)

In the next letter, Mamie, then taking courses in Austin or teaching, touched on familiar themes of missing Frank and the prospects of their future life together as a married couple:

> I am afraid Sweetheart some of these days I won't be able to get along at all without you. Isn't that rather serious? It is going to be awfully hard to live up to the standard on which you have placed me, in fact, I will never, never be able to do it. Sweetheart, please do not think I am better than other girls because I have all their frailties and shortcomings. But it is going to be such a sweet pleasure

> in trying to be in some ways just what my precious sweetheart thinks I am...
>
> Some way a picture will come to my mind this afternoon as I look out into the muddy street of a bright, cozy home which we are going to share together. It is going to be so full of sunshine and happiness, for how could it be otherwise if you are there? How delightful to think that we are young and have the future before us, our plans still to carry out. I often wonder if there is going to be anything to mar the beautiful home we are going to have. I am going to try to be reasonable and not be jealous of those books, and I know you will always be reasonable. You are going to let me study with you, aren't you? We will have the same interests and pleasures and then we always grow nearer to one another. Sometimes a husband and wife live in entirely different atmospheres and then they cannot be happy...
>
> I have learned the new piece and were you here I would promptly make you listen to it. You are going to expect me to do the impossible in music I fear, from the anticipations you expressed. Well it is still raining but the skies are clearer...With fondest love & kisses, Mamie (MW letter to FGG October 24, 1904)

Frank, after returning from a visit to Mamie in Austin, wrote of his feelings and experiences since the conclusion of their last visit:

> My Darling Sweetheart, I have just come back from my dinner and will take a little time to be with you again. But I have been with you, or you have been with me most of the time since I left you...More than ever before, I feel like asking the richest blessings to rest upon you for your devoted love. We will do all we can to keep our love pure and true and tender—won't we, Sweetheart? I imagine you have arrived home by this time and are in a glow of happiness to be with those who love you.
>
> I made a fine reputation as a sprinter the night I left Austin. I had plenty of time after leaving you to get to the station under ordinary circumstances but had to wait for a car for some time when we came to the turn at the capitol. The conductor informed me he had to wait for another car to pass. I looked down the street—no car in sight, my watch told me I had five minutes to train time, without further ado I hopped off that car and then is when I made my reputation. I momentarily expected to hear a policeman cry out, "Halt there!" thinking I might be a fugitive from justice, but I had

> the 'right of way,' got my traps [luggage] at the hotel, and arrived just in time to board the train.
>
> As I was passing down the side of the station, several friendly voices cried, 'You'll have to hurry.' I thought was doing a pretty good job of it. When I got to a seat, I was somewhat out of breath but feeling triumphant. It began to rain soon after leaving Austin, and I think it kept up all the way. I had no trouble going to sleep after that exercise. So after all there was some compensation for it. Today I am feeling finely, classes did well...
>
> Mamie, my Love, though others may love you, yet no one can love you more than I do. I shall eagerly look for your letter. With a loving kiss, Frank (FGG letter to MW April 25, 1905)

In Frank's following letter, he reported on the party he had attended in Waco that he had not really enjoyed:

> I went to a party last night. I was victimized to a certain extent and felt like a real martyr. When I arrived at the young lady's house for whom I was going to do the gallant thing, I was informed that it was to be a phantom party. It was a very warm evening, yet she and her married sister proceeded to envelop me in a sheet, mask and white cap until I looked like a real Ku Klux. Four of us costumed in this style proceeded along the street to the rendezvous of the other phantoms. The most agreeable part about the whole thing was when the time came to unmask and get out to the fresh air, for it was, as I said, a warm night, and any additional clothing made it double so.
>
> Some athletic news: Baylor beat University of Missouri 8 to 5 after that team had beaten the State and Georgetown...We will not meet our classes tomorrow morning on account of the death of Judge Scarborough who was one of the Trustees of the University. (FGG letter to MW May 7, 1905)

Frank's next letter provides a glimpse of the pressures in his new role in the college department at Baylor teaching multiple courses. It also addresses the condition of their relationship, his concern that he not get edged out with Mamie where other suitors are concerned, Mamie's choice of profession, and what they might do for entertainment on his next visit. The letter also suggests a basis for believing that any delay in agreeing on a definite date for marriage had to do with his not feeling as confident with his teaching position as he desired to be. A large plate for one letter:

This had been the most arduous year of teaching I have experienced. I have not missed a single recitation nor been sick a day. I have had to know thoroughly what was in the four thousand pages of textbooks I have studied, besides other collateral study that was necessary. It was a crucial year. I was not overly confident to begin with but knew that if persistence and determination counted for anything, I was ready. I believe I would almost as lief have died as failed in my work, for there has not been a day that I have not thought of you, Sweetheart. I believe that had I not made a success of my work that it would have been my last year as a teacher and I would have tried to obliterate myself from the memory of all my friends and as for you, my darling sweetheart—well, it would have been inexpressible, for I know a girl does not want to have anything to do with a failure. Your love and interest in my success has been my greatest inspiration.

As to losing patience with you, Dear, for letting me know that you are not made of stone and iron, there isn't the least danger for you have been a dear brave girl more than enough times to make up for all the rest if any making up were needed. The only feeling I have ever had when I knew you were in trouble or in low spirits was a great longing to be of some comfort to you in some way.

I would like to be your visitor Mamie but I don't care very much about being one of many. I am a believer in monopolies to a considerable extent. It is not quite right in some respects, but then can you blame me when I see you as little as I do for wanting to be with you as much as possible on those short, sweet visits?

I hope, Sweetheart, you haven't the remotest idea of teaching that school. One teacher in our family will be enough, don't you think so? Yet it was kind of you to make the offer. I am becoming very rapidly a complete convert to the club idea, that is the ladies' clubs. I was the guest of one of them last week and this week enjoyed the hospitality and an intellectual treat at the hands of the Shakespeare club. The intellectual part consisted of a debate on the question: "Resolved that Falstaff was a coward." Poor old Falstaff, fat old Falstaff was pretty well dissected.

When I get through with those examinations, I will feel like taking a holiday in good earnest. I shall be ready for almost any kind of diversion when I come to see you, fishing, picnicking, tennis, circus, nigger camp meeting, or whatever may come along. But the sole source of pleasure will be that I may be with you. You know I do not care for parties when I come to see you; I like them well

> enough and we have had an average of one or two a week for the past two months, but then I feel like we make a very good, in fact an excellent party ourselves.
>
> You will think I am becoming garrulous if I don't condense my letter more.
>
> Devotedly, Frank (FGG letter to MW, May 25, 1905)

Mamie, who was anticipating Frank's next visit, responded to his recent letters, which had been both passionate and insecure, commenting:

> I am so glad that the time for your visit is drawing near. I can hardly await the time even though the days fly by like magic. I am sorry your work has crowded up and been heavy these warm rainy days. I feel sure that was hard enough without those gloomy thoughts of which you wrote. I hope you will not drift into such unreasonable conjectures again for you are generally in a very happy mood...
>
> There is not an hour of the day that my mind does not unconsciously wander to you and I am with you in spirit if not in reality. The more I am with other men, the more I realize that I love only you, and that you are my standard of manhood which no one else could ever attain. In other words, I love you with my whole heart and life, and always will. It is hard to have you always away, and it is natural that I should learn to miss you more were you always near, still you are all essential to my happiness whether I see you every day or only five or six times a year...Lovingly, Devotedly, Mamie (MW letter to FGG May 26, 1905)

Frank attended the summer session for 1905 at the University of Chicago, though he had already received his master's degree. Possibly Frank had embarked on initial efforts to obtain a Ph.D. There is no record indicating his specific plan, but since he always tended to have one, the best conclusion is that he was taking post-graduate work to advance his standing at Baylor. (FGG diary entry for summer 1905)

Frank and Mamie's correspondence that summer shows the difficulty of maintaining a long-distance relationship by mail. Frank, who was under pressure to bring the matter with Mamie to a conclusion by agreeing to a date, was also subject to emotional swings up or down, depending on his interpretation of Mamie's letters on any particular day. When from one of her letters he had wondered whether she regretted their plan to be married, she pointed out:

> You know yourself dear, how differently things sound when they stare at one from a written page, and it never occurred to me once that you would regard it from any other standpoint than from the spirit in which it was written...
>
> After all, there is still this consolation, if we had been together, it never should have occurred. Unpleasant things are never with us when we are not parted as we usually are. It is the inevitable fact that all our intercourse must be made through the medium of a pen, and that the mistakes always originate with me...Lovingly and devotedly, Mamie (MW letter to FGG, August 17, 1905)

Frank's next letter from Chicago shows that Mamie's letter repaired whatever hurt feelings Frank had experienced. It may also indicate that Frank was not the only one under pressure, but also Mamie because of the loftiness with which her fiancée viewed her feminine qualities. Frank wrote Mamie that his feeling of being hurt only lasted a couple of days but were now all over. Further, that:

> You must not think for a moment, my Love, that you are not worthy of my love. You are a queen among women, endowed with all the womanly traits which a man loves and admires. People will misunderstand each other sometimes, and no one is responsible for it, and lovers are probably more prone to do so than other people because they are so jealous of anything that affects their love...

Frank closed this letter with a lament about his waistline:

> I am feeling about 15 or 20% better than when I came here if such matters can be reduced to mathematical calculations. I have developed a suspicious tendency to get fat. There is nothing I would so despise [as] to become as a 'fat man.' However, I have managed to keep my weight at about the same point as when I came...With devoted love, Frank (FGG to MW, August 21, 1905)

In all likelihood, Mamie's friends were counseling her to get married, either to Frank or to one of her other visitors to the Welhausen home in Shiner, i.e., the male competition that concerned Frank. One of her female friends had written her that she had almost concluded that it didn't matter who the man was that went to make up the happiness of a woman's life—just so he wasn't absolutely disagreeable. Another advised her that it was so foolish to let any man know she depended on him for her happiness. However, Mamie continued to feel that the professor from Waco was essential to her happiness and told him so over and over, but occasionally she would need reassurance and would voice her questions to Frank: "Sometimes I wonder if anything could ever estrange us and then I entertain all kinds of gloomy thoughts that I have to banish from me." (MW letter to FGG, October 5, 1905)

As Christmas approached, Mamie's happier thoughts anticipated their time together. Mamie wrote Frank the week before Christmas:

> Next Sunday afternoon at this time you will be with me. I cannot half realize that this can be true. I hope this will be the happiest Christmas we have spent together. I have selfishly wished all friends would postpone their visits until after the holidays. I don't see how I can divide my time when you are here, dear...How many Christmases have we spent together? I believe this is about the fourth. It seems as though we have known each other forever. I am looking forward to the time when we shall spend many more happy times together—in our own home. (MW letter to FGG December 17, 1905)

Frank and Mamie repeatedly returned to certain themes in their letters. Chief among them were the different health issues they were experiencing, especially Mamie's. Mamie wrote Frank:

> I am so very sorry you have been sick and I wish I could do something for you. I know it is a dreadful calamity for a person whose health is so unusually good to have a siege of illness. Those fever blisters seem to denote something more than a cold, and they are such a disagreeable thing. Well, I hope by this time that you are your own sweet self again, just like you always are when you are with me.
>
> I am in a position to sympathize with you very keenly, for I have just had a like experience. Just a few days before Easter I was seized with a cold which made me think –'Life was surely, but a galling load.' I couldn't talk except in the worse squeaking voice imaginable and I barked all day long and half the night. I had boasted so much of my perfect health that I was ashamed to confess that I was feeling miserable and this made matters worse. I am still not altogether recovered, but I am enjoying life as well as ever. I expected it to last several months by the severity with which I was seized, but it didn't take long for it to pass away, which proves that my general health is all right. And I am sure you will recover just as speedily because you are well and strong as a rule...

> Our Sunday school is just out, and I am writing this before noon. The preacher gave me a very unkind glance when I left the church but I didn't want to hear him preach and that was all there is to it... (MW letter to FGG, April 22, 1906)

Another frequent topic of Frank and Mamie's letters was what it took to make a happy home and what they—especially Mamie—thought was essential for that purpose. Neither were fond of boarding houses or hotels. Frank had lived in boarding places for almost twenty years [1886-1906], and Mamie occasionally had to live in a rooming or boarding house when she was not living at her parents' home in Shiner. Mamie wrote Frank concerning a young friend who had just married:

> I sent her a cut glass water set which might be pretty enough, but I fear it is not altogether appropriate since the young people do not intend to have a home. Isn't it strange that so many married people prefer a horrid old boarding house to the sweet atmosphere of a home? J___ tells us that the time is coming when the individual home will pass away. I hope that will not take place in our time and generation, don't you, dear? I should be wretched if I couldn't have a home to claim my time and attention, for it would seem such an aimless kind of existence to be wandering about in eating houses.
>
> I hope the landladies will not be too good to you so that you will never feel like you want to go back to the boarding house. I am going to do all I can, Dear, to make our home just such a place as you would desire it to be, and then you will not long for a return to the boarding house. (MW letter to FGG, April 22, 1906)

In June 1906, six months before his marriage to Mamie in December, Frank purchased a house at 1401 South 7th in Waco for $2,500. It had probably taken years to raise the funds for a down payment considering his salary was only $1,200 annually after a raise in April. The house was one or two blocks from the Baylor campus. Frank always knew that starting married life with Mamie in a rooming house would be a non-starter, nor did he want to live in one himself, especially with a new bride used to living in a large house. Whatever his own feelings were about buying a house versus leasing one, he would write Clarence and Mary Lou almost forty years later:

> You are due congratulations on the purchase of your first home property. All things taken into consideration, I think you made a good purchase. When I planned to give up single life, I was told that it was more economical to rent than to purchase, but I

> considered that the money consideration was not the only matter of importance to be taken into consideration. The feeling of security, the consciousness that you are at night sleeping on your own individual portion of the earth's surface is worth more than can be estimated in dollars and cents. (FGG letter to CAG and MLG, September 10, 1945)

Now that Frank had bought a house within walking distance of the Baylor campus, it was clear to the outside world that a marriage between Frank and Mamie would soon take place. The timing of the purchase of the house was advantageous, as Mamie would advise in her next letter that "I have just heard of a plot to break up our engagement by some meddlesome married parties." Such "married parties," likely Welhausen friends and neighbors in Shiner, probably thought, after so many years, that Mamie's marriage to Frank was a fantasy destined never to become real, and they were concerned that she would miss other opportunities for marriage and family. Mamie also advised:

> Sweetheart, you can't imagine how I long to be with you when you tell me about the little home and your living there alone until I come. I wish I could just walk in and find you sitting there at work at your desk. You should be called upon to surrender your labor immediately for a little while, and I would not be satisfied with a formal greeting either.
>
> Frank dear, you will just have to let me love you all I want to when we are married, for I shall be wishing to be near you and pet you whenever I can, but I shall not be unreasonable and interfere with those histories, economics, and examination papers. (MW letter to FGG, July 22, 1906)

As the Christmas season and the time of their marriage approached, Frank and Mamie continued to process their plans, questions, joys, and doubts. The fact that Frank and Mamie, because of Frank's schedule, did not see each other for the entire summer caused a ripple in their relationship. Mamie, however, smoothed things over, commenting: "That Baylor man who went to visit his sweetheart twice only before the wedding could never have been my sweetheart so his case will admit of no comparisons with ours."

Then, some inevitable tension in their relationship surfaced on Frank's side because of his concern that he not be expected to keep his wife in the style to which she was accustomed, being the daughter of the owner of a bank. Mamie wrote Frank:

> Sweetheart, I don't want you to think you are going to marry a foppish woman who is unreasonable—incapable of understanding a situation. A woman ruled by petty whim and small prejudices. Neither do I expect, Frank, that you will give me all the devotion of your life that I be surrounded with every luxury and comfort and have you only a 'machine' to my wishes without giving anything in return. I want to do all for your happiness that lies in my life to give you—every comfort we shall have will please me in that you are there to enjoy it with me. Everything that I can do to make our home complete will be my greatest effort—I do not want you to do it all for then I could not be happy.
>
> And Sweetheart I shall never want to hear you say anything more about 'amassing property for' my satisfaction. I realize I am not going to have a rich husband; therefore, he will have to love me all the more, and that is just what I want him to do. What are riches anyway if they are not of the heart? Sweetheart I have no worldly possessions to give you, all I have is the pure love of an honest heart. (MW letter to FGG, September 28, 1906)

Katie: Frank seems to have been very close-mouthed about his relationships with Mamie and other women he dated. Did Baylor students ever know what was going on?

Pops: Yes, he kept the subject close to his vest, but his students eventually caught on. Baylor students and faculty alike noted with interest, approval, and amusement that the very proper history professor had a special girlfriend he visited by train on weekends. The *Lariat* reported, date unknown, "Prof. Guittard made a rather suspicious trip somewhere last Friday, returning Monday. He refuses to disclose the place he visited, but it is rumored that it must have been Corpus Christi." The *Lariat* also rumored that gossip had it that he was a candidate for marriage. (*Lariat*, October 10, 1903)

Katie: I have a lot of questions for you. When did Frank first meet Mamie's father? Did they like each other? Did Frank ask him for his daughter's hand in marriage? If so, when? What was Frank's relationship with Mamie's mother? Did he get along with her brothers? And what was the Welhausen family's reaction to Mamie's decision to marry a college professor?

Pops: Taking that last question first, Captain Charles Welhausen was board chair of the Shiner school, which hired Frank as principal for the 1898-99 school year. He was also active in politics and successfully ran for state legislator in 1888.

He was favorably disposed toward Frank, even though Frank did not yet have his bachelor's degree and had only started at the University of Chicago. When Frank was hired in Shiner, Mamie was not quite eighteen and likely had not had any education beyond high school. From all accounts, Frank got on well with Mamie's parents and with her older brothers C.B. (Charles Bismarck), Philip, and Herbert "Peck." C.B. Welhausen was born one week after the end of the Franco-Prussian War in which the Prussians, under Count Otto von Bismarck, defeated the French and annexed Alsace-Lorraine, the home of Frank's father and grandparents. Obviously, the Welhausens admired Count von Bismarck for winning the war, which was disastrous for the French. Philip and Peck would eventually manage Mamie's assets for the benefit of Francis and Clarence. Mamie's mother, Eliza Amsler Welhausen, was also appreciative of her son-in-law.

Frank had to be impressed by Captain Welhausen's career as a soldier, farmer, saddler, rancher, businessman, justice of the peace, county commissioner, and state legislator, along with his success as a banker. Captain Welhausen had emigrated from Hanover, Germany, to the US at eight years of age and grew up in Cat Spring in Austin County, moving to Fayette County to open a saddle shop in 1856 when he was twenty-one. The experience of Frank's father as an immigrant would have resonated with Captain Welhausen, as Francis Joseph Guittard had emigrated from Alsace to the US less than ten years before. That France and Germany fought each other in the Franco-Prussian war in 1870 with Germany annexing Alsace was not a problem in Frank and Captain Welhausen's relationship. Both the Guittards and the Welhausens moved to the US from France and Germany, respectively, for opportunity and personal freedom. Of course, everyone was now an American.

Another subject possibly not raised was the Guittard affiliation with the Union cause in the Civil War, whereas Captain Welhausen served as a Confederate battery officer with Speight's Battalion. Frank's home of Ohio was a hub of abolitionist sentiment, and many important Union generals called Ohio home. The topics of the Underground Railroad and slave catchers in Ohio hoping to catch escaping slaves crossing the Ohio River would not have been safe topics, at least in the early days where one was endeavoring to put his best foot forward. The topic of the Fugitive Slave Law might not have gone down too well with Captain Charlie, even though we have yet to find evidence that he ever owned a slave, took slaves as collateral for loans to planters, or believed slavery was ordained by God. He did fight for the Confederate cause, as many Southerners did for various reasons.

As a student of history, Frank would have been interested in Captain Welhausen's record as a Confederate soldier—then a lieutenant—who played a significant role in the 1863 Battle of Calcasieu Pass, Louisiana. Welhausen's guns were instrumental in shooting away the wheelhouses of two Union gunboats, the Granite City and the Wave. The bravery of Welhausen's battery in the gunfights was noted, especially for remaining at their cannons even after they had incurred serious wounds. The significance of the battle was that it was fought solely by Texas Confederate soldiers and represented the last "significant defeat" of the Union navy for the control of the Texas-Louisiana coast.

Frank, born and raised in a free state and a student of history, would also been interested in hearing Captain Welhausen recall his thinking about the war from the moment he decided to put on Confederate gray to his eventual return to his family. Since Frank likely met Mamie in 1898 and did not marry her until 1906, that left eight years to chat with Captain Welhausen about the Civil War before marrying Mamie. However, we have no reason to believe that Frank and Captain Charlie ever talked about the war. There was no upside for either of them to talk about such a sad chapter that must have affected Captain Charlie's family and business, not to mention countless other Texas sons and their families. Among the many questions Frank could have asked but probably didn't were: Why did you enlist in the Confederate military? Did you feel that slavery was ordained by God? If you had no slaves yourself, why would you support a war to preserve slavery? Would it have been risky for German immigrants to Texas to speak out against slavery? Did you believe the South had a real chance of winning the war? And were you sympathetic with former governor Sam Houston's opposition to the war?

Katie: That makes sense not to talk about the Civil War, but what about whether Frank was prepared financially to get married? Do you think Mamie's family would have been concerned that Mamie was thinking about getting married to a poor teacher? Perhaps Frank was a fortune hunter who was aware of how wealthy Captain Charlie had become.

Pops: Maybe like Montgomery Clift was in *The Heiress* with Olivia de Havilland? I don't think so. If such thoughts passed through their minds, I think they would have been shortly dispelled by the fact that he was an ambitious, likable, mature young man on his own without help from family. Yes, Frank's financial upside was limited, and he was the hard-working bookish type. However, he was raised on a farm and knew how to talk crops and livestock, just as he would prove again decades later when winning over Josie Glenn's mother. However, the financial disparity between Frank and Mamie was obvious as Captain Welhausen was a wealthy man, and, according to the Yoakum Paper November 5, 1916, had accumulated an estate estimated to be worth $250,000, which is over six million in today's dollars. We should add that we have no reason to believe that Welhausen's net worth had ever included the value of any slaves, although slaves constituted nearly half of all taxable property in Lavaca County before the war.

Frank and Mamie married in Shiner on Christmas Eve in 1906. After returning to Waco, Mamie established herself as an energetic worker for various Baylor and Waco-related clubs and projects. The first year Frank took the lead concerning

Baylor homecoming (1909), Mamie was on a faculty wives' committee to support the project. She was also active in the Literary Club with President Brooks's wife and could be relied on for book reviews. She organized the Twentieth Century Club and was its first president. She and Frank enjoyed literature, music, and art together, and she was superintendent of the primary department of the Sunday school at First Baptist in Waco. First son Francis was added to the household in 1907, and Frank, Mamie, and Francis lived happily in Waco without serious worries—at least that we know of—until infant Charles was added in 1915. The year 1916 represented a sad chapter in their lives.

From Altenheim Comfort, Comfort, Texas, which was about 130-140 miles from Shiner, and where Mamie and her mother Eliza were staying for Charles's health, Mamie wrote Frank:

> Dear Frank, I am getting somewhat impatient for news from home and expect to hear from you tomorrow. The rain continues here, and I never saw a 'wetter' place...I would like it better if Charles could be turned loose somewhere to play and romp. We are situated on the 3rd floor in a room 40 x 40 with windows on four sides which makes it cool enough for all purposes...Mama has been making friends too, but I don't seem to get up enough interest in anybody to cultivate acquaintances. There are all kinds of folks here and more young people than older people. Most folks are from San Antonio & Houston...I wish you would get Stella to find the baby's two diaper supports and send them as soon as possible for I need them badly...Also send me a hairbrush, another article I forgot...Lovingly, Mamie (MW letter to FGG July 31, 1916)

Two months after Charles's death in August, Mamie wrote Frank or Francis five times from her parents' home in Shiner:

> Dear Frank, I kept thinking all the while I was coming down that I ought to have stayed at home and looked after you and Francis, and the more I th't it over, the more my conviction grew until I was pretty miserable over it by the time I arrived. I certainly hope you will both stay well and that Francis will not get into trouble. I have visions of him getting overheated on the football field and catching cold. Papa has had a sick spell and is not looking very well but everybody else is alright...With love, Mamie (MW letter to FGG October 15, 1916)

My dear Frank, I went out to Charles's grave [in a Shiner cemetery] this morning with Henrietta and Papa. The agony of seeing it and living over again the memories it brought are too much for words. No flowers are blooming now; we could only find a few forlorn blossoms. Henrietta places fresh showers there every Saturday... [Francis's] stockings are in his small right-hand dresser drawer and if it gets real cold, use some of his cotton union suits. It would not hurt to cut them off at the knees if they are shrunk or tight. Papa is not feeling well, has been lying down all the time...With love for you both. (MW letter to FGG October 16, 1916)

Dearest Frank, I am afraid you are not giving me any details of yourself either. Why do you not say definitely & specifically just how you are? You promised you would you know...Papa seems to be feeling better but does not seem to be in good spirits. Everything is always going wrong. I do not know whether it is politics, financial affairs, or the war in Europe [World War I]. Mama gardens all day long and has a half dozen plants to show for it.

I hope Francis is getting along without any trouble from anywhere. I never feel quite safe about him. In the afternoons, I wonder where he is and what he is doing, and even if I were at home, I could not remedy things much as he wants to be out somewhere anyway. Dr. Gray is moving to Yoakum; and this is an opportunity for a good doctor. I hope you will tell me just how you are today. Does Mariah do as well as Stella did? Much love for you both. Devotedly, Mamie (MW letter to FGG October 16, 1916)

Dear Francis...I received Papa's letter last night, he told me everything you all did but he didn't say a word about how he was feeling. You must let me know how he is and whether he eats like he should. Glade [Glade Welhausen, Mamie's nephew] follows me around all the time and wants me to play with him. He has a little tricycle which he rides all day long. Granma thinks you are very smart to earn an air gun. She is saving you some more buffalo nickels. You ought to be here to ride in the new automobile, it is very nice...Write soon to your Mama. (MW letter to FGG, Jr. October 17, 1916)

Dearest Frank, I hope you all can do without me one more day. We are so lonely here at the house since the excitement has passed.

> We miss Papa at every turn [Captain Welhausen died November 3, 1916, at age 81], & always think we hear his familiar step. It is very hard for Mama. She is just beginning to miss him, and she cannot sleep. Philip is coming today and spend the night with us, which will be good for us especially for Mama. Aunt Julia is gone & so is everyone else that came in for the funeral.
>
> Please phone Mrs. Brooks or Mrs. Poole to explain to the club why I am not there to lead at the Literary Club Thurs. as I was expected to do. Do not forget this. Mama wants us to go to that football game so we may do so, we may feel better by that time. Look for us Thurs. With Love, Mamie (MW letter to FGG November 7, 1916)

At this point, Frank and Mamie's lives in Waco were in the process of absorbing multiple shocks, first the illness and death of infant Charles, then the death of Captain Charlie, and now Mamie's terminal illness—in an advanced stage in early 1917—and death. In April 1917, Frank wrote Francis back in Waco:

> Dear Francis, We took Mama to the Albuquerque Sanatorium. She has a nice room with a sleeping porch all screened in, and canvas doors can be used to close it in when it rains or when there is too much wind. We had a room all to ourselves on the train from Temple and Mama got along nicely. The first day after we came here, Monday, she had considerable fever, which made her feel badly. This morning she has no fever and feels much better. Last night was the first night she has not taken medicine to take the fever away for several weeks. So we are feeling better about her.
>
> The doctors examined Mama yesterday and one of them said that he had found much sicker people than Mama and they had gotten well. But Mama is very sick and it will take a long time for her to get well...I know you are being a nice boy. Write to Mama as soon as you get this letter it will do her lots of good to get a letter from you. One way to help her get well is to keep her cheerful and that is what you can do by writing her a nice letter telling her what you have been doing since she went away...Mama sends her love to you...With love, Papa. I expect to be home by the last of this month.

Mamie's last letter to Frank was written in labored, irregular handwriting, as her strength was fast failing:

> Dear Frank (Monday)...The nurse says I must not write but I am making a desperate effort. Dear, why have you neglected sending Miss Martin's check this week? She wants the money & I have felt quite embarrassed. Forward it at once. I am still the most desperately sick patient in the sanatorium. Miss Martin contracted for another job after May 23 and goes to take charge of a child's welfare station for the town. She made this arrangement before she knew I would need her so long. Dr. Shortle thinks I must still have a special nurse so long as I am so bed-ridden. Now Mama has persuaded him to let her move into the room with me and take the place of a nurse and thereby save the expensive nurse fees.
>
> The past few days I have been thinking the matter over and come to the conclusion that several weeks of nursing such as I require would break her [Mrs. Welhausen] down. She can't lift me around, sponge me off in the night to lower the fever. Sometimes when she comes up the hill and up the steps, she totters a little. We surely must protect Mama. Nursing a patient as sick as I am is a big job. She is very delighted to save a nurse's fee, and I do not know how to persuade her to give up the plans. I am afraid I will have to have a special nurse for several weeks yet. Either until my fever lowers or I am strong enough to be about. I have had some very discouraging days. This letter has been such an effort so don't expect another soon. I wish you would send this to Philip or Peck. They must persuade Mama she can't do a hard job of nursing at her age. Kiss for dear son. Love, from Mamie. (MW letter to FGG, May 14, 1917)

The following is Frank's last letter to Mamie, probably not received in Albuquerque before her death the next day:

> May 16, 1917 (Wednesday) My darling Sweetheart, I hope you will not find it necessary to write again soon. I did not know that the nurse was to be paid in advance. I sent the check Sat. and it should have reached her Mon. I enclose another with this.
>
> Regarding Mama's taking the nurse's place now, that I think would be fatal to both you and Mama. There is no use to talk or think of persuasion. I had already sent telegrams to Mama and to Dr. Shortle when I received your letter about the nurse. I began to

> feel uneasy when Mama first mentioned about the nurse leaving. Have Dr. Peters or Dr. Shortle to secure another nurse immediately to take the place of Miss Martin when she leaves. There is no other plan to be thought of for the present.
>
> Sweetheart, do not do anything to waste your strength, no more writing, Dear. I heard of a patient the other day who was so low that even to read a line would cause her fever to rise. You are far from that, but it shows how careful you should be. That patient is doing well now. With much love, Frank

Frank and Eliza Welhausen had taken Mamie to the Albuquerque Sanatorium for tuberculosis on April 24, when her condition deteriorated from sick and worrisome to terminal in twenty-four days. The family had hoped that a change of climate would be beneficial. L.P. Peters, M.D. and vice president of the Albuquerque Sanatorium for Tuberculosis wrote E.A White, Waco, Texas April 27, 1917 as follows:

> Dear Mr. White, Mrs. Guittard and family arrived here safely, and we have the patient in the sanatorium. Mr. Guittard expects to leave here tonight for home and we have Mrs. Welhausen fixed up only a block away. We were able…to obtain Miss Martin as their nurse, and I am in hopes that we will be able to do something with the case. I need not tell you that she is a very sick woman for that you already know. On the other hand, her pulmonary condition is much better than I expected to find. She is a delightful little woman, and I assure you we shall do all in our power to bring her back to health…

On May 5, 1917, Dr. A.G. Shortle wrote to Frank Guittard:

> Dear Mr. Guittard: Mrs. Guittard's fever had continued so high that we felt it best to try to collapse her left lung. Dr. Peters attempted this today but found extensive adhesions so was unable to get collapse. I shall make another attempt, trying to find space in the back though it is not likely to be successful. I regret this very much as I fear it is her only chance to recover. It is an unfortunate fact that about one-fourth of the cases that we expect to be benefitted by collapse have such extensive adhesions that the operation is not possible. Hoping she may do better than I am expecting, and with kindest regards, A.G. Shortle

On May 16, 1917, Dr. A.G. Shortle sent the following telegram at 11:59 a.m.: "WORSE TODAY COME AS SOON AS POSSIBLE AG SHORTLE."

On May 17, 1917, Mrs. Welhausen sent the following telegram to her son-in-law Frank at 12:57 p.m.: "MAMIE DIED THIS MORNING [May 17] WILL START FOR SHINER 1030 TONIGHT WIRE IMMEDIATELY WHERE YOU WILL MEET ME MOTHER 1257 PM"

Following Mamie's passing, Nurse Elizabeth Martin sent Frank the following response to his letter to her:

> Dear Sir—Please pardon my delay in replying to your letter of inquiry. The immediate cause of Mrs. Guittard's death was due to Tubercular Peritonitis which developed quite suddenly about 36 hours before she died, and progressed very rapidly. The continuous high fever was, of course, exhausting, and that together with the peritoneum becoming so inflamed, soon caused the heart to fail, which already was not very strong. I was sorry you could not get here, but it was not possible for you to have gotten here after she took the turn for the worse. ...With much sympathy, Elizabeth Martin.

<u>Katie</u>: That's a sad story. I'm wondering, since Frank was such a conscientious and introspective guy, did he feel somehow that he could have done more for his partner?

<u>Pops</u>: I think he had to feel very badly that he wasn't present in the hours before she died to comfort her, hold her hand, tell her once again he loved her, that she had been the love of his life, that they would be reunited in heaven, and goodbye. Her mother was there with her, but Frank would have felt strongly he should have been there too. You will remember how badly he felt years before when he learned his mother had died. Realistically, there was nothing he could do for her, or that any doctor or sanatorium could do for her either. There was no cure for tuberculosis in 1917. We have no conclusive information establishing when or how she became infected and whether her exposure to tuberculosis came from her hospital volunteer work many years previously, from one of her club friends in Waco, or another source.

Frank and the Welhausens had all been deeply concerned about Mamie, who was pregnant with Clarence during the year preceding her death. On April 17, 1917, a week before Mamie left for the sanatorium, she executed her last will and testament. Mamie left her entire estate to her husband Frank Guittard so long as he remained unmarried, but in the event he remarried, then to her children Francis and Clarence, the latter being barely a month old when she executed her will. Mamie further appointed her brothers, C.B. and Philip Welhausen, as joint executors charged with delivering any income from her estate to Frank. If he remarried, then the executors would retain control of the estate for the benefit of her two sons, using the proceeds for the education and maintenance of the two children until the youngest arrived at the age of twenty-one and then deliver the remainder of the estate to the two children.

Katie: Mamie was only thirty-seven when she died in Albuquerque.

Pops: Many people died of tuberculosis at Mamie's age. There was no vaccine or cure yet. Mamie was buried in a silver-gray metal casket which was borne to the waiting hearse for delivery to the cemetery in Shiner.

Katie: We mentioned quack medicines awhile back and we will talk more about them in the next chapter. It doesn't sound like those medicines or anything would have helped Mamie, before or after she arrived in Albuquerque.

Pops: No, quack cures could only have only raised the family's hopes temporarily, and then they would have come crashing back down. There is no reason to believe that Frank or the Welhausens ever considered them.

CHAPTER 23

Health Tribulations, Microbial Antagonists (1915-1917)

This chapter arises from the need to focus for a few minutes on a serious health matter in the last decades of the nineteenth century and first decades of the twentieth century. As this work is being completed in the twenty-first century, the COVID-19 virus still rages dangerously out of control in many parts of the world, despite some distribution of effective vaccines. Ironically, though we live in an age when science and medicine are much more advanced than in prior centuries, superstition and politics are able still to frustrate the best plans to defeat a pandemic. Charlie wants to drill down on this one; he likes to look at very small things under a microscope.

Pops: For those readers who may prefer to skip this topic, which has been addressed in depth for members of the Guittard family, and forge ahead to happier chapters, we note that this chapter will be short. Health concerns, setbacks, and tragedies represent essential parts of Frank's life and times. Frank, our immigrant to Texas who had, from early on, a healthy concern about health issues and epidemics, would have never dreamed that infectious disease would impact his small family to the extent it did.

It may be interesting to note that the year of Frank's birth, 1867, nineteen years before Frank's arrival in Texas, has been called the "year of death" for Texas because of outbreaks of yellow fever—with an estimated mortality rate of 85 percent. The disease reached areas close to where Frank would eventually teach and where his first wife would grow up and live as a young woman. The good news is that yellow fever or "yellow jack" was not among the diseases that impacted Frank or his family. Charlie will be in charge of asking questions, if any.

Charlie: Why is the word "antagonists" in your title? I've heard "tribulations" and "lamentations" at church, but not "antagonists."

Pops: An antagonist would be an enemy or adversary. In works of fiction, there is usually a principal character, often a hero or heroine, but then, to create conflict, an adversary or villain appears. Batman has his Joker, Sherlock Homes had his Professor Moriarty, Othello his Iago, and so on. In works of nonfiction or biography, there can also be adversaries, since real people often have enemies. Alexander Hamilton had his Aaron Burr, General Grant his General Lee, Franklin

Roosevelt his Hitler, Mussolini, and Tojo. The antagonist's goals conflict with those of the principal character, who is called the protagonist.

Charlie: Okay, did Frank and his family have antagonists?

Pops: Yes, but not in the sense of other people attacking them, as we see in the cases of Presidents Burleson and Brooks. President Burleson and President Brooks both had to deal with human antagonists. Burleson had William Cowper Brann and Brooks his J. Frank Norris. We have talked about those conflicts elsewhere. Where the Guittards were concerned, the antagonists were of a different sort.

Charlie: I don't get it.

Pops: Their antagonists were infections, both bacterial and viral, caused by tiny microbes spread by coughing, sneezing, hugging, kissing, and other close contacts with infected people. Both kinds of infections can cause similar symptoms such as coughing and sneezing, fever, inflammation, vomiting, diarrhea, fatigue, and cramping, which are all ways that the immune system tries to get rid of infectious organisms.

Charlie: Were the microbes big enough to see?

Pops: Only with a high-powered microscope. Here are the infections which impacted the Guittard family:

Tuberculosis: TB was the greatest killer of nineteenth-century Americans. This disease is caused by a bacterium called *Mycobacterium tuberculosis*. Tuberculosis had ravaged Mamie's body when she died. She likely had this disease for many years before it resulted in her death at the age of thirty-seven at the sanatorium in New Mexico. Edward Snowden notes that "tuberculosis can establish itself as a chronic illness progressing slowly over a period of decades, punctuated by remissions and even apparent recoveries, followed by mysterious relapses and the inexorable advance of the disease." Snowden further observes that "at its peak, tuberculosis may have infected 90 percent of the population...in the United States." On its website, the Center for Disease Control states that "TB disease in adults is usually due to past TB infection that becomes active years later, when a person's immune system becomes weak for some reason" and that "people with TB disease of the lungs or throat can spread bacteria to others with whom they spend time every day." The final days of any sufferer were miserable, "plagued by constant coughing to expel fluid from the lungs, foul-smelling night sweats, and frequent bouts of diarrhea and vomiting...the person's final hours were spent slowly choking to death on his or her own bodily fluids."

Both Mamie's 1901 diary and her correspondence with Frank show much sickness from the age of twenty to her death at thirty-seven. She took care of sick people, probably as a volunteer, although a doctor had warned her of the risk of her doing so. Mamie's death from tuberculosis meant that Clarence was raised without his birth mother for the first four years of his life. Clarence was fortunate not to have contracted tuberculosis from Mamie, as she was not taken to the sanatorium in New Mexico until five weeks after his birth. Frank and Francis were both fortunate for the same reason. No effective treatment for tuberculosis was available until the last half of the twentieth century. Sanatoriums like the one to which Mamie was sent were recommended in the hope that a cool, dry, sunny climate and plenty of rest and nutritious food would help restore a patient to health by "sitting out." New Mexico's sanatoriums were flooded with "lungers" seeking a cure. However, one study showed that nearly 25 percent of patients died in the hospital and another 50 percent of those released died within five years of discharge, combining for a fatality rate of 62.5 percent of those treated in New Mexico sanatoriums.

We will not discuss or describe the available surgical interventions for tuberculosis in 1917. Once the attempt to collapse Mamie's lung was abandoned, it was apparent that her case was so advanced that subjecting her further to other drastic procedures, such as the bloody thoracoplasty procedure, would have been extremely cruel. In 1900, and presumably in 1889 when Frank's mother died at age fifty-eight, the top four causes of death were infectious diseases—pneumonia, flu, tuberculosis, and gastrointestinal infections.

Spinal tuberculous meningitis: Tuberculous Meningitis (TBM) is a form of meningitis characterized by inflammation of the membranes (meninges) around the brain or spinal cord and caused by a specific bacterium known as *Mycobacterium tuberculosis*. Tubercular meningitis was the most widespread form of meningitis at the beginning of the twentieth century. This disease probably killed Frank and Mamie's second son, Charles, the year before Mamie died from tuberculosis. Since Mamie was Charles's mother and primary caretaker, the chances are that his spinal meningitis was related to her tuberculosis and that he was infected during his infancy because of their close contact for a year and some months before his death. Charles was born in 1915 and died in 1916, and Mamie died less than a year after Charles. She had been warned by a physician as early as 1903 that she was risking her health by taking care of sick people. We don't know when she contracted tuberculosis, but we suspect it was years before Charles's death in 1916 and perhaps even before she and Frank were married in 1906. The newspaper article announcing that Charles died from infantile paralysis we discount primarily because there is no indication of a polio outbreak during 1915-1916 in Texas, and we know Mamie died from tuberculosis less than a year later.

Spanish influenza: This disease has been categorized as a pandemic. It was caused by an H1N1 virus with genes of avian origin. The disease killed 675,000 Americans. It reached the US in 1918 after the conclusion of World War I, and it affected the lives of Frank, Francis, and Clarence as it was likely one of the reasons Clarence was mostly separated from his father and brother almost from his birth in March 1917 until they were reunited in May 1921.

Infantile paralysis: Polio, or poliomyelitis, is a disabling and life-threatening disease caused by the poliovirus. The virus spreads from person to person and can infect a person's spinal cord, causing paralysis. This disease was a fact of life during one or more of the summers in California when Clarence and Josie visited Frank in Palo Alto, Frank always being apprehensive that Clarence would be stricken. During the summer of 1927, California had a major outbreak of poliomyelitis which would have contributed to Frank's fears.

Charlie: That's a lot of diseases.

Pops: Yes, the first two bacterial and the second two viral. But despite it all, Frank lived a longer life at eighty-three than either of his parents, and longer—despite all the medical advances made after his death—than all of his sons—64 (Francis), one and a half (Charles), and 81 (Clarence), He was the last of the eight Ohio siblings to die, only his older sister Rosalie lived longer, being ninety-one when she died. His physician brothers Alwin and Virgil died at ages 74 and 67, respectively.

Charlie: How did he do that?

Pops: Must have been something in his genes.

Charlie: What about my genes? How long will I live?

Pops: A long time, I'm sure, but exactly how long, nobody can tell you. But diet and exercise will help, along with periodic medical checkups.

Charlie: You said that there was no cure for tuberculosis until the second half of the twentieth century. It's surprising that doctors and scientists weren't able to find a cure for so long.

Pops: It does seem so; however, in the last half of the twentieth century, medical science literally exploded. Before then, medical quacks pushed their fraudulent medical devices, often advertising to cure every disease known to man. One such quack was Heil Eugene Crum who patented a machine called a "Co-Etherator," which he said could cure anything from an amputated finger to cancer. Crum also claimed that the device could fertilize farmland and treat golf course greens. Can you imagine that? Crum's medical license was eventually revoked, and the Indiana Supreme Court found him guilty of "gross immorality." The helplessness of conventional medicine had ushered in a golden age of patent medicines and quack devices. In addition to the Co-Etherator, there were many others including the David Kidder Magneto, the Magno-Electric-Vitalizer, the Dynomizer, the Oscilloclast, Las-I-Go (impotence cure containing strychnine!), the Radiendocrimator, the Natural Eye Normalizer, goat glands transplants (impotence cure), and many, many others. Popular 1895 and 1902, mail order catalogs contained numerous ads for quack cures and devices to cure disease and physical anomalies from the "Great Russian Corn and Bunion Exterminator"—$0.35 for two bottles, to the "Heidelberg Electric Belt"—$18.00 for the giant power 80-guage belt.

Charlie: Some of those sound pretty weird, and maybe they wouldn't make you feel any better, perhaps worse. Didn't they have things sick people could drink like other oral medicine?

Pops: Indeed, they did. Creators of various patent medicines ran wild, and Congress couldn't catch up to the pushers of such remedies until several decades into the twentieth century. Lack of medical or other scientific education did not hold these quick-buck artists back. Bogus elixirs were popular among patent medicine scam artists from the earliest days of the United States. A creator, to obtain a patent, did not have to establish efficacy, only to list the product's ingredients. Some manufacturers did not seek patents since they didn't want to disclose the product's ingredients to potential competitors. Regardless of the lack of proof of efficacy or a patent, creators of purported cures could advertise in newspapers and other periodicals, handbills, posters, and pamphlets and include preposterous, unproved claims of effectiveness. As a practical matter, nothing could be done about it. *Elixir Salutis* was concocted and promoted by Anthony Daffy, an English clergyman, who said the elixir could be taken for "gout, kidney and bladder stones, languishing and melancholy, shortness of breath, tuberculosis, scurvy, dropsy, rickets, pestilence, ague, a tubercular infection of the lymph glands in the throat." Other products offered to an unsuspecting public accompanied by dubious claims were Anderson Scot's Pills, Dr. Hooper's Female Pills, Dr. Bateman's Pectoral Drops, Kickapoo India Sagwa, Chill and Ague Eliminator, Hamlin's Wizard Oil,

Grove's Bromo Quinine Cold Tablets, The Great Remedy, and the well-known Lydia Pinkham's Vegetable Tablets.

Charlie: I guess we are lucky today we have the FDA and more real medical doctors.

Pops: And the CDC and the WHO. After all of this emphasis on health and disease in the last two chapters, I'll bet you are ready for some lighter stuff.

BOOK FIVE

Homecomings, Football, Josie, & Controversy

Sample questions for the peanut gallery's consideration in this book's chapters:

Baylor was such a serious place back then—how did students unwind, laugh, and let their hair down? Who came up with the idea of homecoming? Why was intercollegiate football banned at Baylor for the 1906 season? Did Baylor's football coach use trick plays? What was the Student Self-Government controversy, and what did Frank have to do with it? How was it resolved? What was the controversy over evolution at Baylor? What was Frank's view on the evolution controversy? Did he teach the evolution theory as part of human history? What was Baylor's position on the KKK? Were any faculty members in the KKK? Was Frank?

Excerpts from Frank's "Funny-Book of Student Bone-heads" on examinations:

Question: "What was the South Sea Bubble?" Answer: "The South Sea Bubble was the name of one of the English ships."

Question: "Describe Romanesque architecture." Answer: "The Romanesque type of architecture consists in building the arches in a square shape."

Examples of Frank's favorite words and phrases from his letters:

"digging" — "It was slow digging [researching] at first...The Digger."

"dandy" — "Have a dandy room, no flies, no roommate."

"little" — "It was a little difficult to follow him at first"; "I get a little hungry for home news"; "I was a little careless taking my last notes."

CHAPTER 24

Comic Relief: Student Wit & Whimsy

We talked earlier about the many rules for students' conduct at Baylor while President Burleson was in charge. So how did the students deal with the closely-monitored, extremely strict college environment mandated by President Burleson and with all the rules he had been enforcing for decades? Particularly those dealing with limitations on social relationships between the sexes? And banning of conversation inside and outside of class except at chaperoned events? And what about Burleson's prohibitions against playing sports like football, smoking and drinking, playing cards or other games of chance, gambling, loitering, and being in the wrong place on campus at the wrong time? Finn is interested in this sort of thing, so he will be helping me.

Pops: One wonders how students fared in this environment which mostly persisted after Burleson passed from the scene. The answer is that the students accessed their funny bones and inborn creativity and vented in campus publications like the *Baylor Lariat* and the *Baylor Round-Up*. We suspect that students also sounded off to each other outside class, passed notes to each other, made jokes about their teachers, President Burleson, and his successors, who only gradually relaxed some of Burleson's rules. Finn, let's start with the students' limericks. Mothers of the world may now relax.

Finn: Why did you say that?

Pops: Some people think the only good limericks are dirty ones, but that's not so. Edward Lear, author of *A Book of Nonsense*, wrote some of the best ones ever written. See what you think of these limericks about Baylor faculty which accompanied student illustrations in the 1906 *Round-Up*:

> And this is our tall Doctor Goodspeed,
> (What teachings and doctrines he does breed!)
> He can pray for an hour
> With such heart-searching power,
> Even music to dreamland he would lead.

Our beloved Kesler, the Dean,
Whose physique is wofully lean,
To dogs and to cats
And even to gnats,
For Science's sake, he is mean.

Oh, our dear, smiling Doctor of Logic,
His mind's filled with many a project;
Through infinite space
His thoughts he does race,
This dear dimpled Doctor of Logic.

There's a dear old Professor D. D.,
He's just as sweet as he can be,
He's so henpecked,
He can't recollect,
The time when his wishes were free.

Here are some more, this time about students:

A senior, whose given name's Carroll,
Kept his very best suit in a barrel,
"It keeps in the crease,
And it keeps out the grease,
And that's what I want," said young Carroll.

Miss Lola May Isbill's a jewel,
She said, "I can never be cruel,
I think it's a shame,
To have such a name,
I'm going to change it to Sewell.

Said a good-looking senior named Bennett,
"I surely have got myself in it,
I've done made my date,
And found out too late,
The girl said she'd rather not been it.

A quiet young person named Lockett,
Carried Duke's cigarettes in his pocket,
When his friends showed surprise,

He answered thus wise,
'For my girl they're much cheaper than choc-lett.'

Miss Graham, a dignified creature,
When courted by many a preacher,
Would frown and say, 'Nay,
You must all go away,
I'm preparing myself for a teacher.'

Pops: So, did you like any of those?

Finn: I liked them all, but especially the ones about Carroll and Bennett. I thought they were the funniest.

Pops: Here are some more bits, this time several student roasts of faculty in the style of the popular "turn over the page" books told in an intentionally cornball kind of way. The mistakes in the writing are for effect. See what you think. Each one of these descriptions had an uncomplimentary picture to go with it drawn by a student.

Now that's Brother Daniels. They say he has been around Baylor for the last part of the last century and all of this. But there's nuthin' like holdin' on, you know. 'It's the plodder that wins,' they say, and it has been kinder intermated around that Brother Daniels has won a housekeeper by stayin' so long. He's very meek and refined, and pertickerly eloquent at prayer-meetin's. I guess, tho' that somebody will take his place when he is gone. Turn over the page.

That's Miss Surratt, the liberrian. It was just a happen-so that her picture came next to Brother Daniels, but it fits all right, don't you think? She's been here a long time; I heard Prof. Poole say exactly, but I've forgot now. But her work is very hard and she's talkin' 'bout making a change for next year.' This year the dust off of the book shelves seems to have affected her lungs and she has made several trips out from town in order to get some fresh air. But she's true to Baylor, all right; even when she was seekin' rest and fresh air she made speeches on Christian education at the educational rallies held mostly at Brother Daniels's churches. Turn over the page.

> Now that is Dr. Reid. You can tell by the lines in his face that he's a hardhearted man. He has breathed in so much bad gas, and acids, and things like that, that it has affected his heart. He's a pretty good chemist, I reckon, but a powerful peculiar man. He likes the women, but women don't seem to like him much, somehow. I thought, maybe, that they didn't like the labertory odor which he generally carries 'round, but I don't know. He gives the girls a whole lot better grades than he does the boys, and he keeps chairs in his office so the girls can come in an' sit by him while he grades their papers. Turn over the page.

Pops: Students obviously loved to make fun of their professors and to publish these irreverent pieces. Don't think you would see much of that in any modern-day college annuals, including Baylor.

Finn: Why is that?

Pops: Well, for starters, back then, students couldn't resist pushing back against the administration and faculty that sought to thoroughly regulate their lives, especially those of the girls in Burleson Hall. It was a different day. Then too, Baylor was not the kind of place where students were allowed to play around for four years, the boys then joining their fathers in the business and the girls preparing themselves to teach school or continuing their searches for husbands. Baylor students were expected to pour themselves into their studies. Rules and regulations were deemed necessary, both to keep the students to their tasks as well as to protect the girls. Baylor men were expected to prepare themselves for the ministry, the law, teaching, or for another occupation in which they could serve as Christians. But, although Baylor was always so earnest about the purpose of the school and Christian education, Baylor students were rarely that serious. An article in the 1908 *Round-Up* summarized the results of a questionnaire allegedly propounded to students containing one question: "Did you ever flunk?" Here are the students' anonymous answers:

The question: Did you ever flunk?
"No, but am confidently expecting to."
"Yes, quite successfully."
"Flunked once in a one credit Latin prose course."
"In no examination did I ever flunk."
"Twice."
"Yes, yes, yes."
"Well, I should smile."
"Almost."

"Flunked once."
"No, I have never failed on any examination."
"Never flunked."
"A few times."
"Yes, I have flunked."
"Have failed on examination."
"I never flunked."
"The Registrar can tell."
"If you care to know this, ask Professor Ragland."
"Haven't flunked in college."
"Yes, indeed."
"Never had the pleasure of flunking."
"Yes, but don't ask me how many times."

Finn: That's funny, but don't tell my parents I said so. They like As and Bs. They are serious about our grades.

Pops: Here's a subject—compulsory chapel—which Baylor students put up with while not being enthusiastic about the hours spent Monday-Friday, usually at ten in the morning. Baylor's presidents (Burleson, Cooper, Brooks, and Neff) presided at chapel; Neff referred to it as "his class," that is, the class he taught. Here are some of the students' comments indicating their disdain for chapel:

1908 *Lariat*: New Rules Adopted Concerning Chapel Talks—

- Any person who begins his speech by saying, 'It is a long-looked for delight to be in this grand University and a joy to look into your smiling young faces,'...shall be removed from the platform by a committee in any way they deem best.
- All persons, before speaking in Chapel, shall promise beforehand that they will not mention the word 'opportunity' throughout their speeches.
- No person will be welcomed in Chapel a second time unless he has a new joke.
- Speakers must not expect much applause. It is getting to be quite irksome.

1908 *Round-Up:*

There was a young sport in Baylor
Who spent much time with his tailor.
When the boys asked him 'why?'
With a wink he'd reply
'Through my clothes I mean to assail her.'

1911 *Round-Up*: From the Baylor Dictionary: "Chapel Talk—A bitter drug administered to Baylor students, compounded of one part 'hot air,' one part egotism, and two parts of platitudes. Treatment compulsory, though sometimes nauseating."

1911 *Round-Up*: Chapel Don'ts—

- Don't smoke on the campus; retire to the Athletic field where you can't be distinguished from a citizen.
- Don't sit on the ground all the time; wait till it rains to cool the grass and softens the earth.
- It's silly for girls to aspire to higher learning and dream of putting their lives in some kind of famous work; the little cottage on the prairie is good enough for you.
- It's perfectly all right for students to study during Chapel, provided the person sitting in front of you is large enough to hide you.

Pops: Students had been aggravated for years, and perhaps still are, by the compulsory chapel requirement, but the Trustees' prohibition against intercollegiate football games represented an open wound, a much more serious aggravation. In the 1907 *Round-Up*, the students lamented the absence of football:

Inscription at the site of Where Our Foot-Ball Lies Buried

Here lies our dear foot-ball,
Long may his ashes rest;
He died by vote of the trustees
And not by our request.

Students not only knocked the faculty and compulsory chapel, but they knocked each other. Juniors mocked seniors, and everyone knocked freshmen and the lowly students at the Prep. Here's an upper-classman ditty making fun of a poor freshman:

A Freshman
I saw him as he came,
And I thought that he was lame
In the foot.
He limped as he walked,
And he stuttered when he talked,
Like a nut.
He looks a perfect 'cad,'

With a green cap on his head—
Solid stone.
You should see him hold it tight,
Fearing that the Soph girls might
Take it home.

Finn: Those upperclassmen writing for the *Round-Up* were pretty mean.

Pops: They were even meaner to the students in the Preparatory Department (the "Academy") who were not ready to be freshmen yet. Here's their advice to the Preps in the 1906 *Round-Up*:

Don't eat anything but soup until your digestive organs develop.
Don't neglect 'Mother Goose.' It is the foundation of all culture.
Don't call seniors by nicknames. It's disrespectful.
Don't spend money on toy balloons.
Don't be afraid of the animals in the museum. They're dead.
Don't try to get on the street car until it stops.
Don't chew gum in Sunday School. It doesn't show good breeding.
Don't snore in the library. Keep your mouth closed and breathe through your nostrils.
Don't throw rocks at your landlady's chickens. The Humane Society will get you.

Pops: Students, whatever class, loved generating nonsense, perhaps because the teachers and adults in charge were so deadly serious nearly all the time. So they also started crazy clubs with strange names that make us today want to say "huh?"—kind of like the names of some modern-day rock groups—but some of the clubs were pretty funny. Some of them were:

1905 *Round-Up*
The Question Girls
Motto: Eat all you can,
And what you can't, can.
Yell:
Toast, toast, toast, toast, toast, to tea,
Muffins, muffins, for you and me;
Rolls, rolls, rolls, gnaw! gnaw! gnaw!
Steak, steak, steak, chaw! Chaw! Chaw!
Biscuit, biscuit, raw! Raw! Raw!

1906 *Round-Up*

The Fat Men's Club

Motto: Good measure in all things.

Advice to Lean People:

> Take life easy—don't think you have to work...Eat six meals a day, and don't think of sleeping less than twelve hours. If you are lean on account of bad temper, take Latin under Prof. Poole [beloved overweight professor in the Prep]—that will cure you. Strive above all things to become fat and handsome.

1909 *Round-Up*

The Ku-Klux Klan [a girls' basketball team]

Motto: "Do it or die!" (So we'll do it.)

Yell:

> Beat us! Beat us!
> Beat us if you can!
> Ku-Klux! Ku-Klux!
> Ku-Klux Klan!

Pops: And no list of the odd clubs at Baylor would be complete without including the Noze Brotherhood.

Finn: What's that?

Pops: That is a complicated subject with a long history. Supposedly, it is a secret society founded in 1924 in Brooks Hall. The Noze was created in reference to the size of freshman Leonard Shoaf's nose, his friends claiming they could form a club around it. Prominent positions at some point in the organization were the Lorde Mayor, bearer of the Enlightening Rod of Elmo, the Cunning Linguist, and the Shekel Keeper, responsible for keeping graft to a minimum to ensure available funds for parties. The Noze has recognized as honorary members George W. Bush, Bill Cosby, John Dean, Kinky Friedman, John Glenn, Billy Graham, Bob Hope, Dan Rather, Robert Griffin III, and the entire 2011-12 Baylor Lady Bears undefeated national championship basketball team. Among the Noze's self-proclaimed contributions to Baylor life have been turning Pat Neff Hall and the fountain pink, attaching giant Noze glasses on Old Main and mud flaps on Waco Hall, and dropping 4,000 ping pong balls in chapel. I myself remember members of the Noze rolling a huge "spirit hairball" down 5th Street and asking a small girl if she would contribute a lock of hair to the "Baylor spirit hairball."

Finn: The Noze Brotherhood sounds cool, but they don't sound like they were very serious about going to class and studying—maybe Frank Guittard wouldn't have liked them very much.

Pops: Maybe not, but—at least according to Steve Guittard, your redheaded first cousin twice removed and a Baylor graduate himself—Frank Guittard was called "Brother VeinNoze" by the Noze Brotherhood, so apparently, he had earned an honorary spot in the Noze because of his nose.

Finn: Good to know, I guess.

Pops: Here's another bit "sending up" the faculty.

1909 *Round-Up*

How to "Stand-in" with the Profs.
[Translation: Brown-nose or Suck up to]

Dr. Newman: Don't disturb his lecture by snoring too loudly.
Miss Jack: Enter the ministry.
B.H. Carroll, Jr.: Tell him that he looks like the Kaiser.
Prof. Guittard: Don't laugh while he is trying to get his mouth off.
Miss Buck: Join her Sunday School class.
Prof. Warren: Call him 'Doctor.'
Prof. Claypool: Eat [Maggie] Houston hash.
Prof. Straton: Buy his syllabus.
Dr. Kesler: Do not tell him he looks like an old fossil.
Dr. Daniel: 'Ne credite equo.' Translation: Do not trust the horse.
Miss Griffith: Unnecessary; she never flunks anyone.
Dr. Eby: Take the course in love.
Miss Scarborough: Smile at her.
Dr. Hargrove: See things like he does.
Librarian: Wouldn't do any good.
Dr. Brooks: Do not get over forty-nine demerits.

And a final group of faculty knocks, mostly from the 1904 *Round-Up*, to wrap up the subject:

How the Faculty Spend Their Idle Hours

Guittard—The Guy who put sys in system. (1915)
Armstrong—Chief inquisitor. (1915)
Trantham—Died in Oxford. (1915)
Eby—Curling his locks.
Hamilton—Chasing Hall [Georgia Burleson] boys.
Daniels—Looking dignified.
Johnson—Sleeping.
Prexy [President Brooks]—Lecturing.
E. Wood—Recording demerits.
Miss Jack—Looking cute.
Miss Griffith—Reading German.
Kesler—Curling his whiskers.
Surratt—Raising Cain.

Finn: Anything further about President Brooks?

Pops: Well, here are some excerpts from a "Baylor Goose Rhyme" which appeared in the *1908 Round-Up* featuring President Brooks:

To Baylor! To Baylor!
To get an education.
Home again! Home again!
To show off in vacation.
Prexy has a little speech
That lies upon the shelf;
And every time we have a rush
This speech displays itself.
Tom, Tom, the rich man's son
Came to Baylor to have some fun;
Tom tried to be cute
But it didn't suit
And Prexy showed him how to scoot.

Finn: I liked those *Round-Ups* you showed me with all the cartoons, poems, and funny stuff. Today's annuals are just heavy books with a zillion photos, most of them very small and not as much fun. I also liked all those students' answers to whether they had ever flunked a course—very funny!

CHAPTER 25

First Baylor Homecomings (1909;1915)

Today we get to tell the story of Baylor's first two homecomings, but especially the initial homecoming parades. Baylor's first parade in 1909 is reported to be the first homecoming parade of any college or university in the US. Frank Guittard played an instrumental role in organizing the parades for the first two homecomings, the parade being a key attraction of homecoming weekend. The other main attraction for returning graduates and their families was the football game. At the parades, the clubs, organizations and their floats, along with the bands, were the draws. At the football games, it was the team and the Baylor band. Katie is onboard to assist with this subject.

Katie: Pops, I know that homecoming is a big deal at Baylor, although I've never been to one. How did it all get started?

Pops: At some point in the fall of 1909, an unusual postcard announcing a homecoming for Baylor graduates—believed to have been the inspiration of President Samuel P. Brooks—was posted from three Baylor professors (George Ragland, W.H. Pool, and F.G. Guittard). The postcard went out to all graduates of Baylor in Waco, all graduates of Baylor at Independence, and all graduates of Waco University. The postcard advised:

> BAYLOR HOMECOMING...It has been the dream for years of the former students and graduates of Baylor University to have at some time a reunion of the large Baylor family...Plans are now being made to have a home-coming of Baylor's former students and graduates on Wednesday and Thursday, November 24th and 25th, 1909...Special rates will be given on all railroads and it would be well for those coming to ask for such rates when buying tickets...A detailed announcement of the program will be sent later or published in the newspapers over the state.

President Brooks's brainstorm of a homecoming for alumni had been developing almost from the beginning of his tenure, predictable from his 1902 inaugural address touching on the need for additional endowment. Increasing endowment was crucial to building a real university, even with the Carrolls' recent gifts, which had made Carroll Science and Carroll Chapel and Library possible. A full year before the professors' postcard went out, Brooks was actively working on funds for buildings and endowment for faculty, one of his ideas being that the literary societies fund "Society Halls." Another idea was for the endowment of a department chair for $50,000.

Katie: Those do sound like ideas that would be near and dear to President Brooks's heart.

Pops: Very near and dear. On Wednesday morning of homecoming week, large delegations arrived by special train from Dallas, Fort Worth, and other parts of North Texas. On Wednesday, there was a band concert featuring a new march composed by Charles Parker, band director, honoring President Brooks; a reception hosted by President Brooks; and a social at Burleson Hall that evening styled as an "old-time soiree." At seven o'clock, there was an athletic rally around an impressive bonfire accompanied by a snake dance of students holding gongs and rattles and shouting college yells and songs. At eight o'clock, after the bonfire, President Brooks delivered an address welcoming all those assembled in Carroll Chapel; the address included the following remarks:

> [Your loving mother] Baylor University...welcomes her children home. Some of you were so good that you never missed a class. Your mother loves you for that. Some of you were so bad you rarely ever went to class, and you never knew a lesson if by chance you went. Your mother loves you well for that. A fond mother never loses her love for any of her children, good or bad. Old Baylor, this loving mother, welcomes you. Right well she knows that some of you who spurned the lessons that she taught you, who trod under foot and spurned the best advice she ever gave you, have been out in the throng of a busy life, teaching to your children the lessons that you learned here. (*applause*).

Katie: You mentioned a band concert. Did Frank play his cornet in Director Parker's band for that concert?

Pops: I would think so since he was playing cornet in a small orchestra under Parker around the same time. Brooks's remarks that night were followed by an address by George W. Truett. Truett was an Erisophian brother of Frank's and the pastor of First Baptist Church in Dallas. His legendary contributions of time and talent to Baylor University were crucial to raising funds for a struggling Baylor in the 1890s. Truett's true genius was in giving inspirational sermons and talks; his talk that night concluded with these lines:

> What a cloud of departed witnesses look down upon this occasion, and beckon us to be true to Baylor!...They make us prouder of our common humanity. They rule our spirits from their sacred urns. Spirits of Baylor's noble dead, Baylor and Graves, and Burleson, and Crane, and Tanner, and Boggess, and Long, and Greer... Let the memories of what you did for Baylor provoke the noblest loyalty and love in the heart of Baylor's every child, today and forevermore. Once more. In the name of all the thousands of Baylor's sons and daughters, now gathered here and scattered throughout the world, let me now gratefully say: 'O Baylor, noble beloved Alma Mater, if ever we forget thee, may our right-hands forget their cunning, and our tongues cleave to the roof of our mouths!' (*long continued applause*)

There was no graduate of Baylor living or dead who could have competed with Truett in inspiring Baptists, especially to open their pocketbooks.

Katie: Sounds like it would have been a good time to take up a collection. Don't Baptists always take up collections after sermons?

Pops: Usually they do, but this happy occasion was probably one of the few occasions where an inspirational speech to Baptists was not followed by passing the collection plate. President Brooks, as part of his pitch to entice graduates to come back for the first homecoming, had promised those returning they would not be solicited for contributions—a wise move. Then, after Truett's address, the Baylor and Calliopean quartettes sang "Our Baylor," and the audience joined [The chorus is excerpted below].

> I love every stone in her stately walls,
> Every brick in her buildings bold.
> I love every plank in her rooms and her halls,
> Every glimpse of the Green and Gold.
> I love every tree, every blade of grass
> That grows on her campus here—
> I love every one, every loyal son
> Who will stand for our Baylor dear.

Many other speeches were made about Baylor heroes of the past, including the late Rufus C. Burleson, who had died the prior year. One speaker recounted a humorous story of President Burleson kneeling with students (always boys) in need of discipline, praying for them, and then administering to their backsides a sound whipping with a handy switch. In one incident, the student knew a whipping was in his immediate future and prudently wore two shirts, two pairs of trousers, and stuffed paper in his trousers "until [he] looked like an animated waste-basket." However, Burleson unexpectedly did not attempt to discipline the student on the day the student was prepared for it; instead, he delivered the delayed thrashing two days later when the student had forgotten to dress appropriately for the session.

Katie: Why were people laughing at a story of the president beating a student? I don't think that sort of thing is permitted anywhere today, and it doesn't seem very funny.

Pops: Maybe the laughter was of the rueful type, but times have changed to be sure. In those days, over 110 years ago, many people still agreed with Edward Eggleston's saying in *The Hoosier Schoolmaster*, "No lickin,' no l'arnin."

Katie: You were going to tell us about those first homecomings.

Pops: Yes, and with those homecomings, we are getting to some of Frank Guittard's big moments. The day after the receptions and the speeches was Thanksgiving, where the two main events were the parade and the football game. The parade featured 130 moving pieces, including automobiles decorated in green and gold and the Baylor band led by the six-foot-six-inch drum major. *The Baylor University Bulletin* reported that:

> The Baylor processions [in 1909] ...under the generalship of the Chief Marshal, Dr. I.L. McGlasson, and his assistants, Messrs. F.G. Guittard, Mordis Falkner, E.R. Nash, Jr., W.L. Prather, and J.K. Strecker, the various features of the pageant were marshaled into line on the cross-streets of the Young Men's Christian Association building. At 2 p.m. the process started west on Washington Street, then proceeded on Eighth to Austin Street, and traversed the principal thoroughfares of the city. The line extended a distance of twenty-five blocks, and all automobiles, carriages, buggies, and other vehicles were tastefully decorated with green and gold bunting and pennants...After the band came sixty automobiles and about the same number of carriages..., the Homecoming speakers, the students of Baylor at Independence and of Waco University prior

> to 1886, the President, Trustees, and Faculty of the present Baylor...Next followed eleven carriages containing the dignified senior class in caps and gowns.

Katie: That must have been wonderful to see. I'm more into parades than football games.

Pops: Well, okay, but this football game on Carroll Field was the first of many homecoming games in which Baylor played Texas Christian University, its cross-town rival. In 1909, five thousand alumni looked on as Baylor won 6-3. Music for the game was provided by Alessandro's Band, a family brass ensemble from Sicily. Seniors wore their caps and gowns to the game. In March of the next year, TCU suffered a catastrophic fire on its Waco campus and eventually relocated to Fort Worth, where it has remained ever since. The rivalry between Baylor and TCU, however, would continue.

Katie: I'm glad the first homecoming worked out well for Baylor and that it has been continued ever nearly every year since those days. Students always need a break from their books. But how did President Brooks feel about the first homecoming and the parade? And what about the next homecoming?

Pops: President Brooks wrote Frank five days after the 1909 parade and homecoming: "I do not think I have ever seen greater loyalty than was manifested by you and the other members of the homecoming committee. Your originality at so many points, coupled with your faithfulness, had much to do with the success of the occasion. Your aid and generalship in the parade cannot be properly estimated by those who were not present to witness it."

Now, about Baylor's second homecoming parade, which did not occur until 1915—it was more exciting and impressive than the first. *The Round-Up* declared that Professor Guittard, taking the part of a cavalier, along with his able assistants, managed the parade in such a splendid manner that it appeared as a symmetrical whole. Frank Guittard's supervision of the details of the 1915 parade is captured in his handwritten instructions for the Baylor Homecoming Pageant. Frank identified the pageant route: "On Austin Ave. to 4th St.; on 4th St. to Franklin St.; on Franklin St. to 5th Street to the Carroll Athletic Field (halt at 1st Baptist Church)." Frank also instructed the students on how to march: "two lines (distance apart); partners on opposite sides of the street; floats between lines; marchers three steps back of those in front; keep that distance; and marshals for each group." Lastly, Frank put down his final admonition to those participating in the parade: "Each of you has been given a role in this pageant which will be a long-remembered event in the history of Baylor and it is earnestly hoped that each one of you will act his part nobly and loyally."

The 1915 game against TCU, Baylor's opponent again, was even more satisfying for the homecoming guests than the first game, the final score being 51-0 in Baylor's favor.

Katie: So it sounds like Frank, his assistants, and the students knocked this one out of the park.

Pops: No question. President Brooks expressed his written thanks to Frank two days after the homecoming: "I would not be true to my own inclinations if I did not in some way express to you my great appreciation of the fidelity with which you assumed the responsibility of the Home-Coming. You have remarkable tact in winning others to your plans and getting them to do the things that ought to be done. I assure you that this letter is not a mere formality, but is written in earnestness. Sincerely yours, S.P. Brooks"

We can't leave the subject of the second homecoming yet, because of the problem that surfaced after Baylor's big victory against TCU. It is unfortunate that President Brooks did not also ask Frank or someone from the faculty to be active behind the scenes in connection with Baylor's football program. Frank Guittard's departmental predecessor, Robert Hamilton—a history and economics professor—was in fact the first of Baylor's football coaches and apparently the last coach to also teach an academic subject. After Baylor's undefeated 3-0 conference season in 1915, it was discovered that Baylor head coach Mosely had, knowingly or unknowingly, played an ineligible player that year, one who had lettered at Carnegie Tech several years before. The failure to discover Baylor was playing an ineligible player that year suggests an obvious weakness in Baylor's athlete recruitment to its sports teams of that era.

I haven't discussed Frank's role at commencement yet. Frank was also responsible for organizing Baylor commencement exercises for forty years, serving as Grand Marshal. Frank left his handwritten notes for how commencement proceedings should take place, including how new graduates should grasp their diploma when handed to them, as well as the measurements for each trustee's height, cap size, and chest. For example, Pat Neff's measurements were 7¼ inches cap, 45 inches chest, and 6 feet, 1 inch height.

Katie: I'm surprised that Frank would have been able to find the time for homecoming and commencement activities considering his commitment to preparation for his classes. After all, I imagine he wasn't paid anything for that time.

Pops: Yes, but his leading these activities makes sense. Although Frank would have done anything within reason to support President Brooks, you are right to question why Frank would have taken on these two large tasks and handled them for decades, at least the commencement exercises. The best answer may be three-fold: first, as the guy who put "sys" in "system" in the students' view, he had a love for organization and planning. Second, the homecomings were the first organized initiatives to bring students back to their alma mater to reconnect with classmates and teachers. The third reason where homecomings were concerned may have had to do with a feeling on his part of the importance of homecoming to the relationship between the alma mater and the former student. It would seem obvious that coming back for a homecoming would keep the ties between Baylor and its graduates evergreen.

Katie: I really want to see one of those parades and all the floats. I've heard about the Baylor Band and those nutty Noze Brotherhood guys who say "Keeko Keeko Muckity Muck." What does that mean?

Pops: I have no clue, but Baylor has the parade every year there's a homecoming planned. I'm ready to see one again myself, maybe from the lawn of Burleson Quadrangle near the end of the parade.

CHAPTER 26

Baylor Football, Baylor Spirit (1899-1920s)

Intercollegiate football at Baylor University in Waco is closely woven into the students' lives during their years on campus. For many students, football is a subject near and dear to their hearts and a source of lifelong pride mixed with some heartbreak. For President Brooks, football was an important link to alumni; it was essential to get graduates back to campus where feelings for their alma mater could be rekindled and fanned into little fires that could result in endowment. The football game and the parade were the centerpieces of homecoming, and the class reunions and other activities were built around those centerpieces along with Pigskin, the annual fraternity-sorority talent show created in the late 1950s being entitled the "Pigskin Review." I've asked Finn, who played a little football in junior high, to go through this chapter with me.

Pops: Finn, why don't we start with any questions you already have?

Finn: I'd like to know what kind of yells the cheerleaders led at football games. My dad did some cheerleading in high school and was really into it.

Pops: College yells in those days tended to be strings of nonsense syllables like this one from 1913:

> K'rip, k'rap, k'ripple-a-tipple-a-tap!
> (Oh-oh)
> Rink-ta, link-ta, Hio-totamus,
> Hop-u-la, skip-u-la, cop-u-la-gotamus;
> Ching-to-lak, Ching-to-lee,
> K'villa, k'valla, k'victory!
> (Oh-oh)
> Hoog-a-la, Tag-a-la, Mellican Man;
> Let 'er go rip, let 'er go roose,
> Ting-a-la, Tang-a-la, turn 'em aloose,
> Zip! Bang!! Baylor!!!!

Finn: Okay. I see what you mean. It does rhyme.

Pops: That's not a bad question, though. Frank Bridges, Baylor's first spectacularly successful coach who we'll be talking about in a minute, thought the lackluster cheering at Baylor games was part of the reason Baylor wasn't winning. Maybe he didn't like yells like that one. Bridges said that when he arrived in Waco in 1920, "the student body failed in organized cheering" and "consequently without a fighting spirit behind them, the teams failed to have the fighting spirit themselves, and the natural results were defeats when victories might have been possible." However, under Bridges's coaching in the 1922 championship football season, "A&M was not only out-played and beaten on the field that year, but their great organized cheering student body was badly out-cheered and beaten by Baylor's student body."

Finn: I also would like to know if Frank Guittard had any interest in football at Baylor. Did he ever have a football himself? Did he throw a football around with Francis or Clarence? Did he take them to Baylor games?

Pops: The answer to all of those questions is yes or probably yes. We know for certain he was a tennis player, and he played tennis with both sons. Francis was a competitive tennis player at Baylor, and Clarence played tennis for the exercise. We don't know what may have spurred Frank's interest in football, but, like nearly everyone who watches a college game, he got into the spirit pretty quickly with the bands playing and the cheerleaders leading the students' cheers. Because of his background as a cornet player and bandsman, hearing the Baylor band or any college band play would automatically have started his heart pumping faster. He may not have seen any college games until he enrolled at the University of Chicago. However, once at Chicago, by the fall of 1900, he must have enjoyed watching Amos Alonzo Stagg's Chicago Maroons compile a 15-6 record that year. Stagg was a legend at Chicago and nationally; he was chair of Chicago's physical education department while Frank was a student. We conclude football eventually became important to Frank because it was the lynchpin of homecoming's appeal to returning alumni. President Brooks had appointed Frank to a committee to plan the first homecoming parades in 1909 and 1915 when football was to be a star event of the homecoming weekend.

Finn: So Frank didn't see a game until he was thirty-three when he was at Chicago?

Pops: Entirely possible, although we would think he might have seen some football before he enrolled at Chicago. No proof either way.

Finn: Tell me about Baylor's early history with football and when Frank would have started attending the games.

Pops: Although football became big on many college campuses from the mid-1880s forward, President Burleson opposed football and other organized sports at Baylor, and he did not step down as president until 1897. However, despite Burleson's opposition, the first documented game was an intramural game played in 1895, the freshman and preparatory men (the "Sunbeams") defeating a team made up of sophomore, junior, and senior men (the "Seniors"). This result may seem a surprising outcome, but preparatory men were not necessarily younger or smaller than collegiate men—they just were not ready for college-level work because of insufficient preparation in high school. The Sunbeams-Seniors game was a muddy one. After the first thirty-minute half, the Seniors were missing two players and wanted to end the game, and the Sunbeams agreed. The umpire called the game for the Sunbeams 6-0 and the victors celebrated at Lavender's Restaurant.

Finn: I'm confused, Pops. If Burleson opposed football and he apparently got his way as president in most things at Baylor, how could this game between the Sunbeams and Seniors have occurred?

Pops: I have absolutely no idea, and that is a sharp question. Maybe his advanced years had softened up the old warrior. Or perhaps he was out of town preaching. Or conceivably, he thought he could conserve his energy for fighting card playing, dancing, drinking, and race-horse gambling, and not publicly opposing an activity so popular on US college campuses. However, Baylor did not play its first intercollegiate home game until 1899 after Burleson had retired, playing Toby's Business College. That year, R.H. Hamilton, history and economics professor, coached the team; he would later serve as chair of Frank's department after Frank began teaching at Baylor. Initially, Baylor faculty members coached football. Baylor's home games in 1899 were played on Carroll Field, where Carroll Science would later be erected. The first Baylor games Frank could have watched would have been in the fall of 1902 when Baylor played Trinity University twice, including once in Waxahachie, Texas; A&M twice; the Texas School for the Deaf in Waco; St. Edward's in Waco; and TCU three times, all in Waco. The next year, Baylor lost two games against Texas A&M, one against Texas, but won two against TCU and one against the Texas School for the Deaf.

Finn: Sounds like with the passing of President Burleson, things started looking up for football.

Pops: Yes, but it was touch and go for a while. In May 1906, Baylor's trustees banned the game for one year after serious football injuries occurred in games involving other colleges. Baylor students protested strenuously as Baylor's school spirit had sagged greatly, and, at last, President Brooks realized football was essential to students' undergraduate years and their feelings of pride in their alma mater. Professor R.H. Hamilton, a strong supporter of clean college sports at Baylor, spoke eloquently about how football develops students mentally and physically. As a result, intercollegiate football resumed in the 1907 season. President Brooks thought long and hard about the risks and rewards of Baylor playing intercollegiate football and came down decisively in favor of resuming the sport. Brooks's decision was supported by a number of rules changes nationally to avoid injuries, including authorizing the forward pass and prohibiting mass momentum plays. These changes all arose from national discussions starting in 1905 following a summit called by President Roosevelt to address injuries in football.

An undated memorandum in Brooks's papers contains the following statement by Brooks: "I regard football as one of the valid college sports...One of the gains that comes to colleges from football games is the return of the old students to the games and, while on the campus primarily to see the game old friends are renewed, old attachments are revived, and old love for the Alma Mater comes to life again. I think it can be said that...Harvard, Yale, Princeton and institutions like them [realized that] intercollegiate athletics [brought about] returns of old graduates and students...and consequently sympathy for Alma Maters...many gifts for the erection of buildings, for endowments, etc., resulted."

Surprisingly, when the football team was reinstated, Baylor's faculty actually urged the student body and its football team to win once games resumed, otherwise "football might meet a still sadder fate." The threat seemed to work, as Baylor won a school high five games in the first year of reinstatement (1907), and the team gained a reputation for fielding gritty players. That year was also dramatic because, although football was permitted in 1907, the faculty had expressly commanded that Baylor not play Toby's Business College team again, perhaps because Toby's teams were comprised of professional players and Waco town athletes. However, a Baylor student recalled in 1913 that despite the faculty's command, "we played [Toby's] at Padgitt's Park...and mopped up with them... The faculty heard about it and was very unhappy, scoring 20 points [demerits against] each of the players."

In 1909, Frank Guittard, who happened to be on the homecoming committee, joined over five thousand other fans in cheering on the team to a 6-3 victory over TCU in the beginning stages of what would become one of the oldest rivalries in all of college football. The 1909 victory under Coach E. J. Mills was greatly savored by Baylorites, as Baylor had already lost twice to TCU earlier in the season. Baylor's rivalry with TCU goes back to 1902, the first year that the two met on the football field. Perhaps the most striking moment in the early history of the schools' rivalry came during Baylor's 1909 Homecoming victory over TCU. "Carroll [Field] was the scene of the greatest demonstration of college spirit that has been manifested for years. On all sides of the field organized bands of 'rooters' rent the air with college yells, while three bands furnished music for the occasion. The grandstands were continuous glares of color, either green and gold or purple and white. Between the halves, the Baylor boys went through a tortuous snake dance in the middle of the field to the accompaniment of the Alessandro and Baylor Bands. Massie of TCU succeeded in counting 'three' on a place-kick. [But Baylor] bucked the ball over in two downs [and then] Robinson kicked a neat goal. The score stood 6 to 3 in favor of the home team."

The 1915 season deserves special mention for several reasons. First, it was the occasion of Baylor's second homecoming celebration and parade; Frank Guittard was largely in charge of the parade. An additional plus for this season was that W.M.J. Balenti, an All-American and a graduate of Carlisle Indian Industrial School, playing on the same team as the legendary Jim Thorpe, coached Baylor's backfield, and as a result, Baylor had one of the greatest football teams in its history. The 1916 *Round-Up* recalled: "The banner game of the year was played on Thanksgiving Day with an old rival, Texas Christian University. This contest served as a fitting climax in a successful season since the final result was 51 to 0." Unfortunately, Baylor, which would otherwise have been the conference champion, was discovered to have played an ineligible player.

The next year, 1916, Baylor had another remarkable year in football. The 1917 *Round-Up* was especially breathless about Baylor's 1916 victory over the Texas Longhorns: "Ever since 1900, the Longhorns have had the edge on the Bears and humbled them in defeat. They looked upon the Baptist team as a small weakling and laughed at its weak attempt to defeat them. But this same little weakling never gave up hope. Under each smarting defeat, it grew and its every wish was to grow up big enough to make the Longhorn herd bite the dust beneath its feet...Never in the history of Baylor football will there be so fond a remembrance for the Bears as when they look back to that memorable day of October 28, 1916. When the Wheel of Time has rolled around and the Bears of today have entered the outside world, they can still point their fingers at the Bears of tomorrow and say: 'Repeat the victory of October 28, 1916.' Thus ended the happiest day in the history of Baylor and the Baylor Bear returned covered with the dust of battle, but a victor, saying: 'Veni, vidi, vici!'"

In 1920, the Bears, in a transformational move after several discouraging years, secured Frank Bridges of Harvard University as their head football coach. The Bears became an offensive force during his tenure, returning to the level of play in their victorious 1916 and 17 seasons. Frank Bridges's work at Baylor was remarkable. According to the 1921 *Round-Up* in its summary of the 1920 season in which Baylor won only half of its games, "Some of the [Baylor players] were not of the best caliber and had to be taught the fundamentals of the game. The Bears next year should have a very prosperous season under the efficient direction of Coach Bridges and...should accomplish feats which will equal the records turned in by the famous elevens of '10, '15, '16, and '17." Regarding the 1921 season, the *Round-Up* further reported: "Frank Bridges has, in the past two years, been largely responsible for Baylor's assuming her rightful place in Southwestern athletics...To him goes the honor of having built up the most efficient scoring machine of the Conference for the 1921 season...His trick plays and rapid shifts made his team the most colorful eleven the Bears have shown in many years. A product of the Harvard school of coaching, Mr. Bridges has developed athletics to a science"...[The 1921 team included W.R. Blailock, W.W. Bradshaw, B.J. Pittman, John S. Tanner, and G.B. Weathers...The season record was 8-3.] The *Round-Up* for 1922 went on to make special mention of quarterback Wesley Bradshaw: "'Brad'...is undoubtedly the greatest quarterback in the South...He is a veritable scoring machine in himself, being able to kick, pass or carry the ball almost at will. No team that the Bears met was able to stop this elusive Bruin... [who] led the conference in scoring by a safe margin and was unanimously selected for 'all-southwestern quarter-back.'"

Under the leadership of Coach Bridges, in 1922 Baylor won its first Southwestern Conference Championship in football. President Brooks honored the team with a feast at the Fish Pond with the old lettermen as honored guests. Those present included the following (along with their wives): Coach Frank Bridges, Frank Guittard, J.M. Dawson (Pastor, First Baptist Church of Waco), and Coach Jim Crow. That year Baylor's only losses were to non-conference teams Boston College and Haskell Institute.

1923 saw Coach Bridges start the season with disadvantages as only six lettermen returned, and Howard Hartzog, one of the stars from the 1922 team, had come down with typhoid fever. Nevertheless, Bridges built a formidable team that was able to tie Texas A&M (0-0) and the Texas Longhorns (7-7), which was considered by many the strongest team in the south. However, in 1924, Baylor got it all together again for another Southwestern Conference Championship. The Bears dominated D.X. Bible's Texas Longhorns 28-10 in the informal opening game at the Texas Memorial Stadium in Austin on November 8 before a crowd of ten thousand. Bill Coffey thrilled Baylorites with his amazing punt returns, and Captain Pittman's plunges into the line were virtually unstoppable. Fakery was also a skill in Coach Bridges's toolkit, put to use when Coffey faked a run around the end but then ran up the middle for forty-five yards and a touchdown. Then Baylor bested Texas A&M 15-7 before a crowd of 25,000. The stars of the 1924 game for Baylor were Pittman, Collier, Walker, Biggs, Sisco, and Coffey.

The Baylor-Texas game in 1924 matched two coaches and teams both accomplished in football tricks and fakes. Bible's team was noted for delayed or spinner plays, reverse shoulder blocks, runners employing a limp leg to evade a tackler, and various other kinds of fakes and reverses. Bridges's teams had their hidden ball trick, eight-man offensive line, a spinner play, and other Bridges's innovations.

Finn: What was Coach Bible's spinner play?

Pops: According to Coach Bible, a delayed or spinner play was one in which the ball goes to a back who hides it from the opponent while executing a full or partial spin, which had the effect of "holding the defensive players in place while they try to locate the ball, or...sending them on a wild goose chase after a player who does not have the ball." Bridges had many plays that he either developed on his own or adapted from other teams' plays. Bridges's plays included the "fake reverse," the "spin play inside short tackle," the "Georgia Tech shift," and the "Princeton '20' formation." Bridges was both a scholar of the game and an innovator. He was also a "systems" guy. He stressed that having a smart quarterback was not enough—the quarterback had to play within a system and that the system itself "develops brains." "Don't let the quarter [back] become superior to the system." We suspect that Frank Guittard and Frank Bridges would have enjoyed comparing their systems for teaching history versus teaching football.

Finn: I don't get what was so dangerous about football in 1905-1906 that President Brooks banned football for 1906 and that Teddy Roosevelt called a meeting at the White House.

Pops: Okay, that requires some explanation. College football in 1905 was of the rugby type. It was extremely dangerous because although it was permissible to run with the ball, passing the ball was not allowed, and there was much more body contact than there is with the modern game. The minimum protective equipment players wore didn't protect. One of the plays in the 1890s was a "flying wedge" or V play where a group of heavier players would start in motion safeguarding a group of lighter players. After the wedge crashed into the other team, the runner would follow his team downfield. This kind of play was so dangerous that the football rule-makers outlawed flying wedges by ruling that only two men could go in motion before the start of the play. "Power plays across the middle or mass plays meant pushing, shoving, or even catapulting the ball carrier, resulting in jarring collisions...and resembled relics of the Theban [or Hoplite] phalanx associated with ancient Greek warfare." The "head harness" or helmet did not come into general use until the early 1900s. In December 1905, representatives of sixty-two colleges and universities met to appoint a rules committee, and such committee met again in January of the following year. Several timely developments came in the wake of the discussion instigated by President Roosevelt, including the allowance of the forward pass. The pass both opened up the game and loosened up the line play, adding considerable excitement to the game. Other changes to the rules included the ten-yard rule, the neutral zone, and stricter measures against unfair play, but the allowance of the forward pass was the most important in reducing injuries.

Finn: So a lot of players got hurt back before the rules changed?

Pops: In 1905, there were, in the rugby-type football games of the times, at least eighteen fatalities and more than 150 severe injuries in football games between US colleges. In 1906, one notorious incident involved a Union College player who was killed in a pile-up in a game against New York University. Another report on fatalities and injuries was that the number killed was twenty-five and the number seriously injured 168.

Finn: Yeah, those pile-ups on the field today still look pretty crazy. It seems like in almost every game, at least one player is removed on a stretcher. And players may stay in the game sometimes even after they get "their bells rung." I've read about CTE—chronic traumatic encephalopathy. That sounds pretty bad, even if no bones are broken and you can't see any blood.

Pops: Modern football from high school to the professional level is a risky sport, even with all the advancements in medicine of today and all the rules to prevent players from injuring each other, like the rule on "targeting." But modern football is lucrative, and a certain amount of risk equals money. People will pay to see a spectacle, especially a dangerous one, like those combats between gladiators in the ancient Roman coliseum or those between a single gladiator and wild animals like leopards and lions. Did you know about those?

Finn: Nope. We still have that 1950s Baylor helmet you gave us. It's pretty solid.

Pops: Yes, it looks okay, but it was not much real protection for the players in those days. Today's improved helmets look more like hockey headgear and the players also wear mouthpieces. Ever watch a hockey game?

CHAPTER 27

Along Comes Josie (1919-1950)

The subject matters of several chapters in this book, all set in the 1920s, have already been addressed at length in *A Ph.D.'s Reverie: The Letters* (2019). Those subjects included Frank's whirlwind courtship of his second wife, Josie Glenn Guittard ("Mama Josie"), told through family letters and editor's notes. Since the earlier book captured this subject, the treatment in this volume will be a brief overview through conversations with Katie.

Pops: Katie, rarely does a man have the good fortune of finding and marrying two compatible, companionable women, but Frank was one of those lucky men. He found Mamie first, and then several years following Mamie's death, Josie. Mamie's story has been fully set out in this volume, from her meeting Frank in Shiner when he was principal of the Shiner school to her last days at the Albuquerque Sanatorium. Josie's story, from her initial noncommittal response to Frank's determined pursuit starting in December 1919 to the couple's close relationship during his Ph.D. sabbaticals in the 1920s was set out in the earlier volume, *A Ph.D.'s Reverie: The Letters.* In this chapter, we will summarize Josie's story since it is an essential piece of Frank's life and times. Make sense?

Katie: Yes, for sure. I'm very interested in Josie and how her relationship with Frank developed, especially considering how cool she was to him at first. It sounds a little like one of those Fred Astaire-Ginger Rogers movies they show on Turner Classic Movies where Fred is pushy but Ginger isn't impressed.

Pops: That's my take, too. Frank and Josie met in Waco sometime in December 1919. Josie, like Frank, had grown up in a large farming family; her parents were William A. and Ollie E. Glenn of Bronte, Texas. She was an unmarried thirty-seven-year-old Houston school teacher who was not thinking about getting married; Josie's mother was also counting on her as the oldest child to remain single. The initial meeting was facilitated by Josie's cousin Katherine Bryan and her husband Tom. The Bryans and Frank were members of First Baptist Church in Waco. When Frank and Josie were first introduced, it had been almost four years since Frank, Francis, and Clarence lost Mamie. Frank needed a life partner who would make a good mother for Clarence, who was not yet four years old and had been living in Shiner since he was a month old. Josie and Frank married June 10,

1920, and Josie moved into the house at 1401 South 8th in Waco, where they would live the rest of their lives.

Josie, like Mamie before her, made an energetic and involved faculty wife. On occasion, Frank referred to her as the "wheel-horse" of the history department when he was chair. Josie had some college education after high school, including possibly some work at Baylor. A gracious hostess who opened up 1401 South 8th for countless faculty wives' gatherings, Josie was popular for her playful sense of humor and happy spirits. Her devotion to Frank, Francis, and Clarence made for a comfortable home for Frank. Based in part on the home support he received from Josie for three decades, Frank was able to earn and retain the confidence of his university president and the admiration of his students. For Frank's five grandchildren, Josie was an especially fun grandmother and companion for the grandchildren on their infrequent trips to Waco.

A single excerpt from one of Josie's letters to Frank, while he was on sabbatical working on his Ph.D. at Stanford, will have to suffice: "I heard a good story the other day. A man was walking along the street and saw a sign 'Woman's Exchange.' He dropped in and when the lady came forward he said 'Is this the Woman's Exchange?' She said 'Yes Sir.' He said 'Be you the woman?' She said 'Yes Sir.' He said 'Well, I believe I'll just keep Sallie.' Would you feel that way about your wifie?" (August 6, 1929 letter from JGG to FGG)

Katie: I'm curious why Frank was so quick to propose to Josie and so slow to propose to Mamie? Frank and Mamie did not get married until seven years after they met, but you say Frank and Josie married in six months?

Pops: That's right. The answer to that question has several parts. It appears from their correspondence that Frank and Mamie had a serious relationship at least since 1902 when he returned from Chicago with his degrees. Although we believe he may have been in contact with one or more other women as late as 1903, nevertheless, there is no hard evidence of that, only rumors in the *Round-Up*. We also know he spent four Christmases with Mamie by 1904. However, in 1902, although Frank now had a position teaching at Baylor—the only job he would have for the rest of his life—he did not feel he was ready professionally or financially to marry anyone. Marrying a woman from a family of substantial wealth and taking her home to live in a boarding house would not have appealed to him or to her, especially considering Mamie must have had other marital options which would have entailed less Spartan living than a Waco boarding house. The primary reason Frank's relationship with Josie developed so rapidly is that not only were there no obstacles, but there was a compelling reason for Frank to find a partner quickly who could mother Clarence. Frank and Josie were also older than Frank and Mamie when they were married. As to how or why Josie changed her mind about marriage to Frank, considering that there was no substantial obstacle to their marriage other than that of Josie's mother initially, the crucial factor seems to have been Frank's persistence and manifest confidence that Josie would come around given time.

Katie: Okay. I get that. I'm curious, though, weren't there ways in which Mamie and Josie were alike and ways that they were different? Was Josie like a lot like Mamie?

Pops: They were certainly both alike in their strong maternal instincts, both being devoted mothers to Francis and Clarence. They each shared an appreciation for good music and for the arts in general. The primary differences lay in their personalities and their families. Mamie and Frank both liked to read, Frank especially so. Josie was more of a social person with a buoyant, humorous personality that attracted others and enabled her to make friends easily. Because Josie grew up on a farm, she was more familiar with home activities like canning peaches and pears and the hard work to be done around the home. The Welhausens were well-to-do financially, whereas Josie's family was a hard-working, hard-scrabble farming family. Does that answer your questions?

Katie: I think so. Did you ever meet Josie or Mamie?

Pops: I knew Mama Josie for more than fifteen years. I liked her a lot. She took my brother and me to old black and white movies they showed at the Student Union in the summertime, like *Arsenic and Old Lace* with Cary Grant and *Mutiny on the Bounty* with Clark Gable. Actually, we saw *Mutiny* at the Melrose Theater, which is no longer there. She also took us to the scary old bear pits, which were cool, and to Cameron Park. Mamie died twenty-five years before I was born, but I learned what Mamie was like through her letters to Frank, her college essays, and her 1901 shipboard diary.

Katie: That shipboard diary gives me an idea. Maybe I could get my dad to take me on one of those big ocean liners, like the Queen Elizabeth.

Pops: It wouldn't hurt to mention it, perhaps for your graduation from college.

CHAPTER 28

The Student Self-Government Experiment (1911-1923)

In tracing Frank Guittard's roles and activities at Baylor, we inevitably come to the origin and aftermath of the Student Self-Government experiment at Baylor. The inspiration for the experiment came initially from President Brooks and then the faculty. The years of that experiment overlapped the first wave of new democratic governments in the twentieth century after World War I. Charlie has expressed an interest in students' democratic organizations on college campuses; we will give him a chance to ask a question or to comment at the beginning and end of this chapter.

Contexts—democracy and intercollegiate athletics.

Charlie: Pops, I can tell by your stack of notes we're going to be here for a while. However, before you get started, I would like to know whether Frank Guittard had anything to do with Baylor's Student Self-Government.

Pops: Yes, he did, and that is one of the primary reasons for this chapter. Frank was there at its beginning and was instrumental in its development. After that, he was involved in monitoring and assisting as needed; and finally, he was involved in bringing about its demise. Be thinking about what you think happened to the Student Self-Government at Baylor and whether the students or the faculty could have avoided the ultimate outcome.

First though, let's back up a moment and consider another essential context of the experiment—the popularity of intercollegiate football across the US and on the Baylor campus. After President Burleson resigned in 1897 and Baylor's literary societies began their three-decade decline, intercollegiate sports at Baylor started to emerge, especially football. Americans enthusiastically embraced an evolving American style of football, a phenomenon *nonpareil* in American life. After a stumble in the first decade of the twentieth century before the new rules emerged to reduce injuries, football—the American institution—arrived with both feet, from pee wee teams to the professional ranks. American football was becoming inextricably woven into our modern world, and, importantly, an inevitable partner in the American educational system. We cannot definitively say why that should have come about, except that athleticism, competitive instinct, a degree of violence, and loyalty to one's college alma mater all came together to capture and hold our imagination in a way like no other sport.

Nowhere would that convergence of forces be more apparent than at Baylor in the 1920s when student spirit rose and fell with the fortunes of Baylor's football team. Baylor's most notable early successes in intercollegiate football were its Southwest Conference Championships in 1922 and 1924 under Baylor coach and Harvard graduate Frank Bridges. As to the relative importance of football to Baylor in these years, effective for the 1922-23 school year, Coach Bridges's compensation was raised from $3,600 annually to $4,800, while the chairs of Baylor's academic departments, including Frank Guittard, topped out at $3,000 annually. President Brooks's salary for the same period was the same as the prior year, $3,600. Since 1923, this sort of disparity has gotten much greater at US colleges.

Baylor creates a Student Self-Government and it begins operations.

In June 1913, the Baylor administration and faculty, at a time of national general interest in increasing the number of democratic institutions and governments, commenced its investigation of the possibility of initiating student self-government at Baylor. Baylor's interest in student self-government began during the administration of President Woodrow Wilson. It extended through the short term of President Warren G. Harding, with both the Harding presidency and student self-government at Baylor collapsing within months of each other, although for completely different reasons. As inspired by President Brooks, a strong proponent of democratic processes, the Baylor faculty desired a shift toward empowering students to take over, in part, certain administrative functions previously exercised by the faculty. The faculty believed that student participation in the school administration would develop college spirit, raise the students' moral tone, develop leaders, and lighten the burden of administrative tasks on the faculty. No one on the faculty enjoyed listening to cases detailing the students' dirty laundry.

Accordingly, Baylor appointed a committee from its academic faculty—Professors F.G. Guittard, Henry Trantham (Baylor's faculty representative to the Southwest Conference), and J.M. Wright—to study the idea of student self-government for a period before approving and setting up such a system. Guittard would serve as the committee's de-facto chair. The committee made an "exhaustive study of all student governments in colleges in the United States and Canada." Fundamental to establishing student self-government was entrusting discipline in many student matters to the students. There were at least three reasons to do this: first, as a vehicle to teach the students the responsibilities of the three divisions of American government, executive, legislative, and judicial; second, to follow the lead of many other colleges and universities; and third, to turn over time consuming and unpleasant fact-finding and disciplinary functions to the students as much as possible.

Some key events in the history of Baylor's Student Self-Government

On June 11, 1911, a committee (F.G. Guittard, Chair) was appointed to investigate incidents of copying.

On January 20, 1913, the committee made its report on student self-government in other colleges and universities following the receipt of answers to the committee's detailed questionnaire from at least thirty or more colleges and universities describing student self-government at their institutions. Questions included: Is there any difficulty experienced in getting students to give their evidence against their fellows? And do students have any interest in ferreting out and disclosing evidence as to offenses alleged? The committee concluded cautiously that if the students met the conditions for creating a student self-government, only a limited degree of student control should be given at first over dishonesty in examinations.

Two years later, in January 1915, Baylor's SSGA (Student Self-Government Association) was organized—legislative, executive, and judicial branches—and described in the student-drafted, faculty-approved constitution for the SSGA. Self-government notably included the implementation of the "Honor System." Additionally, the SSGA took charge of all student affairs, including publications, athletics, and the literary, oratorical, musical, and social schedules of the students.

From May 1918-December 1922, the SSGA functioned in all of its departments and was reported to be a "harmoniously operating little republic." However, over time, despite the initial euphoria over the creation of the SSGA, it unfortunately became clear that all was not tranquil where the SSGA and student discipline were concerned, as witnessed by the following events:

January 1923, the prosecuting attorney for the SSGA resigned.

March 1923, the issue of lax enforcement by the SSGA arose.

March 1, 1923, Professor Guittard and Guy B. Harrison, Jr., Guittard's grader, turned cheating cases that were arising in Guittard's classes over to the SSGA for handling.

Charlie: So what happened to the SSGA? Were the cheaters punished?

Pops: Okay, let's go back a little bit, and then we'll get to those questions.

The early years of Baylor's Student Self-Government

During the eight years the SSGA functioned where student discipline was concerned, the SSGA's judicial arm, vested in one general council and two dormitory councils, heard many types of cases including those involving cheating on examinations. These cases included various unpermitted conflicts between the freshman and sophomore classes—freshmen failing to wear their "slime caps," egg-throwing at a freshman reception, invasion of the other class's reception, and stealing the ice cream designated for another class's reception. The SSGA also prosecuted violations irrespective of class status—hazing at an initiation by yoking and tying initiates to a telephone pole while their tormentors ate hamburgers, forcing initiates to jump Waco creek with their hands tied behind them, smoking cigarettes, misconduct in the library or chapel, car riding without permission, and attending a dance at the Shriners' Hall.

The SSGA also heard allegations that female residents of Georgia Burleson had received unapproved callers, walked with a man in a remote or secluded place, were out of their room after 10 p.m., or failed to wear bedroom slippers.

Charlie: Hold on there, Pops. Failure to wear bedroom slippers was a problem?

Pops: Apparently, bare body parts of a female below the waist were frowned upon, even if no male students were present to view them, since it was unladylike. Dates were closely regulated and female residents were given demerits if they attempted to engage in more dates per week than allowed or attempted other unpermitted contact with the opposite sex; for example, all first-year students were allowed one date a week in the parlor, except during the last quarter when they had the option of attending church; sophomores, one date a week in the parlor or attendance at church; juniors two dates a week, including one to church services on Sunday; and seniors—dates at their discretion.

The faculty minutes from 1913 and after show that Frank took on committee responsibility along with other faculty members to deal with the transfer of student discipline to the SSGA, and after that, with the operation of the SSGA. He served in many cases as committee chair and did a significant amount of the committee's work himself, all of which was discussed, corrected, and approved by other committee members. (Faculty Minutes, November 19, 1920, 41) The crucial part of the Constitution on the Honor System was contained in an appendix:

> [It] is clearly a violation of the system to look upon another's paper or to allow another student to look upon your paper during a quiz for the purpose of getting information therefrom...It is also a violation of the system for a student to fail or refuse to report any

> reasonably clear case of cheating of which he may have knowledge...There are no spies or policemen around the University to detect irregularities. The honor of all the students is at stake, and every loyal citizen of the University community should be glad to help in the elimination of the dishonorable ones among us...As soon as a violation is reported to the President of the Students Association or any other member of the judicial councils, the cases [are] taken up and investigated much the same as a lawyer examines a case in preparation for trial. The council hears all the evidence that can be secured, the accused is given every opportunity to prove his innocence. The council judges the accused either innocent or guilty and in the latter event affixes the penalty. The findings are then reported to the Discipline Committee of the faculty, and if approved, put into execution.

The enforcement problem with student self-government emerges.

In March 1919, it was obvious that questions as to the effectiveness of student government discipline of student offenders were emerging. The Report of the Faculty Committee, appointed to confer with the Judicial Council of the Student Self-Government Association, found "the function of the faculty as an appellate court was interpreted as meaning 1) that the faculty had power to approve or set aside sentences imposed by the Judicial Council. 2) That the faculty has power to retry cases appealed and to modify sentences imposed by the Judicial Council. Faculty Committee—F.G. Guittard, G. Dow, H. Trantham" (Faculty Minutes, March 14, 1919)

A *Lariat* article from the early 1920s subsequently sounded a warning of a possible problem in the future, saying: "Although the students approved the self-government, they did not cooperate with the judicial councils in enforcing the rules. They refused to report violations of the regulations and did not help the student councils secure information concerning cases." A *Lariat* article March 7, 1923 reported: "On Monday, the Grand Jury began a session which will apparently last for several weeks in the investigation of the recent happenings between the freshman and sophomore classes...These include offenses by girls as well as by boys and from all appearances, investigations have only begun." Additionally, an editor of the *Lariat* sounded the alarm regarding the peril the SSGA was in by its lax enforcement of laws passed by its Legislative Assembly, and of the need to rehabilitate the perception of the SSGA:

> Recently, there have been a number of incidents around the University which have grown into a slight insurrection against the

> authority of the Students' Association...The officers of the Association have been too lenient with us. They see their mistake—as do we. The freshman class brought down upon themselves no little criticism for their method of approaching a condemnation of the law enforcing the wearing of their caps...
>
> But the most alarming fact [in the controversy] is the action taken by the student body in general—the Student Association itself. The student body, with the Association officers, has been too lenient on most of us for some time, while it is the well-known duty of everyone to report thieves. Now we must pay for this, which most of us have done.
>
> There is an issue. It is this: are we going to have a Student Self-Government Association or are we not? Are we going to follow the laws or wipe them off in a legal way? Or, are we going to get Bolshevistic and cut our own throats? The officers of the Students' Association say no. What do you say? Let's get right here and fall in behind the Association in its sincere effort to straighten things out. We believe they will as the student body gets right. (*Lariat*, March 7, 1923, 2)

Unfortunately, the editor's call above to straighten out the mess in student discipline caused by the failure and lenience of the Student Association was too late to have a chance of rectifying the damage done to the credibility of the Association. The Association would survive only six weeks longer. On March 10, an article appeared entitled "INDICTMENTS READ FOR JUDICIAL COUNCIL BY MONDAY," and subtitled "Bills are made against 23 freshmen..." The article continued: "Most of the cases to be tried by the Council will be against freshmen for alleged interference in a sophomore reception, which was held at the Raleigh Hotel, March 1. For this particular offense, there will be some 23 of the fish brought to trial, with separate minor charges against some of them. The other cases will include cheating, misconduct at Chapel, and some other offenses." Chairman S___ makes the statement that "the evidence secured will with little doubt convict every culprit, when he calls his counsel together before prosecuting attorneys." (*Lariat*, March 10, 1923, 1)

The cheating cases are filed.

The origin of the cheating cases, in part or in total, is described in the Oral Memoirs of Professor Guy B. Harrison, Jr., who observed instances of cheating in one of Frank Guittard's history classes. Harrison, Frank's student grader at the time and later his faculty colleague, stated that Frank had warned him to watch for dishonesty on tests. Harrison noted that there was a history section he graded in which there were some of the most famous players that Baylor had during its championship years in football and baseball. Harrison sat at the front of the room and tried not to see anything. However, when Frank left the room, he would hear murmuring. When Harrison later graded the papers for this section, the cheating was just flagrant. "You couldn't miss it—the copying from one another. They made similar mistakes, even spelled the words the wrong way...some half dozen of them...I turned them over to Dr. Guittard and I indicated the instances...and said 'those are some of the best players we have, what are we going to do about it?' He said 'there's not anything we can do about it but turn it over to the student government.' And so the papers and all the evidence were turned over and they had their trials. And they merely gave them a few demerits, previously they'd been taking away all their credits and expelling them from school. And this was such flagrant partiality and such flagrant failure to enforce the law."

In a subsequent oral interview with the author, Professor Harrison included with the athletes some members of the SSGA who had cheated, stating, "These were the people supposed to uphold the student government of Baylor University." Harrison said that both he and Frank "thought [the students] were in a spot, but Frank said if they did cheat, the chips will have to fall where they may. He called the boys in [apparently no girls were charged] and showed them their papers and some denied it. It then came up before the SSGA with all that proof" and Frank's word and Harrison's word. Harrison further remembered that Dr. Brooks had looked at the evidence himself and confirmed the Association's recommendation.

On March 14, the SSGA chairman announced in a speech at chapel: "The judicial council is functioning and is dealing out relentless punishment to the lawbreakers of the University, the majority of which are violators of the pledge concerning class rules. With much ready evidence against a freshman who recently entertained prominent sophomore members with auto rides out of the city..., the council has already tried, in sessions yesterday and this morning, five freshmen, convicting all five of them and has charges on file for some twenty more. All of these...having been suspended until the Spring term, when they may return with 45 marks against them...And convicted also in the last session...for disregard of the honor system, the penalty assessed being suspension for the remainder of the school term and 15 marks being accepted upon return of the defendant." (*Lariat*, March 14, 1923, 1)

The honor system convictions were appealed in a dramatic move in which the prosecuting attorney stepped down from his former position as prosecutor, saying he considered it as much his duty to obtain mercy and justice for a particular defendant as to secure a penalty, and then became the defendant's advocate. The general opinion around the university, according to the *Lariat*, was that the verdict had been harsh in light of other sentences for the same offense. When the general council reconvened to consider the case, the student attorney rose before the packed courtroom and his voice shot through with emotion, moved for another consideration of the trial. "The motion passed and the council retired to reconsider its former verdict. After being out for nearly two hours, the verdict [of guilty] was sustained." (*Lariat*, March 14, 1923, 1)

Another highly charged incident involved a case against a sophomore woman and her male companions charged with participating in a scheme to steal the freshmen's ice cream supply for a freshman reception. The female student was charged with "going to a nearby rooming house to swap her feminine attire for masculine clothes to lead her classmen to the storeroom in which the refreshments for the reception were cached by the 'fish.'" Testimony was adduced concerning the arrangement of the rooms at the rooming house where clothes were exchanged and a diagram of their arrangement made for the further understanding of the Council.

The final verdict in the case of the young woman in disguise is not clear, but at some point, the Dean of Women, who had been watching the trial, rose and, with words of conviction, repeated that she knew all the facts of the case, that she knew that "the parties of the case were guilty only of thoughtless impetuosity in striving to lead their classmates in a reckless attempt to thwart their traditional opponents, the Freshmen and that any other implications from the speech of the prosecutor, under great strain from the case, should be ignored." In reply, Attorney B___, in a voice trembling with emotion, said that "he had no intention of casting any reflection on the young lady, that the small pin which he wore was a tie closer than blood and that anyone who should slander the lady, who wore such a pin, should be held responsible for such insult by him." Apparently, no conviction was obtained against the young woman for her participation in the ice cream caper. (*Lariat,* March 17, 1923, 1)

On March 19, the faculty at a called meeting met to discuss and respond to, as needed, the recent actions of the Judicial Council of the Students' Association. President Brooks called the meeting to order, and Mr. B___, president of the Students' Association, made some general remarks to update the faculty on the Association's recent efforts to address various infractions by the students. Reports were furnished, including lists of students punished for various crimes, such as cheating on tests, smoking cigarettes in the dormitory, attending a dance at the Shriner Hall, and participating in a class rush.

Then, a resolution was proposed raising the topic of hazing, saying: "Hazing does develop the gang or mob spirit, which is essentially wrong...Recently there has been too much hazing on the students of Baylor University...The Student Self-Government Association has assessed punishment upon several of their fellow students in obedience to law. Perhaps, if the faculty or some of Baylor's friends had been on the governing body, the results might have been different. Perhaps the punishment would have been more severe or less severe." At that point, the March 19, 1923 faculty resolution ended its comments with the following resolutions: "The judicial council is hereby commended for its recent effort at enforcement of all the laws of the Student Self-Government Association. It is recommended to the Student Self-Government Association that a law be passed at once forbidding any student guilty of cheating on a test from representing the University in any inter-class or inter-collegiate contest. Depending on the proper disposition of this matter, no student guilty of this offense may represent the University." (Faculty Minutes, March 19, 1923)

Following the faculty meeting on March 19, the issues between the students and the faculty worked their way to the painful final resolution. The *Lariat* reported that President Brooks, at chapel the next day, stated the views of the faculty from the meeting the day before. The *Lariat* reported that "President Brooks continued his message to the student body with detailed accounts of the hazing violations. Concerning hazing itself, President Brooks stated, 'Never develops individualism, nor does it remotely educate, except for harm. Hazing does develop a gang or mob spirit which is essentially wrong. Hazing is undemocratic. It partakes of mock aristocracies and fails to recognize the equality of many. There is not known to this faculty any institution in America that encourages it, allows it, or fails to punish students found guilty of it.'" (*Lariat*, March 24, 1923, 1)

Another article in the same *Lariat* issue entitled "Council Ends Most Grueling Sessions; Record Convictions" discussed the most recent work of the Judicial Council: "Forty students were arraigned before the General Council for breach of Association laws, as against 30 the prior week. Sixty out of the 70 were convicted. The charges last week were mainly against freshmen and sophomores for alleged participation in class rushes, all of which were given sentences ranging from 20 marks to suspension. This week shows charges of cheating on examination, 5; car-riding without permission, 7; misconduct in library, 1; misconduct in chapel, 9; sophomore reception committee for not cooperating with authorities, 5; dancing, 10; failure to wear freshman cap, 3. Of this number, only 10 were found not guilty, and all of these in a second week's sitting." *(Lariat* Mar 24, 1923, 1) The *Lariat* then reported significantly that seven cases of cheating would come up before the council upon the opening of the Spring Term next Monday [March 26]. The *Lariat* further revealed that the "Legislative Assembly is now considering a new law which the faculty has proposed. This law will, if accepted by the Association, bar and render ineligible for student activities all students convicted of cheating." Although not mentioned in the *Lariat*, as of March 24, thirteen inter-collegiate games were scheduled between March 24 and May 5 and included those with the University of Oklahoma, the University of Texas, and Texas A&M.

The *Lariat* also called attention to certain features of the deliberations of the General Council upon alleged cheating infractions by students. The first was the fact that the student officials in charge of the deliberations were being asked to punish and correct their fellow students and that it is exceedingly difficult for students to sit in judgment of their fellow students for such a sensitive matter as a cheating allegation. An additional complication, perhaps in meeting the expectations of the faculty, was that the student officials had been deciding charges based not only on the facts of the instant case but also on the past conduct of a defendant. The argument was now made that verdicts should be based upon the evidence in the case at hand and not the prior history of a defendant. The members of the General Council usually knew the record of a student before the trial commences.

Thus, for the *Lariat* editor, the overriding questions were: was the present system of trial, particularly that phase wherein all things were considered by the Council, a just one, and should the form of regular court proceedings be instituted, or was the present system the better? The *Lariat* editor opined further that: "As it stands, the Council is a tribunal before which all alleged offenders are brought to be tried and acquitted or punished according as the laws of the Association instruct. It seems that no special provision has been made in the constitution for the thing now in question. The Council takes the evidence, and when advisable, the past records, and delivers the verdict thereupon. That this is a grave duty to place upon a student is clearly evident. To sit as a judge upon his fellow, often to decide upon past record, whether or not it was best for him and for the school that he should be suspended or expelled—that is a condition which may be questionable as to its advisability. Under regular Court proceedings, the General Council might act in the capacity of Grand Jury. Twelve students from different groups in the University would be impounded as a jury and try the case on the evidence solely." (*Lariat*, March 24, 1923, 2)

The *Lariat* thus identified two potential problems with the method of deciding cases against students: first, the difficulty of fellow students deciding the fate of their fellows; second, the problematic nature of a system under which the Association judges might be already aware of a student's prior record as a troublemaker or for good conduct and could let those improperly influence the outcome. On the other hand, the chief problem with going to the traditional system of grand jury proceedings followed by a separate trial by a jury would be the slowness of such a system.

President Brooks demands the SSGA pass a law.

Regarding the bill for a new law on the penalty for cheating in relation to competition in intercollegiate athletics adopted by the faculty on March 19 and submitted to the Legislative Assembly for their approval, the *Lariat* reported that as of March 24, no definite action had been taken, nor would be taken until March 26 at the time of the opening of the spring term. Further, President Brooks had informed the *Lariat* that should the Students' Association not uphold the faculty in this manner, other means would be taken to secure the inauguration of such a law. "This would be done because such a ruling has long been the custom at Baylor—that is, in regard to cheating—and that this action is but a move of the faculty toward having a written law." Dr. Brooks further explained to the *Lariat*, "pending action by the Association, the law is effective as regards recent convictions for cheating by the General Council." (*Lariat*, March 24, 1923, 1) Presumably, the five convictions for cheating were those cited elsewhere in the same issue of the *Lariat*.

If President Brooks was not clear in his statement to the *Lariat*, or the faculty clear in its faculty resolutions and pronouncements regarding the urgency of the students immediately passing a law barring athletes convicted of cheating from competing in intercollegiate athletic contests, any doubt was conclusively dispelled by Brooks's letter written and delivered to the SSGA president: "Dear Mr. B___, I am to leave town the middle of next [week] and will be gone until after the first of April. I very much hope that the student body will grant the suggestion and make a law, as the faculty has recommended, concerning those who cheat on examination. Yours very truly, [President Brooks]."

In the afternoon of Monday, March 26, the student Legislative Assembly substantially ratified the faculty resolution stating that no student convicted of cheating shall represent the University in any student activities, including intercollegiate athletic competition, but omitting any provision in the faculty resolution disqualifying the students recently convicted of cheating before the passage of the bill. (*Lariat* March 28, 1923, 1) Although President Brooks had reportedly stated to the *Lariat* that the students recently convicted for cheating should be barred from athletic competition, this specific application had not been included in the faculty resolution, nor in President Brooks's letter to the SSGA President. (*Lariat*, March 28, 1923, 2)

The SSGA balks and passes an unacceptable compromise bill.

The problem for the Legislative Assembly of the SSGA was the fact that the cheating students had already been charged, tried, and their punishments determined before the Legislative Assembly had been asked to enact another bill regarding punishment. Now the faculty wanted it to pass a law that would effectively re-determine punishment. To the students' minds, the fact that it may have always been the custom of the faculty, prior to the institution of student self-government, to bar cheating students from competing athletically, or that such a provision had been omitted in error from the student self-government constitution, did not justify such a law. Faculty, administration, and students alike had been given the opportunity to review the proposed constitution before passage and correct any omissions. The students, assisted by those of their number who were law students, could not bring themselves to enact what they considered to be an ex post facto law, which it arguably would have been. (*Lariat*, March 28, 1923, 2)

Charlie: Pops, do you think the students were wrong in not passing the law the faculty requested barring students already convicted of cheating from competing for the university?

Pops: Well, after so much dissension about whether students were being too lenient with their fellow students in all kinds of cases, this request by the faculty came at a bad time and appears to have been the straw that broke the camel's back. But I would say yes, the SSGA should have passed such a law if it desired to keep the Student Self-Government in place. The student newspaper claimed that the merits of such a provision were never in dispute from any quarter. The *Lariat* reported: "That this law was just as it should have been on the books long ago, most of us will agree." (*Lariat*, March 31, 1923, 2)

Following the March 31 *Lariat* was a seventeen-day lull in the matter preceding the inevitable storm April 17 after President Brooks had returned to Waco. At that time, Brooks caught up on the situation before the Legislative Assembly, specifically, his request for a law barring the previously convicted cheating students from intercollegiate competition. Whether any of the convicted students had actually suited up and played is unclear. However, Baylor had played six games post-convictions before the next move by the faculty toward getting the convicted students declared ineligible. (*Lariat,* April 18, 1923)

At the faculty meeting on April 17, the minutes reported that Professor Guittard read the recommended legislation passed by the students' council, and Mr. B___ made some explanatory remarks about the legislation. Thereafter, however, upon recommendation of the faculty committee whose views are attached to the minutes of this meeting, the proposed legislation was not accepted because of certain obscurities in the wording of the proposals. (Faculty Minutes, April 17, 1923) The students' recommended legislation, which was not accepted by the faculty, had read, in pertinent part, as follows: "No student *hereafter* (*emphasis supplied*) cheating shall be allowed to represent the University in any way whatsoever, during the school year in which he is convicted. Signed President, Students Association." The students had stood their ground in declining to pass what they considered to be an ex post facto law.

Thereafter, the recommendation of the faculty committee was read: "We recommend the disapproval [of the Students' bill] because the language is not clear since the purpose of these bills is not adequately expressed." [Signed F.G. Guittard, A.G. Flowers, H. Trantham, Faculty Committee] As an attachment to the faculty minutes was a statement of findings of fact and conclusions of law concerning the cases of the convictions for cheating. Some facts and their sequence related to the cases of certain students convicted by the Student Self-Government of cheating on examination were as follows:

1. Certain students cheated.
2. The Judicial Council convicted them but did not dismiss them from school nor forbid them from representing the university in athletic competition.
3. The faculty approved the findings of the Council (believing that the students guilty of cheating would not insist on playing).
4. About a week later, certain freshmen were dismissed for hazing.
5. The faculty, as in the other case, approved the Council findings but felt there was disparity in the punishment.
6. The President of the university advised with the Committee of the Judicial Council…The President asked them if legislation might not be passed forbidding the students who cheated from representing the University. He stated to the Committee that such a course would be better than for the faculty to make any arbitrary ruling forbidding it. The Committee told the president one by one that he thought it could be done. The Committee retired. The Legislative Assembly thereafter passed a law. This law did not forbid the convicted student from representing the university. *The Assembly felt that to have forbidden the students would have been an ex post facto law.* [emphasis supplied] Notwithstanding, the law did not cover the case as was desired...
7. Before the above law was passed, the faculty passed a resolution forbidding the cheaters from representing the university, pending the proper disposition of the matter.
8. Now comes the difficulty because of technical conflicts:
   a) The records of the faculty show that the judicial findings were approved, therefore the cases could not be remanded for a new trial.
   b) The faculty had declared the convicted students ineligible.
   c) Throughout the history of the university, students who cheated were not only forbidden to represent the university but were usually suspended.
   d) The faculty does not believe its policy in the past had been wrong.
   e) The faculty recognizes the technical conflict in the law as now on the books regarding students who cheated. (Faculty Minutes, April 17, 1923)

Thus, the attachment shows both the technical legal bind the faculty was in and how it hoped to get out of it. The bind being the undesirability of approving and enforcing an ex post facto application of a new law versus the undesirability of not barring identified cheaters from competing for the university. The president and the faculty hoped the bind would prove illusory on the chance that the cheating athletes would voluntarily decide themselves not to compete. Although the record does not provide specifics, and, as a result, will always be unclear in this matter, it appears that such hope may not have been justified by subsequent events, and convicted athletes may have represented the university.

The President and faculty step back in.

At this point, events were moving rapidly toward their conclusion. *The Waco Times Herald* reported following the headline: "BAYLOR FACULTY-COUNCIL BREACH: Student Council Friday Fails to Function First Time Since Organization," and continued: "For the first time since the organization of the student government association at Baylor University about eight years ago, the government failed Friday to function according to [the] president of the Student Self-Government Association. The announcement was read in chapel at 10 o'clock Friday morning. Dr. S.P. Brooks, president of the University, called a meeting of the faculty for 5 o'clock Friday afternoon at which time definite steps will be taken to administer the government in the absence of the cooperative efforts of the student council upon which the faculty has heretofore relied." (*Waco Times Herald*, April 20, 1923)

The faculty met at a called meeting Friday afternoon for the purpose of consideration of the resignations of the officers of the Student Self-Government Association, which had already been accepted by President Brooks at the ten o'clock hour. A motion was made by Dr. J.B. Tidwell that the faculty ratify and commend most heartily the action of the President. After a discussion by several members of the faculty, the motion was carried unanimously as certified by S.P. Brooks, President and C.D. Johnson, Secretary pro tem.

That Saturday, The *Lariat* provided additional clarification as to what happened at the Friday meeting in chapel and the motives of the self-government association in resigning in mass. The headline: "STUDENTS LOSE POWER," subtitled: "Student Officers Tender Resignation in Body, Faculty Takes over Government—Reason for Action not given by Officers; Present Rules Still Apply until Further Changes May be Made by Faculty." The article continued:

> One of the greatest and most surprising upsets which has occurred in the administration of Baylor University occurred yesterday morning in Chapel when [the president] of the Students

> Association...tendered his resignation and that of every one of his fellow officers...and saw it accepted by President S.P. Brooks, who, giving his reasons for not referring the matter to the Students' Association for consideration, declared the Baylor Students' Association dissolved. Since that time, the faculty in meeting assembled have ratified the action of President Brooks and have taken the disciplinary duties over once more into their own hands for the first time in years. President Brooks informed...that the present rules, heretofore of the Association, will be in force but subject to any change which the faculty might at any time see fit.

During the course of the above *Lariat* article, Dr. Brooks pointed out that the student government had gradually grown, but also that the faculty had been criticized by prominent Waco citizens as well as trustees of the University in regard to certain action taken in the past year by the Council. Accordingly, Dr. Brooks said that he found it to be in the best interest of the school to assume absolute control for an indefinite period. SSGA President B___ refused to make any comment on reasons for the action taken. (*Lariat,* April 21, 1923, 1)

The students strongly restate their position.

However, other ex-officials of the Association were more than willing to talk about what has impelled their resignations as officers of the Association. The *Lariat* reported that the chief cause for discontent lay in the students' conviction that the faculty had been usurping the power of the Association and that no single event, such as the problem with the final resolution of the punishment for the students convicted of cheating, precipitated the action of the Council, although some events were more important than others. (*Lariat*, April 21, 1923, 1) The students also expressed their dissatisfaction with the faculty having ratified and approved the students' punishments in the cheating cases and instructed the students to put them on their books as approved. Those found guilty were given, generally, 14 marks active and 35 marks suspended, and the credits for the work of the term automatically removed by the inability of them to take the examination, this being done, according to the *Lariat*, under the law of the constitution which says that the Council in such cases may assess such punishment as it sees fit.

Nevertheless, some weeks later, the *Lariat* reported the faculty now wanted a law passed suspending all those who cheated in the future from all school activities, and the General Council passed such a law. However, "it seems that the faculty wished the law to act upon those cases already closed and as they had approved them they did not see how technically they could submit them back to the Council for another trial." But the Council was not willing to expressly state that the recent law could be applied retroactively to the cheating cases, and the faculty "proceeded to take action themselves to prohibit those guilty from taking part in activities here. In doing this, they waived the technicality by which the constitution says that the Council shall dispose of cheating cases and took the matter into their own hands." (*Lariat*, April 21, 1923, 1)

Those speaking to the *Lariat* on behalf of the ex-officials of the Association saved their most serious complaints regarding the actions by the faculty and the administration and their reasons for resigning for last. The *Lariat* reported: "As a last general statement, the Council feels that the government has been misrepresented to the students. The latter took it to mean they were governing themselves as a democracy in all ordinary matters of discipline such as have arisen. The Association thinks that they have only been able to render verdicts such as would alone please the faculty and at times not in accordance with what they thought best. The government should at least have some semblance of one if it is to be called one, as they would put it, self-government in Baylor [having] been a delusion." (*Lariat*, April 21, 1923, 1) The *Waco News Tribune* offered this headline April 21, 1923: "Rule by Students is Ending—Baylor Faculty Accepts Officers' 40 Resignations—Break Comes Over Disqualifying of Athletes for Cheating; Discipline Now in Teachers' Hands."

In the *Baylor Lariat* for April 21, 1923, immediately below the article entitled "Students Lose Power" is a small box showing the leaders in athletic conference standings, with Baylor in close contention for the baseball championship and four games remaining on its schedule, including games with the conference leader Texas A&M. As of April 21, the Texas Aggies had won 5, lost 2; Baylor had won 4, lost 3; Texas University had won 3, lost 3. The same issue of the *Lariat* quoted Dr. Brooks as saying that abolishing the SSGA because of its failure to sufficiently discipline cheating athletes "was the most embarrassing incident of his 21 years as president." The *Lariat* editor observed "whether or not Students' Self-Government will be instituted in Baylor University again is the main question in the minds of all. It [is the] greatest pity that cooperation is pronounced impossible between faculty and students, which cooperation is in our opinion the only true course for Baylor to follow." (*Lariat*, April 21, 1923, 1)

A fundamentalist sees God's judgment on Baylor for heresy.

As the students and the editors of the *Lariat* and other periodicals pondered the advisability and chances for the revival of student self-government at Baylor, other forces were at work. J. Frank Norris, a Fort Worth Baptist pastor, spread a rumor in his newspaper, *The Searchlight.* Norris claimed the students had asked President Brooks to resign because of his dissolving the student government and that the students were revolting against the administration. The article in *The Searchlight* entitled "Norris Impression of Orderly Conscientious Resignation of Student Officers"—"The Uprising in Baylor" stated as follows:

> Every Baptist and every local citizen deeply regrets the uprising that took place at Baylor University last week...The situation was that the student body rose up in rebellion on one side, and the faculty on the other. The president of the student body and 39 officers resigned. They demanded the resignation of President Brooks. *This is but the natural, inevitable and logical consequence of the character of teaching that has been going on. Deny the authority of the word of God, cheapen it, belittle it, and it is but a step when respect for the authority of the faculty and of the State will be denied. Evolution and Bolshevism are Siamese twins. Baylor is going through the travail of sorrow upon sorrow, and our hope and prayers are that she will emerge a greater Baylor and... uncompromisingly loyal to the whole word of God.* (*The Searchlight*, April 27, 1923) [emphasis supplied}

The *Lariat* stated in response to the above excerpted article in *The Searchlight*: "There are two statements which we wish to correct here, for the enlightenment of all concerned. First the statement that President Brooks was asked to resign is erroneous...President Brooks was not asked to resign...This is all, no doubt, absurd to the majority of the readers of the *Lariat*, but conditions are not to be ignored. Second, there was nothing done at Baylor in the last two weeks that could lead anyone to interpret the resignation as an 'uprising' or 'rebellion.'" The following is a reply by Mr. B—former president of the Students' Association—to the same article in *The Searchlight*:

> In light of what appeared in the April 27 issue of *The Searchlight* concerning the resignation of the officers of the Students' Association, I felt that I, as president of said Association at the time we tendered our resignations, should explain the situation...The officers of the Association DID NOT resign because of the character of the teaching done at Baylor University, for it is the best to be had in all of this fair land of ours. Neither did we demand the resignation of President Brooks, for we quite well know there is not a man at the Southern Baptist Convention who is so anxious to do that which will help Baylor University as is our beloved President. May all of the friends and supporters of Baylor University know that our self-proclaimed friend [J. Frank Norris] has most erroneously represented the matter. Signed J.L. B__. (*Lariat*, April 28, 1923, 1)

Baylor plays baseball following the SSG's dissolution.

As a welcome but ironic footnote to the episode involving the Student Self-Government's dissolution because of the faculty's dissatisfaction with the students' handling of the cheating cases, the *Lariat* reported May 23 regarding the outcome of the 1923 baseball season:

> "Baylor's Southwest Champs—Longhorns Outplayed at Every Angle in Two Thrilling Games with Baylor Masters—Brilliant Play Features Brilliant Attack and Longhorns taken for Two Drumings—Bears' Comeback from Poor Start to Take Second Major Championship for Baylor and Further Lose Only Two Games out of Sixteen After Finding Their Stride and Down Opponents. Staging a sensational comeback after...a bad start, the Baylor University Bears, by virtue of their double victory [over] the prior champion, the Texas University Longhorns, took the Southwestern Championship in baseball yesterday afternoon...After losing three of the first four games, the Bears hit their stride and won 12 straight conference games victories, 12 victories that will be remembered by the fans who have followed the Bears throughout the season." (*Lariat*, May 23, 1923, 2)

Elsewhere in the same *Lariat* issue is another editorial stating: "That Good Old Baylor Line—Baylor Bears bury Longhorns and win baseball conference of the Southwest Conference, the football championship [the 1922 season] being already annexed."

<u>Charlie</u>: That's quite a story. I wonder what Frank Guittard thought about the whole SSGA experiment since he was so involved with its creation and then its collapse.

<u>Pops</u>: Unfortunately, Frank's reaction to the dissolution of the Student Self-Government is not preserved for posterity, but it must have been mixed. He had to be disappointed that the Association, having worked successfully for a number of years, was brought down as a direct result of a drafting omission in its constitution that no one caught. Neither he, nor President Brooks, nor any member of the faculty, including those on Baylor's law school faculty, had thought to include a provision barring students convicted of cheating from representing the university in athletic competitions. Apparently, the sample constitutions received from other colleges and universities drafted by their faculties had the same weakness.

Nevertheless, considering Frank's penchant for planning and avoidance of all manner of sloppiness, it was probably disappointing to him that he had not himself thought of the needed provision in the drafting stage. The fact that attorneys on Baylor's legal faculty and those of other schools had not caught the issue either must have been small consolation for Frank since he was the chair of the faculty committee assigned to explore the pros and cons of establishing a student self-government. Also, the fact that he had felt compelled to turn over students in his class for prosecution must have been sickening. On the other hand, he had to be pleased that student self-government had worked as well as it had for as long as it had and would have no doubt lasted a while longer, absent the problem created principally by the five cheating convictions.

The basic problem for President Brooks and Baylor was that the SSGA failed to fix the problem of convicted cheaters potentially representing Baylor in ball games; to preserve Baylor's academic integrity, Brooks had no alternative but to dissolve the SSGA and for the faculty to take back sole responsibility for student discipline. The faculty, however, if Frank Guittard was a representative example, was not enthusiastic about the transfer of discipline back to the faculty. Frank would tell Josie years after the Student Self-Government experiment had concluded and discipline of the students had returned to the faculty: "Spent all afternoon yesterday to six on the discipline committee meeting. Two cases—one a girl [in a history class] on the front row copied from a neighbor, the other in chemistry brought a bunch of notes with him to use on the test. I always feel like I have been washing dirty clothes when I get through with those cases." (Letter FGG to MJ, February 21, 1935)

Pops: Thoughts, Charlie? Questions?

Charlie: The elephant I see in the room is whether any of the athletes and others in Frank's history class who were convicted of cheating actually played on Baylor's 1923 championship baseball team that beat the Aggies and the Longhorns.

Pops: That is the elephant in the room. There is no record I could find establishing whether any athletes who may have been among the five convicted students played for Baylor after their convictions, although that was part of the faculty's concern. There is simply no available proof and, at this point, the matter is moot. It would be interesting to know if there were any convicted cheaters on Baylor's 1923 championship baseball team and whether any of those were the students caught cheating in Frank's class. But for ninety-eight years now, the responsibility for student discipline has been back where it should be—on the faculty and the administration.

Charlie: Right. I guess the faculty could put up with lax enforcement from time to time for some rules violations, like dancing at the Shriners' Hall, riding in cars at night, and stealing ice cream, but cheating on tests was a much bigger deal. I must say, though, I'm glad the students let that sophomore girl who master-minded that ice cream heist go. Baylor had so many rules those days!

Pops: A final thought: I've never been a school administrator, but I guess it's unrealistic to expect students to judge their fellow students in cheating cases—the stakes are too high for the students and for the university. I think most colleges have come to the same conclusion. President Brooks could have facilitated the adoption of a new constitution for student self-government that included the needed provision forbidding convicted cheaters from representing Baylor in intercollegiate competitions, but he didn't. He had other things he needed to do than worry about, for example, lax enforcement by students of the rule against dancing. One of his chief concerns in the 1920s was fundamentalist Baptist preachers and denominational leaders trying to take him and his faculty down and set Baylor back on its upward climb. We will take all of that up in the next chapter. And, yes, Baylor was overweight with rules in those days, but that has largely changed as times have changed.

Charlie: I'll be interested in why President Brooks would have been worried about those preachers.

Pops: Next chapter, Charlie; bumpy road ahead.

CHAPTER 29

President Brooks & the Evolution Controversy (1920-1931)

The subject matters of several chapters in this book, all set in the 1920s, have already been addressed at length in *A Ph.D.'s Reverie: The Letters* (2019). Those subjects included the evolution controversy at Baylor, told primarily through the editor's notes ("Brooks's Battles") to the family letters featuring Samuel Palmer Brooks, Baylor's president. A brief overview of the evolution controversy at Baylor is included in this book for completeness, and because it is a good topic to discuss with the peanut gallery. Charlie and I will be talking our way through this topic.

Pops: Charlie, we might start by understanding what this chapter is about.

Charlie: Sure. I don't know much about the controversy over evolution.

Pops: I'm going to keep this very basic. First, what is the meaning of "evolution" anyway? Evolution was a scientific theory that came into prominence with Charles Darwin's book, *The Origin of the Species,* published in 1859. The theory created a great deal of controversy, as it was interpreted to mean that human beings developed from ape-like ancestors through the process of natural selection over millions of years. In other words, not according to the literal reading of *Genesis.* The second chapter of *Genesis* in the King James Bible states that God breathed life into a body formed from the dust of the ground, which became Adam, and in the third chapter, God took a rib from Adam and formed it into a woman whom Adam named Eve.

Charlie: Monkeys, baboons, orangutans, and gorillas are very different from us. I've seen them at the zoo. They are scary, except maybe the smaller monkeys.

Pops: Yes, of course, and we'll be talking about the notorious Scopes Monkey Trial in a little bit, but evolution theory is about man's "ape-like" ancestors, not monkeys, baboons, and so on.

Charlie: I didn't know this theory created a problem at Baylor.

Pops: Many Baptists in the 1920s had a major problem with the idea of faculty members at Baptist schools teaching, explaining, or even mentioning evolution. For many pastors and their congregations—not just Baptists, by the way—evolutionary theory seemed to suggest that human beings were not created by God but rather through the notion of natural selection. That view, generally speaking, meant survival of the fittest over eons. This idea conflicted with many Christians' ideas of who we are as human beings, created in the image of God, not just by a natural biological process.

Charlie: Some church people, I guess, might have thought that evolutionary theory should not be discussed at all, especially with children who had been brought up on a literal reading of Genesis.

Pops: A lot of people. The problem came up at Baylor in 1920, the year Baylor celebrated its Diamond Jubilee. Baylor sociology professor Grove Samuel Dow published a college-level sociology textbook through Baylor Press. Although the book was not a biology text, it included a few sentences regarding the age and the first appearance of the human species. Those sentences contradicted *Genesis* in the minds of people who took *Genesis* literally as a record of fact, scientific or otherwise. Dow was chair of Baylor's sociology department and a highly respected authority on sociology.

Charlie: And the president at that time, I guess, was President Brooks.

Pops: Right. Brooks said he believed the evolution controversy reached the Baylor campus the next year (1921) when evangelist T.T. Martin, author of *Hell and the High Schools*, complained about Dow's textbook. Brooks took quick defensive action and asked Southern Baptists to investigate and resolve the charge against Baylor that it taught or advocated evolutionary theory. Brooks's defense was always that evolution theory was discussed appropriately, and that after all, Baylor was a university where ideas were necessarily discussed as part of the student's education. However, Brooks stoutly maintained that evolutionary theory was neither advocated nor taught as fact. After their investigation, the Baptists' report accepted Brooks's position.

Charlie: Maybe that quieted Baylor's critics down.

Pops: I'm afraid not. The controversy was alive on the Baylor campus and across the US during most of the 1920s. J. Frank Norris, the charismatic pastor of Fort Baptist Church of Fort Worth, who took over the attack after Martin started it, got a lot of mileage out of it. Norris used the controversy with Baylor, its faculty, and Brooks to build his church and made them targets for his attacks in sermons and articles in his church magazine, *The Searchlight*. Norris was a master of creating and using controversy to heat things up to draw attention to himself and his ministry. Professor Dow eventually resigned from Baylor under the heat and took a position at another university. Dow turned out to be just one of several notches Norris would carve on his fundamentalist gun belt from attacks on members of the Baylor faculty.

Charlie: Where did the controversy go from there?

Pops: It was just getting started when Professor Dow resigned. In early 1923, the issue cropped up again, this time in the history department chaired by Frank Guittard. A Baylor ministerial student named Dale Crowley complained that Professor Charles S. Fothergill made comments in a European History class that were supportive of evolutionary theory. Crowley claimed Fothergill did not believe the story of Noah's Ark in *Genesis*. Crowley then met separately with Fothergill and with President Brooks to push his complaint about the teaching he claimed he had received.

Somehow Norris got wind of the Fothergill-Crowley dust-up, and his newspaper, *The Searchlight,* reported in April that Baylor students had asked President Brooks to resign. At the end of May, Norris spoke to Baylor students at Waco City Auditorium. Through President Brooks, Baylor denied Crowley's charges and the subsequent attacks by Norris and other fundamentalist Baptist preachers. Brooks argued that Baylor faculty members did not espouse the theory of evolution in their classes but appropriately educated students on the tenets of the theory. In June, Crowley sent out several letters complaining about Professor Fothergill, Baylor, and President Brooks.

Our only record of Frank Guittard's reaction to the allegation against Fothergill is that he told his son, Clarence, he felt strongly against Norris's attack on a member of his department, and that Fothergill was only explaining the theory of evolution. Further, we suspect Frank viewed any discussion of Noah's Ark as of no use whatsoever in teaching or learning European history and that Fothergill had needlessly "stepped in it." Our suspicion is mostly speculative but primarily based on the apparent fact that there was no real reason to talk about Noah's Ark in history courses.

Charlie: So what happened next? Did things settle back down?

Pops: No, unfortunately, they didn't. The conflict between the fundamentalists, principally Norris, and President Brooks kept burning at high heat. Norris continued issuing challenges to Brooks to come to Norris's radio station and debate, answer questions, or say anything to help Norris keep this conflict in front of Baptists. Brooks was a fine debater from his days as a former Philomathesian, but he likewise knew that a public debate on stage with Norris played Norris's game. Norris was a highly skilled debater himself and knew how to work an audience. The subject was a tricky one, at least during the 1920s. On July 9, Norris sent President Brooks a letter challenging him to a public debate on whether the Bible was both scientifically and historically correct. This letter was one of many letters Norris sent to Brooks during the 1920s attempting to provoke Brooks either into a live debate or to make problematic statements on the record regarding the teaching of evolution at Baylor. On more than one occasion, Norris offered Brooks airtime on his radio station.

For example, on July 23, Norris sent a letter to President Brooks referring to Brooks's defense of Baylor botany professor Lula Pace and zoology professor Ora C. Bradbury against Norris's charge of teaching evolution and Brooks's view on God's creation of the world as a "process." In the letter, Norris invited Brooks to appear with him at the public square in Cleburne, Texas, where Norris's topic would be "The Bible vs. Modernism and Evolution." To Norris and other anti-evolutionists, the word "process" was just another word for "evolution." We suppose that it would have been challenging, if not head-scratchingly difficult, for Brooks to explain the difference between "a process" and "evolution."

<u>Charlie</u>: I wonder if Brooks was letting Norris just think he was beating Brooks up, kind of like Brer Rabbit who provoked Brer Fox into beating up the tar baby, but it turned out okay for Brer Rabbit.

<u>Pops</u>: I don't think that metaphor works here since Brer Rabbit fought the tar baby, not Brer Fox. And it turned out okay because Brer Rabbit tricked Brer Fox into throwing him into the Briar Patch after he fought the tar baby. Also, it doesn't work because Brooks finally fought back against Norris, and he fought hard. In August 1923, President Brooks made a strong personal attack on the radio in defense of Baylor. In Brooks's notes for this radio address, he referred to Norris as "the leader of the vaudeville performers in the Texas pulpit." Brooks claimed that Norris didn't care about evolution at Baylor and that "he would drop Baylor and the theory of evolution and attack the theory of gravitation if by it he could get a bigger crowd to hear him." After that, Brooks attacked Norris's church's record of only giving $100 to Baylor, his alma mater, after the Carroll Chapel and Library at Baylor burned.

At that point, the gloves were clearly off between the combatants. In September, Norris preached at Fair Park Auditorium in Dallas against the theory of evolution, Baylor University, and President Brooks. Then in October, Brooks charged that Norris had offered to pay for spies at Baylor. Norris also sent a telegram to Brooks in October claiming that Norris was in the greatest revival campaign of his life at a tabernacle of eight thousand capacity, and he invited Brooks to appear and explain why he expelled [Dale S.] Crowley "for exposing evolution and...why you expelled him without giving him a hearing," but that Brooks would be given "a full, fair and courteous hearing" by Norris.

Charlie: I'm wondering what happened to Professor Fothergill, who mentioned Noah's Ark in his history class.

Pops: Well, at the end of October 1923, Professor Fothergill, who, according to Crowley, had espoused evolution while teaching a history class, offered his resignation, and President Brooks reluctantly accepted. Fast-forward to the spring of 1925 when President Brooks telephoned Guy B. Harrison, Jr., Frank Guittard's grader, to come in and see him. Harrison had no idea why Brooks had called him, but he naturally obliged the president. The meeting turned out to be an interview for the vacancy in the history department created by the resignation of Fothergill. Fothergill had resigned in response to Norris's claims that he was teaching evolution in history classes. Brooks told Harrison that Professor Guittard had highly recommended him. Still, Brooks needed to know "whether [he thought he] can teach History 102 and 103 without getting involved in an [argument] over whether the whale swallowed Jonah or not." Harrison replied that he thought he could and took up his new position at Baylor in June 1925.

Charlie: You mentioned a "Monkey" trial a few minutes ago.

Pops: Yes. It didn't happen in Texas, but it was a significant episode in the controversy over teaching students about evolution theory, especially in state-supported schools. The Scopes Monkey Trial commenced July 10, 1925, in Dayton, Tennessee, and continued until July 21. Substitute teacher John T. Scopes was found guilty of violating a Tennessee law (the Butler Act) against teaching the theory of evolution. This trial was the most highly publicized event of the fundamentalists' holy war of the 1920s. It featured William Jennings Bryan, a gifted orator and thrice-defeated Democratic candidate for US president, for the prosecution and Clarence Darrow, a criminal attorney of national reputation but no professed religious faith, for the defense. The World Christian Fundamentals Association, founded by Reverend William Bell Riley, brought Bryan into the case to lead the prosecution. Riley received his theological training at Southern Baptist Theological Seminary in Louisville, Kentucky. The American Civil Liberties Union offered to pay for the defense of anyone prosecuted under Tennessee's anti-evolution law (the Butler Act) and was likely paying Darrow's fees, unless Darrow donated his time.

Charlie: What was going on back in Waco and with Brooks?

Pops: In September, President Brooks wrote a letter to *The Baptist Standard*, published by the Baptist General Convention of Texas, pushing back against its editorial policy. Brooks felt that *The Baptist Standard* had a practice of occasionally publishing unfounded charges against Baylor without giving Brooks a chance to provide Baylor's view of things before publication. Then, on November 22, the Southern Baptist Convention Radio broadcast an attack on Norris and his actions supporting his anti-evolution views. The program featured President Brooks and others on Baylor's side of the issue. Norris later referred to this broadcast as a "hate-fest." Brooks's mail after the broadcast was mixed, and there was a difference of opinion among his supporters as to whether he had helped or hurt Baylor in regard to Norris's attacks.

From the beginning of the controversy, Brooks attempted to avoid making the controversy personal between him and Norris, and for that reason he had declined to participate in debates on stage with Norris. Brooks finally gave in to the pressure to speak his mind by going on the radio, the broadcast Norris called a "hate-fest." Norris's apparent animus against Brooks suggested the controversy was always partly personal for Norris. At the end of January 1928, Norris mailed President Brooks a letter that Norris claimed he received from an unnamed fellow citizen of Brooks in Waco. The letter contained an off-the-wall personal attack against Brooks, which Norris promised to publish in *The Fundamentalist.* The letter's author, whoever it was, questioned whether Brooks had ever contributed anything to his community, ever written a book or pamphlet, or ever taught anyone anything or made any mark as a teacher. The letter's author further remarked that Brooks had nothing to show for his twenty-five years leading Baylor; that where rebuilding the Carroll Chapel and Library was concerned, Brooks should have been able to immediately rebuild without mounting a fundraising campaign, given his twenty-five years of experience leading Baylor.

The year 1928 closed without as many articles and letters evidencing the controversy. However, at the end of January 1929, *The Dallas Morning News* published a report with the headline, "Anti-Evolution Bill Opposed," relating to efforts in Texas to get such a bill passed into law. 1929 began and ended without any unusual outbreak of the prior hostilities between Norris and President Brooks. The stock market crash in late October 1929 seems to have had no noticeable effect on the Norris-Brooks conflict, or upon Frank Guittard's pursuit of his Ph.D. at Stanford. In all likelihood, Frank and Josie had no investments in the stock market, which the October crash could have wiped out. The only known sources of their income were his salary from Baylor and the handful of rent houses they had accumulated.

But Norris wasn't through with Brooks and Baylor. At the beginning of the following year (1930), Norris effectively reminded President Brooks that he was still on Norris's radar, along with Baylor and certain other prominent Baptists aligned with Brooks and Baylor. Norris informed Brooks by letter that he would be attacking Brooks for modernist views and "Dawsonism" as well. In a show of dubious magnanimity, Norris offered to let Brooks speak on the air for an entire day and night. Joseph Martin Dawson, the longtime pastor of First Baptist Church of Waco, Texas, was a friend of President Brooks and a Baylor classmate of Norris. Dawson claimed that Norris had held a grudge against him that lasted several decades. Norris attacked Dawson by invoking the charge of "Dawsonism" against selected targets.

Finally, by January 1931, just months before Brooks's death in May, Norris was no longer pushing his anti-evolution campaign with the same enthusiasm. However, in April, after a brave and prolonged struggle with cancer, President Brooks succumbed to his terminal illness at the age of sixty-seven. Norris would live another twenty-one years and die of a heart attack in Florida at almost seventy-five.

Charlie: Where does Baylor stand now after Norris's prolonged attack for supporting the teaching of evolutionary theory?

Pops: Today, in 2022, Baylor and most, if not all, public and private universities in Texas not only allow but require the teaching of evolution in biology courses as a foundational and unifying principle. Nevertheless, below the college level, the controversy in the 1920s over the teaching of evolution theory flares up from time to time, especially where public high schools are concerned. The fundamentalist spirit survives in the creationist science and Intelligent Design schools of thought, although at the current time, court cases throughout the United States have generally favored teaching evolution theory. The current issues that occasionally surface, often with the support of conservative politicians running for office, are whether schools should also teach the biblical story of creation and encourage students to criticize or evaluate evolution theory. Non-profit organizations created to support the creationist science or Intelligent Design viewpoint still have a presence in Dallas and Seattle.

One may wonder what the source of the long-lasting Norris-Brooks enmity was. Both Norris and Brooks were trained debaters and writers. Norris was an exceptionally skillful debater of the attacking school, and had he ever debated Pat M. Neff, there would have been standing room only. Brooks, likewise, was a skilled debater, but his strength lay more in his written advocacy, which was generally not of the savage sort. Was there anything personal between them? Was Norris's approach just a calculated strategy arising out of Norris's pugnacious personality but nothing personal? After all, Norris regularly flogged a group of prominent opponents on various subjects, including George W. Truett, L.R. Scarborough, and others.

Charlie: Well, what do you think?

Pops: One source suggests Norris, a Baylor graduate, was bitter at Brooks for not being selected as the most outstanding student during Norris's Baylor days. There is no definite corroborating evidence for this view. Still, there is a great deal of evidence identifying Joseph Martin Dawson as the most outstanding student in Norris's class, as his achievements eclipsed Norris's. It is also true that Norris added Dawson to the list of those he was pleased to flog during the evolution controversy years.

Charlie: I am also wondering about Frank Guittard and what dog, if any, he had in the fight between Norris and Brooks?

Pops: Absolutely. Frank surely had a stake in the outcome of the Brooks-Norris battle over the teaching of evolution theory and Norris's campaign of savage attacks against Brooks and Baylor. Norris's agenda was to stir up controversy for his self-enhancement. He wanted to be perceived by Baptists as a defender of the faith, a St. George fighting a dragon. His attacks on Baylor were dangerous to Baylor's support from Baptists and, therefore, potentially to Frank Guittard. An attack on Baylor would have been worrisome to Frank if he thought there was any significant chance that Norris's followers among the Baptist ranks might be able to obtain control of Baylor. Fundamentalists had attacked the following Baylor faculty members: G.S. Dow (sociology), Lula Pace (biology), Andre Sendon (Spanish), Charles S. Fothergill (history), W.P. Meroney (sociology), A.J. Hall (philosophy), Ora C. Bradbury (zoology), and others. Further, Frank's decision in 1923 to obtain a Ph.D. could have been based in part on a hope that obtaining a Ph.D. from a first-class university like Stanford would provide a measure of job marketability and insulation against unemployment if Norrisites ever obtained control of Baylor. Frank would have been keenly interested in the simmering dispute between Brooks, Baylor, and Norris.

However, we don't think Frank would have been taken with the distinctions between various evolutionary theories or any fine theological point. He was focused on history and historical facts on this earth, not on biological hypotheses about the creation of the universe and the development of life on this planet. With one possible exception, there is no evidence that he ever taught a Sunday school class or attended a Sunday school class as an adult, although he was a faithful church attender. His faith was private and, insofar as can be determined, uncomplicated. In this respect, his faith was markedly different from that of his youngest son, Clarence, who enjoyed the stimulation of discussing different theological perspectives and arguments.

Charlie: I know you are not a theologian or a professional historian, but looking back at the Norris-Brooks conflict, how effective do you think Brooks's strategy was in dealing with Norris?

Pops: Generally effective, although Brooks could have been more effective in some ways. Generally effective because Brooks early on gathered broad support among Baptists who trusted what he said, and because he invited the Baptists to do an investigation into whether evolution was being taught at Baylor, letting the chips fall where they may. He was also effective because of his training as a debater: he knew how and when to go on defense or counter-attack, although it was usually in print and not in person. Brooks also made informal alliances with other denominational leaders whom Norris had attacked similarly. He produced carefully crafted written arguments refuting Norris's allegations that were published in various publications, including the *Baptist Standard* and the *Baylor Bulletin*. Brooks generally declined meeting Norris on terms dictated by Norris. Norris's specialty, in-person debate before a Norris radio audience or another public forum, would have placed Brooks at a distinct disadvantage.

We believe Brooks would have admitted, in hindsight, that his defense against Norris and Baylor's other fundamentalist opponents could have been better. Although Brooks was familiar with Norris and his tendencies before the evolution controversy arose, we think he would have admitted to a failure at the outset of underestimating Norris's tenacity and of not taking his arguments seriously until the dispute was out of the barn and well down the road. After all, Brooks had to have been completely aware that Norris, a student in 1902, had purposely fanned the uproar that resulted in the resignation of President Cooper, Brooks's predecessor. As time went on and the battle lines became clearer, Brooks's defenses and statements in the evolution controversy became sharper and more convincing. Brooks also probably made a mistake waiting three years to publish his article on the evolution controversy in the *Baylor Bulletin*. One could also nit-pick Brooks's handling of Baylor's defense in other ways. Ultimately, however, Brooks's major mistake, if he made one, arguably occurred before the controversy with Norris arose—namely, allowing Dow's sociology textbook to be published by Baylor Press without reading it first and anticipating the attacks from the fundamentalists. But Brooks won the war with most Baptists; a good general may win a war and yet lose a battle or two along the way. George Washington did not win all his battles with the British. Any questions?

Charlie: Nope. I'm passing the witness, Pops.

Pops: One other thing, Charlie. Although Brooks's defense of Baylor and its faculty was eventually successful in fending off Norris's fundamentalist attacks, that success came at a cost to President Brooks in his last years when he was battling both cancer and Norris.

Charlie: Was it smoking that caused President Brooks's cancer?

Pops: I don't know, but he had smoked for years. Brooks, though, had other far-reaching things to worry about besides his health and Baptist fundamentalists; the next chapter reflects potentially one of the most worrisome since it represented a different kind of attack on academic freedom at Baylor, as well as at other colleges and universities.

CHAPTER 30

Waco & the Ku Klux Klan (1920s)

This chapter speaks to a disturbing piece of the 1920s context for the life of Frank Guittard who taught history and for Baylor University. It is a regrettable chapter that should be included along with the football championships and Baylor's transformative growth during the Brooks's administration in the 1920s referenced in other chapters. As everyone in the peanut gallery has expressed a desire to participate in this chapter, they will be interjecting questions or comments as we go along.

Pops: The 1920s, as some of you may know, were not all about the emergence of the jazz age, doing the Charleston until dawn at private clubs awash in illegal booze, or recovering economically after the conclusion of World War I. They were also about the resurrected Ku Klux Klan—the most ruthless white supremacist organization of the Jim Crow era, organized crime, Al Capone and his bootlegging operations, the Bureau of Prohibition, and the scary run-up of the stock market until its collapse in October 1929. We will begin with basic information about the Klan and proceed to events in Waco in the 1920s for which we have oral history memoirs obtained by the Baylor Department of Oral History.

Although Baylor University did not play a major public role in actively opposing the Klan's activities, prominent Baylor figures did publicly oppose the 1920s Klan. Those included President Brooks, Pat M. Neff, and most of the faculty who opposed the Klan's objectives and methods. The Klan had a strong chapter in Waco and in many communities across the South.

Miles: So how did the resurrected Klan get started, and what did this new Klan have to do with the original Klan?

Pops: The first Klan arose after the Civil War in the late 1860s during Reconstruction. It was a white supremacist group targeting primarily African-Americans, but also Catholics, and Jews. The purpose was to compromise efforts to grant equal rights to former slaves, over which the North and the Confederacy fought a war costing six hundred thousand American lives. The first Klan used physical assault and murder to intimidate Blacks and their allies in the south until it was suppressed in the early 1870s. Members made their own robes, masks, and conical hats calculated to be terrifying—they looked like ghosts with pointy hats—

as well as to hide their identities. The fact that they wore masks was frightening, not just because of their bizarre appearance, but because people in masks could get away with doing any crime, including murder, if no one could identify them. Has anyone read H.G. Well's *The Invisible Man*? The same thing, except the character committing crimes couldn't be seen because of his invisibility.

Charlie: So did the original Klan not completely disappear in the nineteenth century?

Pops: The original Klan may have disappeared, but the idea of the Klan and its goals remained, and the human weakness and prejudice that fed the growth of the original Klan remained. When the Klan started up again in the 1920s, called the Second Klan, forty years had elapsed since the disappearance of the original Klan. D.W. Griffith's 1915 silent movie *Birth of a Nation* romanticized the original Klan and was a factor in the second Klan emerging and building to five million members nationwide. The second Klan secured support in part by advocating for prohibition, which was a popular cause with Protestants, including Baptists, and which became the law of the land during the 1920s. The Klan was hostile to Catholics on the premise that Catholics were under the control of the Pope in Rome and to Jews because they were allegedly responsible for helping African-Americans improve their lot and also supporting immigration from Mexico and South American countries. The Klan also castigated Jews for standing apart and allegedly resisting assimilation, notwithstanding the Klan's penchant for recycling old unflattering tropes of Jews. Individual Klan chapters supported themselves through initiation fees and by selling members their white costumes, including their robes. The second Klan burned crosses and conducted large-scale parades to intimidate onlookers. However, toward the end of the 1920s, the Klan substantially declined in numbers and appeal, although we still have Klan chapters today and other white supremacist groups, as well.

Finn: So the Klan is still around today? Why did the Klan burn crosses? And weren't they supposed to be Christians?

Pops: The Klan is still around, along with other white supremacist groups. Reportedly it now has less than 10,000 members. In ideology, it has been called neo-Confederate, white supremacist, white nationalist, anti-Black, anti-immigration, anti-communist, Christian terrorist, anti-Semitic, anti-feminist, anti-atheist, anti-abortion, anti-Zionist, neo-fascist, neo-Nazi, anti-Islamist, and anti-LGBT. The Klan blended xenophobia, religious prejudice, and white supremacy with conservative morality. So were Klan members Christians? If they were, were they Christians in name only? I have my opinion, but you tell me. So why did they burn crosses? The Ku Klux Klan burned crosses to intimidate everyone, African-Americans as well as white people. Burning Klan crosses at night was an act of terror intended to remind the public, whites and Blacks, of the Klan's extra-legal activities, including lynching and beatings to enforce its racist ideology. The Klan succeeded, in part, in intimidating white people because many vocal citizens either joined the Klan or refused to take a stand against the Klan.

<u>Katie</u>: If the Klan was as awful as all that, why would anyone join in the 1920s? The south lost and Reconstruction was finally over.

<u>Pops</u>: I am not an expert on the Klan, but I would say their white supremacist ideologies are like viruses that never completely disappear. Like viruses, they tend to replicate in certain circumstances, and the Klan's ideologies replicate during times of civil or economic unrest, or periods when the average person is unhappy with his lot for whatever reason. At times like these, some people look for scapegoats to take their fury out on; the Klan is there to channel that anger by pointing the finger at its targets, hoping to add to its membership and power to influence others. Then too, in the 1920s the Klan appeared to embrace some Protestant or denominational beliefs and values, including a moral stance against alcohol, which resulted in Prohibition and other values of many Protestants. However, civil rights protections in the 1920s were not what they are today, and Congress had not yet passed the Civil Rights Act; the United States Supreme Court had not yet issued *Brown vs. the Board of Education of Topeka.*

<u>Katie</u>: I heard somewhere that the Klan members in those days were just folks like everybody else, even one's neighbors.

<u>Pops</u>: Yes, the Klan's appeal was very seductive. At times, the Klan could appear fun and wholesome and supportive of traditional values: "The Klan sponsored parades and picnics, baseball teams, and beautiful-baby contests. Klansmen had musical groups that performed public concerts and bands that played at state fairs. It had extensive women's auxiliaries and even several auxiliaries for children, which had names such as the Junior Ku Klux Klan, the Tri-K Klub, and the Ku Klux Kiddies." Klan members showed up in churches on Sunday mornings to donate money, and they ran charity drives for good causes. They threw Christmas parties for orphans and raised money to build Protestant-only hospitals. They made efforts to fight supposed Catholic influence in public schools by donating American flags and Bibles. They created special Klan rites for wedding ceremonies, christenings, and funerals. The Klan also ran candidates for hundreds of state and local offices, and Americans elected countless Klan members as mayors, school-board and city-council members, sheriffs, and state legislators. Klan officeholders in prominent and

powerful positions included Governors Edward Jackson of Indiana and Clifford Walker of Georgia, as well as US Senators Earle Mayfield of Texas and Rice Means of Colorado. The Klan for a period became quite influential politically.

Miles: So were any Baylor teachers members?

Pops: Baylor history professor Guy B. Harrison, Jr. said that many faculty members and students [in the 1920s] were on the KKK's rolls—he doesn't say how many were Klan members. However, Baylor's official position was anti-Klan. Harrison dabbled briefly himself in the Klan for a few months and was a member like his father before him. During the 1920s, the Klan was powerful across the south and in Texas. However, according to Harrison, there came a time when the local Klavern no longer vetted new members and started letting in hooligans and troublemakers. Harrison and his father withdrew at the same time, although Harrison kept his pricey Klan robe for many years before he finally decided to burn it. He was a bit of a history pack rat and was the director of The Texas Collection, which preserved Texas history, for decades. However, he burned his robe because he could no longer stand the idea of keeping it because of what it represented.

Charlie: Was Frank Guittard a Klan member?

Pops: All the evidence is to the contrary. Harrison, Frank's protégé and grader in the late 1910s early 1920s, would have mentioned it to me, as they were very close. Frank could never have been in it as he was a staunch Democrat and a Mason. He grew up in Ohio, which was important to the Underground Railroad before the Civil War. Brooks and Neff were also both known to be hostile to the Klan, although Brooks's position was clearer than Neff's, perhaps because Brooks was not running for public office. Neff, on the other hand, had a complicated set of interests demanding his attention, including law and order as well as Prohibition. According to the primary biography of Pat Neff, "The Klan was, in some areas of the state, the only mechanism enforcing these [Prohibition] laws...A second factor in [Neff] not being explicit about the Klan was that 'good politics' told him that to take a strong stand for or against the Klan before the primary election [1922] would probably not be to his advantage."

Finn: You mentioned a railroad that was underground? How did they do that?

Pops: Yes. It was called the "underground railroad" because it was a clandestine network of anti-slavery sympathizers organized before the Civil War to facilitate the movement of slaves out of slave states into Free states. Ohio was a free state north of its Ohio River boundary with Kentucky, a slave state. Once slaves made it across the river, they were assisted and passed along northerly from station to station until they could relocate in a safer location. Safer, but not completely safe—because Section 7 of the Fugitive Slave Act of 1850 provided a fine of up to $1,000 and imprisonment up to six months for persons assisting slaves in violating the Act. It was risky for citizens of free states to help fleeing slaves. Southern slave catchers could legally cross the Ohio River looking for slaves to capture and return to their owners in the Confederate states.

Finn: What was it like to live in Waco when the second Klan was strong?

Pops: Weird and frightening for everyone, but especially for those opposing the Klan. Baylor Law School Professor Margaret Amsler recalled that the Klan was a "vicious organization" and that her father, Judge Nat Harris, who was a part-time Baylor law school professor, took a strong position against the Klan publicly. The Klan consequently threatened Judge Harris and as a result, the Harris family kept a shotgun near the back door. With a backdrop of burning crosses, lynchings, dragging a burned Black man down Main Street, and masked men noisily marching in bizarre robes and pointed hats, even a peaceful parade down a main street like Austin Avenue was scary. A silent procession could be unnerving as well. Here is an account by a Baylor student of one such chilling march: "Now, the KKK had a silent parade here one time...We went to see the [silent] parade [down Franklin Street in Waco] because we wanted to see what was going on. It was just so silent it seemed like death...I don't know how you would feel. You couldn't hear a sound. Not a sound of anything...This was about '15 or '16...I know one time people were afraid to go out at night for fear they'd get hurt...because you didn't have to be doing anything if you were a Negro. Now, I know the time that Negroes couldn't walk across Baylor campus unless they were working there."

Finn: A silent parade of masked crazy people in white robes wearing pointy hats and carrying a burning cross would be scary, day or night. If your skin was the wrong color, I guess you might think they could snatch you and do whatever they wanted.

Pops: Here is an account of a parade on October 1, 1921, by another Baylor student, this one taking place in Lorena, Texas, less than fourteen miles south of Waco:

> When I was a senior, one day, one of the boys who worked part-time on the Waco newspaper told me and some others that the KKK was going to march at Robinson and that he had been assigned to go out and get a story for them. Wanted to know if we didn't want to go along. Of course we said yes and in those days,

> we weren't even supposed to ride in a car, but we went in this Model-T Ford, open top ...two-seated thing...
>
> And we went out there, and it was a big crowd. There were hundreds of people. Maybe a thousand...just the biggest crowd you ever saw just lining the little street—the railroad track there and the Klan members arrived by train. They all got off the train. They were all in their uniforms and masks over their faces.
>
> And they lit a cross—burning cross to lead the [parade]—and they started parading down the main street and the sheriff of McLennan County [Bob Buchanan] was there with his gun in his hand and he says 'You cannot parade. You cannot pass.' They just kept coming. And he kept hollering and telling them they could not come, and...he fired his gun. I think he fired it up in the air, but we didn't know that.
>
> The boys pushed us down—another girl with me and—to the ground and everybody began running. The crowd, you know, was breaking up—running to the cars...Klan kept marching, but everybody was in a hurry to try to get...out of the way, and the railroad was narrow and there was gravel..."

Katie: Did anyone else see the Lorena parade?

Pops: You bet. The student just mentioned didn't mention some of the crucial details in her interview—she probably was not aware of them. Professor Harrison saw and described the same incident in his memoir, along with other information starting with his initiation:

> My initiation took place on a big hill west of Waco...I got my robe, which I kept for years, and a hood. Of the regalia, I still have the cross which was on the left chest over the heart...I found that there were signs and passwords and signals and all, and we were told to trade only with the KKK people who showed the sign and so on. And I would always look for that in stores and anywhere around and patronize the merchants who showed the Klan sign. [The Waco group] was a large one. It had many thousands of members. I continued in it through...the episode at Lorena.
>
> They were invited out to Lorena. I went out there...to join the parade... [The county sheriff said to take off the KKK masks and Harrison's group] took off our masks...The parade was led by a group of citizens, very prominent citizens here in Waco, one of them bearing a flag...and the sheriff came out and stopped them.

> And the flag bearer, who was a very prominent man here in Waco, was outraged...so cracked down on the head of the sheriff with the flagstaff and knocked him down in the street.
>
> My uncle [Louis Crow], who owned all the laundries in Waco...rushed across to help him up. And the sheriff came to about that time and looked up and saw my uncle and all that white [Louis Crow liked wearing white clothes], and he thought he was a Klansman, that perhaps he was the one who'd knocked him down. He jerked out a tremendous big dirk almost a bowie knife, and stabbed my uncle in the chest, went clear through...
>
> [The Klan group that day was in] the thousands...The whole earth was covered.

<u>Charlie</u>: Didn't you also mention a burning? What was that?

<u>Pops</u>: Yes, that was the Jesse Washington incident which occurred several years earlier in 1916 after a number of other incidents. It was the worst of them all. Jesse Washington, a seventeen-year-old African American farmhand, had been accused of raping and murdering Lucy Fryer. It, as much as anything, set the tone for 1920s Klan activity and the public paranoia about race. Pastor Joseph Dawson of First Baptist Church in Waco witnessed the burning and described it as follows: "It [the Klan] was never as strong in Texas as in other states...In Waco, there were a few such zealots in my own church who sought to enlist me, even came as a committee...which I declined. Fortunately, President S.P. Brooks was very influential and strongly set against the Klan. He was my dearest friend and strongest supporter. I witnessed the event [at the City Hall in May of 1916] where the Negro [Jesse Washington] was burned...five thousand monsters participated...They heaped a pile of wood, they drug him from up on Washington several blocks, and cast him on top of this saturated wood pile and burned him. Now, after his burning, someone tied his mutilated torso to the horn of a saddle and dragged it over the road to Robinson where he disposed of it... [Then later] they discovered they had burned an innocent man."

Another student added more details to this incident: "[The Klan] met quite a bit out on Speight Street...that was...the biggest meeting place.... [One couldn't be both in the Masons and the Klan.] ...I went to the courthouse one time to attend a trial of [Jesse Washington] that was suspected of rape. And in taking him from the courthouse back to the jail the mob took him away from the sheriff and his deputies...They [the deputies] took no real precautions to protect him, bringing him to the courthouse and taking him back. And they took him to the public square and burnt him at a tree. And then tied his body to a car and drug his body up and down Austin Avenue, the main street. The man was later proved to be innocent...

[and another man confessed].The situation involving Jesse Washington went on for an hour or so. And no attempt was made to stop them from dragging his body...The authorities thought it would simply inflame the situation and create a real riot or something, so they just let it die down...There were hundreds—everybody—they knew who the gang leader—who the leaders of the mob were and who actually burnt the man... [The leaders of the mob] were riffraff of the town...known to everybody...during those years in Texas it was impossible to convict anybody or even try anybody for lynching a rape suspect. The first break in really putting the quietus, making people feel they would be responsible, was federal law that came in. But I don't ever remember any local or state laws that were enforced...It was murder really...don't remember...anytime in my life...anybody being convicted in those years because of a lynching."

One final recollection by a Waco resident of the Jesse Washington killing: "[Regarding the Negro that was lynched and dragged] My father didn't want me to see it. And he said, 'Don't go that way home. Go another way.' But it happened and when we came out of school, in the showplace's window, different showcases downtown, had parts of his body—burned body in the showcase window where you could see. We passed by and looked at it like—we didn't know what it was. And after I go home and I got to talking to Papa, and Papa was talking to different people, and they said they had burned this man, and different people got parts of his body as souvenirs. I said, 'Lord have mercy,' that's why Papa didn't want me to go that way because he knew what was happening, but he did not want me to know....the tree where they hanged his body—the tree was still standing there with the burned leaves, but the rope was gone. And they said they took his body and brought it up Sixth Street. Brought it right up, dragging it behind a car, right on up Sixth Street...the last time I heard of it, they still—they know who did it. They know who did the burning...But a lot of people said they knew him. I think they said he lived in East Waco."

With a scene as horrific as the Jesse Washington lynching, murder, and its gruesome aftermath, Waco was naturally on edge throughout the 1920s. However, no one was ever charged for this shameful incident.

Charlie: Awful. Do we know how Frank felt or what he did about it?

Pops: We know a little about what Baylor faculty thought and did, including Frank. The murder of Lucy Fryer occurred on May 8, 1916, and by May 15, one week later, Washington had been arrested, tried, convicted, and taken by a lynch mob away from the authorities. The faculty met at 8:30 a.m. the following day (May 16, 1916). Those present were Dean Kesler and faculty members Wright, Pool, Tidwell, Armstrong, Hawkins, Trantham, Guittard, Pace, Hall, Johnson, and possibly another member. A committee was appointed to draft a resolution on the hanging and burning of Jesse Washington by a mob the day before, May 15. The committee met and produced the following report and accompanying resolutions adopted unanimously by the faculty when it met the next day:

> Whereas on Monday, May 15, 1916, the officers of the law of McLennan County, Texas were proceeding summarily, but proceeding duly with the trial of a Negro prisoner who was accused of a grave crime,
>
> Whereas their proceedings were violently interrupted by a mob of persons who seized the said prisoner, hurried him away through the streets mutilated, hanged and burned him in the city hall square,
>
> Whereas the lifeless remains of the said Negro were thereafter dragged about the streets of our city, and
>
> Whereas we believe that such a manner of publishing crime does not meet the approbation of the citizen body of this community and yet we apprehend that the incident will evoke from the outside world reproaches unmerited by the majority of the people of our fair city and county, therefore
>
> Resolved that we the Faculty of Baylor University do hereby declare that we abhor and deplore the violent act of the mob, although we do not condone the dastardly offense of which the said Negro made confession and we believe that he ought to have received the extreme penalty of the law.
>
> Resolved also that we express our disapproval of every form of mob violence, and that we solemnly call upon our fellow citizens henceforth to allow the regular processes of the law to take their normal course in every case that may arise.
>
> Resolved further that copies of these resolutions be spread upon the minutes of this faculty and furnished to the Lariat and the newspapers of the City of Waco for publication.
>
> Respectfully submitted, J.B. Johnson, A.J. Armstrong, Jas. W. Wright, F.G. Guittard, H. Trantham" (Faculty Minutes, May 16, 1916)

Many of the prominent Waco churches—Baptist, Methodist, Presbyterian—also came out strongly against Jesse Washington's lynching. Pastor J.M. Dawson, First Baptist Church, made a strong outcry against the mob's behavior, and President Brooks drafted resolutions against mob violence that were adopted by the Baptist State Convention.

Charlie: Pops, I don't understand. Did the Baylor faculty and Frank get it wrong? You already said some people were thinking the wrong man had been convicted. So why did Baylor say that Washington should have received "the extreme penalty of the law"?

Pops: Right. This is going to be a mixed answer. The faculty acted as just described the very next day to deplore mob violence, the hanging, burning, mutilation, and dragging of Jesse Washington, the entire day's horrific events before rumors and gossip started circulating about Washington's possible innocence. Those rumors circulated nonetheless. I could find no corroboration of any hearsay statements that someone else had confessed to raping and murdering Lucy Fryer. If there was exculpatory evidence, it should have been introduced at Washington's trial. Of course, that assumes that Washington had access to competent counsel, exculpatory evidence, and a fair trial, those assumptions being extremely dubious under the circumstances. Without a fair trial and access to competent counsel—Washington received neither—the Baylor faculty could not know for sure whether Washington deserved "the extreme penalty of the law." But whether Washington was deserving of death for his actions, nothing could excuse what a Waco mob did to Washington and to the rule of law. Baylor's faculty got that part right.

Charlie: Why would Washington confess to rape if he was innocent? That would have been a bad idea, especially in that day and time.

Pops: Certainly, but Jesse Washington was an illiterate seventeen-year-old African American farmhand. Most people will confess to anything, including rape and murder, including you and me, if subjected to brutal interrogation and physical abuse over an extended period of time, especially when they do not have a lawyer. African American suspects were especially subjected to this kind of treatment in the early twentieth century. As a result of the lynching and the abhorrent conduct of Waco citizens, Waco was perceived as racist for years.

Charlie: I'm glad that such things don't happen these days.

Pops: Unfortunately, Charlie, they do, and sometimes by the sworn officers of the law. In early 2020, George Floyd, an African American man in police custody, was inexcusably killed by a Minnesota policeman before he could be taken to trial. (*Changing the subject*). The next chapter will take us away from the public arena to Frank's mostly private world. Did you know that Frank liked to read the Sunday funnies and that some of them were actually funny? First, though, we all need to take a break and stretch our legs.

Charlie: I like the seventh inning stretch at a baseball game. I'm ready, Pops.

Illustrations 9-15

Spending time with Mamie at the Albuquerque Sanatorium.

Discussing with Josie the pros & cons of pursuing a doctorate.

Adviser Robinson criticizing a draft chapter of Frank's dissertation.

Frank's classroom desktop—pocket watch, text, notes, & gradebook.

Enjoying a lighter moment with his history students.

President Brooks signing diplomas shortly before his death.

Exercising with a sandbag to avoid becoming humpbacked.

SEVENTH INNING STRETCH

A Short Pause for the Peanut Gallery

Pops: (*to the peanut gallery*) How about taking a break after that last chapter? That part about the KKK near the end got intense, didn't you think?

Miles: No kidding.

Pops: Let's take our seventh-inning stretch before getting into the final innings.

Katie: So, Pops, what will the final innings be about?

Pops: Sure—that's where we'll first explore Frank's private sides known only to Mamie, Francis, Josie, and Clarence. Then, we'll look at Frank's stressful days as a much older student at Stanford, climbing an academic mountain and fighting dragons en route to a doctorate. Finally, we'll take a look at what those seventy-five students who sent me their recollections thought about him as a teacher. Then, it will be time for our wrap-up and conclusion. Oh, I should have said after looking at Frank's private sides, we will see what you think the themes of Frank's life were and whether any metaphors or paradoxes come to anyone's mind.

Finn: Okay, but I think I would call it a "third-quarter stretch." We've been talking football mostly, not baseball.

Charlie: Finn has finally come up with a good idea: "Third-quarter stretch."

Pops: Miles? Katie?

Miles: I like "seventh-inning stretch." It fits better. Nobody has ever heard of a "third-quarter stretch."

Katie: I pass; I'm not really into football or baseball. I play volleyball.

Pops: Well, regardless of what we call this break, I thought we could use a pause before beginning the final chapters. Everything we've talked about so far has just been leading up to the last chapters where we will "dig"—to use one of Frank's favorite terms—down deep before we are done. You'll want to hear Professor

Smiley's words about Frank as a teacher of history. And we'll still need everyone's help.

Finn: (*grinning*) When can we look at your bibliography? I may want to check out some of your references.

Pops: (*smiling*) Well, for starters, The Texas Collection is at 5th and Speight, and it's open five days a week.

BOOK SIX

Behind the Scenes at 1401 South 8th

Sample questions for the peanut gallery's consideration in this book's chapters:

What rules did Frank formulate to govern his behavior? Did Frank have a sense of humor or a playful side? What was an ordinary day in Frank and Josie's home at 1401 South 8th? What was Frank like when he was with his family and not in front of his students? What were Frank's eccentricities? What kind of father for Francis, infant Charles, and Clarence was he? Did Frank have an interest in music? What do we know about his religious faith or his relationship with his church? Did expositions and fairs have an attraction for Frank?

Excerpt from Frank's "Funny-Book of Student Bone-heads" on examinations:

Question: "Who was John Hampden?" Answer: "John Hampden was one of the best leaders of his time. He isn't accorded very much in History but when you study his life you find him to be a great deal more than he is supposed to be in History. There were very few men who would have taken up the leadership of his people like he did and fight for their belief."

Examples of Frank's favorite words and phrases from his correspondence:

"amicable relations" — "Glad to know you are maintaining amicable relations as well as laundry connection with Millie."

"agreeable" — "I have an agreeable room."

"private consumption" — "In my last conference with Dr. Robinson—this is for private consumption—"

CHAPTER 31

Frank's Private Sides & Life at Home

This afternoon we pull back the curtain for a few glimpses of Frank's private sides. This chapter is intended to accompany the chapter recounting Frank's public style, personality, and method as a teacher of history. In this chapter, Miles will be helping me look into Frank's "private sides."

Pops: Miles, you may have wondered how I could tell Frank Guittard's story objectively. Actually, I never really worried about this work being considered a hagiographic exercise, as my relationship with my grandfather was brief, infrequent, and remote, with little chance for personal interaction. It did feel presumptuous trying to get into his head seventy years after his death to identify mostly hidden traits, behaviors, and thoughts. In time, however, I became convinced a credible biography could be achieved, my having read, digested, and processed, over a long period, voluminous correspondence from Frank, Josie ("Mama Josie"), Francis, Clarence, and from his former students; Frank's diaries, ledgers, college essays, autobiographies, speeches, miscellaneous writings, and interviews with living relatives, including his youngest son, Clarence, and his oldest grandson, Stephen, along with others who knew him. Although some of my comments are conclusions from the available evidence, I have done my best to avoid going off into the "wild blue yonder" and to acknowledge when an observation might tend in that direction.

Prisms for understanding Frank's private sides

Miles: So, what did Mama Josie, Francis, and Clarence know about Frank that his students didn't know?

Pops: That is a big question, as there was much about Frank that was unknown to his students. Frank, it seems to me, had five fundamental sides, which may be thought of as prisms to view everything that he said or did.

Miles: What do you mean by "prism?"

Pops: A prism is a remarkable piece of glass you look through that gives you a certain view of whatever you are looking at. It is a figure of speech to assist us in distinguishing Frank's different private sides. I could have used the word "lens," but I liked "prism" better.

Miles: So, what are these prisms you are talking about?

Pops: There are five that I see. The first is the moral code Frank lived by. In many ways, Frank's code was similar to the code of chivalry from ages past, which the knights of Arthur's Roundtable were bound by. Interestingly, at the first Baylor homecoming parade that Frank was tasked with organizing, one student observing the parade said Professor Guittard looked like one of the storied knights of legend.

Miles: Did the student mean Frank reminded her of Sir Lancelot and riding a horse with jousting lance in one hand?

Pops: I don't think so, but the student didn't explain what she meant. We don't know what Frank wore at this early homecoming parade or whether he was walking, on a horse, on a float, or in a car. However, Sir Galahad, the "Good Knight" and hero of the grail legends, might have been a better choice than Lancelot. Some of those other knights around King Arthur had serious character deficits, like Gawain, Perceval, Tristan, and, of course, Lancelot, who ultimately betrayed King Arthur.

Miles: I'm wondering if Frank, like Galahad, had a grail. And did he have an Arthur? If he did, was there a roundtable of knights around his Arthur?

Pops: We will get to all of those questions in time, but the short answer for all is a qualified yes. The second prism, which we will discuss with the first prism, is represented by two sets of Frank's personal rules, one for his behavior as a teacher and another as a faculty member. He formulated them soon after he began teaching in the Baylor Academy, which was an extremely challenging, almost overwhelming, experience. The purpose of these personal rules was not simply to perform up to President Brooks's expectations as a teacher, but rather to quell the feelings of panic he must have had as he thought about his first job as a college teacher. After all, he now had to prepare himself to teach multiple subjects he had not studied in Chicago or Sam Houston Normal. The rules tell us a lot about Frank in 1902 and as a mature professor in the later decades of his teaching career. The third prism we can examine comes from his fundamental personality—reserved, introspective, and shy.

Miles: I didn't know teachers were shy. Mine weren't.

Pops: Many teachers are naturally shy but have learned to compensate for their native shyness and can stand in front of a class with confidence to conduct their classes. Knowing that he was shy may help us understand him and some of his decisions. Philip G. Zimbardo, Stanford University psychology emeritus professor and 2002 president of the American Psychological Association, said in his study of shyness that there is a shyness continuum and that at one end of the continuum "are those who feel more comfortable with books, ideas, objects, or nature than with other people." This analysis of shyness seems to fit Frank Guittard and some of his direct descendants. We will talk about Frank's son, Clarence Guittard, elsewhere.

The fourth prism centers on Frank's systematic and methodical mindset, accompanied by his desire to impose order and control on the events of his life, and to some extent, on the lives of those around him in his family circle. This side was partially visible to persons outside his family. We will dedicate an entire chapter later to this side of Frank, as it applied to teaching his students.

Miles: Those four prisms make it sound like he wasn't much fun with his family or students. They make me wonder whether he knew any jokes, or was he always Professor Serious?

Pops: Let's wait a bit before coming to any conclusions—you might be surprised. We have just started exploring his private sides.

The fifth and final prism is our understanding of his spontaneous, playful inner child—he did have one—who could be imaginative, romantic, humorous, affectionate, and generous, and who loved nature and the out-of-doors. This inner child was largely hidden from outsiders and existed in tension with his systematic and bookish sides.

In addition to the five prisms, there are also certain facets of Frank's private sides which we will talk about separately and not under the five prisms.

The first prism: Frank's chivalric moral nature

Pops: Frank recorded, in his handwriting, date unknown, verses from various poems that meant something to him. Here is one: "I dreamed and thought that Life was beauty. I woke and found that life was duty." The duties of knighthood are found in the Knights' Code of Chivalry described in "The Song of Roland." They are sometimes called Charlemagne's Code of Chivalry. Frank consciously and unconsciously internalized concepts from many sources, including the books he read, the Methodist and Baptist churches he attended, and the examples of his parents. These included most of the following core tenets of the Knights' code: "to fear God and maintain his Church; to protect the liege lord in valour and faith; to protect the weak and defenceless; to give succor to widows and orphans; to refrain from the wanton giving of offence; to live by honour and for glory; to despise pecuniary reward; to fight for the welfare of all; to obey those placed in authority; to eschew unfairness, meanness, and deceit; at all times to speak the truth; to persevere to the end in any enterprise begun; never to refuse a challenge from an equal; never to turn the back upon a foe; and to respect the honour of women." Of these, the overwhelming majority relate to acts of chivalry and not to combat, either literally or figuratively. Frank understood and observed the principles of this code instinctively throughout his life.

Miles: Those sounds like the Boy Scout Oath and Scout Law. But who was the liege lord or the scoutmaster?

Pops: Yes, especially the Boy Scout Oath, and the vows regarding God, speaking the truth, protecting the weak and helpless, and not giving offense. Boy Scouts don't swear loyalty to any man, including any king, president, governor, or mayor. Still, in the Middle Ages, knights swore allegiance to their liege lords, who were wealthy owners of manors whose castles the knights protected from invaders. And, of course, knights swore allegiance to King Arthur, at least in those ancient legends.

Miles: All right, so many of Frank's values were in tune with those of the knights of old, but is there any reason to believe that he, in a sense, fancied himself some sort of modern-day knight?

Pops: The evidence is overwhelming that he considered himself a hard-working history teacher toiling at a beggarly wage in a noble profession to inoculate his students with the facts of history. However, there is some evidence that perhaps he did take consolation from the examples of those knights. Eleven years after dropping out of Baylor and now on Baylor's faculty, Frank gave a talk on Christian leadership to a student organization at a prayer meeting. He advised those present that "during the Middle Ages, the noblest warriors were knights on the field of battle," implying that Christians, like knights, must be prepared to do battle. So, I don't think there is any doubt that Frank drew comfort for his persistence and preparation as a teacher not only from his Christian faith, but also from the example of these warrior knights of romantic legends from a thousand years earlier. As to your question, Miles, about who Frank's Arthur was and who was at his roundtable, the evidence suggests that Brooks, in a sense, was the Arthur in Frank's world and that Brooks's loyal faculty was Brooks's roundtable.

The second prism: Frank's original rules for self-regulation

However, consistent with the values from the code of chivalry, Frank formulated, for his private use, two sets of rules [the second prism] for himself governing his conduct as a faculty member and as a teacher. Frank's first set—twenty-six rules—after omitting the rules relating to diet, exercise, and preparing for class the night before, have been consolidated and shortened to eleven:

1. Be careful how you address those in authority or those who have some claim to distinction.
2. Never accuse anyone of falsehood; never speak disrespectfully of things pertaining to religion.
3. Think twice before doing anything that will reflect on your honor.
4. Be careful about changing the subject of conversation or discussion and be thoughtful in conversation.
5. Be honest and truthful on all occasions.
6. Do not express your opinions too emphatically or too positively; control [one's] facial expressions.
7. Greet acquaintances and others pleasantly; take leave of people in a pleasant manner and never abruptly.
8. Avoid flippant conversation; never relate immoral anecdotes; do not speak of your private affairs to strangers.
9. In trying situations, say as little as possible; never speak disparagingly of anyone; hold your tongue when aroused with anger.
10. Do not get too ready to express your own opinion.
11. Get others' views first if possible.

The main takeaway from these rules is that Frank believed strongly he had to be careful about what he said and to whom.

<u>Miles</u>: That's a lot of rules, Pops. I wonder why he was so cautious about what he said?

<u>Pops</u>: We don't know; it may have something to do with his Ohio family or with an inherited trait. But I haven't gotten to all of his rules yet. This second prism also contains a set of rules Frank formulated as reminders for dealing with his students and with faculty and administrators; I have shortened and consolidated these to seven:

1. Do not discuss faculty proceedings with others; do not speak unfavorably of any member of the faculty; never say anything disparagingly about other departments or the relative importance of their work.
2. Cultivate a cheerful manner and expression in the classroom; strive to avoid all evidence of irritability; if necessary to reprove students, do so privately and in kindness, never in anger; strive to gain the love and respect of your students.
3. Be more patient with slow students; let the student make a trial before being assisted in anything.
4. Look after backward students and demote them as soon as possible that they may do themselves justice in work for which they are prepared.
5. Have a definite plan thought out beforehand for each recitation and make it a practice to ask students about their work.
6. Acquiesce to those in authority after stating your own position if you are unable to convince them you are right.
7. Keep all students' attention during a recitation.

The third prism: Frank Guittard's basic personality

Pops: Frank's basic personality, which I am calling the third prism, was itself multi-faceted. Frank was an introspective, ruminating, and reserved guy who, when not in a classroom, spent most of his time in private study, reading and making notes in his notebooks. His handwritten notebooks facilitated his questions to his classes over the assigned readings and were essential to his preparation.

Frank predictably was not a joiner. For a short time, he attended the Friday Kiwanis luncheon. He was also a Mason, but not an especially enthusiastic one, and a lodge member, though he did not encourage his sons to join. Occasionally, he would attend concerts or other social engagements with Josie and invite a few faculty friends over for supper. His younger son, Clarence, who was fond of his father, was introverted himself and understood the constraints that excessive shyness places on those afflicted with it. He remembered his father as self-conscious and lacking assurance in meeting people, characteristics they shared. Further, although Frank had many admirers among his students, his close friends were generally limited to those in Baylor's history department and certain other faculty members. Beyond that relatively small group, he was not especially sociable or outgoing. He escaped being a hermit altogether because he was able to find and marry sociable women, Mamie, and then Josie. Josie, in particular, was Frank's polar opposite in sociability and would provide, as had Mamie before her, their social life by staging dinner parties at 1401 South 8th and by accepting their friends' invitations. Josie would accept the invitations, and she and Frank would go, but Frank often went grudgingly, saying he would rather stay at home.

Frank read a broad mixture of books, periodicals, newspapers, and even comic strips in his quest for knowledge, inspiration, entertainment, and whatever else from the written word. For class or for whatever reason, Frank's need to read broadly was a point of difference and cause of tension between him and both of his wives. Before their marriage, Mamie expressed her concern that she would have limited access to Frank because of his passion for study and books, which now seems to have been justified.

Miles: If it was challenging to get Frank's head out of the books, was he also an "absent-minded professor"?

Pops: Not especially so. Although he did have episodes of absent-mindedness, that subject was more a topic for family kidding than one with actual substance. Frank wrote Josie from Palo Alto about one such episode: "I had a terrible spell of absent-mindedness the other morning—that is, it must have been from results. I noticed that my shaving did not proceed as well as usual and I came to find out I was using tooth-paste for shaving soap." (FGG letter to MJ, August 7, 1929)

Miles: Would any of the books or other things he liked to read tell us more about how he saw himself or his life?

Pops: Yes, I think so. Edwin Alger's [Jay Jerome Williams's] *Ben Webster* was a favorite comic strip of Frank; Dickens's *David Copperfield* was his favorite book. In both of these, and in the Horatio Alger Jr. novels, we have squeaky clean young men trying to solve serious problems or working against great odds, including poverty. The opening paragraph of one of Frank's autobiographies is reminiscent of the first chapter of *David Copperfield*, wherein Dickens takes us to the moment of Copperfield's birth and recounts his birth in the first person, mentioning that "as the clock struck twelve...I began to cry." Guittard similarly starts an autobiography for a class at the University of Chicago: "I do not hesitate to say that up to the present time the most important event of my life was my birth" and goes on to mention his "pretty red cheeks [which he] lost during a spell of fever."

In some respects, Frank himself was an underdog hero, like these favorites of his. Literary themes involving struggle and resolution in times of trouble would have appealed to him. Some of the Alger novels that would most have resonated with Frank, had he read them, would have been *Ragged Dick, The Young Book Agent*, and *Walter Sherwood's Probation*. In *Walter Sherwood's Probation (1890)*, Sherwood's guardian learns that Sherwood is playing around at Euclid College and spending money frivolously. Consequently, he advises Sherwood that a significant portion of the fortune supporting him has been lost and that Sherwood will have to leave school and work for a year. Afterward, Walter's prospects are at such a low ebb that he wonders aloud, "if there is any poorhouse in Chaco...It is not the sort of home I should prefer, but is better than genteel starvation." In *The Young Book Agent (1905)*, a young man is forced, due to his father's misfortunes, to help provide for the family to which he belongs. Additionally, Captain Ralph Bonehill (Edward Stratemeyer] wrote a Horatio Alger knock-off with a title that surely would have caught Frank's attention—*The Young Bandmaster*, which tells the story of a young cornetist who aspires to a career as a bandsman after his father's financial fortunes take a turn for the worse. The *Bandmaster* contains a final episode when young Paul Graham is part of a military brass band accompanying the American Army to Santiago, Cuba, in 1900.

That Frank would have privately seen himself as an underdog, like Ben Webster, David Copperfield, or even an Alger hero like the book agent character—but a well-read, motivated, and patient underdog from an educated family determined to rise in the world—is probable. Frank was not a country rube escaping from an Ohio farm. However, his contemporaries and friends, Samuel P. Brooks and Pat M. Neff, completed college in substantially fewer years than Frank, likely because of denominational and parental assistance or private resources. Brooks's father was a minister, and Neff's mother a property owner of significance. Frank, on the other hand, had to work his way through college over an extended period with no significant help. He could not have helped but see himself as an underdog.

The fourth prism: Frank's systematic and methodical mindset

Pops: The fourth prism is our view of Frank's unusually systematic and methodical turn of mind in all areas of life, from his health practices at home to his teaching style in the classroom. As some of our readers will already know, Frank Bunker Gilbreth Sr.—the central character in the popular, nonfiction *Cheaper by the Dozen*—is widely known today as an early advocate of scientific management and a pioneer of time-motion study. In Gilbreth's early days, he developed more advanced techniques for improved brick-laying efficiency. He had an interest in developing processes eliminating waste motions. Frank Guittard was similarly interested in avoiding wasted time and process steps, notably in the parade process. He was largely responsible for the organization of the first Baylor homecoming parade in 1909 and led commencement parades for decades. Frank's farm work back in Ohio included developing an improved breed of hogs and a system for crop rotation.

Baylor students had opportunities daily to observe their teachers and to discuss them, both between classes and in the *Baylor Lariat* (daily newspaper) and the *Round-Up* (student yearbook). Frank had the reputation of being dedicated to doing things on time, always bringing his pocket watch to class. The 1919 *Round-Up* opined: "Wouldn't it be great if Prof. Guittard was on the other side of the

Atlantic to show them how to get our boys back on time [from fighting overseas in World War I]?" Frank was also known for his interest in time-motion study. A *Lariat* cartoon indicates that Frank, on one occasion, applied his talents to a time-motion study of chapel exit, presumably in the case of fire. Perhaps Frank's early efforts to develop an efficient chapel exit in April 1919 were providential since a catastrophic fire started in Carroll Chapel and Library in February 1922. During this fire, students rushed forward to remove and save most of the books in an efficient and coordinated manner, including those in the world-famous Armstrong-Browning Collection. One student remembers coming up the sidewalk, seeing the fire, and observing that Frank was on the sidewalk advising the people what to do and what not to do. (Student Pugh, January 18, 1980)

How did his systematic nature affect life when Frank was at home? To begin with, the entire day of everyone living at 1401 South 8th was ordered in keeping with Frank's desire for orderliness, predictability, and schedule. Frank would wake Clarence up in the mornings when Clarence slept on the sleeping porch. After they had studied German together one summer, Frank would summon Clarence with "*Steh auf, steh auf, du faule Jager!*" meaning "Get up, get up, you lazy hunter." Everyone at the house got up at the same time—family and roomers began their days in the same way and ate lunch at a predictable time. Meals were served at understood times. Frank dressed and looked the same, with the exception of changing his three-piece suit, tie, and shirt, every work day.

Frank usually had classes in the morning until 12:40 p.m., and then he came home and had lunch at about 1:00. At 1:45 or 2:00, he retired to his room to take a nap, setting his alarm clock for 3:00. Being a heavy sleeper, he was completely inaccessible during his naptime, and his snoring could be heard through the closed door of his room. After his nap, he might study in his room or, in later years, go out two or three days a week to play golf. He spent a lot of time studying at his desk, either upstairs in his bedroom or downstairs in the study, and he frequently studied at night. At mealtimes, Josie would ring a tinkly little silver bell signaling the readiness of the food or for Cleo, the server, to bring the next course. Meals were never hurried. Lounging or resting on the table with one's elbows was discouraged.

<u>Miles</u>: Mabel, Mabel, strong and able…

<u>Pops</u>: Then, around 10:00 or 10:30 p.m., Frank would enter Clarence's bedroom where he was studying and throw him an apple. His penchant for systematizing is nowhere more evident than in his thinking concerning health matters, both for his health and the health of his family. His health views ran to many subjects, including observing an almost inflexible daily routine, eating hearty meals, preserving his speaking and singing voice, avoiding the development of a

decrepit looking humpback, exercising to strengthen his chest and lungs, walking for his overall physical condition, and getting plenty of sleep—he was not given to late-night revelries or activities of any kind as a young man or adult—including daily naps after lunch. Frank may have had in mind that admonition from Cervantes's *Don Quixote*: "With little sleep and much reading [Don Quixote's] brains got so dry that he lost his wits." Last, Frank did not smoke and was abstemious where alcoholic drink was concerned.

Frank would do his voice exercises for five to ten minutes every day at the piano in the dining room. His oldest grandson remembers that he had a medium-high voice, and another grandson remembers it as a medium-pitched voice, perhaps with a bit of an Ohio accent. Another grandson remembered that he had a gentle voice. He did not play the piano, but he would sing notes as he played them on the piano and do simple routines with his voice. He encouraged Francis and Clarence to exercise their voices similarly, but the habit never caught on. In the mornings, Frank did his calisthenics and other exercises, including deep knee bends, grunting, and sputtering for five to ten minutes. When working on his Ph.D. in Palo Alto, he continued his exercise routines, with the possible exception of his voice exercises. He wrote Josie: "The landlady has dedicated an aluminum teakettle to my use for heating my water for tonsorial purposes in the morning down in the kitchen. While it is heating I take my exercises without disturbing the pots and pans or apples and potatoes which look at me wonderingly from various nooks and corners." (FGG letter to MJ, January 5, 1928)

Then there was that odd sack of sand that Frank kept on a bookcase in the study, an exercise prop he brought back from Chicago. It weighed twelve to fifteen pounds and was twelve inches wide, twelve inches long, and four to five inches thick. The sack had the appearance of a small, heavy pillow. Frank was convinced that if he walked around with it on his head for a few minutes each day, he could avoid becoming hump-shouldered in later years. He used the sack regularly himself and encouraged Francis and Clarence to emulate him. There were a few attempts by both sons to walk around with the sack, but no tangible benefits in their cases were observed. There is no direct evidence that Frank, at any point, had the temerity to attempt to encourage either of his wives to walk around with the sack. While he likely suggested the practice to one or both of them, it is not believable either would have been interested. Both of them would have left walking with a sack on the head, voice exercises at the piano, afternoon naps, deep knee bends and chest exercises, and other systematized health routines for Frank to enjoy by himself.

The fifth prism: music—hymns, marches, and opera

Miles: I'm interested in hearing more about Frank and his interest in music. Maybe I inherited that. I played clarinet for a while.

Pops: You certainly could have inherited that from him or another of your Guittard forbears like your own father or his mother. We know that Frank's interest in music was extensive. He loved to sing church music and to take girls to church, singing services being a popular date in the days before movies and ballgames. Singing schools—unheard of these days—were popular, and the Guittard children attended them. We will talk about some of the early hymns Frank liked later. He played in an orchestra at Baylor as a faculty member, before then at the University of Chicago, and no doubt back in Ohio. In Ohio, there were some old horns he would play around on, possibly saxhorns of the "backward blaster" type in which the bell faced the bandsman marching behind. He played cornet, which is similar to a trumpet and plays the same part. President Harper at Chicago was a whiz on the cornet, and we suspect he and Frank met each other in connection with one of the bands at the University of Chicago. We're not exactly sure how Frank managed to play the cornet because the fourth and fifth fingers on his right hand were partially disabled. That hand would have been the one required to manipulate a cornet's valves, but apparently, it wasn't a significant impediment. So, he would have been playing march music from early on, and Sousa marches at least from his days at Chicago.

He also had a lifelong appreciation for classical music, including grand opera and music for the piano, which he encouraged his older son Francis to play. His last musical outing was to a Donizetti opera, which we will talk about later. It is instructive that although Frank's teaching specialty was history, he considered it essential that history students be aware of the great works of art and music. Music was a common interest he shared with both his wives. A number of the most beloved operas, especially those by Puccini and Verdi, spoke to the heart: *Boheme*, *Tosca*, *Butterfly*, and *Traviata*, to name a few. *Boheme* and *Traviata* featured heroines with fatal illnesses, and Tosca and Butterfly died at the end, all of which would have resonated with Frank. Frank's first married love, Mamie, struggled with a deadly disease for years before succumbing. Commitment to principle in *Tosca* and *Madame Butterfly*—Tosca to her lover and Butterfly to her sense of honor—sealed their fates. *Macbeth*, *Boris Godunov*, *William Tell*, *Julius Caesar*, *Mary Queen of Scots*, *The Trojans*, and arguably *Aida*, were all operas that would have appealed to Frank's love of history, if only to note to himself the historical inaccuracies. We can imagine him whispering to Josie, "Well, Josie, you know it didn't really happen that way, don't you?" and Josie replying, "Oh, hush. At least you didn't go to sleep like you do during Sunday sermons."

Miles: What about the popular songs of the day, songs in English that ordinary people could sing? Did he like those?

Pops: We don't know that he sang any of the hundreds of songs popular during his day, but he must have enjoyed listening to most of his era's songs like the following random handful: "O Dem Golden Slippers," "Polly-Wolly-Doodle," "Down by the River-Side," "Clementine," "The Animal Fair," "The Muffin Man," and "Go Down, Moses." "The Animal Fair" and "The Muffin Man" were songs Clarence sang to his children, including the author, and probably heard from Frank.

Frank and his family; mentor to sons

Pops: Miles, there are some other private sides we need to mention.

Miles: We haven't talked much about what it was like between Frank and Mamie or Mama Josie or between Frank and Francis or Clarence.

Pops: You're right. Let's first talk about his relationships with Mamie and Josie. Frank and Mamie were an unusually compatible couple: both were big readers and were interested in history, literature, the arts, and the world in general. Frank was, by any measure, the less social of the two, and Mamie always had a good group of friends, starting in Shiner. Josie and Frank were also quite compatible, although Josie was not the reader—as best as we can tell—that Mamie was. Josie's outlook was also more provincial than Mamie's. Josie, too, was quite different in personality, being highly energetic and blessed with an uncommon ability to make friends and make people laugh. She was affectionate and was what Frank and his boys, especially Clarence, needed after Mamie's passing. The best way to get a feeling for Mamie and Josie's relationships with Frank is to read their letters to Frank. Selected correspondence between Frank and Mamie is included elsewhere in the chapter devoted to Mamie; considerable correspondence between Josie and Frank reflecting their courtship and Frank's years in residence at Stanford is included in *A Ph.D.'s Reverie: The Letters.*

Miles: And the relationships between Frank and his boys?

Pops: Both were good but somewhat different, although the three of them had a lot in common. Starting with Francis; Francis was the firstborn and the namesake. The recent book *The First Born Advantage* (Leman 2008) has some general observations about firstborns which may apply here. We are told that, among other things, firstborns appear to be leaders among siblings, and they tend to be overly sensitive to criticism by others, list-makers, black and white thinkers, goal-setters, perfectionists, and seekers of their parents' approval. For firstborns, getting the job done is the priority over relationships. Francis and Frank bore a strong physical resemblance right down to hair color and mustache. Frank gave up his mustache around the time he started teaching at Baylor, but Francis had one the last four decades of his life. Though not identical to his father's, Francis's interests were strikingly similar: outdoorsmanship, debate, law, stenography, good health and physical fitness, classical music, careful management of his money and his time. The similarity of interests may be explained by both nature and nurture.

Frank and Francis's letters show the dynamics of this father-oldest son relationship, which included a level of fatherly expectation arising from Frank's strong feeling, at least by the 1920s, that he had blundered in the planning of his life's work. Frank felt a duty to provide his sons the guidance he never received from his parents so that they might avoid the mistakes he felt he had made, including lack of early planning and then follow-through.

Professor A.J. Armstrong, a colleague of Frank's and chair of Baylor's English Department, also had a tendency toward self-criticism and was more articulate in identifying personal self-shortcomings than Frank. Armstrong, at one time, strongly criticized himself for "wasting his life" and dropping the ball in helping his son Max make important life decisions. It appears that if Frank and Francis were more on the same page than Professor Armstrong and Max, it was likely because their basic natures were more similar.

The correspondence between Frank and Francis and the choices the latter made with his father's encouragement, strongly suggest Francis's life was in some sense a "what if" project for Frank: *What if I had had the kind of guidance I needed regarding choice of a profession and what if I had had the financial support my parents couldn't give me? What would my life have looked like? Could I have succeeded as an attorney? Or would I have had more opportunities to travel? But then, would I have been less effective as a parent if I had had a career that was more demanding of my time?* Francis was, in some ways, a mirror image of Frank, and Frank did his best, intentionally and unintentionally, to shape Francis into the man he may have wanted to be himself—perhaps a more aggressive and extroverted version of himself, less concerned about how his words might offend others.

Frank's younger son, Clarence, nine years younger than Francis and fifty years younger than Frank, had been separated from his father nearly all of his first four years. Clarence remembered that Frank and Francis would visit him at the Welhausens' home in Shiner, especially at Christmas, and take him to see the families of his three uncles and their families. Clarence, who would become a lawyer in private practice before going on the bench, was a quieter, more philosophical version of Frank. He would have differed markedly from Frank and Francis, neither of whom displayed much interest in asking perennially tricky and unanswerable questions about religion or philosophy. Francis was a fluent and formidable advocate from his days as a debater on Baylor's debate team debating against Oxford to his days as a respected South Texas trial lawyer. As an appellate judge decades later, Clarence was a proficient questioner of the advocates appearing before him and a skillful writer of legal opinions which lucidly analyzed the questions before the court. When Clarence was appointed to serve as a briefing clerk to Justice James Alexander on the Texas Supreme Court, Frank congratulated Clarence but added, "Now don't take any false side steps. Look to the future. Don't be too idealistic in politics or think it is necessary to fight windmills." —advice consistent with Frank's career advice to Francis a decade earlier. Turning from law to sports, Clarence did aspire to play golf and tennis like Francis, although he was never the accomplished athlete Francis was, either at tennis or golf. Moreover, as to music, although Clarence was not the pianist Francis was, he was an enthusiastic French horn player and lover of classical music.

Miles: Since I am a firstborn, will that firstborn stuff, all those characteristics, apply to me?

Pops: Might or might not, or some parts may and some parts not. You won't probably know for sure for many years, if ever. All of that birth order theory is not universally accepted, anyway. You will be pretty much whatever you are going to be, wherever you are in the birth order in your family. You can be the youngest in a family and end up being the leader among the children. Look at Michael Jackson. It's complicated—no rigid rules about this.

A typical day at 1401 South 8th

Miles: What would a typical day have been like for Frank, Mama Josie, Francis, and Clarence at home in Waco? What was their house like?

Pops: If we start with their house, outside and inside, 1401 South 8th was a large, two-story frame house with a multi-landing staircase and a pair of drop-down ladders connecting floors, including an attic used for storage. Although there was no basement, there was a crawl space covered by a lattice of diagonally crossed wooden slats. Behind the house was a three-section garage with heavy tin doors which opened from left to right—a storage section, a shop, and a two-car garage. In the shop, Frank and Josie kept feed for the chickens with a coffee can to scoop the feed out of large bins. The chickens roamed around outside in a fenced-off area near an inside roost enclosure for the roosters. In the backyard was a rose garden, a grape arbor, and occasionally a vegetable garden that Frank puttered around in. There were several pecan trees in the back, as well as a persimmon tree near the southwest corner. Along the driveway leading to the garage, there were plants of bamboo and spear grass which the grandchildren found interesting, the latter inspiring spear grass fights. In the spring and summer, the sounds of rooks and grackles could be heard in the backyard, the rooks either strutting on the ground or sitting high up in the pecan trees.

To enter the northeast-facing house, a series of steps led up the steeply banked front yard to the front door with its large oval glass window and a lace curtain behind it. On the left, as you approached the front door, was a wrap-around front porch painted blue-gray framing the house on the front and right side of the house; there was wooden swing large enough for two people which hung from the porch ceiling; the swing creaked when a person sat swinging back and forth. Once inside the front door and in the foyer with its oriental carpet, and then passing the staircase with its blue runner immediately on the left, you could walk straight down the hall to the back screen door, passing on the right first the parlor with its green carpet, walls and floors, then the dining room with its dark brown woodwork and the oil painting of seaside bathers; and, if you stepped inside the dining room and exited to the kitchen, you passed the refrigerator on the right with its box of Hershey bars. The kitchen itself was not elaborate—a pantry, a gas stovetop, and a table and chairs; you could exit out the kitchen past the back door to a screened-in back porch that contained a high, flat, narrow sideboard for eating breakfast in the mornings—scrambled eggs, bacon, and toast, or maybe cornflakes with bananas, orange juice, and coffee.

On the left, as you entered the foyer at the front of the house, there was a blue loveseat, a built-in L-shaped banquette with the telephone, several bookcases crammed with books, and finally a mantelpiece grandfather clock which had been tolling the quarter hours and playing Westminster in the family home in New Bedford when Frank was growing up in the 1870s and 1880s. Past the bookcases on the left was the study with its oriental carpet and two dark heavy sliding doors. Inside the study on the left was a non-functioning fireplace containing an electric stove, bookcases on three walls with more books, and windows looking out on the front porch swing and the neighbor's house to the east. In front of the first window in the study was Frank's desk with a Baptist quarterly, various books and written materials, and a Kleenex box.

Upstairs were four bedrooms, a large screened-in sleeping porch heated by a cordless steel iron heater, and a screened-in porch over the front entrance. The large master bedroom was Josie's and had an attached bathroom and shower. Frank's small bedroom across the hall was furnished with an enameled iron bedstead, a double bed, a desk for Frank, a rocking chair, and a small, connected lavatory smelling of Bay Rum aftershave. In the lavatory you would find a container of tooth powder, a toothbrush, and a razor and shaving cream in the small cabinet over a small sink. Frank's bedroom was for Frank only and was off limits to others; he used it to prepare for class, read, sleep, and nap after lunch. Frank and Josie had separate bedrooms since Frank, a light sleeper, arose early to begin his day.

Inside Josie's bedroom was a double bed and armoires for clothes, although neither Frank nor Josie had an extensive wardrobe. In his later years, Frank used a truss, probably a plain elastic piece to improve his overweight appearance. On the wall hung an inexpensive black and white print of Pierre Auguste Cot's 1880 oil painting *The Storm* (*La Tempete*), at one point displayed at New York's Metropolitan Museum of Art. The well-known painting shows a couple running from the rain covered by billowing drapery, representing a scene in Bernardin de Saint-Pierre's 1788 novel *Paul et Virginie.* The location of the print in the master bedroom suggests the bedroom served as Frank and Josie's sanctuary from the pressures and problems of the world, whether wars, financial panics, epidemics, or lesser matters.

Despite the absence of air conditioning, the ceiling fans and tall ceilings kept the house reasonably cool in hot weather. According to a master's student who had to take his oral examination in front of a committee at Frank's home, Frank explained to him how he kept his house cool in the summer: at night, he opened the doors and windows to let in the breezes, and in the morning, he closed the house and drew the draperies to hold in the cool.

<u>Miles</u>: What about the other two bedrooms and the sleeping porch on the second floor? Who used those?

<u>Pops</u>: Clarence slept on the sleeping porch, weather permitting, and, weather not permitting, in the middle bedroom. Francis slept in one of the other rooms, and a paying roomer, always a paying female graduate student, slept in the other room. After Francis and Clarence graduated from law school, both middle and front upstairs bedrooms were reserved for roomers. During one or more summers while Frank was in Palo Alto, Josie and Frank discussed Josie taking the middle bedroom because her bedroom could be rented out at a higher rate. However, Frank was opposed to this sacrifice, and there's no proof whether Josie ever moved into the smaller middle bedroom.

<u>Miles</u>: Did the roomers have a separate bathroom like at a bed and breakfast?

<u>Pops</u>: No, and that was a significant complication. There was only one bath in the entire house, and that opened out on Josie's bedroom and the sleeping porch. Roomers had to walk down the hall in robe and slippers and through the sleeping porch to get to the bath when the coast was clear. The bathroom did have hot water and had what was called an "instantaneous heater" above the tub. When its pilot was lit, the water heated up. But there were other inconveniences for the roomers,

who generally stayed several years. They could not use the kitchen or the study on the first floor, but they could use the front parlor, the front door, and the front entrance to receive and entertain their visitors. They did have access to the refrigerator with its Hershey bars for them and their guests.

Miles: I would like to hear more about the bathrooms in those days and also about Frank dying his hair. People take showers these days, even girls.

Pops: All right, but first, let's describe Frank's appearance. For fifty or more years, his appearance was consistent. In the last several decades of his career, he presented himself as a distinguished-looking, rather large, clean-shaven, well-dressed man, about 190-200 pounds and five-foot-eleven inches tall, larger than all of his brothers. In time, he added around fifty pounds since he was weighed by Amos Alonzo Stagg's Department of Physical Culture at the University of Chicago. He had a noticeable paunch which he held in with a waistband type of truss.

He wore conservative pinstriped three-piece suits, typically gray (student Morgan to CFG 1980), and solid shirts with detachable starched stiff collars, and bright-colored ties. He referred to one of these ties within his family as his "flaming youth necktie." His ties were tied in the four-in-hand style, and he wore them all day long, starting at breakfast and up through supper, but he removed his tie and detachable collars for his nap after lunch. Detachable collars were de rigueur among the male faculty at Baylor. One Baylor wit penned the following: "You may live without cooks, you may live without books, and your students will still think you wise; but as leaders of Baylor, please pardon the hint, you can't teach without collars and ties." Frank alternated his three or four suits but kept another good suit for church on Sundays. In the summer, he sometimes wore white linen, pongee, or seersucker suits. The rest of the year, his suits were gray, brown, or blue and usually included a pinstripe. He attached his watch to his vest. Frank often wore tweed suits made by a tailor on South 4th St. in Waco.

He began dying his hair when he commenced Ph.D. studies at Stanford, as he thought he looked too old compared to other students. His hair was white but dyed with a natural henna rinse, giving it a dark brown-reddish tint, almost black on top. Among his family, everyone smiled or chuckled privately because of the decidedly home-job look, although one would never ask him about his hair. His sons thought he should let well enough alone, Francis asking plaintively on one occasion, "Why doesn't he let his hair stay white? It would look so much better." Colleague Guy B. Harrison, Jr. said Frank used walnetta hair color, and Josie would help him do it, leaving some white on the sides to make it look more natural. Where clothes were concerned, Frank generally did not invest in clothes for leisure, and when he wanted to relax, he wore old clothes, which were a little threadbare. Thus, his wardrobe consisted of just two types of clothes, good clothes and old clothes. He would have considered the idea of clothes especially designed for leisure frivolous and wasteful. In the summer around the house, he might wear short-sleeved shirts, but not on campus or to class.

One regular health practice both of Frank's wives supported was regular baths, and they believed in it more strongly than Frank. Frank's stated bath policy for his sons was that they bathed on Saturday night and whenever else they needed one. For most of the time, there was only a bathtub, but later on, a shower was added to Frank's bedroom upstairs. Josie, who came from a large family, had a reputation for taking very quick baths; "she got right in and out and spent very little time on her toilet thereafter."

After his bath, Frank liked to walk before breakfast and pay attention to the animals' antics so he could describe them to Clarence. But during the 1920s, after a shower bath was installed upstairs, the daily shower before breakfast became routine. On Sunday mornings, the family downed waffles with butter and syrup, waffles being one of Frank's comfort foods. While in Palo Alto, he continued his practice of eating waffles on Sunday mornings: "I stopped at the Snow White Creamery for breakfast and tried those waffles. I think I shall make that a regular part of my Sunday program." (FGG letter to MJ, January 28, 1928). On Thursday mornings, pancakes were served to the family. Other mornings it was just the usual bacon, eggs, and buttered toast with jelly. Frank also liked biscuits, and he was usually twenty to thirty pounds overweight. The heaviest meal of the week was Sunday dinner, which came just a few short hours after a big waffle breakfast. While Frank was in Palo Alto, he missed the jelly from the grapes grown on their backyard vines: "I wish I had some of that good jelly out here. I am glad to know that the new grapes are doing something. I think I shall gradually plant other vines around the arbor and eliminate the old vine." (FGG letter to MJ, July 17, 1927).

Frank's preferred activity at home was reading materials in connection with preparation for class, but also history generally, along with unrelated fiction and nonfiction. He enjoyed the Sunday comic strips, at least from the 1920s on. These included *Ben Webster*, *the Bungle Family*, and *The Gumps*. The last two were so widely read in America that their popularity alone would have been enough reason for a well-informed history professor to keep up with them. He also needed mindless diversion and distraction from the usual academic grind.

But he did get out of that upstairs study to do various kinds of things outdoors essential to the overall operation of the household and the household economy. Although he didn't do any of the typical inside chores, there being a maid who provided household services and Josie being in charge of the household, Frank spaded up the flower bed when needed and fed the chickens twice a day. In the earlier days, the chickens were kept for their eggs and not kept to eat. The garden was by a trellis, and Frank would snip vines and rake up. He also, as required, spent time mending the fence with hammer and saw. Although he didn't do much yard work and let others mow the lawn, one summer he and Clarence painted four or five of Frank's rent houses. Clarence did the lower parts, and Frank did the upper parts on a ladder.

Frank's faith life

Miles: I know Frank went to church on Sundays. Did he and Mama Josie pay a church pledge, and did they tithe? I am also curious whether he was a deacon, usher, or a Sunday school teacher.

Pops: In Waco, Frank, Josie, Francis, and Clarence were regular attenders and paid their church pledges. We have no idea whether they tithed. On occasion, Frank and Josie fell behind in their commitment, for example, when Frank was working on his Ph.D. at Stanford and they had additional expenses. When they caught up, Josie was not afraid, as Frank put it, to "look people in the face," when she went to church. Frank's church activities were limited to attending church services on Sunday mornings, never on Wednesday nights, rarely on Sunday nights, and he did not participate as deacon, usher, greeter, or committee member. He did teach a Sunday school class of teenage boys while a student in Baylor and then later another class for a brief period.

Miles: Why no service as a deacon?

Pops: Probably for the same reason he was only lukewarm as a Mason. Being a deacon or Mason meant going to meetings, and Frank thought meetings were usually a waste of time, with a lot of arguing back and forth and expelling of "pious gas." He could be spending that time preparing for class, reading and outlining history texts, or doing other things more important to him. He felt strongly about not wasting time and getting on with his work and life plan. He gave advice to one member of the Baylor history department who was a member of the Christian Church in Waco but had started attending First Baptist. Frank cautioned his colleague, "don't get too involved down there." When First Baptist wanted to make the colleague its chief usher, Frank vetoed it. Frank also told his colleague's wife to "stay in the Christian church so they would have an excuse not to go to First Baptist sometime."

Miles: I'm wondering about his religious background in Ohio? Was he baptized in a creek or river? Did he have religious training?

Pops: Frank's family in New Bedford was Methodist, and his baptism by the Methodists would have been by sprinkling—no river, creek, or baptistery was needed. Later, before joining First Baptist in Waco, he would have had to be baptized by total immersion—the Baptist way—in the church baptistery. Too bad we don't have his account of that experience. I'm sure he had the kind of religious training and baptism for Methodist youths that small rural churches provided in northern Ohio. But as a Methodist, I doubt he participated in any sword drills of the type which are common in Baptist churches.

Miles: I've never heard of sword drills, but they sound pretty cool. What were they?

Pops: Sword drills were an indispensable part of Southern Baptist Sunday schools that Frank missed because he joined First Baptist Waco as an adult after growing up Methodist. Sword drills are timed competitions in which the objective is to find a particular verse in the Bible quickly, the "sword" being the Bible. The standard commands of the leader to the competitors, all standing heels together, shoulders up, hands at their sides, one hand holding a Bible, and facing the leader, are: "Attention," "Sheathe Swords," "Draw Swords," "Matthew, Chapter 2, verse 4 [example]," "Charge," "Time," and "Sheathe swords."

Miles: No real swords then. Methodist kids in Ohio didn't do sword drills?

Pops: I don't believe so, at least not like Southern Baptist kids. Methodists seem not to have been as vigorous in their Bible training of children.

Miles: Did Frank spend a lot of time at church in Waco? What do we know about his Christian faith or commitment to a local church?

Pops: Well, he grew up in a devout Methodist Episcopal household in Ohio surrounded by the Amish and the Pennsylvania Dutch. Frank's father had studied for the priesthood in France, but he had given up the Catholic Church for the Methodist church when he immigrated to the US. His Ohio family had the only organ in the community, and people would convene at their house to sing hymns and popular songs of the day. In Texas, Frank liked singing Sacred Harp hymns from *The Sacred Harp* songbook.

Miles: What was *The Sacred Harp* songbook? Was the harp the one that some say is waiting for a believer in heaven?

Pops: No. The Sacred Harp is a term used for the human voice. *The Sacred Harp* is also the name of the hymnbook containing hymns with the melodies noted in the shaped note style. Singing in this style was a cappella, without accompaniment by piano, organ, guitar, or other musical instruments. In many churches, there was strong opposition to the use of musical instruments in worship, even choir singing had to gain acceptance over time. A cappella singing and then Sacred Harp singing became popular in the early days of choral singing in America.

Miles: I'm curious about what Sacred Harp music sounded like and why Frank liked to sing it. I would like to hear how it sounded.

Pops: Well, it was very loud. Go to YouTube and you can listen to it. Each person had to sing loud enough to drown out his neighbor so he could hear himself sing. Walls of sound. Its loudness was part of why singers—unlike teachers—liked it. A room full of Sacred Harp singers could make a huge sound in a room. Singers weren't trying to blend or harmonize with each other. Before the Civil War, every home contained both a Bible and a *Sacred Harp* hymn book. Music teachers hated singing comprised of loud walls of sound, but Sacred Harp singers didn't worry about their vocal cords.

Miles: Pops, did Frank believe in heaven?

Pops: As a student at Baylor, he attended a Sunday school class taught by Judge W.H. Jenkins, a devout Southern Baptist, who made a strong impression on Frank. Frank's diary entry for 1893-94, his last year at Baylor, said only "Joined the Baptist Church in the fall during Dr. J. [James] M. [Milton] Carroll's meeting at the First Baptist Church." As to how Frank's faith affected his life, coming from a more liberal Methodist home in Ohio, he would have had no objection to dancing—the bête noire of Southern Baptists for many years, the usual party games (poker possibly excepted), or taking an occasional glass of wine. While Frank kept some wine at home, we don't know his or Josie's stance on prohibition. However, we suspect he would have been privately against it while we are confident Josie was a strong supporter. We also guess he would have opposed horse race gambling on moral grounds, but probably would not have thought it advisable to ban it legislatively. However, to answer your question about believing in heaven, we have no reason to think he didn't believe in an afterlife.

Miles: Did Frank ever lose his faith or doubt what he had been taught? What was his view of human nature and the doctrine of original sin? I don't get how we can be blamed for Adam's disobedience in the Garden.

Pops: All we know about those questions is that Frank's view of human nature was that it is largely vain and "what may pass as benevolence is a sort of veneer for men's acts quite often...Get down under that veneer and you will find self and vanity." As to Frank's faith, nothing tells us that he ever abandoned it, even temporarily. He did state publicly that at one point, his faith was shaky and that he drew comfort from Judge Jenkins's Bible lessons. Many years later, after the death of Judge Jenkins, Frank made the following remarks:

> When [Judge Jenkins] addressed the Sunday school [while Frank was enrolled at Baylor]...his words left the impression of a profound belief in the Bible and its teachings which was convincing and comforting to those who heard him. After returning to Baylor as a teacher [ten years later], I enjoyed the privilege for some time of being a member of his Bible Class. At that time, I was passing through a period in my life that nearly every young man experiences. My faith, at times, seemed to be resting on a foundation of shifting sands. While I attended that class, I never heard Judge Jenkins explain God's purposes and interpret the principles and the teaching of Christ without being strengthened in my faith by his own implicit faith. His trust was so complete and his faith so profound that no one could hear him and not be convinced. He became to me the ideal Christian man...He was the example of how the Christ-life may be lived in our own times.

There is much in Frank's life after leaving Baylor—the illnesses and deaths of his second son and first wife, and the early death of his mother before he could set things right with her—that would have been challenging to his faith; also, that he had had to slave so many years making money at low-level underpaid teaching positions to obtain the money to go back to college while the paths of many others, often less deserving, or not as serious as he, were far easier; and that he was not financially able to marry anyone until he was almost forty.

Miles: Were there particular preachers he liked or found inspiring?

Pops: We don't know who his favorites might have been, although he occasionally mentioned outstanding Southern Baptist preachers like Rufus C. Burleson, George W. Truett, Joseph M. Dawson, B.H. [Benajah Harvey] Carroll, and John Roach Straton. Frank also admired the eloquence and wit of Sam P. Jones, a former attorney, reformed alcoholic, and Methodist lecturer, who, for a time, was the most widely known evangelist in the South.

Miles: Tell me more about that Methodist, Sam Jones, and why he might have been one of Frank's favorites.

Pops: Sam Porter Jones's back story is too involved to go into detail, but basically, he read law rather than going to law school and still made high marks on Georgia's bar exam. However, his attempts to make money practicing law failed, and he became an alcoholic. In desperation, he turned to making money by driving a dray wagon, which in status would have been equivalent to driving a garbage truck.

Miles: What was a dray wagon?

Pops: A dray wagon was pulled by mules or other animals and used in the 1800s to transport heavy loads. During this low period in his life, Jones had an emotional encounter with his father at the latter's death bed and promised to give up drinking. After that, he became an itinerant Methodist preacher, despite never having studied the Bible or having preached. Some people said he was, for a time, the most famous man in America. Frank, while a student at Baylor, attended one of Jones's lectures. Frank would have enjoyed Jones for his accomplished storytelling, humorous cutting ridicule, and occasional moments of pathos. In Jones's lecture "Get There and Stay There," which was one of his oft-repeated lectures, he argued that "many men have failed because they gave up too soon. Many men have had pursuit but not persistence...It is the...faithful-until-death fellow that gets there and stays there...he is the man who will win."

Miles: You mentioned his talent at ridicule.

Pops: Ridicule was one of his specialties. There are many examples, but to pick just a few: "What is culture worth if it is but the whitewash on a rascal?"; "I would rather be in heaven learning my ABCs than sitting in hell reading Greek"; "Every barroom is a recruiting office for hell"; and "Whiskey is a good thing in its place, and that place is hell."

Miles: Sounds like Sam Jones made an impression on Frank. Did Frank ever get to hear Jones again?

Pops: We think so. The first time, which I just mentioned, was Jones's "Get There and Stay There" lecture which Frank attended at Baylor. Frank wrote an essay in spring 1894 in W.W. Franklin's class on this lecture. Over six years later, in the summer of 1900 [July 23], Frank composed a touching essay in which the protagonist named "Frank" has a date with a female character named "Bessie." The essay's title was "The Camp-Meeting at Magnesia Springs" and was written for his English III class at the University of Chicago. The essay is included in its entirety in the chapter on Frank's early romances. The beginning of the essay refers to people gathering to hear the "great preacher" Sam Jones. However, because Frank had already heard Jones's lecture at Baylor, his mind was definitely not on the "great preacher" at the Magnesia Springs camp-meeting.

Miles: I don't understand why Frank would take a date to a camp-meeting. That sounds very lame.

Pops: Yes, it may to our ears today. But back in the 1890s, available entertainments for dates, especially in the country, were limited, and a camp-meeting had definite entertainment value for the college educated. Camp meetings in the late 1800s were multi-day, sometimes one to two weeks in duration. People set up tents or stayed in frame cabins, and others just came in for the day. Camp meetings were religious-themed events featuring preachers, choirs, plenty of country food and picnicking, and opportunity for social interaction. They were popular with Methodists, Baptists, and Presbyterians, especially in rural areas, and on the frontier. Magnesia Springs in Arkansas, which was not too far from Magnolia where Frank had been teaching, was a well-known location for camp meetings. Sam Jones estimated he preached a thousand sermons to three million people around the country during the years before Frank came to Texas, in camp meetings, revivals, and other church services. The quintessential revival song was: "Hallelujah, thine the glory, Hallelujah, Amen. Hallelujah, thine the glory, revive us again." Then there were the old faithfuls: "Give Me that Old-Time Religion," "Shall We Gather at the River," "At the Cross," "Blessed Assurance," "Almost Persuaded," "Just As I Am," and many more.

As for the food at camp meetings, it was high calorie, high fat, highly popular country cooking. The dishes would have included home-cooked foods like sunny-side tater salad, Ozarkian taffy apples, George Washington cherry cake, camp meetin' preacher pie, mountaineer dried bean soup, shoo-fly pie, hominy muffins, wild rabbit with vegetables, cinnamon-toast cobbler, chuck wagon boiled coffee, fried cucumbers, fried apple fritters, mock apple pie, green beans with hog jowl, turnip greens, pot likker, and many more.

The meetings would start in a slow, low-key way with a standard sermon and a few hymns, and by stages they would progress to a feverish conclusion, ramping up more passion toward the end of the meeting. At some point, people in the audience would cry out, begin sobbing, and start running through the crowd. As a meeting reached its predictably ecstatic conclusion, several phenomena might be observed, like attendees falling on the floor and appearing to be dead; heads jerking around, backward and forward, or side to side; writhing or rolling on the ground while screaming out as if in pain; dancing in a somber slow way with a blissful smile; and other phenomena, such as barking. Not all the practices at camp meetings were Godly. Camp meetings were also notorious for brothels on the fringe of the campgrounds, and sometimes children born nine months after camp meetings were jokingly called "camp-meeting babies."

Miles: Do you think Sam Jones influenced Frank?

Pops: I think so, at least in one way—Frank definitely believed in "getting there and staying there," and avoiding the demon rum, one of Jones's themes. On the other hand, Jones talked too much about young men who went off to college and returned to their mothers, "graduated into debauchery and ruin" and completely depraved. That kind of talk would have been too much for Frank, and, of course, would have conflicted with his life goals, Jones not being a fan of pursuing a college education.

Miles: Since Frank liked to sing hymns, were there particular ones he liked?

Pops: My answer will have to be an educated guess and perhaps a presumptuous one at that. However, based on how his life went after leaving Ohio, his early experience in the Methodist church, his relatively sophisticated appreciation of classical music and the works of the great composers, his love of singing bass, and his life struggles, I will hazard a few educated guesses. First, we are unsure whether he would have been especially drawn to the old sawdust trail hymns about blood, power of the blood, crimson stain of sin, wearing a crown, being a soldier of the Cross, glory, winning souls, repentance, Christ's Second Coming, the holy city, heaven, resurrection, ascension, and calling the roll up yonder. However, we are not at all confident about this, since Frank's connection with specific hymns would have been personal and depended on factors impossible to assess, such as the hymns he would have sung in the small Methodist church in New Bedford area as a child, and the musicality and emotional power of those hymns.

However, the following kinds of hymns would seem to have resonated with him: hymns about struggle, faith, trusting, grace, mothers, mistakes, being alone, assurance, hymns with memorable melodies, or hymns that were musically interesting to sing like many *Sacred Harp* hymns. As to popular hymns about struggle, Frank's life was an unrelenting battle for his education and then to make a living. Hymns with themes of hope, assurance, comfort, and faith would have been the hymns he would have gravitated toward, especially those that soothed and offered hope and comfort. Admittedly, though, that is almost rank conjecture.

Some of the classic "struggle" hymns in Methodist and Baptist hymnals of the times would include many hymns by legendary hymnodists Isaac Watts, Charles Wesley, Fannie J. Crosby, and Ira D. Sankey. Here are the titles of some of those:

> "When I Survey the Wondrous Cross On Which the Prince of Glory Died"; "When Jesus Calls Us O'er the Tumult of Our Life's Wild Restless Sea"; "Sweet Hour of Prayer! Sweet Hour of Prayer! That Calls me from a World of Care"; "My Hope is Built on Nothing Less Than Jesus' Blood and Righteousness"; "I Need Thee Every Hour...Most Gracious Lord"; "Blessed Assurance, Jesus is Mine!"; "He Leadeth Me! O Blessed Tho't!"; "I Surrender All"; "On Jordan's Stormy Banks I Stand"; "When I Stood at My Mother's Knee, With Her Hand Upon My Brow"; "The Lord's Our Rock, In Him We Hide"; "When the Roll is Called Up Yonder"; and "Amazing Grace."

Miles: Where did you get the names of all those hymns? And how can anyone know what hymns Frank would have been singing in the late 1800s, early 1900s?

Pops: Okay, fair enough. I can only say that the names of the hymns Frank, and everyone else, loved to sing would have been included in widely published hymnals and songsters during those periods. I obtained copies of three old-time hymnals, including Joseph Hillman's 1868 collection, *The Revivalist*; Bigelow & Main's hymnal 1886 hymnal, *Gospel Hymns Consolidated*; and Robert H. Coleman's 1918 compilation, *The Popular Hymnal.*

Miles: Now my big question for you. Did Frank believe that the Old and New Testaments of the *King James Bible* were literally and factually true? No hemming and hawing, please.

Pops: Miles, this is as straight as I can make it. There is no question that Frank believed in the central truths of the Bible, especially the New Testament. He believed that Jesus was a real person born in the first century B.C.E. He also believed in the central theological propositions commonly believed by Baptists, Methodists, and Presbyterians. As to how strongly he believed in the Genesis creation story, the stories of Noah's ark, the parting of the Red Sea or the Tower of Babel in the Old Testament, or the virgin birth, the various recorded miracles, or the Resurrection in the New Testament, it is not possible to know. Frank made it clear that he was a Christian and believed its central articles of faith, but he never talked to the family about the specifics of his faith. It was just a given that he was a Christian and a Southern Baptist in his theological outlook. However, he may not have been on board with all the traditional Southern Baptist doctrines; that's just something we can never know.

Miles: I thought in his history courses he was all about finding out the facts.

Pops: So, you are wondering how he resolved the tension between his understanding of world history as a body of facts and the conclusions that can be drawn from facts, and, on the other hand, his understanding of the history of Biblical characters and events? How did he deal with the supernatural elements in the Bible like the Creation and the Incarnation, Crucifixion, Resurrection from the dead? There are no easy answers to those questions. Still, we think that Frank did not put the Bible to the same test as he did the facts of history and concluded, like most Christians perhaps, that the Biblical story requires faith in its central truths and that any other way of looking at the Bible is a complete waste of time. We don't think he would have wanted to debate whether there were a pair of dinosaurs on the Ark with Noah or in the Garden of Eden before Adam.

Miles: Was it important to Frank what his sons believed?

Pops: Up to a point, yes. Frank had a definite moral and spiritual side. He was Christian and a Baptist in that order. He did tend to be authoritarian in matters of faith because they were not really up for debate or even discussion. However, he did not lecture his children on religious subjects or tell them directly what they should believe. On one rare occasion, he felt compelled to intervene when he heard Clarence saying something unusually off base. Clarence took courses at Baylor in the late 1930s in logic and the history of philosophy from popular professor A.J. Hall. Clarence and Professor Hall discussed questions that Frank was not interested in and were completely settled in his mind. At the time, Clarence was intrigued with philosophical questions, methods, and analysis and inclined to argue certain points. As a young man, he was interested in the differing points of view between Christian denominations and was struggling with the supernatural features of the Christian religion. Though Frank was familiar with the philosophers Clarence was reading, Frank had no interest in arguing philosophy or theology with Clarence. To Clarence's mind, Frank's unwillingness to engage in argument in these matters was conventional and unimaginative.

One occasion stood out for Clarence: "A friend and I were sitting on the front porch on the swing disputing very earnestly some point raised as a result of our philosophical studies. Nearby was an open window which opened on to the stairway inside. The next morning while I was dressing, Pop [Frank] took me by surprise, saying that he had heard what I had been telling my friend and that it was a whole lot of stuff, a whole lot of foolishness. I was taken aback as I fancied myself quite a philosopher. Pop just left it at that and was not opening the subject for argument."

Although Frank shut down invitations to argue points of faith with Clarence, Frank was generally laissez-faire in matters of faith. In another instance, he intervened after learning that Clarence had attended a sermon at a local Episcopal church by a popular preacher. That by itself would not have been alarming to

Frank, but after the sermon, Clarence and a friend went to the pastor's study and engaged the pastor in a series of religious questions. Learning of this, Frank and Josie forbade Clarence from further contact with the Episcopal pastor. Clarence went ahead anyway, and later Frank and Josie told him how disappointed they were in him. Frank and Josie's view was that Episcopalians didn't evangelize the lost, but just proselytized church members from other denominations. They were concerned that Clarence would lose his connection with Baptist denomination. Frank's intervention, in this case, was rare. Josie, on the other hand, had more of a tendency to say what their sons should or should not be doing, whereas Frank reserved his input for more serious occasions.

Frank was a faithful Baptist who regularly attended services Sunday mornings with Josie. He was not personally interested in attending services on Sunday or Wednesday nights. Occasionally, he attended services at night when a protracted revival was going on with a celebrated visiting pastor. On Sunday mornings, consistent with the practice in many Protestant churches, regular attendees sat in the same pews Sunday after Sunday. Frank and Josie sat in the same row with the couple who facilitated their early meeting [Tom and Katherine Bryan]. After Tom and Katherine both passed away, Frank moved down the bench to the seat next to the aisle where "cousin" Tom had sat.

Miles: Was Frank one of those people who took notes on the Sunday services programs to capture the best points of the pastor's sermon? You said he was a big note taker and kept notebooks for his classes. I'm also wondering if he could stay awake during sermons without taking notes.

Pops: (*laughing*) He didn't take notes on sermons. He left no notebooks or church programs with notes. He did have a problem staying awake. Maybe taking notes would have helped. On one occasion while in California, he paid the pastor a back-handed compliment: "I do not sleep very often in church these days...If the pastor ever disturbs my slumbers like he did the man's you [Josie] write about, I shall be inclined to think I can dispense with his preaching, for when I get sleepy, it is a sign that I have been paying him the decided compliment of attention. I never get sleepy when my mind is wandering here and there. The secret of my reading at night is to get my mind fixed on something so I can sleep. Probably that's how I got the habit." (FGG letter to MJ, March 4, 1928) Josie may have been amused but not persuaded by such comments.

Frank said the blessing at meals at home but otherwise did not talk about his faith or about religious matters, likely continuing the pattern of his parents in Ohio. He didn't quote the Bible or theological doctrine for the moral instruction he gave to his sons. He never told his sons what God's will was for their lives. He did occasionally quote scripture, but not to support his own position. Although his sons never doubted that Frank was a firm believer or sincere, he was not completely orthodox in the Baptist tradition concerning dancing, cards, or movies, having no objection to these activities. Frank was raised by his parents in Ohio as a devout Methodist, but he maintained a certain Methodist liberality in some tangential ways external to the core Christian beliefs. As to his moral standards, his personal behavior conformed to the highest standards, and profanity was extremely rare.

As to the consumption of alcohol, Frank was not a teetotaler, and there was a closet at home where bottles of wine were kept, although it was not an actual wine closet. The location of the wine was a matter on which Frank and Josie differed, as she was concerned about Clarence getting into the closet since, on one occasion, he had surreptitiously done so to serve his friends. On a train trip to Niagara Falls in 1925, Clarence remembered that Frank ordered ale at a restaurant. Josie, who came from a stricter family, kidded Frank about that, saying that the ale made his nose look "real red." On the subject of dancing, Frank was definitely not opposed, but said he had lost out getting one teaching position in East Texas because a school trustee thought he went to too many square dances.

Financial matters

Miles: I have some money questions. Was Frank good with money? Did he make enough as a teacher and then as a professor? Were he and Mama Josie ever comfortable financially?

Pops: As a family of four dependent on a college professor's limited income, Frank and Josie were tight with their money. Neither Mamie nor Josie earned an income after marrying Frank. When he was a student at Chicago, Frank kept a ledger in which he recorded all of his expenses, from collars to shoe repair. Josie came from a family that never had much money and, likewise, was always thinking of ways to cut corners. Mamie, before Josie, came from a well-to-do family but understood when she married him that Frank would not be a high earner. Frank appears to have been sensitive about his ability to support a wife financially and, on one occasion, as we mentioned in the Mamie chapter, he advised Mamie emphatically by letter that he did not intend to "amass property" after they married. Of course, as a professor of history at a small Baptist college in Waco, Texas, it must have been obvious he would not be expecting to build up much of an estate. It was a good thing, therefore, that Welhausen money, through the estates of Mamie and Eliza Welhausen, provided an allowance for the sons' welfare for a time. The fact that Frank had committed before marrying Mamie to a low pay, high grind teaching job and that he depended on teaching until he dropped in his tracks resulted in directing his sons to enter the law.

Professor A.J. Armstrong, English department chair, and other Baylor faculty were under similar financial pressures. President Brooks was quoted as saying that Professor Armstrong had a travel agency because he could not afford to live on a college professor's salary and was buying Browning materials and antiques for his home. Frank could not live on the scale he was accustomed to living—a nice big house with a wife and two children who aspired to have college and professional educations—without the funds from the Welhausen estates. Both Professor Armstrong and Professor Guittard would feel compelled to impart their wisdom to their sons about making a living in this world and the blunders they each thought they had made.

Miscellany

Miles: Pops, what did Frank do for fun other than leisure reading the funny papers and playing golf?

Pops: In earlier days, he played tennis, played the cornet in a band or orchestra, and visited with friends. Later, he played honeymoon bridge with Josie, went to an occasional movie or concert, listened to the radio, or invited a few special friends on faculty over for dinner. Before he married Mamie, Frank enjoyed going to a few big-time fairs and some smaller fairs of the type that we don't see as much today. World's fairs and expositions, which were popular in the nineteenth and early twentieth centuries, have largely disappeared in the twenty-first. They were not only entertaining but educational, and for Frank, education was always his first priority. He would have been aware of all the fairs I will mention in a moment and how they influenced or shined a light on the history and culture of the countries which participated. The books chronicling these fairs are fascinating, and the photographs of the fairgrounds and their buildings are stunning, even more than the Disney theme parks of our day.

Miles: What were the big-time fairs he went to?

Pops: Here are the great world's fairs and other fairs in the nineteenth and twentieth centuries we know about, including the national and international expositions, and some of the smaller fairs. I will mention the ones he attended.

1851 *Crystal Palace* in Hyde Park in London was built to house the Great Exhibition in 1851 and was the first real world fair. The Infomart building in Dallas, modeled after the Crystal Palace, counts seven floors and 18.2 acres, opened in 1985, and still stands.

1864 *The Great Central Fair* in Philadelphia was opened during the Civil War.

1876 The US's first national fair—*The Centennial Exposition* in Philadelphia—celebrated the signing of the Declaration of Independence in 1776. Frank would have been interested in the 1876 expo because of its historical significance, but he was only a nine-year-old at the time.

1876-1886 *Ohio State Fairs.* We are confident that Frank, his father, and his large family would have been interested in all of these fairs, staged in Columbus from 1874 to the present. However, the distance (91.1 miles from New Bedford) would have made for a difficult, time-consuming, and problematic journey in a buggy or on horseback. There were railroads at the time, but an excursion by train between those cities would have been unlikely, considering that Dr. Guittard's patients depended on him to be available and the time required for such an excursion. Although we do not believe Frank attended any of the Ohio fairs, we wonder whether his efforts to improve hog breeding or crop rotation on the family farm may have been inspired by an exhibit at an Ohio State Fair.

1886 *Texas State Fairs* commenced in 1886, with the first in November. There is no record Frank attended, and at the time, he would only have been in Texas for a short time. However, after starting to teach at Baylor in 1902, he must have made it to the State Fair in Dallas at some point, by train, Interurban, or car.

1889 *The Exposition Universelle* in Paris, France, celebrated the 100th anniversary of the storming of the Bastille. The Eiffel Tower made its debut at the 1889 *Exposition Universelle.* Frank never went to Europe.

1893 *The Columbian Exposition* in Chicago. Frank would have been envious of anyone who was able to go to this fair, it occurring during his Baylor student years when he was hard up for money. Buffalo Bill's Wild West Show was set up outside the fairgrounds. The Exposition was so spectacular that an entire issue of *The Youth's Companion* was devoted to it. Baylor President Brooks made the trip to the fair before becoming president, commenting that the only thing that was free at the fair was the water. Even President Burleson considered going. If Burleson had been able to attend, he would have had a lot to say about it, no doubt any number of warnings for Baptists. An unfortunate footnote to the spare-no-expense Columbian Exposition was that it, and the spectacular White City, its main feature, immediately preceded a national depression that would last until 1897.

1890 *The Spring Palace in Fort Worth.* In February, Frank went to see this fair and also attended the Southern Baptist Convention. Three months later, the Palace burned.

1894 *The Cotton Palace in Waco.* Frank returned to Waco to attend this fair after dropping out of Baylor in the spring to sell books. Thirty years later, John Philip Sousa's band performed in concert at the Cotton Palace in January 1924. The odds are high that Frank, Josie, Francis, and Clarence were all at the Cotton Palace that Saturday night.

1897 *The Tennessee Centennial Fair* celebrated the 100th anniversary of Tennessee as a state of the Union. Frank attended, possibly on the way to or from his first term at the University of Chicago. While in Nashville, Frank visited General Jackson's home, the Hermitage, Polk's tomb, and the state capital.

1901 *The Pan-American Exposition* in Buffalo, New York. President McKinley was assassinated at this exposition outside of the Temple of Music, dying the day after being shot. He gave a speech that would have resonated with Frank if he had heard it, especially regarding why any student or historian should be interested in attending the fair. Frank did not record having attended this fair, so we assume he didn't go to it.

1901 *Buffalo Bill's Wild West Show*, Chicago. Frank recorded he saw the Buffalo Bill show July 16. Likely, Frank saw the show in Chicago, where he was in school during most of 1901. This show featured an aging Buffalo Bill and a drama from the prior year's Boxer Rebellion in China entitled "The Allied Powers at the Battle of Tien-Tsin and the Capture of Pekin." It was a noisy show, and a Gatling gun (of the type used at Santiago in 1898) mounted on a carriage fired off blanks rapidly with exciting noise. This show was Frank's last opportunity to see fellow Ohioan Annie Oakley, celebrity sharp-shooter and trick-shot artist. Months later, Annie would be seriously injured when the troop's train collided head-on with a freight train, killing 110 horses with the Wild West Show.

1904 *The Louisiana Purchase Exposition* in St. Louis celebrated the 100th anniversary of the 1802 purchase. Frank attended and recorded the event in his diary. This fair is remembered for many things, including the popular song, "Meet Me in St. Louis, Louis." This exposition deserves special comment. For the first time, a world's fair displayed gasoline-powered automobiles. On display were the Studebaker, Ford, Oldsmobile, and Rambler. At the time, Studebaker was the largest manufacturer of cars in the United States. Ford was a newcomer "but was already making a name as an affordable vehicle for the masses." Geronimo, who was in the custody of the US Army, was a regular feature of the 1904 fair. Geronimo liked being at the fair and made more money than he ever had before. In his biography, he said, "I sold my photographs for twenty-five cents and was allowed to keep ten cents of this for myself. I also wrote my name for ten, fifteen, or twenty-five cents...and kept all of that money." Theodore Roosevelt made two visits, and both Will Rogers and Tom Mix performed. The Buffalo Bill Show staged Custer's Last Stand from the 1876 Battle of the Little Bighorn; and a reenactment of a battle from the 1899-1902 Boer War featuring a horse and rider jumping from a thirty-foot cliff into a pool of water. A history professor like Frank would have given his eye teeth to attend this one. The fair also introduced the Dr. Pepper beverage from Waco, hot dogs, and ice cream cones.

If Frank had had the chance to see only one of the big fairs, the St. Louis fair was the one, being grander than the 1893 fair in Chicago and the 1901 fair in Buffalo. There were 1,500 buildings on a 1,200-acre site connected by seventy-five miles of roads and walkways. One building alone (the Palace of Agriculture) covered twenty acres. The fair, which ran from April 30 through November 30, 1904, appealed not only to average attendees, but also to intellectuals in the fields of anthropology, history, art history, and architecture with long-range impact. Nineteen million, six hundred ninety-four thousand, eight hundred fifty-five people attended it, its exhibits staged by sixty-two foreign nations, the United States, and all forty-five of the US's then states. Unlike the Chicago and Buffalo fairs, the St. Louis fair was not about economic or technological progress, but it supported eugenic themes of the alleged superiority of Western and Anglo-Saxon civilization that were criticized as racist. This focus was highly controversial as the African American community was torn on the issue of segregation between the accommodating views of Booker T. Washington and the more hostile and assertive views of W.E.B Du Bois. At all the fairs, Blacks were discriminated against.

A history professor like Frank would have wanted to see the natives from territories acquired by the United States following the Spanish-American War, including Guam, the Philippines, and Puerto Rico. Additionally, various important figures were in attendance, including Helen Keller, Henri Poincare, T.S. Eliot, Geronimo; probably Scott Joplin, whose ragtime music was featured at the fair; and John Philip Sousa, whose band performed on opening day and several other days.

Of the many entertainments and educational opportunities the fair afforded, the Anglo-Boer War was an especially high-grossing concession. Twice a day, visitors could watch thrilling re-enactments of major battles from the Second Boer War in a 15-acre arena. The re-enactments lasted up to three hours and featured generals and six hundred veteran soldiers from both sides of the war. Moreover, although Frank missed the 1893 Exposition in Chicago, and, therefore, the debut of the giant Ferris wheel, the decision was made to bring the wheel out of storage for the St. Louis Fair rather than build an imitation of the Eiffel Tower. We have to assume he took a ride on that Ferris wheel, especially since it had been at the Chicago fair and was a really big deal.

Miles: Those pictures you showed of the St. Louis fairground—there would have been a lot of walking. Did the fair have anything good to eat or drink after all that walking around?

Pops: Oh, sure. The Pike, which was on the northern perimeter of the fair, had many food concessions catering to the fair-goer. That year, two foods were introduced to the international public. I already mentioned the Dr. Pepper beverage, and the second was Puffed Wheat cereal. Frank may have already been familiar with Dr. Pepper since it was created in the mid-1880s in Waco. So he could have tried it when he was a Baylor student in the early 1890s. And didn't I already mention hot dogs?

Miles: Dr. Pepper goes great with hot dogs and corny dogs.

Pops: (*smiling*) So you wouldn't put it on your Puffed Wheat cereal?

Miles: You are joking, right?

Pops: (*smiling*) Of course. I want to warn you and everyone, though, the next chapter may remind you of your high school English class. Hope it won't be a bad memory.

BOOK SEVEN

The Currents in Frank's Life

Sample questions for the peanut gallery's consideration in this book's chapters:

Did the events in Frank's life settle into categories like themes, crossroads, or paradoxes? If so, what were they? Or are there no discernible patterns in his life that you can tell? Was Frank, in any sense, at any time, an underdog? What was the central paradox in Frank's life? What decisions did Frank make that had the most impact on the twists and turns his life took? What themes or plots do you see in Baylor's history during Frank's lifetime? Do any metaphors come to mind for Frank's story? For Baylor's story?

Excerpts from Frank's "Funny-Book of Student Bone-heads" on examinations:

Question: "On what basis did William of Normandy argue that he was the most entitled of all the contenders to the throne of England?" Answer: "William of Normandy claimed he was air [sic] to the throne by inheritance."

Question: "What was humanism?" Answer: "Humanism is a bill passed in Parliament doing away with the use of stocks and bonds and other inhuman modes of punishment in the English government."

Examples of Frank's favorite words and phrases from his correspondence:

"Unreservedly" — "I do not think I could unreservedly give my consent to have Clarence come out here again."

"rather" — "I am under rather severe tension just now."

"determination and persistence" — "but if determination and persistence count for anything, there will not be any lack of either."

CHAPTER 32

Themes & Plots, Crossroads & Turning Points, Metaphors & Paradoxes

Our mission today is to help both the author and the reader focus on Frank Guittard's life from a distance rather than up close. We hope that such an approach will be useful in getting underneath the surface of our story and present the readers, if not with additional insight, at least with a different way of looking at Frank's story. Because this aspect of Frank's story is more abstract than those in other chapters, I have asked my oldest grandson, Miles, to help me with this one. Miles and I will be floating a number of themes, plot lines, metaphors, and paradoxes that may have some application to Frank's life. The reader will have to decide whether these concepts help explain Frank's life, and, if they do, to what extent.

Pops: Miles, in this chapter, we talk about Frank Guittard's life in terms that may help us understand better what he was going through. In reading Frank's letters and studying the events in his life, one cannot help but note that sooner or later, impressions from studying the events and facts of Frank Guittard's journey settle into one or more of the following categories:

Themes
Plots and subplots
Crossroads & turning points
Metaphors
Paradoxes

Related to some of these topics will be the earlier chapter (Chapter 8) on Frank's game plan for obtaining his education, choosing a career, and starting a family; also, the chapter on the twist of fate (Chapter 19) that brought him back to Texas; and finally, the upcoming chapter looks back on Frank's game plan (Chapter 36), which we will talk about later.

Miles: The life of Frank Guittard is starting to sound like the story of *David Copperfield* with all of its plots and subplots.

Pops: Have you read *David Copperfield*?

<u>Miles</u>: Sort of. I read that *Classics Illustrated* comic book you gave us last Christmas.

<u>Pops</u>: I was hoping you might be inspired to read the book someday.

<u>Miles</u>: Maybe I will. I'm pretty busy with my work. The paperback is over a thousand pages. That's longer than most of my dad's Stephen King books.

Theme: Frank as Underdog

<u>Pops</u>: Well, even though it's long, *David Copperfield* was one of Frank's favorite books. We know he identified with young David Copperfield, having as much as said so in an essay he wrote about the book. Let's start with themes, plots, and subplots. What do you think might be a theme for Frank's journey?

<u>Miles</u>: Well, based on the stories of his family packing him off on a train to faraway Texas with just a bag of lunches, and then of his financial struggles after he got off the train, one theme might be that he was an underdog like David Copperfield.

<u>Pops</u>: That's my take as well. Before Frank left Ohio, he had little or no family guidance on his education or a possible career. After 1886, he lost ready access to his family support system, whatever it may have been. He received no financial assistance from his parents, only several small loans at interest from his brothers, which he worked to pay back. He couldn't get a bank loan—he had no collateral to put up to amount to anything. As a result, it took him sixteen years after high school to earn his bachelor's degree since no financial aid for college was available. With some guidance, he could have chosen a career more financially rewarding than teaching or developed a strategy to secure such a career. He was not able to marry until he was almost forty years of age. His collegiate contemporaries Brooks and Neff were able to obtain their degrees in much less time and marry their sweethearts. So yes, Frank, in some respects, started off as a definite underdog compared to people like Samuel Brooks and Pat Neff, especially Neff.

<u>Miles</u>: Sounds like he had a hard, slow grind.

<u>Pops</u>: It certainly was by today's standards with all the grants and loans available to students and career counselors and student advisers who make a living counseling young people. Those sorts of things didn't exist in those days. But, as bad as that may sound, Frank did have certain advantages over the average person faced with similar circumstances in those days. He had unusual persistence, determination,

and stamina, coupled with good health. He had an analytical, orderly, thorough brain and was generally optimistic in his outlook, although his spirits did flag sometimes, though usually not for long. A good night's sleep, a hot breakfast, and an early walk were usually all it took to cheer him up, having ruminated overnight on a plan to deal with whatever issue was bothering him. Frank benefited from working on a farm for a time, which gave him perspective and push. Perhaps one of his advantages was having an energizing purpose beyond himself—he wanted to help students who had faced the same challenges he had faced. All these advantages meant that, although still an underdog, Frank was always progressing on an upward path, however slowly, compared with some of his Baylor contemporaries.

Plots & Subplots in Frank's Story & in Baylor's Story

Pops: Stories in books generally have a primary plot and then some secondary plots. Although the life story of Frank Guittard encompasses both the primary plot of this volume and several secondary plots, I will mention also some plots related to Baylor since the overall book is structured as a life & times. The "& times" part is intended to catch the crucial things going on with Baylor in Waco, beginning with Frank's student days and continuing through his death in 1950. So here are the plots and subplots for you to consider:

> *Primary Frank plot*: Frank's struggle to obtain his higher education, secure a teaching post, establish his family, and teach generations of history students.
>
> *Frank subplots*: Frank's trip to Texas and initial adventures; his Baylor days; his days teaching school, meeting Mamie, and pursuing degrees in Chicago; the initial days teaching in Baylor's Prep; his courtship of, and marriage to, Mamie; grieving the illnesses and deaths of son Charles and wife Mamie; his pursuit and marriage of Mama Josie; his involvement with the establishment of a student self-government at Baylor and his participation in bringing it to an end; his pursuit of a Ph.D. at Stanford; and teaching history to 10,000 students.
>
> *Primary Baylor plots*: For Baylor at Independence, surviving the Civil War and enduring long enough to merge with Waco University to form Baylor at Waco; after that, surviving financially for four-plus decades and facing other crises and challenges while struggling to become a real university.

Baylor subplots: Meeting repeated fundraising crises; adding Carroll Chapel and Library and Carroll Science and finishing out Burleson Quadrangle; working through the challenge to President Burleson's leadership after the unremitting attacks from W.C. Brann on Baylor as a desirable college for young women; responding to jingoistic attacks on Baylor faculty prior to World War I; responding to fundamentalists' attacks on members of Baylor faculty; meeting the crisis associated with the failure of the Student Self-Government to punish academic cheaters; and surviving the peril represented by the Great Depression.

Crossroads & Turning Points

Pops: Miles, I will attempt at this point to identify those possible points in Frank's life when a significant decision had to be made, either going down one road or turning down another. As I run through these, be thinking about the ones you may think represent turning points. Here are some that come to mind from Frank's life; perhaps you can think of some others:

- Deciding to take teacher training in Ohio.
- Taking the train to Texas to scout the land for a possible family move.
- Opting to remain in Texas after his parents decided not to leave Ohio.
- Pursuing additional teacher training in Texas and deciding to become a teacher was his best available career option.
- Enrolling at Baylor and earning two or more years' college credit.
- Attending a service led by James Milton Carroll in which he was converted.
- Dropping out to earn money selling books in Hunt County, Texas.
- Taking teaching positions in Texas and Arkansas with Pat Neff.
- Serving as principal of a school in Shiner, Texas, and meeting Mamie Welhausen.
- Enrolling at the University of Chicago and earning two degrees.
- Accepting President Brooks's offer to return to Texas and teach in Baylor's preparatory department.
- Courting Mamie Welhausen long distance for more than four years and finally marrying her.
- Enrolling at Stanford and pursuing a Ph.D.
- Staying at Baylor University his entire college teaching career.

Well, Miles, what have I left out?

Miles: You left out meeting Mama Josie and putting on a full-court press to court her. You also left out a turning point for Mamie.

Pops: What do you have in mind regarding Mamie?

Miles: Well, Mamie's volunteer job nursing sick people may well have led to her contracting TB and her death.

Pops: You could be right about that; we don't know about that for sure. As to the above decisions Frank made, which of these represented actual turning points or crossroads for Frank?

Miles: Most of them, I guess, especially enrolling at Baylor, deciding to teach, taking the train to Texas, teaching in Shiner, accepting President Brooks's offer, and most of the rest of them.

Pops: Right. Nearly all of them. Maybe selling books in Hunt County did not radically alter Frank's path, but all the rest seem to be important in his life. Hard to imagine his life had he not come to Texas, enrolled at Baylor, taught in Shiner, gone to school with President Brooks, or accepted the offer to teach at Baylor. So many other life paths and destinations were possible.

Metaphors in Frank's story

Pops: Here's another area where I would like your feedback. Possible metaphors seem to jump out of Frank's story; here are some of them:

First metaphor: Frank as a knight-errant on a quest for higher education and ultimately the Ph.D. degree. In one of the *Round-Ups*, he was described as a knight for his demeanor at an early homecoming parade. Perhaps a knight in Arthur's Roundtable, a Parsifal-like character focused on the Holy Grail. Here is what came to mind to tie this metaphor to Frank's story:

- Frank goes on a mission or quest to Texas, a foreign place and its people—a possible Camelot?
- Frank serves along the way as a dining room attendant—Sir Beaumains?
- Frank encounters attractive females in his travels, including Sallie Canon, Cornelia Smith's mother, an unnamed girl in Arkansas, and of course, Mamie and Josie—Lady of the Lake?

- Frank loses his mother and encounters a problematic stepmother—Sir Tristram?
- Frank is elevated to the status of university teacher by the ruler (President Brooks) in the Baylor kingdom—King Arthur dubbing Knights of the Roundtable?
- Frank embarks on his ultimate quest, pursuing the Ph.D. sheepskin, and defeating the German examination and the French examination—Sir Parsifal, Sir Lancelot? Encountering the White Dragon and the Red Dragon?

Second metaphor: Frank as a White Rabbit character in *Alice in Wonderland* who kept disappearing down rabbit holes (low-paid country school teaching assignments), then popping up again, and declaring, "I'm late, I'm late, for a very important date" (completing his higher education or meeting a woman he could marry).

Do you like any of these for Frank?

Miles: Actually, I like all of them and don't like any of them.

Pops: Why is that?

Miles: Well, these metaphors are interesting, but they are cartoonish and too much of a stretch for me. I don't think Frank was blindly pursuing some holy vision. *Spoiler Alert*: As I understand it, he didn't want to start work on a Ph.D., but was under pressure from President Brooks. A David Copperfield or Ben Webster type hero doesn't really work for me, either. I think there was a complicated inheritance backstory in the Copperfield book, and Copperfield became a writer. Ben Webster wasn't real—he was just a comic strip character. The White Rabbit one seems pretty good since Frank always seemed to be out of time, running behind, and he did have a pocket watch like the white rabbit. Still, I don't think Frank was running around like the white rabbit—Frank was thoughtful and deliberate, and the white rabbit was always in a state of panic.

Pops: What would you suggest for a metaphor?

Miles: I like the idea of Frank's pocket watch and the concept of the passage of time as a metaphor for his story, since Frank was obviously aware of the year on the wall calendar. Maybe Frank's story can be tied in some way to his pocket watch.

Pops: How about a railroad metaphor? Similar to a railroad track, Frank's path had been marked by multiple crossings at which he had made choices, incorrect perhaps in some places; at other times, he had strayed off on sidetracks or other diversions which delayed his return to the main line. We know Frank himself used the "sidetrack" metaphor in talking about one part of his Ph.D. saga at Stanford.

Miles: Railroads are cool, especially the dining car and those pull-down beds in the sleeping compartments.

Pops: How about a disappearing staircase as a metaphor? At Frank and Mama Josie's house in Waco, there was a hidden, pull-down staircase that went into an attic with a lot of stuff—like a Samurai sword, old Colt revolvers, and other stuff that you didn't know was there unless you went up there.

Miles: I guess that's okay. How could you use that?

Pops: We could use it in connection with attempting to talk about the various parts of Frank's life, perhaps his private sides, that were hidden away, some even from family.

Miles: How could anything be hidden from family?

Pops: Miles, there will always be hidden things for all of us that we prefer not to talk to our families about, even you, even me.

Miles: How about Frank?

Pops: Yes, definitely. We already included earlier the family crisis in Ohio, which Frank never revealed in detail to his family in Waco.

A few paradoxes

Pops: I want to see if you think there are any paradoxes in Frank's story.

Miles: What do you mean by "paradox"?

Pops: I mean an apparent contradiction or conflict between two ideas, two emotions, or whatever. For example, a "paradox" is a seemingly absurd or self-contradictory statement that when explained, may prove to be true. The comedian Jimmy Durante used to say, "Did you ever have the feeling that you needed to go, but yet you had the feeling that you wanted to stay?"

Miles: Okay. I sort of get it.

<u>Pops</u>: Here's the central paradox of Frank's life as I see it. Frank was the planner, the consummate systematizer, the last guy to want to ride the "winds of chance," or to "go with the flow." He had a conscious game plan for obtaining an education, taking up a career, and starting a family. His students thought of him as the guy who put the "sys" in "system." Yet, paradoxically, often he had no choice except to ride the winds of chance, even when it affected some of the most important issues in his life. For example, Brooks's job offer to teach at Baylor after the dog prank incident; then his first wife's susceptibility, genetic or environmental, to disease; and finally, his second son's exposure to disease. Frank, in fact, would surprisingly admit, four decades after traveling to Texas as a land scout, that insufficient planning—or riding the winds of chance—had been the "bane" of his life. One of the chief challenges in telling Frank's story is to figure out what he meant by "the winds of chance," since he declined to provide the details.

Then too, paradoxes sometimes can suggest other paradoxes. For example, there is a paradox in Frank's view that riding the winds of chance had been the bane of his life when those chance events also brought him his life's greatest and longest-lasting satisfactions. His original connection with Baylor, the opportunity to teach at the Shiner school, and the chance offer from Brooks in 1902 all led to his opportunity to return to Texas and pursue a relationship with Mamie and ultimately marriage and family. It was by no means inevitable that he would meet Josie Glenn, either. Thus, Frank achieved his primary life goals—twice where marriage was concerned—while benefiting from chance events.

<u>Miles</u>: I get that.

<u>Pops</u>: There's another paradox of sorts in the dog prank incident—even without thinking about Frank Guittard—in President Brooks being offered the job of president.

<u>Miles</u>: What's that?

<u>Pops</u>: That a mischievous prank, combined with a moment of sudden impulsive cruelty to an animal, would lead to a new university president who would bring about essential expansions at Baylor, including the addition of a medical school, a college of dentistry, a school of pharmacy, a law school, a school of nursing, and, finally, Baylor's elevation to the ranks of true universities. Also that a mischievous student prank would bring about the presidency of Samuel Palmer Brooks, who would successfully defend Baylor from the deadly serious charge of heresy brought by certain Baptist fundamentalists marketing their brands of the Baptist faith.

<u>Miles</u>: So student pranks in college can sometimes be for the best.

Pops: Sometimes good things unexpectedly come from bad things. But student pranks can worry parents and lead to suspension from school, and that is not a good thing.

Miles: One other thing, Pops. We know that Frank Guittard lived a quiet life, was a mild-mannered guy, and had one job for almost fifty years. You tell us he lived with just one woman at a time and avoided strong drink, tobacco, gambling, and cussing. So, I don't get how there could have been so many of these paradoxes, crossroads, themes, and other things in his life. His life wasn't that dramatic or stressful. With the one exception of those early teachers who whipped him, and that one farmer who refused to pay him for a book, he never had a serious run-in with anyone. Just doesn't figure.

Pops: That is an interesting point of view, Miles, but let's take that "under advisement," as Frank might say. Although "quiet" at times and with very few documented "run-ins," Frank's life could be quite stressful—he had been under great pressure when preparing as a new hire to teach several subjects outside his specialty in the Baylor Academy, and we haven't even reached the chapter I've called "Failure Not an Option." All of the concepts we've talked about in this chapter may shed some light on the way we can understand his life. Themes and metaphors, for example, are the sorts of things that show up in the lives of all of us, but maybe we don't think about them until we are older and inclined to think back on things. Most people probably never reflect on their lives in this way. In the case of Frank Guittard, who was a most private person, he never did exactly say in what way he concluded he had "blundered" in his life planning. My guess is that he could have elaborated at length on many of these themes, metaphors, and paradoxes we've talked about. After all, he lived to a ripe old age of eighty-three, and had eighty-three years to think back on what had been and what could have been throughout his long life.

Miles: Yes, I imagine he kept turning things over in his mind, especially when he was at Stanford, working away as one of the older guys on campus.

Pops: We'll get to those "do or die" years in Frank's life shortly.

Photographs of Guittard Family, Baylor Presidents, and Baylor Campus

Francis "Frank" Gevrier Guittard c. 1901.

Francis "Frank" Gevrier Guittard c. 1927.

Mamie Welhausen Guittard c. 1912.

Francis Gevrier Guittard, Jr. c. 1922.

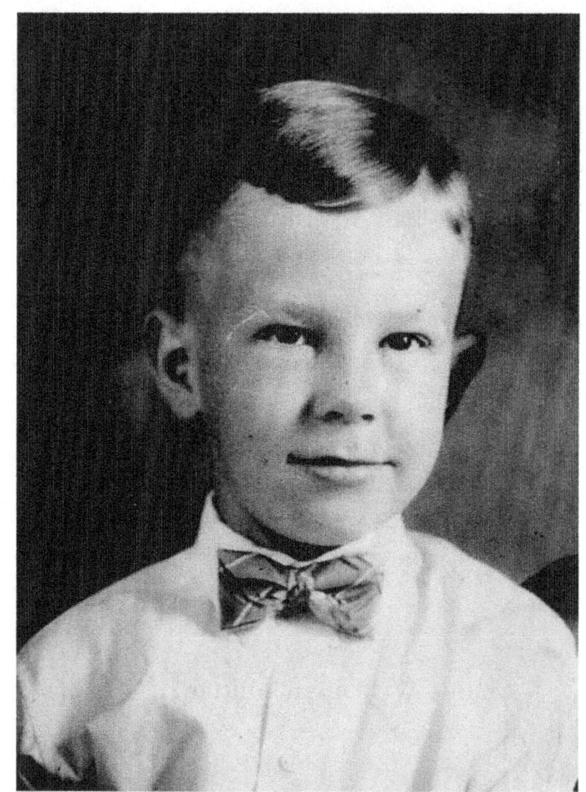

Clarence Alwin Guittard c. 1923.

Josephine Glenn Guittard c. 1940.

Rufus C. Burleson c. 1897 (portrait).

Oscar H. Cooper c. 1902 (portrait).

Samuel Palmer Brooks c. 1894.

Patrick M. Neff c. 1932-1947 (Portrait)

Maggie Houston Hall c. 1890.

Burleson Quadrangle post-1902 and pre-1953.

Georgia Burleson Hall c. 1890.

Main Building c. 1890.

BOOK EIGHT

Quest for the Doctorate, the Final Challenge

Sample questions for the peanut gallery's consideration in this book's chapters:

Who were the Stanfords? What happened to Jane Stanford? Did Frank have misgivings about his thesis topic recognizing the contributions of Theodore Roosevelt to conservation when Frank had been a lifelong Democrat? What was Frank's daily routine at Stanford, and what were Frank's main stressors during his studies at Stanford? How well did Frank get along with his much younger thesis adviser? What was the "mountain" Frank had to climb? What near catastrophe confronted Frank one day at Stanford? What Stanford campus ritual did Frank think Baylor could beat Stanford at after his return to Waco? What was the ultimate payoff to Frank from all the effort he put into earning a Ph.D. in history?

Excerpts from Frank's "Funny-Book of Student Bone-heads" on examinations:

Question: "What were the reforms of Solon?" Answer: "The Reforms of Solon was [sic] that the people ware [sic] the garment of white with a purple hem until he became a man then he should be permitted to ware [sic] a toger [sic].

Question: "What was Pride's Purge?" Answer: "Pride's Purge was revolt in the church lead [sic] by man by the name of Pride. It was to clean and purify the church. This is why it was called Pride's Purge."

Examples of Frank's favorite words and phrases from his correspondence:

"grinding" — "Things are grinding along as usual mostly."

"hot-footed" — "I hot-footed it to the Piggly Wiggly."

"will rejoice" and "keen" — "The new pencil sharpener will rejoice Sonnyboy...for it is a keen one."

CHAPTER 33

Stanford & Palo Alto Days (1923; 1926-1930)

This chapter provides context for Frank's sabbaticals to Stanford to earn a doctorate. Katie and I will focus momentarily on the history of Palo Alto and Stanford University. Then in the next chapter, we'll go on to Frank Guittard's life in Palo Alto and on Stanford's campus as a much older student to earn his degree.

Pops: Before talking about Palo Alto, Stanford, and Frank's life while pursuing his Ph.D., let's talk about the United States in the decade of the 1920s. Frank may have spent most of his waking hours in the Stanford library or studying in his room, but the world outside was in serious upheaval. The University of Houston Digital History Program has described the period this way: "The decade witnessed a titanic struggle between an old and a new America. Immigration, race, alcohol, evolution, gender politics, and sexual morality all became major cultural battlefields during the 1920s. Wets battled drys [the US went dry at midnight, January 16, 1920, and remained dry for the rest of the decade]; religious modernists battled religious fundamentalists; and urban ethnics battled the Ku Klux Klan."

Beginning in the summer of 1923 and for subsequent summers, Frank was engaged in a deadly serious endeavor as a graduate student. Yet during those periods, life on the Stanford campus frequently offered welcome distractions for graduate students like Frank, including ever-present manifestations of college spirit, including that expressed in stirring college songs. "Hail, Stanford, Hail" was one of the most beloved Stanford songs. Although in 1923 Frank was fifty-six years old and long past his college days, he was a sharp observer of traditions at the other schools he attended. He would have heard this song many times as he walked across the campus or sat in his room, the final refrain of "Hail Stanford, Hail" —which you can listen to on YouTube—stirringly evoking the images and sounds of the neighboring foothills and the bay could not have helped but thrill this graduate of the University of Chicago.

Katie: I pulled it up on YouTube. It must have been exciting to hear students sing this song at Stanford's games in a packed stadium. Did Frank go to any football games while he was at Stanford?

Pops: Possibly not, at least we have no record of it, likely because he always had to be back at Baylor teaching each fall. Too bad, though, since Glenn "Pop"

Warner, Stanford's coach, was the winningest coach in Stanford's history. Warner compiled an amazing record in the 1920s, his teams going to the Rose Bowl three times, and winning in 1928 after tying for first in the Pacific Coast Conference in 1927. When Frank arrived for his only long sabbatical in January 1928, the campus must have been electric. Stanford had been the national champion in 1926 after a 10-0-1 season.

Katie: Was Stanford a really old university like Harvard or Yale when Frank went there?

Pops: Oh, no. Stanford and Chicago were both infants as universities in the early 1890s, Stanford opening in 1891—one year before Chicago opened. Stanford was both nondenominational and coeducational. Leland Stanford and his wife Jane decided to establish a university in memory of their only child, Leland Stanford, Jr., who died at fifteen from typhoid fever. The Stanfords would endow their university with twenty million dollars, reportedly four times Harvard's endowment, and like the University of Chicago, Stanford would quickly become a premier destination for students and faculty alike. Despite its status, however, because it was not as well-known as Harvard or Yale or Princeton, Frank Guittard would have to remind people occasionally that Stanford was not a junior college and that his Ph.D. was not from a junior institution.

Katie: So where did the Stanfords get their money? What was the Stanford campus like?

Pops: Railroads. Leland Stanford had also been governor and a US Senator from California. He and his wife, Jane, selected David Starr Jordan as the first president. You will recall that John D. Rockefeller selected William Rainey Harper as the first president of the University of Chicago. Leland would die two years later, but Jane would continue to be influential at Stanford, controlling many matters concerning the school. Their 650-acre country home, horse farm, and their adjoining 8,000 acres became the site of the Stanford campus. The campus buildings and the quad were designed in the Spanish-colonial style common in California called Mission Revival and featured red tile roofs with sandstone masonry. The campus was laid out by famed landscape architect Frederick Law Olmsted, whose name is also associated with designing Central Park in New York, Jackson Park in Chicago, and the Columbian Exposition in Chicago. The original quad and Encina Hall, where US President Herbert Hoover lived as a student, survived the 1906 earthquake. Mrs. Stanford's Memorial Church, however, was seriously damaged by the catastrophe, but was repaired before Frank Guittard's sabbaticals. Hoover was the US president when Frank received his Ph.D.

<u>Katie</u>: What do we know about President Jordan and Mrs. Stanford's relative roles in building Stanford?

<u>Pops</u>: First, I might mention that on one Sunday during the 1920s, Frank went to the beautiful Memorial Church, which was Mrs. Stanford's best-known addition to Stanford's campus. That day, the pews were almost full, but President Emeritus Jordan motioned for Frank and an accompanying friend to sit with him in his row, saying to Frank that "people would think he had guests" and would be impressed, a little Jordan joke. Jordan was an interesting character and, like Frank, would write down rules for himself to remember, including: "Do not discuss with one professor the character or attainments of any other. Do not use any superlatives or over-praise anyone...Never be betrayed into disparaging California. Be very cautious of public utterances of any kind before reporters." Frank would have agreed with each of these rules, which mesh closely with his own rules. We talk about those elsewhere.

President Jordan had been named president of Indiana University at age thirty-five and was an authority on ichthyology, which is the study of fish. In some ways, he was a rising star like William Rainey Harper, who became president of the University of Chicago about the same time. Both were tasked with building universities from scratch and had to deal with wealthy patrons—tycoons Leland Stanford and his wife Jane Stanford on the one hand, and John D. Rockefeller on the other. There were tensions in both relationships, although of a different kind; the tensions between Jane Stanford after her husband's death in 1893 and President Jordan were seemingly more difficult than those between Harper and Rockefeller. Although Mrs. Stanford was a more difficult university patron than Rockefeller, there were crises not of her making which she, Jordan, and Stanford's trustees had to work through, starting with the financial jeopardy in which Leland Stanford's death left the university. Add to that the financial panic of 1893 and the various formidable money problems she and President Jordan had to deal with. There was also the classic tension between Mrs. Stanford's prioritizing building out the campus and Jordan's tendency to emphasize spending money to attract outstanding faculty. However, by the time of her death in 1905, the Stanfords had donated forty million in assets for the benefit of the university, including the endowment. At one point, Mrs. Stanford paid salaries out of her personal assets for several years to avoid financial ruin to the university. But the most dramatic chapter in Mrs. Stanford's life occurred shortly before her death.

<u>Katie</u>: What was that?

<u>Pops</u>: She was poisoned, apparently on two occasions, by persons unknown. In early 1905 in San Francisco, she drank some Poland Spring Mineral Water found to contain strychnine, but she survived. In Hawaii weeks later, a coroner's jury

following an autopsy concluded that Mrs. Stanford died due to strychnine poisoning contained within a bottle of bicarbonate of soda. However, the story that hit the newsstands was that Mrs. Stanford died of a heart ailment. Nevertheless, almost a century later and after a thorough review of all the facts, Robert W. P. Cutler, M.D., distinguished former professor of neurology at Harvard, Chicago, and Stanford, published his book *The Mysterious Death of Jane Stanford* (Stanford University Press, 2003). Professor Cutler concluded that she had been poisoned; he stated that the claim of a "heart failure" was part of an unsubstantiated whitewash of the entire affair by President Jordan. In 1905, disclosure of a poisoning plot involving unidentified third persons would probably not have been in the young university's interest. Today President Jordan's memory at Stanford is still revered, even with the lingering questions concerning the propriety of his efforts to protect Stanford's reputation over a hundred years ago and those involving the identity of the guilty party or parties.

Katie: Did Frank know Mrs. Stanford was poisoned when he was studying for his Ph.D.?

Pops: No—that was not made public knowledge until 2003 when Cutler's book came out. One thing further about President Jordan—in addition to his well-regarded scientific books, in 1899 he published a charming book of fiction for children called *The Book of Knight and Barbara: Being a Series of Stories Told to Children*. In the book, Jordan relates nonsense stories he made up impromptu for his children Knight and Barbara, who produced wacky but charming illustrations to accompany the stories. Your great-grandfather, Clarence, would read these stories to me when I was a young boy. I remember them still, especially the run-on non-sequiturs in the stories and the strange illustrations, all being original and entertaining. Frank or Josie must have bought a copy of Jordan's book to bring home to read to Clarence, as Francis was too old for such stories at the time.

Katie: What were the stories about?

Pops: One was called "The Little Legs That Ran Away"; another, "The Boy That Whacked the Witch's Toadstools"; and another, "The Ghost with the Horsehair Wig." The first of those starts: "Once there was a little girl and she used to take off her little legs when she went to bed at night and put them with her clothes and the rest of her things in a chair. And one night the little legs got uneasy and ran away...so far no one could see them." Nothing in Jordan's distinguished career as a scholar prepared the reader for this book's stories or their popularity with generations of children and their parents.

Katie: Pops, this chapter has been an exciting chapter, with a weird mixture of things—from "Hail Stanford Hail" to death by poison, to charming but odd children's stories. I would like to have a copy of President Jordan's book; it looks like fun.

Pops: President Jordan's book for children is still available. If you want "exciting"—at least for Frank Guittard—that's in our next chapter.

CHAPTER 34

Failure Not an Option—the Struggle for a Doctorate

(1923-1931)

The subject matters of several chapters, all set in the 1920s, have already been addressed at length in *A Ph.D.'s Reverie: The Letters* (2019). Those subjects included Frank's pursuit of his doctorate at Stanford while his family remained in Waco. The chronicling of Frank's efforts through family letters was extensive and supplemented by editors' notes addressing the evolution controversy at Baylor and other events helpful in understanding the letters. Since the current volume, entitled *I WILL TEACH HISTORY, The Life & Times of Francis Gevrier Guittard, professor, Baylor University* necessarily covers Frank's journey to earn his Ph.D., it must reprise the essential correspondence documenting his experience at Stanford. We will include the ups and downs of an older student thrust back into the classroom at age fifty-six when he would have preferred to be home playing golf, fishing, or eating watermelon in the cool of a summer evening. I asked Miles to go with me through this discussion of Frank's pursuit of the doctorate.

<u>Miles</u>: Pops, I'd like to know several things—first, why did he want to go for a Ph.D., why at Stanford, and why did he choose "Roosevelt and Conservation" as his thesis topic?

<u>Pops</u>: Frank's quest for his Ph.D. was an extended one, commencing during the administration of President Harding, continuing during the administration of President Coolidge (two terms), and finally concluding during President Hoover's administration. It was a serious undertaking, and your questions are good ones. First, whatever Frank's aspirations may have been for a Ph.D. before he came back to Baylor to teach, the impetus to get a Ph.D. in the 1920s did not start with Frank. President Brooks made it crystal clear to the entire Baylor faculty, Baylor department chairs especially, that unless they already possessed their terminal degrees, they needed to start working on Ph.Ds. because of the requirements of accrediting associations.

At the time, Frank and Mama Josie doubted that Frank's compensation or rank at Baylor would be impacted if he chose not to work on a Ph.D., as long as Brooks remained president. However, Mama Josie, according to other faculty wives, had a concern about what might happen if President Brooks should retire or no longer be in the picture. Their concerns were prescient as President Brooks's successor, Pat M. Neff, stressed the importance of having the Ph.D. and showed that he was willing to take drastic steps if he perceived them to be necessary. Then too, Frank had always supported Brooks in his efforts to elevate Baylor's standing. Starting Ph.D. work at fifty-six years that would not result in a degree until he was almost sixty-five was an unusual and certainly arduous undertaking for a department chair, especially considering the amount of time required in residence and the absences from his wife and two sons.

Despite all the reasons justifying his undertaking studies at Stanford, it must have been hugely aggravating. He had been committed for many years to obtaining higher education and becoming the most prepared teacher he could be, and now, when his professional and family situations were finally moving along smoothly, he had to return to an even more rigorous grind than the one in Chicago. Why Frank chose Stanford instead of Chicago, where he had obtained his master's and bachelor's degrees, he never said. We are confident it wasn't solely because of the nice weather in Palo Alto. We suspect he went to Stanford because of the depth and reputation of its history department, but he never recorded his reasons.

As to how he chose "Roosevelt and Conservation" for his thesis subject, that decision came about with the guidance of his adviser, Franklin Roosevelt scholar Edgar E. Robinson, who served as Stanford's history chair beginning in 1928. Robinson would have been aware, as Frank states in the preface of his thesis, that although much had been written about Theodore Roosevelt, in the field of conservation "are to be found his most enduring achievements." In his thesis, Frank quotes William Draper Lewis: "Of all the movements which Roosevelt preached and launched and put into practice, perhaps the most far-reaching in its permanent importance was the conservation of natural resources. More than any other, it received his constant and sympathetic attention." Yet, Frank notes, in this one sphere of Roosevelt's interests, less has been written than in any other.

It may seem remarkable that Frank Guittard, a lifelong Democrat who had never voted for Theodore Roosevelt or any other Republican for president, chose a subject in which he would demonstrate substantial enthusiasm for a president he had not supported. However, although Frank always said he was a lifelong Democrat, he had interests in common with Roosevelt. Except that Roosevelt had been fed with a silver spoon, both Frank and Roosevelt had been self-reliant for many years. They both liked the outdoors, and both were inveterate readers. Roosevelt, like Frank, was impressed with the Texas struggle for independence and had written: "The Texans won a striking victory [over the Mexican army] and performed a feat of the utmost importance in our history." Moreover, Roosevelt declared that: "The government of the United States had nothing to do with winning Texas for the English-speaking people of North America. [Rather it was] The American frontiersmen who [took] Texas for themselves, unaided either by the statesmen who controlled the politics of the Republic or by the soldiers who took their orders from Washington."

In Chapter II of Frank's dissertation, he discusses Roosevelt's human interests—"The West and its People," "The Plain People," and "The Farmer." Frank shared all of these interests, going back to his roots on a small farm in Ohio. As to his feeling for the "plain people," Frank quoted Roosevelt as saying in a 1907 letter to Justice W.H. Moody, that: "Very wealthy people...entirely without meaning it...are singularly callous to the needs, sufferings, and feelings of the great mass of the people who work with their hands...Heaven knows how cordially I despise Jefferson, but he did have one great virtue which his Federalist opponents lacked—he stood for the plain people, whom Abraham Lincoln afterwards represented."

Chapter III, however, provides a window into Frank's view of Roosevelt as a man, his personal traits, and his legendary achievements as a naturalist, explorer, hunter, author, and soldier, including as leader of the US Rough Rider volunteer cavalry group who—without their horses—went up San Juan Hill. Frank identifies the personal characteristics of Roosevelt, which he clearly admired in the mid-1920s, after Roosevelt's death in 1919. Frank includes sections on Roosevelt's unique personality, courage, independence, impartiality, love of fairness and justice, sincerity of purpose, capacity for friendship, intense Americanism, keen sense of humor, willingness to take advice, popularity, effectiveness as a public speaker, skillful use of the press, and ability as a great executive. One or two anecdotes from Frank's thesis show his appreciation for Roosevelt's courage and independence. Frank repeats this anecdote from Hermann Hagedorn's *Theodore Roosevelt in the Bad Lands*: "Because he used a tooth-brush and had the habit of shaving, some of the cowboys decided he was a 'dude.' Roosevelt took their gibes in good humor until he concluded that one of them, a Texan, thought he was a coward as well as a dude. One evening when the Texan was unusually offensive, Roosevelt strode up to him and said sharply, 'you're talking like an ass. Put up or shut up. Fight now or be friends.' The Texan stared in astonishment, shuffled his feet, and mumbled, 'I didn't mean no harm. Make it friends.' And they made it friends." As to Roosevelt's sincerity of purpose, Frank quotes Roosevelt's letter to Justice Oliver Wendell Holmes: "It is well to have lived so that at the end it may be possible to know on the whole one's duties had not been shirked, that there has been no flinching from foes, no lack of gentleness and loyalty to friends, and a reasonable measure of success in the effort to do the task allotted."

<u>Pops</u>: To those words in Frank's dissertation about Roosevelt's traits, it should be added that while Frank never aspired to publish his dissertation, or any of his other writings, he must have been highly impressed with Roosevelt's facility of research, writing, and publishing in a wide array of fields, particularly history,

political and social advocacy, and natural science. Roosevelt was an amazing generalist.

Miles: Yet, because Roosevelt was a Republican, Frank had never voted for him. I wonder if Frank was tempted to volunteer to go with Roosevelt on the Rough Rider expedition. Frank knew how to ride a horse, but maybe he wasn't the soldier type.

Pops: Frank said he never voted Republican, but what he says in his thesis about Roosevelt does make me wonder whether he thought he had made a mistake in 1904 by voting for Alton Parker, a lackluster Democrat. Frank was a party man and must have thought it was important for the Democrats to capture the presidency, whether or not their candidate for president was the best choice. As to joining Roosevelt for the Cuba adventure, I doubt Frank received an invitation since he was neither a soldier, a Texas Ranger, nor an Ivy League blue blood—Roosevelt recruited some of those for his expedition. Then too, in 1898, Frank was heading back to Ohio to attend brother Vic's wedding before his second summer at the University of Chicago. Frank didn't have time for a detour now that he was working hard to finish up his first college degree at Chicago. After already working for over ten years and being so close to reaching that degree, going in as an enlisted man for who knows how many months would not have appealed to him. Moreover, in 1898, Roosevelt was just starting to build a national reputation; his success in Cuba is what catapulted him into the national spotlight as a rising star to governor, vice president, and ultimately president.

The decision having been made for Frank to pursue a Ph.D., the resulting summer sabbaticals gave rise to extensive correspondence between Frank and his family members, even with young Clarence, who was six during the summer of 1923, Frank's first sabbatical at Stanford. Because of the family's need to write letters to support each other and stay in close contact, the readers of their correspondence can learn more about Frank, Mama Josie, Francis, and little Clarence and their daily lives than would have been possible otherwise. Francis was fifteen at the beginning of the Stanford sabbaticals and twenty-three at the end; and Clarence (sometimes called "Sonny") was six at the beginning and fourteen at the end.

Miles: Did Frank get on with his adviser?

Pops: He got along well with his adviser, Professor Robinson, after they got to know each other. Robinson was twenty years Frank's junior and Stanford's history chair from 1928 to 1952; he would also establish the Stanford Institute of American History to upgrade the teaching of that subject. Though Frank had taught history more than twenty years at Baylor and Robinson was much younger, the latter cut Frank no slack in his requirements for Frank's studies or his dissertation. Because of the high expectations for Ph.D. students and the worrisome consequences for Frank back in Waco if he failed in his work, Frank ran scared the entire time. If he did not succeed, he would be returning to Baylor as a department head who had not been able to compete with students twenty to thirty years younger. That would have been a complete humiliation. He very well could have imagined that Baylor students might laugh at him behind his back as that ponderous old fuddy-duddy who strutted around in pinstriped suits he too amply filled, flashing his gold pocket watch and society pin. Even though Mama Josie, Francis, and Clarence would be sympathetic, Frank would still know he had failed and now was vulnerable to demotion in favor of a younger man—one with a doctorate.

Frank's initial summer at Stanford was in 1923. Mama Josie's first letter asked Frank: "Am anxious to know how you like Leland S—and if you find the work very heavy." Frank's first letter to Mama Josie describes his impressions of Stanford: "I went through the red tape of registration yesterday. They have the details all worked out to a fine point. Even had my picture taken on the first steps...Immense is the best word to describe the university. I am writing again this morning [before breakfast], for I may get so deeply involved after today that I may not have much leisure."

It wasn't long before the height and breadth of Frank's task became evident. He wrote Josie: "It is certainly nice and kind of you to write so often. Don't expect too much from me. I am a busy man. Wednesday is my busiest day, four hours in the classroom. Then each teacher assigns enough work to keep you entirely employed on his course alone. I am taking four courses under as many teachers. They are all very fine and I am enjoying the work to the fullest extent. One can work all day long and wish the day was longer."

In July, Frank reported to Mama Josie on his use of the shower bath at his lodgings: "I am getting used to the shower bath. Did not like it at first. All bathtubs were taken out some years ago to prevent upper classmen from hazing the freshmen." Frank reported on his exams and that he was looking forward to Mama Josie's trip to Palo Alto: "Try to get here by the 25th of Aug. at least. I can manage the examinations all right. I had one today, and the terrors are somewhat subsided. They are not so bad after all." While Mama Josie, Francis, and Clarence were experiencing a hot Texas summer, it was otherwise for Frank in Palo Alto: "I often wish you could be here when I think of the heat you are experiencing in Texas. I have used those two blankets every night since I have been here and often some cover [in addition,] my overcoat and bathrobe." Among the challenges of obtaining a Ph.D. was the foreign language requirement. Frank noted: "Wednesday I finished reading my paper which was discussed in class longer than any yet presented. My subject was 'The Emancipation of the Slaves in Brazil.' I was given a French book and two French magazine articles as references. In fact, they were the sources of most of my material. It was slow digging at first but I got my French in pretty good working order before I finished it up."

In August, Frank updated Mama Josie on a difficult assignment for which he had just completed a first draft. The subject was the "inexcusable violation of the American flag by the commander of a British war ship." Frank had had to dig "a lot of stuff out of the records of the Congress... and the [British] parliament and present the facts in a fascinating narrative." Frank summed up the experience saying, "You can imagine my problem. I spend hours among musty smelling volumes. Thank goodness it is over but I think it was a valuable experience. I still have to copy my production and be awfully exact about all my references and citations. It will then be given to another student in the same seminar course and I will get his paper, and at the next meeting of the class we will discuss and criticize each other's work. Does it not all sound immensely important?" To which Mama Josie replied promptly: "I am sure you did some digging on your paper. I know it will be favorably received. Then you will forget all about the hard work you did."

The following year (1924), Frank taught three quarters in Baylor and six weeks in the summer. In the summer of 1926, Frank returned to Stanford and described his new room: "I certainly have a quiet room. It is a corner room with four windows on the 2nd floor under one of the towers of the building. The room is furnished for two but I will be the sole occupant. I finished registration and have three courses and of course do not know the nature of the work yet." Two days later Frank requested some of the books in Baylor's history office be sent to him, including Hulme's *History of the British People,* by parcel post, and further complimented his new room: "Have dandy room, no flies, no roommate." Frank was studying the secret negotiations of European chancelleries and meeting with another student to compare notes for a course taught by an Austrian with a thick accent.

Frank distracted himself occasionally from his studies by reading the newspaper but wasn't always able to find local Texas news: "I subscribed for *The Lariat* but after the first copy, it has failed to make its appearance. I get a little hungry for home news. These papers out here are of course full of local and state news. For the first week they were full of large headlines and entire columns and even pages about 'Aimee,' 'Aimee,' 'Aimee.' It looks very much as though Aimee McPherson concocted a scheme to enable her to get some advertising. I suppose you have read about her supposed kidnapping."

At the end of July, Frank commented on his upcoming tests: "I am just in from the library where I have been cramming for a test for next week. All my professors this time believe in tests. Last week I had two and this week one. On these I made two A's and one B." Back in Palo Alto, Frank reported on his progress and the outlook for the year (1927): "I am getting down to a settled stride in my work. I do not feel so much a slave to my books as I did the other two summers I was here. I will have only one final exam at the close. Last summer I had four. The exam will come Thurs Aug. 25th in the morning. That will make it possible to leave here in the afternoon or the next day." In the same letter, Frank wrote Mama Josie about one particular church service he attended: "I attended church as usual this morning and was invited in the pew with President Emeritus [David Starr] Jordan." Frank and two friends at Stanford came to the church entrance just as President Jordan and his wife entered: "We followed them down the aisle and when the old gentleman stopped to lift the cord at the entrance of the pew he looked around and seeing us said: 'Come in here. There is plenty of room and the people will think I have lots of guests,' so we filed in and took our seats very sanctimoniously."

The following year (1928), Frank spent the first six months in Palo Alto. Frank found a room at 527 Waverly Street and told Mama Josie exactly where he was in regard to the university campus so that she could locate his apartment on her map in Waco. After hunting for two days, he found a quiet room at a reasonable price near the campus: "I am settled at the above address. I scouted around a little...The rooms on the campus...were all higher priced...and not more desirable so I came back here. I pay $18 per month. My room is on the second floor and faces the Episcopal Pastor's home...There are no children in this house, only the man and his wife so I think I shall have a quiet place. Waverly Street crosses University St., a block beyond the Russell or Sunset Cafeteria as it is called now. My rooming place is about one block from University St. to the right after passing the cafeteria. Can you locate me?" (FGG letter to MJ, January 3, 1928). However, the stove was not wholly satisfactory to Frank since it was a wood and coal heater rather than a gas stove. Luckily though, since Frank's room was over a room with a Heatrola, he did not need much fire, and then only at night. During the day, he burned his morning paper and *The Literary Digest* for a little warmth. (FGG letter to MJ January 5, 1928)

Frank's daily routine rarely varied: "I walk out to the University every morning and eat breakfast at the Union and get my mail, then spend most of the morning at work in the Library. To clear the cobwebs out of my brain, I then walk to town for lunch and to my room for a rest. I ride back after dinner for library work or a seminar. At 5:30 Belk [Baylor teaching colleague of Frank] and I hit the asphalt for town. In that way, I walk four miles a day. I may later cut out the car ride when my walking machine gets to performing smoothly." (FGG letter to MJ January 5, 1928)

Mealtimes for Frank took on a special significance since he had relatively few acquaintances in Palo Alto and generally took his meals by himself. He gives special attention in his letters to all the restaurants and cafeterias he patronized: "The fare in the eating places is about the same as in the summer with the exception of the melons and berries. I still get my breakfast at the 'Union,' and pass the station nearly every morning at 7:30 when the Sunset Limited goes glimmering by. I eat at least one meal at the Mandarin each day, then I vary the other to keep from knowing what I am going to eat before I get there. I find that I eat more fruit since I do not have to carry it so far and I prefer to eat the desserts in the eating places." (FGG letter to MJ January 11, 1928)

Similarly, Frank's room at his rooming house was important, not only because of the quiet and peace he needed, but also because it was the substitute for his bedroom at 1401 S. 8th. However, Frank discovered in several weeks that his room at 527 Waverly Street was not satisfactory: "I am going to move the 3rd of Feb. I have paid a month here and as soon as it is up 'we vamanose.' I have had leisure to look around, have dashed in and out of all kinds of rooming places, and have interviewed all types, forms, and degrees of landladies and have found a place for the same price I pay here and much more desirable. The lady here has been as nice as could be and doubtless it will shock her terribly to see the transfer man instead of her check the morning of the 3rd but I am going to be here for some time and the chief thing is to get comfortably located. It is a matter of business and not sentiment. I have tried to be nice too and hope we shall part in peace...All the dormitories here have long waiting lists. Since I have tried staying in town, I believe I prefer it. I walk between four and five miles every day, feel fine, and can do more work than I ever have since coming out here. There are many features of dormitory life that do not appeal to me. For example radios, phonographs, banjoes, and vocalizing at all hours of the day and night. I think my new place will be satisfactory. You can't tell though until you try it out. Very innocent looking places I find may develop some alarming nuisances." (FGG letter to MJ January 22, 1928)

He moved to another place within a matter of weeks and commented: "I am liking my new rooming place very much better than the first one. I have a hall on one side of the room, a stairway on the other, and the outdoors on the other two sides. So I am pretty well isolated. This idea of isolation came as a result of my first experience. The landlady's bedroom was next to mine with the bed against my wall. She could out-snore Clarence or Francis without half trying. I do not know how to describe those sounds—probably it sounded somewhat like a snoring hippopotamus basking in the sun on the muddy banks of a turgid river in tropical Africa. My room instead of being a chamber of peace and slumber at night became a chamber of horrors on several nights. But that's all past. I have a quiet room, electric stove in my room and bathroom which opens into my room, as well as into the hall. My stove is not one of those circular radiating electric stoves but looks somewhat like an electric toaster only of course larger. The woodwork and walls have been newly finished. I would not be embarrassed to have you visit me. I am sending the outline for that course in 104(a) which you may send out when Miss Kate sends you the card. Lovingly Frank" (FGG letter to MJ, February 8, 1928)

In 1928, Frank spent eight continuous months in Palo Alto and wrote Mama Josie as to how things were going: "When I 'take out' or 'unhitch' in the evenings and start for town I have three things to make me cheerful. First I have received a letter from home or am expecting one soon; secondly, I know I am going to have something good to eat when I come to the end of my walk; and thirdly I have a comfortable room where I can rest and get ready for another day. I am liking living in town much better than in the dormitory. When I used to leave town in the evening and walk out through the woods in the darkness and solitude, a sort of feeling of depression would get hold of me. I don't experience that with my present program. I get my supper usually at the Mandarin, then leisurely go to my room, enjoying the shop windows as I go. My room is located on the left of University Ave." (FGG letter to MJ, February 12, 1928)

Frank was progressing in his Ph.D. work according to Dr. Robinson. Frank noted: "In my last conference with Dr. Robinson (This is for private consumption) I asked him if I was proceeding properly in regard to these questions; his reply was 'Absolutely, you are going in the right direction just keep on.'" He signed off his letter to Mama Josie with: "How is the garden? How are the flowers? How are the trees? How are the chickens? How are the neighbors? How are you all? Lovingly Frank." (FGG letter to MJ, February 27, 1928)

Mama Josie and Francis were naturally curious how his dissertation work under Dr. Robinson was coming since it took Frank away from Waco. Frank responded to their curiosity as follows: "As to my thesis which he [Francis] inquired about, I have told you about all there is to tell at this time. It is still in an indefinite state of progress. I hope to have some limits for it before a great while. This all sounds very mysterious I know. I would rather have everything clearer myself, but I find it is a process that most sufferers in a like situation have to pass through. Don't imagine, however that I am not doing any work...for quite the contrary is true. I haunt the library. I am becoming an intimate acquaintance with all the library force from the top to lower regions where the old musty newspaper files are stored for those who wish to dig up the records of the past." (FGG letter to MJ March 7, 1928)

Frank's emotional resources to complete his task sometimes flagged; he wrote a week later: "It is certainly great to have you at home to look after things. I could not have undertaken this task in the world if it had not been for you. I appreciate your kindness and helpfulness as well as your words of good cheer and affection more than words can tell. You have been as good and sweet as can be about writing. One thing, you have not written anything to worry me. I hope you will continue to keep all worries from me as I need all time and attention for my work. You know it does not take much to make my spirits rise or fall. I usually try to keep cheerful, but it is hard sometimes." (FGG letter to MJ, March 14, 1928, Wed night)

Mama Josie was also curious in an intervening letter whether he would be home in June, Frank replying: "No, indeed my dear. I hope I have not ever left the impression that I would, for there is not the least possibility of it. If I created any impression like that, it was unintentional. I knew before I came out here it would be a long steep pull. That is why it was so hard for me to leave home. From students here, I learn that most students stay longer than the two years after receiving their master's degree. I will not have been here two years by June. I am just an ordinary hard worker and not a genius. I wonder if you realize what a task of it I have before me. When I stop to think sometimes, it almost overwhelms me and I become terribly blue and discouraged and wonder whether, after all, it is worthwhile. I don't dare to think much about it. I just try to take as big a nibble from the base of the mountains each day as possible without trying to look over, around, or through them."

As to how things were going for him, Frank added: "I am under a rather severe tension here just now in trying to get certain things off my hands, but I do not see much relief until it is all off my hands, mind and heart. I am having a hilarious good time if such a thing is produced by hard work. I have not taken a day off yet, not even an entire Sunday. About the only indulgence I allow myself is to go to the movies occasionally, but I usually come away with a feeling of disgust and wonder why the movie people do not try to educate the people up to something better, yet it gives me two hours of rest and there are times when I need it." Frank had one reason, however, to celebrate: "Now something for home consumption strictly. I have taken my examination in French and passed. I ate up a French grammar and devoured a heap of French history without getting indigestion, but it did get on my nerves somewhat; however, I am rapidly recovering. The evening after I learned I had passed, I dined at the Cardinal to celebrate the event, then I was somewhat curious too as to whether I would know how to act after spending so much time in Chinese restaurants and cafeterias for the past three months. I think I performed all right with the shrimp fork, salad fork, artichoke finger-bowl, and other accessories."

Frank also relayed more good news from Dr. Robinson, which he passed on to Mama Josie: "More for home consumption if you are not 'fed up': Dr. Robinson told me at our last conference that he supposed my quarter's work was of the same character as my previous work and that I would not need to do any more classwork...Still more, if you can hold out: my thesis subject is settled as far as I know...Please do not ask what my subject is because I may have to change it again and the less said, the better. What have I accomplished this quarter? First, the preliminary examination is out of the way. Second I will have no more classwork. Third, the thesis [topic] is settled, and I have done considerable work on it. Fourth, the French exam is off my hands. Fifth, I have an additional seminar to my credit."

Frank then continues his "for home consumption only message": "What is yet before me? First, the examination in German, which will be a steep hill to climb. The French exam was no farce or sham or pretense. It was a written test on some stuff I had never seen. I think I know French better than German. So I have some work to do in German. Second, the final oral examination and preparation in nine fields—this is more than a steep hill. It is a real mountain, a Matterhorn. Third, the completion of the thesis. This is almost a Mount Everest. Well, this will give you some idea of what I have done and what is yet before me. It is not the most cheerful kind of prospect but if determination and persistency count for anything, there will not be any lack of either." If Mama Josie had not already gotten the idea from the preceding that his Ph.D. work was an unmitigated grind, Frank added for good measure: "This week is examination week, but I have none, but it does not relieve me much. Next week will be vacation, all week. However, there will be no vacation for this guy or bird or digger." (FGG letter to MJ, March 21, 1928)

In the next letter, Frank touched on two subjects mentioned previously, their damaged credit at Waco stores and his correspondence students: "I am glad you were able to re-establish our credit at Wood's Bros. We are pulling though gradually...One of my correspondence students...wrote me that he had fallen in his airplane and had not been able to do much on his course lately as he had his leg broken and was otherwise bruised up. I told him he was entitled to a 'lay off.' Lovingly, 'The Digger.'" (FGG letter to MJ, March 25, 1928)

Two weeks later, Frank took occasion to write Francis regarding his attempts to exercise in Palo Alto: "Tom Drake [an acquaintance] picked me up the other day as I was coming from the University...I made an exception and rode with him. I receive many invitations to ride from classmates. I smilingly refuse and they give a sort of incredulous smile in return as though they think I am a queer specimen of genus homo or perhaps a little 'crippled under the hat' as Dr. Brooks expressed it. I can stand that, however, as I am in good health as a result of the exercise. Lovingly, Papa" (FGG to FGG, Jr., April 28, 1928)

A week later, Frank wrote Mama Josie regarding the most recent meeting he had had with his adviser: "Things are grinding along as usual mostly. I do not know whether my Adviser is apprehensive that I am going to get through too soon or whether he is desirous that I should finish up in the right way. He suggested that I 'sit in' on two courses this quarter, that is, not sign up for the courses with a view of getting credit but get the lectures & bibliography. I regarded the suggestion as a sort of requirement, and as he has been very kind and helpful, I followed the suggestion. One course in Chinese history, 'Chinese Civilizations,' the other 'Historiography,' which means the history of history. I find both very interesting. Dr. Martin has the course in Historiography. He wanted me to enroll and become an active member of the class. He presented me to the class or seminar, numbering eight or ten, saying I was head of the History Department of Baylor University, away on a leave of absence. He also added that he hoped I would become a real member of the class not so much for what I would get out of the work but for what I would contribute to it. That was a nice way to put it. I, of course, expressed my appreciation for his view of the matter but had a talk with him afterward and will continue with the class as an 'auditor,' although he said he would like for me to take an active part in the discussions. These two courses will mean five class hours a week and some reading to get any real benefit from the work, but I have found that it is best to follow suggestions." (FGG letter to MJ, April 15, 1928)

Three days later, he would write Mama Josie: "You must have had a presentment that this was a day of celebrating. The box came this morning and I got it at noon when I came home for dinner. Why am I celebrating? Well, I have something for home consumption strictly: I took my German examination this morning and PASSED!

> *Auf wiedersehen* (Ger. For good-bye) to German
> *Au revoir* (Fr. For good-bye) to German
> *Pax vobiscum* (Lat.) Peace be with you—the German.
>
> *Auf wiedersehen* to my German friends of the past few weeks with whom I have gotten pretty well acquainted. Momsen, Lamprecht, Treitschke, Sybel, Otto von Bismarck, Hedwig von Bismarck (Otto's Frau), Emil Ludwig, Jastrow-to all-*pax vobiscum.* Most of them are good enough people but the sentential structure of most of them lacks terminal facilities.
>
> If I had read German history much longer, I think I should have become either a misanthrope, or a cynic or a pessimist of the extremist type. I devoured Joynes-Meissner's German Grammar and between nine hundred and a thousand pages of history. It all hung over me like a lowering cloud. *Jetzt ist es weg fur ewig!* (Now gone forever).
>
> Next Monday night the Department of History gives an 'at home' to its graduate students. Dr. Robinson asked whether you are here. In other words, you have an invitation...I suppose a tuxedo will not be necessary. If all the others do sport theirs, I shall feel perfectly at home with Shaffer suit—which is paid for—and my golf-ball tie."

Having finished the German language requirement and realizing how difficult it was to satisfy, Frank concluded that his college studies in German were woefully inadequate for his purposes: "Reading easy stories, poetry, and plays is a very inadequate preparation for anyone who expects to do anything with German history. I had to learn practically a new vocabulary when I came to the reading of history. So to make German study worthwhile for students who expect to do graduate work, reading along the line of their proposed work should begin soon after acquiring the rudiments of the language...Well I feel terribly relieved. Lovingly, Frank." (FGG to MJ, April 18, 1928)

Four days later, with the immediate push to complete the German requirement finished up, Frank began to doubt his willpower to complete the job. Frank wrote

Mama Josie: "Since I worked at such high tension for a number of weeks to get those language examinations off my mind, I find that after it is over, I am suffering from an attack of a feeling very much akin to laziness at times. The old philosophers held to the theory that the world is governed by two opposing forces such as light and darkness, good and evil, active and passive, industry and indolence, etc., and then man himself is a combination of these forces. I think I am a good illustration of this theory and sometimes it is doubtful which side will win. For half a day at least after my German examination I let indolence prevail. I did nothing but write letters, catch up with my correspondence work, and do more thinking and planning for the next campaign. Thursday morning Mr. Will had some difficulty in whipping me in line again. He is certainly a slave driver. But I am stepping along about as usual with the whip popping over my head occasionally as a gentle reminder that there is to be no letup in this matter."

The period of rest and enjoying the roses in Palo Alto was short lived. Responding to a question from Mama Josie as to his upcoming examinations, Frank continued: "Are the examinations ahead easier than the language exams? I should say not! I have only had a preliminary skirmish or two and they were bad enough. I am now facing an examination in nine different fields of history, must know the bibliography of each field, as well as know the history, besides I am required to know all about Historical Method, Research, and weighing of historical evidence added to his Historiography which involves a knowledge of the historical writers of Greece, Rome, Germany, France, England and the United States. I am almost afraid to go to my conference for fear something more will be heaped upon me. I have become an abject slave. Can you imagine yourself studying eight hours a day, day after day, week after week? I refuse to study Sunday night. That is my only rest time. I wish I could take things as easy as Belk [who was married and living with his wife in Palo Alto.] He goes to work at nine in the morning, takes noon out, of course, then unhitches for the day at 3 and goes home and does not study at night...If I do not put in eight hours I feel as though I have not done much." (FGG letter to MJ, April 29, 1928)

The bills were paid while Frank was in Palo Alto, but payments were sometimes delayed. Frank wrote: "The insurance [invoice] on the South 16th place came as a surprise...I have also paid my church subscription up to date so you can look everybody square in the face when you meet them. I am still digging, digging..." (FGG letter to MJ, May 2, 1928) Sometimes, it wasn't just bill payment that was delayed, but time to refresh his mind with some relaxation. Frank took little or no time for himself, though Mama Josie would encourage him to take some. Frank responded to one such suggestion, saying: "You are very nice and kind to suggest some reading for a time of relaxation but, my dear, there is no relaxation for this guy. I wonder sometimes how it would feel to be in a condition or state of mind without anything impending over me once again." (FGG letter to MJ, May 9, 1928)

No doubt he was lonely and starved for mental stimulation other than that involved in preparing his dissertation. Frank noted in his next letter: "Well, I have nothing new to write about. Each day passes just like the one before. Some days I go the entire day without talking to anyone except a few necessary words to the waiters. I hope you will not measure my love and appreciation for what you do by the length of my letters." (FGG letter to MJ, May 16, 1928)

Regarding whether Mama Josie should economize by releasing their domestic employee for the summer, he wrote: "It seems to me that if you need a servant at all, it is during the summer. There will be little saved when you pay for ironing and cleaning occasionally. So I would say keep your servant. Financially it is not at all necessary for you to do that work and I would rather you would not." (FGG letter to MJ, May 23, 1928)

Then, on a telegram appearing to be dated June of 1928, Frank had exciting news. The telegram read:

> "DA531 10=PALO ALTO CALIF 4 633 pm//MRS. F G GUITTARD=1401 SOUTH 8th WACO TEX//PASSED FINAL ORAL EXAMINATION//HOORAY THREE HOURS OF PUMMELING LOVE//FRANK."

Mama Josie kept Frank up to date with other news from the home front, just as if they were both at the table for lunch or supper. She would write again in August of 1928 as to his prior requests: "I got all the books you wanted, except one, at the Baylor Library and I will try the public library for that one. I looked through the list of Roosevelt books and there are 36 in all. They are sending the books directly from the library and they promised me they would get them off today—I will call Miss N___ tomorrow...I feel like you are making splendid progress on your thesis. I am real proud of you. All things good or bad always come to an end. Sonny and I went to a show this evening and we are just about ready to go to bed. We always like to get your letters. Lots of love, Josie" (MJ letter to FGG, August 15, 1928)

Frank's next letter confirmed Mama Josie's intuition regarding his progress: "I had my first, last and only conference of the summer with Dr. Robinson yesterday. I did not want to intrude on his vacation and then it was not really necessary. He was at the University of Washington the first part of the summer. He commended the amount of work I have done this summer, and approved my plans, and made some valuable suggestions for the future. It, of course, made me feel good after working all summer as I have. I have always believed in praise and commendation in teaching but shall be more careful than ever as I have realized keenly how much it means. Give my love and best wishes to all the folks." (FGG letter to MJ, August 22, 1928)

Though rarely effusive in expressing his feelings, Frank was not afraid to verbalize his appreciation to Mama Josie for her emotional and other support during this period. "You have been great in caring for the situation at home. I could never have accomplished what I did without your help. Then you have been kind and sweet in writing so often. Words cannot express my love and appreciation for the part you have taken this year." (FGG letter to MJ, August 25, 1928)

Frank returned to Baylor to teach at the end of August but was back in Palo Alto in June 1929 before Stanford's commencement for the prior year. Over time, Frank developed a friendly relationship with his thesis advisers, especially Dr. Robinson, and had extended an invitation to the Robinsons to stay with him and Mama Josie should they ever be in Waco. Robinson gave him a ticket to the Stanford baccalaureate services. Frank had already seen Stanford's commencement exercise, tickets to which were in high demand, and did not want to see it again, already having concluded, "I believe we can beat them." (FGG letter to MJ, June 15, 1929). Frank was settling in for the summer of 1929, but he was realizing the worst was not over yet. "I have had two conferences with Dr. Robinson since arriving. I realize more than ever that I have some steep climbing and difficult digging ahead of me. The only thing that affords a little consolation is that perhaps I have gone through ordeals just as bad before and got out in some fashion...As my old room was vacated today, I am back in the old place. You know how I like to do things in the same old way, and to wear the same old coat, etc. Well, I feel more at home in my old room."

Mama Josie, who possibly had not yet received the prior letter, wrote: "I am anxious to know the developments of the conference with Dr. Robinson. I hope the Martins [Dr. Martin being Frank's other faculty adviser] notify me if they are going to stop in Waco. I would like to have them, but I would like to know about it. Love and goodnight, Josie" (MJ letter to FGG, June 21, 1929)

Frank also reported in his next letter on his progress: "I am gathering up the threads where I left off. I had lost some of them. One consolation is that I have not had to register, which means $63.00 to the good. Well, my job gets tedious and tiresome toward the end of the day. I often wonder how long my term of punishment will have to last." (FGG letter to MJ, June 21, 1929)

The topic of whether Frank's dissertation upon completion could be marketed and sold with profit was interesting to Mama Josie, who liked to make a little extra money when she could. She made a few inquiries and advised: "Dr. Allen said that it cost him $500 to get his thesis published. He had to leave 500 copies with the university and he had some extra copies made for sale. I think 100, and he received a 50% royalty from them, so he got some of his money back. He said all but about 10 copies had been sold. They sold $1.50 per copy. Do you know anything about the expense of yours? If it costs that much, we will have to begin saving on many corners." (MJ letter to FGG, June 27, 1929)

Frank responded to Mama Josie's offer to economize at home: "As to the expenses connected with my thesis, the goal is so far off yet, that it seems like a joke to talk about expense. As far as I know, I shall be required to present three or four typewritten copies of the thesis to the Registrar and accompany it with $25.00 to pay the cost of binding. So you need not begin to economize yet for a while. I suppose Dean Allen's thesis represented some new field of work and there was a demand for the results of his investigation. Most theses are not worthy of publication. They are of little use or value to the writer and of still less value to the general reader. In fact, they are a lot of junk. I expect mine to be somewhat of that class. Probably you have heard of the student in Zoology who took as a subject for his learned doctor's dissertation 'A Study of the Organs of Secretion of a South Sea Turtle.' He spent months and months on this investigation; and of what good was it to him or anyone else? There is a whole lot of false value attached to the degree of Doctor of Philosophy. Would I say the same if I had one? Yes, I am pretty sure I would because I have gone through most of the gamut...Your letters are a great help when I have been digging hard all day and feel rather pessimistic as I am afraid you will characterize this letter." (FGG letter to MJ, July 3, 1929)

Both Mama Josie and Frank wrote each other even when there was little or nothing to write about, Frank noting: "You are so nice about writing, I feel that I ought to do better, but there is so little variation in my life these days that I have nothing to write about. Some days I think I am progressing pretty well, then again I get discouraged at the slow rate of progress, and later things clear up again, and so it goes. Once a week I do take time off to go to the movies. It usually gives me a few hours when I get my mind off my work. I don't care much what they have. They are all about alike; I just go when the time comes." (FGG letter to MJ, July 21, 1929)

Frank writing the same day in Palo Alto brought Mama Josie up to date on his pencil sharpener: "The only thing new in my household is that I got a pencil sharpener. It will rejoice Sonny Boy, I know, for it is a keen one. I got tired having my hands forever smeared up with black lead. I wish I had gotten one long ago. This is all the news I have." (FGG letter to MJ, July 24, 1929) Two days later, Mama Josie wrote Frank: "I know you get tired of the grind, but it will be over sometime. I just hope you won't work too hard. Take some time for your friends and take time to make some new friends. There will be other summers to work. You know about all work and no play." (MJ letter to FGG, July 26, 1929). Six days later, Mama Josie received the news regarding the pencil sharpener and responded: "Hurrah! For the new pencil sharpener, we will all use it when you get home. How far along is the thesis? Have you passed the note taking stage? In the last *Good Housekeeping* is an article on the Roosevelt children in the White House. I did not read it but I don't think it would be anything you can use." (MJ letter to FGG, July 30, 1929)

Frank's news to Mama Josie at the first of August was cautiously ambiguous, both hopeful and discouraged: "Sometime ago, my Adviser suggested that I should begin writing and continue my writing and research together. I have followed his suggestion. Up to the present I have ground out about 100 pages of manuscript. This takes up about five chapters and the preface, but there are still six or seven chapters to write and some of them longer than those already written; besides I will be obliged to do considerable investigation for some of them. I have turned in three of the chapters for criticism. The Adviser said it was interesting. That was quite an admission for a 'hard-boiled' professor to make, but he said enough other things to put that all in the shade. The two most discouraging were that it would be well to boil down two of the chapters to one, and that perhaps before I got through, it might be necessary to go to Washington City and do some digging in the archives. If he insists on that, I am 'blowed up' for I do not know when I could get through. As it is I do not doubt but that there will be still a lot left to do at the end of this month. So you can see there is nothing to give out. I have found that I get along better by writing with pencil on lined paper. I write closer even than in a letter and my pages usually make a page of typewritten matter. That gives some idea of what I have done. It is slavish work. I would be tempted at times to give it all up if it were not for the fact that you are so nice and loving about writing and carrying on at home. Probably I should not be discouraged for I was talking to a student the other day who said it took him over three months after he began writing. I have been at it about a month. Then too, I have that delay of three months work on another thesis too, which sets me back considerable or rather prolongs the time for completion. This is not very cheerful news but I thought you ought to know the situation." (FGG letter to MJ, August 3, 1929)

Frank's next letter brought news of a near catastrophe: "The other morning, I missed nearly all the manuscript I had prepared on one chapter of my document. I could not find it anywhere. I had put nearly a whole week on it and some real red blood had gone into it. I looked into all possible and impossible places for it and no manuscript. I began to have visions of having to do all that laborious work over again. Suddenly I remembered that the landlady had been in my room while I was out for a few minutes and had taken the trash basket down. I rushed down the stairs and roused the lady of the house and as calmly as the circumstances would permit, asked to see the trash that had been carried down. Lo and behold, there it was without a wrinkle in it, with some discarded correspondence work. I had been keeping it in the rocker near my right so that I would have it convenient for reference. As to whether I had put it in the waste basket in an absent-minded moment or whether the landlady had absent-mindedly picked it up with the rest of the trash, I did not stop to speculate or theorize but fervently thanked the Lord and ran upstairs with it. You can bet your bottom dollar that when I leave the room now and hereafter, I know exactly where I put my manuscript, so I shall be sure of it when I get back." (FGG letter to MJ, August 7, 1929)

Despite his feelings, Frank was steadily making progress, and his correspondence shows a definite change in mood in the next letter written to Francis. "I do not know when I received a letter that I appreciated more than the last one you wrote. If there is any French in my make-up, I suppose it is manifested in my volatile spirits. They go up and then down. When I received your letter they happened to be down...I have worked hard since coming here, dividing my time between writing and working in the library. So far, I have ground out about a hundred pages of manuscript. As I write closely on lined paper, so when it is typewritten, it makes nearly a page. But I do not know yet whether it is worth anything, and when I have my doubts, then is when I lose heart somewhat. I sure have need of a typist. So far, I have paid out about $20.00 and that is only a beginning. The typist charges from 20 to 25 cents per page including one carbon."

Mama Josie sympathized with Frank's momentary upset from misplacing a manuscript chapter. "A girl friend of mine was sick once and I put cold cream on her tooth brush for her instead of the dental cream. She did not appreciate the mistake very much. I hope the absent-minded professor does not have another hunt for his manuscript." (MJ letter to FGG, August 12, 1929)

In Frank's next letter to Mama Josie, he was unusually expansive about the dissertation. In so doing, he revealed much about his evident determination, including his belief that hard work would eventually accomplish the goal, and that the less said about one's progress toward a goal, the better: "I had my last conference Thurs. afternoon. It was the last because Dr. Robinson will be busy all next week as it is the closing week for the quarter. I feel better since the last conference. At the first one, the Doctor said my work was interesting and then proceeded to land on it with both feet. I did not expect it, of course, but fought back as best I could, however. I came away feeling I had not made much of an impression. At the second meeting, he said the work was interesting and well written and proceeded to land on it pretty emphatically again. I was prepared for him and gave him my interpretation and view of some things as well as my purpose and plan in treating the subject. He was very nice, and I came away feeling I had made some progress. I think they expect you to defend your work; at least, I did some logical talking. In the last conference when I presented two more chapters or had turned them in a week before the conference, there were a few criticisms on diction and construction and one suggestion about arrangement that he thought could be corrected as I went ahead. Then he said again that my paper was interesting and added, 'I like your work. I approve of your plan.' Of course, I felt pretty good, so much so that I took Thurs. night off and went to the movies or talkies. I prefer the movies. They are more restful."

Frank concluded his letter with words of caution: "Of course, this does not mean that my battles are over. They manage to keep you suspended until up close to the end. I have turned in about 120 pages of typewritten material, which has been read and returned. When it is all finished, it will be close to 300 pages. So I am not half through writing but is all outlined, and I know exactly what to do when I start in again. Usually when the Adviser approves the work, it is encouraging, but then a thesis has to run the gauntlet of the graduate committee at the last and a fellow don't know his fate until up to the last moment. So if anyone should make any inquiries about my work, it would be stating the matter conservatively to say that I seem to be making fair progress. That is about all that can be said or should be said; probably it is best to be conservative." These admonitions to Mama Josie were understandable given that Mama Josie was considerably more talkative than Frank and less guarded in her conversation, characteristics that earned her many friends. By 1929, the couple had been married for nine years and Frank knew her very well.

Frank continued: "I have worked hard, scrabbling and digging because both must go along together. I shall enjoy a good rest, but this last week [before returning to Waco] I will put in some good licks...I should add that Sat. Dr. Robinson phoned me to come out to his home Mon. 8 to 10 p.m. 'to meet the visiting teachers in the department and some of the older graduate students.' I have decided to get out a white shirt for the first time this summer and go." (FGG letter to MJ. August 25, 1929)

Mama Josie volunteered facetiously to assist in the typing and brought Frank up to date on Francis's love life: "Hope you got a good typist. Too bad your wife cannot do typing for you. Maybe I should take typing. Francis and C___ seemed to have had a sort of revival of friendship. I thought for a while L____ was the choice. The last time he was here, he took her picture back with him, and now he writes me to send her one of his pictures." (MJ letter to FGG, August 26. 1929)

The same day, Frank privately voiced to Francis two related personal concerns he had for his family, first regarding Mama Josie's blood pressure and the second Francis's driving, especially since Francis was going to be Mama Josie's driver on the trip to Palo Alto to meet up with Frank. Within the family, Francis was notorious for fast driving. Frank wrote Francis: "I received a letter from Mama Josie saying she had called on her doctor and was told that her blood pressure was up and that she should take it easy on her trip. I thought I should tell you this as she might not care to do so. I suppose it is the result of nervousness following the accident, which might have been very much worse. I know you will be careful not to do any hard driving. It seems to be the natural thing for a young fellow to go the limit when he has a good car. But I think there is always more or less risk in speeding. Machinery is not infallible, nor are the human senses nor the common sense of the other fellow. It is, of course, folly to take risks when there is no necessity for it. As for yourself, it would be greatly unfortunate to have to go through life maimed in arm or leg or head or, still worse, have a promising career snuffed out altogether. From the papers the 'speed devil' seems to be getting in his work out here on the coast. Here are a few clippings of what the papers carry daily. I hope you will not take this as 'grandfatherly advice' but as a word of caution from one who is more interested in you than anyone else. My last conference with my Adviser was very encouraging, and I am feeling better. I am glad that you have decided to be with us. With love, Papa" (FGG letter to FGG, Jr., August 26, 1929)

Nine months later, Frank was back at the same rooming house and in the same room in Palo Alto, commencing the final push for his degree. As many times as he had done it before, it was never easy: "It is agreeable to get back to familiar quarters, but as usual I cringe somewhat at getting down to this exacting work. But I shall be in the harness again in a few days." (FGG letter to MJ, June 2, 1930)

Frank commented further on his difficulty getting started in the next letter, and then on an unexpectedly good development where Dr. Robinson was concerned: "I have gotten back into the old routine again. It was somewhat discouraging at first. I had to go back and catch up the various lines of investigation where I left them. Had to do some rereading and find that I was a little careless in taking my last notes, thinking I would be able to use them before I left. So I did not take down references as carefully as I should have. I find it pays to be exact at first, and it saves time in the long run. It was interesting to note how one thing recalled something else until in a few days—I was back where I left off. I think I have had some good luck. Dr. Robinson told me last summer that he would not be here this summer and quite likely I would have to continue my work under someone else. I was certainly glad to learn at the conference I had with him Thurs. (5th) that he would be here this summer. It means much to me. You know I was already set back at least three months with my thesis by changing from Fish to Robinson, so I did not know what was in store for me when I came here this time. I handed him Chapter VII Thurs., as I had completed it before I left last summer but he did not have time to read it. I have nearly another chapter of about twenty pages ready for the typist, so you see I have been working some...If the chickens seem to get along all right, let them stay in their house, but if the heat debilitates them, in other words, seems to affect their laying, then try the open air roost." (FGG letter to MJ, June 7, 1930)

The next day, Frank wrote Francis, who had taken a real interest in his father's work and thesis and who had been allowed to make suggestions for corrections to the manuscript while in Palo Alto visiting his father. Frank confided to Francis: "I looked over your corrections the other night and appreciate them very much. Of course I had caught some of them in looking over the copy I submitted to Dr. Robinson and had not made them in the carbon copy which you read. But there were some I had overlooked. I find sometimes that I miss an error in looking over a page several times. I wish I could submit the dope to you before turning it in. I need you and Mama Josie as proof readers." Frank then returned to the theme of the loss of three months' work associated with efforts made while another adviser [Fish] had been in charge of his thesis, signing off with a reference to the nice weather in Palo Alto that his thesis constrained him from enjoying. (FGG letter to Francis, June 8, 1930)

One morning, Frank was gratified to note: "When I came back from breakfast this morning, what did I find where the folks place my mail? The Anniversary telegram from my Sweetheart! That was sweet and dear of you. I have everything to encourage me to make the most strenuous efforts to get on with my task—your love and interest. It takes something to hearten the victim of this drudgery. At times I am at it from morning till night and part of the night, in fact most of the times. I am making some progress." (FGG letter to MJ, June 10, 1930)

As Frank was coming into the homestretch of the last lap around the track, the outcome was never completely free from doubt, and there was no time that he didn't wish the project was over and that he was back in Waco with Mama Josie, Clarence, and the chickens. He wrote Francis: "To hear from someone at home always relieves the feeling I have while I am out here—that of a sort of an exile. It took a lot of ___, what Mama Josie doesn't like to hear us say, to rush away, and get out here to my task again. I followed my inclinations last year but I find that it is better usually when you have a disagreeable task to finish it up as soon as possible. I pass by one of these miniature golf courses on my way to meals occasionally and stop to watch the 'putting.' I itch to get hold of a club myself sometimes, but I know if I did, I would take the time I should be 'putting' at something else." (FGG letter to Francis, June 15, 1930)

Miles: What word didn't Mama Josie like to hear?

Pops: "Guts." Sometimes Frank felt that his work in Palo Alto was even worse than being exiled: "Just to let you know that I am still 'at it.' Sometimes it gets monotonous, and even worse. I sometimes stand at my window and look out at the deep blue sky, at the eucalyptus trees swaying in the breeze, at the birds as they flit from branch to branch, at the butterflies fluttering from flower to flower and feel somewhat like a prisoner serving out an unjust sentence with a ball and chain [the thesis] to his ankle condemned to sit at my table to dig and write, write, write. Of course, I am making some progress. Gen. Grant said, 'I am going to fight it out on this line if it takes all summer.' I will have to say the same thing, I suppose, and leave the 'if' out." (FGG letter to MJ June 29, 1930)

Frank noted encouragingly that during his first conference with Dr. Robinson concerning the chapter he had submitted, Dr. Robinson said: "It's interesting reading. I have only minor criticisms to make." Frank was encouraged by this response and advised Mama Josie: "I feel better since the conference. I think if it had been discouraging, I would have felt like 'taking out altogether.'" (FGG letter to MJ July 2, 1930)

Frank rarely referred to his somewhat overweight condition, although he commented on other health matters at length, especially where they concerned the health of Mama Josie, Francis, or Clarence. Frank let Mama Josie know: "One thing I have to be thankful for—and that is that I have been in better health than perhaps ever before while I was out here. I think I have been more careful because so much depends on it. I weighed an even 200 when I first came out here, but I am gradually remedying that. Don't think I am doing any desperate stints at reducing for I eat at least two good meals a day and never fail to have a good appetite. Walking, of course, is my chief exercise, and I never fail to get in some each day." (FGG letter to MJ, July 13, 1930)

Sometimes "friendly" busybodies made annoyingly judgmental remarks to Mama Josie, suggesting that Frank's trips to Palo Alto were really vacations. Frank's anger upon learning of such remarks erupted in sarcasm in his letter to Mama Josie: "That was a refreshing remark your friendly neighbor made about your martyrdom and my selfishness in monopolizing this fine climate. Tell her—be sure to tell her—that if she had the choice of taking my job, she would prefer an even still hotter place to live than Waco. In fact, some of the things I have had to go through during the years I have been out here would make h— itself seem a pleasant place to live in. So tell the old gossip that I am not out here for a summer outing. She needs to be set right." (FGG letter to MJ, July 23, 1930)

Frank did get tired of forever answering Mama Josie's questions about when he would be finished with his thesis, especially when he could only describe what kind of work he was doing, the vague usually positive responses of his adviser, and the number of thesis pages produced to date. He had started work on his doctorate seven years previously, and seven years later, he was still dutifully plodding along. There was no understood end date. It was all up to his adviser. Frank wrote Mama Josie in August:

> As to the thesis, yes, it is much more than half finished. When will I get through? Well, I cannot say yet but I think I can finish the writing this summer. I may have to stay somewhat later than usual. I strike a snag occasionally that holds me up.
>
> I do not understand why you should feel as you do about my short letters. I am doing only one thing and see very few people; sometimes I hardly speak to anyone all day. I leave my room only to go to meals and exercise, or I go out to the University and work from 8 A.M. to 10 P.M. and only take out a few minutes for dinner and supper. The document room is a good place to work. Very few students there, often at night I am the only one. I can spread things

> out on the wide tables and it is as quiet as in an underground dungeon. I have a light over me on the ceiling, the rest of the large room is in darkness.
>
> The ghosts of departed statesmen and diplomats hold their conferences in the dark corners while I dig into their reports, speeches, and communications. The ghosts don't bother me. I bother their documents. I find that these departed statesmen were pretty good fellows. They had good intentions for the most part and contributed their share to the progress of the world.
>
> When closing time comes, I take my grip and walk back to my room through the woods. When the old owl hoots 'Who, Who?' I answer back 'when? When will I get through?' And it makes me step a little faster. At night I wake up and the same question comes to me, and I resort to my old friend *The Literary Digest* to divert my mind.
>
> The first thing I think of in the morning is how long will it take to finish and I hurry and shave and dress to see how much I can do for the day. And so my life is going, working to get through and to get back home. So you see there is not much to write about. Just multiply all my words and lines by ten or more and that represents what my intentions and inclinations are. (FGG letter to MJ, August 10, 1930)

Although Frank worked hard to keep his mind free of worries, particularly health worries while in Palo Alto, the subject of health was never far from his mind. The death of Mamie to tuberculosis and the death of infant Charles to tubercular meningitis meant that he was forever on guard against illness or health weakness, in any form, from whatever the source, to himself or any of his family members. The other major worry was a concern about the difficulty of the task ahead of him. He wrote Francis: "You ask about the thesis. Well, I have gone to the top of the mountain and am coming down on the other side. You know, however, that coming down takes careful climbing as well as going up. So my descent is not on a toboggan or on skis. At times it is too much like the progress of a glacier coming through a gorge. But I am pretty well down. With love, Papa." (FGG letter to Francis, August 14, 1930)

At this point, Frank sent telegrams to both Mama Josie and Francis telling them, in substance, that he had finished his thesis. The telegram cannot be located to see what his exact words were, but Mama Josie in Waco and Francis in Victoria received two very different impressions. Francis replied: "Dear Papa—I wish I could be with you today to help you celebrate. It must be a great relief to have all that work off your hands. I know that Mama Josie is overjoyed. It took a lot of guts to go through with it all, & if anybody deserves to be called a 'Doctor of Philosophy' you certainly do...When will I be able to read the completed manuscript? And when are they going to christen you? With love, Francis" (Francis letter to FGG, August 23, 1930)

Mama Josie, however, sent a telegram response to Frank's message that did not explicitly acknowledge Frank's news that he had completed his dissertation, simply saying, "Just received your message." Since Mama Josie's telegram is not available, two interpretations are possible. First, that she did not want to pay the per word expense of a more expansive telegram, or second, more likely, that she did not fully understand his telegram, which is also not available. In any event, Frank, in the following letter, indicates he concluded that she did not understand his telegram and wrote her:

> Awfully glad to get your letter today...It shows that you did not understand my telegram. I sent the same message to Francis and he sent me a rousing letter of congratulation. Your letter merely said: 'Just received your message.' It made me feel awfully bad after working as I have all these years. I did not get over it for hours. But your letter today shows you did not get the real import of the telegram. So you see that I was glad to know that you did not understand my telegram, for you could not blame me for feeling badly after going through everything I have and sending a message telling that I had finished my thesis, 'finished writing,' to be told, 'Just received your message' and nothing more. So my dear, it is not yet too late for congratulations. I know the message was somewhat misleading.
>
> All summer, my plan has been to write a chapter, give it to the typist, get it back and proof-read and correct it. The average has been two chapters a week of from 15 to 24 pages. Each week these two chapters of type written material would be given to the Adviser and those of the preceding week returned. This program was followed each week until last Friday I finished writing the last chapter. At that point I sent the telegram. The great load was off my mind and heart.
>
> I handed the last two chapters to Dr. R. yesterday. Tues. he asked me to let him have all the preceding chapters as he wanted to read it all over a second time. He has the entire thesis now—twenty-two chapters—over 426 pages. I will get it all back tomorrow. Thurs. Then it will be necessary to revise it and have it retyped. The revising is the uncertain element. I do not know how long it will take after I get the thesis back. It depends on how much change is advised and what points have to be looked up. In the meantime I am putting in every minute, so that when I get the document in my hands again there will only be the revision and retyping necessary. I am preparing a biography of the

author—about a page. This is to be handed in with the thesis, also [an] abstract of approximately 1500 or 2000 words on the entire thesis...

I hope to have the biography, the abstract, and bibliography completed by tomorrow morning, Thurs. 28, when I have my final conference, and get the thesis back. My plan is to revise it, turn it over to the typist, and pull out for home. The typist will send me the thesis, I will proof-read it, and send it to Dr. R. He will submit it to the graduate study committee during the fall quarter. He has kindly offered to superintend the binding of the thesis for me, and will return my copy, while the University keeps two copies, one for the library and one for the Department of History.

That is the whole story. I am putting in every minute. I even worked late Sunday night after spending the day in San Francisco and Berkeley, and night and day since. This has been written hurriedly, but I hope I have made everything clear. I was even more disappointed than you that I could not finish sooner, but I have done all a human could. I have never worked so hard and so continuously in my life. The only break during the summer was Sat. afternoon and Sunday of last week. With much love, Frank (FGG letter to MJ, August 27, 1930)

On August 28, 1930, Frank had his very last conference with Dr. Robinson regarding his thesis. Frank wrote Mama Josie: "Had my last conference this morning. The first draft of the entire thesis was returned after Dr. Robinson read it all the second time. Can you imagine how good I felt when he said: 'It is an excellent piece of work.' He told me that Dr. Fish had also read and approved it. My task now is to make some suggested revisions, and have it re-typed. I hope to have it ready for retyping by the middle of next week and then I shall pull out for Texas...Dr. R. said he thought the [Graduate Study] Committee would not make much change in it. With the approval of two hard-boiled professors like Robinson and Fish I am hopeful that the [graduate] study committee will not find much fault with it." (FGG letter to MJ, August 28, 1930)

During commencement exercises the next year, Frank was awarded his Doctor of Philosophy degree from Leland Stanford Junior University. Baylor faculty colleague Henry Trantham noted in the *Baylor Monthly* for November: "On occasion of his graduation there last June, Professor Guittard was accosted by an indiscreet reporter who came right out and asked him his age. It is recorded that Professor Guittard suggested to the youngster that his question was decidedly irrelevant. 'But,' persisted the journalist, 'are you not planning to retire from active teaching, now that you have taken the Ph.D. Degree?' 'Why, no,' replied F.G., 'I am prepared to go to work in earnest!'—a predictable response from Frank Guittard."

As a final note to Frank's Ph.D. saga, one student recalled that Frank was concerned that students might think he had gotten his Ph.D. at an "easy university" because he earned it at Leland Stanford, Jr. University. Mama Josie surely heard the same comment from Frank more than once, yet she had to smile when he complained about the drudgery accompanying his years in Palo Alto. He was proud of his achievement and gratified by the recognition he received from his students.

Miles: Frank must have been excited to get it all over with and be able to go home and sleep in his own bed and get up in the morning to the sound of the rooster in the backyard and have waffles for breakfast.

Pops: Yes, the wheel of fortune was now swinging back in the right direction for a while.

Miles: Wheel of fortune? You mean like on TV?

Pops: No, like the wheel of fortune, which Boethius talked about in his sixth-century book, *The Consolation of Philosophy.* Frank's experiences in the library "dungeons" at Stanford must have reminded him of Boethius's experience, although of an entirely different order of magnitude since Boethius was imprisoned under sentence of death.

Miles: Maybe philosophy would have helped Frank better endure all those lonely months in Palo Alto.

Pops: Maybe, maybe not. In Boethius's work, a character named Lady Philosophy tells Boethius that our world is not created by chance but by a divine creator, and that fortune cannot bring true happiness but only things that are transient, like wealth, power, and honor. Frank wrote home that he considered his room in California was little better than a "dungeon." Frank, who would have been familiar with Boethius, knew that Boethius was eventually tortured and executed in an extremely unpleasant manner and was never able to leave the prison in which he wrote *The Consolation.* Then too, Frank had Mama Josie as his "pepper-upper" to help him ride out his lonely sabbaticals. Boethius was all alone, without an encourager other than Lady Philosophy, a construct of his imagination; he had nothing to look forward to but an assured gruesome fate.

Miles: If Boethius had only known that his book would eventually be published and widely read, maybe that would have been a slight consolation. Maybe if Frank had thought his dissertation had a ghost of a chance of being published, that would have provided some comfort for his labors.

Pops: Well, that's a thought, but it doesn't seem to have worked out that way for Frank, who never intended to publish his dissertation. In the *Consolation,* Boethius quotes Euripides in his play *Andromache*: "O fame, fame! Full many a man ere now of no account hast thou to high estate exalted." So maybe speculating on his own future fame would not have been that consoling to Boethius either.

Miles: That's really heavy stuff. Okay then, thinking back to Boethius would not have been that comforting for Frank. So hopefully, Frank was able to lighten up a bit when he went to movies in Palo Alto. What movies did he see while he was out there in the summers?

Pops: Yes, Boethius's misery would not have made good company for Frank's moods. As for the films he saw, Frank would have been able to watch both silent films, which he called "movies," and films where there was an audio of the actors talking, which he called the "talkies." Frank doesn't name any movies that he was able to see—perhaps he did not want Mama Josie to think he was having a "hilarious good time" while in California working on his Ph.D. Indeed, even if he had been so inclined, nothing good would have come from discussing movies with Mama Josie, who rarely mentions going to a movie in any of her letters to him. However, we know which films came out from 1923 through 1930 that he could have seen. Here are some of the movies in those years that he might have enjoyed if he had seen them but not wanted to admit it to Mama Josie: *The Hunchback of Notre Dame* (silent with Lon Chaney); *The Ten Commandments* (silent directed by Cecil B. DeMille); *The Thief of Bagdad* (silent with Douglas Fairbanks); *Greed* (silent directed by Erich von Stroheim); *Ben-Hur: A Tale of the Christ* (silent with Ramon Novarro); *What Price Glory* (silent with Edmund Lowe); *The General* (silent with Buster Keaton); *The Birth of a Nation* (silent directed by D.W. Griffith); and *Abraham Lincoln* (talkie with Walter Huston directed by D.W. Griffith).

One would think all of these—whether silent or talkie—would have kept Frank awake and, at a minimum, *What Price Glory*, *The General*, and *Abraham Lincoln* would have been engrossing for Frank because of their historical subjects. *Ben-Hur* would have been interesting because of its religious subject, if not because of the chariot race at the end. *The Birth of a Nation*, the 1915 D.W. Griffith classic credited with playing a role in the emergence of the second Ku Klux Klan in the late 1910s-early 1920s, would have been compelling viewing for Frank. However, we believe he would have deplored its fanciful romanticizing of the Old South, its promotion of the Lost Cause Ideology, and the emergence of the Reconstruction Era Ku Klux Klan. We mentioned earlier in the chapter discussing Waco and the KKK that Frank was part of the faculty committee of five condemning the white supremacists' lynching of Jesse Washington in 1916.

Miles: Pops, I would like to go back to all those German professors Frank was saying goodbye to earlier today. Can you tell if any of them influenced his own view of history and how he taught it?

Pops: Miles, that's not a bad question; we can make some solid conclusions here. Most of those German historians he was required to read had no significant bearing on his dissertation subject, or on Frank, or the way he taught history. Some of those historians, like Heinrich von Treitschke, the son of a Saxon general and a member of the Reichstag, had strongly held political agendas and pro-German biases. Treitschke supported authoritarian power politics unchecked by the German parliament and argued for Prussian military power to be used to unify Germany. Because of his lack of objectivity in all matters regarding Germany and its position in the world, Treitschke's failure as a historian was obvious when compared to his contemporary Leopold von Ranke. Ranke came from a family of Lutheran pastors and attorneys, and while he had his own predispositions in certain areas, he argued strongly that the historian's task was to find out and reveal what had actually happened (*wie es eigentlich gewesen*). According to Caroline Hoefferle, "Ranke was probably the most important historian to shape [the] historical profession as it emerged in Europe and the United States in the late 19th century." Professor Leonard Krieger argued that Ranke believed history research should be based on facts, yet he wanted to find universal meaning in the human past.

Miles: It sounds like Frank's views on teaching history would have been more in sync with Ranke than Treitschske, and he was possibly influenced by him.

Pops: I think you are right. Frank taught history primarily as a chronological set of carefully selected and arranged facts involving people, countries, and geographical relationships with causation largely determined from the order and relationship of those facts. Thus, he had much in common with Ranke and little in common with Treistschske, who was an authoritarian as a historian, which would have been anathema to Frank. Frank's method relied heavily on selecting authoritative texts in which he had confidence and then using the recitation method to quiz the students over the facts of history as revealed in the text; in other words, to make sure the students knew what had actually happened. Frank had to have confidence in the authors' selection and arrangement of facts and their stated conclusions as to causation.

Miles: I don't understand what you just said.

Pops: Basically, it's about starting with the facts. Frank's view was that history is finding out, as Ranke said, what the facts are or were—what really happened, not what people would like to think happened or should have happened or what they want people to believe happened to promote some political agenda. We will talk about this more when we get to the students' memories of Frank as a classroom teacher.

Miles: Going back to Roosevelt and conservation, nobody is talking about conservation anymore. It's all about the environment, global warming, fires, floods, and pandemics. How do you think Frank would have come down on these subjects?

Pops: Miles, this is an opinion only. Roosevelt's primary interest was in preserving our natural resources for the general public and for outdoorsmen, including hikers, campers, hunters, and fishermen. In a sense, although conservationists and environmentalists have had strong points of difference, the environmentalism movement is an extension of conservation which emphasized national forests, national parks, wildlife, and national monuments. Frank cared more about the out-of-doors broadly than about hunting and fishing specifically. He would have been sympathetic with many of the goals the environmentalists advocate for, whether it be reforestation, recycling, or pollution control, and would have been leery of letting businesses destroy these national resources just as he would have been sympathetic to Roosevelt's trust-busting program. As for global warming, Frank was never anti-science, and he would have had an open mind where the findings of scientists were concerned. On viral pandemics, Frank probably would have supported masks, testing, social distancing, and scientists' findings, as he was often preoccupied with health concerns.

Miles: Was Frank glad he now had his Ph.D.?

Pops: Well, he was glad his studies were at an end. But if you are asking me whether he would do it all over again, you tell me. Here is the evidence: he told a reporter in Palo Alto when he received his Ph.D. he was now prepared to go to work in earnest [as a teacher]; he told his former student and colleague Guy B. Harrison, Jr. not to go for a Ph.D. and that he [Frank] got nothing from it, didn't go up in rank, didn't get one more dollar, in fact, went into debt, and if he had to do it over again, he would not do it. Nevertheless, according to Harrison, Frank liked being called "Dr. Guittard" and also posing for his portrait in his academic robe. That portrait hung in the Mickle Studio's window for years. So, was he glad he had made the extended effort to obtain his Ph.D.?

Miles: Can't tell. Sounds like he had mixed feelings. But why didn't he send his dissertation off to a publisher to review?

Pops: He told his colleague, Jefferson Bragg, mostly in jest, he was concerned it would get lost in the mail. His real reason came out in his letters—he didn't think anyone would be interested in publishing this sort of academic treatise, as there would be little or no audience for it. Professor Bragg disagreed but didn't want to argue with him. My guess is he thought it would mean a lot more work, more out-of-pocket expenses for typing, more time he wouldn't have to play golf, and that at the end of his effort, no publisher would want it. The self-publishing industry didn't exist yet, and he was probably right that his dissertation, even if reworked for the purpose of sale, wouldn't have generated much revenue in the 1930s.

Miles: I am wondering, too, about how he might have viewed, looking backward, his late-life decision to pursue a Ph.D., considering that he always seemed to be in a race against the clock to obtain his initial degrees so that he could get a college teaching position. You said it took him from 1885 to 1902 (seventeen years) for his education before Stanford. And yet there he was again at Stanford without an end in clear view, the oldest student in the room, not sure when he would be through, or how many summers he would have to spend in that "dungeon" of an archives room at Stanford.

Pops: You are right—the slow pace of progress generally of his academic career and his work on a doctorate must have been depressing, considering the shortness of human life, coupled possibly with feelings that his choice of an academic career was possibly a serious mistake, but that it was too late to do anything about it. I will not repeat it here, but in an earlier chapter I attempted to capture Frank's evolving game plan, setting out some thoughts on his own perception of his progress.

Miles: I remember that chapter. You assumed that Frank might have wondered if he would live about the same number of years as his father. With that assumption, Frank was always behind others in moving forward on his life plan. To be honest, I didn't follow all the math based on that assumption, but I don't need to hear all of that again. What I would like to know is how Frank kept his mind off those heavy thoughts at Stanford and stayed focused on getting his work done and getting home? I'm also wondering how the money part of it worked out for him and Mama Josie. Did they go into the hole?

Pops: It wasn't always easy. Except for 1928, he was only spending summers at Stanford. When he was there, he regularly exercised; took some time off to go to the movies; dined at restaurants he liked, including the Snow White Creamery; and kept up with certain Sunday funnies including "The Bungle Family," "The Gumps," and "Ben Webster." I have some of those strips at home if you would like to look at them sometime. And, of course, he wrote letters to Mama Josie, Francis, and Clarence and read their letters to him, which always gave him a lift. "The Bungle Family" strips from the summer of 1929 when Frank was in California are funny, and Frank would have appreciated them. The June 16 strip for the Sunday after he arrived in Palo Alto would have gotten a chuckle; it showed George Bungle in his lodge costume and with a sword—Frank was a longtime Mason—and he was tripping over his sword. The June 30 strip focused on Bungle thinking he may have forgotten his anniversary, which happened to Frank while in Palo Alto—Frank and Mama Josie married on June 10, 1920. Perhaps the funniest from 1929 is the July 21 strip with George Bungle enthusiastically talking up stewed tripe at the beginning of the strip, but by the strip's final panel, recoiling at the pungent smell.

As for the money part, earning a doctorate was always a dubious financial proposition. Frank's total compensation from Baylor was not raised one dollar and he and Mama Josie went into debt; we don't know the amount. All their sources of income together—salary, rental houses, roomers, correspondence courses, and any trust money for Francis and Clarence—were insufficient to defray the total cost of his sabbaticals, which must have included transportation, lodging, tuition, food, books, typist, and other expenses after being added to all their other expenses. However, Frank retained his position as history chair until he stepped down fifteen years later.

Miles: Wouldn't Frank and Mama Josie's lives together have been very satisfying now that he had already climbed the final mountain and faced all the dragons he would ever encounter?

Pops: Yes, I agree, but it's too bad we don't have many letters for the last nineteen years of his life to know what they had to deal with during that period. A lot of teaching and mentoring of graduate students, catching up with returning students on their lives, families, and careers, and a lot of golf. Probably some additional health problems, too, considering their ages. And, of course, many more students, classes, and commencements.

Miles: Wouldn't it have gotten boring for Frank without a mountain to climb or a dragon to fight?

Pops: (*grinning*) Well, there was always honeymoon bridge with Mama Josie if ever he got tired of reading about Oliver Cromwell, Roosevelt, or Bismarck. Speaking of mountains, I've heard learning to play golf is like climbing a mountain.

Miles: (*smiling*) Well, that's no lie. I'm still trying to get the hang of it.

BOOK NINE

Classroom Teacher & the Grindstone of History

Sample questions for the peanut gallery's consideration in this book's chapters:

What sort of teacher was Frank? What was his method for teaching history, and how did it evolve? What was his usual class routine like? Was he a demanding teacher? Did he tell jokes or funny stories? Did he ever act out scenes from history or impersonate historical figures? Did he lecture—if so, were his lectures lengthy? If he had misplaced his little notebook on any given day, would he have been able to conduct class? Did he assign heavy homework? Why the pocket watch and not a wristwatch? Why did he dye his hair? How effective was his teaching style? What kind of relationship did he have with his students? What did his students think of his classes?

Excerpts from Frank's "Funny-Book of Student Bone-heads" on examinations:

Question: "What were indulgences?" Answer: "This was got [sic] from a treasury of merits and sold to him. This was a sure pass to heaven. He didn't have to work when he got there."

Question: "What was the age of Pericles known for?" Answer: "During the age of Pericles Greece was in a perfect turmoil all the time."

Examples of Frank's favorite words and phrases from his correspondence:

"blowed up" — "If the adviser insists on that, I am 'blowed up' for I do not know when I could get through."

"strenuous" — "I have everything to encourage me to make the most strenuous efforts to get on with my task."

"a bit" — "I feel a bit resentful at the way I was taught German."

CHAPTER 35

The Professor Who Put "Sys" in "System" (1902-1950)

So, what was Frank Guittard like as the teacher of 10,000 students during his forty-seven years at Baylor? Two other sections give a sense of his teaching style: the first is the prologue which included a recreated History 105 class; the second is the final chapter containing Professor David Smiley's tribute. This chapter adds to those other descriptions the following bits of detail: his physical appearance, including his hair and the clothes he wore; his signature classroom props—his pocket watch, notebook, and gradebook; his classroom personality and manner of speaking; his humor; his reaction to cheating on exams; his soft spot for certain students; late-career declining vision and hearing; and the components of his classes—recitation and questioning, occasional class discussion, and a rare debate. Finn volunteered to tag along on this one, and since both Finn and Miles said that they liked the title, Miles may jump in from time to time, too.

Pops: Before I started researching this book, I talked in person to several former students of Frank Guittard. They all liked Professor Guittard and possibly didn't want to say anything negative about him to blood kin. I did wonder, however, if some of these students were pulling their punches. After all, a quirky nursery rhyme about a professor from the late 1600s goes, "I do not like thee, Doctor Fell, the reason why I cannot tell; but this I know, and know full well, I do not like thee, Doctor Fell."

Fortunately, later, when I received written responses from seventy-five former students of Frank Guittard to my inquiries, there was no "Dr. Fell" problem with gathering student responses, mostly positive and some negative, about Frank Guittard. Those students were more than willing to "tell." History professor Ralph L. Lynn, a colleague of Frank's, had advised me to gather all available information I could about Frank Guittard, "warts and all." Another history department colleague, Guy B. Harrison, Jr., said it was not too late to find former students still living, but it soon would be. From 1978 through 1980, I attempted to contact as many of Frank's students as possible by letter and by ad in the *Baylor Line* to send me their recollections of Frank, his history classes, and his teaching method. The students responded eagerly and discussed their memories of the history professor from their college years long past. Insofar as I could tell, they did not hold back negative comments, and both kinds of comments are included in this chapter. I pieced this chapter together from one hundred letters from seventy-five students in

Frank Guittard's history classes between 1914 and 1950. Those one hundred letters made it clear that the students agreed as to Frank's characteristics as a teacher and his method. I will cite some forty or so of those letters from twenty-seven students; for example, "(*D. Applewhite*)." All former students' letters were received between 1978 and 1980.

Finn: That was a lot of stamps to lick, Pops. Did you use one of those gadgets that licks the stamps for you? I would like to hear what his students had to say about Frank's teaching and whether he was B-O-R-I-N-G.

Pops: Nope, I did it myself. Before we get into the students' specific responses, many students viewed Frank as follows: "Then we saw wandering among a vast ocean of books a man who held in his hand a mighty magnifying glass, through which he peered intently. 'It is Prof. Guittard, and he seeketh to bring out the points in the history of the world,' explained our guide." For another perspective on Frank as a teacher, we might contrast his teaching style with that of A.J. Armstrong, Frank's contemporary and legendary English Department professor. Frank, a professor of history, had a distinctly different approach from that of colleague Armstrong, whose lifetime contributions brought important recognition to the school on the Brazos. The most obvious difference was that, although both men inspired their students, they were poles apart in the ways they inspired them. Armstrong, a charismatic peerless motivator with a singular passion to establish the world's foremost Browning collection at Baylor, attracted to his classes unusually enthusiastic adherents. Armstrong, a workaholic of uncommon ambition, required only a few hours of sleep at night. He not only taught English classes, took students on tours to Europe, and purchased Browning items for his collection, but he also taught a large Sunday school class at First Baptist of Waco. In his English classes and his Sunday school class, he preached a strong self-realization message using Robert Browning's poetry as a treasure chest of lofty thoughts poetically expressed. His female students were particularly taken with him; many helped him raise funds to build the Armstrong-Browning Library, considered by many the most beautiful building on the Baylor campus.

Frank, unlike Armstrong, held his cards close to his vest and disdained effusiveness in himself and others. His manner of speaking was soft and deliberate, and his students had to be attentive to hear. (*Ms. L. Blaylock*). Frank's method focused on grilling the students as to the facts of history obtained from their texts and inspired them to draw cautious conclusions from them, particularly the causation of one event or fact by other facts and events. Thus, what Frank imparted to his students was not a challenge to his students to aspire ever higher, or hold fast to one's dreams, but rather a muscular discipline in how to think based on the facts of the past, which they could draw upon for the rest of their lives to interpret the events of the day. Frank strongly felt, along with Professor Edward Hallett Carr, that the benefits from a study of history arise from the study of causes. Herodotus of Halicarnassus, considered the father of history, stated that he intended in his classic work *The Histories*—written in 430 BC—to give the *cause* of the hostilities between the Greeks and the non-Greeks.

In time, Frank's range of knowledge in world history became extremely broad, and, at one point, he taught nearly all the advanced courses at Baylor. Nevertheless, we believe he used the same teaching style for his entire teaching career. The incentive to the student to prepare carefully for class was avoiding embarrassment when Frank called on him or her. Full class periods would consist of rapid-fire questions over the assigned reading. Open books on laps during recitation were discouraged. (*B. Massie*). On one occasion, a student tore out the pages from the text and brought them to class concealed in his notebook. This practice lasted almost all the term, but eventually, the student became careless and was caught; the student being more embarrassed by the class's amusement than by Frank's reproach. (*B. Massie*).

Frank did not lecture, although he would often make extended comments at the end of a day's recitation and questioning. Recitations were commonly used in teaching at many grade levels, from elementary through collegiate. As an inquisitor, Frank Guittard was neither arrogant nor abrasive. He was dignified, courtly, gentle, firm, dependable, controlled, relentless, and, above all, methodical. He addressed students formally as "Mr." or "Miss" and, in return, expected to be addressed formally and with respect. He showed no penchant toward flamboyance and made assertions of fact only after a lengthy and deliberate review of the facts. A characteristic remark of his was "I'll take that under advisement," meaning either that he had insufficient facts to come to a conclusion on the matter at hand, or that he was skeptical of some assertion made by a student. Frank's remark would often have a humorous or sarcastic twist.

Frank prepared for class by outlining the textbook in each course in one or more medium-sized student notebooks. These notebooks, although harmless enough in appearance, obviously provided the rounds he fired at the students. Armed with a gradebook in one hand and his notebook in the other while keeping a close watch on the time remaining in the class period, a locked and loaded Frank Guittard would move down the row one student at a time, firing questions at the student. The students had no idea what was in the professor's notebook. The yellowish color of its ancient pages intrigued them, and it was suspected by some that if Frank ever misplaced his notebook, there was no way class could meet. An unsubstantiated rumor arose of a class cancellation on one occasion involving a supposed payoff to Frank's younger son [Clarence] for hiding the notebook. Students also speculated whether the notebook would last the entire course—it always did—and whether the occasional jokes he told were set out in his notebook—they were not. The students did not know that Frank might have three to seven notebooks in any particular course, depending on the length of the text.

Frank especially emphasized geography and the great figures of history. Every student was required to buy *Shepard's Historical Atlas* and be prepared to locate cities, countries, and rivers mentioned in the daily readings. On tests, the students were responsible for every geographical place-name found in the text. One student recalled that he was always required to locate five geographic features on each test and that the locations had to be exact; Frank did not give obvious features. (*J. Chisholm*). Occasionally, students might be required to draw a map from memory, but most of the time, he instructed them to answer in sentence form; for example, if the question was "Venice" the student should say "seaport," and then, "in northeastern Italy at the head of the Adriatic Sea." That was a sufficient location. If the question was "Danube," then the student might say, "a river rising in the northern slopes in the Alps in southern Germany, flowing generally eastward through southern Germany, Austria, and Hungary and the Balkans into the Black Sea."

Few debates got started or were encouraged, especially in lower-level survey courses. To avoid controversy, Frank seldom said anything which could be quickly challenged; he disapproved of historical theories that amounted to mere speculation. Confronting students regarding their daily assignments was not intended to produce controversy, but only to elicit material from the lesson. The questions that he asked had definite answers to be found in the text. Since practically everything he said came out of the text and he did not offer any interpretations of the text, he did not expect to be challenged by students. On one occasion, he mispronounced the place-name "Michilimackinac" as if it ended in a "k" sound. One student wisely refrained from drawing attention to this error in front of the class and waited until all the other students had left the room at the end of the hour to approach the desk to tell Professor Guittard that he thought he said it wrong. Frank turned bright red but controlled his temper, thanked the student, and the next day corrected himself in class. (*D. Smiley*).

A student of Frank's course in the diplomatic history of the United States distinctly remembered that in "one class session...he departed from his notes and had us debate the quotation, 'My Country, may she always be in the right, but right or wrong, my country'...I was sitting to one side of where he sat at his raised desk near the front, and as emotions grew more heated I saw him put his hand over the lower part of his face in a vain attempt...to hide a broad smile. [Frank] was absolutely delighted at the response he had evoked and vastly amused at some of the intense feelings displayed...I felt closer to him because he obviously viewed history as I did, not as a dry, boring account of past events, but as a living, vibrant story of experiences created by men and women who had preceded the present. People who were as real as our contemporaries, who lived, loved, acted, and reacted to their environment and motivations in a way which culminated in the world as we know it today." (*J. Ronk*).

In advanced courses, Frank encouraged more discussion. One day, knowing that a student was from Louisiana, he indirectly encouraged a debate on the topic of Huey P. Long by looking directly at a student from Louisiana when Long's programs and unorthodox methods were being discussed. There ensued a heated discussion where Frank used current events to generate interest in history. (*G. Hitchcock*). One student, who later became chair of another department at Baylor, remembered the course in US foreign policy he took from Frank when Frank was in his late sixties. He said the class was "one of the most exciting ones he had as an undergraduate" and that Frank raised questions for class discussion and responded to questions raised by students. *(W.J. Kilgore*).

His students remembered Frank's physical appearance. He was neatly attired but not flashy. Always in coat and tie, he wore high, well-starched detachable collars, which contrasted with his pinstriped shirts. There was something about those detachable collars which fascinated some of the students. They were crisp and clean and perfect. Some of his male students sought to emulate him in this respect. One recalled: "My desk-mate in his class...who today is high in the state's judiciary, consequently became thoroughly hipped out over detachable collars. During occasional meetings after these many years, we seldom fail to allude to the collar episode." (*C. Maurer*). Frank also filled his suits well and looked very solid. In later years, he had an expansive stomach or spare tire around his middle, which was, in the opinion of one student, partially obscured by a steel ribbed girdle. One student remembered him as a tall, stocky man with blue eyes. (*B. Macormick*).

Frank's hair began to draw the attention of his students beginning in the 1930s. They remembered his hair vividly, regularly changing color from gray to auburn or reddish to dark brown or black, and then back to gray again before a new application of hair dye. (*W.M. Stoker*). As to the dark-dyed portion of his hair, the students noted when the gray roots started showing and would speculate about how soon it would be before he would come in with a fresh application of dye. One student remembered that, on occasion, he would dye his hair black; another remembered reddish-brown or auburn, and another brown, but safe to say, it was a dark color with a reddish tint. Because Room 202 of Old Main did not have air conditioning, the students would note that as Frank started to sweat, his gray hair would start showing very quickly. (*D. Heard*). Apart from the color of his hair, Frank did one thing that was stylish at the time, combing his hair from front to back, a style called "roaching," in which a roll of hair was pushed up from the forehead or temple on one side or the other or both. (*B. Massie*). In later years, Frank tended to comb his hair straight back without a part. One student remembered that at some point, Frank also dyed his eyebrows. (*Ms. N. LaGrone*).

Finn: All that hair stuff is kind of interesting, but isn't it superficial? Those students, Jeez! I am curious to know why he dyed his hair, but I'm more interested in whether he was a regular guy and had a sense of humor.

Pops: As to why, I'm not sure, but we know he was taught well into his senior years and needed his salary. Baylor did not have a retirement program then. He was also eighteen years older than Josie. Yes, he was a regular guy, and even though he was formal and dignified, his students liked him and believed that he was interested in all of them. Frank's affection for his students reminded one student of author James Hilton's fictional teacher, "Mr. Chips." (*Ms. M. Bigham*). Just before finals, one history major had to have an emergency appendectomy and consequently missed her final exams. Since she was hoping to graduate in May, she approached Frank to schedule a make-up. According to the student, "Dr. Guittard...asked me how many history courses I had [taken] and when I said 'eight,' he said, 'With that many you deserve to get excused from one then.' He was the only one of my professors who did not give me a make-up final!" (*Ms. R.V. Gibbs*).

Despite the natural gulf separating a professor from a student, especially in the first half of the twentieth century, and the formality required by Frank, students felt affectionate toward him. This feeling arose because of his kind and forbearing nature, his focus on the facts of history, and perhaps more than anything else, his devotion to his students. (*D. Applewhite*). Frank told his graders that most students taking survey courses of history could develop an interest in history if not offended or discouraged by an arrogant, harsh-grading, slave-driving professor. Accordingly, he was reasonable in his expectations, and his assignments were consistent with their being enrolled in other classes. For these students, he also sought to intrigue their curiosity to read further in whatever era the students found interesting. For this purpose, he attempted to convey little eccentricities and human frailties of historical figures to pique students' interest. (*D. Heard*).

His regard and affection for his students manifested itself in subtle ways, including his standing by the door with a twinkle in his eye as they passed out of the classroom and by other random acts of kindness. He would often speak to a student as the student was leaving and ask how things were going. (*D. Smiley*). On one occasion, a girl who was reciting in front of the class started to faint, whether from the heat or illness, and Frank left his desk to be sure she did not fall down. (*C. Offerman*). Another time, one student was allowed to take a make-up test because "no way would he take one on Friday the 13th." (*C. Offerman*). Frank had a particular soft spot for country boys like himself, many of whom had managed to make their way to college despite a weak high school education. To many ignorant country boys, Frank represented the best of what they eventually wanted to become—cultured, philosophical, patient, gentle, and kind. One student said he believed that Frank "had a sympathy and understanding for those—like many of the ministerial students—whose knowledge was deficient in background since they came from poor country schools." (*R.G. Winchester*). Often these students had difficulty paying for their education, and where possible, Frank would offer them the opportunity to make a little extra money by being his grading assistant. One student recalled: "I came back in January of 1919 after being dismissed from the Army in World War I. Prof. Guittard offered me a job as student assistant and gave me one class for which I was responsible. That job meant much to me because it helped the poor boy who had no money." (*W.P. Clement*). Another student recalled that Frank's fine letter of recommendation was essential to securing a job. (*D. Gibb*)

Although Frank was generally kind and courteous with his students, situations did arise that could not be ignored and required a harsher response. When students persistently failed to read assignments or continually came into class late, Frank chastised them with mild sarcasm in front of the entire class, accompanied by a certain smile. After a student gave a lame excuse for an inadequate performance, Frank sometimes lifted his eyebrows and asked, "You did?" or "You did not?" or whatever suited the situation.

<ins>Finn</ins>: Pops, I'd like to know whether he was a funny teacher or could act out scenes from history. You know, to keep things interesting for the students.

<ins>Pops</ins>: I don't think so. Except for an occasional joke, Frank did not attempt to get laughs during the class period, but when they came, he was appreciative, along with everyone else. Those instructors in comedy defensive driving courses you may have enjoyed listening to? That was not Frank's style, but he had his moments. The students' letters filled me in on some of them:

> The lighter moments related to the assignment for the day. On one occasion, Frank asked a day-dreamer, "Mr. Harris, who is in control of Egypt?" The student went totally blank, but desperately recalling that Rita Hayworth had been romancing the Khan, answered, "Rita Hayworth?" The class naturally exploded with laughter. After studying the student a second quizzically, Frank chuckled with amusement. (*J. Myrick*).

> On another occasion in European history class, Frank asked a student a question to which the answer was "Austria." The students in this class were sitting in old double desks side by side. The student asked the question was blank and looked to his deskmate for assistance. The deskmate was tired of having to help his deskmate and whispered "Australia," which he immediately blurted out. Frank got a big laugh when, with a twinkle in his eye, he

> remarked dryly: "I congratulate you, Mr. Smith, for performing a miracle. You have moved Austria from Central Europe to the South Pacific in a matter of minutes. Not only that, but Australia had not yet been discovered by Europeans!" At that, the class got an even bigger laugh and the student whispering "Australia" received no further requests for help from his blank deskmate. (*R.G. Winchester*).

Frank also had at his command several mildly humorous anecdotes, which he told about historical characters or to illustrate specific points. In his course on the Middle Ages, when the discussion turned to the knighting ceremony—how a squire was elevated to knighthood and thereby receive all obligations, rights, and privileges of a knight—Dr. Guittard related the conversation allegedly taking place between an Englishman and an American. The Englishman said, "King William struck my ancestor on the shoulder with his sword and made him a knight," to which the American replied, "Well, Sitting Bull hit my grandfather on the head with a tomahawk and made him an angel." Laughs ensued.

On another occasion, Frank told the following story: "A high school class was studying some Greek history, and the teacher asked for volunteers to make a sentence with the name Euripides, only one student raising his hand. When he was called on, he said, 'My mom told me don't you rip i dees pants cause you don't have any more.'" (*D. Gibbs*). When coming to the term "moratorium" in an assignment, Frank told the class of the little boy who snagged his trousers, and the "more 'e pulled the more 'etore 'em." (*R.T. Miller).*

The students enjoyed seeing Dr. Guittard laugh and break out of routine as much or more than the anecdotes themselves. When he laughed, as for example, at an egregiously wrong answer, he laughed all over his body. (*D. Smiley).* In a course on Chinese history, he asked each student to bring a Chinese proverb to class. As he called the roll, each was to respond with a proverb. One particular male student answered smugly, "A beautiful woman needeth no paint." Dr. Guittard and the class laughed uproariously. Then a female student answered, not missing a beat, "Man thinks he knows, but a woman knows better." At this, Dr. Guittard laughed all the harder and was able to continue roll call only after strenuous efforts to regain his accustomed control. (*D. Gibbs*).

On some occasions, Frank departed from the grind of the usual questioning to try out approaches calculated to wake students up. According to one student in the middle 1940s: "A ministerial student named [Jerry] sat two feet in front and to the right of Dr. Guittard. He was an apple polisher and Doc knew it. One day Doc came limping in, leaning on a beautiful straight walking cane. He leaned on the cane as he lectured. Eventually, he stopped directly in front of Jerry, drew a long slender sword from the cane & lunged at Jerry. Jerry fell backward—chair & all—

and moved to another part of the room & remained there for the rest of the term." (*M. Jones*). On another occasion involving Frank and a pointed object, Frank came into class with a bayonet one of his students had sent him, plus a tomato. The tomato Frank had grown in his garden at home. With the bayonet, "Dr. Gitfiddle," as this student referred to him, put on a demonstration involving both the bayonet and the tomato, which sent tomato juice spurting everywhere, much to the delight of his students. (*M. Jones*). Finn, ever see that Gallagher guy on TV?

Finn: Sure—Gallagher's Sledge-o-Matic thing with watermelons. That routine with the tomato and the bayonet must have shocked Frank's class. I never get tired of watching the Sledge-o-Matic routine. That bit must have worked into the assigned reading somehow.

Pops: Probably, but it made a hit with the students because it was totally out of character. Maybe there was a wild guy inside Frank trying to get out. Some of the best stories about Frank Guittard's class came about when he was past his prime during the 1940s and had already been teaching for thirty-eight years. As Frank got older, both his hearing and vision deteriorated noticeably. A little background here: Baylor, as mentioned above, did not have the retirement program for its teachers it has today (*W. David*) and was considerably weaker financially than it became in later decades. As a result, faculty members were compelled to continue teaching beyond age sixty-five, and in some cases, die with their teaching boots on. Frank's son Clarence said that in his later years, Frank's driving was pretty scary because he did not hear well, and on one occasion, he crossed in front of an Interurban train that he did not hear approaching. Frank continued as chair of the history department and teaching a full load of classes into in his early eighties when he partially retired.

Returning to Frank's late-life hearing difficulty, his students learned early to speak clearly and distinctly. Shouting was not necessary. He rarely asked for a repeat, but he would instead turn his head to one side, this movement indicating that the students should repeat whatever they had just said. On other occasions, Frank kept his right elbow on his desk with his right hand casually behind his ear, cupping it to aid his hearing. The deterioration in Frank's hearing and his sight, while no problem in smaller advanced classes (*J. Chisholm*), contributed to occasional student pranks, student dereliction, and various humorous incidents reminiscent of jokes outside the classroom played on President Burleson at Independence.

One frequently repeated story concerns a generally unprepared student who was making a lifetime career of his college work. In one version of this story, the student was a former football player, a back from Waco High School. (*E. Boyd*). This student sat in the back row where he would occasionally make a low-voice comment on something Frank had said, thereby cracking up the class. When Frank would make one of his typically uncontestable statements of fact, this student would declare under his breath in mock amazement and with an exaggerated and sarcastic emphasis, "no shit." This remark was only for the benefit of those sitting in the student's general vicinity in the back of the room. After grades for the quarter had been posted and the career student had received an "F" in the course, he went to Frank's office and asked for a conference on his grade, saying: "Dr. Guittard, I made a passing grade on most of my other exams and don't see how I could have made an F in your course. Would you check and see if there was not some mistake made?" Frank then calmly reviewed the grade sheet and answered, "Yes, Mr. ___, you made an F in this course, and that's no shit." (*B. Massie*).

<u>Finn</u>: Whoops! I was under the impression that Frank didn't use bad language.

<u>Pops</u>: I guess he thought the situation justified an exception. Another student remembered that most of the students who attempted to take advantage of Frank's hearing problem in his last decade were not history majors, but many times athletes. The football players sat in the back of the class, hoping to get by without much effort. Although Frank could not see students in the back very well, he knew they were there and directed many questions toward them. What resulted were many uncomfortable moments. (*M. Morgan*). Some of those athletes in the back of the room were football players who would answer roll call for a buddy. (*M. Morgan*). It was particularly amusing to the other students when Frank would interrogate, in effect, the empty chair of the buddy. Having answered roll call for the missing buddy, the conspirators were hard put to come up with an answer for Frank that would satisfy him. (*D. Willis*).

On examinations, Frank gave essay questions only, no multiple-choice or true/false. He gave tests every two weeks, even before holidays. On test days, students were required to stack their books and all other materials against the front wall upon entering the classroom. Cheating did occur, resulting in some instances when a student had somehow obtained a copy of a test given two years before. On one occasion, in a course which he had taught previously, perhaps many times, he gave a new set of test questions. On test day, a student walked up to the wastebasket and threw in all the answers he had brought to the final with him. (*D. Gibbs*). In courses that he taught less frequently, Frank was less reluctant to use the same test over again. Frank did not upbraid cheaters in class and always settled matters privately. Ironically, cheating was not at all necessary to prepare for Frank's tests since he telegraphed his punches so clearly, and students could tell almost precisely what he would ask on tests because of his emphasis in class.

Discipline of students was rarely needed, and rarer still was expulsion from the classroom. However, it did happen on occasion, with Frank advising the offending student to gather his materials together and to leave the classroom, to return only when he felt he could conduct himself "properly." (*M. Morgan*). A specific instance of cheating was recalled by one of Frank's graders in the 1920s. The grader never knew of Frank's changing his grade on examination papers but suspected he was giving a close look at the grades.

> This was brought home to me during the second quarter (1927). We had several students who obviously never looked at their lessons and never were able to answer any questions in class and their examination papers showed how poorly prepared they were. Then their examination papers started showing near perfect answers. This was a puzzle to me. After a few such good exams, these students and a few others dropped out of his class. After several weeks, my roommate asked why I had reported some of them for cheating. This was a complete surprise to me, as I knew nothing about it. It developed that a group devised some way of getting the examination questions in advance and preparing the answers. I never knew how this was done. I never found out how Dr. Guittard caught them. (*E. Kilgore*).

Frank's graders regularly had memorable one-on-ones with Frank which deserve comment. Frank insisted that all conferences about grading be held in his living room at 1401 S. 8th and not at the university.

Finn: Why not meet in Old Main and close the door for privacy?

Pops: Not exactly sure it was about privacy as much as Frank liked to do special things for his graders. One grader described a session at Frank and Josie's home this way:

> Our pattern was simply this: at the end of class, he would collect the papers and then invite me to his home that afternoon. Each time he went through the formality of an invitation, and I never took this arrangement for granted. On the other hand, he never failed to invite me.
>
> I would block off about two hours in the afternoon to be at his home. When I arrived, only Mrs. Guittard would greet me, take me into the parlor where I would be joined soon by Dr. Guittard. Almost immediately after that, Mrs. Guittard would enter carrying a tray with tea and cookies or cake...[served with] Meissen cups, saucers, and teapot...Dr. and Mrs. Guittard would be highly offended today that some people in similar circumstances drink coffee out of plastic cups. It was certainly not their style.

> Then Dr. Guittard would pick a paper he would say belonged to "some marginal student who may or may not have passed the examination" and then, with a smile, he would pick my paper out of the bunch. We would go over it and discuss the various answers that could be given to each question. He would indicate some of the irreducible, minimal information that he wanted—comments which, if not present, meant that the question was graded either down or out. (*H. Moore*).

Any questions, Finn, before we close this chapter?

Finn: Sure, I have one. You said his students liked him and liked being in his class, but what did they think about him as a teacher? Were they learning history?

Pops: The short answer is yes. But here's a longer explanation. If we consult Professor Ken Bain's book, *What the Best College Teachers Do* (Harvard 2004), we learn that Professor Bain, a history teacher and a Baylor graduate, argues that there is no one profile for the most effective college teacher. Different styles have different strengths and weaknesses. The primary weakness of Frank's teaching, in the view of many of his students, arose inevitably, as did some of its strengths, from his particular classroom teaching method, namely, the student first recited on the facts from the assigned pages and then the teacher questioned her to make sure the student understood the assigned material. (*D. Smiley*). This style militated against class discussions of any depth, especially in lower-level courses, and as a result, Frank was much less disposed to go with the flow of a give-and-take student teacher discussion. (*O. Corey*). Since Frank concentrated on details rather than broad general interpretations, his approach was sometimes frustrating to students "who wanted to understand the snow bank instead of the individual snowflakes" and accordingly left something to be desired for these students. (*D. Smiley*). However, for our final appraisal of Frank's strengths as a teacher, let's wait until our book's conclusion when we will feature Professor Smiley's tribute to Frank's method in a wrap-up of his experience as a master's student.

Finn: I wish someone had recorded one of his classes so I could hear his voice and also what the students sounded like.

Pops: That would have been a good idea. I can't remember his voice myself, although my cousin Steve remembers it as a "medium high" voice. Make sure someone records a conversation of you and your parents talking to each other and your brothers.

BOOK TEN

Final Days & Summing Up

Sample questions for the peanut gallery's consideration in this book's chapters:

Does Frank's story resemble the plot of a Horatio Alger, Jr. novel? What were Frank's principal accomplishments as a teacher, husband, and father? Why, when he was over sixty years of age, did Frank write his son Francis that he had blundered in his early life decision-making? Do you agree with that statement? What can we conclude from Frank's steering both of his sons into the legal profession? What do you think he finally decided about his choice of the teaching profession at the university level for his career?

Excerpt from Frank's file of humorous anecdotes, perhaps used in his classes, with no mention of historical events or characters.

Regarding the husband's use of pajamas, the wife of an old-timer returns from a visit [to see a friend]. Wife: "What kind of a time did you have while I was away?" Husband: "Oh, I had a good time." Wife: "I know—you have been sleeping in your drawers and undershirt."

Examples of Frank's favorite words and phrases from his letters:

"relieve the feeling" — "To hear from someone always relieves the feeling...that of sort of an exile."

"taking out" — "I think if it had been discouraging, I would have felt like taking out altogether."

"the mountain" — "I have gone to the top of the mountain and am coming down on the other side..."

CHAPTER 36

Finale in Dallas; Final Assessment

The peanut gallery (Miles, Charlie, Finn, and Katie) and I have reviewed our notes, conferred, and desire to set out some final thoughts regarding Frank Guittard's life & times. I'm going to attempt to sum up a few things, and then the peanut gallery will have their chance.

Pops: Frank was still teaching students when he had his fatal heart attack after driving to Dallas to attend Gaetano Donizetti's opera *L'elisir d'amore.* He was eighty-three and had lived a long life as a teacher, husband, father, and mentor to generations of history students. The opera he was to attend featured the story of Nemorino, a poor peasant in love with Adina, a wealthy woman who is not interested in him initially, but that is where the elixir of love comes in. Frank never made it to the opera, but he would have surely enjoyed it. He would have sympathized with its thesis that a man should pursue a woman passionately and diligently and not be discouraged by initial signs of female disinterest. We suspect that he would have had a hard time listening to "Una furtive lagrima" without borrowing a hankie from Mama Josie. Go to YouTube and listen to Pavarotti, Caruso, or Andrea Bocelli sing this aria and see what you think.

So, we now take a moment to revisit Frank's hopes, dreams, and ambitions for his life, along with a few of his possible misgivings, and then draw some tentative conclusions. Any "final" assessment in a biography must necessarily be to a degree tentative, mainly because there are nearly always significant aspects of a subject's life that are only partially revealed, and other aspects where descriptions may be debatable.

The prologue asked the question of how a shy young immigrant to Texas from Ohio without a higher education or financial means, one practically stranded without family or friends in a strange southern state during hard times, could have kept soul and body together and found a place where he could achieve something. The chapter addressing his game plan elaborated on his unpreparedness to deal with the fundamental questions of how to make money to live and pay for college, and, importantly, what kind of professional career he might pursue to support a family.

It does appear that whatever romantic appeal the trip to Texas may have had for Frank arising from a naïve expectation of boundless possibilities and the Texas hype must have played out quickly as he came to understand better what he was up against. He developed only one real way to make a living other than hard manual labor (making railroad ties). Teaching at country schools for a meager wage—earning only slightly more than that necessary for his room, board, and a few sundries, at least initially—became that way. He developed no wealthy patron—and probably sought none—desirous of hiring him at a princely wage to tutor his family, or to do some other non-manual labor job. Despite the plot lines of the Horatio Alger stories, all such stories for Frank, if and when he read them, would have amounted to little more than entertainment or a momentary distraction. He certainly never had a wealthy patron. Frank must have recognized Alger's stories for what they were—fanciful, formulaic Pollyanna-ish stories about younger boys he had little in common with other than the fact that he, too, was on his own. Interestingly, such storylines and the predicaments of their heroes did have some appeal for Frank, despite their unrealistic premise. He continued his interest in the Alger-like comic strip "Ben Webster's Career" decades after relocating to Texas. He was always interested in the lives of underdogs whose fortunes might "turn up," as Wilkins Micawber in *David Copperfield* liked to say.

But it is time to look at the entire historical record and judge, as best we can, on what basis did Frank believe—as he apparently did—that he had failed to make adequate plans for his future and, as a result, blundered his way through life on the winds of chance. Then, if we can figure that out, decide if Frank was correct in that view. Frank had written Francis in the 1920s that he felt he had blundered along in life without a plan of action and was driven from moment to moment by circumstance. He wanted Francis, Clarence, and all of his students to profit from his mistakes. However, Frank never concretely identified what he believed to be the mistakes he wished he had not made. Before concluding as to possible errors that Frank probably thought he had made, rightly or wrongly, let us first look at some of his achievements.

Almost entirely from his own efforts, in a day when federal loans were non-existent and grants not generally available, Frank put himself through at least three universities: Baylor University, two years of courses spread out over four years; the University of Chicago, two years of courses spread out over four or five years; and Stanford University, two or three years of courses and thesis preparation spread out over six years. He taught under adverse conditions at ten to fifteen country schools in Texas and Arkansas as he slowly banked the tuition dollars needed to continue his college education. It took him sixteen years after high school to obtain his bachelor's degree from Chicago. He taught an estimated 10,000 students at all different levels, mainly in history. He taught nearly all upper-level history courses at Baylor for many years, facilitated by years of intensive home study. In his early years teaching in the Baylor preparatory department, he taught other courses outside his history specialty, including economics, geometry, and the Romance languages. At a small school like Baylor, any professor who could teach outside his or her specialty was more valuable than one who could not. He successfully married twice and raised two sons to adulthood, first with the assistance of Mamie, the mother of his sons, and then with Mama Josie. His relationships with both wives were solid, devoted, and caring. He survived the blows from the losses of both his first wife, Mamie, and their infant son, Charles, to infectious disease and continued to teach for another thirty years. Frank took on crucial extra projects for President Brooks essential to Brooks's vision for Baylor; he carried them out thoroughly and skillfully. Frank was genuinely interested in all of his students—his twinkle and show of interest in them as they left class each day were appreciated. Frank taught his students the importance of learning the facts of history and the importance of geography to history's ebb and flow. He stressed the importance of understanding the meaning of the words used by authors in their history texts.

So on what basis did Frank conclude that he had blundered his way along and lived too much from day to day without a plan of action? It is instructive that while encouraging his sons to have a plan of action, form a viable career choice early on, and not spend time tilting at windmills (political campaigns and church board discussions), he left no specific road signs for future readers. No warning like, "Caution! —low paying career choice straight ahead—possible lifetime ramifications." Perhaps it would have been painful to write *I should have done this and not have done that* when it was too late to change course. Remember Samuel Johnson who could have been an attorney? Of course, any recitation of those mistakes where his career choice was concerned would inevitably have altered the path of history, including that of the wives and sons he loved. A time-travel speculation without beneficial results.

Nevertheless, as best as can be determined, here are some of his possible-to-probable conclusions about how he thought he or others had misstepped concerning the decisions concerning his education and career. First, it appears that Frank thought his parents could have steered him toward a career that promised greater financial rewards than teaching. Even though he would have had to put himself through college in any event, he would have been going down a path that would have eventually produced a greater financial return. Second, it took him sixteen years after leaving high school to obtain his bachelor's degree based on four years of credit classes. That is a lot of time to get a bachelor's degree, even if one is working his way through school. That is, of course, a fact, but it doesn't necessarily establish that any critical errors of planning were made. Third, if he was thinking he should have been encouraged to think about a professional career other than teaching, we have to doubt how that could have been accomplished in the absence of funds, especially considering the financial straits and upheaval the entire country was going through. Francis Joseph, who had a busy but not especially remunerative practice as a country physician, apparently would have liked to have been able to provide some financial assistance to Frank but could not; in part that was because of some kind of "old claim" he was paying on along with the needs of his large family. Frank had some interest in following in his father's footsteps to medical school, but Francis Joseph already had three of Frank's siblings to send to college before him.

Studying law could have been an option if he had known an attorney who might have encouraged him to go into law. That alternative was available in Texas by studying law in a lawyer's office. A legal education would not have been as financially prohibitive as medical school, but we have no evidence that he ever considered law as a profession or knew anything about getting started as an attorney prior to his encouraging both of his sons to go to law school. Pat Neff, who had the funds to go to undergraduate school and then law school, seemed born to debate with the words "and therefore" on his lips and seemed destined to run for public office. Frank, conversely, did not have the drive to perform in public, whether before a jury or for an electorate that propels people into the public eye. Significantly, where Francis and Clarence were concerned, they had three financial advantages Frank didn't have: they had a parent who encouraged them to become attorneys; they had the benefit of being able to go to Baylor undergraduate and law school at reduced tuition because they were children of a Baylor faculty member; and they had much, if not all, of their costs of living paid for by living at home throughout law school.

Although Frank never said what specific mistakes he had made, one error appearing from our research appears to be not a failure by Frank to plan or make correct decisions, but a forgivable failure of the family process early on before Frank left for Texas. By that, we mean an apparent failure as a large family to work through the subjects of Frank's education, financial, and career issues at family meetings in Ohio before he left for Texas. That way, if Frank were still to be dispatched to Texas with a letter of introduction and bag of lunches, it could have been done with a more cautious, deliberate, and well-considered approach, perhaps with the input of professionals working in different careers. But Frank's family was a large one, and his father, the sole breadwinner, was overworked, underpaid, and limited in the time he had to think about the futures of his seven children considering the time required to care for the health of his many patients. However, where Frank's own decision-making was concerned, Frank had years after arriving in Texas to think through the course he was on—teaching school—and what course corrections were possible. Lack of funds would always have been a crucial factor, but he could have made an adjustment to his plan, and it seems that he recognized his failure to do so. In retrospect, Frank's most apparent mistake—seen from hindsight—was in not developing, in the absence of knowledgeable career counseling from his family group, mentors in Ohio or Texas. Such mentors could have helped him form a more realistic plan to accomplish his primary goals of obtaining his education in a reasonable amount of time and then preparing himself for a career that would offer greater financial rewards than college teaching. But then, life for most people is generally not lived with much hindsight.

In summary, it is not surprising that Frank told Francis he had blundered in planning his education and career, for that is entirely consistent with his systematic ruminating nature and tendency to be self-conscious and overly self-critical. Perhaps he was exaggerating by half to make a point to his sons. Maybe it was the type of exaggeration fathers occasionally make for dramatic effect to get their children's attention in a matter of importance. Possibly his motive was a little of both. Further, since Frank was ultimately happy with the overall arc of his life, with his contributions, achievements, and family, we conclude that his point to Francis about "blundering" was more didactic than confessional. Frank was fundamentally a wise teacher—and he was attempting to provide the kind of counseling to Francis he wished someone had provided to him.

Miles, Charlie, Finn, Katie—do any of you wish to add anything? What sticks with you all?

<u>Miles</u>: We've agreed that Katie can offer our thoughts summing up Frank Guittard's life.

<u>Katie</u>: I will make this very brief. We all had questions that were not answered, and those are summarized elsewhere. As examples, Charlie said he would like to know whether Frank was artistic and could draw good pictures; Finn wanted to learn more about Frank's interests or abilities in sports; Miles said he wanted to hear more about the books Frank read; you, Pops, wanted to know Frank's view on evolution; and I wanted to know more about Frank and Mamie's first meetings and letters. Perhaps there could be further research among family members on these subjects. Finally, all the peanut gallery members are proud of our great-great-grandfather, the kind of guy he was, the life he lived, the devotion he showed to his family and his students, and the obstacles he overcame *en route* to his goals.

<u>Miles</u>: What I will most remember about Frank Guittard is that he was the guy who put "sys" in "system."

<u>Charlie</u>: I liked it when he said he disliked "pious gas" coming from anybody, or what we call "BS" today. And when his students asked him a ridiculous question, or made a crazy comment, he just said, "I'll take that under advisement."

<u>Finn</u>: I thought he was cool when he said in that letter, "I hot-footed it to the Piggly Wiggly." I didn't know that a college professor could loosen up enough to use a little slang. By the way, did any of the rest of you know that the Piggly Wiggly

was the first self-serve grocery in the US? Too bad they're no longer in Texas, but there are still hundreds of stores in over sixteen or so states.

Pops: I can imagine Frank and Mama Josie both smacking their lips on the way to the Piggly Wiggly.

CHAPTER 37

Looking Back at Frank's Life & Times; Conclusion

Pops: (*addressing the entire peanut gallery*) Miles, Charlie, Finn, and Katie, after four decades, it's time to bring this project to an end. You guys and Katie were not around initially, but you are here now and made a big difference in how Frank Guittard's story was presented. I'm sure we have surprised our readers with our conversational approach and using a peanut gallery to develop Frank's life and times. I hope most of them will approve. I do expect they will like Amanda's hand-drawn illustrations for many scenes in our story. She is putting some final touches on them and should be finished in a week or so. I know you want to see them. Maybe our book project will start a trend—biographies told conversationally with a small feedback group like yourselves, and with hand-drawn illustrations. We will see. In any event, you have been part of a brave experiment, and so I thank you.

In conclusion, we can do no better than to adopt a former student's tribute to Frank as a classroom teacher of 10,000 history students—that of the late David L. Smiley, Professor of History at Wake Forest University. Dr. Smiley, who earned his Master's in History under Frank Guittard in 1948, captured Frank as a teacher in a letter to the author in 1980. I have asked Miles to read aloud some excerpts from Dr. Smiley's letter.

Miles: Pops, first, thanks for asking all of us—Charlie, Finn, Katie, and me—to participate in your project. It's been fascinating to learn what you have been able to dig up about Frank Guittard and his times, too. That twist of fate with President Cooper and the dog and everything else—you've given us a lot to think about.

Pops: I wonder—would the peanut gallery consider re-upping in a couple of years to help with an update?

Miles: Maybe, but that might not be easy. It was hard enough to schedule people all these times. It's also difficult to imagine there's much left that anyone can discover about Frank's life. His times...maybe.

Pops: (*smiling*) I was just kidding about that.

Miles: Well then, here are Professor Smiley's words remembering his professor, Frank Guittard:

Francis Guittard was a master of the recitation method of teaching, a practice he followed invariably in all his courses. He prepared himself extremely well for each class, with notebooks of questions and suggestions. For each course he divided the number of class days into the number of pages in the textbook, and at the beginning of each day's class would write on the blackboard the twelve or fourteen or eighteen pages to be covered in the next day's session. Then he sat down at the desk, checked the attendance, and began the interrogation. He used the class roll as a batting order, calling upon six or eight in one class hour, the next group the following day, and [so on] through the roll, when he would begin again at the beginning.

The questions were all factual and from the assigned pages. Some were dictionary questions; as, for example, on page 241, I see the word "oleaginous." "Mr. Smiley, what does that word mean?" Some were geography questions; as, "On page 42, I see the Red River mentioned. Where does it rise, and where does it empty?"

But most of the questions concerned the facts of the past—terms of treaties, contents of bills and laws, candidates and personalities of individual races and administrations, causes and results of whatever the subject. In the students' answers, he would not accept shoddy or vague responses. He wanted it exact and precise and would not let up on a student until he had it.

I remember those classes warmly and yet, when I suspected that it was about my time to be called upon, with some trepidation. I for one dared not go to class unprepared. I looked up and memorized any words I did not know; I checked out all the geographic references, I memorized the facts of the course. For learning the facts there is no better method than the recitation, and in that, Dr. Guittard was a genius. And yet there was a warmth about him, a sudden laugh that made the whole process fun and highly enjoyable.

As a classroom teacher he was a giant among his colleagues. I have not forgotten what I learned from him, that history is fact and person, cause and effect. Thousands there must be in the world who still remember those days when, by the inexorable turn of the roll-call, they were slated to come up for questioning.

CHAPTER 38

Unanswered Questions of the Peanut Gallery

On the divider pages preceding the various books into which this work has been divided, we mentioned some questions that the author ("Pops") suggested for the peanut gallery's consideration. The idea was to prime the peanut gallery's pump, if needed. This chapter gives the peanut gallery—Miles, Charlie, Finn, and Katie—one last opportunity to raise any additional questions about Frank Guittard's life and story they would like answers to, even though they know Pops is already out of answers.

Pops: Everyone, thank you for helping me tell as much of Frank Guittard's story as we can tell. There is always a limit to how much can be found out about anyone given the passage of time, lack of records, and the time needed to do the research. However, if you had just one or two remaining questions that haven't been answered but you would like answers for, what would they be? Katie, why don't you go first?

Katie: I would like to know about Frank and Mamie's first meeting and how long it was after taking the job in Shiner until he sent her his first note. I would like to know about any one-on-one discussions he had with Captain Welhausen and whether Frank actually asked him for Mamie's hand in marriage. I would like to know whether she was merely seasick on the trip she took with her father in 1901, or did she already have some disease she was trying to recover from. What was the reason for the voyage? Why didn't her mother go along? Since Frank was thirteen years older than Mamie, she being only eighteen when they met, when did he start seriously courting her? Did she or her parents throw away his first letters? And did she ever have a paying job and, if so, what was it? I would like to know her favorite books and what courses she took in college.

Pops: Wow, that's a lot of unanswered questions, Katie. Charlie?

Charlie: I would like to know whether Frank was artistic and could draw good pictures. I've seen your cartoons, so I wonder if he could draw. I wonder if he was in a marching band in high school and what his uniform's colors were. What were his favorite marches as a cornetist? Which march did he like best, Sousa's "Stars and Stripes Forever" or Grafulla's "Washington Grays"? Did he ever get in trouble for sassing the band teacher or any other teacher? Did he ever have to serve detentions after school or bring home teachers' notes for his parents to sign? Did he ever flunk a course?

Finn: I would like to know if he ever played football, basketball, or baseball. Did he get to play quarterback, or was he just one of those guys in the line when they picked sides, and did they play tackle or flag football? Did he have a favorite swimming hole in New Bedford? Ever fly a kite? Did a water moccasin or a copperhead ever bite him? What about pets growing up? Did his family have pets? And did he have a girlfriend in high school, and was she pretty? Did they say grace before meals? Did he tithe to his church? Did he have a BB gun or a .22, or ever gig a frog?

Pops: You've been very patient, Miles. What would you like to know?

Finn: *(interrupting)* Pops—I've got one more question. *Huckleberry Finn*, I've learned, came out right around the time Frank left Ohio for Texas. I would like to know what Frank thought about Huck's story of him and Jim, the runaway slave on the Mississippi River, and whether Frank was thinking about Huck and Jim when he escaped Ohio to make a new life in Texas. Also, I've never asked my mom or dad where they got the name "Finn" for me. It's not a family name.

Pops: You're right about the timing of *Huckleberry Finn*—it came out in 1885 before Frank left for Texas. That's a good question about your name; Huckleberry Finn would not be a bad guy to be named after. He was a stand-up sort of fellow—Miles, back to you.

Miles: Pops, Finn's question just now makes me wonder whether I was named after General Miles, who Geronimo surrendered to a few months before Frank came to Texas. We now know Frank saw Geronimo, at least we think he must have, in 1904 at the fair in St. Louis. But getting to my unanswered questions, I would like to know for sure what Frank read in high school other than just those nine books in his father's library and those other things you talked about. Did his father allow dime westerns and Horatio Alger, Jr. novels or similar books in the house? I would like to know about his farm chores, what he had to do, and how early he had to get up. Did he have to milk the cows or slop the hogs? Did he ever step in cow stuff or have to clean up after the cows and horses? Did he have his own horse? Was he good at roping or have a bull-whip? What kind of hat did he wear in Ohio? Was he in a church orchestra? Did he receive any demerits while he was at Baylor? Did he talk to any Baylor girls outside one of those soirees talked about?

Pops: (*grinning*) A lot of those would be great questions to have the answers to. Does anybody have a Ouija board?

Katie: No, and I don't think my parents would like me playing with a Ouija board and trying to talk to a dead person. Besides, Pops, you haven't told us the questions you would like answered.

Pops: No, I haven't. Like you all, it's hard to just come up with just a few. Here are some: What did Frank and his father say to each other on that long ride to the train station in 1886? What were their parting words just before Frank boarded the train? I'd like to know about his years in any band, and how many brass instruments he could play, whether he played any of those Civil War era horns like Saxhorns that faced backward ("backward blasters"); I'd like to know how many times he saw the Sousa band and what he remembers about that band and Sousa himself and whether Sousa was wearing his trademark white gloves. Did he see Sousa's band at the Cotton Palace in Waco? Since he was a cornetist, did he ever see the great Patrick S. Gilmore's band, which was the best-known band before Sousa's? Or Pat Conway and his band? When he was in Chicago and playing in the Chicago band, did President Harper ever sit in with his cornet on a day Frank was also playing his cornet, perhaps share a music stand with Frank? Did Frank and Harper ever have a conversation?

I would also like to know more about his views on the evolution controversy and whether he had any interest in it at all. Did he have any particular theological ideas? If he did, did they more nearly align with those of Rufus C. Burleson, B.H. Carroll, Joseph M. Dawson, or someone else, perhaps a Methodist? And what was the first silent movie he ever saw, and the first talking picture? Did he ever see *The Wizard of Oz*, or did he think that was kid's stuff? Did he see any connection between Baum's first Oz book published in 1900 and the earlier White City in Chicago in 1893? How about *Birth of a Nation* and *Gone with the Wind*? What were his feelings about those movies? Did he sympathize with Jacob Coxey's Army on its trek from Ohio to Washington in 1894 when he dropped out of Baylor? He could have joined Coxey's Army and marched on Washington instead of heading to Hunt County to sell books. Also, exactly how tall was he, and how much did he weigh in his last years? Also, did he envy the speaking ability of his oldest son Francis? Did he ever debate against Brooks or Neff? Oh, one more thing—did he occasionally dip into those Hershey bars Mama Josie kept in the refrigerator for the roomers? Those are just for starters!

Miles: I certainly would like to know what he thought about Coxey's Army which started up in Ohio, and whether he was tempted to join it when he dropped out of Baylor in 1894. I am also interested in whether, after he moved to Texas from Ohio, he could bring himself to sing "Dixie," or maybe he refused to sing it.

Pops: All interesting questions and some I would like the answers to myself. I could make guesses as to many of them, but I won't. If asked which questions I could answer confidently without speculation, it would only be the question about saying grace before meals; the answer to that would have to be yes based on the evidence we have.

EPILOGUE

This epilogue was written after the peanut gallery finished helping Pops with the numbered chapters, and so none of them have been recruited to help. The following information is intended to be straightforward; perhaps clarifying questions and comments will not be needed.

Baylor University History Department (1910—)

The academic subject of history has long been taught at Baylor University at Independence (from 1845), Waco University (from 1861), and at Baylor University in Waco (from 1886). History is currently a humanities department within the College of Arts and Sciences. In 1910, History achieved its distinct department and Frank Guittard was appointed chair. Initially, Baylor's Department of History (DOH) was small, with just the chair and one other instructor. Neither Frank Guittard nor the other instructor had a doctorate, and the department offered only undergraduate level courses.

In the 175 years since Baylor's founding at Independence and the 111 years since the DOH's creation, the teaching of history at Baylor has undergone a dramatic transformation. Today, the DOH includes thirty or more faculty members with doctorates; it offers undergraduate and graduate courses for both the master's and Ph.D. degrees. The doctoral program is characterized by a distinctive emphasis on religion and culture; its concentration of leading scholars in American, British, and Global History is shaping the next generation of religious historians. Additionally, the DOH annually sponsors the Guittard Book Award for Historical Scholarship, which recognizes an outstanding work of original scholarship in any area of history, written by a current or emeritus member of the Baylor Department of History, or by a graduate holding a degree in history from Baylor University.

As of 2022, the Tidwell Building (current home of the Department of History) has been renovated. Additionally, the DOH and the Department of Religion have collaborated to honor Robert L. Gilbert—the first African American graduate of Baylor, a history major, pastor, and Waco civil rights leader. The Robert Gilbert Memorial Endowed Scholarship in History was established in 2021. In 2020, the Department of Religion established the Robert L. Gilbert Scholar in Religion Graduate Stipend.

Renovating Tidwell and honoring Robert Gilbert have represented parallel efforts to reconstruct the past appropriately, reconstruction sometimes unearthing new and occasionally painful stories. Honoring Reverend Gilbert is intended as a significant step in furtherance of the DOH's July 2020 Statement on Racial Justice, acknowledging that Baylor had not been free of racism and repudiating systemic racism in the strongest terms. The DOH's statement followed and supported the Board of Regents' Resolution on Racial Healing and Justice and the American Historical Association's Statement on the History of Racist Violence in the United States.

Career guidance, career selection; scholarships, fellowships, grants, and loans

Resources available for career guidance and selection, virtually non-existent in the last decades of the nineteenth century, have grown exponentially. Resources exist on every college campus, and high schools periodically have days on which college representatives appear on high school campuses to visit with juniors and seniors. Careers in academia generally pay better vis-à-vis those in the corporate world than they did in 1902 when Frank Guittard was hired for $75 a month without health or retirement benefits. Assuming Frank was hired today for the same salary he started at in 1902 with a master's degree and as adjusted by inflation, his nominal pay, before any deductions for insurance and taxes and without modern-day benefits, would be around $27,000 annually. That salary today would hardly be enough to afford a modest apartment and a beat-up car on a borderline set of tires, let alone a wife and family, or a house and medical care. Although colleges and universities compete for research money and more and more students are attracted to science, health, and related careers, money is thankfully still available to history students to fund their graduate educations.

The Guittard Family and the Baylor Department of History

Frank Guittard taught forty-seven years at Baylor. He and Josie Glenn Guittard, by their wills, endowed a fellowship for graduate history students upon Josie's death in 1958, which has been supplemented by the grandchildren of Frank and Mamie Welhausen Guittard. Additionally, descendants of Frank and Mamie Welhausen Guittard have also established the Guittard-Verlander-Voegtle History Endowed Scholarship for undergraduate history majors. A celebration is being tentatively planned for 2022, when the Baylor DOH will recognize the total number of history fellows and scholars reaching more than one hundred. Francis Gevrier Guittard, Jr. attended both Baylor undergraduate and law school and practiced law in Victoria, Texas. Clarence Alwin Guittard attended Baylor undergraduate and law school and practiced law before going on the bench, ultimately retiring as chief justice of the Court of Appeals for the Fifth District of Texas at Dallas. Francis had two sons—Stephen and Philip, the first becoming an in-house attorney for international concerns, the second, a student counselor and public-school teacher who taught

Texas history. Both earned their undergraduate degrees from Baylor. Clarence had two sons and a daughter—Charles, John, and Mary. Both sons became attorneys, and the daughter a law librarian who married an attorney. Only Clarence's older son, the author, graduated from Baylor, and only Francis Jr.'s younger son, Philip, became a teacher of history.

Health crises—Tuberculosis; Influenza; COVID-19 Pandemic

The Albuquerque Sanatorium and other refuges of "lungers" in New Mexico, as well as similar places in California, contended that their salubrious climates contributed to a patient's chances of achieving a cure for tuberculosis. In hindsight, we know that a cure was not available until the BCG vaccines were thoroughly tested and adopted in the 1940s-1950s. However, as to whether climate had any substantial beneficial effect on the course of the disease, that question seems to have been answered negatively at the 1896 annual meeting of the American Climatological Association by Dr. James B. Walker. Dr. Walker presented the findings of a decade-long study that "shattered the view that climate had a direct influence on health and relegated therapeutic climatology to the status of pseudo-science." Thus, "climate was no longer considered a major factor in controlling tuberculosis." However, the belief or hope that mountainous or western climates were beneficial to lungers persisted in the absence of a verifiable cure.

The COVID-19 pandemic and its variants are still with us. A number of vaccines are being administered in the US, Europe, and elsewhere. We don't know what other epidemics, if not pandemics, are on the horizon, including mutations of the existing COVID-19 virus, and may reach the US in the coming months and years. At all levels of government—federal, state, and local—our leadership must be guided by medical science and not political posturing, pandering to the ill-informed, or conspiracy theories peddled around the globe seeking to undercut our confidence in public health measures. While enormous strides have been made in medical science, the current pandemic portends to have as great an impact on the US as the 1918 influenza pandemic or any other epidemic in Frank Guittard's lifetime. The current pandemic was a crucial factor in the election of the Democratic candidate Joseph R. Biden, Jr. for president of the US in November 2020. As of the publication of this volume in 2022, the number of US deaths from COVID-19 has passed one million, which inevitably will be an issue in the 2024 presidential election.

Selling books door to door

In our modern age, few products are sold door to door. The Fuller Brush man has disappeared. Of those products still being sold, religious books and the complete works of Sir Walter Scott are not among them. Even Girl Scouts ringing doorbells selling their cookies seems to be mostly a thing of the past, although we still see them after Christmas outside grocery stores with their mothers. The production of hard copy encyclopedias has gone into decline with the advent of the internet; however, encyclopedias are still sold to readers who want to read them online and who may prefer them to research at Google's website. Frank would have embraced research on the internet for its convenience, even though he would have always preferred holding a book in his hands.

Student Self-Government

In the early decades of the twentieth century, some colleges created student governments with officers elected by undergraduates. Baylor was a denominational school that followed this pattern for a decade. The purpose of college governments was to improve communication between colleges and students, not to turn discipline entirely over to students, since college administrators would still make the rules. The entire subject of discipline of students and faculties' powers in such matters was problematic and complex. Conflicts between university presidents, professors, and students had been widespread for years as to disciplinary judgments by faculty. Because faculties' powers in discipline matters were seen by students as absolute, students at many colleges and universities often felt justified in defending themselves against faculty power, including cheating utilizing cuffs, boots, and rolls of notes in sleeves, sometimes with whole classes cheating on examinations. There was a "code of honor" between college men, and it was unthinkable for a college man to bear witness to a classmate's violation of the rules. This conflict was exacerbated by the cultural war between the goals of eastern colleges and the desire of college men to have a good time for a few years before working in the family business. Because of the code of honor between male students, it became virtually impossible for college authorities to gather evidence against wrongdoers. This difficulty was a predictable part of the war between faculty and college men. Thus, universities' efforts to promote an honor code to accompany a student government conflicted with the code of honor existing between college men. Many nondenominational colleges tended to leave matters of drinking, card playing, and profanity, which were not tolerated by colleges like Baylor, to the students. Denominational colleges, including Baylor, were to some extent exceptions to these overall trends and marketed themselves based on the moral standards they supposedly enforced on their campuses. Nevertheless, the large state schools supported by tax revenue and their greater permissiveness represented the dominant college culture.

Baylor's experiment with student self-government and discipline in the early twentieth century pitted Baylor's desire to inoculate its students with democratic values and citizen responsibilities against the implied code of honor male students owed to each other not to tell on a fellow student. Though Baylor's campus did not resemble the more hedonistic culture on many other campuses, the intense feeling among many students on Baylor's campus that they should not give testimony against their classmates ensured the eventual failure of self-government when cheating was alleged. We suspect that would have been the case at Baylor had the students' self-government constitution made it clear that students convicted of cheating were banned from competing for Baylor in intercollegiate athletics.

In a sense, student self-governments were doomed to failure at least partially because they pitted honor codes promoted by faculties against codes of honor between male students. When disciplinary matters were left totally to faculties and administrators, there were still conflicts between students and administrations, but overall, it made more sense and has seemed to work better.

Acceptance of the Facts of History; Rejection of Racism; and Approval of Changes to the Baylor Campus

This book's title, I WILL TEACH HISTORY, was selected because of Frank Guittard's life-long passion to read, understand, and teach the facts of history. Those facts include certain regrettable aspects of the life of Rufus C. Burleson largely before he became president of Baylor at Waco, including that he had once owned a slave, joined the Confederacy to serve as a chaplain, and after the war promoted the Lost Cause ideology. All of these were on public view in the December 2020 report of the Commission on Historic Campus Representations. The Baylor Regents' decisions, among others, to delete Burleson from the name of Burleson Quadrangle and to remove President Burleson's statue from the Quadrangle were far-reaching. What may be difficult to explain is why it took institutional Baylor many decades to make these changes. I can hear the peanut gallery asking me after reading this whether Frank Guittard was aware that the founders of Baylor at Independence all had owned one or more slaves—Baylor, Tryon, and Huckins, along with William Carey Crane, president of Baylor at Independence, and Rufus C. Burleson, president of Baylor University at Independence, Waco University, and Baylor University at Waco; that President Burleson had encouraged young men at both Baylor at Independence and Waco University to join the Confederacy to fight against "Abolition despotism"; and that after the war's conclusion in 1865 both Burleson and Crane promoted the Lost Cause ideology which, according to the report, honored the memory of antebellum whiteness and Confederate heroes. Did Frank and the other members of the history department, in the first half of the 20th century, impart their knowledge of these facts—assuming they were mostly aware of them—to their students? Since a major theme of this volume has been Professor Guittard's emphasis on teaching students the facts of history—what really happened but some people have declined to acknowledge—this is an interesting question.

There are no completely satisfying answers to these questions, although we are confident that the Baylor faculty must have been aware of the pre-civil war connections between Baylor's founders, most of its board of trustees, and its early presidents with slavery. It is well-recorded that the Baylor faculty, including History Chair Frank Guittard, in the early 20th century promptly put on record their condemnation of the grotesque lynching, burning, and mutilation of Jesse Washington in 1916 as reported in an earlier chapter. The fact that other colleges and universities did have similar issues with their connections to slavery going back a century and a half is well known. Currently, where Baylor is concerned, significant change is already in process on this front. In May 2022, its Board of Regents approved an initial action plan to address strategic priorities identified by the Commission on Historic Campus Representations addressing the area around the Judge Baylor statue, the Quadrangle, the relocation of the Burleson statue, the development of a monument for the unknown enslaved, and other priorities identified following the Regents' unanimous approval of the June 2020 "Resolution on Racial Healing and Justice" and creation of such commission.

Appendix A
Homework Assignment for the Peanut Gallery

The purpose of this piece was to test at the end of this project what the peanut gallery retained from the time spent helping the author go through the chapters of Frank Guittard's life. A secondary objective was to give them a task to complete by consensus rather than competition. Since Miles, Charlie, and Finn have all completed high school and Katie will have her diploma before long, they will all, sooner or later, be writing their profile pages for the inevitable class reunion booklets. This homework assignment will be a practice. Here were my instructions:

> *One of these days, there will be a reunion for your high school graduating class, and you will be asked to fill out and return a questionnaire profile on yourself to inform your curious classmates what you have been doing since graduation from dear old whatever high school. As the years pass, you may be called on a number of times to update your profile. Your task today is to consult with each other and fill out such a form, not on yourselves but for Frank Guittard, based on what you have learned in recent days for a hypothetical reunion of his high school class in New Bedford, Ohio, in March 1950. Frank left high school in 1884. As you know, Frank passed in April of 1950 after his 83rd birthday in January of that year.*

Following receipt of this assignment, the members of the peanut gallery conferred, divided up the questions on the questionnaire I came up with, and determined what to put in the blanks. Katie then emailed me the following completed form for Professor Francis Gevrier Guittard, Class of 1884, New Bedford High School, New Bedford, Ohio:

Graduate's name, graduating class, current address & occupation: Frank Guittard, class of 1884; 1401 South 8th St., Waco, Texas. semi-retired professor of history.

Guilty pleasures: comic strips "Ben Webster" and "The Bungle Family"; an occasional glass of wine; waffles on Sunday mornings; naps during Sunday sermons.

Things no one not in his immediate family would know: did voice exercises at the piano to maintain my voice; walked around with a sandbag on my head to avoid becoming stooped; started dying my hair in the 1920s; secretly wondered if I should have been an attorney; I am partial to peppermint lifesavers.

Favorite expressions: "this is not for public consumption"; "I'll take that under advisement"; "climbing fool's hill"; "working in earnest"; and "hitting the line."

Favorite diversions: golf, travel, reading, reading the newspaper and the funnies; listening to music; going to the opera; honeymoon bridge with Josie.

Favorite hobby: indoor—playing my cornet; outdoor—golf; before golf, tennis.

Favorite preacher: the Carroll brothers, Benajah Harvey and James Milton Carroll.

Most entertaining lecturer, best lecture: Sam Jones, "Get There and Stay There."

Biggest regret: not returning to Ohio before my mother died; haphazard work and college years; following path of least resistance where my career was concerned; not being able to keep my wife and children safe from disease; not going to Europe.

Best decision: leaving Ohio for Texas; staying in Texas; my two marriages.

Most admired person: Samuel Palmer Brooks; Theodore Roosevelt; William Rainey Harper; Judge Warwick Hoxey Jenkins.

Most interesting roommate: Pat M. Neff at Magnolia, Arkansas.

Most agreeable and most disagreeable outdoor chores: feeding the chickens; relocating a swarm of bees to the hive; or anything dealing with hogs.

Most difficult period in your life: starting with the illness of my second son, Charles, and ending with the illness and death of my first wife, Mamie.

Greatest fear: failing in my pursuit of the Ph.D. at Stanford or failing as a teacher early on at Baylor; that disease would take Clarence after taking Charles and Mamie.

Greatest satisfaction: students who achieved something after graduation; students who appreciated their history studies and came back to visit; completing my Ph.D. at Stanford; Francis and Clarence; helping them with their career choices.

Most enjoyable trip: The Louisiana Purchase Exposition in St. Louis, summer 1904.

Most enjoyable diversion from studies in Chicago: The Buffalo Bill Wild West Show featuring Geronimo and Annie Oakley (from Ohio) in 1901.

Biggest disappointment: not being able to go to the Chicago World's Fair in 1893.

Political party: lifelong Democrat; favorite Republican, Theodore Roosevelt.

Pet peeve: gaseous windbags; dull, overly long pastor's sermons; lengthy prayers, especially by pompous deacons; unnecessarily lengthy meetings of any sort; contentious discussions of unimportant matters; impudence in young people.

Favorite work clothes: gray pinstriped suit with vest, stiff detachable collars, colorful tie or bowtie, white dress shirt, watch chain & Erisophian Society pin.

Appendix B

Peanut Gallery's Debate: John Wesley Hardin & Frank Guittard Resolutions

Frank Guittard, despite his days as a debater for the Erisophians at Baylor and as occasional mentor to the Baylor debate team, had counter-intuitively an intense dislike for bickering, particularly religious or scholastic bickering. He distrusted dubious theories that could be easily challenged. Yet, he encouraged occasional classroom debates between his students on points of history to provoke their thinking and, hopefully, learning. One possible topic that came to mind for the peanut gallery to vie over was: Who made the greatest impact upon your life—William Rainey Harper (first president of the University of Chicago), David Starr Jordan (first president of Stanford University), or Samuel Palmer Brooks (president of Baylor University)?

However, on reflection, that topic was too dry, academic, and remote to galvanize the peanut gallery's competitive juices; a livelier topic was needed. Then we made an odd discovery. In glancing through several books on the life of notorious Texas outlaw John Wesley Hardin (1853-1895)—neither an acquaintance nor student of Frank Guittard—the author could not help but notice several odd coincidences, which led to more reading about Hardin. The first coincidence was that both Hardin and Guittard were active members of literary societies and participated in many debates in the early 1890s (the second coincidence), Hardin inside the grim penitentiary walls of the Penitentiary at Huntsville, and Guittard at Baylor in the impressive Erisophian meeting room in Main Building. But that is only where the similarities between their lives start. We decided to give the research on Hardin to the peanut gallery and identify two propositions for them to debate. All of that was done, and they seemed eager to go, all our peanut gallery debaters being experienced debaters in high school or college. They have already agreed on partners and flipped for Affirmative or Negative. Miles and Katie will take the Affirmative and Charlie and Finn the Negative for the following two propositions:

I Resolved: That the similarities between the lives of notorious Texas gunman John Wesley Hardin and legendary history professor Francis Gevrier Guittard substantially outweigh the differences; or, in the alternative,

II Resolved: That the differences between the lives of Hardin and Guittard arose primarily from the fact that Hardin was born into a Confederacy-sympathetic family and Guittard to a Union-sympathetic family.

What follows is a shortened version of the Peanut Gallery debate. The affirmative side (Miles and Katie) of both resolutions is intentionally more sympathetic to Hardin than the negative side (Charlie and Finn). The winning team of this debate and the best individual debater will be decided by votes from readers of the debate received after this book is published. There will be prizes, but I'm not telling what they will be.

Pops: Any questions before we start?

Charlie: Do I have to argue negative with Finn? He'll just goof off. I want to win.

Pops: Well, if he goofs off, that'll just be too bad for him. There will be an award for the best individual debater that you can win, even if the readers vote for Miles and Katie as winning the debate. (*pausing*) Miles will speak first for the affirmative. Miles?

Miles, for the Affirmative: Thank you. Katie and I are excited to present the Affirmative side to the readers as we believe our side of these two propositions is open and shut; the answer to both propositions is clearly "yes." At the outset, we will admit that Mr. Hardin was handier than most of us with a pistol and often was a bit quick to reach for his "peacemaker" when he should have left it holstered. Some might say, but not Katie or I, that most of the twenty-five or more people he is credited with shooting were worthless no-count types who hung out in saloons and deserved it and that Hardin saved the state a lot of hangman's fees. However, in all fairness, Mr. Hardin went through a rough patch in his life before, during, and after Reconstruction in Texas that none of us have had or ever will have in our privileged twenty-first century, big city lives. Further, if this debate is only about how many people Hardin shot versus how many Guittard shot, then there is no point to it, and we might as well stop right here. How many were shot by the outlaw versus by the professor in this debate is irrelevant.

Be all of that as it may, it is undisputed by all the authorities that Hardin had clearly turned over a new leaf after seventeen years in prison. Hardin had rehabilitated himself substantially, if not completely. Katie and I contend that any comparison of Hardin's life with Frank Guittard's should start with his rehabilitation in prison and not dwell on the numerous lapses in judgment that put him in Huntsville. After all, when Guittard was fifteen—the age at which Hardin killed his first man—it was 1882, years after the worst of the Reconstruction years had passed in Texas, and Guittard lived in Ohio anyway, which did not have to suffer from Reconstruction. As to Hardin's rehabilitation, the lawyers in Texas who approved his application to practice law were completely supportive and recommended that he read Hugo's *Les Misérables* for continued inspiration in keeping his life on the right path. They were impressed by the new lawyer named after the spirit-filled John Wesley who founded Methodism.

Katie and I maintain that the similarities between the lives of Hardin and Guittard greatly outweigh the differences. I will discuss the first four similarities and Katie three more. *Argument number one*: Hardin and Guittard were both extremely competitive and believed strongly in perfecting their debating skills. Both were officers in their literary societies. On one occasion, Hardin debated in support of the merits of women's rights and received the judges' verdict. In both cases, their interest in competitive debating in time led to decisions by each of them that the practice of law was a profession for which they were well suited, Hardin by his rigorous course of legal studies inside Huntsville, and Guittard by implication from his letters to his law-school-bound son, Francis.

Argument number two: Both Hardin and Guittard were proficient with the written word, Hardin authoring a 165-page autobiography and Guittard writing several shorter autobiographies as well as a 400-plus page dissertation. Both were big readers—Guittard his whole life, and Hardin after he went to Huntsville and was rehabilitating himself. It is fair to say that his reading in prison and preparing himself to become an attorney by an oral examination by the local Gonzales County Bar Association played a large part in Hardin's receiving a pardon from Governor Hogg. When he died, he had among his possessions three books—The General Laws of Texas, a dictionary, and *The Rise and Fall of the Confederacy*. Guittard was a real bookworm, starting with his father's library in New Bedford and continuing for the rest of his life. Both shared a strong interest in words, the coin of the realm for an attorney and a professor.

Argument three: Both Hardin and Guittard grew up in devout Methodist families, Hardin's father being a Methodist preacher and Guittard's father having been educated to be a priest but who became a Methodist after immigrating to the US. No doubt that early Methodist upbringing was ultimately instrumental in Hardin turning his life around in prison and finding purpose in a lawful and even noble occupation, namely, the practice of law. Guittard was always a Christian, having been brought up as Methodist and then undergoing conversion at a Baptist revival in Texas.

Argument four: Hardin's rehabilitation represented fifteen years of re-education and reprogramming to become a useful citizen and attorney. Guittard took seventeen years to obtain his degrees from college—which was the education he needed to support himself as a college professor. Hardin was forty years of age when he was released from Huntsville, and Guittard was thirty-five when he finished at the University of Chicago. The fifth point of similarity, if you are counting, is that both Hardin and Guittard left their institutions—Hardin the penitentiary and Guittard Baylor University—in the spring of 1894. After that, they both had to apply themselves to making a living, Hardin embarking on a legal career and Guittard on a brief stint as a book salesman. Both endeavors revolved around books.

Katie will discuss several more arguments supporting our position on those two propositions later.

Charlie, for the Negative: It must be completely obvious to any fair-minded person listening so far to this debate who knows anything at all about John Wesley Hardin, even without hearing from Finn and me, that the answer to both propositions must be heck "NO." It must also be clear to all the readers that Miles is trying to cherry-pick his facts, or water down the resolutions, or both—we trust our readers have already caught on to this and are not fooled by any such sophistic reasoning. Honestly, I feel like I should just sit down and let the chips fall where they may, but I know Pops wants us to debate as they did in the literary societies of olden times, and so I will offer a few remarks for the negative position.

First, even if we give the affirmative credit for their dubious contention based on cherry-picked facts that Huntsville rehabilitated Hardin—dubious because he shot and killed at least one person *after* he was supposedly rehabilitated—comparing Hardin to Guittard, whenever you start the comparison, is like comparing a stick of dynamite to a walking stick. That dog just won't hunt. From early in New Bedford, Guittard had a game plan, and it was about education, career, and family. He followed that plan from 1885 through 1931 when he received his Ph.D. Hardin's first real plan for his life was to do whatever was necessary to get the heck out of the pen. However, even after his passing his examination allowed him to practice law, he remained largely unfocused and still motivated by the same passions that got him into trouble to begin with, namely, gambling, drinking, hanging out with assorted lowlifes, an itchy trigger-finger, and generally making poor decisions. As everyone knows who has looked at that photograph of him in his coffin, those decisions after he had his law license resulted in his taking a bullet to the brain while playing poker at the Acme Saloon in El Paso. If Hardin had a game plan and was pursuing it, what the Sam Hill was he doing in that saloon waiting for a shoot-out with someone—John Selman, Sr.—who had told him to go get a gun? Hardin was just a terrible waste of a legal education and a good brain. He was a stick of dynamite, and it was just a matter of time after his release until he was going to get himself blown up.

Books? Let's talk about Hardin's supposed writing skills and his reading books. You've given him credit for writing a 165-page autobiography. Still, you conveniently left out that he had a writing partner, agent, and lover—a former prostitute named Helen Beulah M'rose—who was entitled to fifty percent of the proceeds from any sale of the book. No Helen M'rose, no autobiography. If you have read his crude letters to his wife Jane, then you must know that his writing in those letters was extremely weak and certainly not at the level of his autobiography. Then, did Hardin read widely or deeply? Insofar as anyone knows, Hardin's reading was focused on getting out of jail—who can blame him, I don't—and he became a pretty fair jail-house lawyer.

On the other hand, Guittard was the kind of reader who read at every opportunity and wouldn't have known a jail cell from a preacher's study. Guittard was a constant reader, reading day and night, maybe even while he was supposed to be eating dinner or in the lavatory, I don't know. Growing up, he read the *Youth's Companion* and, in later life, *The Literary Digest* and *The Decline and Fall of the Roman Empire.* Guittard was not addicted to gambling or alcohol or fraternizing with lowlifes, and he, unlike John Wesley Hardin, didn't hawk and spit on the ground. Guittard could not have taught school or college for over sixty years if he had been so addicted. If he had an addiction, it was to books. Okay, who would have been more fun to hang out with in a saloon and drink beer with, you may ask? Hardin, no doubt, unless you p—d him off. Frank, who could tell a few mildly humorous stories and recite numerous bone-headed student examination answers, was not known to be a raconteur or teller of jokes. Hardin, on the other hand, had some terrific stories to tell, including the notorious "death by snoring" anecdote in which he fired off a few lethal rounds through a wall to quiet a snoring sleeper in the next hotel room. But the "death by snoring" story just proves our point. But you already got that.

If Hardin was not about books, what was he about? That's pretty simple—pistols, wagering, shooting people he believed needed shooting, playing cards, pocketknives, drinking whiskey, and betting on horse races. Speaking of pistols, you mentioned a few books Hardin owned on the day he died. However, you left off his five pistols. The only vice he is not as famous for, along with cockfighting and bear-baiting, is consorting with ladies of the evening. However, the jury is still out on that one considering the access he had to prostitutes in those saloons, his extra-marital relationship with Helen M'rose, and his love of strong drink. On the other hand, Frank steered clear of vice, vice being even more prevalent in Waco, Texas, than New Bedford, Ohio, and the saloons and bawdy houses were only a short bike ride away from Frank's dorm.

Finn will now present some additional arguments opposing those resolutions.

Finn, for the Negative: I think Charlie has covered most of the best arguments—he got to speak first—but there are at least two more he forgot about which must be mentioned. First is that Frank Guittard had broad cultural interests, including the art and music of other countries. Frank started playing cornet in high school and played in a band during his years in Chicago. When he was still living at home in Ohio and working on the farm, he and his brothers killed time playing around with old brass horns collected by their father, probably kinds used by community bands during the Civil War. We have no evidence that Hardin had any particular interest in music, although he must have heard many hymns when he was a young boy that didn't make much impression on him. He probably could have sung those drinking songs along with those saloon girls like "Little Brown Jug" and "Barnacle Bill the Sailor."

Another difference between Hardin and Guittard—and this is a huge one—is that Hardin was infected by all that Lost Cause baloney that ran through the south like a malignant virus after the Civil War. On the other hand, Guittard would have understood all too well, as a student of history, the causes of the Civil War and the south's economic dependence on slave labor and its refusal to give it up. Guittard was not into the pseudo-romanticizing of the Confederate states' secession, plantation owners' lifestyles, the lives of the slaves, or the valor of the southern cause.

A minor difference, or perhaps a significant difference depending on your theological point of view, is that Hardin was at best (if he was baptized at all) only sprinkled as a Methodist and not dunked like Guittard, who became a Baptist. For Texas Baptists, Dear Reader, this would be a major difference between the two men. After all, even the legendary Sam Houston could not avoid being baptized in the Little Rocky Creek by that world-class baptizer, Rufus C. Burleson.

So, for these six or seven reasons, the answers to both propositions must be "No."

Katie, for the Affirmative: Pops has signaled that we are short on time so here first are my quick responses to Charlie and Finn's arguments:

First, Hardin most definitely had a game plan when he got out of prison—making a living through the noble practice of criminal defense work—but he was under a lot of stress from the difficulty of attracting sufficient legal business, a problem lawyers have to the present day. Hardin was an ex-con, which couldn't have helped him attract clients except those in trouble with the law. He can't be blamed for looking to relieve some of that stress of making a living and of having to keep an eye out for bad men wanting another notch on their guns by playing a few hands of poker and drinking a few beers. Surely, most of us have participated in that kind of harmless activity. Today, bar associations provide resources to those of their members with various addictions and assistance in building their practices. Hardin had no help along either of those lines. No, although he, like Frank, was trained in the Bible in a Methodist Sunday school, he was no Sunday school teacher. However, in our view, he is more to be pitied than censured. Frank's life was a piece of cake compared to Hardin's.

Second, Charlie dumped on Hardin's reading in prison. However, I dare anyone, including Charlie, to pick up and read Hardin's autobiography and tell me that it is not the work of a well-read mind, just like Frank Guittard's. And Hardin had even more time than Frank to read.

Third, another point of similarity is that both Hardin and Guittard were married twice, their first wives both dying of tuberculosis in their mid-30s. Sadly, Jane Hardin died while Hardin was in prison, bravely waiting for his return to her and their children. His marriage to Jane was a love affair lasting twenty years, and Frank to Josie's lasted thirty years. Additionally, Hardin's first marriage and Frank's first marriage both ended when Jane and Mamie each succumbed to consumption at age thirty-seven. Beat that! Further, while in prison, Hardin wrote to Jane to provide advice and Christian counsel to her and their children, advising them to pursue the right path and not imitate his mistakes. Frank Guittard similarly wrote to his oldest son, Francis, instructing him on the career path he should take to avoid the "blunders" Frank had made in his own life. Good parents want their children to profit from their mistakes. Maybe it's kind of a do-over.

Fourth, and we will not have time to go into this thoroughly, both Hardin and Guittard came from Christian homes, and from early on, had a strong sense of what was just and what was unjust. Hardin once stood up to injustice with a pocketknife when a teacher attempted to whip a schoolmate. Guittard had similar encounters with brutal teachers unjustly flogging him, Guittard not having access to a pocketknife. Hardin and Guittard, in their own ways, were both fighters for justice.

In conclusion, if I may speak both for Miles and myself and Charlie and Finn, I want to thank all the readers for their kind attention to our arguments. Miles and I trust readers will find that the similarities in the lives of Hardin and Frank Guittard outweigh the differences. Please do not let yourself be misled by those obvious differences before Hardin put his life back on a straighter path. Vote Affirmative.

Pops: Miles, would you or Finn like a final word? Sixty seconds.

Finn, for the Negative: Yes, thanks, Pops. Dear Reader, in conclusion, all Charlie and I ask is that you use your good common sense here. John Wesley Hardin, ironically named after a famous Methodist preacher by his not-famous Methodist preacher father—only remembered at all because of the killer son he sired—was not a "fighter for justice" but a prolific killer addicted to multiple vices, and all it got him was a bullet to the brain at the age of forty-two from another killer; perfect karma! Don't buy the Affirmative's argument that you should give Hardin a pass on his at least twenty-five murders—they were, for gosh sake, what got him sent to the Big House! Hardin claimed to have killed more than forty! Frank Guittard, on the other hand, was a kindly scholar of history with a dry sense of humor and a college teacher to thousands, a quiet and introverted man, a wearer of a pocket watch and fraternity key, a reader of Baptist quarterlies, a painter of rental houses, a napper, a golfer, a keeper of backyard chickens, a player of canasta and honeymoon bridge, a fully immersed believer in the birth, death, and Resurrection of Jesus Christ, and a cornet player who died of a heart attack at age eighty-three on the way to a Donizetti opera about love. So these men led similar lives because they both came from Methodist families with a Bible on the kitchen table? I think not. Good try, though, Miles and Katie. But Dear Reader, vote negative.

Pops: Readers, that concludes the debate. You may vote at your leisure for which team and individual team member you think did the best job of presenting their side, but remember, the parties flipped for sides and may have preferred to debate for the other side. Those readers wishing to vote may send their vote for either the affirmative or negative and which team member made the best argument for his or her side to cfguittard@flash.net. Those readers wishing to read further regarding John Wesley Hardin may want to refer to the volumes by Parsons & Brown, Leon Metz, or John Wesley Hardin listed in the bibliography.

Appendix C

Historical Timeline for the Principal Characters

1845 Feb 1: The Republic of Texas charters Baylor University.
1846 Jun: Baylor University opens for college students at Independence.
1846: Francis Joseph Guittard ("FJG") emigrates from France as a family land scout.
1851: Rufus C. Burleson becomes president of Baylor University at Independence.
1856: Oct 2: FJG and Lydia Myers marry; parents of Frank Guittard.
1861: Rufus C. Burleson departs for Waco; becomes Waco University president.
1867 Jan 7: Francis ("Frank") Gevrier Guittard is born in New Bedford, Ohio.
1870 Jan 7: The Waco Suspension Bridge over the Brazos River officially opens.
1872 Sep: The first train to Waco arrives in East Waco.
1880 Oct 11: Mamie Welhausen is born to Charles and Eliza Amsler Welhausen.
1885 Nov 11: Leland Stanford Junior University is founded.
1886 Summer: Frank realizes FJG will not be able to pay for his college education.
1886 Sep: Frank takes a train to Chester, Texas, to scout land for his family.
1886 Sep: Baylor University merges with Waco University and opens in Waco.
1886-1890: Frank teaches twenty-three months in Texas, six schools altogether.
1887 Fall: Frank enrolls at Sam Houston Normal School in Huntsville, Texas.
1889 Mar 23: Lydia Myers Guittard, mother of Frank Guittard, dies in Ohio.
1890 Feb: Frank enrolls at Baylor University in Waco for the spring term.
1891 Oct: Leland Stanford, Jr. University opens for its first session.
1892 Oct: The University of Chicago opens for its first session.
1894 May: Frank's funds run out; he leaves Baylor to sell books in Hunt County.
1897 Jun: Burleson resigns Baylor presidency; becomes president emeritus.
1897 Jul: Frank matriculates at the University of Chicago; stays two quarters.
1898: Frank becomes principal of Shiner School; meets Mamie Welhausen.
1899 Aug: Oscar Henry Cooper is elected Baylor president.
1901 Mar: Frank receives bachelor's degree from the University of Chicago (U of C).
1901 Apr: Frank enters U of C graduate school; commits to teaching history.
1902 Mar: President Cooper resigns following a protest over a chapel incident.
1902 Apr: Samuel Palmer Brooks is elected Baylor president.
1902 May: President Brooks offers Frank a job teaching at Baylor Academy.

1902 Jun 11: FJG dies in Ohio; Frank returns to Ohio to help settle the estate.
1902 Aug: Frank visits Mamie Welhausen in Shiner, Texas.
1902 Fall: Frank begins teaching at the Baylor Academy.
1904: Frank is promoted to faculty in the Baylor collegiate department.
1906 Jun: Frank buys a house at 1401 South 7th Street in Waco.
1906 Dec: Frank and Mamie marry in Shiner on Christmas Eve.
1907 Dec: Francis Gevrier Guittard, Jr. is born.
1910: President Brooks appoints Frank chair of the new Department of History.
1915 Feb: Charles Welhausen Guittard, Frank and Mamie's second son, is born.
1916-1917: Polio pandemic rages; 27,000 cases in the U.S. with 6,000 deaths.
1916 Aug: Charles Welhausen Guittard dies of probable tubercular meningitis.
1917 Mar: Clarence Alwin Guittard, Frank and Mamie's third son, is born in Waco.
1917 Apr: Mamie is admitted to tuberculosis sanatorium in Albuquerque, N.M.
1917 May: Mamie, age thirty-seven, dies, 24 days after admission to sanatorium.
1918-1919: Spanish influenza comes to Waco.
1919 Dec: Frank meets Josie Glenn at Christmas time in Waco.
1920 Jun 10: Frank and Josie marry.
1921 May: Frank and Josie pick up Clarence in Shiner and return to Waco.
1923 Summer: Frank spends his first summer at Stanford pursuing a Ph.D.
1928 Jan-Aug: Frank pursues his Ph.D. at Stanford for eight months.
1931 May 14: President Samuel Palmer Brooks dies in his 30th year as president.
1931 Jun 16: Frank receives his Ph.D. sheepskin at Stanford's commencement.
1931-1950: Frank continues teaching into his 48th year at Baylor.
1947 Jan 7: Frank and Josie execute joint will creating a fund for history fellowships.
1950 Apr 28: Frank dies in Dallas at 83 years of age.
1958 Dec 25: Josie dies in Waco at 73 years of age.
1959-1960: First Guittard History Fellows Ronald Lee Hayworth and Oran Lonnie Sinclair pursue master's degrees in history at Baylor University.
2014 Oct 31: First Guittard Book Award for Historical Scholarship (2013) is presented to Dr. Nancy Beck Young by the Baylor Department of History.
2017: Brendan J. Payne, Guittard History Fellow, receives the first Ph.D. in history from Baylor University.
2017: First Guittard-Verlander-Voegtle Scholarships [undergraduate] are awarded to history majors Michael Lopez and Taylor Kniphfer.
2021: Total number of Guittard Fellowships and Scholarships awarded exceeds 100.
2022: Charles Francis Guittard publishes *I WILL TEACH HISTORY, The Life & Times of Francis Gevrier Guittard*, the 3rd volume of a trilogy.

Author's Postscript

Dear Reader,

A few closing thoughts: This work was researched over several decades before the COVID-19 pandemic took the world by storm in 2020. Research began in 1978 during the second year of the administration of President Jimmy Carter, who is still currently with us in his late 90s. The writing took place almost entirely in apartment 1119 of The Reserve at North Dallas after the virus arrived, and the number of distractions was quickly reduced. Moreover, nearly everyone started staying inside to watch virus updates and unemployment reports. I found that writing was a welcome diversion to watching daily at least three crises unfold simultaneously on television: the presidential race of 2020 and the crisis in our country's leadership; the civil rights and police reform crisis triggered by the death of George Floyd at the hands of the Minneapolis police; and this once-in-a-lifetime pandemic.

One might wonder why we are not reminded of three cautionary, resonating tales of one hundred years ago. Warren G. Harding—acknowledged by historians as one of the worst US presidents because of his scandal-ridden presidency—was elected president of the United States in 1920. Second, the Ku Klux Klan was in its early twentieth-century heyday of intimidating African-Americans and everyone else through blazing crosses, lynchings, and its bizarre parades in masks, robes, and pointy hats. This Klan had widespread outreach and influence, accounting for over five to six million members—roughly five percent of the US population. Finally, Spanish influenza was killing off an estimated 675,000 Americans following the conclusion of World War I. At this writing, despite the achievements of modern medical science, over 1,000,000 deaths from Covid-19 have already been confirmed in the US alone. However, labs around the world, despite an anti-science, anti-vaccine bias in some parts of the world, have fortunately produced several effective vaccines, and the race is on to achieve herd immunity before we have to confront the next pandemic.

May we all live in good health long enough to tell our families' stories, including our college family, while there is still time and memories have yet to fade.

Charles Francis Guittard, April, 2022

SOURCE NOTES

The information in this book comes from a broad range of sources. The initial bibliography contained over 600 books, articles, periodicals, school essays, Baylor's newspaper the *Baylor Lariat* and other newspapers, Baylor's annual *Round-Ups*, master's theses, dissertations, diaries, ledgers, autobiographies, oral memoirs, and personal interviews, as well as online authorities. These sources are in addition to the hundreds of pieces of correspondence which led to beginning research on a possible life & times of Frank Guittard.

The principles I have used to guide my use of citations to source information are summarized below. Originally, the intent was to eliminate numbered citations—and that has been done. Footnotes do not appear at the foot of a page and there are no endnotes at the end of chapters. However, because this book is a life & times requiring extensive research, citations are often appropriate. I have chosen to occasionally include citations in the text itself in certain circumstances. We hope that the limited number of citations embedded in the text will add something to the reader's understanding of Frank Guittard's story.

Here are those principles: source identification will be accomplished in three ways—in the text (already mentioned), in the source notes, or in the bibliography. In either the text or the source notes, the citation may be complete or partial; if the citation is partial, such as "Smith, 33," then readers will need to turn to these source notes or the selected bibliography for the complete reference. Some rough categories may help clarify those three principles:

> *If the material relates to Frank Guittard or his family* and consists of family correspondence or correspondence from Frank's former students or was generated by Frank Guittard himself such as a diary or essay, it will be cited in the text only and no additional reference will be made to it in these source notes or the bibliography.
>
> An exception may be made in a particular instance if the material is unduly lengthy, is not essential to the story line, or may be distracting to readers. In these cases, the material will be contained in the source notes.
>
> *If the material relates to Baylor University or its presidents,* it may be cited in the text in completeness or saved for the source notes, depending on length and whether they add something important which the reader is likely to want to know when reading the text. Source information which would be helpful to an understanding of the text may appear in the text. Source information which is lengthy will be assigned to the source notes.
>
> *All other material including that relating to Waco, to Texas, or to the US generally,* will be cited briefly in the source notes with complete information provided in the selected bibliography.

The source notes below will, at a minimum, generally contain in order the three to ten or so initial words of the sentence in the text for which the source note is intended, the last name where available of the author of the source material, the type of source material, and the page number or other specific identifiers of the source material. In some instances, a particular note will be more extensive and contain the information which is customarily found in a bibliography. In some instances, a note may omit some customary bibliographic information; however, we have endeavored to supply all that was available to us at the time of writing.

Finally, if we have not always consistently applied the "principles" identified above, we hope the final result will serve well enough to document the story of Frank Guittard and his times and leave sufficient bread crumbs to guide anyone who may come after us.

Abbreviations used to refer to various sources include:

CAG Clarence Alwin Guittard
CFG Charles Francis Guittard
FGG Francis "Frank" Gevrier Guittard
GBH Guy B. Harrison, Jr.
JGG or MJ Josie "Mama Josie" Glenn Guittard
MW Mamie Welhausen
SPB Samuel Palmer Brooks
SWG Stephen Wood Guittard
TGF The Guittard Family
TTC The Texas Collection

INTRODUCTION

Unlike the Hoosier Schoolmaster (1871): Eggleston, 9.

PROLOGUE: Master of the Recitation

One student noted that classroom 202: Robert Miller, letters to CFG, January 18, 1980 and February 25, 1980.

At the stroke of 8:00 a.m.: Jefferson Davis Bragg, Oral Memoirs, 127. "Professor Guittard taught more or less sitting...He told me that someone told him once...that all the great teachers sat when they taught."

Couldn't Botchey tackle those guys: Barton "Botchey" Koch, no. 44, was Baylor's All-American guard and football team captain.

Professor, Coach Jennings said after the game: "Morley Jennings was highly regarded by his peers. Legendary Knute Rockne in the *1931 Round-up* said, 'Morley Jennings's work for Baylor has been known far and wide [in football and baseball] ...I heard much of Botchey Koch, your all-American guard, and I know of the record of your Jake Wilson."

The Bears put up a good fight: Jake Wilson was Baylor's undersized all-conference quarterback.

He did like to perform, though: 1980 CFG Interview with CAG.

Chapter 1. His Father Disinherited in Alsace; a Decision in Ohio

Many of the background facts for certain chapters, particularly 1, 4, and 16, and other chapters as well, have been gathered from many sources, but principally those composed by Frank Guittard. Those sources are: a short (legal sized) multi-page autobiographical essay (the "FGG Sketch") composed inside his W.W. Franklin Giant Rhetoric Class Outline and Essay book (sixty-one pages total) at Baylor University in the spring 1894; an eight page essay (the "FGG Theme") composed in the English III class Frank took at the University of Chicago in July 1900; a fifty-seven page autobiographical manuscript (entitled *Reborn'd in Texas* and called "FGG Autobiography" in these notes) written in pencil sometime after the 1908 advent of Henry Ford's Model T automobile mentioned indirectly early in the chapter; and Louise Moore Cagle's *The Life of Francis Gevrier Guittard*, a 120 page Master of Arts thesis, Baylor, a largely hagiographic research paper submitted in 1951 in partial fulfillment of her degree requirements. Professor Cagle, a history student of Frank Guittard, based her thesis on the three autobiographical writings just mentioned but also cited other information she had gathered. She conducted five or more interviews including those with Frank Guittard's surviving spouse, Josie Glenn Guittard, and former President Pat M. Neff, and cited newspaper clippings and other materials in the hands of Josie Glenn Guittard. The relevant chapters of Ms. Cagle's thesis that I have consulted are chapters I-IV, pp. 1-58. The author has occasionally cited both Mrs. Cagle's thesis and the underlying documents footnoted by Mrs. Cagle, which were authored by Frank Guittard, all of which the author has reviewed. Certain other materials generated by Frank Guittard including his diary, ledgers, speeches, and correspondence will also be referenced in these source notes below.

The family's original plan was: Once in America, Joseph, who had been a saddle and harness maker in Alsace, and Catherine, despite never learning English and being homesick for Alsace, remained in America. Francis Joseph and Frank's relationships with Joseph and Catherine in America is lost to history.

Francis Joseph married Lydia Myers: Cagle, 3; FGG Theme, 2.

During the Civil War, Guittard family legend: Harriet Guittard Rentfrow tape 1985.

However, since he was a trained physician: Gwynne, 67.

"*I must say as to what I have seen of Texas, it is the garden spot of the world*": Michael A. Lofaro, "Crockett, David," *Handbook of Texas Online* accessed January 9, 2015.

"*Outlaws. John Wesley Hardin. Sam Bass*": Dan Abrams and David Fisher, "Courtroom drama comes to Dallas," Dallas Morning News, August 8, 2021. "Sam Bass, 'Texas Beloved Bandit,' and his gang had robbed trains and stagecoaches including the Union Pacific 'Gold Train,' " before Texas Rangers killed him in a shoot-out in 1878.

But first, let's start with the beginning: Cagle, 2; FGG Sketch, 58-59.

Francis Joseph Guittard, the father of: FGG Sketch, 58.

Alsace is a largely Roman Catholic region: Cagle, 2; FGG Sketch, 58. The eastern border of France adjoins, from north to south, Belgium, Germany, Switzerland, and Italy. In 1871, at the conclusion of the Franco-Prussian War, Alsace was ceded to Germany and did not return to France until the Treaty of Versailles at the end of World War I. Mulhouse would become known later for the Battle of Mulhouse c. August 7, 1914 which constituted the opening attack of World War I by the French against Germany and was intended to recover Alsace from the Germans.

Around 1854 he began to study medicine: Cagle, 3.

Francis Joseph married Lydia Myers: Cagle, 7-8; Tombaugh, 75.

The Methodist Episcopal Church split into two: Ralph E. Morrow, "Northern Methodism in the South during reconstruction," "Mississippi Valley Historical Review (1954), vol. 41, #2, 197-218.

He did not complete: Cagle, 3; *Holmes County Farmers Hub*, 1902. Given that he received his degree from the University of Wooster in 1971, we have to believe that he and his entire family counted their blessings they had emigrated from Alsace before it was annexed by the victorious Prussians who had crushed the French army the same year. It is interesting that Francis Joseph's son Frank married a daughter of a German immigrant whose family chose to live in the US rather than in the state of Hanover prior to Hanover also being annexed by Prussia several years before the Franco-Prussian war, so Mamie and Frank had much in common when they met in 1898. Nevertheless, Mamie's brother, C.B. Welhausen, was named after Prussia's popular Otto von Bismarck, Chancellor of the German Reich.

Having an excellent small library: Cagle 14; autobiographical statement of JGG, February 16, 1951.

Occasionally there was a taffy-pulling: Cagle, 21; FGG Autobiography, 8.

The choir practices were usually held: Cagle, 22; FGG Autobiography, 6.

Another teacher he remembered with loathing: Cagle, 17; FGG Sketch, 60.

In the Hoosier Schoolmaster, a tough student: Eggleston, 47.

There is also an amusing chapter: Eggleston, 70-89.

When he obtained his teacher's certificate: Cagle, 18; FGG Theme, 3.

As a result of doing farm work: Cagle, 12; JGG statement, February 16, 1951.

Frank took a break from farm work: Cagle, 20; FGG Autobiography, 6.

The horns were probably relics of those militia and community bands: The Garofalo work on civil war musical instruments provides the history of these bands. The beginning of the brass band era in America was 1835, the year the first all brass bands were established, and would have included, in addition to trumpets and valved trombones, keyed bugles, ophicleides, and post horns. In addition to increasing numbers of professional players, there were also large numbers of amateurs who could play these instruments and the brass instruments now being turned out. (Garofalo, 3-5) Common were the over-the-shoulder saxhorns which pointed to the rear to direct the sound of the music to the troops marching behind the band. Woodwinds were excluded from these military bands (Garofalo, 3).

Frank came to a painful realization: Cagle, 19; FGG Sketch, 60.

Around that time a resident of Chester: Cagle, 22; FGG Autobiography, 8.

Francis Joseph had already been: Cagle, 23; FGG Autobiography, 4.

The husband was just as insistent that the doctor: Flexner, 184. A doctor practicing in Cincinnati, Ohio, in the early 1850s carried with him Glauber's salts, Dover's powder, strong paregorics, vermifuges, blisters, Peruvian bark for fevers, dragon's blood, gamboge, and nux vomica. We doubt Francis Joseph would have had better medicines in the 1880s.

Though Francis Joseph had a large and busy country practice: FGG interview, *Baylor Lariat*, May 18, 1949, 1.

Burke's Texas Almanac contained the kind of information: *Burke's Texas Almanac*, Lutcher & Moore, c. 1879, 27-28.

Burke's Almanac also detailed the crops: Ibid., 46.

"Formerly we were liable to visitations": Ibid., 77.

As to educational opportunities: *Burke's Almanac*, Ibid., 77.

"There is also room in Texas for those in the learned professions": Ibid., 78.

"In Texas the railroad boom still continues": Ibid., 75.

And Texas did historically have some detractors: Maillard's *The History of the Republic of Texas*...Maillard's views are set out at length in this volume.

In an 1849 account of his travels through Texas: Ferdinand von Roemer, "German Scientist Concludes Tour of Texas," *Handbook of Texas Online*, Texas State Historical Association, accessed May 9, 2014.

There was one anonymous detractor: Reportedly, English King John died of gorging on peaches, and Henry I after eating lampreys, a kind of eel-like fish. *The History Girls Blog*, November 24, 2013. "A Surfeit of Lampreys and other Misfortunes: The Death of Henry I."

Finally this detractor advised settlers: Anonymous, Muir editor, 170-173.

Another claimed, "Texas had within its borders eight thousand": Gruber, 121.

The solution in 1874 was to reorganize the Texas Rangers: Guinn, 89-91.

And...there were those lethal feuds in Texas: C.L. Sonnichsen, "Feuds," *Handbook of Texas Online*, accessed June 20, 2013.

Bass [Sam], who had been in Waco the week before: *Waco Heritage and History*, "From Waco to Round Rock: The Last Days of Same Bass," September 1989, 53-54.

Soon after saying goodbye to his father: FGG Autobiography, 12-13.

Chapter 2. Frank's Early Schooling; College Days before Baylor

It's hard to say, but in the 1870s: Saffell, 1-2.

"This may come at a bad time": We have no idea what Frank was referring to by "that old claim," but we assume it was a private claim, not a court case, and we have no reason to believe that it related to his medical practice.

Chapter 3. A Bookworm's Mind: Influences, Interests, & Books

Those in his father's library: FGG Autobiography, 59; JGG Statement, February 11, 1951.

There were many points of similarity: Alger, *From Canal Boy to President ...James A. Garfield*, 20, 27, 28, 80, 152; *Peskin*, 14, 20, and 23.

Dime novels were trendy in the US: CAG dictated tape no. 2, 1980.

He would read best sellers with Mama Josie: CAG dictated tape, 1980.

When he was working on his Ph.D.: CAG dictated tape no. 1, 1980.

In the category of "heavy" books: FGG Books Read, 1931-1947 (FGG list).

The books he read that he categorized as "light": Ibid.

Chapter 4. Train Trip to Texas to Enrollment at Baylor (1886-1890)

Frank Guittard's initial adventures in Texas command our attention here, beginning with his 1886 seventy hour train trip: Cagle, 24; FGG Autobiography, 13. Frank Guittard was not the only traveler to Texas in September 1886 beginning a new chapter in his life. On September 13, "under heavy military guard, Apache Indian leader Geronimo arrived in San Antonio…to stand trial in US court. Angry crowds had gathered and were anxious to drag Geronimo away and hang him on the spot." *Texas Landmarks & Legacies*, vol. 8, no. 256.

Frank's destination was Chester: Cagle, 25; FGG Sketch, 61; see also Megan Biesle, "Chester, TX," *Handbook of Texas Online*, accessed July 18, 2020.

In addition, Lawrence Sullivan Ross, the candidate: Hendrickson, 116-117.

Texas experienced a crippling drought: Roy Sylvan Dunn, "Droughts," Handbook *of Texas Online*, accessed July 20, 2012.

"*When the army arrived in Washington D.C., the President ordered*": McMurry, 116-118.

On September 25, 1886, after a tiresome: Cagle, 27; FGG Sketch, 61.

After arriving in Chester: Cagle, 28-30; FGG letter to his father, October 4, 1886 from Chester, Texas.

As of 1890, just a few years later, Chester was reported to have: Megan Biesele, "Chester, TX," *Handbook of Texas Online*, accessed July 18, 2020.

"*In spite of a barking dog*": Cagle, 33.

The Canons received Frank: Cagle, 34; FGG Autobiography, 27.

This tract was for sale: Cagle, 35: FGG Autobiography, 29.

Frank completed his land survey: Cagle, 38; FGG Theme, 5.

He discovered that one of the examiners: Cagle, 39; FGG Autobiography, 32.

When one of the waitresses came over: Cagle 40, FGG Autobiography, 33.

In the morning after a good night's rest: Cagle, 41; FGG Autobiography, 35.

However, since Frank's new school: Cagle, 42-43; FGG Autobiography, 37.

Sundays were rest days: Cagle, 46; FGG Autobiography, 40.

Before school began, Frank made: Cagle, 48; FGG Autobiography, 42.

Parents were often opposed to vaccination: Campbell, *Gone to Texas*, 19.

The first order of business: Cagle, 50; FGG Autobiography, 45.

The furniture was extremely: Cagle, 50; FGG Autobiography, 50-51.

The three R's—reading, "riting": Cagle, 51; FGG Autobiography, 45.

Heating was provided by a potbellied stove: Campbell, Ibid. 17.

Often there was a framed print: Campbell, Ibid. 48.

Recitations were sing-song in spelling, arithmetic: Rice, 8, 83, 94.

Frank had no problem with: Cagle, 51; FGG Autobiography, 45-46.

"*The offenders never knew whether they were cutting*": Poage, *After the Pioneers—Recollections of W.R. Poage*, 80.

The children Frank taught: Cagle, 52; FGG Autobiography, 46-47.

Frank considered that he was "readily adapting": Cagle, 54; FGG Autobiography, 50.

For the 1887-1888 school year: Cagle, 60; FGG Sketch, 61.

During the school months Frank had: Cagle, 59; FGG Autobiography, 57.

He possibly had become aware that as of 1890: Beatty, 85, 105.

After his school closed: Cagle, 60; FGG Autobiography, 57.

Sam advised his brothers to stay in Indiana: Gard, *Sam Bass*, 37-38.

Chapter 5. Short History of Baylor University (1845-1947)

Before talking more about the 1886 merger: Frederick Eby, *The Development of Education in Texas.* New York: The Macmillan Company, 1925, 141-142.

Rufus C. Burleson strongly maintained: early *Baylor Round-Up.*

Baylor University at Waco opened: Walker et al., 1.

At the time of the merger, Waco University: Guemple thesis, 118.

On one occasion in 1900: President Oscar Henry Cooper, Waco, Texas, letter June 29, 1900 to President William R. Harper, Chicago, Illinois.

But it is interesting: hsutx.edu/library/research center/Richardson/chapter.004.

This proposal directly resulted in creating: "In Memoriam, Oscar Henry Cooper," Committee, the University of Texas, Frederick Eby, Chair, c. 1933.

Dr. Eby proclaimed: hsutx.edu/Hall-of-Leaders/Oscar-Henry-Cooper.

The evidence also indicates: Guemple, 118.

Chapter 6. Wild & Woolly Waco, McLennan County, Texas

There were many things about 1890s Waco: Poage, *McLennan County—Before 1980,* 204.

However, when Frank checked into Maggie Houston Hall: Barnes, 61.

We can talk about the Indians who: Wallace, *Waco: A Sesquicentennial..., 13.*

The story of Waco cannot be told...with five depots: 1892 Map of Waco; TTC.

Perhaps the best-known bawdy house [in Waco]: Pylant, 147.

Waco was not unusual: see Richard F. Selcer, *Hell's Half Acre,* for the history of Fort Worth's red-light district.

Let's start with the Indians: Wallace, *Waco: A Sesquicentennial...,* 13, et seq.

The Lover's Leap Legend was about a Waco Indian girl: Ames, 103.

"*Thus is told the wondrous":* W.O. Blount, *1911 Baylor Round-Up,* 270.

About one hundred ninety years: Wallace, *Waco: A Sesquicentennial...,* 115.

"Thus, the Waco that Brann found in 1894": Carver, 39.

[Nevertheless] the law prohibiting the carrying: Brann, vol. iv, 51.

According to one historian, "By the late 1800s the vice capitals": Pylant, 5.

The Methodists and the Baptists competed: Lewis Publishing Company, 161.

The 1900 Waco City directory: Wallace, *Waco: A Sesquicentennial...,* 68.

Waco also had an ordinance: Richard J. Veit, *Waco Heritage and History,* "Law and Order in Six-Shooter Junction," December 1989, vol. 19, no. 2, 31.

Although Waco had: Lewis Publishing Company, 167-169.

"*Waco the Central City of Texas*": Conger, *a Pictorial History of Waco,* 190. George B. Dutton contracted to hoist the cables and install the guy wires and wind anchors for the Waco Suspension Bridge.

"*Yet cotton is master of them all*": Scarborough, x.

"*The mention of abolishing*": Conger, *A Pictorial History of Waco,* 10.

McLennan County voted 586 to 191 for secession: Jones, J., 8.

According to the booklet: Knight, 16. Regarding Add-Ran University, name later changed to Texas Christian University and relocated to Fort Worth, and Baylor University, "the oldest and most famous of Texas colleges," Baylor's original campus [Main Building and Georgia Burleson Hall] and Waco Female College were all designed by local architect W. R Larmour and similar in appearance. In 1896, Waco Female College went bankrupt and Add-Ran moved into its buildings. Add-Ran stayed in Waco until the 1910 fire required it to move to Fort Worth.

An appropriation for such purpose was on the calendar: Knight, 14.

"*This is a river of many faces*": Archer, 2.

The Round-Up went on to declare: 1906 Baylor Round-Up, 294.

"*Saintly Waco fairly ruptures a blood vessel*": Brann, vol. iii, 120.

"*Of course, Waco, like other places, has its drawbacks*": Brann, vol. vii, 293.

"*Waco is the only town in Texas of any consequence*": Brann, vol. vi, 244.

"*Some of the names were the Red Front Saloon*": Pylant, 91-221.

"Another time, two hack drivers": Waco Evening News, January 2, 1894.

After taking his assassin's bullet, however, Brann: Brann, vol. vii, 9.

His grandson one hundred years later admitted: *Waco Tribune Herald*, "Waco's Six-Shooter Journalist," April 1, 1998.

However, when Brann initially arrived in Waco: Wallace, *A Spirit So Rare: A History of the Women of Waco*, 112.

However, where Baylor was concerned: Amanda Norman, "The Tragedy of ...Brann," blogs. baylor.edu/ texascollection/ 2013.04/01. Wallace, Ibid., 114.

Brann's relentless attack on B: Roger N. Conger, "Brann, William Cowper," *Handbook of Texas Online*, Texas State Historical Association, accessed July 27, 2013.

The kidnapping and transport of Brann: Statement of Alva Bryan with respect to the W.C. Brann affair; letters from attorney Cullen F. Thomas to Dr. Carl Lovelace, February 5, 1931. TTC.

The [students'] initial motivation for, or intended resolution: letter from D.K. Martin May 17, 1961 to Guy B. Harrison, Jr. TTC.

Afterward, Brann might possibly: January 12, 1929 letter from Carl Lovelace to Dr. J.M. Dawson and January 15 letter from Dawson to Lovelace. TTC.

George M. Scarborough: Son of Judge Scarborough and brother to Dorothy.

Anyway, after the students reached the campus: Alva Bryan, Ibid.

First Baptist Church pastor J.M. Dawson: untitled publication by J.M. Dawson in The Texas Collection.

The trail was later made famous: Kristina Gaylord, "Chisholm Trail," Kansapedia-Kansas Historical Society, created June 2011.

Captain Shapley P. Ross's ferry connected: Conger, "The Waco Suspension Bridge...," 181.

Then General Joseph Speight and others: Vivian Elizabeth Smyrl, "Waco Suspension Bridge," *Handbook of Texas Online*, accessed April 20, 2013.

Brann asserted without proof that "Waco...": Brann, vol. iv, 1.

The Reservation, called by many "Two Street": Wallace, *Our Lands Our Lives: Pictorial History, McLennan County*, excerpts.

One additional reason for creating the Reservation: Pylant, 6, 73.

During World War I the US Army made Waco a deal: David C. Humphrey, "Prostitution," *Handbook of Texas Online*, accessed June 4, 2013.

The prostitutes were given until August 4, 1917: Pylant, 317.

Over seven hundred cases of flu: Wallace, *Waco: A Sesquicentennial...*, 120.

As for the saloons on Bridge Street: Wallace, *Our Land, Our Lives: A Pictorial History of McLennan County*, Texas, 50.

Kate Ross Padgitt was an 1867 graduate of Waco University: Ibid., 24.

Her father, Shapley P. Ross: Wallace, *Waco: A Sesquicentennial...*, 24.

In 1875 Kate was also instrumental: Ibid., 68-69.

"drought," "parlor," "mantel board": Reagan, 683-684.

Sul Ross we already talked about: Wallace, *A Spirit So Rare: A History of the Women of Waco*, 58.

At the time, Mix said: unidentified Waco newspaper, September 11 & 12, 1927.

Chapter 7. Rufus C. Burleson, his Universities, and Waco (1851-1897)

I think it would have been funny: "Teasips" is a term occasionally used for students of the University of Texas at Austin by students of their primary rival, Texas A&M University.

According to Frederick Eby, Dr. Carroll: It is interesting that although Carroll was a strong believer in preserving the Union, nevertheless decades before, he had joined a group of Texas Rangers under the Confederacy's umbrella. The *1896 Baylor Round-Up* reports that soon "After mustering into the service, he delivered a speech in Arkansas on 'The Delusions of the South.' These delusions were set forth as follows: (1) a speedy victory of the Confederate armies; (2) the supposed cowardice of Northern troops; (3) the reliance on Northern Democrats; and (4) the reliance on European intervention."

At this time, Waco Baptists: Carroll, *A History of Texas Baptists*, 772. Heresy and other church trials in Baptist churches have been abandoned.

Adjudged by Baptist chroniclers: Mathews, pp. 141-42; Eby, chapter 3.

Chapter 8. Frank's Game Plan: Education, Career, & Family (1885—)

Frank's plan for his life: Cagle, 70.

"*I have had much to discourage me but*": Cagle, 68-69; FGG Sketch, 61.

"*It is no satisfactory solution*": Gowin, v.

Gowin's advice was to study the careers: Gowin, 21-28.

A big hat or sombrero to shade him: DVD Series: CR 1993 *American History of the Wild West*, Dan Dalton Productions, insert notes.

Further, Cooper claimed the would-be teacher: article in the January 1890 *Texas School Journal* edited by O.H. Cooper, 25, 32.

In addition to the University of Chicago: FGG Speech—"Students Who Work to Get Through College," FGG Papers, TTC.

Here are a few reasons that would seem to fit Frank: Ferenc M. Szasz, "The Many Meanings of History," *History Teacher*, partially published in the August 1974 issue and partially in the February 1975 issue.

Oftentimes, mentally ill people: Eggleston, 205. In Eggleston's *The Hoosier Schoolmaster* (1871) the central character Ralph Hartsook pays a visit to a local Indiana poor-house for women and their children. "Here were vicious women and good women...And there were...helpless, idiotic women with illegitimate children...people slightly demented and raving maniacs were in the same rooms, while there were also those utter wrecks which sat in heaps on the floor, mumbling and muttering unintelligible words."

Frank would have learned rather quickly that Texas too: Yoakum, 11. For two good works on facilities established to care for the indigent and near helpless, the sick not able to secure medical care, criminals for whom the penitentiary was impractical or inappropriate, and the feeble-minded and insane in Texas, see both C. S. Yoakum's and Williams's books.

To be on charity: Myra H. McIlvain, Myra H. McIlvain blog, "Going to the Poor House in Texas," October 17, 2014.

When the residents were able to work: Williams, 20.

Also disturbing was the fact: Myra H. McIlvain, Myra H. McIlvain blog, "Going to the Poor House in Texas," October 17, 2014.

According to Dana Goolsby, "Poor Farms...": Dana Goolsby, "The Anderson County Poor Farm," TexasEscapes.com. Most of the poor houses and poor farms disappeared with the 1920s social welfare legislation and the Social Security Act of 1935.

His desire to be a physician was despite: Shyrock, 28-36.

As to dentistry, it was reported that: Terkel, 246.

He [Frank Guittard] would have wanted to go to a regular medical school: Wischnitzer, 6-7, set out a criteria for self-evaluation for prospective physicians which were as applicable in the late nineteenth century. Frank would have felt some of them applied to him. However, while it was always clear the was destined for a life of service, it was not clear that medicine's jealous demands of a physician and his family would have been compatible ultimately with his personality and his broad interest in studying all countries' histories. However, Wischnitzer also reminded prospective medical students, if they needed help, to go seek help and use it.

The licensing procedure [for an attorney] required: Robertson, 34.

How well he would have adjusted: Miller, 26-27.

Money was necessary to live: Terry Jo Ryan, "Brazos Past: Toby's Practical Business College Flourished in Waco...," *Waco Tribune*, March 5, 2013.

Because Frank must have known Hardin's history: Here is an overview of the two avenues open to someone like Frank or John Wesley Hardin or any male desiring to study law, putting aside the question of expense for the moment. Entry into the practice of law could be accomplished by the following:

First, a law school education—the law school of the University of Texas was founded in 1883, Pat M. Neff earning his law degree there—which probably required completion of several years of approved undergraduate courses and perhaps an undergraduate degree. Because of the requirement of three to four years of an approved undergraduate course, this route would have had the disadvantage of compelling Frank as of 1894 to undertake at least an additional five years of school, including law school, before he would be qualified to practice. However, if he desired to teach school after earning his undergraduate degree, then a master's degree would take just an additional three years of school; or

Second, reading law with a respected local attorney. At such time as the supervising attorney approved, the applicant would petition an appropriate local court to be admitted to the bar to practice and attach an affidavit of his supervising attorney and whomever else as to his completion of his course of study and his good moral character. There was no written bar exam required by the American Bar Association until the 1920s. Except that Frank was focused on the credibility to be derived from a degree from a recognized institution of higher learning, there seems to have been no insurmountable reason why Frank could not have worked to support himself while reading law in the office of an attorney in Ohio or Texas. If he had commenced such a course in 1886, then he likely he would have been a practicing attorney at least by ten years later at the age of 29. Of course, that would have meant a crucial shift of his focus away from his liberal education to his professional education to make a living other than by teaching.

An additional characteristic needed for success as an attorney, especially in a small town, would have been a personality of the type that would attract clients. Although Frank liked to attend regular church services once a week and occasionally as a destination for a date before being married, he was not interested in mixing and mingling. Nevertheless, the available evidence demonstrates that, despite his basic personality, he would have had enough drive to analyze what he needed to do to attract clients and, thereafter, would have done what was required.

Frank's advice to Francis is consistent: Three years later, Frank would declare in a speech May 23, 1931 to the graduating seniors of Magnolia High School: "The decision as to what calling is to be chosen should not be made without seeking the advice of parents and friends. This vital matter should not be left to caprice or hasty decision. A few leaves out of the book of experience of a sincere friend will often help to avoid many years of useless experimentation."

"Johnson, upon this, seemed much agitated": *Boswell's Life of Johnson.* Editor Charles Grosvenor Osgood, Excerpts, Gutenberg EBook Life of Johnson released May 12, 2006 (EBook #1564).

Similarly, Frank's feeling of having been at the mercy of the forces of chance: In his commencement address ("Making and Investing a Life") to the 1930 graduating senior class of Magnolia High School, Magnolia, Arkansas, Frank appears to have softened his feeling that he had blundered in the planning of his life. He touched on several themes in nuanced remarks to the graduating seniors May 23, 1930. While telling the graduates on the one hand that they should consult parents and friends in the choice of an occupation, thus "taking a few leaves out of the book of experience," he also advised the graduates, "It does not matter so much what occupation or business or profession is chosen," only that the calling should enlist the students' talents, interests, and energies.

Chapter 9. Frank's College Days at Baylor (early 1890s)

"Have a good boarding place [212 Webster Street]": FGG means Webster Avenue in Waco.

The new female student's response: J.W. Bryan, *Baylor University Literary*, May 1893; The Texas Collection.

Soirees came only four or five times a year: Fred Hartman, *Baylor Monthly*, December 1923, 3 & 5. Several years later and in a later chapter, Neff would write his mother that Frank Guittard was guiding him in his approaches to young women in Magnolia, Arkansas.

"We had to march from the Main Building": GBH Oral Memoirs, 220; TTC.

The 1890-1891 Catalogue affirmed: page 44 of this catalogue; TTC.

Student Douglass Scarborough recorded: Douglass Scarborough, "Elocution Course Notes, W.W. Franklin's Elocution Course, June 16, 1890"; TTC.

"The professor of English": President's Page, *Baylor Monthly*, Jan. 1928, 5.

"Teachers of English had no false pride": Ibid.

Chapter 10. "Maggie" for Students of Lesser Means

Frank resided at Maggie: Cagle, 67; Neff, July 2, 1951 interview.

No bath[s] except when: Pat M. Neff, *Baylor Monthly*, August 1927.

The affluent male students: *Baylor Monthly*, March 1929, 3.

"The doctors would come": Sam P. Brooks, *Baylor Monthly*, March 1929.

"Should any grand addition be made": "Demmy" apparently refers to the Athenian orator Demosthenes who allegedly overcame a childhood speech defect by speaking with pebbles in his mouth.

Chapter 11. President Burleson's Rules & Discipline

President Burleson was firm: Pamphlet advertising Baylor University, 1892-1893, Burleson Papers, Texas Collection, quoted by Dickinson in his thesis "Baylor University—A Century of Discipline, 1845-1947," 79. Also see the *Baylor University Catalogue, 1892-1893*, 770-772.

Burleson also came down hard against: Rufus C. Burleson, "Defects in College Discipline," *National Education Association Journal*, 634.

Baptists generally strongly supported Burleson's moral positions: Baptist General Convention of Texas, 1895, 79-80.

For views similar to Burleson's: Reverend Thomas Shepherd, "Advice...to his Son upon the Latter's Admission to Harvard College," Publication of the Colonial Society of Massachusetts, vol. XIV, 192-198, quoted by Professor Cohen in *Education in the United States: A Documentary History*, 667-670.

"Sometimes young women threw notes": Minutes of Faculty Meeting, Baylor University, March 4, 1896, 231.

Apparently, when one is called upon on judgment day: Spain, 11.

Even reading novels: *Baylor Catalogue of 1885-1886*, 41.

"Boys could not converse with girls": Baylor Century, "Judge Pool Recalls Origin Baylor Colors, Yells, Publications," April, 1939, 7; quoted by Dickinson, Ibid, 8, as to the "imaginary line" drawn by President Burleson.

Chapter 12. Literary Societies: Debates, not Athletic Contents

Quoting the 1909 Baylor Round-Up: 127.

The Calliopeans and RCB.'s were: The RCB.s, one of two literary societies for women, took the initials of President Burleson. "Philos" was short for Philomathesians and "Sophies" short for Erisophians. The Philos and the Sophies were the two men's societies, not counting the Adelphian Theological Society made up of ministerial students.

"Oh yes, Sul Ross was a Philo": The illustrious Sul Ross was the former Texas Ranger who ran the Modocs out of East Waco, was elected governor of Texas and served as President of A&M. He attended Baylor at Independence.

In each debate, according to Neff, Brooks: *Baylor Monthly*, August 1927, 11.

The result of Smith and fellow Sophie: Kent Keeth and Harry Marsh, The *Baylor Line*, April 1976, excerpting Jesse Guy Smith's article in the 1929 *Baylor Monthly*.

As bitter as the rivalry was: *1896 Baylor Round-Up*, 173.

Chapter 13. Dropping out & Selling Books to Farmers' Wives (1894)

The 1893 depression and its: Lears, 163; New York Public Library, 295.

In 1894, unemployment worsened: Sperling, *Great Depressions*, 91-104.

"During the fall and winter of 1893": Schwantes, 20-21.

President Cleveland put down the strikes: Ibid., 153-154.

Frank tells the story in an essay: Cagle, 72; FGG Diary, 5.

The typical Talmage sermon: Talmage's style undertook to elevate his audiences by damning those activities he deemed injurious, and which, he warned, led people, step by step, into depravity.

In his letter to his father: Samuel Palmer Brooks. *The Yale Letters from Samuel Palmer Brooks to His Father*. Waco: Baylor University, 1983, 61-62.

First, the section on the doctrine of evolution: Talmage, 67.

Second, the curse of strong drink: Ibid., 121.

Third, the section on dress and dissipation: Ibid., 137.

Fourth, the section on dancing: Ibid., 140.

He also lets fire on bad pictures and bad books: Ibid., 228, 253.

Talmage was delivering his final sermon: Rusk, 74.

I based this scene: The books by Mortimer, Boyce Brothers, and Lindley.

Fourteenth, although it might seem: Mortimer, 201.

Fifteen, the salesperson can always play the "resemblance... ": Lindley, 54.

"Mrs. Smith, I'm here in Greenville today": Ibid., 57.

The most problematic aspect of selling books: Gwynne, 202-203. Many northerners correctly observed that many southerners in the planter class fantasized they were knights a la Wilfred of Ivanhoe fighting for their lifestyle and property rights in slaves against fanatics like John Brown. Mark Twain called this romantic myth sweeping through the south the "Sir Walter Scott" disease, which he considered one cause of the Civil War. Gwynne, 202-203.

There were salesmen—perhaps because: Terkel, 567.

It was estimated that Talmage's sermons: Rusk, 64-65.

It would not be necessary to add: Ibid., 65-66.

However, a line actually used: Butler, 17.

It worked better to pee under a bridge: Boyce, 107, 121.

Chapter 14. Summer 1895 & Family Crisis in Ohio (1895)

You will remember that when: Cagle, 9, 25; FGG Autobiography, 12-13.

According to family legend: Harriet Rentfrow Interview, 1980.

An interview with a cousin: Ibid., 1980.

There was no shame; Most morphine addicts in the 19th century; and *Morphine became a significant problem:* Hodgson, 3-8, 85, and 97.

As late as the early 1930s: Alexander and Selesnick, 4-5.

Chapter 15. Two Bachelors in Arkansas; Rooming with Neff (1895-1896)

Frank accepted and joined Pat Neff: Blodgett, et al., 265.

In fact, Frank and Neff roomed together: Cagle, 113; Neff tribute.

Here are a number of letters: Patrick M. Neff papers; TTC.

"I can almost agree with Talmage": T. DeWitt Talmage; chapter 13 herein.

"We have both felt a great responsibility": Frank likely attended this same social function.

"But the funniest thing was this": Cantwell was principal of the academy and a Baylor and Yale graduate; also a friend of Samuel P. Brooks.

"Prof. C. [Cantwell] & myself were in for a debate": Neff means he thrashed Cantwell soundly, Neff being a formidable intercollegiate debater during his Philomathesian days at Baylor. Samuel P. Brooks had been Neff's roommate at Maggie Houston Hall during their undergraduate days.

"Magnolia is under strict quarantine..., The small pox..., Though the almond-eyed Chinaman": Pat Neff's comments show that associating contagion with China precede similar claims referring to the COVID-19 pandemic in 2020-21.

"Prof. Guittard & myself bought an Encyclopedia": The encyclopedia must be the same one for which Frank Guittard later traded the watch he won selling books Talmage's *Trumpet Blasts* for Neff's half interest in the encyclopedia.

"All the teachers are here except Guittard": See the prior chapter on the difficult summer of 1895 in Ohio.

Neff was a fascinating and enigmatic character: Space does not permit outlining the highlights of his life, career, and personal characteristics. Dorothy Blodgett et al.'s volume *The Land, the Law, and the Lord...* is a first-rate biography of Neff. For a short essay on Neff, the reader is referred to the article "Neff, Pat Morris," by Thomas E. Turner, in the *Handbook of Texas Online* uploaded August 7, 2010 and accessed May 11, 2014.

"So you can see how popular": Lois Smith Strain Interview, Baylor University Institute for Oral History, October 18, 1977.

Chapter 16. Early Flirtations, Romances (1886-1903)

As to your second question: Cagle, 55-56; FGG Autobiography, 51-52.

Okay, we'll get to that, but before we leave: FGG Autobiography, 52-55.

"*Jobe had also descended*": Cagle, 56-58; FGG Autobiography, 52-55.

Frank did not enroll: Cornelia Marshall Smith Oral Memoirs, 6-7.

You will remember in the prior chapter: Neff letter to his mother, March 1895.

According to the one of the Redbooks of that day: *Redbook of Dallas*, Texas, 3, 5, 7, 11. This red book details the rules of etiquette applying to men's hats, cards, dress, conversation, and much more, which guided eight social clubs in Dallas in the 1890s. The men's Idlewild Club was organized in 1884.

If one was really interested in complying with de rigueur social conventions: Holt, 253. Holt's book is 498 pages in length, contains 24 chapters, and provides an alphabetical index of 19 pages.

"*She was the pride of the settlement*": Frank's sentence seems exaggerated. Moreover, the inspiration for "Bessie" may not have been the daughter of a wealthy family, but a teacher at Southwestern Academy.

"*He was now the owner of a large plantation*": Frank here is attempting to enliven the narrative by disguising the fact that the inspiration for the protagonist was actually still a struggling undergraduate student.

"*Roy soon joined the party*": Presumably, Frank means Bessie and Minnie.

"*But I am not satisfied with your love only*": This dialogue resonates with a similar remark made in a letter from Frank to Mamie before their marriage.

Chapter 17. President Burleson's Last Days at Baylor (1895-1902)

Parsons concluded he needed to sign up for the Confederacy: Foner, 28.

"*He [Burleson] 'gave up his desire*": James Lafayette Walker, 247-247.

Parsons, unlike Burleson, agitated for the cause of workers': Jones, J., 93-94.

Burleson remained and ministered: *1896 Baylor Round-Up*, 8.

The good that Burleson did was not interred: *Galveston Tri-Weekly News*, September 20, 1872, 1.

The coming of the railroad, foreseen by Burleson: Reed, 180.

Burleson, called by education historian Frederick Eby: Matthews, 140; Eby, contributor of Chapter 3, "Education and Educators."

The Board of Trustees retired President Burleson: Dickinson, Ibid., 102.

Burleson's loss of influence and control: Guemple, Ibid., 12, citing a letter from Rufus C. Burleson, April 23, 1869, to William Carey Crane; TTC.

Nevertheless, under all the circumstances: J.A. Reynolds, "Rufus Burleson," *Handbook of Texas Online*.

Brann had warned parents [of Baylor students]: Brann, vol. x, 87-88.

Burleson's appeal to the Trustees: Statement ca. 1897 by the Board of Trustees of Baylor University to the Baptist brotherhood of Texas, 2-3.

Returning to the words of Professor Eby: Mathews, 141-142; Eby, chapter 3.

According to Haynes's biography: Burleson, 467.

Chapter 18. Chicago Days (1897-1902)

William Rainey Harper, Chicago's new: Chernov, 317-323; Mayer 63.

The magazine Arena affirmed: Beatty, 269, quoting John T. Flynn's article "The Muckrakers" published by Heath, Boston, 1949, addressing the question whether Rockefeller was a robber baron or an industrial statesman.

Rockefeller not only was responsible: Vehsey, 347.

Further, a new era in American and world medicine: Green, 156.

But beyond Rockefeller's conspicuous: Weinberg, "Exposed," 219 et seq.

Additionally, he was vulnerable to the charge: De Wolk, 62.

Stanford took no interest when young Indian women and children: Ibid., 88.

Where recitations were concerned, Dewey: Cremin, xiii-ix.

One student of Dewey's recalled: Martin, 259.

Frank, although a fact-based teacher: Schevill, *Six Historians*, vii.

Schevill noted that Leopold von Ranke of the University of Berlin: Ibid., 125.

Fifty years later, a later president of the AHA: Ibid., 145.

Frank would have been interested: Carr, 131-135.

The search, perhaps more than the destination: Southgate, 12-18.

Harper was a proficient cornetist: Mayer, 9.

Frank, who played cornet: *Baylor Lariat*, September 13, 1902, announcing an eighteen-member faculty orchestra with Professor Guittard and Mr. Parker who will play lead cornet.

The University of Chicago's Cap & Gown: *Baylor Lariat*, September 13, 1902, interview with FGG.

This scheduling would be convenient: Veysey, 373-374.

Chapter 19. The Twist of Fate, President Cooper Resigns, & a Job Offer (1902)

To make a short story even shorter: Interview of J.E. Hightower by M. Russell, July 15, 1947, quoted by Dickinson at 107. We wonder whether the mischievous Baylor students got the idea for the dog prank from Eggleston's popular novel *The Hoosier Schoolmaster* (1871) in which a student placed a puppy in a drawer of the teacher's desk. The fictitious teacher Ralph Hartsook, unlike President Cooper, maintained his composure, administered harsh language to the perpetrator in front of the class, and directed him to remove the dog from the classroom. Eggleston, 51.

President Cooper had come to Baylor: Mathews, 165; Eby, Chapter 3. Cooper's credentials include his having been the primary advocate for establishing the University of Texas and having aided the legislature in preparing the University Bill. Additionally, he appeared in Austin at the request of the State Teachers' Institute to advocate for founding a normal institute for preparation of teachers. The Sam Houston Normal Institute arose out of his efforts along with monies from the Peabody Fund. Further in 1886, Cooper was elected Superintendent of Public Education in Texas. *Personnel of State Government*, 93-95.

Since his appointment in 1899, he [Cooper] had served: Sinclair, 23.

"We have no endowment, we have no science hall": Ibid., 24.

"May God's blessing rest on Baylor": Ibid., 28.

The future of President Brooks: Ibid., 31-32. See also the article by Tony Riddlesperger, *Baylor Line*, 1992.

Chapter 20. Frank Gives Mamie a Guided Tour of the Campus (imagined)

By the time of his death in 1935: Judith Linsley and Ellen Rienstra, "Carroll, George Washington, *Handbook of Texas Online*, published by the Texas State Historical Association. In his address to the 1930 class of Magnolia High School, Frank Guittard, without mentioning G.W. Carroll's name, told the seniors: "During one of the Texas oil booms a man who made a lucky strike donated a part of his fortune for erecting a building for one of our educational institutions. A few years afterward, he lost his fortune just as quickly as he had made it. Now he has nothing to show of his former wealth except that fine building on the campus of Baylor University. This man tells his friends that the knowledge that young men and young women are being daily benefitted by his gift affords him the greatest satisfaction of his life." TTC.

G.W. Carroll also personally supported: *1945 Baylor Round-Up*, 26.

"*Can I propose to Mamie*": Mosquitoes and mosquito netting are mentioned in an October 1902 of the *Baylor Lariat.*

So, for a while until 1910: *Wallace, Our Lands, Our Lives*, 55, 70.

"*Why did you feel sorry for President Cooper?*": The author acknowledges imagining Frank felt sorry for Cooper; if he did, it was temporary, and Cooper continued on his career of service as a noted educator.

There's a short poem dedicated: *1916 Baylor Round-Up*, author Evans, 13.

Yes, and I was going to say: West, 127.

He also talks about the bullets: Ibid., 98.

Chapter 21. Samuel Palmer Brooks, a Primer

Here are a few of those letters: Samuel P. Brooks's letters; TTC.

"*I have no criticism of the young men concerning*": Sinclair, 117.

One student recalled that: Sinclair, 19.

"*It [Brooks's moustache] had a double twist*": *Baylor Monthly*, August 1927, 10. This article refers to a speech in which Pat M. Neff recounted anecdotes regarding President Brooks filtered through Neff's colorful imagination and way of expressing himself.

"*He stammered and stuttered and after a while*": Ibid., 12.

"*Well, if I have it not in*": *Baylor Monthly*, Pat M. Neff, August 1927, 12.

"*He once invited a group of students*": Sinclair, 42-43.

Speaking again of the suit: *Baylor Monthly*, Pat M. Neff, June 1931, 13.

Fine clothes were not affordable for Brooks: *Baylor Monthly*, July 1926, 2.

He then enrolled at Yale as a senior: For the dates, I relied on those shown in Dr. Sinclair's master's thesis and on his cited authorities; Sinclair, 12-17.

It was also common knowledge that the last president Oscar Cooper: www.Baylor.edu/about Baylor/Oscar Henry Cooper. "According to J.M. Dawson, a student at the time, 'some prankish students sneaked a howling dog into the small upstairs chapel on the lofty third floor of Main. When the perverse little animal disturbed the worship the president became enraged. He (Cooper) leaped down from the platform, seized the dog and hurled it through a window to the ground below. The act appalled everybody, because it showed a lack of control deemed inexcusable, although under most exasperating circumstances.'" A student protest was lodged and Cooper resigned.

On April 24, Brooks advised the Trustees: Sinclair, 31.

The University of Texas at this time did not give: GBH Oral Memoirs, 220.

"*It covered one dollar and seventy-five cents*": Samuel P. Brooks Papers, "Alumni This and That," April 24, 1906.

In his speech he expressed the desire: Sinclair, 34, 38.

In his inaugural address, Brooks additionally pledged: Ibid., 34-40.

Your great-grandfather Clarence: Source, Clarence A. Guittard, c. 1980.

Chapter 22. Mamie—Marriage, Family, & Sad Passing (1906-1917)

Today we will focus on Frank's first lasting: Cagle, 79; FGG Diary, 13-14.

"It took a while for them": Mamie's May 24, 1917, obituary recites that Mamie had attended Victoria College, the Presbyterian College near Austin, and the State University where she had completed her education before the voyage with her father described in her shipboard diary.

We know that marriage and family were always: George Ade, in his 1922 essay "Single Blessedness and Other Observations," observed that: "Next to solitaire, probably the most interesting single-handed pastime is trying to visualize one's own funeral. The bachelor often wonders if it will be an impressive occasion," 19.

Mamie Welhausen's 1901 shipboard diary: For the reader's convenience I have changed unorthodox spellings and occasionally added punctuation. I have not attempted to change word selection. Mamie was well-read and a good writer, though she may not have had a college degree. It is obvious that she was an intelligent and careful observer of the happenings onboard.

We don't know when Frank began courting Mamie seriously: FGG Diary, 10.

He did not want to return from a honeymoon: *Baylor Lariat*, July 23, 1904.

"I shall be ready for most any kind of diversion": Frank had much to think about as he struggled with learning or refreshing, in short order, the subjects he would be required to teach in the Academy: geometry, arithmetic, Latin, modern languages (presumably French or German or both), economics, political science, and history. We also found one reference in the *Baylor Lariat* to Frank giving a final examination in international law. His student and department protégé Guy B. Harrison, Jr. said "He [Frank Guittard] could teach almost any subject, history, philosophy, religion, science, mathematics, with equal facility and was deeply-based in all those." Frank also helped Harrison with a math course he was taking. (GBH Oral Memoirs, 105.) The use of the "n" word in this letter to Mamie is an anomaly and the only known instance in Frank's or his family's letters of the use of words of that nature.

There is no record indicating his specific plan: FGG Diary, 13; summer 1905.

"Just a few days before Easter": Mamie may be quoting Robert Burns's ode "Despondency" which contains the line: "O life! thou art a galling load, Along a rough, a weary road, To wretches such as I!"

The house was one or two blocks: FGG Diary, 13.

Both the Guittards and the Welhausens moved to the US: Tiling, 12.

Another subject possibly not raised: Anonymous articles, Coshocton, County, Ohio.

Then the topics of the Underground Railroad: Bordewich, 196.

He did fight for the Confederate cause: www.familytreedna.com/groups /wellhausen-family

The significance of this battle: W.T. Block, "The Battle of Calcasieu Pass, Louisiana," *Beaumont Enterprise*, May 6, 1977, 1-11.

Among the many questions that Frank might have wanted to ask: Frank would have been interested in whether Captain Charlie had been in communication with any of the German-Texan Unionists and whether he and his wife Eliza were sympathetic with their efforts. German immigrant Julius Schlickum of Fredericksburg, who was imprisoned by the Confederacy on the grounds of general disloyalty, wrote his father December 21, 1862: "This fateful revolution didn't find many supporters among the West Texas Germans. The division of the Union in the interest of the slave holders was not in the interest of the free working Germans in West Texas...They were not inclined to destroy the best form of government the world had every experienced for the sole purpose of establishing a regime whose only purpose was the extension of human enslavement." Spellman, 308, 310.

Frank, born and raised in a free state: See Cutler & Parrish's work on the Civil War letters of the Pierson family for the story of four sons of an educated Louisiana family not owning slaves, but who went off to the fight for the Confederacy to protect their "country" and their homes from invasion and annihilation; David Pierson letter to Wm. H. Pierson, April 22, 1861, 13.

Twenty-one-year-old Sallie McNeill, a former student of Baylor at Independence, born in 1840, like many Southern women, had mixed feelings about the war, particularly because of the potential cost in lives. In May 1861, like others in the South, Sallie initially had an unrealistically rosy view of the Confederacy's prospects in a war: "Virginia has seceded & we confidently hope to gain the other slave states…I trust one battle will be decisive. At the cost of thousands of lives, probably. We believe Justice is on our side. May we not rely on an arm of flesh, but invoke the 'God of Hosts' to fight our battles & protest our homes!" McNeill, 102-103, citing her May 11, 1861 diary entry.

We should add that: Daphne Dalton Garrett, "Fayette County," *Handbook of Texas Online* and bibliography cited, accessed September 27, 2020. Also see Shinertx.com/facts.htm; "Shiner Facts, Figures, and History" from the Shiner Chamber of Commerce downloaded September 26, 2020.

"*I wish you would get Stella to find the baby's two diaper supports*": MW letter to FGG, July 31, 1916. Charles Welhausen Guittard died August 9, 1916 from probable tubercular meningitis. Mamie was pregnant with Clarence at the time. The stay in Comfort, Texas was likely intended to improve either infant Charles's health or Mamie's health, or both, but was unsuccessful in both cases. Mamie would die nine months later in Albuquerque, NM, from tuberculosis, two months after giving birth to Clarence.

"*Papa has had a sick spell*": MW letter to FGG, October 15, 1916.

"*Papa is not feeling well*": MW letter to FGG, October 16, 1916.

Frank and the Welhausens: Cagle, 82; FGG Diary, 19-20.

Chapter 23. Health Tribulations, Microbial Antagonists (1915-1917)

The disease reached areas not far: Cox, *Texas Disasters*, 11-20.

TB was the greatest killer of 19th century Americans: Leavitt, et al., 4.

Edward Snowden notes that "at its peak": Snowden, 275.

Snowden further observes: Ibid., 270.

However, one study showed that: Nancy Olson Lewis, nexmexicohistory.org/people/lungers-and-their legacy. downloaded 3/22/2014.

We will not discuss the available surgical: Murphy and Blank, 95.

Tubercular meningitis was the most widespread form: Kneib, 19-20.

Crum's medical license was eventually revoked: Dary, 285-286.

The helplessness of conventional medicine: Ibid., 273-302.

Elixir Salutis was concocted and promoted: Ibid., 245.

Other products offered to an unsuspecting public: Ibid., 244-272.

Chapter 24. Comic Relief, Student Wit & Whimsy

See what you think of these limericks: The errors in the students' limericks were intended by the students and for effect.

"*Take life easy…Prof. Pool [sic]*": Prof. Poole, a popular overweight professor.

The Ku-Klux Klan [girls' basketball team]: Apparently, the girls liked the way the words "Ku Klux Klan" sounded, perhaps reminding them of girls' sororities called Kappa this and Delta that which Baylor did not have then.

Chapter 25. First Baylor Homecomings (1909 & 1915)

In 1909, five thousand alumni looked on as Baylor: Randy Fiedler, "History of Specific Baylor Homecomings," Baylor History Review, c. July 17, 2013.

After Baylor's undefeated 3-1 conference: Denne H. Freeman, That *Good Old Baylor Line*. Huntsville, Alabama: The Strode Publishers, Inc., 1975, 25.

Chapter 26. Baylor Football, Baylor Spirit (1899-1920s)

"K'rip, k'rap, k'ripple-tipple-a-tap": 1919 Baylor Round-Up, 92.

Bridges said when he arrived in Waco: Coach Frank Bridges, "The Fighting Spirit in Baylor Athletics," *Baylor Monthly*, April 1925, 9-10.

However, under Frank Bridges's coaching: Ibid.

Professor R.H. Hamilton, a strong supporter: Urban, 4-5.

"*I think it can be said that...Harvard*": Brooks Papers; TTC.

"The faculty heard about it": 1913 Baylor Round-Up, 197.

"*Carroll [Field] was the scene of the greatest*": *1910 Baylor Round-Up*, 169.

"*Thus ended the happiest day": 1917 Baylor Round-Up*, 191.

"*The Bears next year should have": 1921 Baylor Round-Up*, 161-163.

"No team that the Bears met"; 1922 Baylor Round-Up, 153-154, 168.

That year Baylor's only losses were: 1923 Baylor Round-Up, 189.

"Nevertheless, Bridges built": 1924 Baylor Round-Up, 135.

The stars of the 1924 game: 1925 Baylor Round-Up, 128, 130.

Bible's team was noted for delayed or spinner: Bible, 14, 37, 43, and 103.

Bridges's teams had their hidden ball trick: LeFever, 33.

According to Coach Bible, a delayed or spinner play: Bible, 37.

Bridges was both a scholar of the game and an innovator: Coach Bridges's "Playbook," Athletics Archive, Baylor University Libraries.

"Don't let the quarter [back] become": Bridges's "Playbook," Ibid., 87.

We suspect that Frank Guittard and Frank Bridges: Bridges had specific ideas for the health of his players and rules for their conduct. It is not known whether the two Franks ever had an extended conversation. However, Bridges's football playbook had both health tips and rules for his players which would have been of interest to Frank Guittard in light of his own health tips and rules for his family. Bridges's health tips included "Don't stand under the hot water very long—It saps the vitality—Always finish with cold water, have shower hit on chest,...should not wet the head." Also, Bridges cautioned his players about boils—"Boils are bad—Couple handfuls of cheap salt in tub to finish bath will keep down boils...Don't put soap on feet. Takes away oil and lets skin crack." (Bridges's Playbook, 8) Rules of psychology for playing football included: "Appeal to the honor of man to keep training," "encourage and praise a man when he does well," and "success comes from drive and mastering fundamentals."

"*Power plays across the middle*": John S. Watterson, The Gridiron Crisis of 1905... "; *Journal of Sports History,* summer 2000, 32-35.

Several timely developments came in the wake: Ibid., 103, 107.

Other changes to the rules: Ibid., 292.

In 1906...a Union College player was killed: Peterson, 45-46.

Another report on fatalities and injuries: Watterson, "Power plays...," 292.

Chapter 27. Along Came Josie (1920-1950)

Josie and Frank married June 10, 1920: Cagle, 88; FGG Diary, 30.

Chapter 28. The Student Self-Government Experiment (1911-1923)

The years of the Experiment overlapped the first wave of new democratic governments: Study.com. CSET Social Science History Course Chapter 13, instructor Greg Hanichak, downloaded September 27, 2020.

As to the relative importance of football to Baylor in these years: President Brook's letter to the Board of Trustees March 14, 1922; TTC. What is not remembered as well is that those years also included the extraordinary gridiron accomplishments of Waco High School and its nationally recognized coach Paul Leighton Tyson, whose coaching career in Waco began in 1913 and led to four state high school championships in 1922, 1925, 1926, and 1927. Tyson's 1927 Waco team was recognized as the unofficial national high school champion after crushing a team from Cleveland Ohio in the post-season 40 to 14. Some of Tyson's stars would later go on to play for Baylor teams. Two members of the Tyson's Waco High team of 1922 would go on to play for Baylor's 1924 Southwest Conference championship team. *Handbook of Texas Online*, "TYSON, PAUL LEIGHTON," accessed November 29, 2018.

As inspired by President Brooks, a strong proponent: Dickinson, 113.

The committee made an "exhaustive study": GBH Oral Memoirs, 107.

"*They refused to report violations of the regulations*": Dickinson, 136-137.

"*On Monday, the Grand Jury began*": *Baylor Lariat*, March 7, 1923, 1.

"*We believe they will as the student body": Baylor Lariat*, March 7, 1923, 2.

The article continued "Most of the": *Baylor Lariat*, March 10, 1923, 1.

"*And this was such flagrant partiality*": GBH Oral Memoirs, 108-109.

"*It then came up before the SSGA*": GBH, Jr. interview by CFG, 1980.

"*And convicted also in the last session*": *Baylor Lariat*, March 14, 1923, 1.

"*After being out for nearly two hours*": *Baylor Lariat*, March 14, 1923, 1.

Apparently no conviction was obtained: *Baylor Lariat*, March 17, 1923, 1.

Following the faculty meeting on March: *Baylor Lariat*, March 24, 1923, 1.

"*This week shows charges of cheating*": *Baylor Lariat*, March 24, 1923, 1.

"*Twelve students from different groups*": *Baylor Lariat*, March 24, 1923, 2.

"*Dr. Brooks further explained*": *Baylor Lariat*, March 24, 1923, 1.

If President Brooks was not clear: President Brooks's letter to SSGA President c. March 24, 1923, S. P. Brooks Papers, The Texas Collection, Box 4c212, Folder 377.

In the afternoon of Monday, March 26: *Baylor Lariat*, March 28, 1923, 1.

Although President Brooks had reportedly: *Baylor Lariat*, March 28, 1923, 2.

The students, assisted by those: *Baylor Lariat*, March 28, 1923, 2.

The Lariat reported "That this law...": *Baylor Lariat*, March 31, 1923, 2.

Whether or not any of the convicted students: *Baylor Lariat*, April 18, 1923; SPB letter April 17, 1923 to Rev. McLinley, SPB folder 377; TTC.

Thereafter, however, upon, the recommendation of the Faculty: Beginning in 1920, Allen G. Flowers was the Dean of the Baylor Law Department.

At this point, events were moving rapidly: *Waco Times Herald*, April 20, 1923.

Accordingly, Dr. Brooks said that he found: *Baylor Lariat*, April 21, 1923, 1.

However, other ex-officials: *Baylor Lariat*, April 21, 1923, 1.

In doing this, they waived the technicality: *Baylor Lariat*, April 21, 1923, 1.

Those speaking to the Baylor Lariat: *Baylor Lariat*, April 21, 1923, 1.

The Lariat editor observed: *Baylor Lariat*, April 21, 1923, 1.

"*Every Baptist and every local citizen*": *Searchlight*, April 27, 1923.

"*May all of the friends and supporters*": *Baylor Lariat*, April 28, 1923, 1.

"*After losing three of the first four games*": *Baylor Lariat*, May 23, 1923, 2.

I guess the faculty could put up with lax enforcement: See Mirrielees, 150-159. At Stanford University in 1908 President Jordan was dealing with the problem of student drunkenness and late night revelers. Stanford had a "student government" of some sort, but all the real power remained in the hands of the faculty. That year the students staged a parade in which they went searching for someone to voice their grievances to, sang offensive songs as they proceeded, and failing to find him at home, changed course and went through the library boisterously singing and yelling. A faculty committee met and issued judgments against 121 students, suspending some and giving demerits to others. Although the parade incident did not involve cheating on examinations, the break in student discipline and the issue of student drunkenness pre-Prohibition were serious and President Jordan had to devise some additional procedures to more nearly ensure orderly behavior. Frank Guittard was dealing with honor code violations and other student misbehavior from 1913-1923 and would have been interested in hearing President Jordan's thoughts about how to deal with misbehaving students although President Brooks had already abolished Baylor's Student Self-Government before Frank enrolled at Stanford.

Chapter 29. President Brooks and the Evolution Controversy (1920-1931)

The problem came up at Baylor in 1920: 1920 represented a highpoint for President Brooks and Baylor, being the year Baylor celebrated its 75th year following its chartering in 1845. Professor Henry Trantham noted in the final couplet of a poem composed for the celebration: "Baylor moves ever on: no storm can overwhelm/ While stalwart Brooks shall hold and guide the helm!"

Harrison replied that he thought: GBH Oral Memoirs, 113.

Fundamentalists attacked the following Baylor faculty members: Charles M. Tolbert, "Meroney, William Penn," Handbook of Texas Online published by the Texas State Historical Association. Meroney published *Introductory Studies in Sociology in 1925 in connection with his views on the evolution controversy with the fundamentalists.*

Chapter 30. Waco and the Ku Klux Klan (1920s)

The Klan also castigated Jews for standing apart: Paraphrasing an email June 7, 2022, from Patricia Bernstein to Charles F. Guittard.

Klan officeholders in prominent: Joshua Rothman, Chair University of Alabama History Department, *The Atlantic*, December 4, 1916.

"*A second factor in [Pat Neff] not being explicit about the Klan*": Blodgett, et al., 125; Bernstein, *Ten Dollars to Hate*, 119-120.

"*Now, I know the time that Negroes couldn't walk*": Lonnie Belle Hodges Oral Memoirs, 2001.

"*When I was a senior, one day one of the boys*": Gladys Jenkins Casmir Oral Memoirs, 1996.

"*I continued in it through*": The Waco Klan was forbidden to parade in masks.

"*It [the Klan] was never as strong in Texas*": Joseph Dawson Oral Memoirs.

An*other student added more details*: Helen Lester Goodman Oral Memoirs.

"*And he said, 'Don't go that way home. Go another way'*": Homa S. Hill Oral Memoirs, 2009.

Many of the prominent Waco churches—Baptist, Methodist: Bernstein, 168.

Of course, that assumes that Washington: Bernstein, 87-126, for the deficiencies in the proceedings.

Chapter 31. Frank's Private Sides & Life at Home

The rules tell us a lot about Frank in 1902: Cagle, 78; FGG Notebook. Also see Bennett, 74, relating to the 54 rules of the young George Washington in his own handwriting c. 1745 which Bennett claims Washington likely copied from an English translation c. 1664 of a book in French. Many of Frank's rules are similar.

Philip G. Zimbardo, Stanford University: Zimbardo, 29, 32-34, 44.

Josie would accept: CAG second interview by CFG, 1980.

"It is not the sort of home": Alger, *Walter Sherwood's Probation* (1890), 144.

In the Young Book Agent (1905): Alger, *The Young Book Agent*, iii.

A Lariat cartoon indicates that Frank: *Baylor Lariat*, April 17, 1919, 1.

One student remembers coming up the sidewalk: U.R. Pugh letter to CFG, January 18, 1980.

While he likely suggested: CAG Interview by CFG, 1980, tape no. 1.

He loved to sing church music: Cagle, 15; FGG Autobiography, 8a.

He played in an orchestra at Baylor: *Baylor Lariat*, September 13, 1902.

In Ohio there were some old horns: Cagle, 20; FGG Autobiography, 6.

We don't know that he sung any: We consulted Rodeheaver's *Sociability Songs* (1928) for the names of these songs, except for the "Muffin Man."

"And the relationships between Frank and his boys?": The conclusions regarding relationships have been reached largely on the basis of family correspondence along with interviews of family members.

The recent book The First Born Advantage: Leman, 12-275.

Armstrong, at one time, strongly criticized himself: Lewis, Scott, 149.

When Clarence was appointed to serve: FGG letter May 23, 1941 to CAG.

In his later decades Frank used a truss: GBH Interview by CFG, 1980.

He wore conservative: M.O. Morgan, FGG student, letter to CFG, 1980.

He referred to one of these ties: CAG tape and interview by CFG, 1980, nos. 1 and 2.

One Baylor wit penned: L.G., "Sudden Attacks," *1915 Round-Up*, 178.

In the summer he sometimes wore: CAG Interview no. 2 by CFG. *In color his suits were grey*: CAG Interview no. 2. *He attached his watch to his vest*: SWG interview by CFG. *Frank often wore tweeds*: Guy B. Harrison, Jr. interview by CFG, 1980.

He began dying his hair: GBH Interview by CFG, 1980.

"It would look so much better": CAG Interview no. 2 by CFG, 1980.

He would have considered the idea of clothes especially: Ibid.

Josie, who came from a large family: Ibid.

"I think I shall make that" and *"On Thursday morning's pancakes"*: FGG letter to MJ January 28, 1928 and CAG Tape no. 1, 1980.

"I think I shall gradually plant other vines": FGG letter to MJ, July 17, 1927.

Clarence did the lower parts: CAG tape no. 1, 1980.

The garden was by a trellis: SWG Interview by CFG, 2012.

He did teach a Sunday school class of teenage boys: Cagle, 72.

Probably for the same reason: CAG manuscript, 1980.

Frank also told his colleague's wife: GBH interview by CFG, 1980.

I'm curious about what Sacred: Sacred Harp was religious folk music composed for unusual four-part harmonies. *The Sacred Harp* (the hymnbook) contained over 500 four-part a cappella hymns. The first choirs in Texas Baptist Churches were not seen heard until the 1870s. B.H. Carroll supported choirs in articles for the *Texas Baptist Herald.* Organs were controversial until about the same time, the main reason being that there is no explicit Biblical authority to use mechanical instruments of music in worship. One hymnbook popular among Texas Baptists was B.F. White and E.J. King's *Sacred Harp* (1847).

As a student at Baylor he attended a Sunday school: Jenkins had a long white beard of the Moses sort making him easily identifiable in group pictures and was chair of Baylor's Board of Trustees many years. Frank and Josie's graves in Waco's Oakwood Cemetery are near those of Judge Jenkins and his family.

"He was the example": FGG essay eulogizing W.H. Jenkins; FGG Papers.

"It is the faithful-until-death fellow": Jones, *Popular Lectures of Sam P. Jones*, 121-122. Frank heard Jones speak twice, once at Baylor and once in Arkansas.

As for the food, at camp meetings: Brumley's *All-Day Singin' and Dinner on the Grounds....* Recipes for the dishes were spread throughout the book.

As a meetings reached its predictably: Gard, *Rawhide Texas*, 131.

"I was taken aback as I fancied myself": CAG interview by CFG no. 2, 1980.

They were concerned that Clarence would: CAG dictated tape no. 2, 1980.

Mama Josie, on the other hand: CAG interview by CFG no. 2, 1980. Clarence and his wife Mary Lou would eventually join a Methodist church in Dallas following the death of George W. Truett, pastor of First Baptist in Dallas.

He was not personally interested: CAG dictated tape no. 2, 1980.

After Tom and Katherine both passed away: CAG manuscript, 1980.

"Probably that's how I got the habit": FGG letter to MJ, March 4, 1928.

Frank said the blessing at meals at home: CAG dictated tape no. 2, 1980.

As to his moral standards, his personal: CAG dictated tape no. 3, 1080.

Josie who came from a stricter family: CAG interview by CFG, 1980 and CAG dictated tape no. 1, 1980.

One the subject of dancing, Frank was: CAG interview by CFG no. 2, 1980.

Both Professor Armstrong: Scott Lewis, 147-149, as to Professor Armstrong.

Here are the great world's fairs: For information on these fairs, see the volumes listed in the bibliography: Appelbaum, *Chicago World's Fair of 1893*; *1901 World's Fair—Pan American Exposition* (a CD collection); Fleming, *Around the "Pan" with Uncle Hank* (1901); Kasper, *Annie Oakley* (1902); and Fox, *Inside the World's Fair of 1904* (St. Louis). The Buffalo Bill Wild West Shows were frequently located just outside the entrances to the world's fairs.

This show was Frank's last opportunity to see fellow Ohioan: Carter, 392.

Ford was a newcomer: Fox, iv, 91.

Geronimo...was a regular feature of the 1904 fair: Geronimo had been on the loose in the months prior to September 1886 when Frank came to Texas. In early 1886, Geronimo was negotiating the terms for his ultimate surrender with the US military. Eight years later, the US military took Geronimo to the world's fair in St. Louis where he stayed for six months, participating in Buffalo Bill's Wild West Shows and on display in a teepee in the Ethnology Exhibit. Several books were written about Geronimo, including a well-written autobiography by the first G-man. Geronimo, after his final surrender to the army, converted to Christianity and came to admire Theodore Roosevelt, President McKinley's vice president.

"I sold my photographs for twenty-five cents": Geronimo, 155.

The Buffalo Bill Show staged Custer's: Jackson, Robert, 17, 82, 108.

The fair also introduced the Dr. Pepper beverage from Waco: Ibid., 87.

Chapter 32. Themes & Plots, Crossroads & Turning Points, Metaphors & Paradoxes

Our mission today is to help: The concepts in this chapter are primarily suggestions to trigger the peanut gallery's thinking and thereby their feedback.

Chapter 33. Stanford and Palo Alto Days (1923; 1926—1930)

The Stanfords would endow their university: Davis, Stanford Album, 11. James, *Fifty Years on the Quad*, 139.

Nevertheless, almost a century: Coincidentally, Wilbur Marsh Rice whose bequest laid the basis for the Rice Institute in Houston, was murdered by chloroform administered by his valet in a conspiracy with an attorney to forge a new will for Rice. Rice Institute opened in 1912 after lengthy litigation.

Chapter 34. Failure Not an Option—the Struggle for a Doctorate (1923-1931)

President Brooks made it crystal clear: Oral History Interview with Professor E.N. Jones August 8, 1973, 56, 70. For the 1924-25 school year, college catalogues and institution studies revealed the following: 82 percent (9) of Rice Institute's faculty had their Ph.D.s; all had degrees. 54 percent (34) of the University of Texas's faculty had their Ph.D.'s and 4 had no degree. 31 percent (10) of Baylor's faculty had their Ph.D.s and 2 had no degree. 28 percent (11) of SMU's faculty had their Ph.D.s and 6 had no degree. 14 percent (3) of TCU's faculty had their Ph.D.s and 1 had no degree.

In his thesis, Frank quotes: Lewis, William Draper, 328.

"*The American frontiersmen who [took] Texas*": Roosevelt, *The Winning of the West*, 261, 279.

As to his feeling for the "plain people": "Roosevelt and Conservation," 40, quoting Roosevelt's 1907 letter to Justice W.H. Moody.

One or two anecdotes: Guittard, dissertation, 49, quoting Hagedorn, 284.

Roosevelt was an amazing generalist: Tilchin introduction, x-xi to Roosevelt's *The Rough Riders*, 2004.

Moreover, Roosevelt in 1898 was just starting: Ibid., xiii.

"*I wish I could take things as easy as Belk*": Belk, unlike Frank, was able to live with his wife in Palo Alto while doing graduate work. Frank was perhaps a bit jealous of his younger Baylor department colleague, or just took the opportunity to grouse further about the drudgery of his days.

"I prefer the movies. They are more restful": Frank means the silent films of that period which did not interfere with napping during the film.

"*I looked over your [Francis's] corrections the other night*": Although future appellate jurist Clarence would arguably be the most accomplished legal writer in the family, Francis being the best oral advocate, he was thirteen at the time and had no input into correcting Frank's dissertation.

Frank returned to the theme of the loss: Peters, 31. Having the wrong adviser can be a real problem in finishing a thesis in a timely manner. According to Dr. Peters, "You can change advisers, but this might be costly in terms of time."

"*Gen. Grant said 'I...propose to fight it out on this line*'": General Grant's famous quote is from the Spotsylvania Campaign. On May 11, 1864, Grant wrote letters with this sentiment to Secretary of War Stanton and Chief of Staff of the Army, General Halleck, near Spotsylvania, Virginia. Gwynne, 63.

Baylor faculty colleague Henry Trantham noted: "Faculty Close-Ups," *Baylor Monthly*, November 1931, 7, 9, quoting Professor Trantham; Cagle, 90.

As a final note to Frank's Ph.D. saga: Gullard & Lund, 82.

Mama Josie surely hear the same comment: History student D. Gibbs, 1980.

In Boethius's work, a character named Lady Philosophy: Boethius, 20-23.

In the Consolation, Boethius quotes Euripides: Ibid., 58.

According to Caroline Hoefferle, "Ranke was probably": Hoefferle, 68.

Thus, he had much in common with von Ranke: *Encyclopaedia Britannica Online.* Encyclopedia Britannica Inc., 2015. Web. 16 Aug. 2015.

Professor Leonard Krieger argued von Ranke: Krieger, xi, xii.

Perhaps the funniest: Tuthill, *The Bungle Family 1929 Sundays,* 27, 29, 32.

Chapter 35. The Professor who put "Sys" in "System" (1902-1950)

"*Then we saw wandering among a vast*": Wilma Green, "Herein Dwelleth the Contentment of all Ages" in the "Campus Camera" section of the *1915 Baylor Round-Up.*

Frank strongly felt, along with: Carr, 113.

Herodotus, considered the father of history: Ibid.

Few debates got started or were encouraged: Cagle, 104, 106.

Frank also had at his command: Cagle, 109; Guittard notebook.

Frank's son Clarence said that in his later: CAG interview by CFG, 1980.

"*Then Dr. Guittard would pick*": His graders were among his best students.

Chapter 36. Finale in Dallas; Final Assessment

Frank was still teaching: Cagle, 16; JGG statement, June 30, 1951.

Almost entirely from his own efforts: The only evidence Frank received financial assistance from any source for his education are a few entries in one of Frank's ledgers showing a several small loans, not gifts, from his brothers.

Chapter 37. Looking Back at Frank's Life & Times; Conclusion

In conclusion, we can do no better: Cagle, 110. All the students' letters received by the author, including the tribute from Professor David L. Smiley, are in the possession of the author; TGF.

EPILOGUE

Dr. Walker presented the findings of a decade-long study: Dary, 223-225.

However, the belief or hope that mountainous or western climates: Ibid., 225.

The purpose of college governments was: Horowitz, *Campus Life…*: 108.

This difficulty was a predictable part: Ibid., 32-42.

APPENDICES

Peanut Gallery's Debate (John Wesley Hardin & Frank Guittard)

He distrusted dubious theories that could easily: Cagle, 103-104.

In glancing through several books: Three volumes furnished the information utilized in the debate, those by Parsons & Brown, Leon Metz, and John Wesley Hardin himself. The bibliography contains the information for these sources.

SELECTED BIBLIOGRAPHY

Books and Treatises

Ade, George. *Single Blessedness and Other Observations.* Garden City, New York: Doubleday, Page & Company, 1922.

Alexander, Franz G., M.D. and Sheldon T. Selesnick, M.D. *The History of Psychiatry: An Evaluation of Psychiatric Thought and Practice from Prehistoric Times to the Present.* New York: Harper & Row, Publishers, 1966.

Alger, Edwin (Alias of Jay Jerome Williams, author of comic strip *Ben Webster's Career*). *Phil Hardy's Greatest Test: The Bound to Win Stories.* New York: Grosser & Dunlap, 1930.

Alger, Horatio, Jr.

---. *Driven from Home.* No publisher indicated, out of copyright protection. Original publication date 1890.

---. *From Canal Boy to President or the Boyhood and Manhood of James A. Garfield.* New York: John R. Anderson & Company, 1881.

---. *Ragged Dick.* Readaclassic.com. Original publication date: 1868.

---. *Walter Sherwood's Probation, or Cool Head and Warm Heart*: Original publication date, 1897.

---. *The Young Book Agent.* Original publication date: 1905. Grosset & Dunlap. New York.

---. *The Young Salesman.* Chicago: M. A. Donohue & Company. Original edition published in 1896.

Allen, Edward. *Selling Door to Door: Alfred C. Fuller.* Chicago: Encyclopedia Britannica Press, 1964.

Ames, Eric S. (editor & author of text). *The Images of America.* Charleston, SC: Arcadia Publishing, 2009. Photos from The Texas Collection and many other sources.

Anonymous. Andrew Forest Muir, Editor. *Texas in 1837: An Anonymous, Contemporary Narrative.* Austin: University of Texas Press, 1986.

Anonymous (or Flora Eleanor Wells). *Sheaf of Baylor Verse.* Nabu Public Domain Reprints. A collection of verses by students who have attended Baylor University. Undated.

Appelbaum, Stanley (ed.). *The Chicago World's Fair of 1893: A Photographic Record.* New York: Dover Publications, 1980. Photos from the Collections of the Avery Library of Columbia University and the Chicago Historical Society and text by Stanley Appelbaum.

Archer, Kenna Lang. *Unruly Waters: A Social and Environmental History of the Brazos River.* Albuquerque: The University of New Mexico Press, 2015.

Bain, Ken. *What the Best College Teachers Do.* Cambridge, MA and London: Harvard University Press, 2004.

Barnes, Agnes Warren. *Postcard History Series: Waco Texas, a Postcard Journey.* Charleston SC: Arcadia Publishing, 1999. Postcards from many sources.

Bates, Barbara. *Bargaining for Life: A Social History of Tuberculosis, 1876-1938.* Philadelphia: University of Pennsylvania Press, 1992.

Beatty, Jack. *Age of Betrayal: The Triumph of Money in America, 1865-1900.* New York: Vintage Books, a Division of Random House, Inc., 2008.

Benson, John T., Jr. (editor). *Old Time Revival.* Nashville: John T. Benson Publishing Co., 1950.

Bernstein, Patricia. *The First Waco Horror: The Lynching of Jesse Washington and the Rise of the NAACP.* College Station: Texas A&M University Press, 2005.

Bible, Dana X. *Championship Football: A Guide for Player, Coach and Fan.* New York: Prentice-Hall, Inc., 1947.

Blodgett, Dorothy; Blodgett, Terrell; and Scott, David L. *The Land, the Law, and the Lord: The Life of Pat Neff, Governor of Texas 1921-1925 and President of Baylor University 1932-1947.* Austin: Home Place Publishers, 2007.

Boethius, Anicius Manlius Severinus. *The Consolation of Philosophy* translated and with an introduction by Victor Watts. London: Penguin Books, 1969. The date of this work is of uncertain origin but predates Boethius' execution in 524 or 525 A.D.

Bordewich, Fergus M. *Bound for Canaan: The Epic Story of the Underground Railroad, American's First Civil Rights Movement.* New York: HarperCollins, Amistad Paperback edition, 2006.

Boyce, Chet, and Scott Boyce (The Brothers Boyce). *Get The Hell Off My Porch: Adventures in Door-to-Door Sales.* Privately published by Chet and Scott Boyce, 2012.

Brann, William Cowper. *The Complete Works of Brann the Iconoclast.* Twelve Volumes. New York City: The Brann Publishers, Inc., 1898. Article index included in Volume XII.

Bridges, Frank. "Football Playbook." Baylor University 1920-1925. Handwritten, presumably while coaching Baylor in Waco.

Brinkley, Douglas. *The Wilderness Warrior: Theodore Roosevelt and the Crusade for America.* New York, London, Toronto and other cities: Harper Perennial, Harper Collins Publishers, 2010.

Brooks, Samuel Palmer. *The Yale Letters from Samuel Palmer Brooks to His Father.* Waco: Baylor University, 1983. Foreword and comments by son Sims Palmer Brooks.

Browne, Charles Farrar. *The Complete Works of Artemus Ward.* New York: G. W. Dillingham Co., 1898.

Brumley, Albert E. *All-Day Singing and Dinner on the Ground.* Camdenton, MO: Albert E. Brumley & Sons, 1972.

Brumley, Albert E. *Olde Time Camp Meeting Songs.* Camdenton, MO: Albert E. Brumley & Sons, 1971.

Bunyan, John. *The Pilgrim's Progress.* Mineola, New York: Dover Publications, 2003. Originally published 1678 (First Part) and 1684 (Second Part).

Burleson, Rufus C. *The Life and Writings of Rufus C. Burleson, Containing a Biography of Dr. Burleson by Harry Haynes; Funeral Occasion, with Sermons, etc.; Selected "Chapel Talks"; Dr. Burleson as a Preacher, with Selected Sermons.* Public domain: Compiled and published by Mrs. Georgia J. Burleson, 1901.

Butler, Ellis Parker. *Kilo, Being the Love Story of Eliph' Hewlitt, Book Agent.* Publisher and place of publication unknown, 1907.

Campbell, Randolph B. *An Empire for Slavery: The Peculiar Institution in Texas (1821-1865).* Baton Rouge: Louisiana State University, 1991 (paperback edition).

Campbell, Randolph B. *Gone to Texas: A History of the Lone Star State.* New York and Oxford: Oxford University Press, 2003.

Carr, Edward Hallett. *What is History? The George Macaulay Trevelyan Lectures Delivered at the University of Cambridge, January—March 1961.* New York: Vintage Books, a Division of Random House, 1961.

Carroll, James Milton. *A History of Texas Baptists,* edited by J.B. Cranfill, Dallas, Baptist Standard Publishing Company, 1923.

Carter, Robert A. *Buffalo Bill Cody: The Man Behind the Legend.* Edison NJ: Castle Books, a Division of Book Sales, Inc., 2005; by permission of John Wiley & Sons, Inc., Hoboken NJ.

Carver, Charles. *Brann and the Iconoclast.* Introduction by Roy Bedichek. Austin: University of Texas Press, 1957.

Cervantes, Miguel De Cervantes (Saavedra). *Don Quixote.* Translated, edited, and abridged by Walter Starkie. New York: A Mentor Book, the New American Library, 1957.

Chernov, Ron. Titan: *The Life of John D. Rockfeller, Sr.* New York: Vintage Books, a Division of Random House, Inc., 1999.

Cobb, Buell E., Jr. *The Sacred Harp: A Tradition and Its Music.* Athens Georgia: University of Georgia Press, 1989.

Cohen, Sol (editor). *Education in the United States: A Documentary History, Volume 2.* New York: Random House, 1974.

Coleman, Robert H. (editor). *The Popular Hymnal: Old Standard Hymns and Popular Gospel Songs for Singing in All Departments of Church, Sunday School, and Young People's Work.* Dallas: Robert H. Coleman Publisher, 1918.

Conger, Roger N. (editor and author of text). *A Pictorial History of Waco with a Reprint of Highlights of Waco History by Roger N. Conger.* Waco: Texian Press, 1964. Photos by F. A. Gildersleeve and others.

Conger, Roger N. *The Waco Suspension Bridge: "First Across and Still Across".* From *Texana*—Vol. 1, No. 3, reprinted by Friends of the Texas Ranger Library, 1992. An article.

Connally, Tom. *My Name is Tom Connally* (an autobiography as told to Alfred Steinberg). New York: Thomas Y. Crowell Company, 1954.

Convis, Charles L. *Outlaw Tales of Texas: True Stories of the Lone Star State's Most Infamous Crooks, Culprits, and Cutthroats (2nd Edition).* Guilford, Connecticut: Morris Publishing, LLC, 2012.

Cox, Mike. Texas Disasters: *True Stories of Tragedy and Survival.* Guilford, Connecticut: Globe Pequot Press, 2006.

Cremin, Lawrence A. *The Transformation of the School: Progressivism in American Education 1876-1957.* New York: Vintage Books, a Division of Random House, 1961.

Crowley, Dale S. *From Oklahoma to this Nation's Capital: My Miraculous Journey via Texas, California & Arkansas.* Mustang OK: Tate Publishing & Enterprises, 2008.

Cutrer, Thomas W. and T. Michael Parrish (editors), *Brothers in Gray: The Civil War Letters of the Pierson Family.* Louisiana State University Press, Baton Rouge, 1997.

Cutter, Charles. *Cutter's Guide to the City of Waco, Texas, 1894.* Charles Cutter, 1894.

Daniell, L.E. *Personnel of the Texas State Government: Sketches of Distinguished Texans.* Austin: L.E. Daniell Publisher, 1889.

Dary, David. *Frontier Medicine: From the Atlantic to the Pacific, 1492-1941.* New York: Vintage Books, 2009.

Davis, Margo, and Nilan, Roxanne. *The Stanford Album: A Photographic History, 1885-1945.* Stanford, California: Stanford University Press, 1989. Text by Roxanne Nilan and photograph selection by Margo Davis.

Davis, Ronald. *Opera in Chicago: A Social and Cultural History 1850-1965.* New York: Appleton-Century, 1966.

Dawson, Joseph Martin. *A Thousand Months to Remember: An Autobiography.* Waco: Baylor University Press, 1964.

Dealey, E.M. (publisher). *Red Book of Dallas, Texas, 1895-96: A Facsimile Reprint.* Dallas: A. H. Belo Corporation, 1966; apparently originally published in 1895.

De Wolk, Roland. *American Disruptor: The Scandalous Life of Leland Stanford.* Oakland, CA: University of California Press, 2019.

Dillon, J.T. *Questioning and Teaching.* New York: Teachers College Press, Columbia University, 1998.

Donizetti, Gaetano. *L'Elisir D'Amore (The Elixir of Love), A Comic Opera in Three Acts.* Unknown translator from the Italian. Melville, NY: Belwin Mills Publishing Corp. No publication date. Composed 1832.

Dow, Grove Samuel. *Classic Reprint Series: Introduction to the Principles of Sociology—A Text Book for Colleges and Universities.* Forgotten Books, 2012: originally published by the Baylor University Press, Waco, Texas, and/or Hargreaves Printing Company, 1920.

Eby, Frederick, Ph.D., L.L.D. *The Development of Education in Texas.* New York: The Macmillan Company, 1925.

Edgerton, Clyde. *The Bible Salesman, A Novel.* New York: Back Bay Books: Little, Brown & Copany, 2008.

Eggleston, Edward. *The Hoosier Schoolmaster: A Story of Backwoods Life in Indiana,* Revised. New York: Grosset & Dunlap, 1892; originally published in 1871.

Evans, Richard J. *In Defense of History.* New York and London: W.W. Norton & Company, 1999, 1997.

Fleming, Thomas. *Around the Pan with Uncle Hank: His Trip Through the Pan-American Exposition.* New York: The Nutshell Pub. Co., 1901.

Flexner, James Thomas. *Doctors on Horseback: Pioneers of American Medicine.* New York: The Viking Press, 1937.

Foner, Philip S. (ed.) *The Autobiographies of the Haymarket Martyrs.* New York: Monad Press, 1983.

Fowler, Thomas B. and Daniel Kuebler. *The Evolution Controversy: A Survey of Competing Theories.* Grand Rapids: Baker Academic, a division of Baker Publishing Group, 2007.

Fox, Elana V. (ed.). *Inside the World's Fair of 1904: Exploring the Louisiana Purchase Exposition,* Volume One. St. Louis (?): 1st Books Library, 2003.

Freeman, Denne H. *That Good Old Baylor Line.* Huntsville, Alabama: The Strode Publishers, Inc., 1975.

Fuller, Robert W. *Somebodies and Nobodies: Overcoming the Abuse of Rank.* New Society Publishers: Gabriola Island, BC, 2004.

Galewitz, Herb (ed.). *Sidney Smith's The Gumps.* New York: Charles Scribner's Sons, 1974.

Garofalo, Robert and Mark Elrod. *A Pictorial History of Civil War Era Musical Instruments & Military Bands.* Missoula, Montana: Pictorial History Publishing Company, Charleston, WVA, 1985.

Gard, Wayne. *Rawhide Texas.* Norman, OK: University of Oklahoma Press, 1965.

Gard, Wayne. *Sam Bass.* Lincoln: University of Nebraska Press, 1936.

Geronimo. *Geronimo His Own Story as Told to S.M. Barrett.* New York: A Meridian Book, Penguin Books USA Inc., 1996, originally published 1906.

Giordano, Ralph G. *Satan in the Dance Hall: Rev. John Roach Straton, Social Dancing, and Morality in 1920s New York City.* Lanham, MD: The Scarecrow Press, Inc., 2008.

Gooch, G. P. *History and Historians in the Nineteenth Century.* Beacon Hill: Beacon Press, 1959. Originally published in 1913.

Gowin, Enoch Burton, and William Alonzo Wheatley. *Occupations: A Textbook in Vocational Guidance.* Boston and other cities: Ginn and Company, 1916.

Grant, Ulysses S. *Personal Memoirs Ulysses S. Grant.* Caleb Carr, series editor. New York: The Modern Library, 1999 paperback edition.

Green, James. *Death in the Haymarket.* New York: Anchor Books, A Division of Random House, Inc, 2007.

Green, John R., M. D. *Medical History for Students.* Springfield, IL: Charles C Thomas Publisher, 1968.

Gruber, Frank. *Zane Grey, a Biography by Frank Gruber.* New York: The World Publishing Company, 1970.

Guinn, Jeff. *The Last Gunfight: The Real Story of the Shootout at the O.K. Corral—And How It Changed the American West.* New York: Simon & Schuster, 2011.

Guittard, Charles Francis (editor). *A Ph.D.'s Reverie: The Letters (a Whirlwind Courtship, A Ph.D. Student's Ordeal).* Sarasota, FL: First Edition Design Publishing, 1919. Letters of the Guittard family. Includes the first and second volumes of a trilogy relating to the pursuit of a doctorate at Stanford University.

Guittard, John Roscoe (compiler). *Carl Conrad Amsler, Texian Soldier at the Storming of San Antonio: Documents and Materials.* Compiled December 26, 1995, Dallas.

Guittard, John Roscoe (compiler). *Jacob Tombaugh, George Tombaugh, and Nathaniel Redd: Revolutionary War Soldiers and Indian Fighters in Pennsylvania and Ohio: Family History Materials.* Compiled December 26, 1995, Dallas.

Gullard, Pamela and Nancy Lund. *History of Palo Alto: The Early Years.* San Francisco: Scottwell Associates, 1989.

Gwynne, S. C. *Hymns of the Republic: The Story of the Final Year of the American Civil War*. New York, London: Scribner, 2019.

Hagedorn, Hermann. *Theodore Roosevelt in the Badlands*. Cambridge, MA: Houghton Mifflin Co., 1930. This is possibly the edition Frank Guittard quoted from in his thesis.

Hankins, Barry. *God's Rascal: J. Frank Norris & the Beginnings of Southern Fundamentalism*. Lexington, KY: The University Press of Kentucky, 1996.

Hardin, John Wesley. *The Life of John Wesley Hardin as Written by Himself.* Norman: University of Oklahoma Press, 1961. Introduction by Robert G. McCubbin.

Hendrickson, Kenneth E., Jr. *The Chief Executives of Texas: From Stephen F. Austin to John B. Connally, Jr.* College Station: Texas A & M University Press, 1995.

Hillman, Joseph (editor and author). *The Revivalist: A Collection (Revised and Enlarged) of Choice Revival Hymns and Tunes*. Troy, New York: Joseph Hillman, 1868.

Hodgson, Barbara. *In the Arms of Morpheus: The Tragic History of Laudanum, Morphine, and Patent Medicines*. Buffalo, New York: Firefly Books, 2001.

Hoefferle, Caroline. *The Essential Historiography Reader*. Boston: Shearson, 2011.

Holt, Emily. *Encyclopaedia of Etiquette: What to Write; What to Wear; What to Do; What to Say. A Book of Manners for Everyday Use*. Garden City, New York: Doubleday, Page & Company, 1901, Revised and Enlarged 1913.

Holt, Marilyn Irvin. *The Orphan Trains: Placing Out in America. Lincoln: University of Nebraska Press*, 1992.

Horowitz, Helen Lefkowitz. *Campus Life: Undergraduate Cultures from the End of the Eighteenth Century to the Present*. Chicago: The University of Chicago Press, 1987.

Jackson, Anna. *EXPO: International Expositions 1851-2010*. London: V&A Publishing, 2008.

Jackson, Robert. *Meet Me in St. Louis: A Trip to the 1904 World's Fair*. New York: HarperCollins Publishers, 2004.

Johnson, Charles A. *The Frontier Camp Meeting: Religion's Harvest Time*. Dallas: Southern Methodist University Press, 1955, 1985. New introduction by Ferenc M. Szasz.

Jones, Jacqueline. *Goddess of Anarchy: The Life and Times of Lucy Parsons, American Radical.* New York: Basic Books, 2017.

Jones, Michael D. *The Battle of Calcasieu Pass and the Great Naval Raid on Lake Charles, Louisiana*. CreateSpace Independent Publishing Platform, 2012.

Jones, Sam. *Sam Jones Sermons*. Chicago: Rhodes & McClure Publishing Co., 1886 copyrighted, published 1895.

Jones, Sam Porter. Edited by Walt Holcomb. *Popular Lectures of Sam P. Jones*. New York: Fleming H. Revell Company, New York, 1909.

Jordan, David Starr. *The Book of Knight and Barbara: Being a Series of Stories Told to Children*. New York: D. Appleton and Company, 1899.

Kasper, Shirl. *Annie Oakley*. Norman and London: University of Oklahoma Press, 1992.

Keeth, Kent. *Looking Back at Baylor: A Collection of Historical Vignettes*. Waco: Baylor University Press, 1985. Articles reprinted from *The Baylor Line*, 1973-1985.

Kneib, Martha. *Epidemics--Deadly Diseases Throughout History: Meningitis*. The Rosen Publishing Group, Inc., 2005.

Knight W.B. *Waco, Texas—the Central City—of the Lone Star State, Illustrated Twentieth Century Edition*. Waco: Knight Printing Co., 1901.

Knowles, Sir James (compiler and arranger of Sir Thomas Malory's version of the Arthurian legends). *King Arthur and His Knights*. New York: Books, Inc., 1923.

Krieger, Leonard. *Ranke: The Meaning of History*. Chicago: The University of Chicago Press, 1977.

Larson, Edward J. *Summer for the Gods: The Scopes Trial and American's Continuing Debate Over Science and Religion.* New York: Basic Books, A Subsidiary of Perseus Books, L.L.C., 1997. Pulitzer Prize Winner 1998.

Larson, Erik. *The Devil in the White City.* New York: Vintage Books, a Division of Random House, Inc., 2003.

Leacock, Stephen. *Too Much College or Education Eating Up Life, with Kindred Essays in Education and Humour.* New York: Dodd, Mead & Company, 1940.

Lears, Jackson. *Rebirth of a Nation: The Making of Modern America, 1877-1920.* New York: HarperCollins Publishers, 2009.

Leavitt, Judith Walzer & Ronald L. Numbers (editors). *Sickness & Health in America: Readings in the History of Medicine and Public Health.* Madison, WI: University of Wisconsin Press, 1997.

Lefever, Alan J. *Fighting the Good Fight: The Life and Work of Benajah Harvey Carroll.* Foreword by Russell H. Dilday. Austin: Eakin Press, an Imprint of Sunbelt Media, Inc., 1994.

Lefever, Alan J. *The History of Baylor Sports (from circa 1893).* Waco: Big Bear Books, an Imprint of Baylor University Press, 2013.

Leman, Kevin. *The Firstborn Advantage.* Grand Rapids: Revell, a Division of Baker Publishing Group, 2008.

Lester, Robin. *Stagg's University: The Rise, Decline & Fall of Big-Time Football at Chicago.* Urbana and Chicago: University of Illinois Press, 1995.

Lewis Publishing Company. *A Memorial and Biographical History of McLennan, Falls, Bell, and Coryall Counties, Texas.* Chicago: 1893.

Lewis, Scott. *Boundless Life: A Biography of Andrew Joseph Armstrong.* Waco: Armstrong-Browning Library of Baylor University, 2014.

Lewis, William Draper. *The Life of Theodore Roosevelt (public domain).* Philadelphia: John C. Winston Company, 1919.

Lindley, Elizabeth. *The Diary of a Book-Agent.* Originally published by Broadway Publishing Company, New York, 1912. Re-published by Loeb Classic Library; undated.

Linsley, Judith Walker; Rienstra, Ellen Walker; Stiles, Jo Ann. *Giant Under the Hill: A History of the Spindletop Oil Discovery at Beaumont, Texas, in 1901.* Austin: Texas State Historical Association, 2002.

Lyman, Henry M., Christian Fenger, H. Webster Jones, and W.T. Belfield. *The New American Family Physician, Giving in Detail the Cause, Symptoms, Treatment and History of all Diseases of the Human Body and Plain Instructions for the Care of the Sick with Full Directions for Treating Emergency Cases: A Description of the Structure and Functions of the Human Body, Hygiene and Rules of Health, Revised.* Chicago: Geo. M. Hill Co. Publishers, 1900.

Mathews, Harlan J., chair of publishing committee. *The Centennial Story of Texas Baptists.* Published by the Executive Board of the Baptist General Convention of Texas, 1936. Chapter Three was authored by Frederick Eby, Ph.D., Professor of the History and Philosophy of Education at the University of Texas and formerly a professor at Baylor University at Waco.

McCoy, Bob. *Quack! Tales of Medical Fraud from the Museum of Questionable Medical Devices.* Santa Monica: Santa Monica Press, 2000.

McGraw, Hugh (editor and chair). *The Sacred Harp, 1991 Revision: The Best Collection of Sacred Songs, Hymns, Odes, and Anthems Ever Offered the Singing Public for General Use.* Sacred Harp Publishing Company, Inc., 1991. Original compilation of songs 1844 by Benjamin Franklin White and revised 1869, 1911, 1936, and 1991.

McMurry, Donald L. *Coxey's Army: A Study of the Industrial Army Movement of 1894.* Seattle: University of Washington Press, 1968.

McNeill, Sallie. *The Uncompromising Diary of Sallie McNeill 1858-1867*. Edited with introduction by Ginnny McNeill Raska and Mary Lynne Gasaway Hill. College Station: Texas A & M University Press, 2009.

Martin, Jay. *The Education of John Dewey: A Biography*. New York: Columbia University Press.

Mayer, Milton Sanford. *Young Man in a Hurry: The Story of William Rainey Harper, First President of the University of Chicago*. Classic Reprint Series. Forgotten Books, 2012.

Metz, Leon. *John Wesley Hardin: Dark Angel of Texas*. Norman: University of Oklahoma Press, 1996.

Miller, Robert H. *Law School Confidential: A Complete Guide to the Law School Experience: By Students, for Students*. New York: St. Martin's Griffin, 2004.

Minnix, Kathleen. *Laughter in the Amen Corner: The Life of Evangelist Sam Jones*. Athens Georgia: University of Georgia Press, 1993.

Mirrielees, Edith R. *Stanford: The Story of a University*. New York: Van Rees Press, 1959.

Montgomery Ward & Co. *Catalogue and Buyers' Guide, No. 57, Spring and Summer, 1895* (an unabridged reprint of the original edition with an introduction by Boris Emmet). New York: Dover Publications, Inc., 1969.

Moore, Jonathan J. *Dreadful Diseases and Terrible Treatments: The Story of Medicine Through the Ages*. London: New Burlington Books, 2017.

Morris, Charles R. *The Tycoons: How Andrew Carnegie, John D. Rockefeller, Jay Gould, and J.P. Morgan Invented the American Supereconomy*. New York: Owl Books, Henry Holt and Company, 2005.

Morris, Edmund. *The Rise of Theodore Roosevelt*. New York: Random House Trade Paperback Edition, 2010.

Mortimer, James Howard. *Confessions of a Book Agent or Twenty Years by Stage and Rail* (Being the Experiences of a man who has sold $1,000,000 worth of books and remembers the characteristics of the people for whom and to whom he sold them; Snapshots of the Agent, the Publisher, and The Purchaser). Chicago: Co-operative Publishing Company, 1906. Reprinted by Forgottenbooks.com.

Murphy, Jim and Alison Blank. *Invincible Microbe Tuberculosis and the Never-Ending Search for a Cure*. Boston, New York: Clarion Books, Houghton Mifflin Harcourt, 2012.

Murray, Lois Smith. *Baylor at Independence*. Waco: Baylor University Press, 1972.

Muzzey, David Saville. *History of the American People*. Boston, New York, Chicago and other cities: Ginn and Company, 1927.

Norris, J. Frank. *Sermons by J. Frank Norris: The Battle of Armageddon and Other Sermons*. Delivered in 1924 and 1947. Printed by unknown publisher on unknown date.

O'Connor, Stephen. *Orphan Trains: The Story of Charles Loring Brace and the Children He Saved and Failed*. Chicago: University of Chicago Press, 2001.

Olmsted, Frederick Law. *A Journey Through Texas, or, a Saddle-Trip on the Southwestern Frontier*. New York: Dix, Edwards & Co., 1857. Reprinted 1981 by Time-Life Books as part of Classics of the Old West.

Optic, Oliver (William T. Adams). *Young Knight-Errant, or, Cruising in the West Indies (American Boys Series)*. Boston: Lothrop, Lee & Shepard Co., 1892.

Parsons, Chuck and Norman Wayne Brown. *A Lawless Breed: John Wesley Hardin, Texas Reconstruction and Violence in the Wild West*. Denton, TX: The University of North Texas Press, 2012.

Penn, W. E. *Harvest Bells: Nos. 1, 2, and 3 Combined—Beautiful Songs Suitable for Sabbath Schools, Revival, and all Religious Meetings*. W. E. Penn Publisher, St. Louis, MO, 1887. Assisted by H. N. Lincoln in connection with No. 3.

Peters, Robert L., Ph.D. *Getting What You Came For: The Smart Student's Guide to Earning a Master's or Ph.D.* New York: Farrar, Straus and Giroux, 1997. First Revised Edition.

Peterson, Robert W. *Pigskin: The Early Years of Pro Football*. New York: The Oxford University Press, 1997.

Peskin, Allan. *Garfield: A Biography*. Kent, Ohio: The Kent State University Press, 1978, 1999.

Poage, W.R. (Bob). *After the Pioneers—Recollections of W.R. Poage.* Waco: Texian Press, 1969. Foreword by Abner V. McCall.

Poage, W.R. (Bob). *McLennan County—Before 1980.* Waco: Texian Press, 1981. *My First 85 years.* Waco: Texian Press, 1985.

Pylant, James, and Knight, Sherri. *The Oldest Profession in Texas: Waco's Legal Red Light District.* Stephenville, Texas: Jacobus Books, 2011.

Rance, Caroline. *The Quack Doctor: Historical Remedies for All Your Ills.* Stroud, Gloucestershire: The History Press, 2013.

Reagan, Patty S. *A Word Atlas of Central Texas,* 1979, submitted to the Graduate School of East Texas State University in partial fulfillment for the degree of Doctor of Education.

Rebok, Barbara (ed.). *Coshocton County, Ohio.* Tucson: A Plus Printing Company, 2000. Published from articles published on the internet.

Reed, S.G.. *A History of the Texas Railroads.* Houston: St. Clair Publishing Co., 1941.

Rice, Joseph Mayer. *The Public-School System of the United States.* New York: The Century Co., 1893, re-published by Forgotten Books. Articles originally published in The Forum Publishing Company in 1892.

Richardson, Ruth. *Dickens & the Workhouse: Oliver Twist & the London Poor.* Oxford: Oxford University Press, 2012.

Robertson, Robert J. *Her Majesty's Texans: Two English Immigrants in Reconstruction Texas.* College Station: Texas A & M University Press, 1998.

Robinson, Armstead L. Robinson. *Bitter Fruits of Bondage: The Demise of Slavery and the Collapse of the Confederacy, 1861-1861.* Charlottesville VA: University of Virginia Press, 2005.

Rodeheaver, Hall. *Sociability Songs for Community-School, Home.* Chicago: Hall-Mack Co., 1928.

Roe, Edward P. *Barriers Burned Away (New and Revised Edition).* New York: Dodd, Mead and Company, 1872, 1885, and 1892.

Roe, Edward P. *A Young Girl's Wooing.* New York: Dodd, Mead and Company, 1884.

Roosevelt, Theodore. *The Rough Riders.* Introduction by William N. Tilchin. New York: Barnes and Noble Publishing, Inc., 2004; originally published in 1899.

Rusk, John. *The Authentic Life of T. DeWitt Talmage, the Greatly Beloved Divine.* Privately published by L.G. Stahl, 1902. Introduction by Russell H. Conwell and John Franklin Talmage.

Russell, Traylor, and Russell, Robert T. *Some Die Twice.* Waco: Texian Press, 1979.

Rydell, Robert W., John E. Findling, and Kimberly D. Pelle. *Fair America: World's Fairs in the United States.* Washington: Smithsonian Institution Press, 2000.

Saffell, John E. *Wake the Echoes: An Updated History of Mount Union College.* New Washington, Ohio: Mount Union College, 1996.

Sankey, Ira, D., R.P. Bliss, James McGranahan, and George C. Stebbins (compilers). *Gospel Hymns Consolidated (Vols. 1-3) for Use in Gospel Meetings and Other Religious Services.* New York: The Biglow & Main Co., 1886 Contains all the hymns and tunes used by D. L. Moody and others found in the consolidated volumes.

Sankey, Ira D., James McGranahan, and George C. Stebbins (editors). *Church Hymns and Gospel Songs.* New York, Chicago: The Biglow and Main Co., 1898.

Scarborough, Dorothy. *In the Land of Cotton.* New York: The Macmillan Company, 1923.

Schevill, Ferdinand. *Karl Bitter, A Biography.* Chicago: The University of Chicago Press, 1917, republished 2012 by Forgotten Books.

Schevill, Ferdinand. *Six Historians.* Chicago: The University of Chicago Press, 1956.

Schwantes, Carlos A. *Coxey's Army: An American Odyssey.* Moscow, ID: University of Idaho Press, 1994.

Sears, Roebuck and Co. *1902 Edition of the Sears Roebuck Catalogue* (introduction Cleveland Amory). New York: Bounty Book, a division of Crown Publishers, Inc., 1969.

Selcer, David (compiler and editor). *Legendary Watering Holes: The Saloons That Made Texas Famous.* College Station: Texas A&M University Press, 2004.

Selcer, Richard F. *Hell's Half Acre: The Life and Legend of a Red-Light District.* Fort Worth: Texas Christian University Press, 1991.

Shyrock, Richard Harrison. *Medical Licensing in America, 1650-1965.* Baltimore, MD: The Johns Hopkins Press, 1967.

Sieber, Harry (ed.). *The Wit and Wisdom of Don Quixote de la Mancha* by Miguel de Cervantes Saavedra as translated by Tobias Smollett. New York: McGraw-Hill, 2004.

Smallwood, James M., Barry A. Crouch, and Larry Peacock. *Murder and Mayhem: The War of Reconstruction in Texas.* College Station: Texas A&M University Press, 2003.

Smith, Alene (ed.). *The Daisy Chain 1928.* Waco: Students of Waco High School, Waco, Texas, 1928.

Smith, Alfred B. *Old Time Revival Songs: A Choice Collection of Enduring Favorites.* Grand Rapids: Zondervan Publishing House, 1950.

Snowden, Frank M. *Epidemics and Society: From the Black Death to the Present.* New Haven: Yale University Press, 2019.

Sonnichsen, C. L. *I'll Die Before I'll Run: The Story of the Great Feuds of Texas.* New York: The Devin-Adair Company, 1962.

Southgate, Beverley. *What Is History for?* London and New York: Routledge, Taylor & Francis Group, 2005.

Spain, Rufus B. *At Ease in Zion.* Tuscaloosa, AL: The University of Alabama Press, 2003.

Spellman, Paul N. (editor). "This Fateful Revolution': Letters of a German-Texan Unionist, 1862-1863." *Southwestern Historical Quarterly,* Vol. CXXI, No. 3, January, 2018. Austin: The State Historical Association, 2018.

Sperling, John. *Great Depressions: 1837-1844, 1893-1898, 1929-1939.* Glenview, IL: Scott, Foreman and Company, 1966. Quotes liberally from source documents.

Stebbins, Genevieve. *Delsarte System of Dramatic Expression.* Forgotten Books. Originally published in New York by Edgar S. Werner in 1886.

Stokes, David. *Apparent Danger: The Pastor of American's First Megachurch AND THE Texas Murder Trial OF THE DECADE in the 1920s.* Minneapolis: Bascom Hill Books, 2010.

Stokes, David R. *The Shooting Salvationist.* Hanover, NH: Steerforth Press LLC, 2011.

Storr, Richard J. *Harper's University, The Beginnings: A History of the University of Chicago.* Chicago and London: The University of Chicago Press, 1966.

Straton, John Roach. *The Menace of Immorality in Church and State.* New York: George H. Doran Company, 1920.

Talmage, T. DeWitt. *Trumpet Blasts or Mountain-Top Views of Life.* Introduction by Russell H. Conwell. Compiled and edited by Rev. J. Ward Gamble and Prof. Charles Morris. Chicago: North American Publishing Co., 1892.

Terkel, Studs. *Working: People Talk About What They Do All Day and How They Feel About What They Do.* New York: Pantheon Books, a Division of Random House, 1972.

Thompson, Ann. *Let's Go to the Opera Guide to The Elixir of Love.* Houston: Ann Thompson, 1999.

Tiling, Moritz. *History of the German Element in Texas from 1820-1850 and Historical Sketches of the German Texas Singers' League and Houston Turnverein from 1853-1913.* Houston: Moritz Tiling Publisher, 1913.

Turner, Thomas E. *Instruments of Providence: Biographical Vignettes of the Charter Trustees of Baylor University.* Waco: Baylor University Heritage Series, Baylor University, 1989.

Tuthill, Harry J. *The Bungle Family: A Complete Compilation—1928.* Westport: Hyperion Press, 1977; originally copyrighted 1928 by McNaught Syndicate, Inc. Introduction by Bill Blackbeard.

Tuthill, Harry J. *The Bungle Family 1929 Sundays.* Public domain material reprinted by Escamilla Comics, 2016.

Twain, Mark and Charles Dudley Warner. *The Gilded Age, a Tale of Today*. New York: A Meridian Book, Published by the Penguin Group, 1994. Originally published 1873.

University of Chicago. *The Cap and Gown, Volume 6*. Managing editors Edward Christian Kohlsaat and Frederic Graham Moloney. Nabu Public Domain Reprint. Originally published under the direction of the Order of the Iron Mask of the University of Chicago, 1901.

Valenstein, Elliot S. *Great and Desperate Cures: The Rise and Decline of Psychosurgery and Other Radical Treatments for Mental Illness*. New York: Basic Boks, Inc., 1986.

Veit, Richard J., Editor. "Law and Order in Six-shooter Junction," *Waco Heritage and History*, a publication of the Historic Waco Foundation, vol. 19, no. 2, December 1989.

Versteeg, John M. *Methodism: Ohio Area (1812-1962)*. Ohio Area Sesquicentennial Committee, 1962.

Veysey, Laurence R. *The Emergence of the American University*. Chicago and London: The University of Chicago Press, 1965.

Walker, James Lafayette and C.P. Lumpkin. *History of the Waco Baptist Association of Texas*. Waco: Byrne-Hill Printing House, 1897.

Wallace, Patricia Ward. *A Spirit So Rare: A History of the Women of Waco*. Austin: Nortex Press, 1984.

Wallace, Patricia Ward. *Our Land, Our Lives: A Pictorial History of McLennan County*, Texas. Norfolk/Virginia Beach: The Donning Company, 1986. Text by Patricia Ward Wallace and photos provided by residents of McLennan County, Texas.

Wallace, Patricia Ward. *Waco: A Sesquicentennial History*. Virginia Beach: The Donning Company Publishers, 1999.

Watterson, John Sayle. *College Football: History-Spectacle-Controversy*. Baltimore: The Johns Hopkins Press, 2000.

Webb, Chloe. *Legacy of the Sacred Harp*. Fort Worth: TCU Press, 2010.

Weinberg, Steve. *Taking on the Trust: How Ida Tarbell Brought Down John D. Rockefeller and Standard Oil*. New York: W.W. Norton & Co., 2008.

Welch, June Rayfield. *The Colleges of Texas: A Survey of the Lone Star State's Institutions of Higher Learning, Past and Present*. Dallas: GLA Press, 1981.

West, John C. *A Texan in Search of a Fight: Being the Diary and Letters of a Private Soldier in Hood's Texas Brigade*. Waco: Press of J. S. Hill & Co., 1901, and Texian Press, 196 (reprint).

White, Michael A. *History of Baylor University 1845-1861*. Waco: Texian Press, 1968.

Wilen, William W. (ed.). *Questions, Questioning Techniques, and Effective Teaching*. Washington, D.C.: NEA Professional Library, National Education Association, 1987.

Williams, Dusty. *The Poor Farm, of Grayson County, TX*. Privately published, undated.

Wilson, Augusta Evans. *Infelice, A Novel*. New York: A.L. Burt Company, 1875.

Winsett, R. E. (ed.). *Camp Meeting Special: Best Songs for Camp Meetings, Revivals and Evangelistic Work*. Dayton: R. E. Winsett Music Co., 1951.

Wolfe, Cameron (ed.) *The Stanford Quad 1931*. Stanford University: Stanford University Press and Associated Students of Stanford University, California, 1931.

Wood, George B., M.D., and Franklin Bache, M.D. *The Dispensatory of the United States of America (10th Edition)*. Philadelphia: Lippincott, Grambo, and Co., 1854.

Yenne, Bill (ed.). *All Aboard! The Golden Age of American Rail Travel*. New York: Barnes & Noble Inc. by arrangement with Brompton Books Corporation, 1989.

Yoakum, C.S. *Care of the Feeble-Minded and Insane in Texas*. Classic Reprint Series, Vol. 16. London: Forgotten Books, 2015. Originally published November 5, 1914.

Yoakum, Henderson K. *The History of Texas from its First Settlement in 1685 to its Annexation to the United States in 1846* (Volume 1). NABU Public Domain Reprint. Originally published by J.S. Redfield, 1856 in New York.

Yoakum, Henderson K. *The History of Texas from its First Settlement in 1685 to its Annexation to the United States in 1846* (Volume 2). Forgotten Books 2012; originally published by J.S. Redfield 1855 in New York.

Young, James Harvey. *The Medical Messiahs: A Social History of Health Quackery in Twentieth-Century America.* Princeton: Princeton University Press, 1967.

Zimbardo, Philip G. *Shyness: What it is; What to do about it.* New York: Jove Publications, Inc. (Harcourt Brace Jovanovich), 1977.

Guittard, F.G., autobiographical & other written documents

Guittard, F.G. autobiographical sketch, handwritten essay 1894, spring session for W.W Franklin's Giant Rhetoric Course, Baylor University.

Guittard, F.G., autobiographical theme, handwritten for English III course, the University of Chicago, July 16, 1900.

Guittard, F.G., autobiographical manuscript "Reborn'd in Texas", handwritten after 1908.

Guittard, F.G., diary; a small leather-bound notebook in which F.G. Guittard recording the main events of each year with his comments.

Guittard, F.G., Funny-Book," a collection of odd, funny, or absurd answers of students on history examinations given by F.G. Guittard. Also cited by L. Cagle.

Guittard, F.G., ledger of expenses.

Guittard, F.G., notebook; a small black book in which F.G. Guittard noted sayings which he liked as well as his favorite poems. Also cited by L. Cagle.

Interviews & Personal Statements

Statement of Mrs. Eugene Sallee in a private conversation with L. Cagle, July 2, 1950. Also cited by L. Cagle.

Statement of Mrs. F.G. Guittard in a personal interview by L. Cagle, February 16, 1951. Also cited by L. Cagle.

Statement of Mrs. F.G. Guittard in a personal interview by L. Cagle, June 20, 1951. Also cited by L. Cagle.

Statement of Pat M. Neff in a personal interview by L. Cagle, July 2, 1951. Also cited by L. Cagle.

Statement of Mrs. W.H. Pool in a personal interview by L. Cagle, July 2, 1951. Also cited by L. Cagle.

Letters, other than from the Guittard Family

Letter from Joe W. Hale, Associate Justice of the Court of Civilo Appeals, Tenth Supreme Judicial District of Texas, May 11,1951. Cited by L. Cagle.

Letter from Guy B. Harrison, Jr., Professor of History, Baylor University, May 14, 1951. Cited by L. Cagle.

Letter from R.T. Miller, Associate Professor of Political Science, Baylor University, May 14, 1951. Cited by L. Cagle.

Letter from Henry Trantham, Baylor University, to L. Cagle, May 14, 1951. Cited by L. Cagle.

Letter from Peck Welhausen, Shiner Texas, to L. Cagle. Peck Welhausen was one of three brothers of Mamie Welhausen Guittard. Cited by L. Cagle.

Minutes of Institutional Proceedings

Minutes of the Board of Trustees of Waco University and Classical School, January 21, 1861 to June 7, 1867. Cited by L. Cagle.

Miscellaneous

Family bible owned by F.G. Guittard. Cited by L. Cagle.
Inscription across the front of Pat Neff Hall, Baylor University, Waco, Texas. Cited by L. Cagle.
Tombaugh, Rene G. *Tombaugh History, 1728-1830.* Cited by L. Cagle.
Unknown author, "Death of F.J. Guittard," a typewritten account filed with the archives of F.G. Guittard, The Texas Collection. Cited by L. Cagle.
Unknown author, "The History of Coshocton County, Ohio," 1881. Cited by L. Cagle.

Periodicals, Baylor University

Baylor University Bulletin, Volume XLIV, Number 4, December 1940. The Texas Collection of Baylor University. Guy Bryan Harrison, Jr., Curator. Waco: Baylor University Press, 1940.
Baylor Monthly, VIII, No. 5, August, 1927, statement on p. 7. Cited by L. Cagle.
Baylor Monthly, VII, November 1931, Professor Henry Trantham, "Faculty Close-ups." Cited by L. Cagle.

Periodicals, other

The Holmes County Farmer-Hub, Millersburg, Ohio, June, 1902. Cited by L. Cagle.
Journal of the Outdoor Life, the Anti-Tuberculosis Magazine. "The Prevention of Tuberculosis", "The Art of Sitting Out", and other articles. February, 1910. Vol. VII, No. 2.
The Literary Digest, August 2, 1902, Vol. XXV, No.5. New York, Whole No. 641.
The Literary Digest, November 22, 1890, Vol. II, No. 4. New York, Whole No. 31.
Searchlight, The, April 27, 1923. (J. Frank Norris publication).
St. Louis Globe–Democrat. Vol. 19, No. 2. April 2004. "Retrospective on the St. Louis World's Fair containing articles from April 1904."
St. Louis Post-Dispatch, Sunday Morning, May 1, 1904.
Waco News-Tribune, May 17, 1937. Also cited by L. Cagle.
The Youth's Companion (Christmas 1890), Boston, Thursday, December 18, 1890, 63rd Volume, No. 51.

Ph.D. Dissertations, Master's Theses, and Research Papers

Adams, Charles Scott. "Twentieth Century Baylor Presidents and Christian Education: The Educational Philosophies of Samuel Palmer Brooks, Pat Morris Neff, and William Richardson White." Master of Arts Thesis, Baylor University, 1964.
Amyett, Paddy Dion Westergard. "A History of Literary Societies at Baylor University." Master of Arts Thesis, Baylor University, 1963.
Barron, Ann. "Dr. Lula Pace." Research Paper for History 3380, Baylor University, 1995. Pertaining to charges that Dr. Pace advocated the theory of evolution.
Bouldin, Donald Glenn. "J.M. Dawson—J.F. Norris Controversy: A Reflection of the Fundamentalist Controversy among Texas Baptists." Master of Arts Thesis, Baylor University, 1969.

Burlison, Benny. "Ecclesiology and Strategy of J. Frank Norris from 1915 to 1950." Master of Arts Thesis, Baylor University, 1950.

Cagle, Louise Moore. "The Life of Francis Gevrier Guittard." Master of Arts Thesis, Baylor University, 1951.

Dickinson, William Calvin. "Baylor University—A Century of Discipline, 1845-1947." Master of Arts Thesis, Baylor University, 1962.

Guemple, John Robert. "A History of Waco University." Master of Arts Thesis, Baylor University, 1964.

Guittard, Francis Gevrier. "Roosevelt and Conservation." Ph.D. Dissertation, Stanford University, 1930.

Renberg, James Bernard. "Samuel Palmer Brooks: President of Baylor University, 1920-1931." Master of Arts Thesis, 1963.

Sinclair, Oran Lonnie. "Samuel Palmer Brooks: President of Baylor University, 1902-1920." Master of Arts Thesis, 1961.

Smith, Lisa. "Francis Gevrier Guittard." Research Paper, English 1304, Baylor University, 1991.

Smythe, Sarah Belle. "History of the Literary Societies in Baylor." Term Paper, English 247, Baylor University, no date.

Tilden, Susan. "A Man Loves His Home: Waco and Madison Cooper's *Sironia, Texas.*" Term Project, Geology A-T 1405, 1979.

INDEX

H

I

J

K

L

T

U

V

W

Guide for Classroom Discussion

of

I WILL TEACH HISTORY, the Life & Times of

Francis Gevrier Guittard, Professor, Baylor University

1. In which of the following ways does the book take the reader into a classroom-like setting? Give your reason(s) for your answer.

   (a) the prologue which includes a History 105 class in 1930;
   (b) the questions on the book dividers and the unanswered questions at the book's end;
   (c) the employment of the peanut gallery throughout to raise and answer questions in connection with Pops's remarks as narrator-lecturer;
   (d) Professor Smiley's tribute to Frank Guittard at the conclusion;
   (e) all of the above.

2. What was the twist of fate in Frank Guittard's life and how important was it in the way his life played out? Which had the greatest impact on Frank's life—the winds of chance or careful planning and waiting? Explain your answers.

3. State who you think had the greatest impact on Frank, directly or indirectly, and why. You may name more than one person.

(a) Rufus C. Burleson	(e) Mamie Welhausen Guittard
(b) Oscar H. Cooper	(f) John D. Rockefeller
(c) James Milton Carroll	(g) Samuel P. Brooks
(d) F.L. and G.W. Carroll	(h) Josie Glenn Guittard

4. Which of the following perspectives of Frank do you feel best explains his private sides? Please explain your answer.

(a) chivalric moral nature	(e) addiction to golf
(b) passion for reading	(f) secret romantic
(c) belief in self-control	(g) systematic, methodical mindset
(d) dry sense of humor	(h) sympathy for the underdog

5. Do you see Frank's life as a sort of Horatio Alger story? Whether your answer is yes or no, state the reason(s) for your view.

6. Which nickname best fits Waco as of the 1890s when Frank attended Baylor? Please state your reasons in your answer.

(a) Buckle of the Bible Belt
(b) Vice Capital of Texas
(c) Six-Shooter Junction
(d) Geyser City
(e) Athens on the Brazos

7. Identify Frank's greatest challenge(s) from the list below and provide your reasons:

(a) making a new start in Texas, a new land, with little or no family support;
(b) teaching in an ungraded piney woods school and other country schools;
(c) working his way through the University of Chicago to earn two degrees;
(d) despite a limited teacher's income, persuading two women to marry him;
(e) relearning subjects outside his major to teach in Baylor's Academy;
(f) surviving the losses of his second son and first wife to disease;
(g) pursuing a Ph.D. over six years at Stanford as the oldest guy in the room;
(h) teaching history into his 80s for lack of adequate retirement income.

8. Which of the following events mentioned in the book do you think was most important, directly or indirectly, to the development of Baylor at Waco as a university in the second half of the 19th century/first half of the 20th? Include your reasons. You may choose more than one.

(a) the leadership of President Rufus C. Burleson;
(b) the coming of the railroads to Waco;
(c) the merging of Waco University and Baylor at Independence;
(d) the resignation of President Burleson;
(e) the Spindletop Oil discovery and the east Texas oil boom;
(f) the election and administration of President Samuel P. Brooks;
(g) the resumption of intercollegiate football in 1907;
(h) the resolution of the evolution controversy on campus;
(i) the building of the Armstrong-Browning Collection.

9. Do you agree with Professor Leopold von Ranke that the purpose of the study of history is to find out what actually happened? If you disagree, why do you think people should study history?

Charles Francis Guittard, Author

Charles Francis Guittard, a graduate of Baylor University, was born in Austin, Texas. He followed the career path of his father, Justice Clarence Alwin Guittard, who was steered into law by his father, Francis "Frank" Gevrier Guittard, professor of history at Baylor and the ultimate subject of this work. Ten years after completing law school, Charles began researching the life of his grandfather, who left his parents' Ohio home in 1886 and boarded a train to Texas. The incentive for Charles's research was reading 250 family letters from the 1920s. After retiring, Charles aspired to publish a "trilogy" on Frank Guittard's life & times, starting with an illustrated poem entitled *A Ph.D.'s Reverie*, with original illustrations by a Baylor art student and accompanied by historical notes. Next, Charles published *A Ph.D.'s Reverie: The Letters*, which added excerpts from the 250 letters to the illustrated poem and told the contemporaneous story of the fundamentalists' assault on Baylor. The current work—*I WILL TEACH HISTORY, the Life & Times of Francis Gevrier Guittard, Professor, Baylor University*—comprises the trilogy's third volume and was completed during the COVID-19 pandemic. It was edited and illustrated by Baylor students. Charles's four grandchildren assisted him in bringing forth the stories of Frank Guittard's life & times from the past's dark vault.

Cole Niles, Editor

Cole Niles is a writer from Dallas, Texas. A 2019 graduate of Baylor University, Cole earned a degree in professional writing and rhetoric from the Department of English and is currently pursuing a master's degree in divinity from Princeton Theological Seminary in Princeton, New Jersey. He worked as a staff writer for the Baylor Line Foundation, focusing on sports and book reviews for the publication before recently setting out on more independent writing projects. He currently serves as editor-in-chief of the Unorthodoxy Christian Blog, which examines the synthesis of ancient faith with the modern world. The current book is the first full-length volume he has edited.

Amanda Hope Smith—Illustrator

Amanda Hope Smith is an artist based in College Station, Texas. Amanda recently graduated from Baylor University with a bachelor's degree in Fine Arts and is currently pursuing her master's at Savannah College of Art and Design. Her work was selected for the juried Baylor Art Student Exhibition in 2020, 2021, 2022, and won Best in Printmaking for 2022. Amanda enjoys hiking, card games, and spending time with friends and family.

Made in the USA
Monee, IL
25 November 2022